GENDER AND DISORDERED BEHAVIOR
Sex Differences in Psychopathology

Gender and Disordered Behavior

Sex Differences in Psychopathology

Edited by

EDITH S. GOMBERG, Ph.D.
School of Social Work, University of Michigan

and

VIOLET FRANKS, Ph.D.
Department of Psychology, The Carrier Clinic
Belle Mead, New Jersey

BRUNNER/MAZEL, Publishers • New York

SECOND PRINTING

Library of Congress Cataloging in Publication Data

Main entry under title:
Gender and disordered behavior: sex differences in psychopathology.
    Includes bibliographies and index.
    1. Psychology, Pathological.   2. Sex differences (Psychology)   I. Gomberg,
Edith S., 1920-   II. Franks, Violet.

RC455.4.S45G46   616.8'9   78-27390
ISBN 0-87630-188-X

Dedicated to the memory of our parents:

Dorothy and Barnet Silverglied, and Sarah and Joseph **Greenberg,**

And to the future, our children:

Judith, Eugene, Stephen and Susan Lisansky, Robert, Pamela, Richard and Sara Gomberg, and Steven and Sharon Franks

PREFACE

In approaching the topic of men, women and disordered behavior, the editors recognized from the start that gender comparison was one of several different types of analysis which could be made of disordered behavior. Until recent years there have been few publications relating the incidence of disturbed behavior to gender, perhaps because subject characteristics—sex, age, social class, ethnicity, etc.—have not been a traditional concern of research workers in the behavioral sciences. The editors of this volume, a clinically trained research psychologist and a research-minded clinical psychologist, are both interested in and aware of subject characteristics.

The book will be helpful to social workers, psychologists, psychiatrists, nurses and others in the helping professions. It may also be used as a supplementary text in courses on psychopathology or abnormal psychology. Some chapters cover sex differences in traditional diagnostic categories; others deal with comparisons of the sexes at various crisis points in the life cycle. We have also given consideration to various problematic behaviors shown by men and women to varying degrees.

We have invited qualified experts from a variety of professions to contribute to this volume in order to cover the complex issues of gender and psychopathology. The professions of the authors of various chapters include clinical psychology, psychiatry, sociology, experimental psychology and social work. The chapter authors represent different and often controversial points of view on some theoretical, methodological and political issues. While each contributor was requested to write of "the current state of knowledge," the request was interpreted in individual ways by the different chapter authors. Some chapters emphasize empirical findings, some attempt to integrate findings and develop hypotheses, and several report new data. The heterogeneity of the chapters means that some are more closely related to clinical work with clients, and others are more closely related to research activities.

vii

The first chapter begins, delightfully enough, with a quotation from Maeterlinck. Ethel Tobach's quotation about the sexual identity of the chief bee relates to a current question raised about some species by animal behaviorists: Is the kingdom really a queendom? Dr. Tobach's discussion of the applicability of animal research to persons confronts the difficult question of the generalizability of any research with non-human subjects. In the second chapter, Walter R. Gove considers sex differences in the epidemiology of mental disorders and demonstrates the provocative and interesting findings which emerge from epidemiological data. His work is always interesting, sometimes controversial.

The next section of the book focuses on *Life Cycle Crises*. There is a greatly increased awareness of developmental issues in current research, an awareness that development does not end with infancy, childhood and adolescence. We have touched upon three points in the life cycle. Anne Locksley and Elizabeth Douvan open a number of interesting questions in their exploration of the different ways in which boys and girls cope with the problems of adolescence. Marriage and divorce are not universal experiences, but the chapter on divorce by Prudence Brown and Hanna Fox presents some interesting findings on marital status, mental health and sex differences, consistent with the view of marriage and divorce as different experiences for men and for women. Lillian E. Troll and Barbara F. Turner write on sex differences in aging and in dealing with the problems of old age. The mental health problems of aging persons are a new frontier of research.

The third section of this volume deals with *Problem Behaviors*. Our definition of problem behaviors probably comes closest to the classical sociological definition of "deviant behavior." These are not the functional disorders, neuroses, psychoses and psychosomatics, but problematic behaviors which involve acting-out behavior and which are disturbing to society. First, Rosemary Sarri presents startling differences in our legal conception of permissible behavior for female and male adolescents, a true double standard. One of the editors (ESG) examines problem behavior relating to alcohol and drug use; clearly, society views men's and women's drug-related behavior differently. Richard B. Stuart and Barbara Jacobson find both physiological and psychological differences in the way men and women gain or lose weight and the way their obesity affects self-image. Again, the similarities and differences in problem behaviors are pointed up by the review of homosexual behaviors among men and women by Bernard F. Riess and Jeanne M. Safer, both well known for their work in this area. David Lester examines the possible reasons why men complete suicide more often and women attempt suicide more often. The final problem behavior explored in this section is rape—an illuminating, new way of looking at a very old problem is presented by two sociologists, Joseph A. Marolla and Diana H. Scully.

Section IV on *Functional Disorders* opens with a chapter on schizophrenia; the organization of the material on schizophrenia for gender comparison was a challenge which Florence Schumer meets with éclat. Pauline B. Bart and Diana H. Scully have written a provocative and most interesting chapter on hysteria, focusing on psychiatry's role in defining and treating this "woman's disorder." In the chapter on sex differences in depression, Myrna M. Weissman and Gerald L. Klerman bring systematization to a mass of material on depression and a clarification of some of the issues raised in looking at gender and depression. Anne M. Seiden, in the final chapter of this section, brilliantly examines the relationship between gender and psychosomatic disorder.

In the final section, one of the editors (VF) considers the relationship between gender and the processes of psychotherapy. This is an area where the practical value of gender comparison is most evident, i.e. the implications of such comparison for treatment. The final chapter of the book contains the editors' reflections on the subject of gender comparison and the vast amount of work that remains to be done.

Special thanks are due many of the chapter authors who met deadlines and then waited patiently for the others to catch up. The encouragement and support of staff members and colleagues at the places we work, the University of Michigan and the Carrier Clinic Foundation, was invaluable. Without time made available by these institutions, there would be no book. Cynthia Sansom did a fine and patient job of editing, and Susan E. Barrows has been most helpful in bringing the work to completion.

Finally, we would like to thank our patient husbands, Henry J. Gomberg and Cyril Franks, each busy with his own life work, for listening, encouraging, inspiring.

EDITH S. GOMBERG
VIOLET FRANKS

CONTENTS

xi

CONTRIBUTORS

PAULINE B. BART, Ph.D.
Associate Professor, Department of Psychiatry, The Abraham Lincoln School of Medicine and University of Illinois at the Medical Center, Chicago, Illinois

PRUDENCE BROWN, Ph.D.
Assistant Professor, School of Social Work, Columbia University, New York

ELIZABETH DOUVAN, Ph.D.
Professor, Department of Psychology, University of Michigan, Ann Arbor

HANNA FOX
Princeton, New Jersey

VIOLET FRANKS, Ph.D.
Department of Psychology, The Carrier Clinic, Belle Mead, New Jersey

EDITH S. GOMBERG, Ph.D.
Professor, School of Social Work, and Research Scientist, Institute of Gerontology, University of Michigan, Ann Arbor

WALTER R. GOVE, Ph.D
Professor of Sociology, Vanderbilt University, Nashville, Tennessee

BARBARA JACOBSON, M.Ed.
Counselor, Merrimack College, North Andover, Massachusetts

GERALD L. KLERMAN, M.D.
Administrator, Alcohol, Drug Abuse and Mental Health Administration, Rockville, Maryland and on leave from Professor of Psychiatry, Harvard University Medical School, Massachusetts General Hospital, Boston

DAVID LESTER, Ph.D.
Professor of Psychology, Richard Stockton State College, Pomona, New Jersey

ANNE LOCKSLEY, Ph.D.
Assistant Professor, Department of Psychology, New York University, New York

JOSEPH A. MAROLLA, Ph.D.
Assistant Professor, Department of Sociology, Virginia Commonwealth University, Richmond

BERNARD F. RIESS, Ph.D.
Director of Graduate Training in Professional Psychology, New School for Social Research, New York, and Director, Housatonic Mental Health Center, Lakeville, Connecticut

JEANNE M. SAFER, Ph.D.
Associate Director of Research, Postgraduate Center for Mental Health, New York, and private practice in New York City

ROSEMARY C. SARRI, Ph.D.
Professor, School of Social Work, University of Michigan, Ann Arbor

FLORENCE SCHUMER, Ph.D.
Private practice of Psychotherapy and Psychodiagnosis, New York, Former Senior Research Scientist, Institute for Developmental Studies, New York University

DIANA H. SCULLY, Ph.D.
Assistant Professor, Department of Sociology and Anthropology, Virginia Commonwealth University, Richmond

ANNE M. SEIDEN, M.D.
Director of Research, Institute for Juvenile Research, State of Illinois Department of Mental Health, Chicago, Illinois

RICHARD B. STUART, D.S.W.
Professor of Social Work and Psychology, University of Utah, Salt

Lake City, and Psychological Director, Weight Watchers International

ETHEL TOBACH, Ph.D.
Curator, Department of Animal Behavior, The American Museum of Natural History, New York; Adjunct Professor, Department of Biology, City College of New York, and Adjunct Professor, Department of Psychology, Hunter College

LILLIAN E. TROLL, Ph.D.
Professor and Chair, Department of Psychology, University College, Rutgers University, New Brunswick

BARBARA F. TURNER, Ph.D.
Associate Professor of Education and Psychology, School of Education, University of Massachusetts, Amherst

MYRNA M. WEISSMAN, Ph.D.
Associate Professor of Psychiatry and Epidemiology, Yale University School of Medicine, and Director, Depression Research Unit, Connecticut Mental Health Center

GENDER AND DISORDERED BEHAVIOR
Sex Differences in Psychopathology

Part I

PERSPECTIVES

1

FEMALENESS, MALENESS AND BEHAVIOR DISORDERS IN NONHUMANS

ETHEL TOBACH

> The real history of the bee begins in the seventeenth century, with the discovery of the great Dutch savant, Swammerdam. It is well, however, to add this detail, but little known: before Swammerdam a Flemish naturalist named Clutius had arrived at certain important truths, such as the sole maternity of the queen and her possession of the attributes of both sexes, but he had left these unproven. Swammerdam founded the true methods of scientific investigation; he invented the microscope, contrived injections to ward off decay, was the first to dissect the bees, and by the discovery of the ovaries and the oviduct definitely fixed the sex of the queen, hitherto looked upon as a king; and threw the whole political scheme of the hive into most unexpected light by basing it upon maternity (Maeterlinck, 1903).

New knowledge continually impinges itself on the interpretation foisted by human values on animal behavior, but it rarely has such a dramatic effect as Swammerdam's discovery. The comparative study of different species, including the human species, is still dominated by anthropomorphism (the view of animals as models of human behavior) and zoomorphism (the view of people as significantly more similar than dissimilar from other animals*) (Tobach, 1976). Studies of the behavior of women and men also reflect societal values, and these are frequently justified by allusions to animal behavior (Tiger & Shepherd, 1975; Wilson, 1975). A discussion of the implications of research with animals for understanding human behavior disorders must deal with the consequences of these philosophical and societal phenomena.

---

* To simplify the writing, the word "animal" will refer to species other than humans.

RATIONALES FOR ANIMAL RESEARCH

For example, a curious situation in animal research complicates an analysis of the relevance of such research for understanding gender differences in behavioral disorders.* In the psychiatric literature much of the explanation offered for gender differences is based on hormonal functions of women in contrast to those of men. Animal studies dealing with behavior disorders generally use male subjects. The typical reason given for this procedure is that males do not have an estrous cycle. This is reminiscent of the statement that men are more suited for certain kinds of societal roles because they do not menstruate. So our societal conceptions of human behavior have influenced the direction of animal research.

Other aspects of the rationale for using animals rather than people for research in behavioral disorders are also relevant to this discussion. The usual reasons for such a choice are: (a) The history of the animal is easily

---

* The levels of integration approach (Schneirla, 1971; Tobach, 1970) to the issues in this chapter differentiates between the concepts of "sex" and "gender." There are five structural and functional expressions of organismic specialization in reproduction: chromosomal (including genetic processes involved; see McKusick & Ruddle, 1977; Wachtel et al., 1976); gonadal (neural and glandular variations related to the five aspects of reproduction discussed below); endocrine and exocrine (biochemical secretions that vary in proportion and type according to reproductive specialization); gamete production (carriers of different types of genetic configurations. e.g., ovum and sperm). These four expressions are found in various patterns and relationships in all animals including humans, and are generally referred to as "sex." Sex does not always mean female and male. In the case of some unicellular and lower invertebrates, organisms with different chromosomal configurations may fuse: "Femaleness" and "maleness" are not involved on this level of organismic organization. The fifth expression of specialization is that of "gender," which can only be applicable to people. This is the assignment of a societal role that is in some way related to sex but has nothing to do with reproduction. There are five phases of reproduction, each with related behavioral patterns: zygote formation (e.g., fertilization of ova by sperm; fusion of two different breeding strains of paramecia); incubation of the zygote (internally or externally to one or another of the sexes); birth of the offspring (establishment of individual identity of offspring); nurturance of the immature offspring (not present in all species); organismic social interaction particularly related to zygote formation (sex behavior). The assignment of women to desk jobs at lower salaries rather than to a machine shop in a technologically industrialized society is an example of gender—the assignment of a societal role based on "sex" but having nothing to do with reproduction. In animal social organizations behavioral differences in reproductive specializations are complexly derived from the integration of many physiological and biochemical processes in the context of developmental experiences (Lehrman, 1961); the role played is not "assigned." Sex differences in other aspects of behavior that are indirectly related to differences in reproductive function (e.g., play; responses to predators; approach to unfamiliar objects in familiar or unfamiliar situations) are similarly complexly derived but the behavior in such non-reproductive situations is not prescribed by the decisions of conspecifics based on reproductive characteristics.

controlled both in terms of individual experience and genetic background; (b) they can be studied throughout their lifetimes, which are usually shorter than those of humans; and (c) one can perform operations (e.g., biochemically, surgically, experientially) which could not be performed on people. Let us consider these.

The animal's history is usually considered relevant only insofar as its not having been used in other behavioral or related experiments. Other experiences, e.g., how it was reared, the behavioral characteristics of the litter in which it was born, how it was maintained before the experiment, are rarely considered significant. The strain of the animal or its taxonomic identity is being designated more frequently today; in previous years general descriptions such as "albino" or "hooded" were used. In increasing numbers of articles the source of the population (where purchased or bred) is being given. Nonetheless, the genetic history of the populations studied is usually considered of little importance. The use of animals in order to have subjects with well-defined histories does not seem to be supported in practice.

Also, little advantage is taken of the feasibility of studying animals throughout their life spans. Usually the effects of experimental manipulation during one stage of development are assayed at later stages of development (sexual maturity is a typical endpoint). Longitudinal lifetime studies are rare. However, the recent interest in gerontology and geriatrics has led to studies of longer duration with laboratory species.

As for the wider range of treatments available to the experimenter when dealing with animals rather than people, recent philosophical developments around which various citizens' groups have rallied have challenged the ethics of this rationale.

THE CONCEPT OF NORMALITY IN ANIMAL RESEARCH

The concept of disordered behavior in humans is derived in great part from the formulations of other processes, such as typicality, normality, orderliness, emotion, health and disease, or ease and dis-ease. How are these dealt with in animal studies?

Two concepts of normality, typicality, or orderliness are evident in animal research. One is derived from hereditarianism, that is, the premise that causal explanations of all behavior are ultimately reducible to genetic processes. Behavior is preprogramed, wired in, phylogenetically adaptive, encoded, and so on. To define the program, the behavioral repertoire of the animal is described in varying detail by different authors and termed an ethogram. Most of the features of the ethogram center around reproduction, social behavior, and predator-prey relationships. The behavioral program leads to the survival of the species and the individual. This is normal, typical, orderly, and healthy. When circumstances of catastrophic dimensions, such as social deprivation or other situations in which the programed responses are not expressible for extrinsic reasons, pertain, the program may be disrupted, and the behavior may become deviant, abnormal, atypical, and disordered.

The other concept arises from experimental design and practice. The effects of experimental manipulation are contrasted with the lack of experimental manipulation, the tacit assumption being that the behavior of animals not so treated is "normal, typical, and orderly." Interest in behavioral development has resulted in a number of reports of typical behavior, but no attempt has been made to derive criteria for normality, health, or ease in the animals studied.

EMOTION

The elucidation of emotion as a phenomenon, process, or construct through the study of animals has been more a reflection of the dimness of the present insights into human emotion than a beacon to those seeking answers. In a conference held in 1967 in which scientists from a variety of disciplines participated, and which concentrated on animal research primarily, several traditional formulations were found to be unchallenged: " (a) Emotion is an innately organized drive (instinctive); (b) anatomical relationships in the adult are equivalent to those at earlier stages in the development of emotional behavior; (c) emotional behavior in the hands of the experimentalist is still defined in operational terms rather than in terms of process; and (d) emotion is a disorganizing response or a disorganized response, primarily. In much of the work with emotional behavior, either phyletic or ontogenetic considerations, or both, are ignored. It is also evident that the laboratory is the typical ecological setting for most investigations of emotional behavior, and that when 'natural' behavior patterns are studied, the traditional 'instinctive' conceptualization prevails" (Tobach, 1969). A survey of three representative volumes more recently published reveals that the same formulations predominate in the consideration of research with animals in regard to emotion. (Arnold, 1970; Eibl-Eibesfeldt, 1971; Levi, 1975).

An alternate evolutionary and developmental view of emotion is derived from Schneirla's theory of biphasic processes underlying approach and withdrawal. The theory stems from a consideration of the relationships among phylogeny, ontogeny, and motivation ("causation of behavior"):

> . . . behavior, from its beginning in the primitive scintilla many ages ago, has been a decisive factor in natural selection. For the haunts and the typical niche of any organism must depend on what conditions it approaches and what it moves away from—these types of reaction thereby determine what future stimuli can affect the individual, its life span, and the fate of its species.
>
> The principle may be stated roughly as follows: *Intensity of stimulation basically determines the direction of reaction with respect to the source, and thereby exerts a selective effect on what conditions generally affect the organism.* This statement derived from the generalization that, for all organisms in early ontogenetic stages, *low intensities of stimulation tend to evoke approach reactions, high intensities withdrawal reactions with reference to the source* (Schneirla, 1971, p. 299).

Emotion evolved as a process in relationship to other phylogenetic and ontogenetic processes, such as approach-withdrawal. The well-known formulation of fight-flight, as well as the significance of bond formations in discussions of emotion, attest to this notion. The adjustments of individual organisms vary along a continuum extending from activities which promote the integrity of the individual (euphoric) to those which lead to the disintegration of the individual (dysphoric) (see Rioch, 1955; Tobach, 1970), within the level of organization and integration of the species and within the stage of development of the individual.

The concepts of euphoria and dysphoria are of adaptive significance (species related) as well as of adjustive significance (related to survival of the individual). For the individual, dysphoric behavior (in the case of animals) consists of not avoiding electric shock in an avoidance conditioning situation, not feeding under stress when being pushed out of a troop of monkeys, and self-mutilation when in social deprivation situations. In the case of humans, it is manifested by anorexia when depressed; also, suicide clearly does not promote integrity. In the case of the species, dysphoric behavior leads to negative selection for the individual which would soon disappear from the population, especially if it affects the individual so as to prevent reproduction. Dysphoric behavior of this type would include an animal's eating food that did not promote its health or the health of young which it was incubating or nurturing, or inability to detect a predator. However, there would always be the likelihood of the expression of some degree of dysphoria, or type of dysphoria, as well as euphoria, in most populations.

Although such dysphoric activities as tics, poor grooming interactions, and self-mutilations have been reported in various groups of mammals and primates studied in laboratories and natural habitats, these have been viewed as aberrations of behavior related to frustration or deviation of a drive, motivation, or instinct. The appearance of these behavior patterns might rather be viewed as the intensification of "normal" behavior patterns such as grooming, locomotion, or postural adjustments in response to social or situational stress. Stress in this instance might be related to intensity of stimulation to which approach-withdrawal processes are ineffective. When approach-withdrawal processes are functional, euphoric behavior, that is, behavior promoting the integrity of the organism, results.

The formulation of emotion according to these principles permits the study of these processes in all organisms, human and non-human, without anthropomorphism and zoomorphism. Each species expresses euphoria or dysphoria within the context of its level of hormonal and neural integration and organization, within its level of social organization, and in the pattern of its typical developmental history. A fight between two male fish is an intensified approach response in a positive-feedback situation. This analysis does not require any assumptions about intention to perpetuate the species or pass on its genetic material. The intensity of stimulation provided by the female and the male in the vicinity of the female, within the context of the fighting male's experience with animals of its own species, brings about the reaction to approach the one and withdraw from the other.

From these behavioral events in fish one cannot predict whether a teenage boy will or will not fight another boy who asks "his girl" to dance. In this situation the processes that result in a fight or no-fight are formed by a socialization process and a level of neural integration which produce a set of phenomena far removed from those produced in the fish. Nevertheless, the principles of approach-withdrawal in the context of phyletic and ontogenetic differences are useful in analyzing the behavior of both species and comparing them, without overlooking the differences or emphasizing the similarities (Tobach & Schneirla, 1971b).

BEHAVIORAL HEALTH AND DISEASES

The concepts of behavioral health and disease also reflect fundamental theoretical commitments on the part of the investigator. An often-heard formulation among those who bring nonlaboratory-bred animals into human settings is to evaluate the effects of such operations on the animals by asking: "Do they grow and reproduce successfully?" If so, the situation cannot be seriously disruptive for the species. Nonetheless, there has been some discussion about the deleterious effects of laboratory-generated "domestication" on "natural behavior" (Tobach, Adler, & Adler, 1973). Such arguments are derived from the notion that animals in such settings do not have the opportunity to display their instinctive behavior patterns which have proved phylogenetically adaptive. The "nature" of the laboratory animal, however, may be viewed as a variant of the population of conspecifics which are in their nonlaboratory environments. Laboratory species are populations with their own behavioral, physiological, and genetic characteristics. They are as valid a population for study as any other population. Laboratory rats are derived from *Rattus norvegicus*, for the most part, and they differ in some ways from those populations found in the streets of large cities all over the world. But in both cases, their health, or behavioral ease, is considered to be demonstrated by reproductive success of the population. Populations of animals that are studied in their natural habitats are most usually not described in terms of infection, pathological physiology, or morphology unless they are studied by scientists of those disciplines focusing on such phenomena (virologists, physiological ecologists, taxonomists, etc.). The same type of evidence of ease or health is tacitly accepted for all feral populations as for the laboratory populations.

A recent paper (Freeland, 1976) has suggested that disease affects behavior, and behavior affects disease within the processes described by sociobiological principles (Wilson, 1975). Basing his analysis on the dynamics of group organization derived from altruism (behavior designed to guarantee transmission of the genes of nearest relatives), Freeland concludes that group organization has evolved to permit the primate male most likely to be free of disease to mate with a female who is most likely to choose males that are least likely to bring new pathogens into the group. This suggestion requires research to substantiate the analysis as there are obvious problems with it. For example, the animal with a communicable viral infection and preclinical symptom status may infect the other animals during the fighting and interaction which leads to the success of one or another animal. It is important also to note that the disease processes under discussion are physiological, not behavioral. Nonetheless, Freeland's formulation demonstrates the impact of sociobiological thinking on concepts of disease.

The study of species other than humans, of course, not only has intrinsic merit in the general search for knowledge but clearly is a mark of the growing sophistication in human methods of understanding the world. The domestication of animals, their use in religious and other ritualized forms of dealing with the mysterious phenomena of nature and the value of animals as a source of labor are evidence of the ancient significance of the relationship between humans and animals. Such activities were responsible for much of the earliest knowledge about animals. But it was not until Darwin brought together a body of information and formulated the theory of evolution that the relationship between animals and people assumed a significant role in the growth of scientific knowledge. The second theory that had a profound effect on the use of animals in research was the formulation of the cell theory by Virchow (Simpson, Pittendrigh, & Tiffany, 1957), which states that all living systems arise from other living systems and the cell is the fundamental element of life, a unifying concept for the study of all living things. This theory is fundamental to all the life sciences. Facts gathered from research with many nonhuman species in biochemistry, anatomy, physiology, endocrinology, neurology, and other sciences form a protean substrate for studying human physiology and function.

It is understandable, then, that a psychiatrist states, "The rest of medicine has long used animal models to advance knowledge, and there is no logical reason why psychiatrists should not do the same" (McKinney, 1974). As examples he reviews the experiments of social deprivation in monkeys, separation phenomena in dogs (removing puppies from littermates), and learned helplessness in a variety of species (inability to learn to avoid shock because of previous experience with random shock which cannot be controlled by the animal's behavior). The resultant dysphoric behavior is considered analogous to human depression, and the author cites biochemical agents which have had salutory effects on the animals after such treatment. Extrapolating from these physiologically induced results in animals, the author then proposes that animals be used for socially induced rehabilitation procedures which could then be applied to humans.

It is difficult to accept these proposals in light of the nosological controversies in discussions of depression. Further, the implication of hormonal dysfunction in various types of depression would seem to indicate that research with animal models should seriously consider hormonal processes (Prange, Lipton, Nemeroff, & Wilson, 1977). Murphy (1976) also raises serious questions about animal models for studying depression, although he concludes that the research should be encouraged. He points out that, "Major limitations impeding the discovery of useful animal models come from our inexact understanding of the etiology and even of the precise phenomenology of the human disorders. . . . Available animal models for depression (e.g., the behavioral separation models, and pharmacologic models . . .) have some partial validity, but also have major limitations" (p. 271).

The need to consider the limitations to valid extrapolations from animal behavioral pathology to human psychopathology is echoed by a few writers (Broadhurst, 1973; Hinde, 1976; Zubin & Hunt, 1967). The majority of writers on the subject, however, under the impact of Lorenz and Tinbergen, find more to be gained than gainsayed from such endeavors, as can be seen in the following:

> The ethologist, on the other hand, brings a fresh, new appreciation of animal behavior, which can indeed be useful for interpreting the human behavioral mechanism (Serban, 1976, p. 2).

> I was struck by the overlap of subject matter between ethology and psychoanalysis. Both were interested in species-specific behavior, especially that meditating affectional bonds between parent and young and between mates; both were interested in the effect of early experience on later development, in conflict arising in social situations, in redirection of behavior, and in displacement activities (Bowlby, 1976, p. 28).

It is significant to note that in a footnote in the article by Bowlby cited above, he makes the following statement:

> It is recognized that, in the case of humans, separation from the father and deprivation of paternal care can also be of great importance. Since the role of the father in the development of a nonhuman primate is very different from what it is in the case of the human child, discussion of this variable is omitted from this paper (p. 29).

Additional support for the study of animals in order to understand human behavioral disorders comes from the geneticists. An example of the approach in this discipline is the work with audiogenic seizures in mice (Schlesinger, 1968). It was reported that rats subjected to key jangling would show a classical tonic-clonic convulsion. This led to experimental investigation which found the phenomenon in a variety of vertebrate species. The behavior was amenable to selective breeding techniques as well as to various chemical, nutritional, and experiential agents and situations. Schlesinger discusses it in regard to the phenomena and conceptualization of central nervous system excitability. He sees animals showing this behavior as "useful tool(s) for investigating genetically determined differences in central nervous system excitability. It is this possibility, as well as the fact that dilute, seizure-susceptible animals resemble human phenylketonurics in certain respects, which has prompted great interest in audiogenic seizures; it is hoped that these animals will come to serve as experimental prototypes for investigating the central nervous system correlates of this disease" (p. 273).

The value of studying organisms other than humans to understand genetic processes has been well documented in plants, bacteria, and many animals. The complexity of these processes has been frequently overlooked in attempts to understand behavior through application of those processes (Hirsch, 1967). This has also been true of physiological disease entities such as Kuru (Ehrman & Parsons, 1976) and pellagra (Chase, 1977). These two diseases were thought to be genetic in origin, but were discovered to be the result of viral transmission in the first case and faulty nutrition in the second.

Another example of the complexities of the relationship between genes and behavior is evident in the work done by Hamilton, Walter, Daniel, and Mestler (1969) on fish with XYY chromosomes and by Jacobs, Brunton, Melville, Brittain, and McClemont (1965) and Wiener, Sutherland, Bartholomew, and Hudson (1968) with men in prisons.

It is well-known that the chromosomal characteristics of fish are complicated and highly variable. It is in this family of vertebrates that sex role is changed by social factors as in reef fish (Fishelson, 1970; Robertson, 1972), and the difficulties of karyotyping fish to understand genetic processes are formidable. The roles of the Y and X chromosomes have been persistently investigated, and Japanese investigators have been well represented in this area of research. Medaka male fish ordinarily have XY chromosomes, but Yamamoto (1962) was able to produce males with YY chromosomes by treating young males with estrogen. In 1965, a group of researchers suggested that men with a double YY chromosome were likely to be aggressive and end up in prisons. As a result, Hamilton, et al. (1969) undertook to study the behavior of Yamamoto medaka fish: "The writers have observed unusually well-developed male secondary sex characters in YY male fish, *Oryzias latipes*. It seemed possible that the behavior of YY males might also be unusual, especially since men with double Y chromosomes (XYY) have been reported to be aggressive and to be much more common among men in prisons than in the population at large (Jacobs, et al., 1965; Wiener, et al., 1968)." Despite the fact that the data relating to men have since been the subject of much statistical controversy (Jarvik, 1976; Owen, 1972), the initial response of the press was to cite the animal data as supporting the human data (Stock, 1968). Although there was a profound reaction among scientists to the societal effects of this research (Beckwith & King, 1974), behavioral research with mice with double Y chromosomes continues (Selmanoff, Jumonville, Maxson, & Ginsburg, 1974; Selmanoff, Goldman, Maxson, and Ginsburg, 1977).

Jarvik (1976) points out that the general public and the scientific community seem more likely to accept the finding that deleterious behavioral effects are linked with the X chromosome (societally unacceptable behavioral characteristics in Turner and Klinefelter syndromes) than that unacceptable behavior is linked with the Y chromosome. Nonetheless, the issue remains one of understanding the relationship between genes and behavior. For example, aggression is also evidenced by female mammals, particularly when in nonestrous state and approached by males, or when with newly born young. One of the earlier hypotheses advanced was the effect of estrogen (Birch & Clark, 1946). More recently Svare and Gandelman (1976) have shown that the fighting behavior may be a function of stimulation provided by the suckling young, rather than levels of circulating estrogenic hormone or progesterone.

In a perceptive discussion of the relationship between the nature-nurture argument and its relevance to concepts of disease, Childs (1977) makes a strong plea for the medical practitioner to become more alert to genetic processes in disease. He bases this on the widely accepted idea that ultimately genes control the mechanisms contributing to processes which account for disease. But he recognizes that the proper way to approach the problem of genetics and disease is not in the individual but in the traditional population genetics approach: "An epidemiological approach might be the way to begin . . . to obtain the data necessary to understand the nature of the genetic contribution to such diseases as allergy, cancer, hypertension, gout, responses to drugs and mental illness, and other behavioral characteristics" (p. 11). Further, "neither genes nor environment 'cause' disease, it is simply that the organism is unsuited for adaptive action in one, or several, environments" (p. 16). "For example, phenylketonuria is an 'hereditary' disease, but without an 'environment' of excessive dietary phenylalanine there is no disease" (p. 6). Childs' concept of disease "recognizes disease as one part of a continuous distribution of adaptive states varying from robust good health to just short of death and reveals its connection with the biological and cultural structure of a society, transcending the conventional restrictive concept of etiology" p. 6).

GENDER DIFFERENCES

The concept of genetic destiny as a prime determiner of behavioral differences and particularly of gender differences has had a profound effect on research with animals in regard to sex differences, as well as on the inferences made about gender differences from animal work. As indicated above, most of the research done with animals in regard to emotional behavior has been with males (Hutzell & Knutson, 1972; Knutson & Hynan, 1972; Weiss, Glazer, & Poborecky, 1976). Further, when males and females are studied, the cyclical nature of hormonal functions in both sexes is overlooked despite experimental results which would seem to indicate the possible relevance of such biochemical factors. For example, in experiments on taste threshold the animals were maintained in constant light which affects the cycle in females (effects on male gonadal function have not been studied): yet significant differences were found between females and males (Hamilton & Timmons, 1976; Krecek, Novakova & Sibral, 1972). A survey of introductory psychology textbooks revealed that in all the methods and techniques reviewed as inducing disordered behavior (experimental neurosis [Pavlovian]; conditioned emotional response [Skinnerian]; social deprivation; crowding; avoidance conditioning), the sex of the animals was never discussed, although all books discuss the value of animal work in the elucidation of human behavior, and give significant space to gender differences in abnormal behavior.

There are some outstanding exceptions to this state of affairs. Gray, Drewett, and Laljee (1975) have continued the initial investigations of Burke and Broadhurst (1966) on the differences between females and males in the open-field situation. When rats are placed in an unfamiliar place, they tend to become inactive and urinate and defecate. With repeated exposures to this previously unfamiliar area, the eliminative behavior decreases and activity increases. Male rats usually defecate more and locomote less than females. These investigators have been exploring the hormonal processes related to this behavior which has been considered analogous to fearfulness, although this has been challenged (Birke & Archer, 1975; Tobach & Schneirla, 1971a). Other investigators have found differences in the behavior of female and male rats either treated with dexamethasone (Joffe, Mulick, & Peterson, 1976) or subjected to stress during earlier stages of development (Syme, 1974) when they were observed in an open-field situation. In the first case the role of hormones was investigated; in the second, it was not. Gray (1977) has also been investigating the differences in avoidance conditioning in female and male mice.

The relevance of these differences to the often cited gender differences in psychopathology is indirect at best and irrelevant at worst. The rationale for much of the work, sometimes explicit but more often implicit, is that the circulating hormones have differential effects on different parts of the brain. This in turn is expressed in differences in thresholds for stress or change and in differences in response patterns to such changes. Hormones, as biochemical entities, are more clearly related to the genetic processes which differ in the two sexes. Accordingly, the indebtedness of behavioral difference to genetic destiny is apparent.

Genetic destiny is expressed not only in writings about gender differences in behavior (Clancy & Gove, 1974; Gershon, Bunney, Leckman, Van Eerdewegh, & DeBauche, 1976; Lerner, 1974; Noyes & Kolb, 1963) but also in discussions of the evolutionary processes which have brought about sex and gender differences (Crook, 1972; Hutt, 1974), as well as in discussions about the inferences about human behavior gathered from animal behavior (Cleghorn, 1968; Sugarman, 1977). Most explicit in this respect are the comments by Serban (1976): "One of the present cultural contentions is that the woman throughout history has been dominated and exploited by man. This situation allegedly started with the physical superiority of man and continued because of a 'general male conspiracy' to control women for their own economical and social benefit. The evolutionary biological findings do not support this conclusion" (p. 282-283). Rather it is the need for women to be able to take care of the children that has been supported by animal studies as the explanation of male domination of women.

> The females take care of the offspring, while the males, based on a hierarchical dominance order, control the members' interaction, protect the territory, and look for better feeding grounds. . . . Primitive human society follows the same patterns, while in more advanced ones, the social differentiation between sexes becomes less well defined. . . . Nevertheless, the basic differential function remains un-

changed. Women still are in charge of child rearing while men are involved in the policy and strategy of defending territory and providing food. . . . Indeed, the psychopathology of modern marriage appears to be produced by the lack of clear identification of sex roles in family interaction (Serban, 1976, p. 283).

The relationships among the five aspects of sex and gender is extremely complicated, and the significance of societal, cultural factors in determining what is to be considered aberrant and what is considered normal is exemplified by the following quotation from Serban (1976) and recent data from the Dominican Republic. Serban states: "The reevaluation by ethologists of the old concept of instinct in the light of its environmental influences, namely, that of misdirection of instinctual patterns when activated by inappropriate social releasers at critical periods for that instinct, offered us a plausible understanding of some sexual deviations" (p. 281).

The definition of sexual deviation is at present a controversial discussion in our culture. It is interesting to note how another culture responds to a change in gender role. In the Dominican Republic, a group of individuals with a common ancestry has been found to possess a steroid imbalance which results in profound changes in secondary sex characteristics at puberty. These individuals are usually considered to be "females" at birth, and therefore assigned gender roles as women (Imperato-McGinley, et al., 1974). At puberty, however, they evidence all the secondary sex characteristics of males and are able to assume male gender roles in the society, although they are physiologically not capable of inseminating their wives. The community adjusts to those who undergo gender role change as well as to those who do not. In a follow-up study by an anthropologist (Vélez, 1977), it was found that the first factor that had to be dealt with was the effect of the endocrine screening procedure which made it possible to determine at birth whether the "female" child was likely to become a "male'" at puberty. Whether the family would continue to do what it had always done or modify its socialization of the child was dependent on economic factors, on the status of the family in the village or township in which it lived, and on other factors that remain to be analyzed.

The many studies done on changes in reproductive function as a result of early administration of steroids to animals would not have shed light on any of the phenomena described in the Dominican Republic population. The effects of human observation on the behavior of animals have been well documented, but in no case can the reproductive processes of the animals undergo a change because of the knowledge gained by humans, unless the humans bring about those changes. The reproductive processes of the humans described above are not now being treated so that the gender role change will be accompanied by reproductive changes. However, the variability in gender role change and response of the community is not equaled in any population of animals, including primates.

Despite the limitations imposed on inferences by the significant phyletic differences between humans and other animals, one must carefully evaluate the possibility of significant information being gathered from such studies beyond the simple fact of the necessity for knowledge. Two opposing theoretical positions support the view that the study of animal behavior has much to contribute to the understanding of human behavior. They are the hereditarian position and the integrationist position (Schneirla, 1971) referred to above. Between the two are the "interactionist" and "epigenetic" theories of behavior. All are derived from the fundamental apposition of two concepts: nature-nurture; heredity-environment; instinctive-learned; innate-acquired, and other such terms. The consequences of these views for consideration of gender differences and sex differences are reflected in the research rationale, methods, and interpretations of comparative studies of behavior.

The usual dichotomy between the so-called ethologists and environmentalists (sometimes referred to as the European and American schools; ethological and psychological schools; ethological and behaviorist schools) is no longer viable. Beginning with an article in 1966, and continuing with a paper in 1975, Skinner has made it clear that his schema for contingency as the fundamental process in ontogeny and phylogeny of behavior is compatible with Lorenz's (1965) concept of the preprogramed limitation of the modification of behavior. This rapprochement has been underscored by the recent article by Herrnstein (1977) in which he states: "Thus refined, behaviorism appears to merge with the main lines of ethology as a more complete science of behavior than either one alone has been" (p. 593). (See Tobach 1976.) Accordingly, the two remaining schools are those of the ethologists or hereditarians and the integrationists.

The hereditarian view has been explicated repeatedly throughout this chapter. The integrationist view has been referred to in the work of Schneirla primarily. This view rests on the concept of level of integration and organization (Schneirla, 1971; Tobach, 1972). This concept of a hierarchical arrangement of matter, including animate and inanimate matter, is further derived from a reliance on historicity, change, and process. Integral to the concept is the phylogenetic and ontogenetic history of any organism, as well as the hierarchical organismic ordering or structure (molecules, enzymes, cells, tissues, organs, systems, organism) and function (biochemical and biophysical phenomena, physiological phenomena, behavioral phenomena, social phenomena, and ecological phenomena) as well as the hierarchical ordering of behavior processes (levels of modification of behavior, levels of social organization, levels of cognition).

For example, an individual organism with a particular configuration of biochemical history (genes), in a particular species-typical environment during all stages of development, is likely to develop behavioral, morphological, and physiological characteristics, that are expressions of those biochemical systems, called genes. The demonstration of the gene's existence lies in the expression of the gene's function in a variety of situations. These will be different for different species and for different stages of development, but comparisons are possible as long as the similarities are not overemphasized while the differences are overlooked. The value of such comparative studies is the possible derivation of generalizations and principles which will help organize explanations of process and causality. One example of such a principle is that of the approach-withdrawal theory (see above). Another is the concept of reciprocal stimulation proposed by Schneirla as the fundamental process whereby bonds are formed between members of the same species. The stimulation may occur at many levels. For example, it may be that the feeding of one organism (A) by organism (B) not only stimulates organism A, but for organism B also provides relief of tension from the gut or other organ which produces the food given to B, as in the case of ants in an ant colony, or a nursing situation between a mammal and its offspring. The type of bond formed by such reciprocal stimulation is dependent on the level of organization and integration of the nervous system, endocrine system, and level of plasticity of behavior. Plasticity of behavior is defined in terms of the ability to receive a variety of stimuli of different energy forms (complexity of photic reception), to store and integrate experience, to project consequences of behavior and store such consequences, to initiate and solve problems in regard to interaction with the environment as well as with other organisms, conspecifics or heterospecifics. The species which are most able to show such plasticity are able to form bonds that do not have a base in reciprocal stimulation of particular sensory modalities; rather such bonds can be formed through language, symbolic relationships or economic exchange.

In all these bond formations the physiological levels are functioning, as are all other levels, and the history of the behavior of the individual on all those levels is pertinent. This is equivalent to the relationship among the five aspects of reproductive behavior and specializations for reproduction known as sex. Although the physiological, hormonal, and other levels are obviously at work, the dominant relationship of behavior to the social level of organization is evident in consideration of the peak of that hierarchy, gender.

However, the concept of levels suggests that the causal explanation of events on any one level will require the integration of preceding, subsumed levels of integration at lower levels. For example, if a child has experienced certain treatment in a particular societal setting and then evidences behavior that is not acceptable to society, analyses on all levels subsumed by the societal level would have to be made in order to understand the psychosocial problem presented.

The levels concept also prevents the scientist from trying to predict from one level of organization to another. Knowing that circulating hormones affect different parts of the brain in various fashions is not sufficient to predict the gender role to be undertaken by an individual in the Dominican Republic sample.

These considerations make it possible to evaluate the contributions of studies with animals to the understanding of gender differences in behavior disorders. Beginning primarily with the females and males of vertebrates, one becomes aware that, for the most part, biochemical and biophysical phenomena (related to sex and reproduction) are most amenable to generalization across species. The second inference one can make is that, beyond that, the answer to the relationship between gender and psychopathology lies only in the study of human beings and the ways in which they function in regard to gender and society.

REFERENCES

ARNOLD, M. (Ed.). Feelings and Emotions. New York: Academic Press, 1970.

BECKWITH, J. & KING, J. The XYY syndrome: A dangerous myth. New Scientist, 1974, 474-476.

BIRCH, H. G. & CLARK, G. Hormonal modification of social behavior. II. The effects of sex-hormone administration on the social dominance status of the female-castrate chimpanzee. Psychosomatic Medicine, 1946, 8, 320-321.

BIRKE, L. I. A. & ARCHER, J. Open-field behavior of oestrous and dioestrous rats: Evidence against an "emotionality" interpretation. Animal Behavior, 1975, 23, 509-512.

BOWLBY, J. Human personality development in an ethological light. In G. Serban and A. Kling (Eds.), Animal Models in Human Psychobiology. New York: Plenum Press, 1976.

BROADHURST, P. L. Animal studies bearing on abnormal behavior. In H. J. Eysenck (Ed.), *Handbook of Abnormal Psychology*. London: Pitman, 1973.

BURKE, A. W. & BROADHURST, P. L. Behavioral correlates of the oestrous cycle in the rat. *Nature*, 1966, 209, 223-224.

CHASE, A. *The Legacy of Malthus*. New York: Alfred A. Knopf, 1977.

CHILDS, B. Persistent echoes of the nature-nurture argument. *American Journal of Human Genetics*, 1977, 29, 1-13.

CLANCY, K. & GOVE, W. Sex differences in mental illness: An analysis of response bias in self-reports. *American Journal of Sociology*, 1974, 80, 205-216.

CLEGHORN, R. A. Endocrine order and disorder basic to mind. In C. Rupp (Ed.), *Mind as a Tissue*. New York: Hoeber, 1968.

CROOK, J. H. Darwinism and the sexual politics of primates. *Social Science Information*, 1972, 12, 7-28.

EHRMAN, L. & PARSONS, P. A. *The Genetics of Behavior*. Sunderland, Mass.: Sinauer Associates, 1976.

EIBL-EIBESFELDT, I. *Love and Hate*. New York: Holt, Rinehart & Winston, 1971.

FISHELSON, L. Protogynous sex reversal in the fish. *Anthias squamipinnis* (Teleostei, Anthiidae) regulated by the presence or absence of a male fish. *Nature*, 1970, 227, 90-91.

FREELAND, W. J. Pathogens and the evolution of primate sociality. *Biotropica*, 1976, 8, 12-24.

GERSHON, E. S., BUNNEY, JR., W. E., LECKMAN, F. J., VAN EERDEWEGH, M., & DEBAUCHE, B. A. The inheritance of affective disorders: A review of data and of hypotheses. *Behavior Genetics*, 1976, 6, 227-261.

GRAY, J. A., DREWETT, R. F., & LALJEE, B. Effects of neonatal castration and testosterone injection on adult open-field behavior in rats with atypical sex difference in defecation. *Animal Behavior*, 1975, 23, 773-778.

GRAY, P. Effect of the estrous cycle on conditioned avoidance in mice. *Hormones and Behavior*, 1977, 8, 235-241.

HAMILTON, J. B., WALTER, R. O., DANIEL, R. M., & MESTLER, G. E. Competition for mating between ordinary and supermale Japanese Medaka fish. *Animal Behavior*, 1969, 17, 168-176.

HAMILTON, L. W. & TIMMONS, C. R. Sex differences in response to taste and post-ingestive consequences of sugar solutions. *Physiology and Behavior*, 1976, 17, 221-225.

HERRNSTEIN, R. J. The evolution of behaviorism. *American Psychologist*, 1977, 32, 593-603.

HINDE, R. A. The use of differences and similarities in comparative psychopathology. In G. Serban and A. Kling (Eds.), *Animal Models in Human Psychobiology*. New York: Plenum Press, 1976.

HIRSCH, J. Behavior-genetic, or "experimental" analysis: The challenge of science versus the lure of technology. *American Psychologist*, 1967, 22, 118-130.

HUTT, C. Sex: What's the difference? *New Scientist*, 1974, 62, 405-407.

HUTZELL, R. R. & KNUTSON, J. F. A comparison of shock-elicited fighting and shock-elicited biting in rats. *Physiology and Behavior*, 1972, 8, 477-480.

IMPERATO-McGINLEY, J., GUERRERO, L., GAUTIER, T., & PETERSON, R. E. Steroid 5α-Reductase deficiency in man: An inherited form of male pseudohermaphroditism. *Science*, 1974, 186, 1213-1215.

JACOBS, P. A., BRUNTON, M., MELVILLE, M. M., BRITTAIN, R. P., & McCLEMONT, W. F. Aggressive behavior, mental subnormality, and the XYY male. *Nature*, 1965, 208, 1351.

JARVIK, L. F. Genetic modes of transmission relevant to psychopathology. In M. A. Sperber and L. F. Jarvik (Eds.), *Psychiatry and Genetics*. New York: Basic Books, 1976.

JOFFE, J. M., MULICK, J. A., & PETERSON, J. M. Sex difference in the effect of desamethasone on open-field behavior in rats: Gonadal hormones. *Physiology and Behavior*, 1976, 16, 543-546.

KNUTSON, J. F. & HYNAN, M. T. Influence of upright posture on shock-elicited aggression in rats. *Journal of Comparative and Physiological Psychology*, 1972, 81, 297-306.

KRECEK, J., NOVAKOVA, V., & SIBRAL, K. Sex differences in the taste preference for a salt solution in the rat. *Physiology and Behavior*, 1972, 8, 183-188.

LEHRMAN, D. S.: Gonadal hormones and parental behavior in birds and infrahuman mammals. In William C. Young (Ed.), *Sex and Internal Secretion*. Baltimore: Williams & Wilkins Co., 1961.

LERNER, H. E. The hysterical personality: A "woman's disease." *Comprehensive Psychiatry*, 1974, 15, 157-164.

LEVI, L., Emotions: Their parameters and measurement. New York: Raven Press, 1975.

LORENZ, K. Evolution and modification of behavior. Chicago: University of Chicago Press, 1965.

MAETERLINCK, M. *The Life of the Bee*. New York: Dodd & Mead, 1903.

McKINNEY, JR., W. T. Animal models in psychiatry. *Perspectives in Biology and Medicine*, 1974, 17, 529-541.

McKUSICK, V. A. & RUDDLE, F. H. The status of the gene map of the human chromosomes. *Science*, 1977, 196, 390-405.

MURPHY, D. L. Animal models for human psychopathology: Observations from the vantage point of clinical psychopharmacology. In G. Serban and A. Kling (Eds.), *Animal Models in Human Psychobiology*. New York: Plenum Press, 1976.

NOYES, A. P. & KOLB, L. C. *Modern Clinical Psychiatry*. New York: W. B. Saunders, 1963.

PRANGE, JR., A. J., LIPTON, A. M., NEMEROFF, C. B., & WILSON, I. C. The role of hormones in depression. *Life Sciences*, 1977, 20, 1305-1318.

OWEN, D. R. The 47, XYY male: A review. *Psychological Bulletin*, 1972, 78, 209-233.

RIOCH, D. McK. Certain aspects of conscious phenomena and their neural correlates. *American Journal of Psychiatry*, 1955, 11, 810-817.

ROBERTSON, D. R. Social control of sex reversal in a coral-reef fish. *Science*, 1972, 177, 1007-1009.

SCHLESINGER, K. Experimentally induced seizures in mice. In C. Rupp (Ed.), *Mind as a Tissue*. New York: Hoeber Medical Division, Harper & Row, 1968.

SCHNEIRLA, T. C. *Selected Writings*. L. R. Aronson, E. Tobach, J. S. Rosenblatt, and D. S. Lehrman (Eds.). San Francisco: Freeman Press, 1971.

SELMANOFF, M. K., JUMONVILLE, J. E., MAXSON, S. C., & GINSBURG, B. E. Evidence for a Y chromosomal contribution to an aggressive phenotype in inbred mice. *Nature*, 1975, 253, 529-530.

SELMANOFF, M. K., GOLDMAN, B. D., MAXSON, S. C., & GINSBURG, B. E. Correlated effects of the Y-chromosome of mice on developmental changes in testosterone levels and intermale aggression. *Life Science*, 1977, 20, 359-366.

SERBAN, G. New perspectives in psychiatry. In G. Serban and A. Kling (Eds.), *Animal Models in Human Psychobiology*. New York: Plenum Press, 1976.

SIMPSON, G. G., PITTENDRIGH, C. S., & TIFFANY, L. H. (Eds.). *Life: An Introduction to Biology*. New York: Harcourt, Brace, & World, Inc., 1957.

SKINNER, B. F. The phylogeny and ontogeny of behavior. *Science*, 1966, 153, 1205-1213.

SKINNER, B. F. The shaping of phylogenic behavior. *Journal of the Experimental Analysis of Behavior*, 1975, 24, 117-120.

STOCK, R. W. The XYY and the criminal. *The New York Times*, October 29, 1968. (Sunday Magazine Section).

SUGARMAN, M. Paranatal influences on maternal-infant attachment. *American Journal of Orthopsychiatry*, 1977, 47, 407-421.

SVARE, B. & GANDELMAN, R. Suckling stimulation induces aggression in virgin female mice. *Nature*, 1976, 260, 606-608.

SYME, L. A. Influence of age and sex on the behavior of rats deprived of the rearing response. *Developmental Psychobiology*, 1974, 8, 35-39.

TIGER, L. & SHEPHERD, J. *Women in the Kibbutz*. New York: Harcourt, Brace, & Jovanovich, 1975.

TOBACH, E. Introduction to experimental approaches to the study of emotional behavior. *Annals of the New York Academy of Sciences*, 1969, 159, 623-624.

TOBACH, E. Some guidelines to the study of the evolution and development of emotion. In L. R. Aronson, E. Tobach, D. S. Lehrman and J. S. Rosenblatt (Eds.), *Development and Evolution of Behavior*. San Francisco: W. H. Freeman & Co., 1970, pp. 238-253.

TOBACH, E. The meaning of the cryptanthroparion. In L. Ehrman, G. S. Omenn, and E. Caspari (Eds.), *Genetics, Environment and Behavior*. New York: Academic Press, 1972.

TOBACH, E. Evolution of behavior and the comparative method. *International Journal of Psychology*, 1976, 11, 185-201.

TOBACH, E. & SCHNEIRLA, T. C. Eliminative responses in mice and rats and the problem of "emotionality." In L. R. Aronson, E. Tobach, D. S. Lehrman, and J. S. Rosenblatt (Eds.), *Selected Writings of T. C. Schneirla*. San Francisco: W. H. Freeman & Co., 1971. (a)

TOBACH, E. & SCHNEIRLA, T. C. The biopsychology of social behavior in animals. In L. R. Aronson, E. Tobach, D. S. Lehrman and J. S. Rosenblatt (Eds.), *Selected Writings of T. C. Schneirla*. San Francisco: W. H. Freeman & Co., 1971. (b)

TOBACH, E., ADLER, H. E., & ADLER, L. L. Comparative psychology at issue. *Annals of the New York Academy of Sciences*, 1973, 223, 1-198.

VÉLEZ, S. M. *Gender Role of Male Pseudohermaphrodites in the Dominican Republic*. Master of Arts dissertation, Hunter College, the City University of New York, 1977.

WACHTEL, S. S., KOO, G. C., BREG, W. R., THALER, H. T., DILLARD, G. M., ROSENTHAL, I. M., DOSIK, H., GERALD, P. S., SAENGER, P., NEW, M., LIEBER, E., & MILLER, O. J. Serologic detection of a Y-linked gene in XX males and XX true hermaphrodites. *The New England Journal of Medicine*, 1976, 295, 750-754.

WIENER, S., SUTHERLAND, G., BARTHOLOMEW, A. A., & HUDSON, B. XYY males in a Melbourne prison. *Lancet*, 1968, 1, 150.

WEISS, J., GLAZER, H. I., & POBORECKY, L. A. Coping behavior and neurochemical changes in rats: An alternative explanation for the original "learned helplessness" experiments. In G. Serban and A. Kling (Eds.), *Animal Models in Human Psychobiology*. New York: Plenum Press, 1976.

WILSON, E. O. *Sociobiology: The New Synthesis*. Cambridge, Mass.: The Belknap Press, Harvard University Press, 1975.

YAMAMOTO, T. Hormonic factors affecting gonadal differentiation in fish. *General and Comparative Endocrinology*, 1962, 1, 341-345.

ZUBIN, J. & HUNT, H. F. Preface. In J. Zubin and H. F. Hunt (Eds.), *Comparative Psychopathology—Animal and Human*. New York: Grune & Stratton, 1967.

2

SEX DIFFERENCES IN THE EPIDEMIOLOGY OF MENTAL DISORDER: EVIDENCE AND EXPLANATIONS

WALTER R. GOVE

The history of science has shown that an essential ingredient in the development of science is the grouping of phenomena under investigation into homogenous categories (Kuhn, 1970). Different classification schemes often yield different results and different conclusions. In the investigation of the relationship between any variable and mental illness, perhaps the most basic question that must be resolved is what is meant by mental illness.

This paper will explore sex differences in the rates of mental illness. It will focus first on boys and girls and then on adult men and women. The early attempts of Dohrenwend and Dohrenwend (1965, 1969) and Manis (1968) to clarify these relationships among adults produced inconsistent and contradictory results. Probably the major reason that there are contradictory results is that, as Scheff (1966) has so cogently argued, mental illness is treated by society as a residual category into which diverse and unrelated disorders have been grouped. Most sociologists who have looked at mental illness have, in fact, simply looked at the incidence or prevalence of psychiatric treatment. To treat all phenomena that receive a psychiatric label as the same disorder makes about as much sense as a doctor treating all persons admitted to a general hospital (including those admitted to the psychiatric ward) as suffering from the same disease.

In contrast, in this paper, mental illness will be treated as a fairly

---

The research for this paper was supported in part by NSF Grant #73-05455A01.

specific phenomenon—a disorder that involves personal discomfort (as indicated by distress, anxiety, depression, etc.) and/or mental disorganization (as indicated by confusion, thought blockage, motor retardation, and, in the more extreme cases, by hallucinations and delusions) that is not caused by an organic or toxic condition. The two major categories that fit this definition are the neurotic disorders and the functional psychoses. The chief characteristic of the neurotic disorders is anxiety in the absence of psychotic disorganization. The functional psychoses (schizophrenia, involutional psychotic reaction, manic-depressive reaction, psychotic depressive reaction and paranoid reaction) are psychotic disorders with no (known) organic cause (American Psychiatric Association, 1968).

There are two other categories which also fit this definition that are relatively infrequently used. The transient situational disorders are acute symptomatic responses to overwhelming situations where there is no underlying personal disturbance. When the situational stress diminishes, so do the symptoms. This diagnosis is applied mainly to children and adolescents but it is also occasionally used with adults. The other category is comprised of the psychophysiological disorders, which are characterized by somatic symptoms that appear to be the consequence of emotional tension, although the person may sometimes be unaware of the emotional stress. The psychophysiologic disorders do not fit within the definition of mental illness being used here as clearly as the other disorders. However, they are included because (a) they are functional disorders, and (b) they do reflect a fair amount of distress, albeit in a somewhat masked form. There are a number of reasons for grouping these disorders together under a relatively narrow definition of mental illness. First, there is a similarity in symptomatology: Persons in all these diagnostic categories are typically severely distressed. Second, these disorders respond to the same forms of therapy, namely drug therapy and psychotherapy. Third, cross-cultural and historical evidence suggests that the concept of mental illness does not typically include the disorders we are excluding.

There are two frequently used diagnostic categories that do not fit under the definition of mental illness being used—the personality disorders and the acute and chronic brain syndromes. The brain syndromes are caused by a physical condition, either brain damage or toxins, and are not functional disorders. Most investigators clearly believe it is important to distinguish between the brain syndromes and the disorders we are classifying as mental illness. We should note, however, that the brain syndromes make up approximately 25% of the first admissions to public mental hospitals, a fact which emphasizes the need to distinguish between the incidence of psychiatric treatment and (types of) mental illness.

Persons with a personality disorder do not experience personal discomfort, being neither anxious nor distressed, nor are they suffering from any form of psychotic disorganization. They are viewed as mentally ill because they do not conform to social norms and are usually forced into treatment because their behavior is disruptive to others. These persons are characterized by aggressive, impulsive, goal-directed behavior which is either antisocial or asocial in nature and creates serious problems with (and for) others (American Psychiatric Association, 1968; Dohrenwend, 1975; Klein & Davis, 1969; Rowe, 1970). Not only are the symptoms associated with the personality disorders different from those associated with mental illness (as defined here), but the forms of therapy effective in the treatment of mental illness are not effective in the treatment of the personality disorders. Data from nonwestern societies are consistent with the distinction between the personality disorders and what I am labeling mental illness. According to these data, although there are persons in nonwestern societies who manifest the behavior that would lead to a diagnosis of a personality disorder in our society, and such persons are viewed as deviants, they are not viewed as ill, and shamans and healers do not believe that such behavior can be cured or changed (Murphy, 1976). In fact, it is only recently that the personality disorders have come to be considered within the domain of psychiatry (e.g., Robbins, 1966), a fact which probably should be attributed to historical accident and the successful entrepreneurship of the psychiatric profession (Gove, 1976).

Almost all psychiatric patients are classified under the diagnostic categories we have discussed here. Three remaining categories—"mental deficiency," "without mental disorder," and "undiagnosed"—are largely self-explanatory, very infrequently used, and not relevant to this chapter.

In this chapter the term mental illness refers to a functional disorder in which there is manifestation of distress and sometimes psychotic disorganization. The reader should understand quite clearly that under this definition not all persons treated in a psychiatric facility are "mentally ill." It is not important whether one agrees that it is correct to exclude the personality disorders and the brain syndromes from an overall concept of mental illness. What is important is to recognize that it is necessary to distinguish between mental illness, as defined here, and the other disorders.

We will now turn to a discussion of mental illness among children.

A COMPARISON OF RATES OF MENTAL ILLNESS AMONG BOYS AND GIRLS*

A review of the literature on both the biological attributes of boys and girls and the social expectations they confront leads to the conclusion that (a) life tends to be more stressful for young boys than for young girls, but (b) with advancing age the sex difference in experienced stress tends to disappear, and by late adolescence the situation of girls appears to be at least as stressful, if not more stressful, than that of boys. Although this pattern is consistently supported by the literature, the pattern itself has gone virtually unnoticed, with the partial exception of Bardwick (1971). We will begin with a statement of why this pattern occurs. Then, on the assumption that these stress differences should be reflected in rates of mental illness, we will look at national data on persons receiving psychiatric treatment in four different settings—public mental hospitals, private mental hospitals, general hospitals, and outpatient clinics.

Young Boys and Girls

One of the clearest problems confronting young boys is this: Their intellectual and physical development is slower than that of girls, but they are expected to perform as well as girls. Kagan and Lewis (1965) found girls to be ahead of boys developmentally even at the age of six months, and throughout the first year males manifest a greater vulnerability to stress and trauma (Bentzen, 1963). Perhaps most of the evidence on sex differences in development comes from studies of language acquisition. Virtually all the evidence indicates that girls not only say their first word sooner and are able to articulate at an earlier age than boys, but once having reached this stage, they tend to progress verbally at a more rapid rate than boys. Parallel differences appear in perception, cognition, and emotions (Anastasi, 1958; Bardwick, 1971; Bentzen, 1963; Kagan & Lewis, 1965; Maccoby, 1966; McCarthy, 1953; Sapir, 1966; Terman & Tyler, 1954; Thompson, 1962; Witkin, Dyk, Faterson, Goodenough, & Kaup, 1962). In short, as Bentzen (1963) states, "at the chronological age of six . . . girls are approximately 12 months ahead of boys in developmental age; by the time they are nine years of age this difference has increased to about 18 months" (p. 97). The only area where girls do not tend to surpass boys is in spatial and mechanical reasoning. But, as Bardwick (1971) notes, there is not much demand for this skill in the elementary grades.

This developmental difference suggests that boys would experience more difficulty than girls in the academic role in the elementary grades.

---

*This section on children is adopted, with some modification, from Gove and Herb (1974).

The evidence uniformly indicates that this is the case. For example, Mills (1947) found that in the first three grades, 46.1% of the boys showed articulatory errors as compared to 28.3% of the girls. In a study of referrals to clinics for reading disabilities, Kopel and Geerded (1933) found that 78% of the referrals were male. Bentzen (1963), in a study of 28 elementary schools (grades 1-7), reported that approximately three times as many boys as girls were referred for language disorders and vision, hearing, and speech defects, and two times as many boys as girls were referred for reading problems (see Gates, 1961; Sarason, 1959).

It is likely that most parents are not particularly aware of these developmental differences and that they generally expect boys to perform as well as girls. Furthermore, it is clear that in our public school system there is little or no recognition of the developmental age differential between the sexes (Bentzen, 1963). Thus, it would appear that boys experience a greater difference between their ability and the expectations of others than do girls, and it should follow that boys experience more stress than girls.

A second factor which we feel probably creates problems for boys is their aggressiveness. Virtually all the evidence indicates that boys have a lower frustration threshold, that they are more impulsive and more aggressive* and that they get into quarrels and fights more often than girls (e.g., Bardwick, 1971; Cohen, 1966; Hartup & Zook, 1960; Maccoby, 1966; Santrock, 1970; Scott, 1958; Sears, 1961; Sears, Maccoby, & Levin, 1957; Terman & Tyler, 1954). Such behavior creates problems for parents and teachers (e.g., Bardwick, 1971), and teachers view boys as more troublesome, seeing them as more likely to get into arguments and fights and generally as being defiant, rude, cruel, and bullying (Davidson & Lang, 1960; Scott, 1958; Terman & Tyler, 1954). It would seem that boys would be more likely to get into conflicts with parents and teachers because of their aggressiveness** and that this, in turn, would increase the amount of stress they experience.

---

*Normatively appropriate verbal responses aimed at enforcing rules, which Sears (1961, p. 471) has referred to as "prosocial aggression," are perhaps more common among girls, but in our view it is misleading to label such behavior aggression.

**Sears and Feldman (1966) indicate that, controlling for achievement, there is a trend for teachers to favor girls in grading and in making other evaluations. Meyer and Thompson (1970) found that teachers display significantly greater disapproval of boys and Goodenough (1933) found that more disciplinary actions are directed toward boys and that boys are usually handled more harshly than girls (also see Davidson & Lang, 1960; Lippitt & Gold, 1959). Similarly, teachers see girls as more responsible and girls receive more affection, praise, and companionship from their parents while boys are subjected to more physical punishment and achievement demands (Bronfenbrenner, 1961).

A third factor creating problems for young boys is the character of their sex role. The literature consistently indicates that sex role expectations are more stringent for young boys than for young girls. At an early age the boy learns that he is expected to be masculine and that he must earn his masculine identity. In contrast, young girls are allowed and sometimes encouraged to succeed in traditionally masculine activities, and it is only in adolescence that behaving in a feminine manner becomes a serious issue (e.g., Bardwick, 1971; Brown, 1958; Cohen, 1966; Hartley, 1959-60; Hartup & Zook, 1960; Hartup, Moore, & Sager, 1963; Kagan & Moss, 1962; Maccoby, 1966; Rabban, 1950). As Bardwick (1971) states, "girls can be tomboys without undue notice, (but) boys can never be sissies" (p. 92).

Furthermore, not only is the range of appropriate behavior narrower for young boys, but they are also more likely to find it difficult to acquire and maintain appropriate sex role behaviors, for both at home and in school young boys are immersed in a feminine world (Anastasi, 1958; Faggot & Patterson, 1969; Kagan, 1964; Kellogg, 1969; Maccoby, 1966; Pintler, Phillips, & Sears, 1946; Sears & Feldman, 1966; Sears et al., 1957; Vener & Snyder, 1966). In this environment both males and females may be unconsciously rewarded for feminine behavior. For example, a study by Faggot and Patterson (1969) found that female nursery school teachers rewarded boys a total of 232 times for sex-preferred behaviors and, of these reinforcements, 199 were for feminine behaviors. In comparison, girls were reinforced 363 times for sex-preferred behaviors, with 353 of the reinforcements being for feminine behaviors. In general, the evidence suggests that children learn appropriate sex role behaviors primarily as a consequence of contact with persons of the same sex and that young boys have a much more limited amount of such contact (see Faggot & Patterson, 1969; Lynn, 1959). Pintler et al. (1946) go so far as to suggest that because of their feminine environment boys may encounter obstacles in adopting a masculine identity instead of receiving guidelines. Boys do initially prefer aspects of their mother's behavior to their father's behavior (Brown, 1956; Lynn, 1961; Parsons & Bales, 1955; Vener & Snyder, 1966) and Sears et al. (1957) suggest that boys, having been brought up in a feminine environment, may find that the shift to masculine behavior produces feelings of ambiguity and frustration as to how they should act. The fact that young boys live in a predominantly feminine world may explain why the identification process occurs earlier for girls, while it is more complex for boys and proceeds at a slower pace (Ward, 1969).*

In summary, the evidence suggests that the physical immaturity of boys, their temperament, the expectations for their behavior, and the feminine environment in which they live work both separately and in concert to increase the amount of stress experienced by boys as compared to girls. Furthermore, the boy's lack of cognitive and social skills, his impulsive nature, and his limited range of maneuverability make it more difficult for him to overcome the problems he confronts. In Bardwick's (1971) words, "the stress from the culture is greater for boys and the capacity for resolution is less" (p. 105).

Adolescent Boys and Girls

By midadolescence there is reason to believe that there has been a considerable change in the relative stress experienced by the two sexes. For one thing, boys are performing better academically and are finding school more rewarding. As noted earlier, girls get off to a faster start in language learning and other aspects of cognitive development. But boys start to catch up during the middle school years, and by high school they begin to forge ahead in some ability areas (Bardwick, 1971; Maccoby, 1966; Sontag, Baker, & Nelson, 1958). Another reason for the improved academic position of boys is the change in the character of academic work which increasingly requires analytic problem-solving skills and focuses on mathematics and science. Not only are such academic subjects seen as masculine, but they are fields in which boys seem to be able to outperform girls (Kagan, 1964). Furthermore, with the change in academic focus, boys tend to see their schooling as relevant to their careers and to take an instrumental, vocational orientation to it. In contrast, girls tend to be less adept and less interested in these academic areas and not to see the relationship between their school activities and their long-range goals (Bardwick, 1971; Douvan & Adelson, 1966; Kagan, 1964).

As we have indicated, the parameters of appropriate behavior are quite narrow for young boys, and their ability to conform to the sex role expectations is somewhat problematic. But the adolescent world is more masculine than the world of young children, and the literature suggests that

---

*Being brought up in a feminine environment is probably not the only factor which makes it difficult for boys to adopt the appropriate sex role behavior. For example, Bardwick (1971) has argued that although dependency is a normal behavior for both young boys and young girls, parents will be likely to accept such behavior only from girls.

adolescent boys by this time have acquired a masculine identity and have relatively few problems meeting the sex role expectations. The situation for girls is quite different. At adolescence there is marked pressure for the girls to adopt the traditional feminine role and not to compete in the masculine world. However, for many years she has been permitted to participate in what are now treated as masculine activities, and such activities are likely to have been integrated into her personality and to be reflected in her repertoire of behavior (see Bardwick, 1971; Cohen, 1966; Coleman, 1961; Crandall, 1969; Kagan, 1964; Kagan & Moss, 1962; Lynn, 1959; Rabban, 1950; Veroff, 1969). It is likely, as Bardwick (1971) indicates, that "the sudden pressure to conform to a rather specific sex role stereotype is bound to induce some role conflict and anxiety" (p. 144). And it is clear that girls who once sought and were rewarded for academic success find, in adolescence, that they should not surpass men, and they come to fear success and to feel anxious over competitive behavior (Bardwick, 1971; Friedan, 1963; Kagan & Moss, 1962; Komarovsky, 1946; Maccoby, 1966; Steinmann & Fox, 1966; Veroff, 1969).

Not only does the sex role of adolescent girls tend to be narrower than that of boys, but it is marked by other problems. First, a very basic assumption of our society is that adolescent and adult females will defer to men and adopt the traditional feminine aspirations and behavior. Yet women are told that they are the equals of men and have equal opportunities. Thus, the female confronts the choice of competing in the masculine world, presumably at the cost of denying herself as a woman, or of responding to the covert message by deferring to men (Bernard, 1971a; Seward, 1964). Second, the feminine role, which focuses on developing and maintaining interpersonal ties with males, depends on the actions of others, i.e., males. Thus, unlike males, females perceive their career as depending on the actions of others and see their roles as entailing adjustment to and preparation for contingencies (see Angrist, 1969; Epstein, 1970; Rose, 1951). It is likely that females find the uncertainty and lack of control over their future to be frustrating. Furthermore, unmarried females, perceiving their state as transitional, probably find it difficult to commit themselves emotionally or intellectually to a vocational career. Third, adult women appear to find their role more frustrating than do adult men (Bernard, 1971a, 1971b; Epstein & Goode, 1971; Gornick & Moran, 1971; Gove & Tudor, 1973; Reeves, 1971), and it would be surprising if adolescent girls were unaware of this and did not feel ambivalent about their future role. One indicator that they are ambivalent is the fact that males show a much stronger preference for the masculine role than females show for the feminine role (Bardwick, 1971; Brown, 1958; Kagan, 1964; Lynn, 1959; Rabban, 1950; Rudy, 1968-69; Seward, 1964).

Just as young boys have a personality trait—aggressiveness—that tends to get them into trouble, girls have a trait—dependency—that would appear to create problems for them in late adolescence. Research uniformly indicates that boys are much more independent and autonomous than girls and that by adolescence they have become fairly self-sufficient. Girls, in contrast, are generally quite dependent on others and tend not to establish an independent identity and self-esteem. Furthermore, they tend to lack confidence in their ability to meet goals and are relatively unwilling to attempt new or difficult tasks (see Anastasi, 1958; Bardwick, 1971; Cohen, 1966; Coleman, 1961; Crandall, 1969; Crandall & Rabson, 1960; Douvan, 1960; Douvan & Adelson, 1966; Kagan, 1964; Kagan & Moss, 1962; Komarovsky, 1950; Maccoby, 1966; Murphy, 1962; Veroff, 1969; Winterbottom, 1953). Since in late adolescence one makes the transition into adulthood, acquiring a new social identity and a new set of problems, it seems to us, as it has to others (Bardwick, 1971; Crandall, 1969; Kagan & Moss, 1962; Komarovsky, 1950; Seward, 1964), that girls will tend to be anxious about the transition and find it difficult to handle.

In summary, while the literature suggests that young boys experience more stress than young girls, the situation appears to be quite different among adolescents. Boys are catching up with girls developmentally and the focus of academic activities has shifted in a manner favoring boys. In adolescence girls have to go through a process boys went through earlier, that of adjusting to a set of expectations that limit their behavior and may run counter to their predispositions. Because of their characteristic dependency, girls probably find the transition to an independent status, which starts to occur in adolescence, more difficult than boys do. Furthermore, as adolescents prepare for and start moving into adult roles, they become aware that males are favored in our society and girls start experiencing the stress associated with their adult sex role. Hence, it would appear that girls, by late adolescence, would experience as much stress and probably more than boys.

If our analysis of the relative degree of stress experienced by boys and girls is correct, we would expect young boys to have higher rates of mental illness than young girls, while by late adolescence girls would have as high if not higher rates of mental illness. To test this expectation we will look at the national data on children in psychiatric treatment.

Before turning to the national statistics, we might note that the scattered results from the studies of normal populations are generally consistent with our formulation. Most studies of children in the elementary grades indicate that boys have higher rates of emotional disturbance than girls (Beilin, 1959; Cumming, 1944; Epstein, 1941; Glidewell, 1968; Glidewell, Mensh, & Gildea, 1957; Goldfarb, 1963; Griffiths, 1952; Rogers, 1942; Sarason, 1959; Ullman, 1952), although at least one study (Mac-Farlane, Allen, & Honzik, 1954) indicates little difference between the sexes. Furthermore, studies of young school children referred to guidance centers also indicate that boys in the elementary grades have higher rates of emotional disturbance (Bentzen, 1963; Gilbert, 1957). The evidence for a shift in rates, with girls being higher in adolescence, is not quite as clear. The studies by MacFarlane et al. (1954) and Gilbert (1957) show at most only slight evidence of such a shift. However, both of these studies suffer from methodological problems.* In contrast, the study by Matthews (1923) shows boys at age 10 to have slightly higher rates of neurotic symptoms than girls, while in the middle and late teens girls have markedly higher rates than boys. Brenner (1970) found that junior and senior high school girls manifest more anxiety than comparable boys, and Schubert and Wagner (1936) report a similar finding among high school seniors (see also Terman & Tyler, 1954). Furthermore, there is considerable evidence that women in college have a more negative image of themselves and are more likely to manifest neurotic symptoms (McKee & Sherriffs, 1957, 1959; Rosenkrantz, Vogel, Broverman, & Broverman, 1968; Sherriffs & McKee, 1957).

Treatment for the Functional Mental Disorders

For the analysis we will look at persons 19 years old and younger receiving psychiatric treatment in the United States in public mental hospitals (NIMH, 1967a), private mental hospitals (NIMH, 1967b), general hospitals (NIMH, 1967c), and outpatient clinics (NIMH, 1967d). The data from public and private mental hospitals deal only with first admissions, while the data from general hospitals deal with all discharges, and the data from the outpatient clinics deal with all terminations from treat-

---

*The study by MacFarlane et al. (1954) is longitudinal and it suffers from a very marked attrition. Gilbert's (1957) study does not deal with cases but with complaints (there is interaction between sex, age, and complaints which make the published results misleading).

ment. These data were used to calculate the rates* of persons in treatment per 100,000 persons in the population for the age categories 5-9, 10-14, and 15-19. These rates were then used to calculate the ratio produced by dividing the female rate by the male rate to get an index of the sex differences in rate of treatment. Before five years of age, the rates tend to be unreliable due to the very low proportion of persons receiving psychiatric treatment. Between the ages of five and 14, the data published by NIMH are grouped by five-year categories. The data are then presented for the ages 15-17 and 18-19. However, the five-year grouping has been retained because it provides symmetry and using the two subcategories in no way changes the results.

We would expect that the functional disorders would differ somewhat in the degree to which they respond to the types of stress outlined in the first section of this paper. As the stresses under consideration are transient and are not as serious as those produced, for example, in a seriously disrupted and impoverished home, we would expect the neurotic and transient situational disorders, which are relatively mild and short-lived, to be the most sensitive to these stresses. In contrast, we would expect the psychotic disorders, which tend to be severe and chronic, to be produced by a very seriously disturbed environment, while the stresses with which we have been concerned would make up only a part of such an environment. Finally, as to reactivity to the stresses considered, the psychophysiological disorders have been placed between the neurotic and the transient situational disorders and psychotic disorders. There is relatively little discussion of the psychophysiological disorders in the literature; one of the reasons for categorizing them in this manner is that this is where the analysis suggests they fit.

The rates and the ratios are presented in Table 1. Let us look first at the rates. They show that both sexes experience a dramatic increase in the proportion of persons receiving treatment in all settings and for all disorders as we shift from the ages of 5-9 to 10-14. Furthermore, this pattern of a marked increase in rates of treatment continues as we shift from the ages 10-14 to 15-19, except for males with neurotic and transient situational disorders receiving treatment in outpatient clinics. Note that

---

*The reports from the hospitals and outpatient clinics are not entirely complete. For the public mental hospitals, private mental hospitals and outpatient clinics, the rates were corrected for the missing data by using the estimates provided by NIMH. We have corrected for the nonreporting general hospitals by assuming their rate was the same as the hospitals which reported. For an earlier use of similar data, using very different age categories, see Lynn's (1961) paper on sex differences in identification development.

TABLE 1

A Comparison of Boys and Girls in the United States Receiving Treatment for the Functional Mental Disorders

| | Place of Treatment | | | | | | | | | | | |
| | Public Mental Hospitals rate/100,000 | | | Private Mental Hospitals rate/100,000 | | | General Hospitals rate/100,000 | | | Outpatient Clinics rate/100,000 | | | |
Age	Male	Female	Ratio F/M	Male	Female	F/M	Male	Female	F/M	Male	Female	F/M	Average Ratio
Part A: Disorders that are Highly Reactive to Situational (Role) Stress													
1. The Neurotic Disorders													
5-9	.38	.11	.29	.12	.03	.25	.98	1.06	1.08	27.13	11.73	.43	.51
10-14	1.54	1.14	.74	.77	.86	1.12	5.26	8.94	1.70	38.73	25.40	.66	1.06
15-19	5.21	7.75	1.49	4.73	7.72	1.63	35.37	77.29	2.19	35.75	62.66	1.75	1.77
2. The Transient Disorders													
5-9	3.26	.66	.20	.21	.01	.05	2.50	1.05	.42	154.42	60.94	.39	.27
10-14	9.16	5.65	.62	1.60	1.44	.90	7.48	8.88	1.19	212.60	106.12	.50	.80
15-19	16.30	14.28	.88	5.04	6.05	1.20	25.05	36.49	1.46	136.99	135.70	.99	1.13

TABLE 1 *(continued)*

Part B: Disorders that are Moderately Reactive to Situational (Role) Stress
1. The Psychophysiologic Disorders

Age													
5-9	Too few cases for reliable rates			Too few cases for reliable rates			1.08	1.37	1.27	1.72	1.07	.62	.95
10-14							1.49	2.22	1.49	2.67	1.64	.61	1.05
15-19							3.36	6.38	1.90	1.87	2.56	1.37	1.64

Part C: Disorders that are Only Somewhat Reactive to Situational (Role) Stress
1. The Psychotic Disorders

Age													
5-9	2.45	.51	.21	.12	.10	.83	1.23	.66	.54	12.18	3.77	.31	.47
10-14	3.92	3.55	.91	.74	.77	1.04	5.90	5.24	.89	16.30	9.17	.56	.85
15-19	21.76	16.64	.76	7.73	8.42	1.09	45.12	51.04	1.13	39.34	34.60	.88	.97

Part D: All Functional Disorders

Age													
5-9	6.09	1.28	.21	.45	.14	.31	5.79	4.14	.72	195.45	77.51	.40	.41
10-14	14.62	10.34	.71	3.11	3.07	.99	20.13	25.28	1.26	270.30	142.33	.53	.87
15-19	43.27	38.67	.89	17.50	22.19	1.27	108.90	171.20	1.57	213.95	235.52	1.10	1.21

these two exceptions involve relatively mild disorders in the least inten-sive treatment setting.

The pattern of children experiencing marked increases in the rate of treatment with advancing age has gone virtually unnoticed. In fact, a fairly thorough search did not produce a reference to this phenomenon in the psychiatric, psychological, or sociological literature. This pattern may reflect basic developmental processes, with young children simply being less susceptible to mental illness, perhaps because their personality structure is less clearly developed. A second possible explanation is that life for children becomes more stressful with advancing age.* A third possibility is that, as expectations for behavior become more clearly de-fined with advancing age, the manifestation of mental illness becomes more obvious. Another possibility is that, since adults typically play a key role in the referral process, they become less tolerant of disturbed behav-ior in children as the children grow older. At present we have no em-pirical base from which to assess these or other possible explanations.

Let us now turn to the ratios produced by dividing the female rate by the male rate, which provides an indicator of sex differences in treated mental illness. Looking at Table 1, Part D, where the disorders are grouped together, we see first that between the ages of 5-9 males have higher rates of disorder than females in all four treatment settings. Second, with increasing age there is a monotonic increase in the size of the ratio in each of the four treatment settings, which indicates, as anticipated, that with increasing age females develop higher rates of mental disorder. Third, in the age group 15-19, the female rates have tended to catch up with the male rates and, in fact, an average of the ratios from the dif-ferent treatment settings indicates that, overall, the female rate is slightly higher than the male rate. Since it appears that more children receive psychiatric treatment in general hospitals and outpatient clinics than in public and private mental hospitals, and given the pattern of the values, this average ratio probably minimizes the extent to which females in this age category are receiving more psychiatric treatment than males.**

---

*For some evidence bearing on this possibility, see Simmons, Rosenberg and Rosen-berg (1973).

**Between the ages of 15 and 19, the calculated rates show almost six times as many persons being treated in general hospitals and outpatient clinics as in the mental hos-pitals. This is not a legitimate comparison, as the mental hospital rates deal only with first admissions whereas the other rates deal with both first admissions and readmis-sions. However, it seems unlikely to us that if readmissions were included in the men-tal hospital admission rates the additional cases would be numerous enough to make up the difference between the treatment settings.

Turning to the individual disorders, we find that the pattern remains consistent with our expectations. First, looking at the average ratios for each of the disorders, we find that, at ages 5-9, the male rate is higher than the female rate and in three of the four comparisons the differences between the sexes is substantial. Furthermore, looking at the individual ratios for this age group, we find that in 12 of the 14 comparisons the male rate is larger than the female rate. Second, for each type of disorder, the size of the average ratio increases monotonically with age. Furthermore, looking at disorder by treatment setting, we find that in 12 out of the 14 comparisons the increase remains monotonic and that one of the two exceptions (the drop from .62 to .61 in the psychophysiological disorders is trivial.* Third, the greatest shift in the size of the ratio occurs with the neurotic and transient situational disorders, which we anticipated would be the disorders most sensitive to the stresses we have considered, while the smallest shift occurs in the psychotic disorders which we anticipated would be the disorders least sensitive to the stresses considered. Fourth, the average ratio of three of the five disorders indicates that by the ages 15-19 the female rate is higher than the male rate, and 12 of the 18 individual comparisons show the same trend, which suggests that, by this age, the rate of disorder among females is at least as high as that among males.

In summary, when we look at the rates of mental illness of boys and girls, we find, as anticipated, that young boys have higher rates of treated mental illness than young girls, but by late adolescence girls have as high, if not higher, rates as their male counterparts. The marked variation by age suggests that a number of factors affect the rates, and it is possible that the differences between the sexes are due to some intervening variable and do not reflect actual differences in experienced stress. With children the most obvious intervening and potentially biasing variable is that apparently most are placed in treatment by their parents. The actions of the parents may be affected by the stereotypes and concerns of the parents as well as by the disorder of the child. Yet, while such biasing effects are clearly possible, we would tentatively conclude that they have not produced the pattern found. First, as noted earlier, studies of children in the community generally show a similar pattern.

---

*The other exception is the drop that occurs with psychotic disorders in public mental hospitals from .91 for ages 10-14 to .76 for ages 15-19. This group may be explained by the fact that serious mental illness (i.e., psychosis) is more likely to produce a prompt negative response when it occurs in males than when it occurs in females (e.g., Tudor, Tudor, & Gove, 1977).

Second, and more important, the methodological study by Glidewell (1968) strongly indicates that the parents' perception of the degree to which the child is disturbed is not affected by the sex of the child. It is, of course, clearly possible to develop other explanations of the sex differences in treated mental illness, but at present such explanations rest on untested assumptions. Given the available evidence, obviously the most parsimonious position is to view the data on psychiatric treatment as providing fairly strong corroboration for the literature on sex differences in experienced stress among children.

Summary

The pertinent literature on childhood and adolescence strongly suggests that young boys experience more stress than young girls, while by late adolescence girls experience as much stress as and probably more stress than boys. This pattern is strongly supported by national data on psychiatric treatment and it appears that the sociological and psychological literature focuses on real and serious problems. But at present we have only a very rudimentary understanding of the processes involved, and further work needs to be done before we can be sure the pattern of stress noted above really exists. Research on childhood points to a number of factors that might be producing this pattern but, at present, we are not in a position to evaluate the importance of these factors. Furthermore, our investigation has demonstrated that young children are much less likely to receive psychiatric treatment than older children, but we have virtually no understanding of why this is the case. Related to this issue is the fact that we know relatively little about the factors which determine whether a disturbed child enters treatment. In short, while we have clarified some of the basic parameters involved in understanding the relationship of role stress to mental health and psychiatric treatment, particularly as they vary by age and sex of child, a great deal of research is needed.

A COMPARISON OF MENTAL ILLNESS RATES
AMONG ADULT MEN AND WOMEN*

We now turn to a discussion of the characteristics of adult sex roles which may be related to mental illness. Again, implicit in the analysis is the assumption that stress can lead to mental illness. It should be em-

---

*The first part of this section on adult men and women is adopted, with some modification, from Gove and Tudor (1973).

phasized that this discussion of sex roles is limited to modern industrial nations of the West, particularly the United States.

Sex Roles

In Western society, as elsewhere, sex acts as a master status, channeling persons into particular roles and determining the quality of their interaction with others (Angrist, 1969; Hughes, 1945). There are several reasons to assume that, because of the roles they typically occupy, women are more likely than men to have emotional problems. First, most women are restricted to a single major societal role, that of housewife, whereas, most men occupy two such roles, those of household head and worker. Thus, a man typically has two sources of gratification—his family and his work, while a woman usually only has one—her family. If a male finds one of his roles unsatisfactory, he can frequently focus his interest and concern on the other role. In contrast, if a woman finds her family role unsatisfactory, she typically has no major alternative source of gratification (Bernard, 1971b, pp. 157-63; Gavron, 1966; Gove & Geerken, 1977; Langner & Michael, 1963; Lopata, 1971, p. 171; Radloff, 1975—for some modification of this argument see Fidell & Prather, 1975 and Pearlin, 1975).

Second, it seems reasonable to assume that a large number of women find their major instrumental activities—raising children and keeping house—frustrating. Being a housewife does not require a great deal of skill, since virtually all women, whether educated or not, seem to be capable of being at least moderately competent housewives. Furthermore, it is a position of low prestige.* Because the occupancy of such a low-status, technically undemanding position is not consonant with the educational and intellectual attainment of a large number of women in our society, we might expect such women to be unhappy with the role (Arnott, 1972; Birnbaum, 1971; Poloma & Garland, 1971; Safilios-Rothschild, 1970).

Third, the role of housewife is relatively unstructured and invisible. It is possible for the housewife to put work off, to let things slide, in sum, to perform poorly. The lack of structure and visibility allows her to brood over her troubles, and her distress may thus feed upon itself. In contrast, the job holder must consistently and satisfactorily meet demands that constantly force him to be involved with his environment. Having to

---

* Most authors routinely assume that the role of housewife has little prestige (e.g., Bardwick, 1971; Bernard, 1971b; Friedan, 1963; Harrison, 1964; Parsons, 1942; Rossi, 1964); however, I have been unable to locate any systematic evaluation of this assumption.

meet these structured demands should draw his attention from his troubles and help prevent him from becoming obsessed with his worries.*

Fourth, even when a married woman works, she is typically in a less satisfactory position than a married man (Rapoport & Rapoport, 1965). There has been a consistent decline in the status of women relative to men since 1940, as measured by occupation, income, and even education (Knudsen, 1969). Women are discriminated against in the job market, and they frequently hold positions that are not commensurate with their educational backgrounds (Coser & Rokoff, 1971; Epstein, 1970; Harrison, 1964; Knudsen, 1969; Kreps, 1971; Perrucci, 1970; Veroff & Feld, 1970). Furthermore, working wives are typically viewed by themselves and by others as supplementing the family income, which makes their career involvement fairly tenuous (Almquist & Angrist, 1970; Bailyn, 1970; Davis & Olsen, 1965; Epstein, 1970, pp. 3-4; Harrison, 1964, p. 79; Hartley, 1959-60; Safilios-Rothschild, 1970; Sobol, 1963). Perhaps more important, working wives appear to be under a greater strain than their husbands. In addition to their jobs, they apparently typically perform most of the household chores, which means that they work considerably more hours per day than their husbands** (Blood & Hamblin, 1958; Blood & Wolfe, 1960; Farmer & Bohn, 1970; Hoffman, 1960; Lamousse, 1969; Myrdal & Klein, 1956; Nye & Hoffman, 1963).

Fifth, several observers have noted that the expectations confronting women are unclear and diffuse (Angrist, 1969; Epstein, 1970; Goode, 1960; Parsons, 1942; Rose, 1951); many have argued that this lack of specificity creates problems for women*** (see especially Cottrell, 1942; Parsons, 1942; Rose, 1951; Rossi, 1967). Rose (1951), Angrist (1969), Epstein (1970) and Bardwick (1971) note that the feminine role is characterized by adjusting to and preparing for contingencies. Rose (1951), Block (1973) and Freeman (1970), for example, found that women tend to perceive their career in terms of what men will do, whereas men perceive their career in terms of their own needs. At best,

---

*Although this analysis is somewhat speculative, evidence consistent with it is provided by Langner and Michael (1963, pp. 301-57), Phillips and Segal (1969), Gove (1967), and especially Bradburn and Caplovitz (1965, pp. 95-127).

** The evidence indicates this is the case in Europe (Dahlstrom & Liljestrom, 1971; Haavio-Mannila, 1967; Prudenski & Kalpakov, 1962), in Greece (Safilios-Rothschild, 1970) and it appears to be the case in the United States (Hartley, 1959-60).

*** Some investigators (e.g., Bardwick, 1971; Frieden, 1963; Komarovsky, 1946; Mead, 1949; Steinmann & Fox, 1966) have suggested that the expectations confronting women are not merely diffuse but in fact contradictory and that women are placed in a serious double bind.

it is likely that many women find the uncertainty and lack of control over their futures frustrating (Kando, 1972).

Many authors (Friedan, 1963; Gavron, 1966; Komarovsky, 1950; McKee & Sherriffs, 1959; Mead, 1949; Mednick & Tangri, 1972; Rossi, 1964; Seward & Williamson, 1970) have viewed the difficulties confronting women as being a result of recent changes in the woman's role in industrial societies. According to this argument, women previously had a more meaningful role. Families were large, and during most of their adult life women were responsible for the care of children. Without the conveniences of modern industrial society, housework required more time and skill and was highly valued. Since the family's economic support was frequently provided by a family enterprise, the wife played a role in supporting the family. With the development of industrialization and the small nuclear family, the woman's child-rearing years were shortened, her domestic skills were largely made unnecessary by modern conveniences and she was no longer part of a family enterprise supporting the family. During this time, both sexes were receiving more education: For the male, education produced occupational advancement and diversity; for the female, while she was receiving more education her role was shrinking in importance. These changes in women's roles were accompanied by changes in the legal and ideological structure, which held that the same standards should apply to men and women. However, instead of being treated as equals, women remained in their old institutionalized positions. If this analysis is correct, much of the presumed stress on women is a relatively recent phenomenon. Furthermore, from this framework it seems likely, given the present changes that are occurring in the roles of women, that their roles will become more commensurate with the roles of men and that the two sexes will (again) experience similar amounts of stress, with the consequence that their rates of mental illness will become relatively similar.

To summarize, there are ample grounds for assuming that women find their position in society to be more frustrating and less rewarding than do men and that this may be a relatively recent development. Let us then postulate that because of the difficulties associated with the feminine role in modern Western societies, more women than men become mentally ill. Our analysis of roles has focused primarily but not exclusively on the roles of married men and women, and it is within this group that we might expect to find the greatest difference in the rates of mental illness of men and women. Unfortunately, most existing data are presented by sex and not by sex and marital status.

Before we turn to an analysis of the data on mental illness, we might note two types of evidence that appear to support our framework. First, there is considerable evidence that women have a more negative image of themselves than men have of themselves (Baruch, 1973; Broverman, Vogal, Broverman, Clarkson, & Rosenkrantz, 1972; Gurin, Veroff, & Feld, 1960; McClelland, 1965; McKee & Sherriffs, 1957, 1959; Rosenkrantz, et al., 1968; Sherriffs & McKee, 1957). Second, the available evidence on depression uniformly indicates that women are more likely to become depressed than men (e.g., Bullock, Siegel, Weissman, & Paykel, 1972; Chesler, 1971; Silverman, 1968; Weissman & Klerman, 1976).

Rates of Mental Illness for Adult Males and Females

To evaluate rates of mental illness for males and females we will look at community surveys, first admissions to mental hospitals, psychiatric admissions to general hospitals, psychiatric care in outpatient clinics, private outpatient psychiatric care and the prevalence of mental illness in the practices of general physicians. The National Institute of Mental Health (NIMH) provides data for the United States on first admissions to mental hospitals, psychiatric admissions to general hospitals, and psychiatric care in outpatient clinics. Because these data are much more comprehensive than any provided by individual investigators, our discussion of such treatment will be limited to these data. For community surveys and private outpatient care, we will, of course, have to depend upon information from individual studies.

*First admissions to psychiatric hospitals.** There are three types of psychiatric hospitals in the United States—public mental hospitals (state and county), private mental hospitals, and VA psychiatric hospitals. NIMH reports yearly on first admissions to public and private mental hospitals. According to their definition, first admissions include only persons with no prior inpatient psychiatric experience. Their definition thus excludes not only persons who have previously been in a mental hospital but also those who have received inpatient psychiatric treatment in a general hospital. Using these reports, we calculated age-adjusted rates of admissions to public and private mental hospitals in the United States by diagnosis for persons 18 and over. The only relevant information available on the VA psychiatric hospitals is the total number of psychiatric admissions (first admissions and readmissions) with no diagnostic break-

---

*The details of the procedures used in calculating these rates are presented in Gove and Tudor (1973), as are the details with regard to the data on pyschiatric care in general hospitals and psychiatric outpatient care.

down. We therefore have to estimate the number of first admissions to the VA hospitals. Because VA patients are predominantly male, and we have predicted that more women than men would be mentally ill, the VA rates have been overestimated to avoid favorably biasing our results.

The data are presented in Table 2. They indicate that women have higher rates than men for mental illness as we have defined it. The difference between men and women is particularly marked for the neurotic disorders but is also discernible among the psychotic disorders. However, among the two infrequently used categories the differences are not in the predicted direction: There is absolutely no difference between the sexes in the psychophysiological disorders, and males have a slightly higher rate on the transient situational disorders.

Psychiatric care in general hospitals. About as many persons receive inpatient psychiatric treatment in general hospitals as are cared for in mental hospitals. Such treatment is generally quite brief, and most of those persons return to the community, although a few go on to become patients in mental hospitals. As with the public mental hospitals, the NIMH reports have been used to calculate age-standardized rates by diagnosis for men and women for the United States as a whole. The only data available from the VA hospitals are total admissions, so in calculating these rates, estimates had to be made for two parameters.* From the Public Health Service we had discharge data on public health general hospitals by sex and diagnosis.

These data are presented in Table 3. They show that women are much more likely than men to receive treatment for mental illness in general hospitals. As before, the differences between the sexes are particularly marked for the neurotic disorders; but they are also very substantial for the psychotic disorders as well as for the transient situational disorders and the psychophysiological disorders.**

Psychiatric outpatient care (excluding private practice). The NIMH reports terminations for outpatient psychiatric facilities by age, sex, and diagnosis. Again, this information has been used to compute age-stan-

---

*To estimate the proportion of men and women who were discharged we used the proportion of men and women who were psychiatric residents in the VA hospitals in 1967 (NIMH, 1967e). To estimate the diagnostic distribution of admissions to the VA hospitals we used the diagnostic distribution of men and women discharged from the nonfederal general hospitals.

**General hospitals are the only treatment settings where many persons receive psychiatric treatment for the psychophysiologic disorders and, thus, the overall rate of psychiatric treatment for the psychophysiologic disorders is much higher for women than for men.

TABLE 2

First Admissions to Mental Hospitals in the United States (Persons per 100,000)

	State and County	Private	Combined	Ratio F/M	VA Hospitals Overestimate	All Hospitals	Ratio F/M
Functional Psychosis							
Male	293	89	382	1.27	61	443	1.10
Female	322	162	484		2	486	
Neurosis							
Male	107	99	206	1.68	22	228	1.53
Female	165	182	347		1	348	
Transient Situational Disorders							
Male	26	5	31	.94	5	36	.81
Female	23	6	29		0	29	
Psychophysiologic and Psychosomatic Disorders							
Male	2	2	4	1.00	0	4	1.00
Female	2	2	4		0	4	
TOTAL							
Male	428	195	623	1.39	88	711	1.21
Female	512	352	864		3	867	

dardized rates for persons 18 and over. These data are presented in Table 4. The rates for men and women are quite similar to those dealing with inpatient treatment: There are many more women than men classified as mentally ill. The differences between men and women are very large for both the neurotic disorders and the transient situational disorders, substantial for the psychotic disorders and small for the psychophysiological disorders, but the number of cases in this last category is also very small

It should be noted that the NIMH report does not include facilities where a mental health professional other than a psychiatrist directs the mental health program and assumes responsibility for the patients. However, a study by Zolik and Marches (1968) indicates that the proportions of men and women who are treated as mentally ill in such facilities are very similar to the proportions presented here.

Private outpatient psychiatric care. To discover the relative proportion of mentally ill men and women in private outpatient psychiatric care we have to turn to studies conducted by individual investigators. Unfortunately, there are only a few studies which indicate the sex distribution of the practices of psychiatrists. None of these studies presents a breakdown by diagnosis, and, thus, the patients have probably included some with personality disorders and a few with brain syndromes. These studies are presented in Table 5. All the studies indicate that more women than men received private outpatient psychiatric care, and in all but one study the differences between the sexes were very substantial.

Most persons who receive treatment for mental illness are treated by physicians in the community who lack special psychiatric training. These physicians also play a major role in channeling persons into more specialized psychiatric care (e.g., Susser, 1968, p. 246). Most of the mentally ill persons treated by general physicians are suffering from a psychoneurotic disorder. Table 6 presents some of the findings regarding the proportion of men and women being treated for mental illness by general practitioners. Table 6 does not present all the relevant studies but is limited to those that are relatively recent and readily available. For a discussion of the earlier and less easily located studies see Ryle (1960) and Watts (1962). In all of these studies more women than men received treatment, and in all cases the differences between the sexes was substantial. The finding by Shepherd, Cooper, Brown, and Kalton (1964, p. 1361) that psychiatric disorders ranked third among presenting conditions for women and seventh for men suggests that this relationship cannot be

TABLE 3

Psychiatric Care in General Hospitals in the United States
(Persons per 100,000)

	Nonfederal Hospitals*	VA General Hospitals**	Public Health Hospitals*	All General Hospitals	Ratio F/M
Functional Psychosis					
Male	816	109	6	931	
					1.44
Female	1,334	3	0	1,337	
Neurosis					
Male	959	128	11	1,098	
					1.89
Female	2,068	4	4	2,076	
Transient Situational Disorders					
Male	65	9	—	74	
					1.62
Female	120	0	—	120	
Psychophysiologic and Psychosomatic Disorders					
Male	70	9	2	81	
					1.69
Female	137	0	0	137	
TOTAL					
Male	1,910	255	19	2,184	
					1.68
Female	3,659	7	4	3,670	

*Rates based on discharges
**Rates based on admissions

explained by assuming that women simply go to physicians more frequently than men.

In summary, all the data on the treatment of mental illness (as defined
here) show higher rates of treatment for women than for men. In the
beginning of this section it was argued that these differences between the
sexes might be a product of different sex roles. One might anticipate that
the problems caused by role strains would be reflected more in the neurotic disorders, which are largely reactions to situational stress, than in the
psychotic disorders, which have a substantial genetic component and
which are generally thought to be reactions to severely "pathological"
situations. The breakdown by diagnosis supports this view, with the

Table 4

Care in Psychiatric Clinics in the United States (Persons per 100,000) Rates Based on Terminations

	All Outpatient Clinics (Except VA)	VA Outpatient Clinics	All Clinics	Ratio F/M
Functional Psychosis				
Male	573	114	687	
				1.21
Female	832	2	834	
Neurosis				
Male	433	122	555	
				1.73
Female	956	3	959	
Transient Situational Disorders				
Male	166	0	166	
				1.63
Female	271	0	271	
Psychophysiologic and Psychosomatic Disorders				
Male	20	6	26	
				1.04
Female	27	0	27	
TOTAL				
Male	1192	242	1434	
				1.46
Female	2086	5	2091	

differences between the sexes being much greater for the neurotic disorders than for the psychotic disorders.

The role framework proposed suggests that the differences between the sexes might change over time as the roles change. As is indicated in Gove and Tudor (1973), a preliminary analysis indicates that prior to World War II men appear to have had higher rates of treatment for mental illness. Similarly, as Seidler (1975) notes, in the last few years the rate of psychiatric treatment of men has been increasing more rapidly than that of women, which is consistent with the view that as the roles of men and women become more comparable the sex differences in rates of mental illness will diminish.

Let us end the discussion of rates of psychiatric treatment by noting that if one uses a different definition of mental illness than the one used here, the patterns are not as clear. In all settings for which NIMH provides data

TABLE 5

Contact with a Psychiatrist—All Types of Mental Disorders

Source	Men (%)	Women (%)	Patients (N)
Private office practice:			
Gordon and Gordon (1958, p. 544):			
Bergen	41	59	746
Ulster County	34	66	264
Cattaraugus County	37	63	239
Bahn,, Gardner, Alltop, Knatterud, and Solomon (1966, p. 2046)	—	a	270
Ryan (1969, p. 15)	about two-thirds are female		2,500[b]
Marmor (1975, p. 29)[c]	43	57	4,347
Referred to psychiatrist:			
Watts, Caute, and Kuenssberg (1964, p. 1355)			
Referrals	39	61	4,452[d]
Innes and Sharp (1962, p. 449)			
Referred from general population in given year	0.5	0.6	2,003
Outpatients:[e]			
Hagnell (1966, p. 46)	2.9	7.6	2,550

a. Rates higher for females.
b. Estimated figures for persons treated in Boston, Mass. For estimates see Ryan, 1969, p. 10, and Appendix A.
c. Based on a national survey of psychiatrists.
d. Based on a study of 261 general practices.
e. Persons from the general population who saw a psychiatrist as outpatients over a 10-year period.

TABLE 6

Treatment of Men and Women for Mental Illness by General Practitioners

Source	Men (%)	Women (%)	Patients (N)	Practices Studied (N)
A. Percentage in Specified Population Being Treated				
Hare and Shaw (1965, p. 26) :				
New Adam	3.0	7.5	990	—
Old Butte	3.4	7.4	875	—
Taylor and Chave (1964, p. 118)	5.5	9.4	2,826	—
B. Percentage of Mentally Ill Patients in Practice				
Fry (1960, p. 86)	7.1	16.3	5,471	1
Ryle (1960, p. 324)	1.4	7.1	2,400	1
Logan and Cushion (1958, pp. 69-70)	3.0	6.4	114,294	106
Kessel (1960, p. 18)	11.1	15.8	670	1
Martin, Brotherston, and Chave (1957, p. 199)	3.5	7.5	—	—
Shepherd, Cooper, Brown, and Kalton (1964, p. 1361)	5.9	12.6	14,697	40
Cooper (1966, p. 9)	17.4	27.2	7,454	—
Cooper, Brown, and Kalton (1962)	6.9	15.6	743	—
C. Sex Distribution of Patients Receiving Treatment for Mental Illness				
Watts et al. (1964, p. 1355)	32.0	68.0	6,123	—
Mazer (1967)	31.8	68.2	154	—
Ryan (1969, p. 156)	two thirds women		145,000[a]	—

a. These figures are estimates for all persons receiving treatment for an emotional disturbance by general physicians (see Ryan 1969, p. 10 and Appendix A for basis).

on the United States as a whole, men are more likely than women to receive treatment for the brain syndromes and for the personality disorders. If, instead of looking at particular diagnoses, we use the incidence of psychiatric treatment as our measure of mental illness, the data show that men are more likely than women to receive treatment in public mental hospitals (including, of course, VA hospitals), whereas women have higher rates of treatment in all other settings and have a higher overall rate of treatment than men (Seidler, 1975). In short, the finding that women have higher rates of mental illness is only unambiguously supported when we limit mental illness to functional disorders where there is a personal distress and/or psychotic disorganization.

Community surveys. In 1969, Dohrenwend and Dohrenwend reviewed the sex differences in mental illness found in community surveys. From their review they concluded that there were no sex differences in overall rates of mental illness. Given our role framework, Jeannette Tudor and I (Gove & Tudor, 1973) focused on the community studies conducted in Western industrial nations following World War II. Of the 17 relevant and usable studies, all showed women to have higher rates of mental illness than men. In contrast, an analysis of Dohrenwend and Dohrenwend's review showed that, of the studies conducted in Western industrial nations before World War II, three showed higher rates of mental illness for women and eight showed higher rates for men.

Subsequently the Dohrenwends (1976) updated their review, focusing on our ordering of the studies. As is noted in Gove and Tudor (1977), they included a number of studies inappropriate for the analysis of adult sex roles in Western society after World War II,* and excluded a number of relevant studies. Nevertheless, as is shown in Gove and Tudor (1977), their studies presented a pattern that is consistent with the present formulation of changing sex roles over time.** Table 7 presents all the relevant studies*** that could be found which were conducted in Western indus-

---

*They included studies of mental illness occurring before World War II and studies of inappropriate populations (e.g., an Indian Village, the Hutterites, the aged, etc.).

**They, however, state that their data are inconsistent with our formulation. As is shown in Gove and Tudor (1977), they manage to reach this conclusion by distorting the position taken in Gove and Tudor (1973) and in the present paper. As there is obviously some controversy over what the data show, the reader may want to look at Dohrenwend and Dohrenwend (1976) and Gove and Tudor (1977).

***Five other community surveys (Blumenthal & Dielman, 1975; Engelsmann, Murphy, Prince, Leduc, & Demers, 1972; Gaitz & Scott, 1972; Kasl & Harburg, 1975; Roberts, Forthofer, & Fabrega, 1976) which do not deal with a representative population also found women to have higher rates of mental illness.

TABLE 7
Community Surveys

Part I: Women Higher than Men

A. Percentages Based Solely on Responses to Structured Interview

Source	Male	Female	Sample Size
Martin, Brotherston, and Chave (1957, p. 200)	25	Over 40	750
Phillips and Segal (1969, p. 61)	21.2	35.5	278
Phillips (1966)	21	34	600
Bradburn and Caplovitz (1965, p. 30)	31	54	2,006
Tauss (1967, p. 122)	18.4	38.0	707
Taylor and Chave (1964, p. 50)	22	43	422
Gurin et al. (1960, p. 189) [c,k]	22	40	2,460
Haberman (1969):			
Washington Heights	18.2	25.3	1,865
New York City	14.9	33.3	706
Hare and Shaw (1965, p. 25):			
New Adam	15.6	22.9	1,015
Old Butte	13.1	26.3	924
Public Health Service (1970, p. 27) [a,c]	14.9	34.2	6,672
Bradburn (1969, p. 119) [f]	20.3	38.9	2,375
Meile and Haese (1969, p. 289)	16.4	[g]	5,498
Warheit, Holzer, and Arey (1975)	8.7	29.2	1,645
Holzer, Arey, Warheit, and Bell (1975)	21	12.2	3,674
Brunetti (1964)	18	30	102
Denis, Tousignant, and Laforest (1973)		26	1,158
Hughes (1973):			
(a) Rural	5.0	15.5	581
(b) Urban	12.50	23.0	300
Pearlin (1975) [a]		[h]	2,300

TABLE 7 (continued)

Source	Male	Female	Sample Size
Clancy and Gove (1974)	24.6	32.5	402
Ilfeld (1977)	8.5	19.0	2,299
B. Mean Scores Based Solely on Responses to Structured Interview			
Radloff (1975) [a]	7.33	9.54	1,709
Gove et al. (1976) [b]	2.74	4.58	94
Gove and Geerken (1977) [c]	5.94	6.61	2,248
Gove and Galle (1977)	6.91	8.21	2,035
C. Percentages Based on Clinical Evaluation			
Pasamanick et al. (1959, p. 188):			
Diagnosis:			
Psychosis	.6	.3	
Neurosis	3.6	6.8	
Psychophysiologic	1.9	5.2	
Total	6.1	12.3	809
Primrose (1962, pp. 18-24) [1]			
Diagnosis:			
Psychosis	.3	1.1	
Neurosis	4.4	13.6	
Total	4.7	14.7	1,701
Essen-Moller (1956, pp. 148-9)			
Diagnosis:			
Psychosis	.3	1.3	
Neurosis	1.4	2.4	
Psychophysiologic	18.2	30.7	
Total	19.9	34.4	2,550

TABLE 7 (continued)

Source	Male	Female	Sample Size
Hagnell (1966, pp. 99-103)[i,j]			
Diagnosis:			
Psychosis	.5	.5	
Neurosis	5.5	15.1	
Total	6.0	15.6	2,550

D. Percentages Based on Several Scores[l]

Leighton et al. (1963, pp. 507-9)			
Diagnosis:[d]			
Psychosis	1.0	2.0	
Neurosis	44.0	64.0	
Psychophysiologic	66.0	71.0	1,010

Part II: Men Have Higher Rates than Women

A. Percentages Based on Informants and Some Clinical Interviews

Brunetti (1973)	2.5	2.4	683

a. Measure of depression
b. Mean on Langner scale, two other scales showed the same pattern
c. National sample
d. Gave multiple diagnoses, so percentages not summed
e. Rate indicates persons with three or more symptoms
f. Rates of persons high on symptoms of anxiety
g. 2.5 times male rate
h. There are almost 20% more women in the two highest depression categories (Pearlin 1975, pp. 194-5)
i. Study involved the complete survey of an entire community and excludes psychosis due to organic disorder.
j. Rates for neurosis calculated by author from data on pp. 99-102. (Child neurosis was not considered when calculating the rates).
k. Gurin et al. (1960) present their data along four symptom factors, psychological anxiety, physical health, immobilization, and anxiety factor. Women also scored higher than men on the other three factors.
l. Rates combine psychosis and neurosis and are based on interviews, observations of interviewer, hospital and other institutional records, impressions of physicians in contact with respondent, and impressions of community informants.

trial societies since World War II. These studies range from examination of prevalence at a particular point in time (e.g., Essen-Moller, 1956) to investigations of incidence over a specific proportion of time (e.g., Hagnell, 1966), to an attempt to identify an incident of mental illness at any time in the respondent's lifetime up to the time of the study (Leighton, Leighton, Hardin, Macklin, & MacMillan, 1963). However, most of the studies focused on prevalence at the time of the study. In all of the studies that do not provide a diagnostic breakdown the measures of mental illness relate very well to our conception of mental illness since they focus primarily on the symptoms associated with neurosis.

Of the 35 studies all but one* found women to have higher rates of mental illness than men. As with the data on treatment we would expect the difference between the sexes to be substantial for the neurotic and psychophysiologic disorders and relatively modest for the psychoses. Looking at the few studies that provide diagnoses, we see that, as anticipated, women tend to have markedly higher rates for the neurotic and psychophysiologic disorders. There is no sharp pattern with the psychotic disorders. One reason the psychotic disorders do not reflect a clearer pattern is that the rates are relatively unstable due to the fact that they are based on very few cases.** However, the majority of the studies show women to have higher rates; furthermore, if the rates are averaged, the rates of treatment for women are twice those for men (women 1.0% versus men 0.5%).

In summary, all the data on mental illness (as defined here)*** indicate that in modern western industrial societies more women than men are mentally ill. It is especially important to note that this finding is not dependent on who is doing the selection. For example, if we look at admissions to mental hospitals, where the societal response would appear to be of prime importance, women have higher rates; if we look at treatment by general physicians, where self-selection would appear to be of prime importance, women have higher rates; and if we look at community surveys, where the attempt is to eliminate selective processes, women have higher rates.

---

*The one exception (Brunetti, 1973) was a small, rather unsophisticated methodological study in rural Quebec which found almost identical rates for men and women (with one more mentally ill woman or one less mentally ill male, women would have had higher rates).

**For example, Pasamanick, Roberts, Lemkau, and Krueger's (1959) rates are based on only 17 cases and Primrose's (1962) rates are based on only 12 cases.

***Just as with the data on treatment, the community studies indicate that in all places men are more likely to have a personality disorder.

Further Evidence for the Role Explanation

Reviewing the argument presented above about why women are more likely to be mentally ill than men, one will note that we focused primarily on the roles of married men and women. We noted first that the housewife, unlike her husband, typically has only one major source of gratification—her family—and she thus has a narrower structural base from which to find both gratification and support. Second, the occupation of housewife is of low prestige and frustrating in its demands, with poorly defined expectations and standards of excellence. Third, the housewife's role is isolated and unstructured, which gives her too much time to dwell on her problems. And fourth, even when a married woman works, she still tends to be in a less satisfactory position than a married male; not only is she likely to hold a low-status job, but in addition she will still typically perform most of the household chores, which means she will confront very heavy time and energy demands.

In contrast to the roles of married men and women, the roles of single men and women appear to be more similar. Single persons generally have only one major societal role, that of job holder. On the job, the visibility and structure of the demands confronting men and women are relatively similar. Furthermore, both single men and single women tend to lack close interpersonal ties and are relatively isolated. It should be noted that such ties appear to be a major source of a feeling of well-being and that married persons, regardless of sex, are much happier than single persons (Glenn, 1976; Gurin, et al., 1960, pp. 231-32). An analysis of the roles of never-married, divorced, and widowed men and women indicates that it is not clear whether one should expect men or women to have higher rates of mental illness in these unmarried statuses (Gove, 1972a, 1973a). Gove (1972a) reviews all the studies in Western industrial nations conducted after World War II that present the relationship between marital status and mental disorder. These studies use quite varying definitions of mental disorder. It was found that the married of both sexes tended to have lower rates of mental illness than the unmarried. This relationship would appear to be due to the nature of the different roles of the married and unmarried and to the selective processes which keep unstable persons from marrying. Next, the differences between the sexes within the various marital statuses were investigated. All the studies indicate that married women have higher rates of mental illness than married men. In contrast, when never-married men are compared with never-married women, divorced men with divorced women and widowed men with widowed women, in each instance a substantial majority of the studies found that it was the men who had the higher rates.

Gove (1972b) explores the possibility that the patterns found between mental illness and sex and marital roles would be reflected in data on suicide. Because men commit suicide more frequently than women in virtually all societies while women attempt suicide much more frequently than men, a simple comparison of the suicidal behavior of men and women invariably gives ambiguous results. This, of course, has long been known and, at least since Durkheim (1951), investigators who wished to draw conclusions about the roles of men and women have not simply compared their rates, but have instead looked for patterned variations. Since the data on mental illness show married men to have lower rates of mental illness than married women and never-married (and divorced, and widowed) men to have higher rates than comparable women, it follows that if suicidal behavior displays the same pattern as mental illness, then the following ratios—$\frac{\text{never married,}}{\text{married}}$ $\frac{\text{divorced,}}{\text{married}}$ and $\frac{\text{widowed}}{\text{married}}$ should be larger for men than for women. Durkheim (1951) called the ratio created in this manner the "coefficient of preservation" and, in his pioneering work, he was able to show that the sex which had the largest coefficient varied from society to society and that these variations were related to the nature of the marital roles in those societies.

Gove (1972b) looks at data on completed suicide, attempted suicide and, in one case, threatened suicide in various western industrial nations. The data virtually invariably showed men to have a larger ratio than women and are thus consistent with the data on mental illness. In a subsequent paper (1973b), Gove expands upon the suicide paper. He looks at mortality patterns for a wide number of causes of death in which a person's psychological state would appear likely to affect his/her life chances. Using national data, this paper analyzes: (a) mortality involving overt social acts (suicide, homicide, automobile accidents, pedestrian accidents and "other" accidents), (b) mortality associated with the use of socially approved "narcotics" (cirrhosis of the liver, which is associated with alcohol use, and lung cancer, which is associated with smoking), and (c) mortality associated with two diseases requiring very prolonged, methodical treatment (tuberculosis and diabetes). The data for these types of mortality are consistent with the data on mental illness, for they uniformly indicate that the difference between being married and being single (or divorced or widowed) is much greater for men than for women. These results do not appear to be the result of a methodological artifact, for among those causes of mortality which one would not expect to be affected by a person's psychological state, such as leukemia, the relationship between sex and marital status disappears. Furthermore, internal patterns within the data suggest a role explanation (e.g., the "protection" of marriage is greater during the ages young children are present in the home), and it appears to be possible to virtually rule out the two major alternative explanations of the differences, namely, socio-economic factors and marital selection.

In summary, the data on mental illness and on selected types of mortality clearly suggest that in modern Western industrial society marriage is more beneficial to men than women, whereas being single is, if anything, more stressful for men than for women. This finding of substantially different patterns for men and women across the various marital statuses is consistent with the view that the sex differences in mental illness are largely a product of societal roles.

Alternative Perspectives

The labeling perspective. During the past decade the labeling perspective has been the most pervasive and influential sociological approach to deviance (Cole, 1975). Scheff (1966), in particular, has used this approach to explain stabilized mental illness. According to this perspective, a person comes to occupy the role of the mentally ill primarily because of the actions of others. It is Scheff's formulation that (a) virtually everyone at sometime commits acts that correspond to the public stereotype of mental illness; (b) if these acts become public knowledge the individual may, depending on various contingencies, be referred to the appropriate officials; and (c) the person will then be routinely processed as mentally ill and placed in a mental institution. In short, a person becomes mentally ill primarily because others perceive him as mentally ill and act accordingly.

In a recent paper, Tudor, Tudor and Gove (1977) review the literature on the characteristics of the roles of men and women and the relationship of these characteristics to the reactions to mental illness. The relationship clearly suggests that mental disorders among housewives are likely to be seen as less disruptive than similar disorders among working males. Furthermore, it is suggested that there are generalized role expectations for males and females which reflect the roles they typically occupy, and that because of these expectations mental disorder is more readily recognized among males and more severely reacted to. Both the literature and the national data on treatment suggest that these suppositions are correct, as mental illnesses (as defined here) are more readily identified among males and are reacted to more quickly and severely. Thus, if the rates of manifest distress and disorganization were equal for males and females, more males than females would be reacted to and labeled mentally ill. Furthermore, the labeling perspective could not readily be used to explain the patterned variations reflected in the statistics on mental illness and mortality discussed in the previous section. In short, the labeling perspective does not provide a satisfactory explanation for the higher rates of mental illness among women.

Women as expressive. Parsons and Bales (1955) consider that the critical functional distinction between men and women lies in their social orientation, with men being more fundamentally "instrumental" and women more fundamentally "expressive." As the recent review by Seidler (1975) indicates, this is a very popular position among social scientists, apparently in part because it corresponds to one's intuitive feeling. Furthermore, the presumed expressiveness of women has been used to "explain" the apparent higher rates of mental illness among women. Perhaps the most important and explicit case has been made by Phillips and Segal (1969). It is their position that community surveys, which are based on self-reported symptoms and which find women to have higher rates of symptomatology, do not reflect real sex differences in frequency of disturbance but only the greater reluctance of men to admit to certain unpleasant feelings and sensations (Phillips & Segal, 1969, p. 69). They argue that "men are more reluctant because it is culturally more appropriate and acceptable for women to be expressive of their difficulties" (Phillips & Segal, 1969, p. 59). Although their paper is replete with data tangentially related to their argument, they have no data bearing directly on this main premise.

A very similar argument is proposed by Cooperstock (1971) in an article devoted to explaining the results of two studies which show that psychotherapeutic drugs are much more likely to be prescribed for women than for men. In essence, her argument is that "contemporary Western women are permitted greater freedom than men in expressing feelings" and that therefore "she feels freer to bring her perceived emotional problems to the attention of a physician" (Cooperstock, 1971, pp. 240-41). However, like Phillips and Segal, Cooperstock has no evidence that bears directly on her theoretical explanation.

Building on the work of Dohrenwend and Dohrenwend (1969) and Phillips and Clancy (1970, 1972), who have shown that reports of psychiatric symptoms were affected by a set of response biases, including the extent to which the respondent saw the symptoms as desirable or undesirable, Clancy and Gove (1974) investigated the relationship between the respondent's sex and reports of psychiatric symptoms while controlling for response bias. It was found that, contrary to the position of Phillips and Segal (1969) and Cooperstock (1971), there were no differences between men and women in the degree to which they saw the symptoms as undesirable. Furthermore, when three forms of response bias (yeasaying/naysaying, need for approval and perceived desirability of symptoms) were controlled for, the differences between the sexes did not diminish but increased. Two subsequent studies (Gove & Geerken, 1977; Gove, McCorkel, Fain, & Hughes, 1976), which used somewhat different techniques and measures, also showed that the higher rates of psychiatric symptoms reported by women were not an artifact of response bias.

These results, which used the procedures developed by some of the very persons who argue that the high rates of symptoms reported by women are an artifact of a response set, provide fairly convincing evidence that the differences are real. There remains the possibility that although there are no differences in response set which predispose women to report more symptoms in community surveys, if a woman is symptomatic she may be more likely than a man to seek professional help. However, the available data clearly indicate that, controlling for level of disorder, there are no marked sex differences in help-seeking, and men are fully as likely as women to seek help (Gove & Tudor, 1977; Gurin, et al., 1960, pp. 372-400). In short, the data clearly indicate that women are no more likely than men to articulate their symptoms.

SUMMARY

It has been argued that the role and capabilities of young boys in our society make for a stressful situation relative to that of young girls, and that by late adolescence the situation has changed and, if anything, this period is more stressful for girls than for boys. With the shift into adulthood the situation continues to be more stressful for females, with probably most of the differences between the sexes in experienced stress being found in the roles of married men and women. It has been assumed that these stresses will be reflected in rates of mental illness of males and females. In the analysis a fairly precise definition of mental illness has been used, limiting it to a functional disorder characterized by distress and/or psychotic disorganization. The data on first admissions to mental hospitals, psychiatric treatment in general hospitals, psychiatric outpatient clinics, private outpatient care, the practices of general physicians, and community surveys all uniformly indicate that young boys have higher rates of mental illness than young girls, that by adolescence girls tend to have slightly higher rates than boys, and that higher rates for females then persist through adulthood. Furthermore, there is strong evidence that the higher rates of mental illness in adult women are primarily due to the relatively high rates of mental illness in married women as compared to married men.

REFERENCES

ALMQUIST, E. & ANGRIST, S. S. Career salience and atypicality of occupational choice among college women. *Journal of Marriage and the Family*, 1970, 32 (2) , 242-249.

American Psychiatric Association. *Annual Report, 1967*. Washington, D.C.: Government Printing Office, 1968.

ANASTASI, A. *Differential Psychology*. New York: MacMillan, 1958.

ANGRIST, S. The study of sex roles. *Journal of Social Issues*, 1969, 25, 215-232.

ARNOTT, C. C. Husbands' attitudes and wives' commitment to employment. *Journal of Marriage and the Family*, 1972, 34, 673-684.

BAHN, A., GARDNER, E., ALLTOP, L., KNATTERUD, G., & SOLOMON, M. Admissions and prevalence rates for psychiatric facilities in four register areas. *American Journal of Public Health*, 1966, 56, 2003-2051.

BAILYN, L. Career and family orientations of husbands and wives in relation to marital happiness. *Human Relations*, 1970, 23, 97-113.

BARDWICK, J. *The Psychology of Women: A Study of Bio-Cultural Conflicts*. New York: Harper & Row, 1971.

BARUCH, G. K. Feminine self-esteem, self-ratings of competence, and maternal career commitment. *Journal of Counseling Psychology*, 1973, 20, 487-488.

BEILIN, H. Teachers' and clinicians' attitudes toward the behavior problems of children: A reappraisal. *Child Development*, 1959, 30, 9-25.

BENTZEN, F. Sex ratios in learning and behavior disorders. *American Journal of Orthopsychiatry*, 1963, 33, 92-98.

BERNARD, J. The paradox of the happy marriage. In V. Gornick and B. Moran (Eds.), *Women in Sexist Society: Studies in Power and Powerlessness*. New York: Basic Books, 1971. (a)

BERNARD, J. *Women and the Public Interest*. Chicago: Aldine-Atherton, 1971. (b)

BIRNBAUM, J. Life patterns, personality style and self-esteem in gifted family oriented and career committed women. *Dissertation Abstracts International*, 1971, 32, 1834B.

BLOCK, J. H. Conceptions of sex role: Some cross-cultural and longitudinal perspectives. *American Psychologist*, 1973, 28, 512-526.

BLOOD, R. O. & HAMBLIN, R. C. The effect of the wife's employment on the family power structure. *Social Forces*, 1958, 36, 347-352.

BLOOD, R. O. & WOLFE, D. M. *Husbands and Wives: The Dynamics of Married Living*. Glencoe, Ill.: Free Press, 1960.

BLUMENTHAL, S. & DIELMAN, T. Depressive symptomatology and role function in a general population. *Archives of General Psychiatry*, 1975, 32, 985-991.

BRADBURN, N. *The Structure of Psychological Well Being*. Chicago: Aldine, 1969.

BRADBURN, N. & CAPLOVITZ, D. *Reports on Happiness*. Chicago: Aldine, 1965.

BRENNER, B. *Social Factors in Mental Well-Being at Adolescence*. Unpublished doctoral dissertation. American University, 1970.

BROFENBRENNER, U. The changing American child—a speculative analysis. *Journal of Social Issues*, 1961, 17, 6-18.

BROVERMAN, I. K., VOGAL, S. R., BROVERMAN, D. M., CLARKSON, F. E., & ROSENKRANTZ, P. S. Sex role stereotypes: A current appraisal. *Journal of Social Issues*, 1972, 28 (2), 59-78.

BROWN, D. Sex-role preference in young children. *Psychological Monographs*, 1956, 70, 1-19.

BROWN, D. Sex-role development in a changing culture. *Psychological Bulletin*, 1958, 55, 232-242.

BRUNETTI, P. M. A prevalence survey of mental disorders in a rural commune in Vaucluse: Methodological consideration. *Acta Psychiatrica Scandinavica*, 1964, 40, 323-358.

BRUNETTI, P. M. Prevalance des troubles mentaux dans une population rurale du Vaucluse: Donnés nouvelles et recapitulatives. *L'Hygiene Mentale*, 1973, 62, 1-15.

BULLOCK, R. C., SIEGEL, R., WEISSMAN, M., & PAYKEL, E. S. The weeping wife: Marital relations of depressed women. *Journal of Marriage and the Family*, 1972, 32, 488-495.

CHESLER, P. Women as psychiatric and psychotherapeutic patients. *Journal of Marriage and the Family*, 1971, 33, 746-759.

CLANCY, K. & GOVE, W. Sex differences in mental illness: An analysis of response bias in self-reports. *American Journal of Sociology*, 1974, 80, 205-216.

COHEN, M. Personal identity and sexual identity. *Psychiatry*, 1966, 29, 1-14.

COLE, S. The growth of scientific knowledge. In R. L. Coser (Ed.), *The Idea of the Social Structure: Papers in Honor of Robert K. Merton*. New York: Harcourt, 1975.

COLEMAN, J. *The Adolescent Society*. New York: Free Press, 1961.

COOPER, B. Psychiatric disorder in hospital and general practice. *Social Psychiatry*, 1966, 1 (1), 7-10.

COOPER, B., BROWN, A. C., & KALTON, G. G. A pilot study of psychiatric morbidity in general practice. *Journal of the College of General Practitioners*, 1962, 5, 590-602.

COOPERSTOCK, R. Sex differences in the use of mood-modifying drugs: An explanatory model. *Journal of Health and Social Behavior*, 1971, 12, 238-244.

COSER, R. L. & ROKOFF, G. Women in the occupational world: Social disruption and conflict. *Social Problems*, 1971, 18, 535-555.

COTTRELL, L. The adjustment of the individual to his age and sex roles. *American Sociological Review*, 1942, 7, 617-620.

CRANDALL, V. & RABSON, A. Children's repetition choices in an intellectual achievement situation following success and failure. *The Journal of Genetic Psychology*, 1960, 97, 161-168.

CRANDALL, V. Sex differences in expectancy of intellectual and academic reinforcement. In C. Smith (Ed.), *Achievement Related to Motives in Children*. New York: Russell Sage Foundation, 1969.

CUMMING, J. The incidence of emotional symptoms in children. *British Journal of Educational Psychology*, 1944, 14, 151-161.

DAHLSTROM, E. & LILJESTROM, R. The family and married women at work. In E. Dahlstrom (Ed.), *The Changing Roles of Men and Women*. Boston: Beacon, 1971.

DAVIDSON, H. & LANG, G. Children's perceptions of their teacher's feelings toward them related to self-perception, school achievement and behavior. *Journal of Experimental Education*, 1960, 29, 107-118.

DAVIS, F. & OLSEN, V. The career outlook of professionally educated women. *Psychiatry*, 1965, 28, 334-345.

DENIS, G., TOUSIGNANT, M., & LAFOREST, L. Prevalence de cas d'interet psychiatrique dans une region du Quebec. *Canadian Journal of Public Health*, 1973, 604, 387-397.

DOHRENWEND, B. Sociocultural and social-psychological factors in the genesis of mental disorder. *Journal of Health and Social Behavior,* 1975, 16, 365-392.

DOHRENWEND, B. & DOHRENWEND, B. S. The problem of validity in field studies of psychological disorder. *Journal of Abnormal Psychology,* 1965, 70 (4) , 52-69.

DOHRENWEND, B. & DOHRENWEND, B. S. *Social Status and Psychological Disorder.* New York: Wiley, 1969.

DOHRENWEND, B. & DOHRENWEND, B. S. Sex differences in psychiatric disorders. *American Journal of Sociology,* May, 1976, 81, 1447-1459.

DOUVAN, E. Sex differences in adolescent character processes. *Merrill-Palmer Quarterly,* 1960, 6, 203-211.

DOUVAN, E. & ADELSON, J. *The Adolescent Experience.* New York: Wiley, 1966.

DURKHEIM, E. *Suicide: A Study in Sociology.* New York: Free Press, 1951.

ENGELSMANN, F., MURPHY, H. B. M., PRINCE, R., LEDUC, M., & DEMERS, H. Variations in responses to a symptom check-list by age, sex, income, residence and ethnicity. *Social Psychiatry,* 1972, 7, 150-156.

EPSTEIN, C. *Woman's Place.* Berkeley: University of California Press, 1970.

EPSTEIN, C. & GOODE, W. (Eds.) . *The Other Half: Roads to Women's Equality.* Englewood Cliffs, N.J.: Prentice Hall, 1971.

EPSTEIN, L. J. An analysis of teachers' judgments of problem children. *Journal of Genetic Psychology,* 1941, 59, 501-511.

ESSEN-MOLLER, E. Individual traits and morbidity in a Swedish rural population. *Acta Psychiatrica et Neurologica Scandinavica,* 1956, Suppl. 100, 1-160.

FAGGOT, B. & PATTERSON, G. An *in vivo* analysis of reinforcing contingencies for sex-role behaviors in the preschool child. *Developmental Psychology,* 1969, 1, 563-568.

FARMER, H. & BOHN, M. Home-career conflict redirection and the level of career interest in women. *Journal of Counseling Psychology,* 1970, 17, 228-232.

FIDELL, L. & PRATHER, J. The housewife syndrome: Fact or fiction. Mimeographed, 1975.

FREEMAN, J. Growing up girlish. *Trans-Action,* 1970, 8, 36-43.

FRIEDAN, B. *The Feminine Mystique.* New York: Norton, 1963.

FRY, J. What happens to our neurotic patients? *Practitioner,* 1960, 185, 85-89.

GAITZ, C. M. & SCOTT, J. Age and the measurement of mental health. *Journal of Health and Social Behavior,* 1972, 13, 55-67.

GATES, A. T. Sex differences in reading ability. *Elementary School Journal,* 1961, 61, 431-434.

GAVRON, H. *The Captive Wife: Conflicts of Housebound Mothers.* London: Routledge & Kegan Paul, 1966.

GILBERT, G. M. A survey of referred problems in metropolitan child guidance centers. *Journal of Clinical Psychology,* 1957, 13, 37-42.

GLENN, N. The contribution of marriage to the psychological well-being of males and females. *Journal of Marriage and the Family,* 1975, 37, 594-604.

GLIDEWELL, J. Studies of mothers' reports of behavior symptoms in the children. In S. B. Sells (Ed.) , *Definition and Measurement of Mental Health.* Washington: Government Printing Office, 1968.

GLIDEWELL, J., MENSH, I., & GILDEA, M. Behavior symptoms in children and degree of sickness. *American Journal of Psychiatry,* 1957, 11, 47-53.

GOLDFARB, A. Teachers' ratings in psychiatric case finding. *American Journal of Public Health,* 1963, 53, 1919-1927.

GOODE, W. Norm commitment and conformity to role status obligations. *American Journal of Sociology,* 1960, 66, 246-258.

GOODENOUGH, F. L. Anger in young children. *Institute of Child Welfare Monograph,* Series 9. Minneapolis: University of Minnesota Press, 1933.

GORDON, R. & GORDON, K. Psychiatric problems of a rapidly growing suburb. *American Medical Association Archives of Neurology and Psychiatry*, 1958, 79, 543-548.

GORNICK, V. & MORAN, B. (Eds.). *Women in Sexist Society: Studies in Power and Powerlessness*. New York: Basic Books, 1971.

GOVE, W. Types of psychiatric patients. Master's thesis, University of Washington, Seattle, 1967.

GOVE, W. The relationship between sex roles, mental illness and marital status. *Social Forces*, 1972, 51, 34-44. (a)

GOVE, W. Sex roles, marital status and suicide. *Journal of Health and Social Behavior*, 1972, 13, 204-213. (b)

GOVE, W. Psychological status and social correlates. Grant application to the National Science Foundation, 1973. (a)

GOVE, W. Sex, marital status and mortality. *American Journal of Sociology*, 1973, 79, 45-67. (b)

GOVE, W. Deviant behavior, social intervention and labelling theory. In L. Coser and O. Larsen (Eds.), *The Uses of Controversy in Sociology*. New York: Free Press, 1976.

GOVE, W. & GALLE, O. Unpublished data, 1977.

GOVE, W. & GEERKEN, M. Response bias in community surveys: An empirical investigation. *American Journal of Sociology*, 1977, 82, 1289-1317.

GOVE, W. & HERB, T. Stress and mental illness among the young: A comparison of the sexes. *Social Forces*, 1974, 53 (2) , 256-265.

GOVE, W., McCORKEL, J., FAIN, T. & HUGHES, M. Response bias in community surveys of mental health: Systematic bias and random noise. *Social Science and Medicine*, 1976, 10, 497-502.

GOVE, W. & TUDOR, J. Adult sex roles and mental illness. *American Journal of Sociology*, 1973, 73, 812-835.

GOVE, W. & TUDOR, J. Sex differences in mental illness: A comment on Dohrenwend and Dohrenwend. *American Journal of Sociology*, 1977, 82, 1327-1336.

GRIFFITHS, W. *Behavior Difficulties of Children as Perceived and Judged by Parents, Teachers, and Children Themselves*. Minneapolis: University of Minnesota Press, 1952.

GURIN, G., VEROFF, J., & FELD, S. *Americans View their Mental Health*. New York: Basic, 1960.

HAAVIO-MANNILA, E. Sex differentiation in role expectations and performance. *Journal of Marriage and the Family*, 1967, 29, 368-378.

HABERMAN, P. Cross-survey analysis of psychiatric symptomatology: A corroborative report on subgroup differences. Paper presented at the annual meeting of the American Sociological Association, San Francisco, 1969.

HAGNELL, O. *A Prospective Study of the Incidence of Mental Disorder*. Stockholm: Svenska Bokforlaget Norstedts-Bonniers, 1966.

HARE, E. H. & SHAW, G. K. *Mental Health on a New Housing Estate*. London: Oxford University Press, 1965.

HARRISON, E. The working women: Barriers in employment. *Public Administration Review*, 1964, 24, 78-85.

HARTLEY, R. Some implications of current changes in sex role patterns. *Merrill-Palmer Quarterly of Behavior and Development*, 1959-60, 6, 153-164b.

HARTUP, W. & ZOOK, E. Sex-role preferences in three- and four-year-old children. *Journal of Consulting Psychology*, 1960, 24, 420-426.

HARTUP, W. W., MOORE, S. G., & SAGER, G. Avoidance of inappropriate sextyping by young children. *Journal of Consulting Psychology*, 1963, 24, 467-473.

HOFFMAN, L. W. Effects of the employment of mothers on parental power relations and the division of household tasks. *Marriage and Family Living*, 1960, 22, 27-35.

HOLZER, C. E., AREY, S. A., WARHEIT, G. J., & BELL, R. A. Sex, marital status and mental health: A reappraisal. Paper presented at the annual meeting of the American Sociological Association, San Francisco, 1975.

HUGHES, E. Dilemmas and contradictions of status. *American Journal of Sociology*, 1945, 50, 353-359.

HUGHES, D. Morbidity statistics from population surveys. In J. K. Wing and H. Hafner (Eds.), *Roots of Evaluation: The Epidemiological Basis for Planning Psychiatric Services*. New York: Oxford University Press, 1973.

ILFELD, F. Sex differences in psychiatric symptomatology. Mimeographed, 1977.

INNES, G. & SHARP, G. A study of psychiatric patients in Northeast Scotland. *Journal of Mental Science*, 1962, 108, 447-456.

KAGAN, J. Acquisition and significance of sextyping and sex-role identity. In M. Hoffman and L. Hoffman (Eds.), *Review of Child Development Research*. New York: Russell Sage Foundation, 1964.

KAGAN, J. & LEWIS, M. Studies of attention in the human infant. *Merrill-Palmer Quarterly*, 1965, 11, 95-127.

KAGAN, J. & MOSS, H. *Birth to Maturity*. New York: Wiley, 1962.

KANDO, T. Role strain: A comparison of males, females and transsexuals. *Journal of Marriage and the Family*, 1972, 34, 459-464.

KASL, S. & HARBURG, E. Mental health and urban environment: Some doubts and second thoughts. *Journal of Health and Social Behavior*, 1975, 16, 268-282.

KELLOGG, R. L. A direct approach to sex-role identification of school-related objects. *Psychological Reports*, 1969, 24, 839-841.

KESSEL, W. I. N. Psychiatric morbidity in a London general practice. *British Journal of Preventive Social Medicine*, 1960, 14, 16-22.

KLEIN, D. & DAVIS, J. *Diagnosis and Drug Treatment of Psychiatric Disorders*. Baltimore: Williams & Wilkins, 1969.

KNUDSEN, D. The declining status of women: Popular myths and the failure of functionalist thought. *Social Forces*, 1969, 48, 183-193.

KOMAROVSKY, M. Cultural contradiction and sex roles. *American Journal of Sociology*, 1946, 52, 184-189.

KOMAROVSKY, M. Functional analysis of sex roles. *American Sociological Review*, 1950, 15, 508-516.

KOPEL, D. & GEERDED, H. A survey of clinical services for poor readers. *Journal of Education and Psychology Monographs*, 1933, 13, 209-224. Baltimore: Warwick & York.

KREPS, J. *Sex in the Market Place: American Women at Work*. Baltimore: Johns Hopkins Press, 1971.

KUHN, T. *The Structure of Scientific Revolutions* (2nd ed.). Chicago: University of Chicago Press, 1970.

LAMOUSSE, A. Family roles of women: A German example. *Journal of Marriage and the Family*, 1969, 31, 145-152.

LANGNER, T. & MICHAEL, S. *Life Stress and Mental Health*. New York: Free Press, 1963.

LEIGHTON, D., LEIGHTON, A., HARDIN, J., MACKLIN, D., & MACMILLAN, A. *The Character of Danger*. New York: Basic Books, 1963.

LIPPITT, R. & GOLD, M. Classroom social structure as a mental health problem. *Journal of Social Issues*, 1959, 15, 40-50.

LOGAN, W. P. D. & CUSHION, A. A. *Morbidity Statistics from General Practice* (Vol. 1). Studies on medical population subjects, No. 14. London: Her Majesty's Stationery Office, 1958.

LOPATA, H. *Occupation Housewife*. New York: Oxford University Press, 1971.

LYNN, D. A note on sex differences in the development of masculine and feminine identification. *Psychological Review*, 1959, 66, 126-135.

LYNN, D. Sex differences in identification development. *Sociometry*, 1961, 24, 372-383.

McCARTHY, D. Some possible explanations of sex differences in language development and disorders. *Journal of Psychology*, 1953, 35, 155-160.

McCLELLAND, D. C. Wanted: A new self-image for women. In R. J. Liftron (Ed.), *The Women in America*. New York: Houghton Mifflin, 1965.

MACCOBY, E. *The Development of Sex Differences*. Stanford: Stanford University Press, 1966.

MACFARLANE, J., ALLEN, L., & HONZIK, M. *Behavior Problems of Normal Children*. Berkeley & Los Angeles: University of California Press, 1954.

McKEE, J. & SHERRIFFS, A. The differential evaluation of males and females. *Journal of Personality*, 1957, 25, 356-371.

McKEE, J. & SHERRIFFS, A. Men's and women's beliefs, ideals and self-conceptions. *American Journal of Sociology*, 1959, 64, 356-363.

MANIS, J. The sociology of knowledge and community mental health research. *Social Problems*, 1968, 15, 488-501.

MARMOR, J. *Psychiatrists and their Patients: A National Study of Private Office Practice*. Washington, D.C.: American Psychiatric Association, 1975.

MARTIN, F. M., BROTHERSTON, J. F., & CHAVE, S. P. Incidence of neurosis in a new housing estate. *British Journal of Preventive and Social Medicine*, 1957, 11, 196-202.

MATTHEWS, E. A study of emotional stability in children by means of a questionnaire. *Journal of Delinquency*, 1923, 8, 1-40.

MAZER, M. Psychiatric disorders in general practice: The experience of an island community. *American Journal of Psychiatry*, 1967, 124, 609-615.

MEAD, M. *Male and Female*. New York: Morrow, 1949.

MEDNICK, M. & TANGRI, S. New social psychological perspectives on marriage. *Journal of Social Issues*, 1972, 28, 1-16.

MEILE, R. & HAESE, P. Social status, incongruence and symptoms of stress. *Journal of Health and Social Behavior*, 1969, 10, 237-244.

MEYER, W. & THOMPSON, G. Teacher interaction with boys as contrasted with girls. In R. G. Kuhlens and G. G. Thompson (Eds.), *Psychological Studies in Human Development* (3rd ed.). New York: Appleton-Century-Crofts, 1970.

MILLS, A. W. Reports of a speech survey in Mount Holyoke, Massachusetts. *Journal of Speech Disorders*, 1947, 7, 161-167.

MURPHY, J. Psychiatric labeling in cross-cultural perspective. *Science*, 1976, 191, 1019-1028.

MURPHY, L. *The Widening World of Childhood*. New York: Basic Books, 1962.

MYRDAL, A. & KLEIN, V. *Women's Two Roles: Home and Work*. London: Kegan Paul, 1956.

National Institute of Mental Health. *Patients in State and County Mental Hospitals, 1967*. Washington: Government Printing Office, 1967. (a)

National Institute of Mental Health. *Patient Characteristics Private Mental Hospitals, 1967*. Washington: Government Printing Office, 1967. (b)

National Institute of Mental Health. *General Hospital Inpatient Psychiatric Services, 1967*. Washington: Government Printing Office, 1967. (c)

National Institute of Mental Health. *Outpatient Psychiatric Services, 1967*. Washington: Government Printing Office, 1967. (d)

National Institute of Mental Health. *Veterans with Mental Disorders, 1963-67*. Washington, D.C.: U.S. Government Printing Office, 1967. (e)

NYE, F. I. & HOFFMAN, L. W. The socio-cultural setting. In F. Nye and L. Hoffman (Eds.), *The Employed Mother in America*. Chicago: Rand McNally, 1963.

PARSONS, T. Age and sex in the social structure of the United States. *American Sociological Review*, 1942, 7, 604-616.

PARSONS, T. & BALES, R. *Family, Socialization, and Interaction Process.* Glencoe: Free Press, 1955.

PASAMANICK, B., ROBERTS, D. W., LEMKAU, P. W., & KRUEGER, D. B. A survey of mental disease in an urban population: Prevalence by race and income." In B. Pasamanick (Ed.), *Epidemiology of Mental Disorder.* Washington: American Assn. for the Advancement of Science, 1959.

PEARLIN, L. Sex roles and depression. *Life Span Developmental Psychology: Normative Life Crisis.* New York: Academic Press, 1975.

PERUCCI, C. C. Minority status and the pursuit of professional careers: Women in science and engineering. *Social Forces,* 1970, 49, 245-259.

PHILLIPS, D. Rejection of the mentally ill: The influence of behavior and sex. *American Sociological Review,* 1966, 29, 679-687.

PHILLIPS, D. & CLANCY, K. Response biases in field studies of mental illness. *American Sociological Review,* 1970, 35, 503-515.

PHILLIPS, D. & CLANCY, K. Some effects of "social desirability" in survey studies. *American Journal of Sociology,* 1972, 77, 921-940.

PHILLIPS, D. & SEGAL, B. Sexual status and psychiatric symptoms. *American Sociological Review,* 1969, 34, 58-72.

PINTLER, M., PHILLIPS, R., & SEARS, R. Sex differences in the projective doll play of preschool children. *Journal of Psychology,* 1946, 21, 73-80.

POLOMA, M. & GARLAND, T. N. The married professional woman: A study in the tolerance of domestication. *Journal of Marriage and the Family,* 1971, 33, 531-540.

PRIMROSE, E. J. B. *Psychological Illness: A Community Study.* London: Tavistock Publications, 1962.

PRUDENSKI, G. & KALPAKOV, B. Questions concerning the calculations of non-working time in budget statistics. *Problems of Economics,* 1962, 6, 12-31.

Public Health Service. *Selected Symptoms of Psychological Distress.* Public Health Service Publication No. 1000, Ser. 11, No. 37. Washington, D.C.: Government Printing Office, 1970.

RABBAN, M. Sex-role identification in young children in two diverse social groups. *Genetic Psychology Monographs,* 1950, 42, 81-158.

RADLOFF, L. Sex differences in depression: The effects of occupation and marital status. *Sex Roles,* 1975, 1 (No. 3), 249-265.

RAPOPORT, R. & RAPOPORT, R. Work and family in contemporary society. *American Sociological Review,* 1965, 30, 318-394.

REEVES, N. *Womankind: Beyond the Stereotype.* Chicago: Aldine-Altherton, 1971.

ROBBINS, L. A historical review of the classification of behavior disorders and one current perspective. In L. Eron (Ed.), *The Classification of Behavior Disorders.* Chicago: Aldine, 1966.

ROBERTS, E. R., FORTHOFER, R. N., & FABREGA, H., JR. The Langner items and acquiescence. *Social Science and Medicine,* 1976, 10, 69-75.

ROGERS, C. R. The criteria used in the study of mental health problems. *Educational Research Bulletin,* 1942, 21, 29-40.

ROSE, A. The adequacy of women's expectations for adult roles. *Social Forces,* 1951, 30, 69-77.

ROSENKRANTZ, P., VOGEL, S., BEE, H., BROVERMAN, I., & BROVERMAN,, D. Sex role stereotypes and self-conceptions in college students. *Journal of Consulting Psychology,* 1968, 32 (3), 287-295.

ROSSI, A. Equality between sexes: An immodest proposal. *Daedalus,* 1964, 93, 607-652.

ROSSI, A. The roots of ambivalence in American women. Unpublished paper presented at the Continuing Education Conference, Oakland University. Michigan, 1967.

ROWE, C. *An Outline of Psychiatry*. Dubuque, Iowa: Brown, 1970.

RUDY, A. J. Sex-role perceptions in early adolescence. *Adolescence*, 1968-69, 3, 453-460.

RYAN, W. *Distress in the City: Essays on the Design and Administration of Urban Mental Health Services*. Cleveland: The Press of Case Western Reserve University, 1969.

RYLE, A. The neurosis in a general practice. *Journal of the College of General Practitioners*, 1960, 3, 313-328.

SAFILIOS-ROTHSCHILD, C. The influence of the wife's degree of work commitment upon some aspects of family organization and dynamics. *Journal of Marriage and the Family*, 1970, 32, 681-691.

SANTROCK, J. Paternal absence, sex typing, and identification. *Developmental Psychology*, 1970, 2, 264-272.

SAPIR, S. Sex differences in perceptual motor development. *Perceptual and Motor Skills*, 1966, 22, 987-992.

SARASON, S. *Psychological Problems in Mental Deficiency* (3rd ed.). New York: Harper & Row, 1959.

SCHEFF, T. *Being Mentally Ill: A Sociological Theory*. Chicago: Aldine, 1966.

SCHUBERT, H. J. P. & WAGNER, M. E. The relations of individual personal data responses and transiency: Place among siblings and academic ability. *Journal of Abnormal and Social Psychology*, 1936, 30, 474-483.

SCOTT, J. *Aggression*. Chicago: University of Chicago Press, 1958.

SEARS, P. & FELDMAN, D. Teacher interactions: With boys and with girls. *National Elementary Principal*, 1966, 46, 30-36.

SEARS, R. Relations of early socialization experiences to aggression in middle childhood. *Journal of Abnormal and Social Psychology*, 1961, 63, 466-492.

SEARS, R., MACCOBY, E., & LEVIN, H. *Patterns of Child Rearing*. New York: Harper & Row, 1957.

SEIDLER, D. Sex differences in psychiatric epidemiology: A critique and inquiry. Unpublished dissertation, 1975.

SEWARD, G. Sex identity and the social order. *Journal of Nervous and Mental Diseases*, 1964, 139, 126-137.

SEWARD, G. & WILLIAMSON, R. C. *Sex Roles in Changing Society*. New York: Random House, 1970.

SHEPHERD, M., COOPER, B., BROWN, A. C., & KALTON, G. W. Minor mental illness in London: Some aspects of a general practice survey. *British Medical Journal*, 1964, 2, 1359-1363.

SHERRIFFS, A. & McKEE, J. Qualitative aspects of beliefs about men and women. *Journal of Personality*, 1957, 25, 450-464.

SILVERMAN, C. *The Epidemiology of Depression*. Baltimore: Johns Hopkins Press, 1968.

SIMMONS, R., ROSENBERG, F., & ROSENBERG, M. Disturbance in the self-image at adolescence. *American Sociological Review*, 1973, 38, 553-568.

SOBOL, M. G. Commitment to work. In F. Nye and L. Hoffman (Eds.), *The Employed Mother in America*. Chicago: Rand McNally, 1963.

SONTAG, L. W., BAKER, C. T., & NELSON, V. L. Mental growth and personality development: A longitudinal study. *Monographs of the Society for Research in Child Development*, 1958, 23 (2).

STEINMANN, A. & FOX, D. Male-female perceptions of the female role in the United States. *Journal of Psychology*, 1966, 64, 265-279.

SUSSER, M. *Community Psychiatry: Epidemiologic and Social Themes*. New York: Random House, 1968.

TAUSS, W. A note on the prevalence of mental disturbance. *Australian Journal of Psychology*, 1967, 19, 121-123.

TAYLOR, L. & CHAVE, S. *Mental Health and Environment*. London: Longman's Green, 1964.

TERMAN, L. & TYLER, L. Psychological sex differences. In L. Carmichael (Ed.), *Manual of Child Psychology*. New York: Wiley, 1954.

THOMPSON, G. *Child Psychology*. Boston: Houghton-Mifflin, 1962.

TUDOR, J., TUDOR, W., & GOVE, W. R. The effect of sex role differences on the social control of mental illness. *Journal of Health and Social Behavior*, 1977, 18, 98-112.

ULLMAN, C. Identification of maladjusted school children: A comparison of three methods of screening. *Public Health Monograph No. 7*. Washington: Government Printing Office, 1952.

VENER, A. & SNYDER, C. The preschool child's awareness and anticipation of adult sex roles. *Sociometry*, 1966, 29, 159-168.

VEROFF, J. Social comparison and development of achievement motivation. In C. Smith (Ed.), *Achievement-Related Motives in Children*. New York: Russell Sage Foundation, 1969.

VEROFF, J. & FELD, S. *Marriage and Work in America*. New York: Van Nostrand Rheinold, Co., 1970.

WARD, W. Process of sex-role development. *Developmental Psychology*, 1969, 1, 163-168.

WARHEIT, G. J., HOLZER, C. E., & AREY, S. A. Race and mental illness: An epidemiologic update. *Journal of Health and Social Behavior*, 1975, 16, 243-256.

WATTS, C. A. H. Psychiatric disorders. In *Morbidity Statistics from General Practice* (Vol. 3). Studies on Medical Population Subjects No. 14. London: Her Majesty's Stationery Office, 1962.

WATTS, C. A. H., CAUTE, E. C., & KUENSSBERG, E. U. Survey of mental illness in general practice. *British Medical Journal*, 1964, 2, 1351-1359.

WEISSMAN, M. & KLERMAN, G. Sex differences in the epidemiology of depression. Mimeographed, 1976.

WINTERBOTTOM, M. The relationship of childhood training in independence to achievement motivation. Unpublished doctoral dissertation, University of Michigan, 1953.

WITKIN, H. A., DYK, R. B., FATERSON, H. F., GOODENOUGH, D. R., & KAUP, S. A. *Psychological Differentiation*. New York: Wiley, 1962.

ZOLIK, E. & MARCHES, J. Mental health morbidity in a suburban community. *Journal of Clinical Psychology*, 1968, 24, 103-108.

Part II
LIFE CYCLE CRISES

3

PROBLEM BEHAVIOR
IN ADOLESCENTS

ANNE LOCKSLEY and ELIZABETH DOUVAN

Analyses by Gove and his associates of sex differences in the incidence and forms of psychopathology (Gove & Herb, 1974; Gove & Tudor, 1973) have stimulated a lively exchange concerning the methodological problems inherent in such work—problems of response bias, for example (Clancy & Gove, 1974; Dohrenwend & Dohrenwend, 1975). When we move from an adult population to a concern with adolescent pathology, problems proliferate, particularly with regard to "objective" indices.

Questions about the meaning and sources of sex differences in the distribution of psychopathology among adolescents obviously presuppose that such a distribution can be determined. For several reasons, however, this information is difficult to obtain. Forms of psychopathology are ordinarily defined by prevailing psychiatric diagnostic categories. Distributions of these forms usually consist of distributions of diagnoses sampled from psychiatric clinics, psychiatric hospitals, and similar organizations. But the complex sequence of events which culminates in a diagnosis of an adolescent by an authority of the mental health professions cannot be assumed to function in such a way that the sample of diagnoses could serve as a representative estimate of the distribution of all possible diagnoses among adolescents in the population. Some of the factors responsible for this conclusion can be outlined:

First, adolescents rarely initiate contact with mental health professionals. Adults, whether parents, school authorities, or legal authorities, are usually responsible for the adolescent's referral. Hence, the problems

The research reported in this paper was supported by a grant from the National Institute of Mental Health (MH-15606). We would 'like to think Richard Kulka for his helpful comments on the first draft of this paper.

which precipitate adult intervention tend to be either forms of psycho-pathology which are accompanied by extreme behavioral disturbances (such as schizophrenia or anorexia nervosa), or behavioral disturbances which may be as indicative of situational difficulties in the adolescent's home or school environment as symptomatic of underlying psychody-namic problems. Examples of the latter category are repeated truancy or running away from home, drug abuse, delinquency, and promiscuity and illegitimate pregnancy for girls. Referrals for such problems can reflect breakdowns in the ordinary modes of social control which adults exercise over adolescents. And such problems are not necessarily coextensive with psychopathology. "Silent" psychopathology, or symptoms, like persistent depression or anxiety, which are problematic for the adolescent but not excessively so for adults, are unlikely to precipitate adult intervention.

This point is central to the issue of sex differences in the incidence of psychopathology. Insofar as distributions of diagnoses serve as the em-pirical base for theoretical explanations of sex differences, it is essential to consider the nature and role of adults' judgments in the interactional process by which an adolescent is referred for diagnosis and treatment. For what is perceived to be problematic behavior for girls, such as sexual promiscuity, can be perceived to be acceptable for boys. Yet social norms are not equivalent to a psychological theory of mental health and illness.

Secondly, diagnoses are most easily sampled from psychiatric clinics and hospitals. But there are other points of contact between adolescents and mental health professionals. Children of affluent parents, for example, are more likely to see psychotherapists in private practice, unless the problem is so extreme that it warrants hospitalization. Children of lower-class parents may see therapists or counselors in reform schools or other juvenile delinquency correctional programs, or, in the case of girls, in homes for unwed mothers. Therapists working in private practice or in nonpsychiatric organizations and programs are difficult to sample, may not compile diagnostic histories, or, particularly in the latter arena of practice, may not make formal individual diagnoses at all. Since class, race, and sex characteristics of the adolescent influence the locus of con-tact with mental health professionals, these factors bias the distribution of diagnoses sampled from psychiatric clinics and hospitals.

We have not yet considered the adequacy of psychiatric diagnostic categories to represent or indicate psychopathology. This is a complex issue and lies beyond the scope of this paper. Nonetheless, it should be noted that criteria for specific diagnoses may affect their distribution by sex even when there is reason to suppose the basic syndrome occurs in both males and females. For example, no male adolescent could have been diagnosed as anorexic as long as amenorrhea was included in the list of diagnostic criteria for anorexia nervosa.

Recently, explanations of sex differences in the incidence of forms of psychopathology have considered the role of sex-linked socialization and of situational stress characteristic of largely female or largely male populated social niches in the development of psychopathology (Bart, 1971; Chesler, 1972; Dube, 1974; Fodor, 1974; Nathanson, 1975; Schwab, 1974; Wolowitz, 1972). These studies often rely on distributions of diagnoses for empirical evidence of the differential impact of situations, norms, and demands more commonly experienced by members of one sex than another. However, the leap from diagnostic distributions to daily life events is largely conjectural. In particular, such an approach raises the question of why other people experiencing the same stress do not wind up in clinic or hospital, or on a couch. Do they evidence similar symptoms?

In light of these considerations, the explanation and significance of sex differences in the incidence of psychopathology among adolescents may require an alternative empirical base to that established by sampling diagnostic distributions from psychiatric clinics and hospitals. Indeed, in spite of their own limitations, direct surveys of samples of the general population may provide better estimates for epidemiological statistics. Although national surveys of the incidence of psychopathology among adolescents have not been conducted as yet, this may be a direction for research ultimately as profitable as those directions heretofore pursued.

In the absence of data it was natural enough for people to assume that adolescent pathology was more common in males than in females. The data which were available and seemed the closest launching place for generalizing—data on childhood incidence—were clear and clearly indicated a higher incidence of problem behaviors among boys. From preschool through grade school a disproportionate number of behavior problems of all kinds presented to school authorities and child guidance clinics occur in boys. At the beginning of kindergarten girls generally score higher than boys on school readiness indices, on rough measures of specific social and verbal skills, and on overall ratings of capacity to endure separation from the family and to adapt and cooperate with peers in a new social setting. Boys are more disruptive in school throughout the elementary grades. They show a higher incidence of learning disabilities and have more serious separation problems than girls do.

Recently, however, Gove and Herb's (1974) examination of data specific to the adolescent period has raised the possibility that around prepuberty girls begin to show an increase in symptoms and that by adolescence they have either caught up with or overtaken boys in the incidence of behavior problems and psychopathology.

To those of us who have worked in the area for some time, the Gove and Herb data and conclusions came as confirmation of impressions and hunches built up over the years but previously unsupported by clear systematic data. The adolescent developmental tasks of our major theories imply larger ambiguities and complications for females, interviews and diaries from female adolescents reflect these problems, and we know from data on adults that women report more symptoms than men in both the psychological and physical realms. Somewhere between childhood and adulthood a reversal occurs, and developmental theory would seem to make a compelling case for adolescence as the shifting point. Gove and Herb's work confirmed a view that can be developed abstractly on the basis of theory.

It is this theoretical argument which we will present, along with some data from our own research on normal adolescents in high school. The theoretical view would predict both a higher incidence of problems in females during adolescence and also specific sex differences in the particular behaviors and symptoms through which stress will be expressed.

DEVELOPMENTAL THEORY

A careful reading of the developmental theories of childhood which encompass social and emotional growth leads to the view that there are two central crises of childhood which outweigh other developmental tasks which occur during the period between birth and adulthood. These are (a) the crisis of becoming a child and leaving infancy behind, and (b) the crisis of adolescence, that is, yielding childhood to become adult. The two crises share characteristics: They both mark radical discontinuities in behavior and the acquisition or potential acquisition of new powers. They both signal a new relationship to a developing self and to the social structure.

In early childhood, about the middle of the third year of life, the child enters what Erikson designates as the stage of autonomy. In part the stage is precipitated by a social demand on the child for adherence to the society's standards of cleanliness. This demand, in turn, is timed to correspond with the child's muscular development: Now acquiring facility in the use and control of both large and fine muscles (including the sphincters), the child is asked to curb expression of body functions, to alter his relationship to his body. He is asked to learn to recognize internal cues surrounding body functions and to bring performance under conscious control—all in the service of conformity to social demand. At the same time the child meets restrictions on the exercise of his newly acquired power of locomotion and large muscle coordination. The society demands both conformity and self-control from the child.

Several features of the child's development and the society's norms lead to greater potential hazards for the boy child at this juncture. At the most abstract level we can capture some of the reasons for this by noting that in the vocabulary of conventional sex roles, all babies are feminine. That is, all babies are passive and dependent. The girl can maintain these central themes throughout childhood (and indeed, in traditional circles, throughout life) without threatening her own social acceptance or the norms of her society. But the boy cannot. In order to become an acceptable male, the little boy must make a decisive break from infancy. He must abandon the passivity and dependency of babyhood and make himself into a boy in order to be accepted and regarded by his parents and in order not to frighten them.

In concrete and specific terms, the boy is likely to have more conflict with socializing agents because of developmental pacing and because of the culture's narrower prescriptions regarding acceptable male behavior. There is, first of all, the differential rate of muscular development and of those other skills which facilitate self-control. Boy babies are larger and have more developed large muscle mass than girls, they have a lower threshold for aggressive behavior, they are less early and less adept in the acquisition of language, and perhaps of other skills closely tied to language—in the interpretation of verbal cues and other social cues like facial expressions, in empathy and the leaning into other people's social space to catch meaning.

Their muscle development and aggressive potential insure that little boys will experience confrontations with adult authority, while little girls are more facile at figuring out what adults want, and have less intense internal pressure to explore forbidden acts. The litle girl continues to find dominant satisfaction in the response of others and exercises her finer skills in divining what it is that those important people want who supply her satisfactions and sense of self.

But there is a further complication in the boy's development: The culture defines acceptable masculinity more narrowly than it defines acceptable femininity. Both boys and girls are sanctioned for aggressive or explicitly sexual behavior (though boys are probably in fact more likely to provoke the sanctions), but little boys are also sanctioned for passive and dependent behaviors which are acceptable in girls.

So the male child is more likely than the female to have relatively direct confrontations and conflict with adult authorities trying to impose cultural norms for control. Their musculature and their relatively unrefined social skills make running, jumping, climbing, and hitting more focused and central sources of pleasure and of a sense of self. Their biological sexuality—external and specific—is more likely to put them in direct conflict with adult prohibition against masturbating and other forms of open sexual curiosity and expression.

An even more important source of conflict for the boy comes from the social norms which impose restrictions not only on his freedom, aggressiveness, and sexuality, but also on his dependency. When the boy is about two or two-and-a-half, his parents begin to expect him to give up his baby ways and become both more self-controlled and more self-sufficient. Parents are concerned about a little boy who clings to his mother, needs the reassurance of her presence, and cannot participate freely in a play group or stay alone (i.e., without a parent) at nursery school. Parents are more concerned about the little boy who shows these signs of dependency than they are about similar behaviors in a little girl, even though boys are less socially developed than girls and are more likely to exhibit these specific dependent behaviors. Developmental facts and norms of performance to the contrary notwithstanding, parents expect greater autonomy from the boy than from the girl.

It is no wonder, then, that boys exhibit more symptoms of conflict and more behavior problems in early childhood than girls do. Having just discovered his new powers—for locomotion, sexual stimulation, and self-assertion—the boy finds that his expression of these powers is carefully hedged in and restricted by adults, and that they expect him not only to give up these pleasures but also to master certain feats of self-control (i.e., for cleanliness) which he can only roughly understand and inadequately perform.

If the little boy manages to weather the period of early childhood, he will emerge with a relatively well developed sense of self, a rudimentary conscience, and a relatively close knowledge of the pleasures to be had from the body, from the exercise of its powers. The girl emerges from a less hazardous passage into childhood without so strong a sense of self but with a more refined and highly developed ability to detect the meanings and desires of important adults and the ability to get what she needs (including a sense of self) by depending on adults and receiving rewards from social exchange.

The second major developmental crisis occurs at puberty. Both the boy and the girl child must come to terms with emerging adult sexuality and integrate sexuality into a new concept of self. Radical body changes and the demands of society for performance of new roles must be worked into a new and coherent concept.

Sexuality for the boy is explicit and knowable through the external genitalia which are both familiar and familiarly pleasurable. The girl's sexuality is more ambiguous and hidden and is issued into her consciousness initially with blood and often with pain. The boy's sexual task during adolescence consists of detaching cathexis from the family and developing heterosexual friendships in which he can eventually find a suitable love relationship. The girl has all of these tasks but she has in addition to come to know the nature of her more ambiguous and obscure sexuality. This understanding is traditionally achieved through close sharing relationships with other girls.

For this and a number of other reasons, adolescence is probably a more subtle and complicated period for the female than for the male. In early childhood the boy is asked to give up old patterns and make a clean break from infancy; at puberty the girl is required to yield old and customary ways of behaving and sources of satisfaction. Up to puberty the girl has, in Bardwick's terms, experienced bisexual socialization. She is expected to be compliant, feminine, and charming, thoughtful, helpful, and giving; but she has also been taught in school that it is legitimate and good for her to seek personal achievement in school and to compete actively to reach that goal.

At adolescence, however, she is confronted with the sex-role norms of her society which define the central goals for a woman as the traditional affiliative ones of marriage and motherhood. She discovers through the peer group that, to be a desirable and acceptable woman, she must restrict her competitive and achieving behavior, that boys don't like "brains" and assertive-competitiveness in their girlfriends, and that they do not want to be bested in competition by a girl. High school norms are demonstrably conservative regarding sex roles. Popular girls value being in school activities and being social leaders, and devalue academic performance.

What this means to the bright, high achievement female is that she has been trained in school in behaviors that now have no payoff in the world of peer activities and peer acceptance. The individualistic skills and values of grade school will get her none of the rewards of adolescent society, and, in addition, they have little relevance to what she is now told are the central roles by which she is to define her adult self—the roles of wife and mother. The training in independence, autonomy, and achievement which has defined her formal schooling through elementary school and junior high school must be yielded in favor of deference, dependency, and definition of the self by attachments to others rather than by individuated, autonomous behavior.

One final point about the situation of male and female adolescents: We expect on the basis of both theory and previous empirical findings that males will assert their autonomy from adult authority during this developmental phase and that they will use peers as allies in their thrust for freedom and as a reference group in defining their progress on the path to autonomy and adulthood. Female adolescents, on the other hand, will continue to look to adults for evaluation of their developing self. For most females the thrust for autonomy will not occur until after adolescence—when the young woman leaves home for college, or to marry, or perhaps not until the birth of her first child (when she establishes herself decisively as her mother's peer in the critical area of feminine realization). In most cases, the female will work through her autonomy without direct confrontation, and during adolescence she will not use peers as reference anchors or comparison figures in the way that males do.

PROBLEM BEHAVIORS IN A POPULATION OF NORMAL ADOLESCENTS

Our interest in sex differences in the forms and incidence of psychopathology among adolescents developed out of a social psychological, rather than clinical, perspective. We were concerned about relationships between behavioral and symptomatic manifestations of stress and contemporaneous problems of adolescence, rather than with links between intrapsychic conflicts and early childhood experiences. For several reasons, an investigation of adolescents' experience of high school appeared to be an important way to pursue this interest.

First, the high school is the formal organization for the preparation of students to become adult members of society, presumably responsible for facilitating their integration into the work force through transmission of skills and clarification of capacities. Stinchcombe (1964) has pointed out that the high school functions within the context of the community and society at large. He argues that students' responses to the high school can be understood in terms of their anticipation of its significance for their future status in the work world. Although he focuses on the implications of anticipated socioeconomic class as a major predictor of students' attitudes and behavior in high school, he acknowledges that sex segregation of roles and jobs within class must be considered in interpreting sex differences in attitudes towards school and extent of rebellious behavior.

Given the world outside of high school is largely sex segregated, teachers, counselors, and other school adults may selectively attend to those aspects of their students which are congruent with future role prospects. Their articulation of the significance of achievement and participation in high school for students' futures may vary for female and male students. The assumption that girls will be primarily invested in family roles creates an attitude of benign neglect toward female students. On the one hand, immediate social control interests of school authorities reinforce their expectations that girls behave appropriately and perform well in the classroom. On the other hand, selective socialization interests of school authorities reinforce their expectations that girls' futures are largely a function of their marriage prospects and only secondarily a function of the talents and skills evidenced by their academic performance. In this way, high school adults are involved in the transmission of information about contingencies and values of sex-role acquisition.

Second, sexual and biological maturation during adolescence catalyzes the task of developing a sense of adult sexual identity. Sexuality can be extremely salient and laden with anxiety during adolescence, creating vulnerability to behavioral norms of masculinity and femininity. And whether or not an adolescent winds up marrying a high school sweetheart, the peer group functions as a more reliable source of information about standards of sexual acceptability and desirability in interpersonal relationships than adults.

Thus, the high school, unlike the family, is an organization which is simultaneously characterized by interactions with adults who function as links to the students' futures in the world of work, and by interactions with peers who function as links to the students' futures in the world of sexuality, friendship, and family. Processes of sex-role acquisition and gender identity consolidation are implicated in adolescents' experience of peers and adults in the high school setting.

Differential Foci of Conflict for Male and Female Adolescents

Research on the stressful impact of the high school has usually focused either on problems all students encounter (e.g., Buxton, 1973; Jackson, 1968), or on problems male students encounter (Sexton, 1967, 1970). The focus on male students' problems is partly attributable to the fact that males characteristically outnumber females in discipline referrals, expulsions, and so on. It has been accordingly inferred that males experience more conflict in the high school setting than females. One theory which attempts to explain sex differences in the stressful impact of high school extends Kagan's (1964) and others' (Grambs & Waetjen, 1966; Peltier, 1968) characterization of elementary school environments as feminine to the high school (Sexton, 1967, 1970). The basic argument may be stated as follows:

> *Proposition 1*: The structure of opportunities and expectations in high school is such that rewards are most easily achieved by verbal, compliant, and introspective students, and punishment administered to independent, energetic, and assertive students.
>
> *Proposition 2*: In general, girls are verbal, compliant, and introspective, and boys are independent, energetic, and assertive.
>
> *Conclusion*: Thus girls are more likely to be rewarded in school than boys, and boys are more likely to be punished.
>
> *Prediction*: Since boys are punished more frequently than girls, they experience high school demands as conflictful and consequently evidence more stress in such forms as aggressive behavior.

The theory may sound persuasive at first reading. Academic achievement requires compliance, verbal fluency, and competence, and academic achievement is the primary standard for administration of rewards in high school. However, there are several questionable assumptions underlying this argument. The first assumption is that the high school environment is uniform with respect to the nature of formal and informal tasks it imposes upon both male and female students. But it was suggested earlier that teachers, counselors, and administrative staff have very different expectations about appropriate male and female student behavior, and different assumptions about the significance of such behavior as academic achievement for male and female students which influence their responses to such behavior. In addition, sex segregation exists in most coeducational high schools in extracurricular activities (notably athletics) and vocational curricular programs (notably home economics and typing versus auto mechanics and shop).

The second assumption is that discipline referrals, expulsions, and similar indicators of disruptive behavior are representative of manifestations of stress. However, such indicators are subject to the same limitation as diagnostic distributions, as explained earlier in this chapter. They are the consequence of adult intervention and clearly limited to custodially relevant manifestations of stress. Other indicators of stress, like depression, anxiety, or psychosomatic symptoms, are irrelevant to the social control interests of school authorities. Evidence (Bardwick, 1971) suggests that adolescent girls are more likely to express stress in custodially irrelevant forms. Furthermore, aggression is considered to be masculine behavior. Adolescents' heightened concerns about their own sexuality and sexual identities may facilitate a tendency to respond to problematic situations with stereotypic sex-role appropriate behavior in an attempt to maintain or develop a secure sense of sexual identity. As a result, the failure to consider both custodially relevant and irrelevant indicators of stress can create misleading impressions about the sex differential impact of the high school.

Third, the feminine high school theory neglects the realistic fears students experience in anticipating and planning their lives after graduation from high school, and anxieties and problems involved in the process of mastering sexual impulses and developing interpersonal attachments. Studies have demonstrated that adolescent students distinguish areas of achievement in terms of masculinity/femininity categories (Stein, 1971; Stein & Smithells, 1969), and that females value achievement in feminine areas over achievement in masculine areas (Battle, 1965, 1966; Stein, 1971). Although academic achievement in courses in the humanities and social sciences may be less incongruent with respect to a category of femininity than achievement in courses in mathematics and the natural sciences, college admissions requirements consider overall grade point average. Boys who plan to attend college need to earn good grades in all of their courses, and girls do as well. However, overall achievement, success, and intelligence are more congruent with masculinity categories than with femininity categories. Thus, even though girls may be capable of or actually achieve good grades in high school, they may experience conflicts between academic achievement and peer expectations for feminine behavior. Because grades are distributed to all students, they serve as a basis for social comparison and public accomplishment. The results of several studies suggest that girls experience academic achievement as conflictual with respect to their interactions with their male peers and may either reduce their effort or conceal their accomplishment (Horner, 1972; Stein & Bailey, 1973; Weiss, 1962).

In light of these considerations, the feminine high school theory of differential foci of conflict for female and male students appeared to be theoretically untenable. In the absence of data on the incidence of both custodially relevant and irrelevant forms of stress, however, and on their relationship to high school environmental factors, a systematic alternative theory was difficult to compose. Consequently, we decided to conduct an exploratory study which would be guided by schematically formulated propositions rather than rigorous hypotheses. The net had to be spread widely enough to catch the fish.

The schematic propositions with respect to sex differences in foci of conflict for female and male students have already been presented in our criticisms of the feminine high school theory. Essentially, we expected that girls would experience conflict over academic achievement with respect to planning for their futures, to sex-role identity, and in relation to male peers. We expected that boys would experience conflict over issues of compliance with school authorities, but that academic achievement would not be conflictful otherwise.

STRESS

The indicators of conflict to be reported in this chapter can be grouped under the general heading of manifestations of stress. Given an emphasis on the stressful impact of contemporaneous problems, diagnostic categories would not be useful indicators in this regard. Their distributions are too limited for use in a nonclinical population. The reader should note, therefore, that the indicators of stress are not equivalent to psychopathology, nor do they necessarily suggest psychodynamic conflicts. They are assumed to be manifestations of ongoing conflicts, experienced in interactions with high school adults and peers and in the activities into which the high school draws its students.

For reasons already stated, both custodially relevant and custodially irrelevant indicators of conflict were operationalized. In addition, both masculine-congruent and feminine-congruent indicators of conflict were operationalized. Disruptive behaviors which precipitate adult intervention may be more characteristic of males because they are congruent with stereotypes of masculinity and expressive as assertions of autonomy. Girls may express stress in ways which do not precipitate adult intervention because challenging authority and aggressive behavior are incongruent with femininity. Schematic propositions with respect to stress have also been presented in the context of our criticisms of the feminine high school theory. It was expected that females and males would generally express stress in sex-role congruent forms and that the extent of stress would relate differentially to academic achievement in the ways formulated above.

Findings from a Study of Normal Adolescents

Because it appeared to be necessary to bypass the process by which certain adolescents become identified as difficult or mentally ill by adults, it was decided to survey students directly about the incidence of indicators of stress which are both relevant and irrelevant to school adults' interest in social control and maintaining order in the high school. To minimize the effects of response bias and other limitations of self-report data, students were asked, on an item-by-item basis, to rate the frequency of specific behaviors, perceptions, sensations, and experiences within a specified time period. No global terms, such as depression or aggression, were used in item wording.

The data for this study were generated by the administration of a pretested questionnaire to a random sample of sophomores, juniors, and seniors attending a Midwestern, urban, lower-middle-class high school in the spring of 1973. The population of students was predominantly Caucasian.

The variables used as indicators of stress are scales constructed by factor analysis of item responses. The set of variables comprises (a) a measure of aggression, a scale composed of students' ratings of the frequency with which they engaged in a variety of aggressive behaviors ranging from physical, to verbal, to passive aggression; (b) a measure of psychosomatic symptoms, a scale composed of students' ratings of the frequency with which they experience sleeping difficulties (either insomnia or excessive sleeping), headaches, eating problems (either overeating or loss of appetite), and upset stomachs; (c) a measure of depression; (d) a measure of tension, and (e) a measure of resentment. All five scales met acceptable criteria for inter-item reliability coefficients and six- or eight-week retest reliability coefficients (Klingel, 1973; Kulka, 1975; Locksley, 1974).

Sex Differences in Distributions of Stress Indicators

Table 1 presents the means of male and female students on the five indicators of stress. Analyses of variance generated F-tests and Eta values to estimate the significance of sex differences in mean ratings of stress, and to estimate the proportion of variance of the stress indicators explained by the sex of the respondent. It can be seen in the table that, on the average, males report a significantly higher frequency of aggression and of feelings of resentment towards others than females do. On the average, females report a significantly higher frequency of feelings of

TABLE 1

Mean Ratings on Indicators of Stress by Sex

Indicators of Stress	Males[1]	Females[2]	F[3]	Eta
Aggression	35.4	21.0	20.9***	0.19
Tension	8.4	9.3	22.4***	0.20
Depression	18.2	18.8	NS	—
Resentment	4.8	4.4	10.1**	0.14
Psychosomatic symptoms	9.9	11.2	24.7***	0.21

[1]$N = 272$
[2]$N = 280$
[3]NS = not significant
** $= p < .01$
*** $= p < .001$

tension and of psychosomatic symptoms. The sexes do not differ on reported feelings of depression.

These findings are consistent with the hypothesis that males and females
express stress in different ways, although the proportion of variance in
the stress indicators explained by sex of the respondent is relatively small.

If males and females express in sex-role appropriate ways, then one
would expect differential cross-time consistency in the stress indicators,
as well as mean differences at one time point. Longitudinal data on reported stress were generated by a readministration of the questionnaire
to a subsample of the sophomores during their senior year in the spring
of 1975. Table 2 presents the longitudinal correlations between students'
ratings on the stress indicators sophomore year and their ratings senior
year, by sex. For males, only reported frequency of aggression sophomore
year is significantly correlated with reported frequency of aggression
senior year. None of the other indicators of stress evidence consistency
over the two-year experience of high school. Contrary to expectations,
reported frequency of aggression sophomore year is significantly correlated
with reported frequency of aggression during senior year for females as
well as males. But it is also the case for females that reported frequency
of psychosomatic symptoms during sophomore year is significantly correlated with reported frequency of psychosomatic symptoms during senior
year.

Several implications of these findings should be noted. First, the five
indicators of stress are not comparable. One unit of aggression is not
equivalent to one unit of tension. Thus these results cannot be used

TABLE 2

Longitudinal Correlations on Indicators of Stress by Sex

	Longitudinal Correlations	
Indicators of Stress	Males[1]	Females[2]
Aggression	.40**	.55**
Tension	.13	.26
Depression	.17	.26
Resentment	.27	.25
Psychosomatic symptoms	.20	.58***

[1]$N = 41$
[2]$N = 48$
** $= p \leq .01$
*** $= p < .001$

to make a comparative statement about how much stress male and female adolescents experience during the high school years. Nonetheless, the finding that females report a greater frequency of feelings of tension and of psychosomatic symptoms, whereas males report a greater frequency of aggression and feelings of resentment towards others, suggests that both sexes experience stress. The distribution of mean differences explains why boys are more likely to be subject to discipline referrals and other forms of adult intervention than girls. They express stress in ways hostile to others. However, this should not be interpreted to mean that boys experience high school as a more stressful environment than girls.

Second, the longitudinal correlations are somewhat ambiguous with respect to the expectation that adolescent boys and girls express stress in sex-role appropriate ways. For boys, the pattern emerges as expected. However, girls evidence consistency in both aggression and psychosomatic symptoms. This finding suggests a revision of our expectations and interpretation of the significance of longitudinal correlations. For one thing, it could be argued that aggression evidences cross-time consistency in both males and females because aggressive sophomores are likely to precipitate positive adult intervention, and positive adult intervention has the effect of contributing to the consolidation of a specific mode of response to problems simply because it exacerbates the hostility towards authorities such students already feel. As far as the issue of sex-role congruent expression of stress is concerned, it would appear to be a contributing factor to this consolidation process in boys but not in girls. An untabulated finding of relevance to this issue is that reported frequency of aggression sophomore year tends to predict reported frequency of psychosomatic symptoms during senior year for girls ($r = 0.27$, $p < .06$, $N = 49$), but not for boys. Given the strong cross-time correlation in aggression, this trend could probably not be interpreted as indicative of a shift in stress expression towards a more sex-role congruent form. It could suggest that the costs of aggressive behavior for girls increase from sophomore to senior year.

Thus, whereas boys appear to be consistently other-directed in expressing stress and frustration, girls are not only consistently self-directed, but they are also other-directed. Though less so, on the average, than boys, girls who are aggressive sophomore year tend to remain aggressive throughout high school. Perhaps the costs of sex-role incongruent behavior are less high for girls during the high school years than for boys. Alternatively, the costs of sex-role congruent expressions of stress may be greater for girls than for boys and so girls are less likely to confirm to sex-role prescriptions than boys are, particularly girls who experience punitive behavior on the part of school adults.

Stress and Academic Achievement

Two measures of academic achievement were used. The first measure is the respondents' cumulative grade point average, obtained from high school records. Grade point averages presumably mean several things to students. They indicate the extent to which the student's teachers judge the student's performance to meet the teachers' criteria of academic performance. However, they also serve as the basis for social comparison with peers, and as the basis for decision-making about one's plans for work and further education after high school graduation. It was expected that boys would find compliance with teachers' criteria and expectations conflictful because of autonomy norms, but that success relative to peers, and success relative to future planning for college or work, would reduce conflict. With respect to girls, it was expected that meeting teachers' criteria would not be conflictful, but that academic success relative to peers and to future planning would be conflictful because of its ambiguous status with respect to standards of femininity.

In order to tease out these effects, a subjective measure of academic achievement was used. This measure is one of ten operationalizing French's (French, Rodgers, & Cobb, 1974a, 1974b) concept of person-environment fit as a predictor of stress, (Kulka, 1975). French's concept of fit distinguishes categories of personal attributes and environmental properties. The measure in question, entitled Student Role Fit, distinguishes between personal abilities and environmental demands. Respondents were asked to rate the extent to which they considered themselves capable of various academic tasks, including earning good grades, putting effort into their school work, participating in class discussions, and staying alert and attentive throughout class sessions. They were also asked to rate the extent to which their parents and teachers expected them to be capable of these tasks. Student Role Fit is an index derived from subtracting respondents' average scores across environmental demands items from their average score across personal abilities item. Thus it is a subjective measure of the extent to which students perceive themselves to be capable of meeting the expectations of significant adults for academic achievement and academic behavior. The degree of perceived fit is not simply a function of objective academic achievement (that is, grade point average), because increasing grade point average predicts both increasing ratings of abilities and increasing ratings of perceived expectations for both boys and girls. Indeed, even though girls on the average achieve a higher grade point average than boys do ($2.8 > 2.4$, $F = 23.6$, $p < .001$, $Eta = 0.21$), they experience a greater mean discrepancy between their own abilities as students and adult expectations for academic success ($F = 8.1$, $p < .01$).

The Student Role Fit scale is a categorical variable with seven levels. Respondents classified as level one have the greatest discrepancy between personal abilities and adults' expectations for academic achievement and behavior. Respondents classified as level four have the least discrepancy, and respondents classified as level seven report more abilities than they perceive adults to expect.

Analyses of variance between the student-role abilities-demand scale and the five indicators of stress were computed separately for male and female respondents. Tables 3 and 4 present the results of the analysis, for males and females respectively. For boys, the only significant relationship between degree of student role fit and stress was obtained for resentment. In Table 3, the distribution of mean frequencies of feeling resentful across the fit groups demonstrates that increasing fit is associated with fewer feelings of resentment. Table 4 shows that for girls student role fit is significantly related to three indicators of stress: aggression, depression, and resentment. Girls who perceive themselves to be less capable of meeting academic expectations of teachers and parents are more aggressive, more frequently depressed, and more resentful than girls who perceive themselves to be capable.

TABLE 3

Impact of Student Role Abilities-Demands Fit on Males' Reported Frequencies of Stress

Student Role Abilities-Demands Fit Groups	N	Indicators of Stress				
		Aggression Mean	Tension Mean	Depression Mean	Resentment Mean	Psychosomatic Symptoms Mean
1	10	68.7	9.6	21.5	5.5	10.8
2	14	58.6	8.8	19.9	5.8	9.5
3	28	41.3	8.0	18.1	5.4	11.1
4	110	33.1	8.4	18.1	4.9	9.7
5	60	31.2	8.2	17.3	4.4	9.6
6	22	21.6	8.6	18.5	4.0	10.1
7	15	36.1	8.0	18.1	5.1	9.6
F		2.1	0.9	1.8	3.5**	1.3
Eta		0.22	0.14	0.20	0.28	0.17

** $= p < .01$

TABLE 4

Impact of Student Role Abilities-Demands Fit on Females' Reported Frequencies of Stress

Student Role Abilities-Demands Fit Groups	N	Aggression Mean	Tension Mean	Indicators of Stress Depression Mean	Resentment Mean	Psychosomatic Symptoms Mean
1	19	42.7	9.8	21.3	5.7	12.4
2	17	39.1	10.6	22.0	5.1	12.6
3	33	20.9	9.6	20.0	4.9	11.1
4	131	20.1	9.3	18.5	4.1	11.4
5	58	11.6	8.7	17.4	4.1	10.6
6	10	10.9	9.9	17.8	4.6	10.1
7	5	12.8	8.2	15.8	4.4	8.8
F		6.7***	2.1	3.9***	3.8***	1.9
Eta		0.36	0.21	0.29	0.28	0.21

*** = $p < .001$

These findings are consistent with the proposition that meeting adults' expectations for academic achievement would not necessarily reduce conflict in male adolescents. The degree to which meeting adults' expectations is associated with reduced conflict in female adolescents is striking. The Student Role Fit scale explains 13% of the variance in aggression scores for girls, and about 9% of the variance in depression and resentment scores.

There are two interesting implications of these findings. The first is that even though girls are, on the average, less aggressive and less resentful than boys, and even though no mean sex difference obtains for reported frequencies of depression, girls' experience of failing to meet adult expectations for academic achievement is associated with aggression, feelings of depression and feelings of resentment. Thus, mean differences alone can be misleading.

The second implication is that high school is as stressful, if not more so, for girls than for boys. More girls perceive themselves to be less capable of meeting the academic expectations of their parents and teachers than boys. Since meeting adults' expectations for academic achievement is associated more strongly with more indicators of stress for girls than for boys, it would appear that the high school experience is at least as conflictual for girls as it is for boys.

Finally, these findings contradict the proposition that the sexes respond to stress in sex-role appropriate ways. Only one of the three indicators of stress related to student role fit among girls is a self-directed measure of stress, namely depression.

In order to determine sex differences in the impact of grade point average on the five stress indicators, we used a technique called analysis of covariance (Blalock, 1970; Kerlinger & Pedhazur, 1973; Moser & Kalton, 1972). Analysis of covariance essentially computes regressions of the predictor variable (in this case, grade point average) on the dependent variables (in this case, the five indicators of stress), for the entire sample (both males and females) and within groups defined by a categorical variable (in this case, for males and females separately). It enables the data analyst to determine whether or not prediction of the indicators of stress by grade point average is significantly improved by computing regressions within sex groups. Thus, it is a method which can be used to evaluate the statistical significance of sex differences in patterns of relationships between variables.

In this paper we will restrict our presentation of the results of this analysis to those which meet the following criteria: (a) the prediction of an indicator of stress by grade point average is significant for at least one of the two sexes, and (b) the F test for the sex difference in regression lines is significant. Three of the analyses between the five indicators of a stress and grade point average met these criteria. The results are graphed in Figures 1-3. The graphs demonstrate that grade point average has a significant effect on reported frequencies of aggression, depression, and psychosomatic symptoms for boys but not for girls. Boys who achieve high

FIGURE 1

Grade Point Average and Aggression by Sex[1]

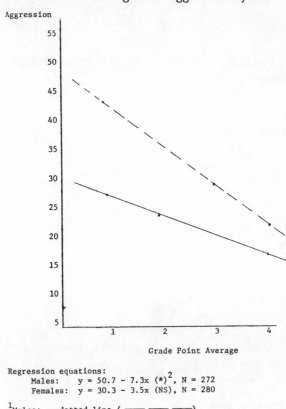

Grade Point Average

Regression equations:
Males: $y = 50.7 - 7.3x$ (*)[2], N = 272
Females: $y = 30.3 - 3.5x$ (NS), N = 280

[1]Males: dotted line (—— —— ——)
Females: solid line (——————)

[2] NS = not significant
   * = $p < .05$
  ** = $p < .01$
 *** = $p < .001$

grade point averages report less aggression, less depression, and fewer psychosomatic symptoms than boys who achieve low grade point averages. Further, Figure 1 shows that the size of the difference between male and female reported frequencies of aggression decreases as grade point averages increase. Figures 2 and 3 show that for each level of grade point average girls are more depressed and have more psychosomatic symptoms than boys.

Thus actual academic achievement reduces conflict for males but not for females. Indeed, girls with high grade point averages are more depressed and report more psychosomatic symptoms than boys do. These findings are consistent with the proposition that actual achievement is

FIGURE 2

Grade Point Average and Depression by Sex[1]

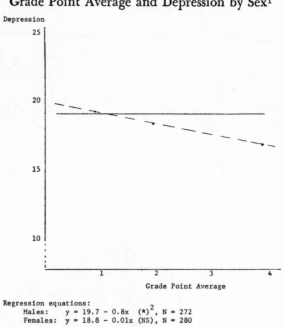

Regression equations:
Males: $y = 19.7 - 0.8x$ (*)[2], N = 272
Females: $y = 18.8 - 0.01x$ (NS), N = 280

[1]Males: dotted line (— — —— ——)
Females: solid line (————)

[2] NS = not significant
* = p .05
** = p .01
*** = p .001

conflictful for girls because grades provide a basis for social comparison with peers, and because high grades create problems in anticipating future work and family commitments. Academic achievement reduces conflict for boys because success in relation to one's peers, and success in preparation for one's future, are congruent with sex-role norms of masculinity.

Other Findings Supportive of the Argument

If the interpretation of the obtained sex differences in relationships between indicators of stress, academic achievement, and subjective perceptions of meeting adults' expectations for academic achievement is correct, then one can derive predictions for sex differences in relations between academic achievement and future plans.

FIGURE 3

Grade Point Average and Psychosomatic Symptoms by Sex[1]

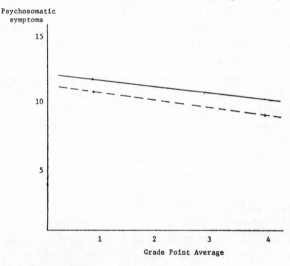

Regression equations:
  Males: $y = 11.1 - 0.6x$ $(*)^2$, N = 272
  Females: $y = 12.8 - 0.5x$ (NS), N = 280

[1]Males: dotted line (—— —— ——)
  Females: solid line (————)

[2] NS = not significant
  * = p .05
  ** = p .01
  *** = p .001

The questionnaire administered to the respondents asked them to in-dicate their anticipated occupations and plans for further education after high school. Tables 5 and 6 present mean grade point averages for planned education and occupation categories, respectively, by sex. Table 5 demonstrates that for each category of education planned after high school, females achieve a significantly higher grade point average than males. Similarly, Table 6 demonstrates that for each category of occupa-tion planned, females achieve a significantly higher grade point average than males. Of interest in Table 5 is that girls who plan no education after high school earn a higher grade point average than boys who plan some college or a vocational school. Similarly, in Table 6, the data show that girls who anticipate working in the lowest status occupations earn a higher grade point average than boys who anticipate working in medium status occupations. These findings suggest that girls underplan for their future work and education relative to boys.

Items also included on the questionnaire were used to construct two scales, one entitled Family Role Orientation and one entitled Family Plans. Family Role Orientation is a measure of attitudes about family roles. The higher the score on this measure, the more conventional are the students' attitudes about family roles. Conventionality refers to a division of labor and tasks within the family, in which the man essentially functions as the breadwinner, protector, and mediator with the world outside the family, and the woman functions as the mother and domestic caretaker. Family Plans measures the salience of both number of children the student expects to have, and the number of years by which the student expects to be married (the latter is corrected for grade effects). Salience is assumed to be indicated by temporal proximity. The more children expected, and the sooner marriage is planned, the smaller value of the variable score (that is, the less time between the date of questionnaire administration and the onset of family experience). Figure 4 and Table 7 present the results of analyses by sex of the relations between grade point and Family Role Orientation and Family Plans respectively. Figure 4 demonstrates that the relationship between Family Role Orientation and grade point average is not significant for males, but is significant for females. The higher the grade point average, the less conventional are the girls' attitudes about family roles. In Table 7, it can be seen that the small correlation between family plans and grade point average for girls is nevertheless in the expected direction. Girls who earn high grade point averages are somewhat more likely to put off families than girls who do not.

TABLE 5

Education Plans and Grade Point Average

Education Plans	Males (N = 266)	Females (N = 265)	t	(df)
No education after high school; undecided	2.1	2.5	—34.48***	(241)
Some college; trade or technical school	2.4	2.8	—37.14***	(165)
Graduate from 4-yr. college; graduate or professional school	3.0	3.3	—20.99***	(119)
F	25.9***	21.2***		
Eta	0.41	0.37		

*** = $p < .001$

TABLE 6

Occupation Plans and Grade Point Average

Occupation Plans	Males (N = 255)	Females (N = 262)	t	(df)
Occupations requiring no further training[1]	2.2	2.6	—21.88***	(172)
Occupations requiring non-academic training[2]	2.3	2.5	—6.6***	(124)
Occupations requiring more academic training[3]	2.8	3.0	—19.4***	(215)
F	11.2***	10.4***		
Eta	0.29	0.27		

[1]Undecided; housewife, military service; service worker; laborer; semi-skilled; clerical worker; sales clerk
[2]Protective service worker; skilled worker; foreman; manager or administrator; self-employed.
[3]Professional
*** = $p < .001$

TABLE 7

Grade Point Average and Family Plans by Sex

	Family Plans	
	Males (N = 260)	Females (N = 275)
Grade point average	NS	0.12*[1]

[1]NS = not significant
* = $p < .05$

Finally, we computed the relationship between grade point average and a modified version of Rosenberg's (1968) Self-Esteem scale. The results of this analysis are presented in Figure 5. Figure 5 shows that for each level of grade point average, girls report significantly less self-esteem than boys do.

These findings offer only circumstantial evidence for the argument about different foci of conflict within the high school for male and female adolescents. Nonetheless, they are consistent with the argument. The obtained sex differences in relations between Family Role Orientation and Family Plans and grade point average suggest that girls anticipate ramifications of academic achievement for their interpersonal lives

FIGURE 4

Grade Point Average and Family Role Orientation by Sex[1]

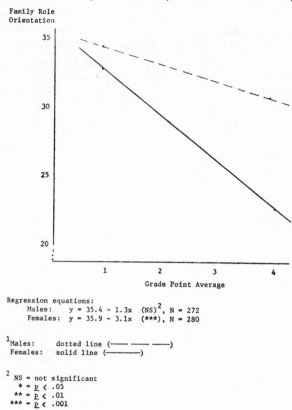

Regression equations:
    Males: y = 35.4 - 1.3x   (NS)[2], N = 272
    Females: y = 35.9 - 3.1x   (***), N = 280

[1]Males: dotted line (——— ——— ———)
Females: solid line (—————)

[2] NS = not significant
    * = p < .05
    ** = p < .01
    *** = p < .001

after high school. The sex difference in relationships between grade point average and educational and occupational plans suggests that girls may be responding to conflicts over achievement in high school by underplanning work and education relative to boys. And the sex difference in the relationship between grade point average and self-esteem suggests that girls do not experience achievement as an unambiguous basis for generally positive self-regard as much as boys do. Such findings are consistent with the interpretation of the differential impact of grade point average on indicators of stress. They are also consistent with the differential impact of subjective perceptions of meeting adults' expectations for academic achievement on indicators of stress. For inasmuch as high achiev-

FIGURE 5

Grade Point Average and Self Esteem by Sex[1]

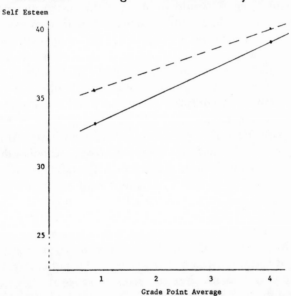

Regression equations:
    Males: $y = 33.7 + 1.4x$ (**)[2], N = 272
    Females: $y = 31.4 + 1.8x$ (***), N = 280

[1]Males: dotted line (——— ——— ———)
   Females: solid line (————————)

[2] NS = not significant
    * = $p < .05$
    ** = $p < .01$
    *** = $p < .001$

ing girls remain oriented towards adult expectations, postponement of family plans and more liberal attitudes towards family roles can absorb some of the conflict between achievement, relations with peers, and pressures to conform to sex-role norms of behavior.

SUMMARY AND CONCLUSIONS

Recent work in sex differences in the incidence of psychopathology has led to the suggestion that differences in socialization and role tasks may account for the increasing amount of mental stress in adolescent and adult women relative to men. Such work has often relied on sex differences in distributions of diagnostic categories. Problems with relying on diagnostic distributions for this purpose were noted. It was suggested that surveying nonclinical populations may generate more appropriate information to address this issue.

Developmental theory would imply that the increasing proportion of mental stress among adolescent women relative to men is indicative of greater conflicts between the assumption of an adult sexual identity and general developmental tasks of adolescence. Attention was drawn to the high school as the formal organization linking adolescents to their future positions in the worlds of work and family life. Within the high school, girls are simultaneously confronted with peer and adult expectations for sex-role congruent behavior, and with adult expectations for academic achievement which conflict with standards of femininity. Although boys have conflicts over the issue of autonomy relative to school authorities, success in school activities is more congruent with standards of masculinity, as are the implications of academic achievement for future plans. It was also suggested that one way in which adolescents might handle such conflicts would entail the expression of stress in sex-role congruent ways. Boys would be more likely to express conflict through aggressive behavior and resentful feelings towards others, both because such behavior is considered masculine and because it represents a struggle for autonomy. Girls would be more likely to evidence internal stress because it does not threaten norms of femininity.

Research findings from a study of adolescents enrolled in a largely white, lower-middle-class, Midwestern urban high school were reported. Although mean differences on the five indicators of stress used in the study were generally consistent with the proposition that female and male adolescents express stress in sex-role congruent ways, the proportion of variance explained by sex of the respondent was small, and other findings were inconsistent with the proposition. Girls' failure to meet adult expectations for academic achievement was associated with aggression, resentment, and depression. Boys' grade point averages were negatively correlated with aggression, depression, and psychosomatic symptoms. Thus analysis of relationships between indicators of stress and sources of conflict failed to yield any consistent pattern of sex differences in expression of stress.

However, the research findings were consistent with the proposition that males and females experience different foci of conflict within the high school. Meeting adult expectations for academic achievement and behavior was associated with less stress for girls, but did not significantly reduce stress for boys. Objective academic achievement was associated with less stress for boys, but not for girls. Indeed, girls with high grade point averages were more depressed and reported more psychosomatic symptoms than boys with high grade point averages, and were not significantly less aggressive than girls with low grade point averages. It was suggested that the reason why actual academic achievement did not reduce stress in girls is that grades constitute a basis for social comparison with peers, precipitating conflicts over standards of femininity and sexual desirability, and that the anticipated ramifications of academic achievement for future work and family plans are conflictful for girls. Other findings affording circumstantial support for the interpretation were cited.

REFERENCES

BARDWICK, J. *The Psychology of Women*. New York: Harper & Row, 1971.

BART, P. Depression in middle-aged women. In V. Gornick and B. Moran (Eds.), *Woman in Sexist Society*. New York: Basic Books, 1971, Chapter 6.

BATTLE, E. S. Motivational determinants of academic task persistence. *Journal of Personality and Social Psychology*, 1965, 2, 209-218.

BATTLE, E. S. Motivational determinants of academic competence. *Journal of Personality and Social Psychology*, 1966, 4, 634-642.

BLALOCK, H. M. *Social Statistics*. New York: McGraw-Hill, 1970.

BUXTON, C. E. *Adolescents in School*. New Haven, Conn.: Yale University Press, 1973.

CHESLER, P. *Women and Madness*. New York: Avon, 1972.

CLANCY, K. & GOVE, W. R. Sex differences in mental illness: An analysis of response bias in self-reports. *American Journal of Sociology*, 1974, 80 (July) ; 205-216.

DOHRENWEND, B. P. & DOHRENWEND, B. S. Sex differences and psychiatric disorders. *American Journal of Sociology*, 1975, 81 (6) , 1447-1463.

DUBE, K. C., et al. An epidemiological study of hysteria. *Journal of Biosocial Science*, 1974, 6 (Y) , 401-405.

ERIKSON, E. *Childhood and Society*. Norton, 1950.

FODOR, I. G. The phobic syndrome in women: Implications for treatment. In: V. Franks and V. Burtle (Eds.) , *Women in Therapy: New Psychotherapies for a Changing Society*. New York: Brunner/Mazel, 1974. Chapter 6.

FRENCH, J., JR., RODGERS, W., & COBB, S. Adjustment as person-environment fit. In G. V. Coelho, D. A. Hamburgh, and J. E. Adams (Eds.), *Coping and Adaptation*. New York: Basic Books, 1974, 316-334. (a)

FRENCH, J., JR., RODGERS, W., & COBB, S. A model of person-environment fit. Paper presented at the W.H.O. Symposium on Society, Stress, and Disease, Stockholm, June, 1974. (b)

GOVE, W. R. & HERB, T. R. Stress and mental illness among the young: A comparison of the sexes. *Social Forces*, 1974, 53(2), 256-265.

GOVE, W. R. & TUDOR, J. Adult sex roles and mental illness. *American Journal of Sociology*, 1973, 78 (Jan.), 812-835.

GRAMBS, J. B. & WAETJEN, W. Being equally different: A new right for boys and girls. *National Elementary School Principal*, 1966, 46, 59-67.

HORNER, M. S. Toward an understanding of achievement-related conflicts in women. *Journal of Social Issues*, 1972, 28, 157-176.

JACKSON, P. W. *Life in Classrooms*. New York: Holt, Rinehart & Winston, 1968.

KAGAN, J. Acquisition and significance of sex typing and sex role identity. In M. L. Hoffman and L. W. Hoffman (Eds.), *Review of Child Development Research*, Vol. 1. New York: Russell Sage, 1964.

KERLINGER, F. N. & PEDHAZOR E. J. *Multiple Regression in Behavioral Research*. New York: Holt, Rinehart & Winston, 1973.

KLINGEL, D. M. The aggressive behavior of eleventh grade boys in two suburban high schools. Paper presented at the meeting of the International Society for the Study of Behavioral Development. Ann Arbor, Michigan, August, 1973.

KULKA, R. A. Person-environment fit in the high school: A validation study. Unpublished doctoral dissertation, University of Michigan, 1975.

LOCKSLEY, A. Towards unsexing stereotypes of the high school environment. Paper presented at the 82nd Annual Meeting of the American Psychological Association, New Orleans, La., September, 1974.

LOCKSLEY, A. Sex differences in correlates of future plans. Working paper #10, Opinions of Youth Project, Survey Research Center, Institute for Social Research, Ann Arbor, Michigan, 1976.

MOSER, C. A. & KALTON, G. *Survey Methods in Social Investigation*. New York: Basic Books, 1972.

NATHANSON, C. A. Illness and the feminine role: A theoretical review. *Social Science Medicine*, 1975, 9 (2), 57-62.

PELTIER, G. L. Sex differences in the schools: Problem and proposed solution. *Phi Delta Kappan*, 1968, 50, 182-185.

ROSENBERG, M. *Society and the Adolescent Self-Image*. Princeton: Princeton University Press, 1965.

SCHWAB, J. J., et al. The epidemiology of hysterical disorders. *Psychosomatics*, 1974, 15 (2), 88-93.

SEXTON, P. C. *The American School*. Englewood Cliffs, New Jersey: Prentice-Hall, Inc., 1967.

SEXTON, P. How the American boy is feminized. *Psychology Today*, 1970, 3, 23-29, 66-67.

STEIN, A. H. The effects of sex-role standards for achievement and sex-role preference on three determinants of achievement motivation. *Developmental Psychology*, 1971, 4, 219-231.

STEIN, A. H. & BAILEY, M. M. The socialization of achievement orientation in females. *Psychological Bulletin*, 1973, 80, 345-366.

STEIN, A. H. & SMITHELLS, J. Age and sex differences in children's sex role standards about achievement. *Developmental Psychology*, 1969, 1, 252-259.

STINCHCOMBE, A. L. *Rebellion in a High School*. Chicago: Quadrangle Books, 1964.

WEISS, P. Some aspects of femininity. *Dissertation Abstracts*, 1962, 23, 1083.

WOLOWITZ, H. Hysterical character and feminine identity. In J. Bardwick (Ed.), *Readings on the Psychology of Women*. New York: Harper & Row, 1972, 307-313.

4

SEX DIFFERENCES
IN DIVORCE

PRUDENCE BROWN and HANNA FOX

Sex differences express themselves in three aspects of the divorce process: (a) the stresses that men and women confront during divorce; (b) the ways in which they cope with these stresses, and (c) the physical and mental health outcomes they experience. The goal of our chapter is to review the current state of knowledge regarding sex differences in divorce. The question is not which sex does better or worse but what is the configuration of stresses and coping strategies that differentially characterizes both positive and negative outcomes of divorce for men and women.

We present our findings in the context of two major assumptions: first, that sex differences in divorce are more the result of socialization for gender-linked social roles and coping styles than innate characteristics; and second, that divorce is a life crisis involving a series of social and psychological stresses, instead of a symptom of individual pathology, which earlier research implied.

In addition to sex differences, several other demographic variables have a significant impact on the process of divorce. Race, class, and age or stage in the life cycle combine with sex to define not only the conditions under which divorce is likely to occur but also the nature of post-divorce stress and adjustment. Our focus here is sex differences. We do not examine the possible interactive effects of sex with race, class, or age due to both the lack of research in the area and the lack of space. We are primarily concerned with divorces involving children, which constitute more than 60% of all divorces granted in the United States each year.

The authors extend their appreciation to Linda Garnets, Gay Kitson, Joe Pleck and Robert Weiss for helpful comments on an earlier version of this chapter.

The presence of a child in a dissolving family system influences the economic, legal, and psychological impact of a divorce to such an extent that the breakup of a marriage may be quite different for couples with and without children.

Our review parallels the chronology of a divorce. We begin with an investigation of the different ways men and women initiate the breakup of a marriage and proceed to discuss various aspects of divorce from the perspective of sex differences: the economics of divorce; relationships with children; social relationships; and the emotional separation and redefinition of identity during divorce. We then examine epidemiological data on sex differences in the physical and mental health consequences of divorce over time, ending with a summary of the findings and a discussion of their implications for future research.

MARITAL DISSATISFACTION AND BREAKDOWN

The decision to end a marriage produces a life crisis of considerable magnitude. In national samples Holmes and Rahe (1967) found that divorce and marital separation consistently ranked second and third in the 42 stressful life events in their scale. Death of spouse was the only event considered to require more readjustment. Ross and Sawhill (1975, p. 38) hypothesize that "individuals implicitly weigh social, economic, and personal benefits (or costs) of marriage and that they choose to divorce only when the future expected net benefits of a marriage compare unfavorably to its perceived alternatives" over an extended period of time. There is general agreement in the literature that, at least on the surface, women are more likely than men to initiate steps toward the dissolution of a marriage, regardless of the way the decision to end the marriage is conceptualized.

Women file for divorce about three-quarters of the time (U.S. Dept. of HEW, 1973). This figure is influenced by the fact that a woman usually files for divorce to obtain child support once her husband has left. Nonetheless, both Goode (1956) and Brown (1976) found that women were more likely than men to first think of and seriously suggest divorce and to want the separation and divorce more than their husbands. The husbands in Brown's sample also perceived their wives as more desirous of ending the marriage. Hill, Rubin, and Peplau (1976) report more women than men precipitated the breakup of dating relationships which the investigators followed over a two-year period. Obviously, a marriage is different from a dating relationship, especially if children are involved. But

Hill et al.'s findings can be interpreted as evidence for a pattern established in pre-marital dating and continued into marriage.

Additional evidence supports the fact that women more frequently initiate steps to end a marriage. Wives tend to report more marital problems than husbands, both when married and when applying for divorce. It is noteworthy that both wives and husbands tend to locate the source of the problem in the husband more than in the wife. Among 600 applicants for divorce in Cleveland, Levinger (1966) found that wives listed two times as many complaints as husbands. Gurin, Veroff, and Feld (1960) and Brown (1976) found that both marital partners were more likely to blame the husbands for the problems in the marriage than vice-versa. Brown found that 45% of the problems described by 429 respondents in the process of divorce were attributed to the husbands as compared to 19% to the wives. Whereas 57% of the complaints described by the women were "blamed" on the husband, only 32% of the men's complaints were considered by the men to be the wife's fault. Levinger (1976) further points out that divorce is generally the end product of a long interactive process of estrangement. Rarely can one spouse's behavior be isolated and identified as the "cause" of the breakup. More men than women (one in four compared to one in five) oppose divorce as a solution to a marriage that is not working out (Roper Organization, 1974). Furthermore, 19% of the men versus 10% of the women in this national survey felt that a couple should stay together for the sake of the children. Fifty-five percent of the women felt that the children would be better off if the couple separated, while only 38% of the men felt this way.

Three theories on these sex differences in marital dissatisfaction and breakdown follow. They are largely speculative due to the dearth of research into this question.

1. The relationship between marital and overall life satisfaction is much stronger for women than men (Bradburn, 1969). In other words, marital satisfaction contributes more to overall happiness for women than for men. This may be due, in part, to the fact that men have greater access to a community organized around their work which in turn can act as a supplement to an unsatisfying home. Ross and Sawhill (1975) argue that women's greater investment in marriage causes them to expect a higher return and be more disappointed if these expectations are not met. This is consistent with findings by Hill et al. (1976) that a much higher proportion of highly invested women than men found it necessary

and possible to terminate a serious dating relationship. Apparently, the only men initiating breakups were the less involved partners who wanted to move on to better alternatives. Although many women ended relationships on this basis also, a significant number of the women who were the more invested partners precipitated the breakup when they realized that their commitment was not reciprocated. If more involved men tend not to initiate breakups, Goode's finding (1956) that when they do initiate, they do it more quickly suggests that their speediness may be related to their lack of involvement in the relationship. The median time between the first serious suggestion of divorce and the final decree was 5.4 months for men and 12.9 months for women. Other economic and social factors may play a part in this sex-linked time difference, but Brown's data (1976) are consistent with Goode's in that women were more likely to first seriously suggest filing for divorce yet took longer to actually initiate the divorce than men. Men in the sample reported first thinking that problems in the marriage could lead to divorce on the average of 39 months before separation or filing had actually occurred; the parallel amount of time for women was 54 months.

2. Bernard (1972) and Gove (1972) speculate that the social role of housewife has inherent frustrations stemming from its relatively unstructured and invisible nature, its low prestige, and the limited alternatives in the extrafamilial world. Bernard asserts that marriage has a "dwindling" effect on women whereby they become less competent, have lower self-esteem, and feel unhappier as the marriage proceeds. Women's most valuable social function is to protect, nurture, and foster the growth of other family members. The marital adjustment literature indicates that in a happy or adjusted marriage the wife does most of the changing and that her adaptability is more crucial than the husband's for marital stability. Although the role stress theory has some empirical support (Gove, 1972), recent research indicates the need to specify dimensions of the married women's role that are differentially associated with psychiatric disability or marital dissatisfaction (Campbell, 1974; Radloff, 1975). The link between stressful aspects of the housewife role and the propensity to initiate divorce is still speculative.

3. Gurin et al. (1960) discuss women's role in the family as the socioemotional "expert" requiring them to be more sensitive than men to the "psychological facets of experience," more in touch with their own feelings and those of other family members. Hill et al. (1976, p. 164) speculate that this greater sensitivity to the quality of interpersonal rela-

tionships may result in "women's criteria for falling in love—and for staying in love—to be higher than men's and they may reevaluate their relationships more carefully."

ECONOMICS OF DIVORCE

One of the few areas in which fairly consistent sex differences emerge involves the post-divorce economic adjustment of men and women: women experience more downward economic mobility and simply have less income than men after a divorce (Carter & Glick, 1970; Ross & Sawhill, 1975). This finding is dramatically illustrated in Hampton's report (1975) of the Michigan survey of income dynamics of 5000 families from 1967-1971. While intact families experienced an average increase in family income of 35.3%, divorced/separated/widowed women showed a family income drop of 16.5% as compared to an income increase of 10.4% during the same period for comparable men. After separation or divorce, women's position in the income distribution fell such that 35% found themselves in the lowest third of the economic distribution while only 19% of the men were in this same position, even after alimony and child support payments were taken into account. Similarly, 47.5% of the husbands as compared to 23.4% of the wives were in the top third of the economic distribution after marital dissolution.

Perhaps the most important aspect of the divorced woman's economic situation is her relatively low earning potential as compared to that of the divorced man. Hoffman and Holmes (1976) found that the most frequent change in economic activity for divorced and separated women is increased labor force participation rather than reliance on welfare. They report that nearly 80% of the divorced and separated women in their longitudinal national survey were employed in 1973 although 30% of these same women had not worked as married women in 1967. Problems faced by women in the labor market then become critical for the divorced woman trying to assume the primary breadwinner role in her family. Job and wage discrimination, lack of job training, difficulty obtaining credit, and inadequate day care opportunities result in a highly stressful work situation for many divorced women. Bane (1976) points out that women's average earnings for full-time year-round work are only 58% of their male counterparts'. Women's rates of unemployment are higher; when they are employed, the occupational levels available to them are limited: More than three-quarters of employed female family heads work as clericals, operatives, and service and private household workers (U.S. Bureau of Census, 1974).

Other aspects of the post-divorce status are problematic for women. Over 90% of the children involved in a divorce are awarded to the mother, yet child support payments are often inadequate and irregular. The Citizens' Advisory Council on the Status of Women (1972) reports that less than 40% of divorced mothers receive regular child support payments in full one year after divorce. Although a new amendment to the Social Security Act, known as the 4-D program, is expected to locate delinquent fathers and increase enforcement of court-ordered support payments, only one divorcee in every seven was awarded alimony and less than one in two was granted child support in 1975 (Lake, 1976).

Continued economic dependence on the ex-husband, relatives, or welfare can be a source of psychological stress. Respondents in Brown, Feldberg, Fox, and Kohen's (1976) sample of 30 divorced or separated mothers described the constraints and strings attached to these outside sources of income and support, demonstrating that economic dependence affects the woman's ability to determine her life after marital dissolution. Even if she is able to assume a self-supporting head of household role as a result of divorce, she may not feel comfortable or satisfied in this role. Brown and Manela (1976) found that a number of women who assumed primary breadwinner roles during the process of divorce reported anxiety about not fulfilling deeply internalized traditional sex-role expectations, worry about being "unfeminine," or guilt over leaving the children during work. Accompanying this source of distress may be a sense of inadequacy or anger generated by the downward economic mobility and the poorer housing, neighborhoods, and schools with which the divorced woman and her children may be confronted. Campbell (1974) found that 58% of the divorced men in his national sample never worried about meeting bills, while only 30% of the divorced women were so confident about their financial circumstances.

Despite the man's economic advantage after divorce, there are unique stresses which confront him as a result of court-ordered alimony or child support. A divorced man's income simply may be inadequate to support two households, especially if he remarries. He may feel outraged at the fact that he must support his children financially but has less chance than his wife to receive custody of the children and little opportunity to determine how the child support money is spent if his ex-wife does receive custody (Weiss, 1975). Thus, the divorced father's compliance with court-ordered support payments over time seems to be less related to his actual ability to pay (Ross & Sawhill, 1975) than to the nature of his relationship with his ex-wife (Goode, 1956) and the degree to which legal sanctions are brought to bear on his delinquency (Chambers, 1976).

Neither spouse can expect to profit economically from a divorce, at least in the short run. Divorce is more common among low-income as compared with high-income families (Norton & Glick, 1976). Many divorcing couples are barely able to cope financially while the household is intact, let alone when two households are created.

RELATIONSHIPS WITH THE CHILDREN

Over 60% of all divorces involve children under the age of 18 (Norton & Glick, 1976). Much of the earlier research on divorce and children has focused retrospectively on the child's often negative adjustment to the family change. More recent longitudinal studies indicate that assimilation of divorce-related changes is a process lasting several years which can have positive as well as negative consequences for the adjustment of both child and parent (Kelly & Wallerstein, 1976; Wallerstein & Kelly, 1976). The stresses and opportunities for growth which divorce differentially confers on men and women have not been adequately studied. Both sexes may experience a heightened sense of their children's importance to them, accompanied by feelings of guilt, sadness, failure, and anxiety about successfully fulfilling the parent role after the divorce. But because children are awarded to their mothers in more than 90% of divorce cases, men and women are likely to face quite different problems and challenges regarding their relations to the children. These differences may become significantly decreased as the courts grant custody to more and more fathers. At present, however, actual household composition dictates many of the coping tasks confronting parents following divorce.

The relationship of a divorced parent with his or her children is in part defined by the parent-child relationship before the divorce, both in terms of the individuals involved and in terms of the parent's role in the family as father (family head, protector and source of financial support) or mother (homemaker, nurturer and source of emotional support). Although there has been little research into the relationship of non-custodial divorced fathers and their children, Finkelstein (1976, p. 279) suggests that newly divorced fathers often experience parenting as "a conscious role dimension requiring new learning, new social supports, new planning." A number of men in his sample reported that they had trouble just "being" with the children as opposed to "doing" something with them. Pleck and Sawyer (1974) discuss the lack of training which the competitive and emotionally repressed masculine role affords to men

attempting to relate to children. The limits of traditional sex-role socialization may be exacerbated by the necessity of visiting with the children
on a prearranged schedule with the specific purpose of having fun together or getting to know each other better. The pressures to relate inter-
personally and be available emotionally to his children during visitation
periods may create a great deal of anxiety for a man who never felt comfortable in this role before the divorce.

> Frightened by the enormous sense of loss, the presence of unsus-
> pected feelings of love and tenderness, and a wracking guilt, . . .
> many fathers may quell their real feelings and settle for being footers
> of the bills, weekend baby-sitters, off-stage parents wheeled in only for
> crises, holidays, graduations and weddings (Krantzler, 1973, p. 222).

In addition to new emotional demands, Weiss (1975) points out that
the fundamental changes in the relationship between a father and his
children after divorce involve a stripping of his traditionally vital functions as head of household and prime authority in the family to financial
supporter robbed of actual inputs into the way that financial support is
spent. Divorced fathers, then, may experience a deep sense of loss at no
longer living with the children, combined with anger at the mother's
having obtained what is perceived as full control of the situation. Bohannan (1970) refers to the father who feels that his children are being made
into different kinds of adults from what he himself is or from what he
wants them to become. Hetherington, Cox, and Cox (1976) found that
their sample of 49 divorced fathers were having almost as much face-to-
face contact with their children two months after the divorce as were a
control group of fathers in intact homes. This interaction declined steadily
over the next two years with the researchers finding that the divorced
fathers became less nurturant, more detached, and less salient in the
social, cognitive, and personality development of their children (p. 426).
Nevertheless, a significant subgroup of fathers did report that their relationship with the children improved following divorce, especially when
there had been a high degree of husband-wife conflict in the home.

The life change of divorce, then, seems to present men both with the
danger of increased constraints on the fathering roles and bases for interaction available to them and their children and with the opportunity
to consciously mold and expand the relationship to involve more personal satisfaction and intimacy. Clearly, men do not have to experience
divorce as a prerequisite to working beyond the traditionally defined
limits in fathering; divorce, however, may stimulate a more direct con-

frontation with these limits and enable the father to adopt new ways of relating to his children. As divorced fathers increasingly receive joint or full custody of their children, a variety of new parenting roles (and their accompanying strains and satisfactions) will become options for men. A recent issue of *The Family Coordinator* (1976, 25, 335-520) on fatherhood contains several studies devoted to single-parent fatherhood as an emerging life-style.

Like the divorced father, a mother confronted with single parenthood has to assume new roles, which go beyond her traditionally defined sex role. She is expected to become head of the household, mediating the family's needs with those of the larger society, and assuming authority and ultimate decision-making power in the family. Just as there are constraints (both internal and external) on the divorced father's attempt to redefine his role with his children, the single-parent mother may confront difficulties in being solely responsible for the children. These demands are quite different from the father's constraints. Whereas fathers may worry about the lack of a relationship with their children, mothers may find their lives inextricably (sometimes irritatingly so) bound up with those of their children. Brown (1976) found that over 60% of her sample of 253 women in the midst of marital dissolution responded to the question, "How did you manage to keep yourself going?" with "for the children." The demands of being a single parent and the lack of social supports for this role may cause the mother to feel angry, guilty, or overwhelmed by her new responsibilities. Brandwein, Brown, and Fox (1974) document the delibilitating practical and emotional stresses with which the divorced mother must deal without the support and feedback from another adult. Hetherington et al. (1976) found that the lack of control divorced parents (especially mothers) experienced over their children one year after divorce was associated with "very different patterns of relating to the child for mothers and fathers" (p. 425). Divorced mothers started out more authoritarian and became less restrictive over the two years after divorce. The opposite trend existed for divorced fathers. Positive mother-child interactions were associated with the frequency of the father's contact with the child when there was low parental conflict, high emotional maturity, and agreement concerning child-rearing on the part of the parents.

Finally, the divorced woman's need to work and have a social life may conflict with her full-time child care function. Her heavy investment in the children cannot fulfill her need for emotional support, and she may report a "sense of being locked into a child's world" with little opportunity for adult social contact (Hetherington et al., 1976, p. 422). Brown et al. (1976), however, found that the majority of their sample of single-parent mothers reported a great deal of satisfaction in their relations with their children. This satisfaction, a compensating factor, was the freedom to "mold the parent-child relationship without interference" (p. 127).

SOCIAL RELATIONSHIPS

The breakup of a marriage is likely to be accompanied by significant disruption in the individual's social network and a need to redefine general relations with family, friends, members of the larger social community, and intimate relations with the opposite sex. There has been little research on how men and women differentially approach the task of establishing a new social identity and what social support systems aid them in this endeavor.

Most families rally together, at least temporarily, to support their members during stressful life transitions such as divorce. The nature of the support and the relationships that ensue may differ somewhat for divorced men and women. Families are more likely to encourage daughters as opposed to sons to move in with them after divorce and may be likely to try and direct their lives more than they would those of their sons. They may view their daughter as "having tried adulthood and failed" (Weiss, 1975, p. 140), whereas their son may be experienced more as a temporary boarder. While living with her parents may benefit the divorced mother both emotionally and practically (companionship, support with child-rearing responsibilities, and financial aid), Weiss points out that the risk is reduced autonomy. Spicer and Hampe's (1975) interviews with 62 divorced males and 42 divorced females revealed that women had more contact than men with both their own families and their in-laws, even when the presence of children was held constant. They were also more likely to receive financial aid from their parents and in-laws than were divorced men.

A major coping task facing all newly divorced people involves establishing a new social life as a single person in a couples-oriented society. Borenzweig (1976) asserts that one aspect of the "punishment of divorced mothers" involves social ostracism resulting from the fears the divorced woman arouses in others as a "symbol of the potentiality of the dissolution of one's marriage" (p. 295). The divorced woman becomes viewed as a seductress or as "fair game" sexually. The degree to which men undergo similar social ostracism is not clear, although Hetherington et al. (1976) found that divorced men were less likely than divorced women to experience dissociation from married friends over time. Hetherington et al. also report that both men and women experienced a restricted social life and loneliness after divorce although they tended to define the problem somewhat differently. Divorced women were more likely to feel trapped and isolated from adult contact, while divorced men reported "feeling shut out, rootless, and at loose ends," needing to engage in social activities even if they often were not pleasurable (p. 422).

Knupfer, Clark, and Room (1966) cite evidence that, in this culture, single women have a greater tendency to form and maintain close interpersonal ties, while single men are more apt to be independent and isolated. If men in general tend to rely heavily on the marital relationship as the sole source of intimate bonds, whereas women find it easier or are more adept at forming close interpersonal relationships, divorce may leave a man potentially more emotionally isolated or lonely. "Being unmarried creates 'expressive hardships' for a man at least as important as a single woman's economic hardships" (Knupfer et al., 1966, p. 846). Powers and Bultena (1976) report that, among their elderly sample of 234, men had more frequent social contacts than women, but a smaller proportion of their interaction was with intimate friends. Perhaps divorced men have more opportunities for socializing than divorced women but they may be less able to transform casual social activities into encounters that meet their needs for intimacy.

Sex differences in post-divorce sexual activity also emerge from Hetherington et al.'s data (1976). They found that, for both divorced men and women, frequency of sexual intercourse in relationships characterized by a high degree of intimacy was significantly associated with happiness and self-esteem at two months, one year, and two years after the divorce. Frequency of intercourse in low intimacy relationships was, on the other hand, negatively correlated with happiness and self-esteem. The one exception to these findings was that males in low intimacy relationships two months after the divorce seemed to be "pleased at the increased opportunity for sexual experiences with a variety of partners" (p. 423). The authors note that, by the end of the first year following the divorce, both men and women reported a desire for intimacy which was not satisfied in casual sexual relations. Weiss (1975) puts more emphasis on the differences between the sexes, arguing that divorced men are more likely than women to be motivated to have many casual sexual relations to augment their self-esteem, whereas divorced women may find such relations less reassuring and experience considerable guilt in relation to their children.

The only other studies on post-divorce sexual activity tend to be focused solely on women. Brown et al. (1976) found that divorced women were likely to feel more satisfied with their post-divorce sexual activities because they felt able to control the decision on when and with whom to engage in sexual relations. Gebhard (1970) and Hunt (1966) offer data indicating that the majority of divorced women find their sex life post-maritally to be more intense, less inhibited, and more satisfying than their marital sex life. Gebhard found that the divorced women in his sample had significantly higher orgasm rates than they did while married or as compared with wives of the same age.

Little is known about the formal sources of support used by men and women in the process of divorce. Gurin et al. (1960) found that 22% of the divorced or separated men in their national survey sought professional help for personal problems, whereas 40% of the divorced or separated women sought similar help. More recently, Brown and Manela (1977) observed that women in the midst of marital dissolution were more likely than men to seek professional counseling and to evaluate the counseling as helpful. Their research with 429 men and women who attended a counseling agency at least once also indicated some sex differences in the function which counseling served. Men were more likely than women to find counseling improved their communication skills, whereas women were more likely than men to say they obtained emotional support from the counseling. These differences are predictable given the socialization in this culture for women to turn to others for help and talk about personal problems and for men to feel inhibited about expressing feelings and talking about problems. Not surprisingly, a self-help organization, Parents Without Partners (PWP), also attracts more women than men for its social and educational activities. Furthermore, Weiss (1973) reports that, while both men and women tended to seek new emotional cross-sex attachments in PWP, women were likely to form close friendship with members of the same sex while men exhibited little interest in forming such relationships.

EMOTIONAL SEPARATION AND REDEFINITION OF IDENTITY

People mourn every loss of a meaningful relationship or attachment (Bohannan, 1970). The process of mourning the end of a marriage involves grief not only over the loss of the attachment figure or spouse but also over the end of the relationship which primarily defined one's social role and ways of looking at and living in the world (Parkes, 1971). When divorced people say life no longer has any meaning, they are saying that the relationship that principally defined who they were and what they had to do is gone (Marris, 1974). Divorce requires the individual not only to "let go" of the spouse but also to relinquish one particular set of social roles and identities and to restructure a new identity and life-style. Weiss' (1975) research with separated and divorced people has led him to conclude that it takes two to four years to "recover" from a divorce. The first year is a transitional period, characterized by shock and then by a relinquishment of the marital identity, a sense of social dislocation, and emotional turmoil. This is followed by a longer period of "recovery" in which an integrated new identity and stable life pattern emerge.

Although the task of separating emotionally from one's spouse is defined in part by the degree and length of attachment, whether one was the "leaver" or the "left," and the nature of alternative relationships available, people experiencing loss tend to describe their feelings in quite similar ways. Weiss (1975) discusses the "erosion of love and the persistence of attachment" even with an intellectual desire for the end of a marriage. The lack of the partner's emotional accessibility tends to create anxiety and depression, anger and guilt.

Little research has been directed to the question of how men and women differentially experience the tasks of emotional separation and redefinition of identity during divorce. The similarities between the sexes may far outweigh the differences. Kitson and Sussman (1976) found no sex difference in extent of attachment to the former spouse following divorce. Attachment was defined as a preoccupation with or pining for the loss of the spouse characteristic of the mourning process during bereavement. But there are two areas in which sex differences are suggested: (a) the meaning and place of the marital role in the adult's role structure; and (b) sex role socialization regarding coping styles.

In this culture, the role of wife is seen as a major source of identity, esteem, and status, as a full-time career to which employment outside the home remains secondary. Bardwick (1971) argues that differential socialization patterns restrict female development of an independent sense of self and make women more dependent on others for their self-esteem. Peele and Brodsky (1974) note the addictive quality of such overinvested love. Keller (1974) points out that, in their exchange of autonomy for security, women tend to live through and for others rather than for themselves. Thus, the loss of the wife role through divorce is all the more stressful, frequently to the point of feeling desperate since it is the key role through which the woman's identity has been fabricated and sustained.

The sex-role socialization process is further reinforced by the institution of marriage and the roles available to married women in this culture. Parkes (1972, p. 120) cites four components of human relationships which help determine the nature of grief at their dissolution: strength of attachment, security of attachment, reliance or dependence, and involvement or the "extent to which one person's role, plans, and repertoire of problem solutions depend upon the presence of the other person for their relevance and practicality." Consider a middle-aged married women in a traditional marriage whose children have left home. Marris (1974) points out how much the meaning of her life is constructed around her relationship to her husband: Most of her purposes, anxieties, resentments, and satisfactions involve that relationship. The dissolution of the marriage can be expected to reopen unresolved identity issues which may have been tabled for such a woman during the marriage (Wiseman, 1975).

Although marital status is incorporated into the identities of both men and women, it seems to occupy a more central place for women than for men. As cited earlier, Brown (1976) found that the question, "How did you manage to keep yourself going?", elicited different post-divorce responses from men and women. Women responded that their still existent role within their familial world, that of mother, provided a critical sense of support and continuity. Twice as many men as women reported that working fulfilled that same need. The occupational role affords a man structure, an opportunity to engage with others socially, and a self-definition to which his marital status is largely irrelevant (Weiss, 1975).

A closely related source of potential sex difference in marital dissolution is coping styles. As discussed earlier, sex-role socialization experienced early in life and reinforced throughout the life cycle tends to result in sex-linked coping modalities: Boys are encouraged to cope through environmental mastery and autonomous problem-solving; girls are reinforced for employing an affiliative mode of coping, using their affective relationships to elicit the help and protection of others (Hoffman, 1972).

Divorce confronts men and women with mastery demands requiring autonomous instrumental coping strategies (such as setting up a new household and managing child care and finances in new ways) and with demands to resolve feelings of grief and anger and reestablish a new sense of self. Men are better trained in this culture to have confidence in their ability to accomplish mastery tasks. At the same time, they are discouraged from "being caught doing anything traditionally defined as feminine" such as acknowledging feelings of vulnerability, weakness, or tenderness (Hartley, 1959, p. 458). Carlson (1971) suggests that it is not simply the expression of negative affect that distinguishes men from women but also the experience and awareness of such affect.

Brown (1976) classified her respondents in the midst of marital dissolution on the basis of coping styles and found that men were much more likely than women to employ denial or avoidance coping styles. Use of denial under stress is adaptive in the short run but it may "cause trouble in the long run because it contains no provision . . . for learning anything new about the sources of danger. Closing the cognitive field is a static solution" that impedes personal growth and does not make the individual any less reactive to future stress (White, 1974, p. 65). White's point is consistent with Brown's (1976) findings in answer to the question to respondents, "Sometimes in times of change, we learn things about ourselves we never knew. Have the changes in your marriage given you any insights or taught you anything about yourself?" Fifty-three percent of the women versus 15% of the men were coded on the "personal strength" dimension of this question with the following kinds of responses: "I'm stronger than I thought I was," "I don't need my spouse to survive," or "I'm a person with my own mind." Men were more likely than women to respond with "I didn't have things under control as well as I thought," or "I didn't really learn anything."

Although their respondents were bereaved rather than divorced, Glick, Weiss, and Parkes (1974) found that men and women experienced similar grief reactions but coped with the emotions and life changes brought about by the loss in different ways. They report that men were more likely than women to inhibit their expression of feeling, to maintain a rational and self-controlled outlook on their situations, and to be more confident in their ability to recover from the loss.

Thus, while coping with the similar task of emotional separation, men and women appear to confront different dangers and opportunities. The danger for women stems from their lack of training for autonomous coping and results in low self-confidence or depression, conceptualized by Seligman (in press) as learned helplessness. To relieve severe distress, women may become highly motivated to cope with the loss in new and more effective ways, thus promoting a sense of efficacy and enhancing self-esteem. Similarly, men are afforded the opportunity to expand their primarily instrumental mode of dealing with stress and incorporate more affective, bonding strategies into their coping repertoire. As sex-role social-ization becomes less rigid and boys and girls are encouraged to develop and use both instrumental and expressive coping modalities, the experi-ence of divorce may become more similar for men and women.

HEALTH AND MENTAL HEALTH CONSEQUENCES OF DIVORCE

Epidemiological data on the relationship of marital status to physical and mental health reveal some consistent sex differences: While marriage appears more advantageous to men, being single or widowed is associated with poorer health and mental health outcomes for men than for women (Bachrach, 1975; Gove; 1972, Gove, 1973). The relative impact of divorce on men and women is less conclusive. Evidence that men are harder hit by divorce comes from rates of mortality and mental illness among the divorced as compared to married populations. Gove (1972, p. 24) reviews 11 studies all reporting higher rates of mental illness for divorced as opposed to married men and women but concludes that "in all but one case the difference between being married and formerly married is greater for men than for women and in most cases this difference is quite large." Similarly, Robertson (1974) found that of the eight sex/marital status groups, divorced males had the highest rate of psychiatric referral (almost twice as great as the next highest group, divorced females), while married males had the lowest rate (nearly 10 per 1,000 lower than the married females). Waldron (1976, p. 2) reports that the sex differential in mortality (males having a higher mortality rate) varies significantly by marital status: "The excess of male mortality is lowest among married adults, it is 10% greater among single and widowed adults, and it is 50% greater among divorced adults." Gove (1973) makes the assumption that one's emotional state (generated in part by one's marital status) affects the etiology and potential effectiveness of treatment for at least certain types of illness. Analyzing age-specific mortality rates for a number of illnesses, Gove found that mortality rates were significantly higher for divorced versus married adults and that the differences between the mar-ried and divorced statuses were much greater for men than for women.

Conflicting evidence on the relative impact of divorce on men and women comes from national surveys of the psychological well-being and overall life satisfaction of divorced men and women. Campbell (1974, p. 12) concludes that "divorce is a more disturbing experience for women than it is for men" using the criteria of life satisfaction and propensity to "always feel rushed," to worry about having a nervous breakdown, and to describe their lives as difficult. While married men and women did not differ consistently, divorced women scored much less favorably than divorced men on these items. Similarly, Gurin et al. (1960, p. 236) take the position that "women experience more disruption, more distress in their lives after a breakup of a marriage" as indicated by their reports of worrying "all the time" and feeling an impending nervous breakdown much more frequently than divorced men. Radloff (1975) and Spreitzer, Snyder, and Larson (1975) also found that divorce contributed relatively more to decreased life satisfaction and increased depression for women than for men.

The contradictory findings reported in previous epidemiological research raise important methodological and conceptual issues which have yet to be resolved satisfactorily. Even if consistent patterns of association between the status of divorce and various health and mental health outcomes can be established, efforts to draw causal links between the two sets of variables are premature (Bachrach, 1975). Perhaps men and women are differentially selected into the status of divorce so that sex differences in mental health among the divorced are more reflective of premorbid personality characteristics than any differential reaction to the divorced role and stresses it generates. Briscoe, Smith, Robins, Marten, and Gaskin (1973, p. 125) offer some evidence that "psychiatric illness is probably a significant cause of marital breakdown" as well as a consequence. It is important to remember that the status of divorce is a transitional one usually lasting five or six years for women and three to four years for men, and that the large majority of both sexes remarry eventually (Ross & Sawhill, 1975). Men tend to remarry more often and more quickly than women. Surveys which fail to control for length of time in any particular marital status will affect this important variable. According to Overall (1971), marital history rather than current marital status may be the salient variable. The role of sex differences in response bias to mental health surveys is still unresolved. Sex differences in self-reported symptom scales may be, in part, artifactual. Women may have a greater propensity to acknowledge and express negative feelings (Clancy & Gove, 1974; Cooperstock & Parnell, 1976; Phillips & Segal, 1969).

There are at least two ways in which future epidemiological research could yield more useful findings for the study of sex differences in divorce. First, Dohrenwend and Dohrenwend (1976) and Radloff (1976) advocate the differentiation of specific diagnostic categories and population subgroups rather than studying "unidimensional concepts of psychiatric disorder" and asking "false questions about whether men or women are more prone to 'mental illness'" (Dohrenwend & Dohrenwend, 1976, p.

1453). Secondly, on the question of why men and women respond so differently to the stress of divorce, possible confounding variables often overlooked in current research need to be examined. The presence or absence of children, living arrangements, and resources (particularly economic) are three such variables.

Divorced and separated females are more likely to be heads of families than their male counterparts (Kramer, 1967). About 50% of the women versus 10% of the men who are divorced or separated between the ages of 25 and 44 occupy this position. Divorced or separated men are more likely to live alone, with parents or non-relatives, or in group quarters (military or institutional settings primarily). Women who are divorced or separated, then, may be: (a) more likely to be "found" by the conventional sampling techniques of survey researchers than males in group or transient settings (Radloff, 1976); (b) more "protected" in the Durkheimian sense as heads of households and child caretakers against the anomie and lack of support/normative regulation associated with living alone (Gove, 1976); and (c) less likely to engage in "inappropriate use" of mental institutionalization in terms of longer and more frequent hospitalizations than are clinically justified but occur due to the lack of other viable alternatives and regulative controls (Bachrach, 1975).

Male inpatient psychiatric facility admissions exceed female admissions among the separated and divorced, whereas female rates are greater than male rates at outpatient facilities. This may indicate that divorced and separated women are pressured to "keep themselves together" for the children (Kramer, 1967). Whether the actual state of mental health of divorced men and women is any different is clearly a different, and unanswered, question. Sex differences in divorce adjustment may be greatly diminished if men and women who have custody of the children are compared.

In addition to living arrangements and the presence or absence of children, the economic resources available to the individual may be related to post-divorce adjustment. In an earlier section, women were shown to have less income and to experience more downward economic mobility than men following divorce. The significance of this sex difference pertains to the possibility that low income is associated more severe life stress and with more psychiatric disability (Dohrenwend & Dohrenwend, 1969; Myers, Lindenthal, & Pepper, 1973). Berkman (1969, p. 330) reports that socioeconomic status and spouseless motherhood are "additively or cumulatively associated with physical morbidity among mothers." Brown (1976) and Kitson and Sussman (1976) found that anticipated income for the coming year was related to physical and mental health measures for both men and women following divorce: The lower the anticipated income, the less favorable the individual's physical and psychological well-being. We may speculate that, because they can generally expect a lower income than men after divorce, women are more likely to experience a greater amount of post-divorce stress with fewer resources to facilitate the process of adjustment. This stress, coupled with a lack of mastery training, may contribute to the depression and life dissatisfaction reported by women more often than men following divorce.

CONCLUSION

The studies reviewed here present a complex picture of the ways in which men and women cope with marital separation and divorce. Both differences and similarities appear to exist in the nature of the post-divorce stresses faced by men and women, the ways in which they cope with these stresses, and the mental and physical health outcomes they experience. Separating out the variance in post-divorce adjustment explained by sex alone is difficult, partly because a number of other critical variables such as economic resources and custody of the children tend to be sex-linked.

The review indicates that women experience both more situational stress and more conscious feelings of subjective distress than men during a divorce. Their economic situation is more disadvantaged, and they worry more about it. Often they have to assume a whole new set of work and economic roles as a consequence of divorce. In contrast, men are more likely to find their financial conditions less deprived and their work roles largely unchanged. Instead of undergoing increased stress and additional role demands, divorced men are stripped of a visible economic role in the family. They must give up the decision-making power and respect that often characterizes the family breadwinner.

A similar situation exists for the parenting roles available to divorced men and women. While mothers tend to assume the additional child-rearing responsibilities of the single parent, fathers often find a narrowing basis for interaction with their children. For men, there is both less day-to-day stress and responsibility and more opportunity to feel cut off from vital social roles and a sense of social meaning or purpose. This sense of alienation or lack of control may be enhanced by the fact that women actually initiate the process of divorce more often than men do.

The changes in economic and parenting roles brought about by a divorce have further consequences for the ways in which men and women cope with the new marital status. Women are more likely to be tied into family networks that involve economic and social support because of the children. The demands of being a single parent (and often a working mother) may put severe limitations on the amount of time, energy, and money the divorced woman can devote to her own social life. Divorced men may have more opportunities and resources for socializing but actually feel more rootless and emotionally isolated (Hetherington et al., 1976). Here the impact of sex role socialization seems more important than the extent of the available social opportunities. In this culture women are trained to cope through eliciting the help and support of others and receive better emotional preparation for establishing intimate relations with both men and women. They are more likely to seek professional help and join informal groups and social organizations to meet their social and emotional needs during divorce. Men are less likely to be in touch with feelings of helplessness and the terror of being alone, so frequently reported by women.

Divorce appears to take a greater toll on the health of the divorced man. His early socialization which discourages the development of "intimacy skills" combined with the decreased amount of normative regulation of his divorced status could be responsible. The woman's early socialization, which is weak in mastery training, along with the greater amount of practical stress during the divorce, may contribute to her greater subjective distress and poorer sense of well-being. These factors exist on a continuum. Additional research is needed to determine to what degree sex differences in divorce are governed by different post-divorce situations and to what degree they are a function of sex-linked early socialization processes.

REFERENCES

BACHRACH, L. *Marital Status and Mental Disorder: An Analytical Review.* DHEW Publication No. (ADM) 75-217. Washington, D.C.: U.S. Government Printing Office, 1975.

BANE, M. J. Marital disruption and the lives of children. *Journal of Social Issues,* 1976, 32, 103-117.

BARDWICK, J. *Psychology of Women: A Study of Bio-Cultural Conflicts.* New York: Harper & Row, 1971.

BERKMAN, P. Spouseless motherhood, psychological stress, and physical morbidity. *Journal of Health and Social Behavior,* 1969, 10, 323-334.

BERNARD, J. *The Future of Marriage.* New York: Bantam Books, 1972.

BOHANNAN, P. (Ed.). *Divorce and After.* New York: Doubleday, 1970.

BORENZWEIG, H. The punishment of divorced mothers. *Journal of Sociology and Social Welfare,* 1976, 3, 291-300.

BRADBURN, N. *The Structure of Psychological Well-Being.* Chicago: Aldine, 1969.

BRANDWEIN, R., BROWN, C., & FOX, E. Women and children last: The social situation of divorced mothers and their families. *Journal of Marriage and the Family*, 1974, 36, 498-514.

BRISCOE, C. W., SMITH, J., ROBINS, E., MARTEN, S., & GASKIN, F. Divorce and psychiatric disease. *Archives of General Psychiatry*, 1973, 29, 119-125.

BROWN, C., FELDBERG, R., FOX, R., & KOHEN, J. Divorce: Chance of a lifetime. *Journal of Social Issues*, 1976, 32, 119-133.

BROWN, P. Psychological distress and personal growth among women coping with marital dissolution. (Doctoral dissertation, University of Michigan, 1976). *Dissertation Abstracts International*, 1976, 37, pp. 947-B. (University Microfilms No. 76-19, 092.)

BROWN, P. & MANELA, R. *Changing Family Roles: Women and Divorce*. Paper prepared for the American Jewish Committee. Ann Arbor, Mich.: Program for Urban Health Research, 1976.

BROWN, P. & MANELA, R. Client satisfaction with marital and divorce counseling. *The Family Coordinator*, 1977, 26, 294-303.

CAMPBELL, A. *Are Women's Lives More Frustrating and Less Rewarding than Men's?* Unpublished manuscript, University of Michigan, Institute for Social Research, 1974.

CARLSON, R. Sex differences in ego functioning: Exploratory studies of agency and communion. *Journal of Consulting and Clinical Psychology*, 1971, 37, 267-277.

CARTER, H. & GLICK, P. C. *Marriage and Divorce: A Social and Economic Study*. Cambridge, Mass.: Harvard University Press, 1970.

CHAMBERS, D. Child support enforcement process. Study in progress at the University of Michigan Law School, Ann Arbor, Michigan, 1976.

Citizen's Advisory Council on the Status of Women. *The Equal Rights Amendment and Alimony and Child Support Laws*. Washington, D.C.: Author, 1972.

CLANCY, K. & GOVE, W. Sex differences in respondent's reports of psychiatric symptoms: An analysis of response bias. *American Journal of Sociology*, 1974, 80, 205-216.

COOPERSTOCK, R. & PARNELL, P. Comment on Clancy and Gove. *American Journal of Sociology*, 1976, 81, 1455-1458.

DOHRENWEND, B. P. & DOHRENWEND, B. S. *Social Status and Psychological Disorder: A Causal Inquiry*. New York: Wiley, 1969.

DOHRENWEND, B. P. & DOHRENWEND, B. S. Sex differences and psychiatric disorders. *American Journal of Sociology*, 1976, 81, 1447-1454.

FINKELSTEIN, H. Fathering and marital separation. In D. McGuigan (Ed.), *New Research on Women and Sex Roles*. Ann Arbor, Mich.: Center for Continuing Education of Women, 1976.

GEBHARD, P. Postmarital coitus among widows and divorcees. In P. Bohannan (Ed.), *Divorce and After*. Garden City, N. Y.: Doubleday, 1970.

GLICK, I., WEISS, R., & PARKES, C. M. *The First Year of Bereavement*. New York: Wiley-Interscience, 1974.

GOODE, W. J. *Women in Divorce*. New York: The Free Press, 1956.

GOVE, W. The relationship between sex roles, marital status, and mental illness. *Social Forces*, 1972, 51, 238-244.

GOVE, W. Sex, marital status, and mortality. *American Journal of Sociology*, 1973, 79, 45-67.

GOVE, W. Personal communication, September 1976.

GURIN, G., VEROFF, J., & FELD, S. *Americans View their Mental Health*. New York: Basic Books, 1960.

HAMPTON, R. Marital disruption: Some social and economic consequences. In G. J.

Duncan and J. N. Morgan (Eds.), *Five Thousand American Families: Patterns of Economic Progress*, Vol. 3. Ann Arbor: Institute for Social Research, 1975.

HARTLEY, R. Sex role pressures in the socialization of the male child. *Psychological Reports*, 1959, 5, 457-468.

HETHERINGTON, E. M., COX, M., & COX, R. Divorced fathers. *The Family Coordinator*, 1976, 25,, 417-428.

HILL, C., RUBIN, Z., & PEPLAU, L. Breakups before marriage: The end of 103 affairs. *The Journal of Social Issues*, 1976, 33, 147-168.

HOFFMAN, L. W. Early childhood experiences and women's achievement motives. *Journal of Social Issues*, 1972, 28, 129-155.

HOFFMAN, S. & HOLMES, J. Husbands, wives, and divorce. In G. J. Duncan and J. N. Morgan (Eds.), *Five Thousand American Families: Patterns of Economic Progress*, Vol. 4. Ann Arbor: Institute for Social Research, 1976.

HOLMES, T. & RAHE, R. The social readjustment rating scale. *Journal of Psychosomatic Research*, 1967, 11, 213-218.

HUNT, M. *The World of the Formerly Married*. New York: McGraw-Hill, 1966.

KELLER, S. The female role: Constants and change. In V. Franks and V. Burtle (Eds.), *Women in Therapy: New Psychotherapies for a Changing Society*. New York: Brunner/Mazel, 1974.

KELLY, J. & WALLERSTEIN, J. The effects of parental divorce: Experiences of the child in early latency. *American Journal of Orthopsychiatry*, 1976, 46, 20-32.

KITSON, G. & SUSSMAN, M. *The Process of Marital Separation and Divorce: Male and Female Similarities and Differences*. Unpublished paper. Case Western Reserve University, Cleveland, Ohio, November 1976.

KNUPFER, F., CLARK, W., & ROOM, R. The mental health of the unmarried. *American Journal of Psychiatry*, 1966, 122, 841-851.

KRAMER, M. Epidemiology, biostatistics, and mental health planning. In R. Monroe, G. Klee, and E. Brody (Eds.), *Psychiatric Epidemiology and Mental Health Planning*. Washington, D.C.: American Psychiatric Association, 1967.

KRANTZLER, M. *Creative Divorce*. New York: M. Evans & Co., 1973.

LAKE, A. Divorcees: The new poor. *McCall's*, September 1976, 103, pp. 20, 22, 24, 152.

LEVINGER,, G. Sources of marital dissatisfaction among applicants for divorce. *American Journal of Orthopsychiatry*, 1966, 36, 803-807.

LEVINGER, G. A social psychological perspective on marital dissolution. *The Journal of Social Issues*, 1976, 32, 21-48.

MARRIS, P. *Loss and Change*. New York: Pantheon Books, 1974.

MYERS, J., LINDENTHAL, J., & PEPPER, M. *Social Class, Life Events, and Psychiatric Symptoms: A Longitudinal Study*. Paper presented at the Conference on Stressful Life Events, New York, June 1973.

NORTON, A. & GLICK, P. Marital instability: Past, present and future. *The Journal of Social Issues*, 1976, 32, 5-20.

OVERALL, J. Associations between marital history and the nature of manifest psychopathology. *Journal of Abnormal Psychology*, 1971, 78, 213-221.

PARKES, C. M. Psycho-social transitions: A field for study. *Social Science and Medicine*, 1971, 5, 101-115.

PARKES, C. M. *Bereavement: Studies of Grief in Adult Life*. New York: International Universities Press, 1972.

PEELE, S. & BRODSKY, A. Love can be an addiction. *Psychology Today*, August 1974, pp. 22-26.

PHILLIPS, D. & SEGAL, B. Sexual status and psychiatric symptoms. *American Sociological Review*, 1969, 34, 58-72.

PLECK, J. & SAWYER, J. (Eds.). *Men and Masculinity*. Englewood Cliffs, N. J.: Prentice Hall, 1974.

POWERS, E. & BULTENA, G. Sex differences in intimate friendships of old age. *Journal of Marriage and the Family*, 1976, 38, 739-747.

RADLOFF, L. Sex differences in depression: The effects of occupation and marital status. *Sex Roles*, 1975, 1, 249-265.

RADLOFF, L. *Marital Status and Depression*. Unpublished manuscript. Center for Epidemiologic Studies, National Institute of Mental Health, Washington, D.C., November, 1976.

ROBERTSON, N. The relationship between marital status and the risk of psychiatric referral. *British Journal of Psychiatry*, 1974, 124, 191-202.

ROPER ORGANIZATION, INC. *Virginia Slims American Women's Opinion Poll*, Vol. 3. New York: Author, 1974.

ROSS, H. & SAWHILL, I. *Time of Transition: The Growth of Families Headed by Women*. Washington, D.C.: The Urban Institute, 1975.

SELIGMAN, M. Depression and learned helplessness. In R. Friedman and M. Katz (Eds.), *The Psychology of Depression: Contemporary Theory and Research*, in press.

SPICER, J. & HAMPE, G. Kinship interaction after divorce. *Journal of Marriage and the Family*, 1975, 37, 113-119.

SPREITZER, E., SNYDER, E., & LARSON, D. Age, marital status and labor force participation as related to life satisfaction. *Sex Roles*, 1975, 1, 235-247.

WALDRON, I. Why do women live longer than men? *Journal of Human Stress*, 1976, 2, 2-14.

WALLERSTEIN, J. & KELLY, J. The effects of parental divorce: Experiences of the child in later latency. *American Journal of Orthopsychiatry*, 1976, 46, 256-269.

WEISS, R. The contributions of an organization of single parents to the well-being of its members. *The Family Coordinator*, 1973, 22, 321-326.

WEISS, R. *Marital Separation*. New York: Basic Books, 1975.

WHITE, R. Strategies of adaptation: An attempt at systematic description. In G. Coelho, D. Hamburg, and J. Adams (Eds.), *Coping and Adaptation*. New York: Basic Books, 1974.

WISEMAN, R. Crisis theory and the process of divorce. *Social Casework*, 1975, 56, 205-212.

U.S. Bureau of the Census. *Female Family Heads* (Current Population Reports, Series P-23, No. 25). Washington, D.C.: U.S. Government Printing Office, 1974.

U.S. Department of Health, Education and Welfare. *One Hundred Years of Marriage and Divorce Statistics: United States 1867-1967* (#74-1902, Series 21, Number 24). Washington, D.C.: U.S. Government Printing Office, 1973.

5
SEX DIFFERENCES IN
PROBLEMS OF AGING

LILLIAN E. TROLL and BARBARA F. TURNER

It is possible to grow old without any more distressing problems than beset some humans at any time of life, and there are women and men who are lucky enough to do so. Furthermore, the definition of what are problems associated with aging varies with each society and even subgroups within our society (Binstock & Shanas, 1976; Gutmann, 1977). At each point in history there are variations in what is normal and what is deviant. Many social and demographic characteristics that are associated with old age in present-day America—such as relatively poor health, relative poverty, widowhood—are indeed viewed as "social problems" by our society and are shared by both women and men. Both can suffer from debilitating illnesses, both may be poor or near poverty, and both have probably lost their spouses, as well as many other people who were close to them. Not only that, but both women and men are affected by prevailing ageist stereotyping and bias. However, sex status is so powerful an influence in the life chances and life-styles of individuals throughout all of life that patterns of aging tend to be very different for women than for men. Sexism—systematic institutional discrimination against women—continues to operate in old age, compounding the "social problem" status and the social problems of older women. The following pages will attend to these sex differences in aging.

First, we will turn to demographic and physiological factors that differentially distribute life chances by sex: mortality, health or morbidity, and economics.

MORTALITY AND HEALTH

In the first place, females of our species (and of many other species) tend to live longer than do males. At the present time, the sex difference in life expectancy is about seven years, to the advantage of women (76.6

124

for women and 68.9 for men at birth, in 1974), and this differential has been steadily increasing (Retherford, 1975; U.S. Bureau of the Census, 1976). This means that with each decade past 50, there are more older women alive than there are older men. In 1974, for example, 60% of all people over 65 in the United States were women (U.S. Government Printing Office, 1975). In 1890 there were 102 men aged 65 and over for every 100 women of that age group. By 1974, the ratio was sharply reversed to 100 men for every 143 women. The life expectancy for men born in 1900 was 48 years, for women 51 years—only a three-year difference, but one heralding the trend to come. To the extent that health is related to distance from death, then, among women and men of the same age (65, for example), women are likely to be in better health than men. Common experience corroborates Kalish's (1975) report that older men are much more likely than older women of the same age to report limitation of major work and maintenance activities due to chronic health problems. At any older age, apparently, men are more likely to suffer from life-threatening conditions (terminal illnesses) while women are prone to more chronic disorders that are not immediately lethal (Verbrugge, 1975). In almost any group of older people, the women display more vitality and verve than the men, even when the women are as old as the men. This sex difference is accentuated in groups of married couples by the typical age differential between spouses in which the husband is older than the wife. Thus, due to the sex difference in life expectancy and the social expectation that women will marry men older than themselves, the ratio of unmarried to married women increases sharply in the later years. Over the age of 65, 73% of men but only 37% of women are married (U.S. Bureau of Census, 1976). Singled women find fewer men available for remarriage, but singled men have many women from whom to choose. The sex difference in health and longevity has many behavioral and interpersonal consequences. And these consequences are exaggerated by the differential interpretation of good and poor health for the two sexes.

One important consequence of good health in later years is the opportunity to remain active. Remaining active—both in physical and social activities—is generally associated with higher morale, happiness, and life satisfaction (Neugarten, 1968). Thus, older women, by virtue of having a greater chance for better health, should enjoy a happier, more vigorous outlook on life than older men. On top of this, poor health for men in our society, particularly during the transition years of middle age, is equated with passivity and the "feminine" characteristics they wish to deny in themselves (Huyck, 1976, 1977). Throughout adulthood, many women have experienced at least occasional periods of reduced vigor as a consequence of menstruation, pregnancy, and childbirth, and while the reduction in vigor at such times may have been neither as universal nor as extreme as some writers state (cf. Bardwick, 1971), women are not perceived as defeminized. Less than "top form" is contrary to the stereotype of the masculine sex role. Women past menopause often feel healthier than they have for years and experience an extra sense of buoyancy and morale (Weg, 1977). At this time, though, the men their age are threatened by the possibility of illness for which they have no psychological preparation. Loss of strength is equated by many men with loss of virility or manliness and can be seen as destructive to their whole view of themselves.

Some of the concomitants of this reversal in general health status will be discussed below under personality and androgeny. At this time, though, the consequences for marital interaction will be suggested. If a wife is in good health and her husband is showing dangerous symptoms which he is ignoring, she can easily be drawn back into a repetition of the mother-nurse role she experienced while raising children. It becomes her responsibility to see to it that he goes to the doctor, watches his diet, takes his medication, and alters his activities as indicated. The end result for women of the differential in health can be a paradoxically continued servitude and caring function instead of new freedom and individuation. Lopata (1973) found to her surprise that most widows had been the primary nurse for their ill husband for months and even years, and had not been "out of the house" all during that time. Lieberman and Lakin (1963) found that women's fantasies around entering an institution for the aged had centered on the opportunity for a new lover; men's fantasies had centered around the availability of nursing and mothering. It is not unusual for older singled women to complain that the men whom they date want them to be a nurse—and "who needs that?"

A related consequence of this health differential is the absence of a healthy spouse to nurse the older woman who is unlucky enough to become ill. Just as young mothers are not supposed to become sick when their children are, so old women try to nurse themselves as best as they can—until their situation becomes so extreme that their children must step in with extreme solutions, such as professional (read nursing home) care. It is not surprising that many older women try to turn to the medical profession for the attention they cannot find at home. Unfortunately, as Butler and Lewis (1973) point out:

Old women cannot count on the medical profession. Few doctors are interested in them. Their physical and emotional discomforts are often characterized as "post-menopausal syndromes" until they have lived too long for this to be an even faintly reasonable diagnosis. After that, they are assigned the category of "senility." Doctors complain about being harassed by their elderly female patients, and it is true that many are lonely and seeking attention. Yet more than 85% have some kind of chronic health problem, and both depression and hypochondriasis commonly accompany the physical ailments (Butler & Lewis, 1973, p. 91).

In other words, many older women may be healthier than their male contemporaries, but the attitudes of others (and themselves) force them into a hypochondriacal condition which negates the positive benefits of their advantage. What Butler and Lewis have said about the medical profession in general is perhaps even more true of the psychotherapists who might be helping them. Reliance on the "medical model" for interpreting the problems of older people—particularly older women—prevents both older people and therapists from providing the kind of help which would allow such older women to enjoy their later years instead of becoming more anxious, depressed, and passive than they had been earlier.

ECONOMIC STATUS

Equal in importance with health is economic security. Again, as for health, sex differences are striking. A recent study of selected "problem groups" of old people in Chicago (Bild & Havighurst, 1976) found that the women were much more "disadvantaged" than the men, even when the data were corrected for the fact that the man's income usually supported husband and wife. More than 45% of single, divorced, and widowed women have incomes below poverty level, compared to 33% of the men (Cutler & Harootyan, 1975). The reasons for this differential are multiple and cumulative and reflect the traditional sex roles under which the men and women who are now old were socialized and led their lives.

Sex-role stereotypes assume that men are employed on jobs outside the home and "bring home the bacon" while women remain at home and receive whatever money their husband considers adequate for household management. While many older women of today have been employed for a while before marriage, they are likely to have "retired" to the home when they married to keep house and raise a family. There has recently been an upswell of middle-aged and younger women returning to the job market (see Table 1), but this movement has reached only a small proportion of those women who are now past 65 or 70 (Huyck, 1977).

So long as women did not outlive their husbands and continued to bear and raise children throughout their fertile years, the traditional plan of women relying on men for financial support had some justification, though even then it was rarely free of abuses. However, over the last three-quarters of a century, women have stopped bearing children while they were still young and have limited the number of children to two or three instead of six or more (see Table 2 and Figure 1). They are thus likely to be finished with child-rearing while they are in their thirties or forties and can then find themselves left without a reason for existence. This is made even more acute for widows and other singled women. The rising tide of divorce, coupled with differential longevity, has left many older women not only without children to care for, but also without a husband to care for—and also without a legitimate means of support. While the media celebrate the grasping divorcee who gets all her ex-husband's money, this is rarely true for middle-aged and older divorced wives. No-fault divorces and lack of enforcement of alimony or child-support judgments contribute to the financial abandonment of most ex-wives and their children (Bernard, 1974, p. 218).

Singled men are much more likely to remarry than are singled women. Not only are there more women than men available, but remarriage is more imperative for the older singled man of today than for the older singled woman. Most older men have relied on their wives for intimacy, for basic care, and for linkages with family, friends, and social life in general (Bernard, 1972; Troll, 1971, 1975). After 30, singled husbands

TABLE 1

Labor Force Participation Rates by Age and Sex: 1970

	Women	Men	Index ratio women/men
45-54	54%	93%	.58
55-64	43%	82%	.52
65 and over	9%	26%	.35
70 and over	5%	17%	.29

Adapted from: Atchley, 1977, p. 235, and Schulz, 1976, p. 40.

TABLE 2

Median Age of Mothers at Selected Stages of the Family Life Cycle

Stage of the Family Life Cycle	80-Year Average	Period of Birth of Mother / Approximate Period of First Marriage							
		1880's / 1900's	1890's / 1910's	1900's / 1920's	1910's / 1930's	1920's / 1940's	1930's / 1950's	1940's / 1960's	1950's / 1970's
Median age at:									
First marriage	20.9	21.4	21.2	21.0	21.4	20.7	20.0	20.5	21.2
Birth of first child	22.6	23.0	22.9	22.8	23.5	22.7	21.4	21.8	22.7
Birth of last child	31.3	32.9	32.0	31.0	32.0	31.5	31.2	30.1	29.6
Marriage of last child	53.5	55.4	54.8	53.0	53.2	53.2	53.6	52.7	52.3
Death of one spouse	62.8	57.0	59.6	62.3	63.7	64.4	65.1	65.1	65.2
Difference between age at first marriage and:									
Birth of first child	1.7	1.6	1.7	1.8	2.1	2.0	1.4	1.3	1.5
Birth of last child	10.4	11.5	10.8	10.0	10.6	10.8	11.2	9.6	8.4
Marriage of last child	32.6	34.0	33.6	32.0	31.8	32.5	33.6	32.2	31.1
Death of one spouse	41.9	35.6	38.4	41.3	42.3	43.7	45.1	44.6	44.0
Difference between:									
Age at birth of first and last children	8.7	9.9	9.1	8.2	8.5	8.8	9.8	8.3	6.9
Age at birth of and marriage of last child	22.2	22.5	22.8	22.0	21.2	21.7	22.4	22.6	22.7
Age at marriage of last child and death of one spouse (empty nest)	9.3	1.6	4.8	9.3	10.5	11.2	11.5	12.4	12.9

Source: U.S. Bureau of the Census Reports (Glick, 1977).

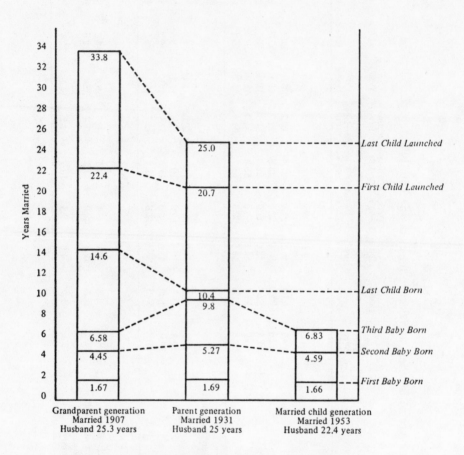

Figure 1. Profile of the timing of family composition changes by generation. From *Family Development in Three Generations* by R. Hill, N. Foote, J. Aldous, R. Carlson, and R. Macdonald. Copyright 1970 by Schenkman Publishing Company. Reprinted by permission.

are much more likely to replace a wife than singled women a husband (Troll, 1975). This is illustrated in Figure 2, both for divorced and widowed men and women.

Even if women remain married until the death of their husbands in old age, they may then find themselves without any income (Schulz, 1976). Further, many men choose a retirement option that yields them more money while they are alive instead of one that insures the support (even though minimal) of their widow. And since there is no obligation for men to consult with their wives or to inform them of such decisions, a widow is often cruelly confronted with the fact that she has no income only after her husband's funeral.

Finally, traditionally women are not generally involved in the handling

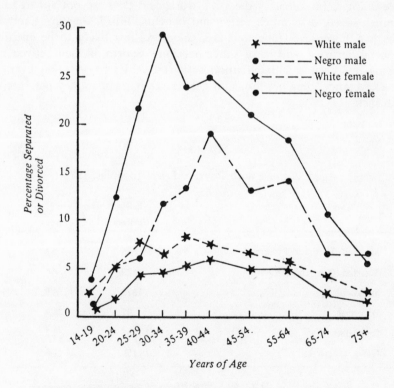

Figure 2. Percentage separated or divorced, by age. From U.S. Bureau of the Census Subject Report: Marital Status, PC(2)-4C, 1972.

of money matters while their husbands are alive. They know little about budgeting, investments, taxes, or other aspects of economic management, even if they themselves have been employed. They are at a loss when they have to take over these matters, and particularly vulnerable to fraudulent advisors. Table 3 shows the differential effects of sex and marital status on poverty.

Not all women have remained housewives exclusively. Many have held jobs outside their home, either intermittently during their child-rearing years, or some even throughout those years. Yet their employment history, on the average, does not make them as economically secure as the average older man (Atchley & Corbett, 1977). Most women have worked fewer total years and have thus accumulated less retirement benefits. Second, they are likely to have received lower pay than men, even when they were doing approximately the same work, and thus are not apt to have as much saved or as much retirement benefits. Third, they are likely to have had lower-level jobs, and are, therefore, less likely to be entitled to Social Security benefits or other pensions. Fourth, if their retirement income has been calculated upon actuarial tables based upon average life expectancy, they are going to get less retirement money per month than men.

TABLE 3

Aged Women with Poverty Level Incomes, 1973

Marital Status	Below Poverty Level	
	Number[a]	Percent
Married, Husband Present	375	8.3
Married, Husband Absent	29	•[b]
Widowed	1578	24.9
Divorced	97	31.4
Separated	55	54.5
Never Married	165	21.6

Source: U.S. Bureau of the Census, *Characteristics of the Low-Income Population: 1973*, Current Population Reports Series P-60, No. 98. (Washington, D.C.: U.S. Government Printing Office, 1975).
[a]Thousands.
[b]Base less than 75,000.

As Huyck (1976) sums up:

A specially disadvantaged group are the "displaced homemakers"—women who entered marriage at a time when they believed, in good faith and with full social support, that marriage would provide a lifetime of economic and social security. As older women, they find themselves divorced or widowed, too young for retirement benefits of former husbands, too old to stand much chance of remarriage, and usually considered undesirable employees in the paid work force. "Survivor benefits" may be minimal or nonexistent. They find they have no credit rating of their own. Many such women face financial disaster (Huyck, 1976).

It is hoped that future generations of old women will not be so disadvantaged. Equal education and equal opportunities for employment, equal payment and benefits for equal work should all help even out existing sex discrepancies in economic security. New definitions of sex-role appropriateness should also enable women to take money and financial management more seriously so that they acquire more experience in sharing financial management with their husbands while they are married and are able to take care of themselves better if they are single or singled.

SEXUALITY

Since there are gender differences in both fertility and sexual behavior, it would follow that there would be gender differences in problems relating to both aspects of sex during the process of aging. These aspects tend to be confounded in most treatments of the subject; problems of sexuality are considered related to problems of fertility. They are, however, independent events.

Fertility

Fertility declines in middle age for both men and women, due to gonadal deterioration (Weg, 1977). For women, it ceases relatively abruptly with the menopause. For men, it continues longer, though at a reduced level, and diminishes gradually rather than abruptly. The male climacteric occurs, on the average, five or ten years later than the female. Because the male climacteric has fewer physiological consequences or concomitants, it is less noticeable and is seen as having less effect on behavior than the menopause, even though some popular writers are glibly using the misnomer "male menopause" to refer to problems men may experience during the middle years.

Women are commonly, and traditionally, perceived in terms of their body and its biological functioning. From the menarche on, they are supposed to be under the control of their menstrual cycle and, thus, impulsive and nonrational. Menopause is usually perceived from this kind of perceptual stance. Since women's function is considered primarily sexual and reproductive, the end of fertility is assumed to be the end of their useful life. Both women and men take it for granted that women will suffer and mourn at this time (Neugarten, Wood, Kraines, & Loomis, 1963), and the medical profession has usually followed suit and ascribed all the ills of middle-aged women to menopausal symptoms (e.g., "involutional melancholia"), as the aforementioned quote from Butler and Lewis testified.

That most of these assumptions are more mythical than necessary (cf. Janeway, 1971) is attested to by the wide variation in symptomatology and reactions across individuals within a culture and across cultures (Datan, Maoz, Antonovsky, & Wijsenbeek, 1970). Apparently, without societal prescriptions for discomfort, leading to anxiety arousal and secondary troubles, most menopausal women report few problems, either biological or psychological. One of the few studies that tried to test out some of the clinicians' hypotheses about menopausal disorders interviewed a large number of "normal" women—married, mothers (Neugarten et al., 1963). Only about half of all the women interviewed agreed that menopause was an unpleasant experience, and these tended to be younger women who were looking forward to it apprehensively, largely worried about its unpredictability. Three-fourths of those actually in menopausal age (45-55) felt that it does not change a woman in any important way and that those who have trouble with it are usually those who "have nothing to do with their time."

It is true that some women do have both medical and psychological difficulties during the menopause. Some of these seem to be women who are particularly vulnerable to psychosexual changes, who are apt to have had crises at the time of menarche, and who have had trouble with sexuality, pregnancy, childbirth, nursing, and menstrual periods. After all, the significant effects of cultural norms and beliefs as well as long-standing personality characteristics are clear in reactions to all life crises including menopause (Kimmel, 1974; Neugarten, 1968). Such women are thus particularly in need of psychotherapeutic help at this time, and should not have their problems dismissed as trivial or humorous concomitants of menopause. Others seem to be those women described as having too much time on their hands, though this is more likely to be the result of having concentrated their adult life work upon child-rearing. As Bart (1971) points out, they are the "super-mothers" who do not, like most middle-aged women, wait impatiently for the departure of their last child from the nest (cf. Lowenthal, Thurnher, Chiriboga, and associates, 1975), but find themselves lost when their children no longer need their concentrated mothering. Few women want to keep on bearing children throughout their lives, but some don't know what else to do.

Since men can continue to fertilize women well into old age, they are less concerned with waning of this ability—at least in our culture. Male climacteric is probably seen more as a threat to sexual activity than as a threat to fertility.

Sexual Activity

An extrapolation from our current inadequate data which, besides, are heavily influenced by traditional sex-role stereotypes, would show that men reach their peak of sexual power in late adolescence and gradually decrease from that time on, while women do not peak until at least the late twenties and may continue to increase after that (Kinsey, Pomeroy, Martin, & Gebhard, 1953; Masters & Johnson, 1966; Pfeiffer, 1969; Pfeiffer, Verwoerdt, & Davis, 1972). On the other hand, men in today's older cohorts report greater interest in sex and more sexual activity than women their age (Pfeiffer, 1969; Pfeiffer et al., 1972). Since the women who are old now were socialized to sexual activity in a traditional way, the loss of their husbands or the loss of their husbands' interest in sex puts an end to their own activity. The best predictors of continued sexual functioning in old age for men are past sexual experience, age, health, and social class; the best predictor for women is marital status (Palmore, 1970, 1974), though age and past experience are also relevant. Most of today's older women assume that anybody knows that without a husband (or, for a few, a lover), there is no sex. Kinsey et al. (1953) report that before the middle years of life, wives report more activity than interest in marital intercourse, while afterward they report more interest than activity. In all studies, spouses agree that the husband was responsible for any decline or cessation in sexual intercourse (Pfeiffer et al., 1972). As Huyck (1976, p. 13) wryly comments: "There is nothing less responsive to compulsion and command than a limp penis." Bossard and Boll (1955) explained the increased marital dissatisfaction of wives in their forties, not by the "empty nest" or the menopause, but by sexual frustration due to their husband's waning potency. It seems that just when they are able to feel free in their sexual expression without fear of getting pregnant, their husband withdraws.

It is notable that life-span studies of marital sexuality have focused only upon vaginal intercourse, indicating a phallocentric bias in researchers, and undoubtedly also in the older respondents. It may be that as other sexual practices gain more acceptance, investigators will broaden the scope of sexual practices which they study. At the present time, most old women do not even consider masturbation after they lose their sexual partner.

Both Kinsey, Pomeroy, and Martin (1948) and Kinsey et al. (1953) employed cross-sectional designs, as did Masters and Johnson (1966), so that their findings must be taken with caution. The younger of the old cohorts—those closer to 60 than to 80—may already have moved away from the kinds of situations the older ones were reporting in the 1940s and 1950s. Furthermore, they included few subjects over 60. The Kinsey studies concluded that men were sexually most active between 16 and 20, with a gradual decline but no cessation till past 70. However, impotence increased from 20% at 60 to 75% at 80, and older married men were only slightly less active than singled or never-married men. In contrast, singled or never-married older women were much less sexually active than men in the same marital status groups. Men and women over 60 in the Masters and Johnson (1966) laboratory sample had slower reactions at all phases of the sexual response cycle as compared with younger men and women. For those women who had had regular sexual activity throughout adulthood, however, orgasmic capacity was as high as for younger women. For both sexes, the prescription for a happy sex life in old age is "use it or lose it."

Longitudinal studies of men and women between 60 and 94 at Duke University (Pfeiffer, 1969; Pfeiffer et al., 1972) generally replicated the cross-sectional data above. Older men reported greater interest and more activity in heterosexual intercourse than did older women. Among men, the median age of stopping sexual activity was 69; among women, 60. Interestingly, about one-quarter of the men and even a few women showed not declining but rising sexual interest and activity with advancing age. How can we explain these apparently discrepant conclusions? Are the older men turning to other, younger women, for sexual partners? Is women's increased sexual interest true for those who are now middle-aged rather than for those who are now old? Does the increase in women's interest start from a lower base so that they still do not match the somewhat decreased level of their husband? It is likely that we are dealing not only with cohort and period differences (Bengtson & Cutler, 1976) but also with wide individual, social class, and ethnic differences.

FAMILY

Family relationships in later life include those between spouses, between parents and children, and between extended kin. These are considered below.

Marital Relations

The discussion above dealt with a number of different aspects of husband-wife relationships in old age: with effects of differential health status, differential economic status, and differences in sexual responsivity. It did not deal directly with the reports by men and women of their marital satisfaction or happiness, nor with mental health concomitants of marital status.

In spite of constant criticism of its validity, the index of marital satisfaction used by Blood and Wolfe (1960) has been the one used most consistently by investigators of marital interaction. Also, because women— particularly housewives—are more ready to talk to interviewers than are men, most of the studies of marital satisfaction are based on their reports. Almost all these studies, both cross-sectional and longitudinal, find a decline in satisfaction from the peak of the honeymoon to the nadir of middle age (e.g., Blood & Wolfe, 1960; Feldman, 1964; Paris & Luckey, 1966; Pineo, 1961).

The array of findings are reviewed by Rollins and Cannon (1974), Spanier, Lewis, and Cole (1975), and Troll (1971, 1975). That this drop in marital satisfaction with length of marriage may be associated with child-rearing is suggested by its acceleration after the birth of the first child, its relative absence in couples without children, its greater strength and consistency among women than among men, and its possible reversal—at least temporarily—after the children are "launched." Data derived from husbands are not only rarer, but also less consistent than those derived from wives. Some studies show no life course change in husband's marital satisfaction (Hamilton, 1929; Luckey, 1961; Paris & Luckey, 1966), while other studies show different time patterns in marital satisfaction for husbands and wives (Bossard & Boll, 1955; Hicks & Platt, 1970; Lowenthal et al., 1975; Rollins & Feldman, 1970). In the Lowenthal et al. (1975) study, sex differences in marital satisfaction were primarily confined to the launching stage subjects (men and women whose youngest child was a senior in high school). While four-fifths of the men of all ages (newlywed through retired) reported high marital satisfaction and positive regard for their wives, as did newlywed and pre-retired women, the "launching-stage" women were much more critical. Only two-fifths gave predominantly positive portrayals of their husbands and their marriages. These middle-aged women mentioned the most difficulties in getting along with their husbands. On the other hand, when they were asked, "How do you think your spouse would describe you?" over half expected positive responses, compared with only one-third of the men of that age (the men and women in the sample were not married to each other), who expected predominantly negative descriptions of themselves. While the men stressed their wives' virtues, they knew that they did not meet their wives' expectations. Thurnher (1975) notes, "In terms of fulfilling emotional needs, these sex differences appear to mirror actuality. Middle-aged men, by and large, did not question their adequacy as family providers but seemed aware—though not necessarily contrite about it nor moved to change—that they were often inconsiderate and unheeding of their wife's desires for attention, companionship, or diversion." In describing daily activities, these women spoke about their husbands more than the men spoke about their wives. In fact, the men tended not to mention the everyday domestic interactions that the women described. Similar to the working-class and upper-middle-class fathers described by Rubin (1975), then, these lower-middle-class middle-aged men tended to be psychologically absent from their homes even when physically present in them.

Many of the launching stage and pre-retired women in the Lowenthal et al. (1975) study (average ages about 48 and 58, respectively) felt that their husbands were overdependent. (Among newlyweds, it was the men who were more likely to feel that way about their wives.) Like the young men, the middle-aged women were looking forward with a certain amount of impatience to expressing themselves autonomously in the world outside of the family. However, any emotional support they might be seeking from their husbands in making such big changes did not seem likely to be forthcoming. Instead, they were being drawn into mothering their husbands—and few of them seemed to want this.

Responses of these subjects to the Thematic Apperception Test (TAT) showed discrepancies between the middle-aged men's interview description of their wives and their fantasies about them. In the interview, these men usually focused upon their wives' instrumental role performance, how well they did their housewifely activities, but in fantasy they revealed a need for more reciprocal nurturance—they covertly wanted their wives to love them and help them and in turn express tenderness toward them. The women of the same age were more aware of their feelings and more able to express them. Like their overt interview statements, their TAT responses indicated that their husbands were failing to meet their emotional needs, and that they anticipated more dependency mixed with more closeness in the future. Where the men used words like "tender," the women talked about "clinging." Thus, while the fantasies of both women and men at this stage yearned for warmth and intimacy in the marital relationship, the women seemed less hopeful of its promise, expecting at best some support and a staving off of loneliness.

In the same study (Lowenthal et al., 1975), the men and women who were a decade or so older and whose youngest child had generally "left the nest" felt that their marital relationship had improved. However, these men also were more satisfied than the women their age and looked forward more than did the women to increased sharing of activities after their anticipated retirement. The older men's fantasies differed from those of the men in the somewhat younger group ("launching stage") in that they stressed comfort more and nurturance and warmth less. The women of this stage, on the TAT, portrayed fewer consolation and dependency themes and more stoicism and "leaning on one another."

In two mailed questionnaire studies of older married men and women (again, not married to each other), Stinnett, Collins and Montgomery (1970) and Stinnett, Carter, and Montgomery (1972) found somewhat similar results. Both samples were cross-sectional and probably more traditional than the American average (Oklahoman and Mormon respondents). Even though these older people said that they were happily married and even though both men and women stressed the importance of love in marriage, the needs that they felt marriage should or did fulfill were different for each sex. For example, the men felt that respect was the area in which they received least satisfaction, and the women felt that communication was the area in which they received least satisfaction. The theme of respect does not appear in other data, and its presence here may be related either to the fact that these subjects were retired and thus had increased need for respect in general, or it may come from the unique sample. The theme of the women—the sense of isolation—recurs in all the literature on married women.

That marriage is different for men and for women has been eloquently documented by Bernard (1973), who speaks of "his" and "her" marriages. She stresses particularly the difference in advantages (and disadvantages). In general, marriage is good for men and bad for women. This is partly related to its greater importance, socially and personally, for women. Being married is so important for women that they put up with a lot just to get and stay that way. A man who is not satisfied with his marriage is likely to leave it; a woman who is not satisfied is less likely to do so—if she acknowledges it at all. Even present massive changes in sex-role values do not seem to have led to impressive changes in this picture, at least among older people. While those older people who are married are better off in health, mental health, economic status, morale, etc., than those who are not married, the men are better off than the women on all these indices. In fact, married women are not notably better off than unmarried women, though married men are clearly better off than unmarried men. Again, we must remind ourselves that older men who are in relatively good shape can much more easily find a new wife than can older women, and practically no demographic or empirical reports separate out those older married people who have stayed married to the same spouse throughout their married life from those who are now married to their second, third, or even fourth wife. This omission is particularly important in trying to understand the scanty research findings on very old couples.

Household division of labor is notoriously unequal between the two sexes. Even among couples dedicated to equalitarian values, housework becomes the woman's responsibility following the birth of the first child (Hoffman, 1977; Walker, 1970). Even where women are employed—and this refers to more than half of middle-aged women today (see Table 1)—they just add on the work of the job to the work of the home. Time-motion studies like Walker's indicate no differences between husbands of employed and homemaker wives in household task participation (including child care). They show that husbands spend one-and-one-half hours per day in household work, on the average, compared with five hours per day for employed wives. The wives are responsible for, and actually perform, almost all janitorial services, child care tasks, and meal preparation; husbands are responsible for, and actually perform, a very few "masculine" tasks that, in any case, require infrequent performance, such as minor repairs, shoveling snow, and mowing the grass. Emptying the garbage is an exception, requiring frequent performance.

These lists do not even consider the major responsibility of women for kin-keeping activities—visiting, helping, and keeping in touch with all relatives, their husbands' as well as their own. Blood and Wolfe (1960), in an earlier cross-sectional study, found that household task specialization by sex increased over the life span, reaching its highest point during retirement. Departure of children from the home and even retirement did not increase the husband's share of household work. Lipman (1961, 1962) reported that many retired husbands participated in chores that required little specialized skill and knowledge, and which could be done jointly with their wives, like washing dishes and shopping for groceries. On the other hand, Ballweg (1967) did not find that retired husbands shared more work with their wives than employed husbands of the same age. Instead, the retired husbands were slightly more likely to assume full responsibility for a few tasks already socially defined as "masculine"; they did not perform any "feminine" tasks. That this sex-role defined division of labor fits in with the values of both marital partners is attested to by Ballweg's respondents. At least among these older couples—more likely to be from a "traditional" background—the women had mixed feelings and some even resented the perceived intrusion of their husbands into their territory. We will discuss sex-role ideology somewhat more fully in a later section of this chapter.

In very late old age, when both partners to a marriage may find the tasks of household maintenance beyond their strength, they may shift to what has been called a "symbiotic" relationship (Troll, 1971), in which each contributes what best she or he can. If this is so, we need much more study of this condition than we have had so far. The fact that people who have been married many years tend to die within a short time of each other suggests that they are holding each other up as in the form of an arch, which collapses when either side falls.

Parent-Child Relations

Although many writers about the family still assert that the nuclear family—a husband and wife and their immature offspring—exists, and must exist, in almost complete isolation from extended kin, this position seems to be based more upon wish than upon reality. Data accumulating from a host of major and minor studies since the late 1950s point strongly to a continuation of family relationships throughout life. It is true that there are few three-generation households (and perhaps always have been few). However, grown children and their parents commonly live near each other, visit each other frequently, and help each other in countless ways (e.g., Adams, 1968; Bengtson, Olander, & Haddad, 1976; Hill, Foote, Aldous, Carlson, & Macdonald, 1970; Litwak, 1960; Shanas, Townsend, Wedderburn, Friis, Milhoj, & Stehouwer, 1968; Sussman & Burchinal, 1962; Troll, 1971).

It has been mentioned that it is the wife's function to maintain kin relationships. Most data show that while there may be little sex difference in parents' influence upon their children (Troll & Bengtson, in press), mothers tend to live nearer to their children than do fathers (if they are currently singled or remarried) and are more likely to move in with a daughter than a son. There is more visiting among the female line of kinship, between grandmother, mother, and daughter, than between grandfather, father, and son, and, while there is no research evidence for this, there may be more help exchanged among the women in a lineage than among the men. Because kin-keeping is a female-preponderant function, widowers tend to be more at a loss than widows. They lose not only their spouses, but also with them their ties to friends, children, and even their own parents and siblings. It was the wife who called relatives to make arrangements for getting together and to find out how everybody was. As will be noted later in the discussion of friendship, women tend to find it easy to self-disclose and maintain close ties with a number of people, both friends and kin, but men generally restrict such intimacy to their wives. The special loneliness of the widower, not only his greater opportunities, is a strong propellant to his remarriage.

SEX ROLES

At least three major studies suggest that gender-linked personality characteristics are most differentiated in early adulthood and that women and men become progressively more "androgenous" as they move from middle to old age (Livson, 1976; Lowenthal et al., 1975; Neugarten & Gutmann, 1964). This age shift is most frequently associated with measures of intrapsychic functioning (e.g., projective tests); less often with measures involving conscious material, such as self-image; and least often in role behavior itself. Gutmann (1964, 1974, 1975) suggests that a normal developmental shift occurs in middle-aged men from an intrapsychic stance emphasizing active mastery of the environment to a passive-receptive mode. When older American respondents (40-70) were administered a TAT-type card depicting a family scene, they described the old man as more passive, submissive, and easygoing than had younger respondents. Conversely, the older respondents said the old woman was a dominant authority figure; younger ones ascribed a subordinate role to her. The conclusion was:

> For both men and women respondents, it is almost always the old woman, not the old man, to whom impulsivity, aggressivity, and

hostile dominance are ascribed. This consistency cannot be explained by chance. The assumption seems warranted that there is something common to the actual role behaviors of older women that elicits this consistency in respondents' fantasies (Gutmann, 1964, p. 88).

Gutmann—and his colleague Neugarten—were careful to note that the behavior attributed by older respondents to the old woman and man in the TAT stimulus was not apparent in the social behavior of these respondents, and warned against applying their findings directly to actual behavior.

In summarizing his later studies, Gutmann (1975) reported that, compared with younger men, the fantasies of older ones are less aggressive, more affiliative, more interested in love than in power, more diffusely sensual, and more likely to see power as located outside themselves. Conversely, even in patriarchal societies, women in later life become covertly more aggressive, less sentimental, and more domineering. He suggests that each sex in young adulthood represses characteristics ascribed to the other sex so as to provide an environment maximally conducive to survival of offspring. After the children reach adulthood, their parents are free to release and express these repressed characteristics. There is some support for his theory from the Berkeley longitudinal data (Livson, 1976) which show little difference in sex-typed personality characteristics at the beginning of adolescence (around 12), a dropping out of opposite sex attributes during adolescence to a peak of sex-role differentiation by late adolescence, and a "bringing back" of these purportedly repressed characteristics in middle age.

To the extent that such an age shift in sex-typed characteristics does occur, there is evidence that the middle age transition is more problematic for women than for men. Huyck (1976) points out that jokes and social unease accompany tales of strong, dominant old women. "The old battle-axe" is deprecated; more acceptable is the meek, kindly, "feminine" old man who poses no threat either to his own generation or to the ones following. On the other hand, Livson reports that clinical psychologists who evaluated the mental health of the longitudinal subjects rated those women who had "taken back" the assertive characteristics (some women had not) they had discarded in early adolescence as much healthier. All the men—and they had all made the transition described—were rated highly, but those women who had remained determinedly "feminine" were described clinically as anxious and dependent and less able to cope with their life circumstances. Data from at least one longitudinal (Maas & Kuypers, 1974) and one cross-sectional study (Lowenthal et al., 1975) suggest that the late-life personal adaptation of highly feminine, other-oriented women is dependent upon their marital status and proximity to children. With no interests and involvements outside the family circle, such women are more vulnerable than more autonomous women to the changes in life-style and life focus wrought by widowhood, for example. Bart (1971) has pointed to the fragility of the super-mothers at the time of middle-age changes in physiology and household responsibilities (menopause and empty nest).

But, as Goodchilds (1977) so graphically demonstrates, older women now are damned if they do and damned if they don't. There are few legitimate social channels outside the family circle that are open at present to middle-aged and older women's expressions of self-assertion. In the Lowenthal et al. (1975) sample, long-employed lower-middle-class women were as bored with their jobs as long-employed lower-middle-class men. If they are in a leadership role on the job, they are damned as bitches if they exert authority and damned as ineffectual if they don't (Goodchilds, 1977). Even if they are fully enjoying a new career, they are likely to find retirement looming just when they are reaching their stride (Atchley & Corbett, 1977). Among the "androgenous" women nearest to retirement, a common solution was to cater to their husbands' growing dependency needs, becoming more of a mother and less of a wife in the marital relationship. If they cannot find substitute solutions (see Feldman, 1977), the only solution left to them may be the adoption of hypochondria, as indicated above.

ROLE STRESS

Among the consequences of the influx of women into the labor market, and especially of middle-aged and older women, has been the problem of synchronizing job and marital roles (Neugarten & Hagestad, 1976). The periods of greatest role stress resulting from multiple demands differ between men and women. Most of the literature suggests that for men the stresses are greatest during the period preceding retirement (Reichard, Livson, & Peterson, 1962). At least, this seems to be true for those men who have been socialized to identify themselves with their job role and who must redefine themselves during the process of anticipatory socialization for loss of that role. This, of course, is likely to be true largely for a small percentage of middle-class men, like professionals, academicians, and artists, as will be discussed more fully below.

The period of greatest role stress for women would be during the forties and fifties. At this time, women may be characterized as pursuing the "Cassandra function" (Troll & Turner, 1976). They are doing the "work of worry." Bernard (1972) has suggested that the supportive or stroking function is the quintessential social psychological sex-role function of women. Socialization shapes personality and behavior patterns in girls so that, as women, they will assume a nurturant role in interaction with others: Women comply, understand, accept, allay the anxiety of others, and promote solidarity and emotional bonds. During middle age, their worries extend in multiple directions. They worry about their children who must comply with the norms for young adults: starting a job or career and getting married and having children. The mothers of college left-wing activists, who themselves were "forerunners" of their generation in terms of values (Troll & Bengtson, 1978) were generally satisfied with their children when they were re-interviewed after seven years (as indeed they had been seven years earlier), unless these children were not fulfilling job and family norms (Angres, 1975). The cry "I wish I had grandchildren!" reflects not so much a desire for grandchildren as such—on the whole, grandparenting for most middle-aged women seems to be a peripheral function (Troll, 1975)—but rather worry about the normality of their children (and thus their own adequacy as parents).

Both psychoanalytic personality theory and social role theory shed light on the propensity of mothers to worry about their high-school-aged and young adult children. Benedek (1959, 1970) points out that in normal development, parents identify with their children as well as vice versa— parents aim at self-realization, according to current cultural standards, through the development of their children; and they hope to be "good parents." Current cultural standards require completion of a minimum educational level, dependent on parental socioeconomic class; the establishment of economic independence, including occupational stability and establishing an independent household, and marriage, followed by parenthood. Adolescent children's academic difficulties—dropping out of school, alcohol or drug addiction, premarital pregnancy, brushes with the law, desultory progress toward occupational choice, postponement of marriage, and once married, of parenthood—any of these may threaten both parental self-realization and the self-definition of "good parent," with consequent parental depression and at least covert parent-child conflict.

According to social role theory (Lopata, 1973), many social roles have a life cycle which is expectable and foreseen by those entering the role. In somewhat analogous terms, Back (1976) points out that the departure of children from the parental household is a developmental event that is part of the identity of parents; it is an expected development. People expect to have children, raise them to adulthood, watch them leave home and establish their own families, and live independently in old age without children. Although the "full house" stage of the parental role—with all the children at home—is viewed as the cultural ideal for mothers, the "full house," according to social expectations (internalized by parents), contains subadult children only. Mothers whose adult children live in the parental household are suspected of inculcating excessive dependency in their children: Such mothers may be regarded not as having "succeeded" as mothers, but as having failed; their children, too, have "failed" in the task of achieving adult independence. There is evidence that the average age (and, therefore, the socially normative age) of leaving the parental home has decreased since 1950 (Glick, 1977). Before 1950, children left home to go to college, join the military, or marry. In the working class, economic circumstances required even many newlyweds to live with parents (Komarovsky, 1964). General increasing economic affluence in the last two decades has permitted increasing numbers of youth to establish households independent of their parents, so that the average age of departure from the parental household has dropped to 18 years (Glick, 1977). Conversely, parents are less likely to need the additional income provided by the contributions of working adult children who live in the parental home. The interlocking of the cohort effect of increasing economic affluence with social role theory and psychoanalytic personality theory explains both the general relief of mothers when their children depart and parental tension regarding subsequent signs of their children's failure to achieve full adult independence.

Middle-aged women worry about their young adult children's marital problems, about their health, about their romantic difficulties, and about their job problems (Lowenthal et al., 1975). At the same time, they worry about their husbands—about their health, their love, even their job problems (Lowenthal et al., 1975). Although, according to folklore, it is the tribulations of the menopause and the empty nest that make women between 40 and 59 particularly unhappy, Huyck (1975, p. 34) notes that "many 'old wives' tales' about the menopause . . . turn out not to be true of most old wives." As indicated earlier when Neugarten et al. (1963) interviewed women in various stages of the menopause, few of the respondents attached much significance to that event. They were concerned about health issues, but it was more the health of their husbands that worried them than their own health. Further, rather than being upset about the emptying of the nest, most studies show that middle-aged mothers can hardly wait for that event and show greater marital and general happiness once their children are launched (Glenn, 1975; Lowenthal et al., 1975). In fact, it is the nonemptying of the nest that worries and bothers most mothers today, as their supposedly grown children, who may even have nominally moved out, continue to fill the parental closets, use their laundry and cooking facilities, and drop in repeatedly for shorter or longer stays (Troll, 1975). Not only do the women feel frustrated at the disruption of the peace and privacy they had expected, but the normative issues mentioned in the last paragraph bother them.

Thus, it is neither menopause nor loss of mother role that is salient for middle-aged women, but the fact that their friends' husbands are having heart attacks or leaving them for other women that arouses their anxiety. They do not want to be widowed or divorced, even though they may be "fulfilling themselves" in new jobs and careers. Because others' stresses are experienced as their own, they also are disturbed if their husbands become depressed around approaching retirement or loss of strength or health.

On top of all these worries, middle-aged women face the declining health of their aging parents and parents-in-law, and its consequences. Remember, it is the woman who assumes the responsibilities for kinship ties and obligations, and the care and arrangements for both their own and their husbands' parents (and sometimes aunts and uncles in addition). At the same time, many of them are involved with their own jobs, and the anxieties of achieving often delayed career goals in the face of their looming retirement which can come hard on the heels of their return to the labor market. It is surprising, indeed, that more middle-aged women are not severely anxious and depressed.

What we have not considered in the preceding discussion is the difference in the importance of appearance and attractiveness for men and women. Susan Sontag (1975) has used the terms the "double standard of aging" to characterize this difference. The masculinity of older men may be threatened by the slowing of their sexual response cycle or the diminution of strength and health (although many women appreciate the slower sexual activity) (Huyck, 1976). Women's self-esteem rests in part upon affirmation of their "femininity" and "femininity" includes the ability to attract men. Sex-role socialization of girls focuses upon the cultivation of charm, but every little girl recognizes, from the frequency of comments upon how pretty she is (or, unfortunately, is not), that physical beauty is the critical ingredient in attracting males. Beautiful girls can use their beauty to marry up (Elder, 1969), and studies of college dating indicate that women's physical attractiveness is the most important determinant of man's satisfaction with dates (Coombs & Kenkel, 1966).

Our standards of physical attractiveness are based upon the physical attributes of women aged 18-25, and are unrealistic even for most women that age. To the extent that physical attractiveness is dependent upon looking young, a woman's looks, and her appeal to men, must steadily diminish with age. Indeed, Nowak and Troll (1974) found that middle-aged women were more concerned with youthfulness than with attractiveness per se, and Nowak (1975) later found that they even had difficulty distinguishing between youthfulness and attractiveness. If middle-aged women judge a person—particularly another woman—to be attractive, they say she is years younger than if they judge her to be unattractive, and if they see her as older, they say she is unattractive. This does not happen with either younger or older women, nor with men of any age group.

The signs of aging in the appearance of men, however, do not lead to their loss of attractiveness to women. In fact, young women, as compared with older women, overestimated the attractiveness of older men, just as older men overestimated the attractiveness of young women.

FRIENDSHIP

Up to now, most of the gender differences we have been discussing have favored the surviving older man over the older woman. There is one important difference in favor of the women, however, and that is her relatively greater ease in self-disclosure, in establishing intimate (as distinguished from sexual) relationships with other people (Jourard & Lasakow, 1958). Since intimate relationships may be the strongest survival mechanism possible (Lowenthal & Haven, 1968), most older women's long-lasting ties with family or friends should stand them in good stead. During most of adulthood, social life is largely based upon couple friendships (Babchuck & Bates, 1963), and such friendships tend to fracture when one of the couples becomes unmated, either by widowhood or divorce (Lopata, 1973). However, many women maintain close personal friends apart from their couple friends who have mostly been derived from the husband's occupational associations (Troll, 1975). They may not see these personal friends often or for long periods of time, but when their couple friends disappear, they can turn back to sisters, cousins, or nonrelated friends for comfort and companionship. Many men, on the other hand, find it difficult to reveal their secret thoughts to others, and rely chiefly upon their wives for such service. Thus, when men lose their wives, they also lose their best friends and find it difficult to make new ones; consequently, they are more vulnerable, in general, to loneliness and anomie.

The array of studies on disengagement theory in aging (Neugarten, 1968) found that older people, with each added decade, are progressively less involved in the world around them. They play fewer social roles and participate less in each of the roles they are still playing. The one arena where there is little evidence for disengagement, though, is the family. Some gerontologists conclude that the older years are characterized by disengagement into the family rather than from the family (Neugarten, 1968; Troll, 1971). Though this process may be partly in the service of help-seeking, it is likely that it is also in the service of intimacy. In fact, a factor analysis of functions of friendship (Candy, 1977) found that intimacy and mutual assistance are part of the same function, and that this function is the most salient one for both women and men from adolescence to old age.

JOB AND RETIREMENT

A man's job can mean to him anything from hours of drudgery that yield him the money he needs to do the things he wants—even if it is sitting in front of a TV with a can of beer in his hand—to the total absorption of a creative endeavor. Obviously, therefore, retirement from a job can also mean different things to different people. For some, it means freedom; for others, poverty. For still others, it means being cut off from the core meaning of their existence. Early studies of retirement (e.g., Reichard, Livson, & Peterson, 1962) found that for most men there was a period of unease, and that this "crisis" tended to come about five years before actual retirement rather than at the time of retirement itself. The folklore that retirement is followed by death tends to be viewed more cautiously by such industrial gerontologists as Sheppard (1971) and Parnes, Nestel, and Andrisani (1972), who suggest that the reality is the other way around. When men feel in poor health and unable to carry on their work, they tend to retire; retirement is the consequence of poor health, not the other way around. Other investigators have looked more carefully at the concomitants of retirement and pointed to diversities (Atchley, 1976; Friedmann & Havighurst, 1954; Lowenthal, 1972) in adjustment to it. In general, if there is a period of crisis, most men adjust to it and tend to continue their earlier life-style. Those who have been "engagers" and active, find new avenues in which to pursue activities.

Many of those who have worked primarily for the money enjoy their well-earned passivity in retirement—provided they have enough money to live on. Those who tend to plan ahead have already planned out their lives after retirement, often far beyond reasonable need. One of the main intervening variables in post-retirement status is economics. When retirement signifies poverty or, at least, drastically reduced income as, unfortunately, it does for most older people today, it is understandably viewed with fear. It is the money, not the occupational participation that is the keystone to much dissatisfaction with compulsory retirement.

Yet, we should not forget the men whose job identity is their major personal identity—and this cuts across economic levels. It is they who perhaps find the transition most difficult. The fact that most compulsory retirement laws specify the age of 65 (or now, 70), an age when most workers are still competent and healthy, seems particularly arbitrary and unwelcome. Preretirement programs that purport to prepare people for their coming retirement are generally unsuccessful and inadequate. They tend to focus upon financial investment or give advice on how to "adjust" to poverty. Above all, they come too late. Retirement will not be alarming when little children are asked not "What will you be when you grow up?" but "What different things will you do in your life?" An acceptance of a norm of multiple careers and pursuits should aid flexibility for all job or leisure career changes.

The above paragraph dealt largely with men. However, it has been mentioned earlier that a majority of older women are also in the labor market and subject to the same compulsory retirement laws as those for men. Atchley and Corbett (1977) point out that for older women of the present generations, who have had interrupted careers and who probably have gone back to work just because there was nothing to do at home, retirement can be much more painful than for most men. Most people writing about retirement say that women find it easier than men because they can always go back into the home, a territory that is more congruent for them than for men.

> Retirement is typically seen as a man's life crisis. He is more often seen as a "breadwinner" and his job as providing both income and meaning to life. Since the primary female roles are those of wife, housekeeper, and mother, the woman's work outside the home has been considered less significant . . . There are several flaws in this line of reasoning. First . . . a job may be just as important for a woman as a man. She is just as likely to be highly committed to it. Retirement could therefore result in "withdrawal symptoms" for

women as well as for men. Second, the assumption that women can easily refocus to "in-home" roles ignores the fact that it was partly because of the loss of such roles in middle age that they initially became involved in jobs. Most women at retirement have no children living at home and 30% are widows (Atchley, 1976). It is therefore no surprise that women tend to take longer than men to adjust to retirement (Atchley & Corbett, 1977, p. 124-5).

Part of the problems of retiring men and, to some extent, women is our society's valuation of work and achievement, the "Protestant ethic." In comparing the adjectives used by middle-aged and older men to describe themselves with their self-reports of feelings of self-worth, Lowenthal et al. (1975) found that the characteristics of vigor and achievement were associated with high morale and self-esteem among the middle-aged men but were associated with feelings of low morale among the older men. Men who are most successfully socialized for the valued behaviors of adulthood find it the hardest to make the transition to the role of "old man" which carries an opposite definition. If you have always been rewarded and reinforced for high achievement and effort and suddenly get punished for these same attributes, you have every reason to feel unfairly treated. It is these same people who find adapting to the leisure norms of retirement most difficult. Those people in our society, however, who have always focused more on fun and games find the leisure ethic that is normative for old age "a natural." Only when our social norms can incorporate more of a valuation of leisure will older people find the transition to retirement welcome rather than frightening. That this may be happening among the youngest adult generations has been suggested by a number of recent writers (Troll & Bengtson, 1978). If so, when our present youth generation becomes old, it will look to a different set of problems.

CONCLUSION

Ignoring individual and subgroup differences, we can conclude that there are significant sex differences in the processes of aging and the problems that may arise consequent to these events and conditions. These differences cannot be said to favor either sex outright. Rather they form the kind of pattern familiarly known as "pilpul" or point-counterpoint. On the one hand, women have the advantage in some ways, but on the other hand, men have the advantage in other ways.

Thus, on the one hand, the modal aging woman has the advantage of longer life expectancy and greater chances for longer health and vigor. On the other hand, because the present generations of older women are living longer than they expected or their socialization prepared them for, the modal older woman may not know what to do with herself during these extra years and may end up as a hypochondriac. On the one hand, the modal older man is better off economically than the modal older woman, but on the other hand he may not live as long to enjoy this advantage. On the one hand, the modal older woman loses her attractiveness when she loses her youthfulness, all at a relatively young age, but on the other hand, she may gain autonomy and feelings of self-confidence and power. On the one hand, the modal older man is upset when his strength and vigor and health deteriorate, but on the other hand, he gains in sensitivity and spontaneity. On the one hand, the modal older woman loses her role as mother when the children grow up, but on the other hand, she is free to "do her own thing." On the one hand, the modal older man is bereft when his wife dies because she is his chief and probably only confidant, but on the other hand, he should have little difficulty replacing her. On the one hand, the modal older woman, when she is singled, has little chance of remarrying, but on the other hand, she has personality and housekeeping skills to survive on her own, to make friends easily and to take care of herself.

This kind of point-counterpoint could be continued another few pages, but the point should be obvious. The tally sheet comes out closer to equal instead of being heavily weighted in favor of either sex.

REFERENCES

ADAMS, B. N. The middle-class adult and his widowed or still-married mother. *Social Problems*, 1968, 16 (1) , 50-59.

ANGRES, S. *Intergenerational Relations and Value Congruence Between Young Adults and Their Mothers.* Unpublished Ph.D. dissertation, University of Chicago, 1975.

ATCHLEY, R. *The Sociology of Retirement.* New York: Shenkman Publishing Co., 1976.

ATCHLEY, R. *The Social Forces on Later Life,* Second Edition. Belmont, Calif.: Wadsworth Publishing Company, 1977.

ATCHLEY, R. & CORBETT, S. Women and work. In L. Troll, J. Israel, and K. Israel (Eds.), *Looking Ahead: A Woman's Guide to the Problems and Joys of Growing Older.* Englewood Cliffs, N. J.: Prentice-Hall, 1977.

BABCHUCK, N. & BATES, A. P. Primary relations of middle-class couples: A study of male dominance. *American Sociological Review*, 1963, 28, 374-384.

BACK, K. W. Personal characteristics and social behavior: Theory and method. In R. H. Binstock and E. Shanas (Eds.) , *Handbook of Aging and the Social Sciences.* New York: Van Nostrand, 1976.

BALLWEG, J. A. Resolution of conjugal role adjustment after retirement. *Journal of Marriage and the Family*, 1967, 29 (2), 277-281.

BARDWICK, J. *Psychology of Women: A Study of Biosocial Conflicts.* New York: Harper & Row, 1971.

BART, P. B. Depression in middle-aged women. In V. Gornick and B. K. Moran (Eds.) , *Women in Sexist Society.* New York: Basic Books, 1971, pp. 99-117.

BENEDEK, T. Parenthood as a developmental phase. *Journal of the American Psychoanalytic Association*, 1959, 7, 389-417.

BENEDEK, T. Chapters 4, 5, 6, & 7. In E. J. Anthony and T. Benedek (Eds.), *Parenthood*. Boston: Little, Brown, 1970.

BENGTSON, V. & CUTLER, N. Generations and intergenerational relations: Perspectives on age groups and social change. In R. Binstock and E. Shanas (Eds.), *Handbook of Aging and Social Sciences*. New York: Van Nostrand, 1976.

BENGTSON, V., OLANDER, E., & HADDAD, A. The "generation gap" and aging family members: Toward a conceptual model. In J. F. Gubrium (Ed.), *Time, Roles, and Self in Old Age*. New York: Human Sciences Press, 1976.

BERNARD, J. *The Sex Game*. New York: Atheneum, 1972.

BERNARD, J. *The Future of Marriage*. New York: World Press (Bantam Books), 1973.

BERNARD, J. *The Future of Motherhood*. New York: Dial Press, 1974.

BILD, B. R. & HAVIGHURST, R. J. Senior citizens in great cities: The case of Chicago. *The Gerontologist*, 1976, 16(1).

BINSTOCK, R. H. & SHANAS, E. *Handbook of Aging and the Social Sciences*. New York: Van Nostrand Rheinhold Company, 1976.

BLOOD, R. O. & WOLFE, D. M. *Husbands and Wives*. Glencoe, N. Y.: The Free Press, 1960.

BOSSARD, J. H. S. & BOLL, E. S. Marital unhappiness in the life cycle of marriage. *Marriage and Family Living*, 1955, 17, 10-14.

BUTLER, R. N. & LEWIS, M. I. *Aging and Mental Health*. St. Louis: C. V. Mosby, 1973.

CANDY, S. What do women use friends for? In L. Troll, J. Israel, and K. Israel (Eds.), *Looking Ahead: A Woman's Guide to the Problems and Joys of Growing Older*. Englewood Cliffs, N. J.: Prentice Hall, 1977.

COOMBS, R. H. & KENKEL, W. F. Sex differences in dating aspirations and satisfaction with computer-selected partner. *Journal of Marriage and the Family*, 1966, 28, 62-66.

CUTLER, N. E. & HAROOTYAN, R. Demography of the aged. In D. Woodruff and J. E. Birren (Eds.), *Aging: Scientific Perspectives and Social Issues*. New York: Van Nostrand, 1975.

DATAN, N., MAOZ, B., ANTONOVSKY, A., & WIJSENBEEK, H. Climacterium in three cultural contexts. *Tropical and Geographic Medicine*, 1970, 22, 77-86.

ELDER, G. H., JR. Appearance and education in marriage mobility. *American Sociological Review*, 1969, 34, 519-533.

FELDMAN, H. *Development of the Husband-Wife Relationship: A Research Report*. New York: Cornell University Press, 1964.

FELDMAN, H. Penelope, Susan, Molly, and Narcissus. In L. Troll, J. Israel, and K. Israel (Eds.), *Looking Ahead: A Woman's Guide to the Problems and Joys of Growing Older*. Englewood Cliffs, N. J.: Prentice-Hall, 1977.

FRIEDMANN, E. A. & HAVIGHURST, R. J. *The Meaning of Work and Retirement*. Chicago: University of Chicago Press, 1954.

GLENN, N. D. Psychological well-being in the postparental stage: Some evidence from national surveys. *Journal of Marriage and the Family*, 1975, 37, 15-27.

GLICK, P. Updating the family life cycle. *Journal of Marriage and the Family*, 1977, 39(1), 5-13.

GOODCHILDS, J. The older woman and power. In L. Troll, J. Israel, and K. Israel (Eds.), *Looking Ahead: A Woman's Guide to the Problems and Joys of Growing Older*. Englewood Cliffs, N. J.: Prentice-Hall, 1977.

GUTMANN, D. An exploration of ego configurations in middle and later life. In B. Neugarten (Ed.), *Personality in Middle and Later Life*. New York: Atherton, 1964.

GUTMANN, D. Alternatives of disengagement: The old man of the highland Druze. In R. LeVine (Ed.), *Culture and Personality: Contemporary Readings*. Chicago: Aldine, 1974.

GUTMANN, D. Parenthood: A key to the comparative study of life cycle. In N. Datan and L. H. Ginsberg (Eds.), *Life-Span Developmental Psychology: Normative Life Crises*. New York: Academic Press, 1975.

GUTMANN, D. The cross-cultural perspective: Notes toward a comparative psychology of aging. In J. E. Birren and W. Schaie (Eds.), *Handbook of the Psychology of Aging*. New York: Van Nostrand Rheinhold Company, 1977, pp. 302-326.

HAMILTON, G. V. *A Research in Marriage*. New York: Boni, 1929.

HICKS, M. W. & PLATT, M. Marital happiness and stability: A review of the research in the sixties. *Journal of Marriage and the Family*, 1970, 32, 553-574.

HILL, R., FOOTE, N., ALDOUS, J., CARLSON, R., & MACDONALD, R. *Family Development in Three Generations*. Cambridge: Schenkman, 1970.

HOFFMAN, L. W. *Influences of the Child on Marital Quality and Parent-Parent-Inter-action*. Paper presented at Conference on Human and Family Development, Pennsylvania State University, April 1977.

HUYCK, M. H. *Friendships and Coping Among United States Adults 18-65*. Presented at International Congress of Gerontology, Jerusalem, Israel, June 1975.

HUYCK, M. H. *Sex, Gender, and Aging*. Paper presented at the 29th Annual Scientific Meetings of the Gerontological Society, New York, October 1976.

HUYCK, M. H. Sex and the older woman. In L. Troll, J. Israel, and K. Israel (Eds.), *Looking Ahead: A Woman's Guide to the Problems and Joys of Growing Older*. Englewood Cliffs, N. J.: Prentice-Hall, 1977.

JANEWAY, E. *Man's World Woman's Place*. New York: Dell Publishing Company (Delta Books), 1971.

JOURARD, S. & LASAKOW, P. Some factors in self-disclosure. *Journal of Abnormal and Social Psychology*, 1958, 56, 91-98.

KALISH, R. *Late Adulthood: Perspectives on Human Development*. Monterey, Calif.: Brooks Cole, 1975.

KIMMEL, D. C. *Adulthood and Aging*. New York: John Wiley & Sons, Inc., 1974.

KINSEY, A. C., POMEROY, W. B., & MARTIN, C. E. *Sexual Behavior in the Human Male*. Philadelphia: Saunders, 1948.

KINSEY, A. C., POMEROY, W. B., MARTIN, C. E., & GEBHARD, P. H. *Sexual Behavior in the Human Female*. Philadelphia: W. B. Saunders, 1953.

KOMAROVSKY, M. *Blue-Collar Marriage*. New York: Random House, 1964.

LIEBERMAN, M. & LAKIN, M. On becoming an institutionalized person. In R. H. Williams, C. Tibbetts, and W. Donahue (Eds.), *Processes of Aging: Social and Psychological Perspectives*, Vol. 1. New York: Atherton Press, 1963.

LIPMAN, A. Role conceptions and morale of couples in retirement. *Journal of Gerontology*, 1961, 16, 3, 267-271.

LIPMAN, A. Role conceptions of couples in retirement. In C. Tibbetts and W. Donahue (Eds.), *Social and Psychological Aspects of Aging: Aging Around the World*. New York: Columbia University Press, 1962.

LITWAK, F. Geographic mobility and extended family cohesion. *American Sociological Review*, 1960, 25, 385-394.

LIVSON, F. B. *Coming Together in the Middle Years: A Longitudinal Study of Sex Role Convergence*. Paper presented at the 29th Annual Scientific Meetings of the Gerontological Society, New York, October, 1976.

LOPATA, H. Z. *Widowhood in an American City*. Cambridge, Mass.: Schenkman, 1973.

LOWENTHAL, M. F. & HAVEN, C. Interaction and adaptation: Intimacy as a critical variable. *American Sociological Review*, 1968, 33, 20-30.

LOWENTHAL, M. F. Some potentialities of a life-cycle approach to the study of retirement. In F. Carp (Ed.), *Retirement*. New York: Behavioral Publications, 1972.

LOWENTHAL, M. F., THURNHER, M., CHIRIBOGA, D., & ASSOCIATES. *Four Stages of Life*. San Francisco: Jossey-Bass, 1975.

LUCKEY, E. B. Perceptual congruence of self and family concepts as related to marital interaction. *Sociometry*, 1961, 24, 234-250.

MAAS, H. S. & KUYPERS, J. A. *From Thirty to Seventy*. San Francisco: Jossey-Bass, 1974.

MASTERS, W. H. & JOHNSON, V. E. *Human Sexual Response*. Boston: Little, Brown & Co., 1966.

NEUGARTEN, B. L. (Ed.). *Middle Age and Aging*. Chicago: University of Chicago Press, 1968.

NEUGARTEN, B. L. & GUTMANN, D. Age-sex roles and personality in middle age. A thematic apperception study. In B. L. Neugarten and associates (Eds.), *Personality in Middle and Late Life*. New York: Atherton Press, 1964, pp. 44-90

NEUGARTEN, B. L. & HAGESTAD, G. Age and the life course. In R. Binstock and E. Shanas (Eds.), *Handbook of Aging and the Social Sciences*. New York: Van Nostrand Rheinhold Co., 1976.

NEUGARTEN, B. L., WOODS, V., KRAINES, R., & LOOMIS, B. Women's attitudes towards the menopause. *Vita Humana*, 1963, 6, 140-151.

NOWAK, C. A. *The Appearance Signal in Adult Development*. Unpublished Ph.D. Dissertation, Wayne State University, 1975.

NOWAK, C. A. & TROLL, L. E. *Age Concept in Women: Concern with Youthfulness and Attractiveness Relative to Self-Perceived Age*. Paper presented at the 29th Annual Meeting of the Gerontological Society, Portland, Oregon, October, 1974.

PALMORE, E. (Ed.). *Normal Aging: Reports from the Duke Longitudinal Studies, 1955-1969*. Durham, N.C.: Duke University Press, 1970.

PALMORE, E. (Ed.). *Norman Aging II: Reports from the Duke Longitudinal Studies, 1970-1973*. Durham, N.C.: Duke University Press, 1974.

PARIS, B. L. & LUCKEY, E. B. A longitudinal study of marital satisfaction. *Sociology and Social Research*, January 1966, 50, 212-223.

PARNES, H. S., NESTEL, G., & ANDRISANI, P. *The Pre-Retirement Years: A Longitudinal Study of the Labor Market Experience of Men*, Vol. 3. Columbus, Ohio: Center for Human Resources Research, 1972.

PFEIFFER, E. Sexual behavior in old age. In E. Busse and E. Pfeiffer (Eds.), *Behavior and Adaptation in Late Life*. Boston: Little, Brown & Co., 1969.

PFEIFFER, E., VERWOERDT, A., & DAVIS, G. Sexual behavior in middle life. *American Journal of Psychiatry*, April, 1972, 128 (10), 1262-1267.

PINEO, P. Disenchantment in the later years of marriage. *Marriage and Family Living*, February 1961, pp. 3-11.

REICHARD, S., LIVSON, F., & PETERSON, P. G. *Aging and Personality*. New York: John Wiley, 1962.

RETHERFORD, R. D. *The Changing Sex Differential in Mortality*. Westport, Conn.: Greenwood, 1975.

ROLLINS, B. C. & CANNON, K. L. Marital satisfaction over the family life cycle: A re-evaluation. *Journal of Marriage and the Family*, 1974, 36, 271-282.

ROLLINS, B. & FELDMAN, H. Marital satisfaction over the family life cycle. *Journal of Marriage and the Family*, 1970, 32 (1), 20-28.

RUBIN, L. B. *Worlds of Pain*. New York: Basic Books, 1975.

SCHULZ, J. *The Economics of Aging*. Belmont, Cal.: Wadsworth, 1976.

SHANAS, E., TOWNSEND, P., WEDDERBURN, D., FRIIS, H., MILHOJ, P., & STEHOUWER, J. *Older People in Three Industrial Societies*. New York: Atherton, 1968.

SHEPPARD, H. L. *New Perspectives on Older Workers.* Washington, D.C.: The W. E. Upjohn Institute for Employment Research, 1971.

SONTAG, S. The double standard of aging. In Institute of Gerontology, University of Michigan-Wayne State University, *No Longer Young.* 1975, pp. 31-41.

SPANIER, G. B., LEWIS, R. A., & COLE, C. L. Marital adjustment over the family life cycle: The issue of curvilinearity. *Journal of Marriage and the Family,* May 1975, 37, 263-276.

STINNETT, N., CARTER, L. M., & MONTGOMERY, J. E. Older persons' perceptions of their marriages. *Journal of Marriage and the Family,* November 1972, pp. 665-670.

STINNETT, N., COLLINS, J., & MONTGOMERY, J. E. Marital need satisfaction of older husbands and wives. *Journal of Marriage and the Family,* 1970, 32 (3) , 428-434.

SUSSMAN, M. B. & BURCHINAL, L. Kin family network: Unheralded structures in current conceptualizations of family functioning. *Marriage and Family Living,* 1962, 24 (3), 231-240.

THURNHER, M. Family confluence, conflict and affect. In M. Lowenthal, M. Thurnher, and D. Chiriboga (Eds.), *Four Stages of Life.* San Francisco: Jossey-Bass, 1975.

TROLL, L. The family of later life: A decade review. *Journal of Marriage and the Family,* May 1971, 33, 263-290.

TROLL, L. *Development in Early and Middle Adulthood.* Monterey, Cal.: Brook/Cole Co., 1975.

TROLL, L. & BENGTSON, V. Generations in the family. In W. Burr, I. Reiss, R. Hill, and G. Nye (Eds.) , *Contemporary Theories about the Family.* New York: The Free Press, 1978.

TROLL, L. & TURNER, B. F. Impact of changing sex roles on the family of later life. In C. Safilios-Rothschild (Ed.), *The Effect of Changing Sex Roles on the Family,* Ford Foundation Conference, Detroit, 1976.

U.S. Bureau of Census. *Current Population Reports.* Series P-23, No. 59. Demographic aspects of aging and the older population in the United States. Washington, D.C.: U.S. Government Printing Office, 1976.

U.S. Bureau of the Census Subject Report: Marital Status. PC (2) —4C, 1972.

U.S. Government Printing Office. *Developments in Aging,* 1975 and January-May, 1976. Washington, D.C., 1975.

VERBRUGGE, L. *Sex Differentials in Morbidity and Mortality in the United States.* Paper presented at the Annual Meeting of the Population Association of America, 1975.

WALKER, K. Time spent by husbands in household work. *Family Economics Review,* June 1970, pp. 8-11.

WEG, R. More than wrinkles. In L. Troll, J. Israel, and K. Israel (Eds.) , *Looking Ahead: A Woman's Guide to the Problems and Joys of Growing Older.* Englewood Cliffs, N. J.: Prentice-Hall, 1977.

Part III

PROBLEM BEHAVIORS

6

CRIME AND THE FEMALE OFFENDER

ROSEMARY C. SARRI

To anyone familiar with the problems of sexism in the United States the situation of female offenders comes as no surprise. The inequities faced by the majority of women in this society are magnified a hundred-fold in the lives of female offenders. Female crime has received more attention recently in both the popular and the professional literature, but it is typically referred to as the "dark side of the feminist movement." Publicity received by a few women because of notorious incidents has led others to suggest that women's liberation is associated with increases in female crime, particularly violent, aggressive crime. As shall be noted subsequently, these authors provide no data to support their assertions. The one systematic analysis of comparable data provides no support for assertions about significant increases in violent crime by women (Simon, 1975b).

Concern for the plight of the female offender has just begun to emerge and, interestingly, that concern is expressed most often by feminist lawyers, journalists, and selected personnel in the criminal justice sys-

Most of the survey data reported here were obtained by the National Assessment of Juvenile Corrections project supported by a grant (76JN-99-0001) from the Juvenile Justice and Delinquency Prevention Operations Task Group, Law Enforcement Assistance Administration, U.S. Department of Justice, under authorizing legislation of the Omnibus Crime Control and Safe Streets Act of 1968 and the Juvenile Justice and Delinquency Prevention Act of 1974. The project was sponsored by the Institute of Continuing Legal Education and the School of Social Work of the University of Michigan; codirectors, Robert D. Vinter and Rosemary Sarri.

The author wishes to acknowledge assistance and comments from members of the NAJC staff: Elaine Selo, Josefina Figueira-McDonough, William Barton, and Paul Isenstadt.

tem.* One can surmise many reasons for the neglect of female crime and female offenders. Compared to male crime, it is vastly less in quantity. In 1974, 5,185,110 males were arrested and 994,296 females or a ratio of nearly six to one. (U.S. Department of Justice, 1975.) Moreover, women offenders are arrested for less serious crimes than males, and they are perceived as less dangerous or threatening than their male counterparts. Female criminal behavior more often is viewed as deviant with respect to the traditional sex roles assigned to women in the society. (Clark & Haurek, 1966; Datesman, Scarpetti, & Stephenson, 1975). It should not be assumed, however, that merely because female crime and offenders have been neglected that they have been dealt with justly, fairly, or humanely. As we shall note in this chapter, nearly the opposite is closer to reality. The entire criminal justice justice system for all offenders in the United States could not be characterized as a just or humane system, but in the case of the female offender its ineffectiveness and inhumanity are even more apparent (Mitford, 1973).

This chapter will summarize some of the major theoretical orientations about the etiology of female crime, characteristics of female offenders, mechanisms for processing women in and through the criminal justice system, laws which govern the operation of that system, and conditions of incarceration. It will attempt to address what appear to be some of the more problematic issues of sexism in the justice system. This perspective is adopted because crime is clearly problematic behavior which is influenced by values, economics, social structural patterns, temporal characteristics, and so forth.** Not only do the definitions of what crime is change over time and in different societies, but even within the United States today what is defined as crime varies by sex, social class, race, and age, within as well as between states.***

Greater attention will be directed in this chapter to the adolescent female offender than to the adult offender, because the criminal justice

---

*Interest in and concern about the female offender parallel more general concern about civil rights of the mentally ill, handicapped, and children. Professionals who serve these populations have often been less concerned about their individual rights than lawyers who have become advocates for individual civil rights and better social services.

**The likelihood of being apprehended and subsequently processed through the criminal justice system varies widely because of individual staff discretion, time of the day or year when a particular offense is committed, resources available to the organization to implement an initial decision to apprehend, and so forth.

***For a comparative analysis of female crime in a number of developing and industrialized countries see Simon (1975a).

system is far more problematic for the former. Moreover, understanding the problems and socialization of the adolescent is necessary if we are to comprehend fully subsequent adult behavior. It also can be expected that if the women's movement is having a significant effect on female crime, the adolescent population should be more sensitive to that influence than the older adult population whose sex roles are more likely to be stabilized. Adler (1975) has suggested that the feminist movement is having a pronounced effect on female crime in that women are less satisfied with petty or so-called victimless crimes. If her proposition were to be supported, adolescent criminal behavior should manifest some significant changes. The focus on youth is also appropriate because it has received relatively less attention in the recent literature on female crime despite the fact that a larger number of youth are apprehended, processed, and institutionalized in the United States. In fact, the majority of criminal behavior in the United States occurs between the ages of 12 and 25 years for both males and females. Failure to consider some of the critical problems of that age group is most unwise if one wishes to understand motivations toward deviance and the particular form of illegal behavior that may be selected.

WHY WOMEN COMMIT CRIMES

Explaining crime and delinquency has long been of interest to social practitioners (psychologists, psychiatrists, social workers, educators), as well as to social scientists. Only recently, as information has become more widely available, have questions been asked about why crime rates vary among certain societies, cultures, or ethnic groups. And, in the case of females, an even more interesting question arises but has not been answered: Why is it that women commit fewer crimes than males overall, and why are their criminal behavior patterns so different from those of males? Unfortunately, because of the relative political and social power of males, there is a tendency to consider how and why women are likely to behave more like men than vice versa. This orientation persists despite the fact that female behavioral patterns may be far more appropriate in a complex, crowded, post-industrial society.

As with male criminality, a review of the historical, scientific, and practice literature reveals that no single theory has been adequate at any time to explain female criminality. Comprehensive reviews of the etiology of crime by Klein (1973), Scutt (1976), Rasche (1974), and Hoffman-Bustamante (1973) conclude that multiple factors are involved in female criminality; therefore a multi-factor theory is necessary for adequate explanation and prediction. One can profitably examine the study of female criminality from a historical perspective. At least six major stages of development can be identified and, while each is distinct, those which emerged first influenced all subsequent study and elements of each can be identified today in both practice and research directed toward the female offender (Rasche, 1974).* The earliest theorists contended that female offenders were evil, immoral, or possessed by demons, but they were viewed only as a minor problem. The social movement which culminated in the establishment of early prisons and the Houses of Refuge were strongly influenced by moral-ethical perspectives about criminality. In the second stage there was a search for constitutional or physiological causes for female crime. Lombroso's theories were the first attempts at distinguishing male/female behavior related to crime (Lombroso, 1895).** He argued that female criminality was an inherent tendency which would wither away if atavistic persons were not permitted to reproduce. Contemporary theorists such as Cowie, Cowie, and Slater (1968) have incorporated related assumptions about delinquency and physical characteristics. Freud's theory emphasized psychological traits but these were related to physiological characteristics inherent in women. Others emphasized genetic factors, asserting that criminality was inherited (Fernald, Hayes, & Dawley, 1920; Healy & Bonner, 1926).*** Both emphasized the inferiority of women with respect to crime but they also emphasized that those who were intellectually inferior or retarded were more susceptible to criminal influence.

The third stage, represented by the work of the Gluecks (1934), viewed female crime in terms of individual characteristics, but as a product of the interaction of constitutional and environmental factors. They failed to consider temporal factors which influenced both their independent and dependent variables. Thus, characteristics of the population changed greatly, but their conceptions were limited to the absolute variables such

---

*Rasche (1974) identifies five stages of development, but examination of her latter stage reveals that it is very comprehensive, and subdivision seems appropriate.

**Lombroso's description of female behavior is both amusing and appalling. Nonetheless, his work had considerable influence on many later writers such as Fernald et al. (1920), Glueck and Glueck (1934), Pollak (1950), and Thomas (1923).

***Even today one finds references to inherited traits as explanatory variables for criminal behavior (Cowie, Cowie, & Slater, 1968; Pollak, 1950; Pollak & Friedman, 1964).

as being foreign born, having parents of certain ethnicity, physical size and body build, and so forth.*

During World War II interest grew in explanations based on analysis of socio-demographic characteristics and offense patterns, but it was limited far more to males than females. In the latter part of the fourth stage Otto Pollak (1950) published his treatise on female criminality, which had a significant impact on subsequent research and writing. Pollak argued that there were no "real" male/female differences in criminality. He coined such phrases as "hidden crime" and deceitfulness of the female as an inherent attribute. He argued that the low rates of official female crime were due to the covert behavior of women—"their deceitfulness." Like Freud, he emphasized sexual factors as paramount, for he saw criminal women as attempting to extend their sexual role. The emphasis on sexism grew rapidly and pervaded the literature about female crime (Konopka, 1966; Sarri, Propper, Selo, & Scutt, 1975; Vedder & Somerville, 1970). Interest in other socio-psychological aspects of female crime led to a number of studies with a social interactionist perspective. In contrast to Sutherland (1947), who focused on the peer group and neighborhood in his theory of differential association, theorists who wrote about female delinquency emphasized family interactions and relationships (Morris, 1964). In W. I. Thomas' work on adolescent female deviance, behavior was viewed as the result of ineffective social regulation by the family (Thomas, 1923). More recent literature emphasized discipline (Gilbert, 1972), family tension (Morris, 1964), and loneliness (Konopka 1966, 1976; Riege, 1972).

In the fifth stage interest emerged in studying the processing of females in and through the justice system. Most attention was directed toward prisons rather than courts or probation agencies, and this choice affected the behavior that was studied and the conclusions reached. Studies of inmate social systems are characteristic of this period, and attempts were made to distinguish male/female differences (Giallombardo, 1966, 1974; Heffernan, 1972; Tittle, 1972; Ward & Kassebaum, 1965). Relatively little interest was shown in pre- or post-institutional behavior or toward organizational factors of the justice system which produced the prison population. Because most of the research involved case studies and participant observation, generalizations were necessarily limited. How-

---

*Glueck and Glueck (1934) also incorporated into their analysis behaviors which are no longer a basis for criminal action—"common night walking"; "lewd and lascivious behavior"; "information"; and "crimes against chastity." However, they still have meaning, especially with reference to status offenders.

ever, the literature incorporated the researchers' findings about qualitative differences in homosexual behavior between males and females and other forms of accommodation learned in closed institutions. Propper's (1976) recent comparative study of homosexuality in female institutions illustrates the advantages of a methodology where several organizations are studied simultaneously.

The late sixties might be referred to as a transition period to the sixth and final state. There were numerous efforts to delineate the distinguishing features of female crime and female offenders. From these studies a profile of the female offender emerged as a young adult, likely to be poor and undereducated, reared in a disturbed or problematic family situation with abusive or neglecting parents (Velimesis, 1975). The emphasis on interpersonal, moral, and sexual behavior as more characteristic of female offenders resulted in two major strains in theories of female and male crime. Male crime was viewed as provoked by utilitarian motives and as a result of social structural factors such as social class, access to legitimate opportunities, and differential association. Female crime, on the other hand, was explained almost wholly in socio-psychological terms despite the fact that socio-demographic characteristics of female and male offenders were similar. Given the traditional sex-role definitions, such results are to be expected.

The sixth stage and the contemporary period began in the early seventies and reflects the influence of the feminist movement as well as growing societal concerns about the human rights of offenders. In this decade the women's and human rights movements have stimulated a number of studies, reports, and essays about female crime (Burkhart, 1973; Crites, 1976; McDonough, 1976; Mitford, 1973; Simon, 1975a). From these, two theories have emerged about female criminal behavior—"equal opportunity" and "discriminatory control." The former approach suggests that with greater equality females are more likely to engage in more criminal behavior because they have the opportunity to do so (Adler, 1975; Simon, 1975a). The "discriminatory control" argument is that women receive biased treatment from social control agencies in arrest, detention, and disposition (Armstrong, 1977; Chesney-Lind, 1973, 1977; Hoffman-Bustamante, 1973). A fuller understanding of female crime, others argue, requires that elements of both arguments be taken into consideration (McDonough, 1976). Obviously, full documentation requires data presently unavailable from offenders, law enforcement, and judicial agents.

The contemporary scene is also influenced by three major theories about criminal behavior in general: strain, subculture, and control.

These apply differentially to females, and, unfortunately, many researchers accept a theoretical formulation developed for males and apply it directly to females. For the "strain" theory, the lack of access to opportunities is the major rationale for deviant behavior; however, the opportunity structure for females varies markedly from that for males because of the social welfare system as well as the employment market. The "subcultural" school views criminal deviance as a result of the internalization of contracultural values. "Control" theorists address the lack of commitment to or involvement with legitimate groups and institutions. It is possible that each of these theories would help to illuminate selected aspects of female crime, but how and in what ways is insufficiently documented. Much of the research continues to be dominated by implicit or explicit assumptions about human nature and "natural" sex differences. The null hypothesis of "no difference" between the sexes remains untested.

Little is known today about how broad social change in sex roles may be affecting deviant behavior, but one cannot assume that the only direction of influence is from males to females. Elements of that modeling and influence may be present in some deviant behavior, but it also is possible that males will model females in selected areas where such behavior may be more widely accepted. Likewise, the emergence of new sex roles and sex-role balances may result in new patterns of deviance. The very rapid increase in all types of substance abuse by males and females in the 1960s and 1970s is one possible example of a new pattern which is more closely linked to age and economic opportunity than it is to sex. Wiersma's recent study of working class adolescents in a juvenile court indicates that many females wholly reject the model of the female presented in the "middle-class women's movement" (Wiersma, 1974), and yet they evidenced increasing criminal behavior.

More recently, economists have attempted to employ econometric models to explain criminal behavior. Although they explicitly take environmental factors into consideration, they are lacking in sophisticated analysis of socio-psychological factors. Given the fact that the definition of crime is broad and ambiguous, changing with time and place, any simple explanation is bound to be insufficient. If proposals for decriminalization of status offenses, alcohol and drug use, prostitution, and gambling were implemented in law, there would be a tremendous reduction in the numbers of women processed through the criminal justice system, and theories about female criminal behavior would undoubtedly be modified substantially.* As Quinney (1975) indicates, crime must be understood in its social and political contexts so that one's theory takes into consideration why and how certain behaviors come to be defined as criminal and are applied to selected persons.

WHICH WOMEN COMMIT CRIMES

Given the local, state, and federal statutes and systems of justice, all of which are variable, the definition of crime and the female offender is imprecise, to say the least. Perhaps most useful for our purposes here is the definition provided in Section 601 (a) of the Comprehensive Employment and Training Act of 1973.**

> Offender means any adult or juvenile who is confined in any type of correctional institution and also includes any individual or juvenile assigned to a community-based facility or subject to pretrial, probationary, or parole or other stages of the judicial, correctional or probationary process where manpower training and services may be beneficial . . .

The data on offenders and offenses are imprecise for a variety of reasons. Many crimes are not reported; others do not result in arrest or conviction. The official crime reports include only those persons arrested regardless of the subsequent outcome. Only recently have there been attempts to correlate data from self-reports and victimization surveys with official data (Hindelang, Dunn, Sutton, & Amick, 1976). Another problem arises from variable definitions of criminal behavior—particularly in crimes for which women are frequently arrested. Thus, national data which speak about incidence of criminal behavior must be viewed cautiously. For example, in the case of drunk and disorderly behavior in one single year, Massachusetts had 50% of all females charged with drunkenness and New York had nearly 50% of all charged with disorderly behavior. Differences of this magnitude can also be observed among counties within a single state. Criminality, therefore, must be viewed as recorded behavior rather than merely as legal deviance. These records are built from information provided by offenders, other citizens, all levels of police, courts, and other criminal justice agencies. Crime statistics

---

*It is possible to assume that in the future when the conservation of environmental resources will be highly valued, abuse of such might be the basis of a serious criminal charge. As Durkheim (1947) long ago suggested the definition of crime reflects the society's values and priorities.

**Public Law 93-203; 87 Statutes 839; 29 United States Code 3801.

reflect differentials in the administration of criminal law, not differences in the incidence of criminal behavior (Gold & Reimer, 1975; Hindelang, 1971; Short & Nye, 1970).

With the above qualifications we will attempt to comment briefly on recent patterns—focusing more attention on changes rather than findings at a given point in time.* Simon's analysis of official data provides the most complete picture of female crime in America. Overall she shows that crimes of violence have been remarkably stable at about 10%, but that larceny/theft, drunkenness, disorderly conduct, and narcotics violations have shown the greatest increases. However, Uniform Crime Reports indicate that the rate of arrests rose three times faster for females than males between 1960 and 1972. The most dramatic increases involved property crimes—larceny, embezzlement, forgery, and fraud. Simon attributes this largely to women's increased participation in the labor force through employment outside the home.

Dramatic reports are available in much of the literature about large increases in female arrests, especially of younger women. When these percentages are compared with males, typically a smaller percentage increase is noted for males, but few of the authors comment on the vastly different totals on which these percentages are based. The data in Table 1 provide us with comparative female/male data for 1960 and 1974. Substantial increases are noted in the case of property crimes primarily because even in the "index" crime category most of the increase is due to larceny, rather than crimes against persons. Attention to the problem of the juvenile female offenders is particularly important for they contribute disproportionately in all categories, but especially in the areas of property and serious person crimes. When one recognizes that the category "under 18" refers primarily to three to four years between the ages of 14 and 18 whereas the adult category covers the entire period from 18 years through adulthood, these findings are most significant. Table 1 presents a picture of crime that is referred to as "serious" crime, and the differences are noteworthy, but not outstanding. Crimes which have shown increases of great magnitude for females between 1960 and 1974 are: narcotics violations (860%), "driving under the influence" (340%), and "buying, receiving, or possessing stolen property" (767%). Much less concern is expressed by various public officials about these patterns.

---

*Simon's analysis (1975, pp. 49-63) was limited to Federal District Court data and to selected information from California and Ohio courts. Thus one cannot generalize to the country from these data about court actions.

TABLE 1

Arrest Patterns in the United States 1960 and 1974

Offenses	Total Arrests 1960	Female Percent Total	Female Under 18 Percent	Total Arrests 1974	Female Percent Total	Female Under 18 Percent
Property[a]						
Females	29,292	10.6	43.2	139,169	22.5	43.7
Males	244,562			497,676		
Index[b]						
Females	36,957	10.6	37.0	159,011	19.4	41.0
Males	311,855			660,351		
Violent Crime[c]						
Females	7,563	10.3	11.1	19,720	10.9	22.0
Males	66,220			161,803		
Total						
Females	259,038	10.7	19.1	540,987	16.9	31.6
Males	2,155,159			2,655,339		

Source: *Crime in the United States, 1974*. Uniform Crime Reports (Washington, D.C. Federal Bureau of Investigation, 1975), pp. 184-186.

a. Includes burglary and auto theft.

b. Includes criminal homicide, rape, robbery, aggravated assault, burglary, larceny and auto theft.

c. Includes criminal homicide, rape, robbery, aggravated assault.

At every step in the criminal justice process, female offenders are a minority. In 1974 one out of every six persons arrested was a female and one out of every ten in jail was female. As we shall note subsequently in the discussion of incarceration, adult females are incarcerated far less than are juvenile females, resulting in a popular view that women are dealt with benignly by the justice system. Rogers' (1972) data on Connecticut's processing of juvenile females and that from Pennsylvania about adults should readily dispel such views. Rogers shows conclusively that females are processed and sentenced more often than males for minor crimes, and once institutionalized, they remain longer.

A survey in 1975 in Pennsylvania of 150 women in nine "representative" county jails revealed that 69% were awaiting trial, 14% were serving sentences and 17% were held for other reasons (Pennsylvania, 1975). The observers noted that the most serious problem was the overuse of jails in large urban counties, not in the rural counties. Many women were detained for a few days and then released without a trial. Family life, however, was seriously disrupted, since 65% were held for more than ten days and 35% for more than a month. Strangely, of those held for more than a month, more were awaiting trial than were serving a sentence. Women held in these jails were charged as follows: 32% were held for felony charges; 36% for misdemeanors; and 29% for other reasons. Clearly, the need for detention in jail can be justified only for those charged with felonies, and not even for that entire group if the criteria for detention is protection of the public from dangerous behavior or the probability that the female will abscond prior to her trial. These findings take on greater import when considered with those from the Manhattan Bail Project and several home detention experiments (Sarri & Hasenfeld, 1976). Offenders who are detained prior to trial are more likely to be convicted than those not held but charged with the same offense, and, if convicted, they are more likely to be institutionalized.

Information about socio-demographic characteristics of arrestees and of women processed by the courts is sorely lacking (Bertrand, 1967; Cloninger & Guze, 1970; Haft, 1974, and Singer, 1973). Far more data are available about incarcerated females, but we lack needed knowledge of how the system operates in selection, processing, conviction, and disposition of women from various racial, ethnic, and social class backgrounds.

Homicide is perhaps the crime for which the strongest sanctions could be expected. There have been a few studies of women who murder, and from these some data are available about characteristics of offenders and about critical factors in the event (Boudouris, 1971; Totman, 1970; Wolfgang, 1958). Women who commit homicide differ significantly from males in that the homicide almost always involves a family member or close friend. Totman's study of female murderers produced findings similar to those of Wolfgang, but she provides us with further information about these women and their lives. They are disproportionately urban poor and from minority groups. The female homicide rate in the United States is far higher than in European countries, probably because of the greater availability of guns.

Fifty-three percent of the victims of female homicide are husbands or lovers; 19% are their children; and 16% were female friends or relatives. Frequently there was evidence to suggest that the husband or male friend had physically abused the female so that the homicide may have been an act of self-defense in some instances (Boudouris, 1971). Most women were readily apprehended because they confessed or remained at the scene of the crime. Totman's observations about female homicide was noteworthy and in contrast to some earlier psychological interpretations of violence in women:

> Women murder their mates (or their children) when their relationship is felt to be directly and overtly destructive to them and their sense of identity as a woman, when they feel they cannot share their concerns and thus get adequate support and help from other significant relationships or community resources, when they have exhausted all other alternative courses of action, either actually or in fantasy and find them not viable, and finally, when they have redefined and reinterpreted their negative situation so it calls for action not previously considered possible (Totman, 1970, pp. 128-129).

Examination of conviction rates where data are available reveals patterns similar to those for arrest. Adult females are less likely to be convicted than their male counterparts. However, Simon (1975b) shows that between 1961 and 1971 there was an increase of 62% in female convictions compared to a 20% increase for males. The probability of conviction was highest for fraud, embezzlement, and forgery. Patterns of conviction did not follow the increases in arrest categories nor were they related to probable consequences of growth in the women's movement. Particularly noteworthy in state data from Ohio and California were the high proportion of convictions for narcotics law violation. These convictions were in accord with the large increases in arrests for narcotics violations and in contrast to property arrests for which there was almost no increase in conviction rate.

Sentencing is particularly problematic for females, because of the way in which indeterminate sentences may be interpreted and applied (Armstrong, 1977; Conway & Bogdan, 1977; Haft, 1974; Singer, 1973; Wheeler, 1976). Unfortunately, the fact that female prison populations declined for a number of years meant that more "free beds" were available. As a result the average time spent was longer in those instances, regardless of the person's offense.

It seems quite clear that the average female offender is not a person presented with numerous opportunities. Instead, she is seriously disadvantaged and becomes involved in criminal behavior as an unhappy solution to serious pressures and problems within her home and her community.

LAW AND THE ADMINISTRATION OF JUSTICE

In myriad ways statutes governing the criminal justice systems have discriminated against females. Any historical examination of law in the Western world documents sexism in both law and legal practice. Which comes first—the perspectives about female criminality, or statutes defining female crime—matters very little, because once the ideology and law are established, each reinforces the other. The processing of females into and through the justice system manifests some marked contrasts between males and females. It is frequently observed that adult females have been treated more leniently by the system, when comparisons can be made with males for the same offenses (Arditi, Goldberg, Hartle, Peters, & Phelps, 1973; Simon, 1975b; Singer, 1973). For example, the population of state correctional facilities was 97% male in 1974 when the male proportion of all adult arrests was 85% (U.S. NCJISS, 1975, 1976). At the same time, women are arrested, tried, convicted, and incarcerated for behavior (e.g., promiscuity and prostitution) for which men are not prosecuted in the vast majority of jurisdictions.

In contrast, juvenile females are dealt with more stringently by the juvenile justice system than juvenile males, for the arrest ratio of males to females is approximately four to one, but the ratio of detention to incarceration is three to one (Sarri, 1974). Obviously such contradictions are not the result of rational decision-making about criminal justice processing, nor are they based on systematic knowledge about criminal careers, deterrence, and recidivism. But as we shall note subsequently, this society is ambivalent in its perspectives toward adolescent females. On the one hand they are to be socialized in a nurturant manner; on the other hand they are viewed as disruptive persons to be controlled by adults. This section will refer primarily to statutory and case law pertaining to juvenile females since there has been more activity in this area recently.

Courts have applied a "reasonableness" test in matters of alleged sex discrimination, and as it is relatively easy to justify a law on the grounds of reasonableness, most sex-discriminatory laws have been upheld. The Fourteenth Amendment has been invoked to constrain racial discrimination in voting, employment, social welfare, education, and other areas, but only very recently have attempts been made to employ it to prohibit or discourage discrimination against women. Nowhere is this discrimination more apparent and of greater importance than in the administration of justice. Sexism is a pervasive phenomenon. It is only recently, for example, that in some states delinquency laws discriminating against females have been struck down as unconstitutional.

In recent years some sex-based discrimination, particularly in military benefits and in some areas of criminal law, has been ruled unconstitutional by the courts. For example, it has been held that laws permitting a longer sentence for a woman than a man for the same crime contravene the Fourteenth Amendment (*Robinson* v. *York,* 1968, in Connecticut; *Commonwealth* v. *Daniels,* 1968, in Pennsylvania; and *State* v. *Chambers,* 1973, in New Jersey; and *Commonwealth* v. *Butler,* 1974). Similarly, it has been held that longer sentences for female juvenile delinquents violate the equal protection clause (Armstrong, 1977; Temin, 1973). Until recently a New York juvenile delinquency statute (the PINS law) provided that girls who were "persons in need of supervision" could be institutionalized until the age of 18, but the age for boys was 16. This law was held to violate the equal protection clause (*In re Patricia A.,* 1972). Similar laws have been held unconstitutional also in Connecticut (*Sumrell* v. *York,* 1968) and Oklahoma (*Lamb* v. *Brown,* 1972).

Juvenile delinquency laws have long discriminated against females (Davis & Chaires, 1973) but a further problem remains, namely, the attitudes and ideologies of persons administering it (i.e., judges, probation officers, or other court staff) may result in violations of the Fourteenth Amendment equal protection clause by inducing them to award females longer sentences than males under the guise of "protection of the female." Or the so-called double standard of morality may lead to longer terms of institutionalization for females than males committing the same acts. Even when laws appear to be nondiscriminatory, they are, from an operational point of view, discriminatory. One example of prima facie discrimination was the Connecticut law that until 1972 made it a crime for an unmarried woman to be in manifest danger of falling into habits of vice; it was not applicable to males in the same position.

Statutory Law

Any examination of sexism in the administration of justice must inevitably include the legal definitions outlined in the codes and the provisions established in statute and case law to govern juvenile court behavior vis-à-vis these phenomena. Of particular consequence in the processing of females are provisions assigning jurisdiction to the juvenile court for behaviors that are not violations for adults (e.g., incorrigibility, truancy, curfew violations, promiscuity, running away). Females are disproportionately processed in and through the juvenile justice system for these behaviors, usually referred to as "status offenses."

Statutory differences in jurisdiction of the juvenile court are startling with respect to age, definitions of delinquent and status offenses, offense limitations on the court's powers, jurisdictional conflicts, and permissible interaction with the adult system (Levin & Sarri, 1974). At present all 50 states and the District of Columbia include status offenders within the purview of the juvenile court. In 1972, 24 states and the District of Columbia had a separate category for status offenders (PINS, CINS, MINS, etc.), with eight other states having mixed categories.

Four states (Alabama, Michigan, New York, and Vermont) set a higher maximum age for original juvenile court jurisdiction for those charged with status offenses. Some states also have sex-age differences for status offenses, but these are generally considered unconstitutional today because of the New York family court decision in *In re Patricia A.* (1972) and the U.S. Supreme Court decision in *Stanton* v. *Stanton* (1975).

Three states have lower maximum ages for males than females but state courts in these states (Illinois, Oklahoma, and Texas) have declared such distinctions unconstitutional (Levin & Sarri, 1974). Similarly, statutes with disparate sentences for female juvenile offenders have been struck down as being unconstitutional, such as the Connecticut law that provided for girls under 21 to be sentenced for three years but boys under 21 and convicted for the same offense to be incarcerated for only two years (*Sumrell* v. *York*, 1968).

Fourteen states now have fairly stringent prohibitions against placement of status offenders with other delinquents in correctional facilities. Often, however, status offenders may violate probation requirements or be classified as not amenable to rehabilitation. In such cases the youth often are declared delinquent and in no way differentiated from other delinquents. Thus statutory provisions do not control the negative labeling and stigmatizing processes.

Litigation

Where laws are enforced in a discriminatory manner despite their apparently neutral nature, the reason is often that the laws are vague or overboard, so that the double standard of morality may be applied with impunity. Terms used in such statutes as being applicable to juveniles are *immoral, in danger of becoming immoral,* and *moral depravity.* Use of such terms gives no standards for determining the type of behavior prescribed; neither the person accused nor the judge has any standard on which to base or judge behavior (Davis & Chaires, 1973). In fact, some states' statutes framed in these or similar terms have been struck down as vague (*Gonzales* v. *Maillard,* 1971, in California). However, other courts in other states have upheld such laws, stating that no question could be raised about what the terms of the statute meant. For example in *E.S.G.* v. *State* (1969, Texas), the section provided that a youth who "habitually so comports himself as to injure or endanger the morals of himself or others" may be classed as a juvenile delinquent by the court and committed to an institution up to the age of 21. *Morals,* the court held, conveys a concrete impression to the ordinary person; there could be no question as to what the term meant. Here the girl in question had been found with a young male adult in what was classified as a "transient apartment"; she had been keeping the company of a reputed prostitute and was away from home for more than a week. Although one might say that for a 14-year-old girl to be in such a position would not be in her best interests, placing the girl in an institution for up to seven years would seem to require a more definitive standard for such a drastic action.

Challenges that affect the processing of female status offenders are of particular concern, because this category includes 50-70% of the female offenders in the various states. These challenges have been based most frequently on vagueness, status charges that violate the Eighth Amendment, and overbreadth.*

---

*See Conway and Bogdan (1977) for similar data on New York. They note that from the time of W. I. Thomas's original study in 1923 there has been little change in the processing and incarceration of adolescent females for status offenses except that vastly increased numbers have been processed and increasing percentages of females are institutionalized, whereas the percentage of males committed to institutions declined. Clearly a double standard has prevailed in decision-making, especially with respect to sexual behavior.

Void for vagueness. The Supreme Court has struck down as vague statutes which "either forbid or require the doing of an act in terms so vague that men of common intelligence must necessarily guess at its meaning and differ as to its application" (*Connally* v. *General Construction Co.,* 1926).

More recently, the Court, in vacating a California federal district court decision, held that the California juvenile statute was void because it granted juvenile court jurisdiction over children who were "in danger of leading an idle, dissolute, lewd or immoral life." Such a statute was void, the Court said, because it failed to give fair warning of proscribed conduct or information to the factfinder to enable him to accurately recognize such conduct (*Gonzalez* v. *Maillard,* 1974).

Punishment of a Condition. In 1962 the United States Supreme Court, in *Robinson* v. *California,* reversed a conviction for violation of a California penal code making it a criminal offense to "be addicted to the use of narcotics." The Court held that Robinson manifested a condition—addiction—which he was not able to control; thus the defendant maintained a particular "status." Mr. Justice Douglas, in his concurring opinion, stated:

> We would forget the teachings of the Eighth Amendment if we allowed sickness to be a crime and permitted sick people to be punished for being sick. This age of enlightenment cannot tolerate such barbarous action. (p. 678).

The effect of *Robinson* v. *California* was to support the argument that a status must be differentiated from a criminal act and that punishment for a status is in violation of the Eighth Amendment. This argument has continued to surface in cases involving convictions of chronic alcoholics for public intoxication—*Easter* v. *D.C.* (1966), *Driver* v. *Hinnant* (1966), and the ultimate Supreme Court decision that upheld the constitutionality of convictions of chronic alcoholics for public intoxication, *Powell* v. *Texas* (1968).

The previous constitutional arguments attacked adult system practices punishing status rather than behavior. The last few years have seen similar attempts to confront statutes applicable to juveniles. In a case involving an adolescent female—*Gesicki* v. *Oswald* (1971)—the Wayward Minor statute of New York was declared unconstitutional. The act granted adult criminal jurisdiction over youth 16-21 who were punished for being "morally depraved" and "in danger of becoming morally depraved." The court stated that the Wayward Minor statute permitted the "unconstitutional punishment of a minor's condition rather than of any specific action."

However, two recent decisions have supported statutes that were applicable solely to status offenders and that were challenged by the "void for vagueness" doctrine. In *Mercado* v. *Rockefeller* (1974) the New York State PINS statute was upheld as constitutional.

In *Blondheim* v. *State* (1975) the Washington Supreme Court upheld the constitutionality of the state's incorrigibility statute and ruled that punishment for this offense was not cruel and unusual. (In this particular case a 17-year-old female had run away from home and various placements eight times in three months.) The statute read:

> An incorrigible child is one less than 18 who is beyond control of his parents, guardian, or custodian by reason of the conduct or nature of said child.

The girl contended that the statute punished the "status" of being incorrigible, in violation of the Eighth Amendment. The court, although not denying that incorrigibility is a condition or state of being, justified the statute's legitimacy by stating that one acquires such a status only by reason of one's conduct or a pattern of behavior proscribed by the statute. Engaging in conduct that placed her beyond the lawfully exercised control of her mother was felt to be sufficient basis for support of an adjudication of incorrigibility. The court, however, did not show awareness of parental involvement nor did it acknowledge that the parents also could have been charged.

Overbreadth. Overbreadth may be another basis for an attack on status offense statutes. In the case of *State* v. *Mattiello* (1966) the court upheld a conviction of a female juvenile for violation of the Connecticut statute "forbidding walking with a lascivious carriage." The appellate division upheld the statute as valid under the concept of *parens patriae,* that the proceeding was civil rather than criminal, and that its end was not to punish but to rehabilitate the child through guardianship and protection.

The recency of legal changes is apparent in the U.S. Supreme Court decision in *Stanton* v. *Stanton* (1975). The Court reversed the decision of the Utah Supreme Court which, in the case of child support payments, differentiated minority ages for males and females. The Utah statute had provided that the period of minority for males extended to 21 and for females to 18. But the U.S. Supreme Court qualified its reversal by saying,

"We find it unnecessary in this case to decide whether a classification based on sex is inherently suspect." Thus, further decisions on statutes are required to clarify this matter.

Sex-Related Behavior

Prostitution and promiscuity are two behaviors for which women almost exclusively are prosecuted despite the obvious injustice of such processing. In the majority of American states prostitution is defined as the "engaging, offering or agreeing to engage in sexual intercourse for a fee."* Discrimination may arise in two ways: Some laws confine "prostitution" to the activities of females—male prostitutes are not covered; second, in most jurisdictions the customer is not penalized at all. In regard to the latter, some states are now enacting, or have enacted, "john laws" or "customer laws" specifically to veto the activities of the person keeping the prostitute in business—the customer. For example, New York has recently enacted a law that states that "patronizing a prostitute" is a violation, with a maximum sentence of imprisonment for 15 days. Even here, however, the effect of the double standard is obvious, in that in New York the penalty for the prostitute is far more severe with a maximum prison sentence of three months.

Data reported by Dorsen (1970) for New York City in 1968 indicate that there were 3,500 convictions of prostitutes, but only two convictions of patrons out of the 112 arrested. Thus, far more prostitutes are arrested and convicted than customers. "Pimping," or living off the proceeds of prostitution, is also a crime; however, it seems that here too the vigilance of the police is not as rigorous as in relation to the prostitute herself. New York City, 1968, had 3,500 *convictions* of prostitutes, but only 182 arrests of pimps and fewer than 50 convictions. Even though there are more prostitutes than pimps, it would be reasonable to suppose that because the prostitute is more obvious in her activities she would be more likely to be proceeded against than the pimp, who may be able to conceal his activities with greater ease.

One of the most problematic aspects of sex-related behavior and the law for adolescent females has been the prohibition against their obtaining treatment in their own right. Under the common law interpretation

---

*In the United Kingdom, Australia, and Canada the actual act of prostitution—exchange of the body for money—is not a crime; it is the solicitation that is prohibited. Several states have similar proposals under consideration, and in Iowa, Michigan, Missouri, Montana, Nevada, Rhode Island, and the District of Columbia, prostitution is not a crime, but solicitation is illegal.

the consent of parents or a guardian has been required before a physician or agency would provide any kind of treatment, even on an emergency basis. Moreover, the court has supported the right of parents to make decisions contrary to the wishes of their children. In *In re Smith* (1972) the juvenile court judge placed Cindy Lou Smith in the custody of her parents and ordered that she submit to a termination of pregnancy despite her desire to have the child. On appeal the appellate court reversed the lower court judge and ruled that he did not have the power to order an abortion merely because the youth's mother wished her to have the pregnancy terminated.

In recent years there have been a number of decisions affecting the right of adolescent females to obtain sex-related medical care on their own consent (Paul 1974/75; Paul, Pilpel, & Wechsler, 1976). Changes in age-of-majority laws have had a marked positive effect for those youth 18 and older, but younger youth in the majority of states still find it difficult to obtain medical contraceptive services or termination of a pregnancy without parental consent. By the end of 1975, 26 states and the District of Columbia permitted youth under 18 to obtain contraceptive care and 25 states permitted termination of pregnancy decisions without parental consent (Paul, Pilpel, & Wechsler, 1976, p. 16).

In the landmark decisions *Roe* v. *Wade* (1973) and *Doe* v. *Bolton* (1973), the U.S. Supreme Court held that states may not restrict the right to abortion unless the restriction can be justified by a "compelling state interest." Many courts have now interpreted that to mean that parental consent requirements are no longer necessary. In *Poe* v. *Gerstein* (1975) the Court pointed out that there were explicit limits on the conditions under which parental consent could be required. Most recently the Supreme Court ruled in a state of Utah case that family planning services could be made available to minors by the Planned Parenthood Association without parental consent (*Jones* v. *T.H.*, 1976).

The general principle involved in these cases and in other related ones is the extension of constitutional rights to minors. In *Tinker* v. *Des Moines Independent Community School District* (1969), the Supreme Court ruled that minors are "persons" under the Constitution with "fundamental rights which the state must respect." Nonetheless, agencies as well as courts have been reluctant to proceed with the extension of rights to adolescents, even when the request is for medical or psychological treatment. Instead, parental rights are supported and reinforced under the presumption that youth are unable to make the proper decision (Lee & Paxman 1974/75). The problem is particularly significant in the case of adolescent female offenders because substantial proportions are referred to the court for behavior objectionable to their parents, i.e., promiscuity, incorrigibility, ungovernability, and so forth. Obviously such females might encounter difficulty in obtaining parental consent for treatment—psychological, medical, or social work.

Other Supreme Court decisions that have import regarding this question involve more general extensions of rights to youth such as *In re Gault* (1967) and *Goss* v. *Lopez* (1975). These decisions have not been applied explicitly to programs for adjudicated youth, and if they were, there is little doubt that arbitrary actions by many agencies would be constrained substantially. A lower court in Wisconsin ruled in *Kidd* v. *Schmidt* (1975) that a juvenile may not be committed without a hearing on the basis of a parental or guardian signature. Unfortunately, until very recently less diligence has been shown in protecting adolescent females from abuse by parents as some tragic cases reveal (*In re Rebecca Oakes, Minor,* 1974; see also *Commonwealth* v. *Brasher,* 1971). Nevertheless, it can be expected that courts will gradually acknowledge greater rights to youth in decision-making affecting their own person, not necessarily their general status.

Equal Rights Amendment

As the words imply, the purpose of the ERA is to oust laws based on sex as being discriminatory. If the amendment is indeed ratified and become law, all laws determining rights and responsibilities on the grounds of sex as a sole determinant will be unconstitutional. This would mean that contrary to the present position, females would no longer be punished for crimes not applicable to males. For example, prostitution provisions framed to make the offense applicable only to females—e.g., "the engaging, by a *woman,* in the act of sexual intercourse for a fee is punishable . . ."—will offend the ERA. Similarly, sexual delinquency laws that make it a crime to be an unmarried girl between 16 and 20 in "manifest danger of falling into habits of vice" (unmarried boys are not mentioned!) would be constitutional.*

Modifications in many civil and criminal statutes will be necessary to achieve conformity with constitutional requirements (Benjamin, 1975; Frankel, 1973). Historically females have been doubly disadvantaged under the criminal law. In the case of most rape, they were supposed to be protected as victim but typically were not. In the case of prostitution,

---

*Conn. General Statute Am., see 17-379, 1958; repealed in 1972, P.A. 38, see 2.

only females were prosecuted, when both sexes were involved in the behavior at issue. Our earlier discussion regarding juvenile runaways and detention practices clearly documents the fact that females are more readily processed by both police and courts for behavior identical to that of males.

WOMEN IN CUSTODY

Despite the discrimination or inequities which may exist among police, judges, prosecutors, and others in the law enforcement and judicial systems, the most serious problems exist in residential facilities: jails, prisons, reformatories, lockups, and other facilities. Journalists' reports by Mitford (1973), Burkhart (1973), Wooden (1976), and others do not exaggerate the conditions for these have been corroborated by substantial recent research which clearly demonstrates consistent inequities: in programs and services available to women offenders; in incarceration for behavior for which males are not incarcerated; and in longer sentences for identical or lesser crimes.

The incarceration of adult women in separate prison facilities developed within the past century, since 1880; for adolescent females the use of separate institutions is even more recent, dating from the early 1900s. Only in the state of Vermont has the juvenile state training school always been coeducational since its establishment in the mid-19th century. Prisons structured for females were purportedly established to provide female inmates with the same benefits of rehabilitation given their male counterparts. Prisons were built to comply with the reformists' beliefs that women prisoners needed sexual morality and sobriety if they were to resume their "predestined roles as homemakers, mothers and wives." They were located in isolated rural areas, and the public knew very little about the persons or events inside, in contrast to a voluminous popular and scientific literature about male prisons.*

Population

As of 1976 there were approximately 275,000 adults in state and federal prisons (U.S. Dept. of Justice, LEAA, NCJISS, 1976b). Of that population approximately 16,000 were females. There were about 990 females housed in six Federal and 7437 in 40 state facilities in contrast to 25

---

*There are several biographies and autobiographies written by inmates about conditions and life-styles in women's prisons. Perhaps one of the most compelling descriptions is that written by Elizabeth Gurley Flynn (1963) who spent more than 25 years at the Federal prison for women in Alderson, West Virginia.

Federal and 260 state facilities for men. Of the 160,863 persons in more than 4,000 local jails in the recent LEAA census (U.S. Dept. of Justice, LEAA, NCJISS, 1971), 7739 were adult women. In addition, the juvenile total is even larger despite the fact that there was nearly a 25% decline between 1971 and 1975. As of June 30, 1974, there were 10,139 females in state and local public detention and correctional facilities and 9,645 in privately operated correctional units (U.S. Dept. of Justice, LEAA, NCJISS, 1976a). Moreover, there were an estimated 2,600 juveniles in local jails for adults, for a grand total of 22,384. Thus, approximately 38,000 women are held in the United States in some type of correctional facility on any given day in the mid-1970s. The rate is far higher for juveniles than for adult women since the age range is relatively small (13-17) for juveniles as compared to adult women (17-60). Furthermore, the female juvenile population is 25% of all incarcerated juveniles whereas for adult women the rate of incarceration overall is 3.6%—a dramatic difference. Given the fact that the juvenile arrest rate is less than 25% of the total, these data suggest that chivalry is certainly not being shown to juvenile females. However, in the case of adult women, the incarceration proportion of 3.6% falls below that which would be expected given the arrest ratio of five male to one female in 1974.*

Women, as well as men, are disproportionately incarcerated in Southern states rather than in the more populous states of the North and West or the rural areas of the Middle West. Hindelang et al. (1976) note that overall rates of incarceration vary from 27.9 in North Dakota and 50.4 per thousand in Illinois to 173.2 in Georgia and 182.8 in North Carolina. Even in the Federal system the six Southern states in the Fifth Circuit District contributed 33% of all the female Federal prisoner commitments in 1973.**

Because of their relatively smaller number, females in prisons, jails, and training schools have received much less attention, but lack of interest is also due to the fact that females have done little to attract attention. Unfortunately most correctional reform has been preceded by disruption or violence. Prisoners who riot, destroy property, and threaten lives are far more likely to be listened to in terms of their complaints

---

*It still should be noted that many of the behaviors for which women continue to be arrested do not result in arrests for men. Thus, there is no reason why the correspondence should be identical unless comparisons are made between comparable offenses. As Simon (1975) indicates, these differences do persist in some of the comparisons, but they are not as outstanding as many writers imply.

**The southern states are also less populous than other regions which contributed far fewer females (e.g., Mid-Atlantic).

and requests than are those who passively accept the institutional environment as it is.

Women offenders also have received less attention because the crimes which they commit are far more often "victimless" and do not threaten society. Since 1970, however, there has been greater concern, particularly about the long institutionalization of juvenile females who are charged as status offenders. Thus, there have been concerted efforts toward reform by national and local interest groups such as the Junior League, National Council on Crime and Delinquency, the National Council of Jewish Women, the Children's Defense Fund, the National Coalition for Children and Youth, and the League of Women Voters. It is not accidental that the majority of these groups are women's organizations. In fact, most interest groups working for prison reform in the past two centuries have been women's organizations. The payoff for their efforts, however, has been far greater in male than in female programs and services. Citizens groups of women have been particularly active in Pennsylvania, and they have had a profound effect there both on deinstitutionalization of female programs and on the quality of programs. Most recently they submitted a set of ten goals and standards for female correctional programs throughout the state.*

Several recent surveys have been completed of females in adult prisons and juvenile institutions. (Citizens Task Force, 1970; Foster, 1974; Glick, 1975; Hendrix, 1972; Hindelang et al., 1975, 1976; McGowan & Blumenthal, 1976; Sims, 1976; U.S. Dept. of Justice, NCJISS, 1976; Vinter, 1976.) Although there are some variations in findings among these several surveys because of differences in sampling procedures and methodologies, the basic findings about population characteristics of females in residential correctional facilities are essentially similar, as the following summary indicates:

Adults

1. Two-thirds of the incarcerated females are under 30 years. The median age for misdemeanants is 24 years and 27 for felons.

---

*See Pennslyvania (1975) for a cogent statement of standards for female correctional programs developed by the Pennsylvania Program for Women and Girl Offenders, Inc. This is the first time such a statement of standards has been prepared at any level of government—local, state, or federal. It does rather clearly argue that there are distinctive needs of females, but these in no way would be jeopardized by the passage of ERA. On the other hand, passage of that amendment would not be sufficient to insure the implementation of program standards for men and women in the areas of medical care, educational handicaps due to past inequities, and so forth.

2. Fifty to fifty-five percent of the women are Black, but Chicanos and Native Americans are also overrepresented in selected states.

3. Nine out of ten women report that they expect to support themselves upon release. Seven out of ten were heads of households and two-thirds had an average of 2.4 dependent children. However, 25% of the mothers reported that the children were not residing with them at the time of their arrest and detention. More than half are not married (55-60%), further indication of the problematic situation for minor children since these women must rely on extended family support or lose their children to the state.

4. The majority are unskilled and educationally handicapped. Although most have been employed (70%), that employment was sporadic and insufficient in most cases. About a third have received public welfare benefits. Forty-five percent have not completed secondary school and 14% completed only elementary school.

5. The offenses for which women were incarcerated are not systematically available for all of the states, but in terms of frequency, substance abuse of all types, theft and other property violations, and prostitution are the largest categories, with only small percentages of women offenders incarcerated for homicide, assault, or robbery. It is clear from the data which are available that there have been no significant increases in commitments for violent crime since the women's and equal rights movements became widely known in the late sixties and early seventies.

Juveniles. Data compiled by the National Assessment of Juvenile Corrections as well as by federal agencies and many other students of juvenile justice clearly indicate that females are overrepresented in critical areas of the justice system. One of the most critical areas pertains to placement in adult jails, lockups, and detention facilities. Females have a greater probability of being detained and held for longer periods than males, even though the overwhelming majority of females are charged with status offenses. Moreover, in the juvenile jurisdictions reporting a ratio of one female to four male arrests, the ratio for placement in detention is typically on to three (Sarri, 1974).

1. The data in Table 2 were obtained by the NAJC survey of juvenile correctional programs in 1974. They clearly indicate the variation among males and females in commitment offense, that is, the offense which was the basis for adjudication and assignment to a correctional program. Moreover, females were institutionalized disproportionately for status and other minor offenses.

2. The median age of institutionalized juveniles was 15.5 years

TABLE 2

Commitment Offense, by Program Type and Sex (In Percentages)

	Status Offense[a]	Probation or Parole Violation	Misdemeanor	Drugs or Alcohol	Property	Person	(n)
Institution							
Male	23	4	2	6	46	18	(832)
Female	50	1	3	18	14	14	(349)
Community Residential							
Male	50	3	1	10	26	10	(70)
Female	67	3	0	14	12	3	(58)
Day Treatment							
Male	45	3	4	6	30	12	(164)
Female	87	0	0	5	3	5	(37)

Source of Data: National Assessment of Juvenile Corrections, University of Michigan, Ann Arbor, Michigan, (Sarri & Hasenfeld, 1976).
Note: Determination of commitment offense was based on youth response to the question, "Why were you sent here?"
a. Status offenses include incorrigibility, dependent and neglected, truancy, running away, curfew violations, disorderly, etc.

with younger females in the closed institutions rather than in community-based programs (Vinter, 1976). Males and females were essentially similar in age at the time of commitment but because they remained longer, the females' median age increased.

3. Fifty-seven percent of the populations were non-white, vastly overrepresenting minority groups.

4. Over half of the females came from working and lower-class families, and a substantial proportion (22%) reported that their parents were on welfare or were unemployed. Less than 25% had parents in white collar occupations.

5. Most females lived with one or both parents prior to incarceration, as did the male offenders. However, 13% of the females who committed more serious offenses reported that they lived independently. Although living patterns did not differ significantly between males and females, family relationships were reported as more problematic by females. Given the fact that about 20% of the referrals to juvenile court of females are by their parents, this result might be expected. In other words, the nature of the relationship with one or both parents was a more influential factor than was the fact that the home had one or two parents present. Youth, both males and females, reported that relationships with their mothers rather than fathers were more significant to them.

6. Discrepancies between age and school grade completed were greater for females than males although both groups were educationally handicapped two to four years relative to their ages.

7. Overall, approximately half (55%) of the females were committed for status offenses; 17% for drugs; 13% for property; and 12% for person crimes. For only the latter group of 12% might institutionalization be required in order to protect society and yet it is a small and relatively unchanging proportion of institutionalized female delinquents.

The punitiveness of the juvenile justice system toward females is particularly apparent in the handling of status offenders. It was recently reported by HEW that 68% of all runaways were females. Their data were based on police apprehension of youth. However, Gold and Reimer's (1975) national survey of youth in 1972 indicated no significant differences between males and females in self-reports of running away, nor did they observe any pattern of increase between 1967 and 1972. Clearly, the differential processing of females is a factor producing the variations in these two sets of data.

The survey of cases of "ungovernability" in the New York Family Court indicates that 62% of these youth were females in midadolescence, disproportionately nonwhite, and from large, poor, and single-parent or broken families (*Yale Law Journal,* 1974). They further observed that 37% of these females were "neglected" but were classified as "ungovernable" in order to expedite processing. Sixty-eight percent were held in secure detention despite its obvious impropriety. Finally, they observed that higher proportions of these youth were adjudicated and committed to residential facilities than youth who committed serious property or person crimes.

Placement of juvenile females in jail is increasing more rapidly than that of males, in several states (Skoler & McKeown, 1974). In Wisconsin there were 2,875 males and 768 females in adult jails in 1961. In 1972 there were 7,032 males and 2,892 females—a 277% increase for females versus 145% for males (Sarri, 1974). Some will undoubtedly assert that these increases are due to more rapid increase in serious criminal behavior by females. However, such assertions cannot be supported if systematic and comprehensive data are used, as the most recent report from Wisconsin indicates (Wisconsin, 1976). The National Survey of Youth shows increased use of marijuana, alcohol, and other drugs but no increase in other delinquent behavior by females (Gold & Reimer, 1975).

Table 3 presents the average number of previous correctional experiences reported by youth in the National Assessment of Juvenile Corrections survey. As would be expected, females generally report fewer prior correctional contacts than males, with the exception of the number of times in group or foster homes. Yet, considering the median age of 15.5 years, and that females much less frequently commit serious crimes, it is noteworthy that they report so much correctional contact. Forty-five percent of the females have been arrested more than twice, and 50% have been in detention more than twice; only 31% have never been on probation, and only 42% have never been in an institution. Clearly, the concept of "lesser penetration" into the justice system is not being implemented for these females.

The data just presented indicate that thousands of adult and juvenile females are institutionalized each year, primarily in state public facilities but also in local, private, and federal programs. What are some of the problems faced by women in correctional institutions?

Endemic Problems for Females in Institutions

Views differ about the relative advantages and disadvantages of female inmates. It has been noted that penal institutions for women are usually more attractive physically because they do not have cell blocks, gun

TABLE 3

Prior Correctional Experience of Juveniles in Correctional Programs[a]
(By Mean Number of Times)

	Female	Male
Arrest	4.6	8.7
Detention	3.8	4.6
Jail	2.0	3.2
Court	4.7	5.6
Probation	1.4	2.1
Group or Foster Home	1.5	0.9
Institution	1.3	1.6
N in ranges[b] =	476-488	1162-1237

Source: National Assessment of Juvenile Corrections, *Time Out*, (Vinter, 1976, p. 45).
a. Based on the question "How many times in your life has each of the following things happened to you?"
b. Number of respondents differs for each item.

towers, and other overt signs of maximum security.[*] The Yale survey of 15 states indicates that female prisons are smaller, have more privacy and higher staff-client ratios. The relatively smaller size of the female prisons results in less differentiated programming and fewer programs that are related to the variable needs of clientele. The 1973 survey found that male prisons had an average of 40 vocational training programs per institution while female facilities had only 2.7. Academic education and work-release programs were also poorer in quality as well as quantity. Recreation, medical, and dental services were likewise fewer, but this was not always a disadvantage since women then might have had greater access to local community programs. The mean expenditure per female inmate was $9,439 in 1973 while for males it was $4,850.[**] Most of this difference can be attributed to higher numbers of custodial staff in the female programs.

Because female prisons are more often remote from urban centers and thus lack access to work-release and employment opportunities, rehabili-

---

[*] Women offenders, however, often complain about physical isolation, lack of family contact, and being treated as if they were young children (Hendrix, 1972).

[**] See American Bar Association Correctional Economics Center *Community Programs for Women Offenders: Costs and Economic Considerations* (1975).

tation is further handicapped. All ex-offenders have problems in obtaining employment but a female ex-offender often has three strikes against her—sex, race, and criminal record. That the institution can do nothing to mediate the effects of these handicaps is especially problematic.

As was noted earlier, the majority of adult female prisoners are mothers of minor children. Incarcerated mothers and children face a myriad of special problems, the most obvious of which is separation. Given the fact that some women may be hundreds of miles from their children, the maintenance of family ties is nearly impossible; yet most report that they expect to live with their children upon release. Very few prisons in the United States have adopted programs that allow mothers to keep their children. In Europe, however, such practice is relatively routine. Norway has a variety of provisions for mothers of infants and young children to remain with their children. In France a mother serving a prison sentence may keep her children until they are 18 months old. One experiment in West Germany, "the Kinderheim Program" has been reported as particularly successful. The mothers—most of whom were convicted for prostitution, substance abuse, or shoplifting—are allowed to have their children with them in prison. The women work in the prison factory 40 hours per week and then are with their children the remainder of the time.

McGowan and Blumenthal (1976) queried mothers about program changes for inmate mothers.* They clearly indicate that the inmates perceive that the state has a responsibility not to destroy whatever family life existed through ignorance or indifference.

Foster's findings from a survey of programs for female offenders in the federal system only corroborates those of other observers of state facilities (Foster, 1974). However, these problems are aggravated in federal facilities because of their location in remote areas of the United States relative to the population. Particularly noteworthy in this study was the high proportion of females committed for nonviolent crimes. In 1973, 35% of all the females committed to federal facilities were sent for property crimes, and 40% for substance abuse crimes of all types. According to this report, not one federal commitment of a woman in 1973 was for an assault or homicide; yet, these women remain in prison longer on the average than do those committed to state facilities.** Clearly, Federal

---

*McGowan and Blumenthal (1976) report that women inmates identified many programs and situations which could be readily implemented to facilitate the maintenance of family responsibilities and relationships.

**Length of stay in federal prisons is often longer because there are more beds available and greater program resources than in the states.

judges were more punitive in their sanctioning of women than in earlier years, given comparisons with arrest and conviction rates.

Federal female prisoners like those in the states are disproportionately poor, undereducated, and from minority groups. Most of the Federal prisons lack academic, vocational, and work-release programs which will prepare these women for subsequent successful achievement in their home communities.

According to the Supreme Court decision in *Frontiero* v. *Richardson*, 1973, the state must show a compelling interest before it may afford different treatment to persons on the basis of sex. Thus, women should have equal access to the full range of programs available to males, but this guarantee is not presently available in the majority of states. Recently, however, in the state of Mississippi women won the right to conjugal visiting by threatening legal action because such visits had been available to men for many years. The courts have also stated that the lack of resources is not a satisfactory excuse for denying opportunities to females. In *Barefield* v. *Leach*, 1974, the Federal Court in New Mexico held that female prisoners are entitled to equal treatment—and that one interpretation of such was equal expenditure of program funds. Thus, it is no longer legitimate to assert, the court said, that women can only be trained in traditional blue collar female occupations or that less money should be spent because women are less of a threat.

Racism and the justice system. The literature on female criminality largely ignores the distinctions in the status of black and white women in the United States (Crites, 1976). It further assumes that law enforcement agencies may operate with a "sex" bias in their identification and handling of criminal behavior, but it is silent on how that bias may interact differentially with race. As Iglehart (1977) suggests in her review of black and white female criminality, the history of black women in the United States would caution against such an assumption. Stereotypes define the feminine role in terms usually associated with white Euro-American women—as obedient, docile, passive, attractive, and dependent. In contrast, the cultural image of the black woman is that she is the head of the family, aggressive, independent, self-reliant, and morally permissive. It might very well be expected that law enforcement personnel would respond quite differently to the same behavior given those role images of black and white women.

As long ago as 1904, Dubois, and as recently as 1975, Quinney, have reported research findings which indicate that the status of being black involves a far greater probability of being arrested, jailed, convicted, imprisoned, and executed. Although females have a far lower probability than do males of being arrested and processed through the criminal justice system, it could be expected that black females would be at greater risk than white females. Throughout this chapter we have noted the disproportionate numbers of minority group members in most steps of the processing. Sims' recent account of her observations of Southern jails provides clear support for this proposition (Sims, 1976). Moreover, she reports frequent incidents of gross sexual and physical abuse of women offenders and arrestees in most of the states she visited.

Iglehart (1977) analyzed female prison populations from 1890 to 1970 where data were available. She is able to show conclusive data as follows:

1. Black women are substantially overrepresented in prison populations (50-55% of the total population). They are committed more often to state facilities whereas white women more often are placed on probation or in local facilities in their own communities.
2. Most female prisoners fall into the 25-34 age category, but black women tend to be consistently younger than whites. Selo (1976) noted a similar age pattern in juvenile facilities.
3. Although black women more often reported their marital status as single, higher proportions had children for whom they were responsible.
4. Although there were variations among black and white women in commitment offense patterns, theft and victimless crimes predominated for both races. Black women committed more serious person crimes than did white women, but the former still constituted a small proportion of the total (5-20%). In the federal prisons 52% of the females were black and more than 75% were committed because of substance abuse or property crimes. Even among women charged with homicide, Boudouris (1971) observed that a majority reported that physical abuse and battering by their male spouse or friend was a precipitating factor in their subsequent act of homicide.
5. Until recently the criminal justice literature has given little attention to females as victims of crimes. With the availability of information from the national victimization surveys (U.S. Dept. of Justice, LEAA, NCJISS, 1977), it is now clear that females are less involved in crime than are males—both as offenders and as victims. The one expected exception occurs in the case of rape where women are the victims almost exclusively. Observation of the victimization data also reveals that black females are far more often the victims of crime than are white females—with one exception—that of theft, excluding personal larceny. Reports of victim assistance programs indicate that these are meager programs at best and usually they have as their primary aim the

obtaining of witnesses and corroborating evidence for prosecutors. The black female is thus further handicapped by the operation of the criminal justice system as a victim as well as an offender.

In contrast to the situation for males, relatively little data is available about racial factors in other stages of the criminal justice processing system so it is difficult to know where and how racial biases operate to produce the disproportionate numbers of black women in institutions. Data for Detroit 1930-1970 suggest that police processing may be far less stringent today than it was a quarter of a century ago. The arrest rate declined in this period, dropping from 29 to 12 per thousand black women while for whites it remained constant at two per thousand. This shift occurred during the period when Detroit was undergoing a massive black-white population change in the inner-Metropolitan area. Nevertheless, in 1970, 79% of all females arrested in Detroit were black when the total percentage of blacks in the city was 40%.

The inmate subculture. Sociologists have long been concerned with the significance of the informal inmate subculture as a critical factor in socialization of offenders to subsequent criminal behavior, and in social control of correctional facilities. Only recently has there been systematic study of the inmate social system in adult and juvenile female programs (Giallombardo, 1974; Heffernan, 1972; Propper, 1976; Rochelle, 1965; Tittle, 1972). Their findings, taken together, reveal that it is not a monolithic social system, but it varies with differences in organizational characteristics of programs and individual characteristics of inmates. All are in agreement, however, about the importance of knowledge of the structure and dynamics of this system if inmate behavior is to be understood—both within the correctional facility and in the external environment. Most of the literature on inmate subsystems has been developed in studies of institutions. As a result we are limited in our ability to characterize these phenomena comprehensively.

Although one might consider many facets of the inmate subculture, there are two which have been studied more thoroughly and enable one to illustrate some of the critical dimensions with respect to the female offender. These two facets are homosexual behavior and the informal social organization of "girl gangs."

"Girl gangs." There have been many statements made about the increase in acting-out, aggressive behavior by females and particular reference has been made to female gangs as an increasing factor in female crime. The most thorough and systematic surveys of gangs have been

reported by Miller (1975) in his survey of major United States cities. Miller reported that autonomous female gangs continue to be a rare phenomenon and, even where they exist, their criminal behavior falls far below that of male gang members. Females instead continue in urban blue collar neighborhoods to function as auxiliaries to male gangs or occasionally in sexually mixed gangs. Overall their membership equals about 10% of the total gang membership.

Miller's staff did complete some participant observation research on girl gangs in one city. They found that the female gang usually took members at age 13 and girls left voluntarily at about 16. The average size of the gangs was 11. These "corner gang girls" did engage in considerable illegal behavior and were arrested almost as frequently as boys in their neighborhoods (45%). Their offenses, however, were quite different from those of the males. Truancy, petty thefts, use of alcohol, petty property damage, and sexual promiscuity were the most frequent offenses they reported. Their self-report offense rate was approximately 10% of that reported by male gang members. This differs sharply from the nearly equal arrest rate noted above, but other self-report data (Gold & Reimer, 1975; Short & Nye, 1970) corroborate the self-reports obtained by Miller in this study. Again, in the case of juvenile females, the justice system is more rather than less punitive in its processing of females. The girl gang itself manifested variations in organizational structure from that of male gangs. There were more dyadic subgroups with far less stability in group functioning. Miller noted that female gangs had equal opportunities to be criminal but were not. He concluded:

> Despite claims by some that criminality by females, either in general or in connection with gang activity, is both more prevalent and violent than in the past, what data were available did not provide much support for such claims (1975, p. 23).

Homosexuality. Because sexuality has been a significant factor in the processing of 30% or more of the female offenders into and through the criminal justice system, it is not surprising that concern with this variable continues throughout the criminal career. However, most correctional programs have been little concerned with "normal" sexuality and, instead, have focused on various types of abnormal behavior and, in particular, on homosexuality.

Homosexual behavior is variously defined by researchers who have studied the female offender, but more interest has been shown in trying to explain its emergence rather than its form. Two theoretical perspectives predominate among those which have been conceptualized to explain inmate subculture and the prevalence of homosexuality in correctional facilities: (a) deprivational model and (b) importation model. The deprivation model views the inmate subculture of which homosexuality is an important aspect as a consequence of the conditions of prison life (Giallombardo, 1966, 1974; Sykes & Messinger, 1960). Giallombardo suggests that differences in direction and focus of male and female subcultures can be understood by recognizing that the culture which emerges within the prison reflects the way in which sex roles are defined externally. Homosexual dyads and "make believe" family groups are more prevalent in female facilities because of inmates' perceptions about female roles. This assumption has been challenged by Tittle (1972), Heffernan (1972), and Propper (1976). They observe more varied patterns of informal social organization and fewer differences from male behavior in male facilities. Ward and Kassebaum (1965) assume that homosexual behavior in prison is an indicator of the likelihood of subsequent deviant behavior in other situations and roles. They do not, however, provide supporting data for that assumption.

In the NAJC study of juvenile correctional institutions, youth and staff were asked to report on various behaviors classified as homosexual. Relative to the deprivation model, Propper observed that importation theory was more important in predicting homosexual behavior.

> Previous homosexuality was the only one of the 29 variables examined which showed a strong and statistically signfiicant relationship to homosexuality scores. Previous homosexuality explained a large part of the variance (31%) in homosexuality scores . . . while previous homosexual experience explains a lot of the variation in institutional homosexuality it does not explain all of it. Only 37% . . . reported previous homosexual experience. More girls . . . reporting homosexual experiences report their first homosexual experience in prison (24%) (1976, p. 201)

Based on self-reports, the overall rates of homosexuality were 14% for "going together or being married"; 10% for passionately kissing; and 7% for having sex. The total percentage of youth reporting at least one experience ranged between 5% and 29% among the institutions, with an overall rate of 17%. Coed institutions had as high rates as institutions with only females. The overlap between homosexual behavior and participation in ersatz families was very small. Most staff reported that ersatz families were a reflection of the adolescents' needs for security, affection, and companionship. Adolescence is a critical period for developments of one's adult identity. Being in a single-sex environment handicaps that development. In the NAJC survey, 3% of the females said that they would probably have sex with girls after they left the institutions. This substantial number, plus the fact that the majority reported that their first homosexual experience took place in a correctional institution, suggests that these facilities have played a significant role in the adult sexual socialization of these females.

Sexism among correctional staff. As has been noted earlier, racism and sexism in the criminal justice system are not likely to be eliminated easily, despite the passage of ERA, because of powerful political and social forces for the maintenance of the existing system. Both Titles VII of the Civil Rights Act and Title IX of the Education Act have had only minimal effect on correctional programs in contrast to other human service organizations such as schools, colleges, and hospitals. In the NAJC surveys of juvenile courts and correctional programs, staff characteristics were examined in relation to those of the clientele in the respective programs. Table 4 reveals that minority group representation was low in juvenile courts (10%) where the ratio of nonwhite to white referrals is three to one.* In the correctional programs 27% of the staff were nonwhite and 51% of the youth were nonwhite. The findings in Table 4 reveal considerable homogeneity among the staff in all juvenile justice programs and further suggest that there are marked discrepancies between staff and client characteristics. Given the fact that most of these staff have broad discretion in defining, labeling, and dealing with criminal behavior, this discrepancy can be expected to have significant effects on the processing of offenders.

When the characteristics of executive level staff are examined, the effects are even more pronounced. Most minority group staff and women tend to occupy line positions at the lowest or middle levels of hierarchy in the organization. Six out of seven executives in the NAJC surveys were white and five out of six were male. Male administrators in corrections predominate even in the female and coed programs. The presence of female staff in leadership positions cannot guarantee a reduction in sexism, but it does appear to be one of the essential preconditions.

CONCLUSION

Our review of the female offender literature demonstrates conclusively that the justice system arrests, processes, and sentences females—both

---

*See Sarri and Hasenfeld (1976) for more detailed information about differential referral and detention rates for minorities and women.

TABLE 4

Staff Characteristics by Occupational Subgroups

| | Juvenile Courts | | | | Juvenile Correctional Programs | | | | | |
	Judge	Court Admin.	Prob. Super.	Line Prob.	Detention Superv.	Executive	Treatment Staff	Teachers	Living Unit Staff	Clerical & Maint.
Median Age	a	44	40	32	42	34	30	35	34	39
% Male	97	79	72	61	82	80	68	56	52	43
% White	94	89	93	89	86	84	68	70	68	76
% Married	93	85	82	68	81	61	55	66	59	73
N =	(274)	(237)	(119)	(388)	(171)	(52)	(233)	(218)	(302)	(197)

Source: National Assessment of Juvenile Corrections: See *Brought to Justice* (Sarri & Hasenfeld, 1976, 108) and *Time Out* (Vinter, 1976, 54).

a. Data unavailable.

adult and juvenile—differently than it does males. Unfortunately, the balance of the differential handling is negative for women. The ineffectiveness is partially due to the tremendous overload of the whole criminal justice system, but perhaps even more to our expectations about the probable positive consequences for the society from these forms of social control of deviance. Nowhere are these control mechanisms more apparent than in the handling of female youth. They are the more significant victims because so often they are charged and held for offenses which involve ambiguous interpersonal relationships rather than property or person felonies.

Theories of female crime continue to emphasize the "natural" differences between males and females. Few theorists seem interested in investigation of why it is that so few women commit personal or other serious crimes. Instead, more place emphasis on the increasing numbers of females being arrested (without controlling for differences in the sizes of the cohorts being compared). These increases are attributed without hesitation to the effects of the feminist movement on the rapid changes in sex-role definitions in the recent decade. Examination of longitudinal data as well as those from other countries reveals that stability has been at least as significant as change in behavior. What is needed now is far more research about the dynamics in the operation of the justice system as it selects and processes women. Such research, however, must be done by persons who are sensitive to their own ideological orientations toward women and their behavior.

Discrimination and sexism are serious and pervasive problems in statutes, law enforcement, courts, and correctional agencies. Obviously, society thinks its action will have positive consequences in the long run. Such reasoning is clearly fallacious. All society is being harmed by a serious overkill in the processing of females and by the inhumane conditions which continue to prevail in correctional agencies.

REFERENCES

ADLER, F. *Sisters in Crime: The Rise of the New Female Criminal*. New York: McGraw-Hill, 1975.

ALGAN, A. Study of delinquent and maladjusted girls in the Department of the Meure-France. *Annales de Vauenessan*, 1973, 11, 49-71.

American Criminal Law Review. Sex discrimination in the criminal law: The effect of the Equal Rights Amendment, 1973, 11, 469, 489-491.

ARDITI, R. R., GOLDBERG, F., JR., HARTLE, M., PETERS, J. H., & PHELPS, W. R. The sexual segregation of American prisoners. *Yale Law Journal*, 1973, 82 (6), 1229-1273.

ARMSTRONG, G. Females under the law—protected but unequal. *Crime and Delinquency*, 1977, 23 (2) , 109-120.

BARDWICK, J. *The Psychology of Women: A Study of Bio-Cultural Conflict.* New York: Harper & Row, 1971.

BARKER, G. H. & WILLIAM, T. A. Comparison of the delinquencies of boys and girls. *Journal of Criminal Law, Criminology and Police Science,* 1962, 53, 470-475.

BAZELON, D. L. Beyond control of the juvenile court. *Juvenile Court Journal,* 1970, 20 (Summer), p. 44.

BEAVER, H. W. *The Legal Status of Runaway Children: Final Report.* Washington, D.C., Educational Systems Corporation, April, 1975.

BENJAMIN, A. *A Commentary on the Effects of the Equal Rights Amendment on State Laws and Institutions.* Sacramento, Cal.: California Commission on the Status of Women, 1975.

BERTRAND, M. The myth of sexual equality before the law. Quebec: Society of Criminology, *Proceedings of the 5th Research Conference on Delinquency and Criminality,* 1967.

BISHOP, C. *Women in Crime.* London: Chatham & Windus, 1931.

BOUDOURIS, J. Homicide and the family. *Journal of Marriage and the Family,* 1971, 33 (November), 667-676. (Based, in part, on Dissertation "Trends in Homicide, Detroit: 1926-1968." Wayne State University, 1970).

BRENNAN, T., BLANCHARD, F., HUIZENGA, D., & ELLIOTT, D. *The Incidence and Nature of Runaway Behavior,* Final Report for DHEW, Boulder, Colorado: Behavioral Research and Evaluation Corporation, May 30, 1975.

BURKHART, K. *Women in Prison.* New York: Doubleday, 1973.

CARLSON, R. Understanding women: Implications for personality and research. *Journal of Social Issues,* 1972, 28, 2, 17-33.

CAVAN, R. *Juvenile Delinquency: Development, Treatment and Control.* Philadelphia: Lippincott, 1962.

CHESLER, P. *Women and Madness.* New York: Doubleday, 1972.

CHESNEY-LIND, M. Judicial enforcement of the female sex role: The family court and the female delinquent. *Issues in Criminology,* 1973, 8, 51-59.

CHESNEY-LIND, M. Judicial paternalism and the female status offender. *Crime and Delinquency,* 1977, 23 (2), 121-130.

CITIZEN'S TASK FORCE. Report on State Correctional Institutions at Muncy, Pennsylvania. Philadelphia, Pa.: Pennsylvania Program for Women and Girl Offenders, 1970.

CLARK, J. & HAUREK, E. W. Age and sex roles of adolescents and their involvement in misconduct: A reappraisal. *Sociology and Social Research,* 1966, 31, 516-523.

CLONINGER, R. & GUZE, S. B. Female criminals: Their personal familial and social backgrounds. *Archives of General Psychiatry,* 1970, 23, 554-558.

CONWAY, A. & BOGDAN, C. Sexual delinquency: The persistence of a double standard. *Crime and Delinquency,* 1977, 23 (2), 131-135.

COWIE, J., COWIE, V., & SLATER, E. *Delinquency in Girls.* London: Heinemann, 1968.

Crime in the United States, 1974. Uniform Crime Reports. Washington, D.C.: F.B.I., 1975.

CRITES, L. (Ed.). *The Female Offender.* Lexington, Mass.: Lexington Books, 1976.

DATESMAN, S. K., SCARPETTI, F. R., & STEPHENSON, R. Female delinquency: An application of self and opportunity theories. *Journal of Research in Crime and Delinquency,* 1975, 12, 107-123.

DAVID, L. The gentle sex? I'd rather meet a cougar. *Today's Health,* 1972, (July), 47-49.

DAVIES, J. & GOODMAN, N. *Girl Offenders Aged 17 to 20 Years.* London: Her Majesty's Stationery Office, Home Office Research Study, 1972.

DAVIS, J. A. Blacks, crime and American culture. *American Academy of Political and Social Science,* 1976, 423 (January), 89-98.

DAVIS, S. & CHAIRES, S. Equal protection for juveniles: The present status of sex-based discrimination in juvenile court laws. *Georgia Law Review*, 1973, 7, 494-532.

DINEEN, J. *Juvenile Court Organization and Status Offenses: A Statutory Profile.* Pittsburgh: National Center for Juvenile Justice, 1974.

DOLESCHAL, E. The female offender. *Crime and Delinquency Literature*, 1970, 2, 639-670.

DORSEN, N. Women, the criminal code, and the correction system. In City of New York: *The Report of the New York City Commission on Human Rights*, 1970.

DUBOIS, W. E. B. *Some Notes on Negro Crime.* Atlanta: Atlanta University Press, 1904.

DURKHEIM, E. *The Division of Labor in Society.* Glencoe, Ill.: Free Press, 1947.

ELLIS, D. & AUSTIN, P. Menstruation and aggressive behavior in a correctional center for women. *Journal of Criminal Law—Criminology and Police Science*, 1971, 62, 388-395.

FERNALD, M., HAYES, M. H. S., & DAWLEY, A. *A Study of Women Delinquents in New York State* (1968 Edition). Montclair, N.J.: Patterson Smith, 1920.

FIELD, X. *Under Lock and Key: A Study of Women in Prison.* London: Waterlow & Sons, 1963.

FLYNN, E. G. *My Life as a Political Prisoner.* New York: International Publishers, 1963.

FORER, L. *No One Will Listen—How Our Legal System Brutalizes the Youthful Poor.* New York: John Day, 1970.

FOSTER, E. *The Federal Female Offender.* Washington, D.C.: Federal Bureau of Prisons, 1974.

FRANKEL, L. J. Sex discrimination in the criminal law: The effect of the equal rights amendment. *American Criminal Law Review*, 1973, 11, 469-510.

GAGNON, J. H. & SIMON, W. The meaning of prison homosexuality. *Federal Probation*, 1968, 32, 23-29.

GIALLOMBARDO, R. *Society of Women: A Study of a Women's Prison.* New York: Wiley, 1966.

GIALLOMBARDO, R. *The Social World of Imprisoned Girls.* New York: Wiley, 1974.

GILBERT, J. Delinquent and non-delinquent girls. *British Journal of Criminology*, 1972, 325-356.

GIPSER, D. Women take to crime with a will. *The German Tribune*, 1976, 731, 14.

GLICK, R. *A Survey of Women in Prison.* Paper presented at the National Conference on Crime and Delinquency, Minneapolis, June, 1975.

GLUECK, S. & GLUECK, E. *Five Hundred Delinquent Girls.* New York: Alfred Knopf, 1934.

GOLD, M. & REIMER, D. J. Changing patterns of delinquent behavior among Americans 13 through 16 years old: 1967-1972. *Crime and Delinquency Literature*, 1975, 7, 483-517.

GOLD, S. Women, the criminal code, and the corrections system. In S. Gold (Ed.), *Women and Social Services.* New York: Discus Books, 512-515.

GOLD, S. Equal protection for juvenile girls in need of supervision in New York State. *New York Law Forum*, 1971, 57 (2).

GOODMAN, M., MALONEY, E., & DAVIS, J. *Further Studies of Female Offenders.* London: Her Majesty's Stationery Office, 1976.

GREENE, N. B. & ESSELSTYN, T. C. The beyond control girl. *Juvenile Justice*, 1972, 23, 13-19.

GRICHTING, W. *The State and Fate of Status Offenders.* Ann Arbor, Mich.: National Assessment of Juvenile Corrections, 1975. Unpublished paper.

HAFT, M. G. Women in prison: Discriminatory practices and some legal solutions. *Clearinghouse Review*, 1974, 8, 3.

HEALY, W. & BONNER, A. *Delinquents and Criminals: Their Making and Unmaking:*

Studies in Two American Cities (Judge Baker Foundation, Publication No. 3). New York: Macmillan, 1926.

HEFFERNAN, E. *Making It in Prison: The Square, the Cool and the Life.* New York: Wiley-Interscience, 1972.

HENDRIX, O. *A Study in Neglect: A Report on Women Prisoners.* New York: Women's Prison Association, 1972.

HENTIG, H. VAN. The criminality of the colored woman. University of Colorado, Series C, I No. 3, 1942.

HERMANN, M. & HAFT, M. G. *Prisoner's Rights Sourcebook.* New York: Clark Boardman, Co., 1973, pp. 341-355.

HINDELANG, M. J. Age, sex, and the versatility of delinquent involvements. *Social Problems,* 1971, 18, 522-535.

HINDELANG, M. J., DUNN, C. S., SUTTON, L. P., & AMICK, A. A. *Sourcebook of Criminal Justice Statistics—1974.* United States Department of Justice, LEAA NCJISS. Washington, D.C.: U.S. Government Printing Office, Report Nos. SD-5B-2 and SD-5B-3, 1975.

HINDELANG, M. J., DUNN, C. S., SUTTON, L. P., & AMICK, A. A. *Sourcebook of Criminal Justice Statistics—1975.* United States Department of Justice, LEAA NCJISS. Washington, D.C.: U.S. Government Printing Office, Report Nos. SD-5B-2 and SD-5B-3, 1976.

HOFFMAN-BUSTAMANTE, D. The nature of female criminality. *Issues in Criminology,* 1973, 8, 117-136.

IGLEHART, A. *Differences in Black and White Female Criminality.* University of Michigan, School of Social Work, March, 1977. Unpublished paper.

INSTITUTE OF JUDICIAL ADMINISTRATION. *The Ellery C. Decision: A Case Study of Judicial Regulation of Juvenile Status Offenders.* New York: Institute of Judicial Administration, 40 Washington Square So., 1975.

JUVENILE JUSTICE DIGEST. Discrimination shown against female juveniles in Louisville. *Juvenile Justice Digest,* 1976 (January 30), 9-10.

KANOWITZ, L. *Women and the Law: The Unfinished Revolution.* Albequerque: University of New Mexico Press, 1969.

KATZ, S. *When Parents Fail: The Law's Response to Family Breakdown.* Boston: Beacon Press, 1971.

KLEIN, D. The etiology of female crime. *Issues in Criminology,* 1973, 8 (2), 3-30.

KONOPKA, G. *The Adolescent Girl in Conflict.* Englewood Cliffs, N.J.: Prentice-Hall, 1966.

KONOPKA, G. *Young Girls: A Portrait of Adolescence.* Englewood Cliffs, N.J.: Prentice-Hall, 1976.

LANDAU, B. Adolescent female offenders: Our dilemma. *Canadian Journal of Criminology and Corrections,* 1975, 17 (April), 146-153.

LEE, L. & PAXMAN, J. M. Pregnancy and abortion in adolescence: A comparative legal survey and proposals for reform. *Columbia Human Rights Law Review,* 1974/75, 6, 307-355.

LERMAN, P. *The New Jersey Training School for Girls: A Study of Alternatives.* Rutgers University, 1974. Unpublished report.

LEVIN, M. & SARRI, R. C. *Juvenile Delinquency: A Comparative Analysis of Legal Codes in the United States.* Ann Arbor: University of Michigan, National Assessment of Juvenile Corrections, 1974.

LOMBROSO, C. & FERRERO, W. *The Female Offender.* New York: D. Appleton & Co., 1895.

MacLEOD, C. Street girls: If nobody wants you, where do you go? *Nation,* 1974, 218 (16), 486-488.

McDONOUGH, J. F. *Female Delinquency: A Review.* Unpublished paper. East Lansing, Michigan: Michigan State University, 1976.

McGOWAN, B. & BLUMENTHAL, K. Children of woman prisoners: A forgotten minority. In L. Crites (Ed.), *The Female Offender.* Lexington, Mass.: Lexington Books, 1976.

MEYER, J., et al. One hundred girls in suburban courts. *Mental Hygiene,* 1967, 51, 254-260.

MILLER, W. B. Race, sex and gangs: The molls. *Society,* 1973, 11, 32-36.

MILLER, W. B. *Violence by Youth Gangs and Youth Groups as a Crime Problem in Major American Cities.* Washington, D.C.: Office of Juvenile Justice and Delinquency Prevention, U.S. Government Printing Office, Stock No. 027-000-00499-7, 1975.

MITFORD, J. *Kind and Usual Punishment: The Prison Business.* New York: Alfred Knopf, 1973.

MITTWOCH, U. *Genetics of Sex Differentiation.* New York: Academic Press, 1973.

MONAHAN, F. *Women in Crime.* New York: Ives Washburn, 1941.

MORRIS, R. Female delinquency and relational problems. *Social Forces,* 1964, 43, 82-89.

NAGEL, S. & WEITZMAN, L. Woman as litigants. *The Hastings Law Journal,* 1971, 23, 171-198.

New York State Department of Corrections. *Annual Report,* 1973.

NORTH DAKOTA LAW REVIEW. *Female Offender: A Challenge to Court and the Legislature,* 1975, 51, 827-853.

OFFORD, D. R., FREI, J. F., & CROSS, L. A. A study of recidivism among female juvenile delinquents. *Journal of Corrective Psychiatry and Social Therapy,* 1968, 14, 166-174.

O'REILLY, C. CIZON, F., FLANAGAN, J., & PFLANICZER, S. Sentenced women in a county jail. *American Journal of Corrections,* 1968, 30, 23-25,

PAUL, E. W. The legal rights of minors to sex-related medical care. *Columbia Human Rights Law Review,* 1974/75, 6, 357-377.

PAUL, E. W., PILPEL, H. F., & WECHSLER, N. F. Pregnancy, teenagers and the law. *Family Planning Perspectives,* 1976, 8, 16-21.

PAUMIER, K. Serving time family style. *Ms.,* 1976, 4, 47.

PAYAK, B. Understanding the female offender. *Federal Probation,* 1963, 27 (4), 7-12.

Pennsylvania Program for Women and Girl Offenders. Proposed Pennsylvania criminal justice standards and goals. Philadelphia, Pa.: 1530 Chestnut Street, 1975.

POLLAK, O. *The Criminality of Women.* New York: Barnes & Co., 1950.

POLLAK, O. & FRIEDMAN, A. S. *Family Dynamics and Female Sexual Delinquency.* Palo Alto, California: Science and Behavior Books, 1964.

PRICE, R R. The forgotten female offender. *Crime and Delinquency,* 1977, 23, 101-108.

PROPPER, A. *Importation and Deprivation Perspectives on Homosexuality in Correctional Institutions: An Empirical Test of Their Relative Efficacy.* Ph.D. Dissertation. Ann Arbor: University of Michigan, 1976.

QUINNEY, R. *Criminology: Analysis and Critique of Crime in America.* Boston: Little Brown & Co., 1975.

RASCHE, C. F. The female offender as an object of criminological research. *Criminal Justice and Behavior,* 1974, 1, 301-320.

REEVES, M. *Training Schools for Delinquent Girls.* New York: Russell Sage, 1929.

RIEGE, M. G. Parental affection and juvenile delinquency in girls. *British Journal of Criminology,* 1972, 12, 55-73.

RIBACK, L. Juvenile delinquency laws: Juvenile women and the double standard of morality. *UCLA Law Review,* 1971, 19 (2), 313-342.

RIS, H. W. The integration of a comprehensive medical program in a juvenile correctional institution. *JAMWA,* 1975, 30, 367-378.

ROCHELLE, P. A. *A Study of the Social System of an Institution for Adolescent Delinquent Girls.* Ph.D. Dissertation. Berkeley, Calif.: University of California, 1965.

ROGERS, K. For her own protection: Conditions of incarceration for female juvenile offenders in the state of Connecticut. *Law and Society*, 1972, 7, 223-246.

ROSENBERG, C. & PAINE, H. Female juvenile delinquency: A 19th century followup. *Crime and Delinquency*, 1973, January, 72-78.

ROSENBLUM, K. F. Female deviance and the female sex role: A preliminary investigation. *The British Journal of Criminology*, 1975, 26, 169-185.

ROSENWEIG, M. & BRODSKY, A. *The Psychology of the Female Offender: A Research Bibliography.* University of Alabama: Center for Correctional Psychology, Report No .32, 1976.

SANDERS, H. & IRVING, L. H. Female offenders and marital disorganization: An aggressive and retreatist reaction. *International Journal of Criminology and Penology*, 1974, 2, 35-42.

SARRI, R. C. *Under Lock and Key: Juveniles in Jails and Detention.* Ann Arbor: University of Michigan, National Assessment of Juvenile Corrections, 1974.

SARRI, R. C. & HASENFELD, Y. *Brought to Justice: Juveniles, the Court and the Law.* Ann Arbor: University of Michigan, National Assessment of Juvenile Corrections, 1976.

SARRI, R. C., PROPPER, A., SELO, E., & SCUTT, J. *The Female Offender: An Annotated Bibliography.* Unpublished paper. University of Michigan, School of Social Work, 1975.

SCUTT, J. Role conditioning theory: An explanation for disparity in male and female criminality. *Australian and New Zealand Journal of Criminology*, 1972, 9, 25-35.

SCUTT, J. *Crime and Sexual Politics.* Unpublished manuscript. Sydney, Australia: Australian Law Reform Commission, 1976.

SELO, E. A comparative study of juvenile correctional institutions. In L. Crites (Ed.), *The Female Offender, op cit.*, 1976.

SHORT, J. F. & NYE, F. I. Extent of unrecorded juvenile delinquency. In J. E. Teele (Ed.), *Juvenile Delinquency: A Reader.* Itasca, Ill.: F. E. Peacock, 1970.

SILBERT, J. D. & SUSSMAN, A. The rights of juveniles confined in training schools. In M. G. Hermann and M. Haft (Eds.), *Prisoner's Rights Sourcebook.* New York: Clark Boardman, 1973, pp. 357-381.

SIMON, R. J. *The Contemporary Woman and Crime.* NIMH Crime and Delinquency Issues, DHEW Publication No. (ADM) 75-161. Washington, 1975a.

SIMON, R. J. *Women and Crime.* Lexington, Mass.: Lexington Books, 1975b.

SIMS, P. Women in southern jails. In L. Crites (Ed.), *The Female Offender.* Lexington, Mass.: Lexington Books, 1976, pp. 137-147.

SINGER, L. R. Women and the correctional process. *American Criminal Law Review*, 1973, 11 (2), 295-308.

SKOLER, D. L. & McKEOWN, J. C. *Women in Detention and Statewide Jail Standards.* Clearinghouse Bill #7, March, Washington, D.C.: American Bar Association, Commission on Correctional Facilities and Services, Statewide Jail Standards and Inspection Systems Project, 1974.

STILLER, S. & ELDER, C. PINS—A concept in need of supervision. *American Criminal Law Review*, 1974, 12, 33-60.

STROUSE, J. To be minor and female: The legal rights of women under 21. *Ms.*, 1972, 70, (ff).

SUTHERLAND, E. H. *Principles of Criminology* (Fourth Edition). Chicago: Lippincott, 1947.

SYKES, G. & MESSINGER, S. The inmate social system. In R. Cloward (Ed.), *Theoretical*

Studies in Social Organization of the Prison. New York: Social Service Research Pamphlet, No. 15, 1960, pp. 14-23.

TEMIN, C. E. Discriminatory sentencing of women offenders: The argument for ERA in a nutshell. *The American Criminal Law Review,* 1973, 2 (2), 355-372.

THOMAS, W. I. *The Unadjusted Girl.* New York: Harper & Row, 1923.

TITTLE, C. R. *Society of Subordinates: Inmate Organization in a Narcotics Hospital.* Bloomington: Indiana University Press, 1972.

TOTMAN, J. M. *The Murderess: A Psychosocial Study of the Process of Criminal Homicide.* Ph.D. Dissertation. Berkeley, Cal.: University of California, School of Social Work, 1970.

UNITED STATES DEPARTMENT OF JUSTICE, LEAA NCJISS. *National Jail Census, 1970.* Washington, D.C.: U.S. Government Printing Office, 1971.

UNITED STATES DEPARTMENT OF JUSTICE. *Crime in the United States, 1974 Uniform Crime Reports,* Federal Bureau of Investigation. Washington, D.C.: Government Printing Office, 1975.

UNITED STATES DEPARTMENT OF JUSTICE,, LEAA NCJISS. *Children in Custody: A Report on Juvenile Detention and Correctional Facility Census of 1974.* Washington, D.C.: Government Printing Office, 1976a.

UNITED STATES DEPARTMENT OF JUSTICE, LEAA NCJISS. *Survey of Inmates of State Correctional Facilities—1974.* Washington, D.C.: U.S. Government Printing Office, 1976b.

UNITED STATES DEPARTMENT OF JUSTICE, LEAA NCJISS. *Criminal Victimization in the United States: A Comparison of 1974 and 1975 Findings.* Washington, D.C.: Government Printing Office, No. SD-NCP-N-5, 1977.

UPSHUR, C. Delinquency in girls: Implications for service delivery. In Y. Bakal (Ed.), *Closing Correctional Institutions.* Lexington, Mass.: Lexington Books, 1973, pp. 19-30.

VEDDER, C. & SOMERVILLE, D. *The Delinquent Girl.* Springfield, Ill.: Charles Thomas & Co., 1970.

VELIMESIS, M. L. The female offender. *Crime and Delinquency Literature,* 1975, 7, 94-112.

VERA INSTITUTE OF JUSTICE. *Programs in Criminal Justice Reform.* New York: Vera Institute of Justice, 1972.

VINTER, R. D. (Ed.). *Time Out: A National Study of Juvenile Correctional Programs.* Ann Arbor: University of Michigan, National Assessment of Juvenile Corrections, 1976.

WARD, D. & KASSEBAUM, G. *Women's Prison: Sex and Social Structure.* Chicago: Aldine, 1965.

WHEELER, G. R. The computerization of juvenile corrections: Demystification of the therapeutic state. *Crime and Delinquency,* 1976, 22, 201-210.

WIERSMA, J. K. *Sex-Typed Offense Patterns in Juvenile Delinquent Girls: The Role of Feminine Identity and Self-Esteem.* Unpublished paper. University of Michigan, Department of Psychology, 1974.

WISCONSIN DEPARTMENT OF CORRECTIONS. *Offenders Resident in Wisconsin Juvenile Correctional Institutions.* Madison: Wisconsin, 1975, 8 pages.

WISCONSIN DEPARTMENT OF HEALTH AND SOCIAL SERVICES. *Juvenile Detention in Wisconsin.* Madison: Wisconsin, 1976, 170 pages.

WOLFGANG, M. *Patterns of Criminal Violence.* Philadelphia: University of Pennsylvania Press, 1958.

WOODEN, K. *Weeping in the Playtime of Others.* New York: McGraw Hill, 1976.

WOODS, C. H. *Women in Prison.* New York: Hurd and Houghton. 1969.

YALE LAW JOURNAL. *Ungovernability: The Unjustifiable Jurisdiction,* 1974, 83 (June), 1383-1409.

LEGAL CASES

In re Patricia A., 1972, 31 N.Y. 2d 83, 286 N.E. 2d 432.

Barefield v. *Leach,* 1974, #102-82 (D.N.M. Dec. 19).

Blondheim v. *State,* 1975, 529 P. 2d 1096, 84 Wash. 2d 874.

Commonwealth v. *Brasher,* 1971, 270 N.E. 2d 389 (Supreme Judicial Court of Bristol).

Commonwealth v. *Butler,* 1974, 458 Pa. 289, 328A 2d 251.

Commonwealth v. *Daniels,* 1968, 430 Pa. 642, 243A. 2d 400.

Connally v. *General Construction Co.,* 1926, 269 U.S. 385.

Doe v. *Bolton,* 1973, 410 U.S. 179.

Driver v. *Hinnant,* 1966, 356 F.2d 761 (4th Cir.).

Easter v. *D.C.,* 1966, 361 F.2d 50 (D.C. Cir).

E.S.G. v. *State,* 1969, 447 S.W. 2d 225 (Civ. App. Tex.).

Frontiero v. *Richardson,* 1973, 411 U.S. 677.

In re Gault, 1967, 387 U.S. 1.

Gesicki v. *Oswald,* 1971, 336 F. Supp. 365 (S.D.N.Y.).

Gonzalez v. *Mailliard,* 1971, Civil No. 50424 (N.D. Cal., Feb. 9). 1974 Vacated, 416 U.S. 918.

Goss v. *Lopez,* 1975, 419 U.S. 565.

Jones v. *T.H.,* 1976, 44 U.S.L.W. 3663 (May 25).

Kidd v. *Schmidt,* 1975, No. 74-C-605 (E.D. Wis., Aug. 15).

Lamb v. *Brown,* 1972, 456 F.2d 18 (10th Cir.).

Mercado v. *Rockefeller,* 1974, 502 F.2d 666 (2nd Cir.).

In re Oakes, 1974, 220 N.W. 2d 53 Mich. App. 629, 188.

Poe v. *Gerstein,* 1975, 420 U.S. 918.

Powell v. *Texas,* 1968, 392 U.S. 514.

Robinson v. *California,* 1962, 370 U.S. 660.

Robinson v. *York,* 1968, 281 F. Supp. 8 (D. Conn.).

Roe v. *Wade,* 1973, 410 U.S. 113.

In re Smith, 1972, 16 Md. App. 209, 295 A. 2d 238.

Stanton v. *Stanton,* 1975, 421 U.S. 7.

State v. *Chambers,* 1973, 13 Cr. L. 2330 (E.D.N.J.).

State v. *Mattiello,* 1966, 4 Conn. Cir. 55, 225 A. 2d 507.

Sumrell v. *York,* 1968, 288 F. Supp. 955 (D. Conn.).

Tinker v. *Des Moines Independent Community School District,* 1969, 393 U.S. 503.

7

PROBLEMS WITH ALCOHOL
AND OTHER DRUGS

EDITH S. GOMBERG

INTRODUCTION

Terms like "substance abuse" are widely used, yet there are a number of different meanings which attach to that term. Some, for example, are:

1. Buying drugs through criminal or quasi-criminal channels, usually on the street;
2. Using drugs which are legally forbidden, e.g. heroin;
3. Using a medication ordinarily prescribed, which has not been prescribed for the user;
4. Formation of a "dependence, psychic or physical or both, of the individual on a chemical agent" (Eddy, Halbach, Isbell, & Seevers, 1965);
5. Use of a socially acceptable and sanctioned substance like alcohol in an excessive way which causes problems for the user and for society.

Drugs in American society can be classified in a number of ways, such as: drugs which are totally proscribed or tabooed, drugs which are not to be used unless prescribed by a physician, socially sanctioned drugs sold over-the-counter, and "social drugs" like alcohol, nicotine and caffeine.

This chapter will be focused primarily on alcohol, the substance most widely used in Western societies for recreational, social, or even medicinal purposes. Other substances have, historically and at the present time, competed with alcohol for popularity as the social drug par excellence: In the last century, some opiates and anesthetics were drugs of pleasure, and cocaine has been a social pleasure drug for some groups in the last century—and it still is. Some Amerindian tribes have used peyote and mescaline. Marijuana was available to a few groups, e.g. jazz musicians, a generation ago but is available to almost everyone, including adolescents, now. A variety of substances—benzine, glue, nutmeg, etc.—may be sniffed and abused.

Drug usage is a highly complex subject area which encompasses the biomedical and psychopharmacological effects of drugs on body function and behavioral response of the user; variations in drug effects depending on the amount, the user, the context in which the drug is used; drug effects on efficiency, on mood, on sexual response, on aggressive behavior, on social interaction; field studies in which the use and effects of a substance are studied as they occur in natural settings; social attitudes toward use of different substances; the economics of substance production and distribution; and the laws and policies of government which determine which drugs will be legal and obtainable and which will not be (Brecher, 1972).

The three "social drugs" are alcohol, nicotine and caffeine; of these, the one known longest to man and most universally used has been alcohol. Alcohol has been used as tonic, sedative, soporific, anesthetic, tranquilizer, and stimulant, and it is almost universally used in celebrations and in rites. My own view was best stated by Myerson (1940), a psychiatrist writing of the conflict between hedonism and asceticism in attitudes toward alcohol:

> Men drink in celebration as well as for relief. They drink to lend ceremony, color and fellowship to life, just as surely as to banish anxiety, dread and frustration. . . . The amount of social damage done by alcoholism is enormous and if drinking is used as a way of escape, it is a futile one and overcostly. But even these facts . . . do not alter the fact that the alcoholic beverages serve useful functions in society (p. 311).

SEX DIFFERENCES IN GENERAL USE OF SUBSTANCES

Think of a continuum of drug substances ordered along a dimension of social acceptability. At one end are the most socially sanctioned drugs of all, medicine prescribed by a very high status person, a physician. Next on the spectrum come socially sanctioned and legally obtainable drugs, advertised by the media and easily purchasable: aspirin, cough syrups, some sedatives, antacids, laxatives, tonics. The next class on the spectrum are "the social drugs"; alcohol, caffeine and nicotine are not ordinarily used for medication and one can choose whether to abstain or to use. They are part of the scene, not ordinarily thought about as "drugs." And finally, at the other end of our continuum of social acceptability, there are the disapproved, illegal drugs, sometimes "soft" drugs (more easily obtainable and almost acceptable) like marijuana and sometimes "hard" drugs like heroin.

If we start with *the most socially sanctioned drugs,* medically prescribed substances, women are larger users than men. A survey in New York State showed housewives to be the most frequent users of relaxants, minor tranquilizers, barbiturates, diet pills, antidepressants and hypnotics (Chambers, 1971). Among regular users of antidepressants, for example, housewives constitute 46% of all regular users and the other 54% are divided among professional and technical workers, clerical, skilled and unskilled workers, salesworkers, farmers, unskilled workers and the unemployed. A survey in California showed large sex differences: Almost twice as many women as men were frequent users of stimulants, sedatives and tranquilizers (Manheimer, Mellinger, & Balter, 1968). A national study shows the same pattern: 13% of the men and 29% of the women report use of "psychotherapeutic" prescription drugs during the past year (Parry, Balter, Mellinger, Cisin, & Manheimer, 1973).

The 1976 Drug Alert Warning Network (DAWN) report, based on information from emergency rooms and drug crisis centers in major American cities, indicates that a widely abused prescribed drug is diazepam or Valium. Of persons being reported to the Network by these centers, 70% are women.

A Canadian study (Cooperstock, 1971) reports consistently higher prevalence of use of "mood-modifying" drugs by women in Canada, the United States and the United Kingdom. This study also reports that when 68 general practitioners are asked to describe "a typical complaintive patient" (no sex mentioned), 4% describe a male patient, 24% do not mention the sex of the patient, and 72% describe a woman patient. There is evidence that, regardless of diagnosis, women patients are prescribed psychoactive drugs more often. Cooperstock cites a British study which found that the only types of treatment that distinguished male and female neurotic patients were the proportions of tranquilizers, stimulants and sedative drugs given them. A more recent report (Cooperstock, 1976) finds a consistent 2:1 ratio of women to men "in the receipt of prescriptions for psychotropic drugs."

In another Canadian study, on drug use among adolescents and their parents (Smart & Fejer, 1972), students report parental drug use by *only mother* most frequently and the mothers' use of tranquilizers, barbiturates and stimulants was reported much more frequently than fathers' use.

The greater female use of prescribed, mood-modifying drugs is apparently a universal pattern. In a cross-national study of "anti-anxiety/sedative" drug use in nine European countries, Belgium, Denmark, France, Italy, Germany, Netherlands, Spain, Sweden and the United Kingdom, the percentage of women who used such psychoactive drugs during the past year was approximately twice the percentage of men (Balter, Levine, & Manheimer, 1974).

There is also some suggestion that *nonprescribed socially sanctioned medication sold over the counter* is more widely used by women. A household survey reports female rates of use to be higher than male use, among age groups between 15 and 44 (Bush & Rabin, 1976). We think that this sex difference may become less as people age.

The question is why the greater preponderance of women taking the prescribed, psychoactive, mood-modifying drugs? There seem to be two important aspects of women's lives and socialization which make it more likely that they will use such medication. The role of physicians and their prescribing practices have been discussed (Cooperstock, 1971, 1976) but what about the concerns and motivations of women themselves? First, there is evidence that women are more health concerned and more involved in somatic concerns than are men (we will avoid the question whether they are born that way, whether clearly visible somatic events like menstruation or childbirth are the basis or whether women learn from others to be more concerned about their bodies). Second, we think that women are socialized to look to medication as a way of relieving physical and mental discomfort more than men are. In response to the question, *When you feel worried, tense or nervous, do you ever take medicines or drugs to help you handle things?*, a recent replication of *Americans View Their Mental Health* (Gurin, Veroff, & Feld, 1960; Veroff, 1978) yields Table 1 which shows women responding affirmatively more than men in every age group. This is consistent with the American ideal of male as stoic.

The greater female concern with health and greater tendency to turn to medication are reflected, we believe, in substance abuse data. In a nationwide survey, men cite a number of drinking-related problems as major ones (Cahalan, 1970); these problems are not mentioned significantly by women drinkers. The drinking-related problem most often cited by women is "health problems." There is some support for the idea that women alcoholics, more than men, are likely to use alcohol medicinally, and women alcoholics, more than men, are likely to be concerned with alcohol-related health problems.

TABLE 1

Male and Female Response About the Use of Medication
for Tension or Anxiety

QUESTION: When you feel worried, tense or nervous, do you ever take medicines or
drugs to help you handle things?

	Percent responding Many Times or Sometimes Ages					
	21-24	25-34	35-44	45-54	55-64	65+
Male	6.9	7.5	9.7	12.8	11.6	19.8
Female	8.6	14.1	19.1	20.0	25.1	23.3

Data from Veroff, J. Personal communication, March 1978. Replication of *Americans View their
Mental Health*. Survey Research Center Project 462283, Institute for Social Research, University
of Michigan, 1976.

The fact is that more men than women use certain drug substances
(alcohol, heroin) and more women than men use other substances (e.g.
tranquilizers). This difference appears in a number of surveys, for example in a recent survey of drug use and abuse in Michigan (Alcohol and
Other Drug Abuse in the State of Michigan, 1975). For all prescribed
drugs, use by women was almost twice that for men. But twice as high a
percentage of men report illicit narcotics use during the past year and
three times as high a percentage of men than women report use of hallucinogens during the past year. The sharp contrast—more women than
men using tranquilizers and other prescribed drugs and more men using
street drugs—leads to the conclusion that the more legal and sanctioned
the substance, the greater the likelihood of women using it. The more
illegal and unsanctioned the substance, the greater the likelihood that
male usage will be greater. It is of historic interest that before the passage of the Harrison Act in 1914, the major users of opiates (in tonics
and medicines) in the United States were women.

This does not answer the question of male/female usage of the "social
drugs." As far as alcohol goes, national and cross-cultural surveys indicate quite clearly that more men use alcohol and use it in larger quan-
tities in every society about which we have information. This appears to
remain true even in the face of changing customs relating to women's
drinking.

SOCIAL DRINKING

What is the relevance of social drinking to alcoholism? With rare exceptions, alcoholism begins with ordinary social drinking and it is defined, as it develops, in terms of deviance from accepted social norms. This is a good place to note that alcoholism is a progressive, phasic disorder which usually begins with ordinary social drinking. Of those who drink, about 5% to 6% will probably develop alcoholism and another percentage will develop problems related to drinking serious enough to get them into difficulty, although they will not be diagnosed as alcoholics.

In the United States, as in most countries, normative drinking behavior for men and for women is different. More men drink, they begin earlier, they drink more and they become alcoholics more frequently. Nonetheless, the gap between the sexes in the precentage of people who drink (nonabstainers) has narrowed in the last quarter century. The percentage of American men who drink rose from 75% to 77% while the percentage of women rose from 56% to 60% (Cahalan, Cisin, & Crossley, 1969). This 60% figure will vary with age: The percentage is higher with college-age women and lower with elderly women. The percentage also varies with income, social class, ethnic group, religion and region of the country.

When Americans are compared with others, a larger percentage of male drinkers persists. Canadian figures for Ontario are 86% male and 75% female, and in Norway, percentages are 79% and 62% (Keller and Gurioli, 1976). Cross-cultural research on preliterate societies shows the same: A majority of such societies have similar sex differences in drinking norms. It is an interesting, provocative finding that sex difference is more associated with aboriginal use of alcohol and lack of sex difference in norms about drinking is more associated with postcontact introduction of alcohol (Child, Barry, & Bacon, 1965).

The relationship between increase in percentage of American women who drink and the statistics of problem drinking and alcoholism is less clear. In the 1969 survey (Cahalan, Cisin, & Crossley, 1969), 21% of the men and 5% of the women interviewed were classified as "heavy drinkers." The variability with age is interesting: Both men and women show the highest proportion of heavy drinkers in the age group 45 to 49 but women show another peak at ages 21 to 24, attributed to dating and mate-seeking behavior.

The recent second survey of *Americans View Their Mental Health* (Veroff, 1978) included a question about "escape drinking," i.e. drinking to minimize anxieties. The question did not ask about quantity, only about the use of alcohol as a substance used in times of stress. When men and women respondents are compared, there are more men in each age group. Note in Table 2 that the percentage of women who use alcohol as tension-reducer peaks in the 21-24 year age group and again in the 45-54 age group is consistent with the findings of the 1969 survey. Note, too, that there are more men and women in each age group but that the difference is smallest in the 21-24 age group. The peak in heavy-escape drinking for men appears in the forties but the rise in percentage is a gradual one from early childhood. Women, on the other hand, show a peak in their early twenties, the percentage then drops and rises gradually to the forties.

Recent surveys of adolescent alcohol and drug usage have caused a good deal of uneasiness. Yearly surveys of junior and senior high school students in San Mateo County, California, from 1968 to 1977 show large increases in the percentage of girls who drink. The largest percent increase among girls is in the use of marijuana but there are increases in the reported use of most drug substances (Blackford, 1975, 1976, 1977). Another study of junior and senior high school students reports similar findings: Although a smaller percentage of girls in the study drink and although they drink less than the boys, 17.8% of the girls are classified as moderate/heavy and heavy drinkers. The comparable figures for the boys was 31% (Rachel, Williams, Brehm, Cavanaugh, Moore, & Eckerman, 1975). A third study finds, "the margin of difference between the proportion of both sexes who report drinking is decreased, and, in fact, girls report a significantly greater proportion as using multiple drugs

TABLE 2

Male and Female Response About the Use of Alcohol to
Reduce Tension and Nervousness

QUESTION: When you feel worried, tense or nervous, do you ever take medicines or drugs to help you handle things?

	Percent responding Sometimes Ages				(Many times: very small N)	
	21-24	25-34	35-44	45-54	55-64	65+
Male	9.8	12.4	14.6	18.3	10.3	5.8
Female	8.6	4.3	6.9	7.8	1.6	2.0

Data from Veroff, J. Personal communication, March 1978. Replication of *Americans View their Mental Health.* Survey Research Center Project 462283, Institute for Social Research, University of Michigan, 1976.

(Wechsler & McFadden, 1976). There is, clearly, a normative change in the drinking behavior of adolescents: It begins at a younger age than was true a generation ago, and the sex difference in percentage of users has decreased. And while the reported increase in frequency of intoxication is greater for girls than for boys, Knupfer and Room's (1964) caveat still seems appropriate:

> While the younger generation, showing almost no sex difference in the proportion of abstainers, reflects the effects of the emancipation of women, this emancipation does not include an extension to women of the young man's license to drink heavily (p. 235).

Emancipation has apparently moved further since Knupfer and Room wrote these words and license-for-intoxication has apparently increased among young women. Nonetheless, intoxication and alcoholism are not synonymous and the interpretation of the various survey findings as indicating an epidemic of adolescent alcoholism seems unwarranted. It is true that adolescents with drinking problems do appear at treatment facilities but the changes in drinking behavior in recent years seem to reflect two phenomena: increases in alcohol consumption in general, and adult ambivalence in lowering (and then, in some cases, raising) the legal drinking age. The standards of adolescent behavior have changed in many ways—economic, sexual and familial—and drinking and substance use seem to be part of that change. Double standards of behavior for boys and for girls are questioned and shrinking differences in the percentage who drink is part of the challenge of social change. Sexual activity as well as drinking behavior begins earlier than it did a generation ago. It seems important that we follow up with a study of the survey adolescents as they become adults; some will probably become alcoholic but others may not because they have already tried out some "wild" behavior and not found it rewarding.

Although there is a good deal of epidemiological information about drinking, there is remarkably little about the drinking behavior itself or about the customs and contexts of drinking. Is the drinking reported in the adolescent surveys done at parties, in peoples' homes, in small groups, in mixed sex groups, at school, in cars, with parents?

There has been more research interest in the *effects* of drinking than in the reasons for drinking. One study which compared the sexes in motivation for drinking (Edwards, Hensman, & Peto, 1973) utilized a 17-item questionnaire, and women rated as significantly lower these reasons for drinking: thirst, boredom, habit and job demands. Both sexes were similar in "ataractic" motivation, and for men, this factor is a good predictor both of the quantity drunk and the related troubles. For women, a second factor, drinking for "sophisticated" reasons, was a better predictor of quantity, and a third factor, social pressure to drink, was important as a predictor of alcohol-related troubles. This third factor may link to the frequent report that women alcoholics have a problem-drinking spouse and/or alcoholic relatives more frequently than do male alcoholics. Is that what women mean by social pressure to drink?

Research on the effects of drinking has not, until recently, differentiated between male and female subjects, avoiding the whole question usually by using only male subjects. Recently, there have been a few alcohol experiments which involve some measurement of sexual response of young male and female subjects (Wilson & Lawson, 1978), but the complexities of sexual behavior, with or without alcohol, have been little explored. A recent review:

> Research on alcohol and sexual behavior, the little that has been done, has emphasized copulation or elements of it. . . . What is the role of alcohol in the dating-courtship-mating pattern? When two activities (drinking, dating-courtship-mating) occur in a large portion of society, the chances are that some individuals engage in both, possibly at the same time. (Carpenter & Armenti, 1972, p. 525)

In the work of Marlatt and his colleagues on alcohol and its relation to stress and aggression, there is one study which involves an equal number of male and female college student subjects, identified as "heavy social drinkers" (Marlatt, Kosturn, & Lang, 1975). Some subjects were provoked to anger, some were angered and given an opportunity to retaliate and both groups were compared with a no-provocation, no-retaliation control group to see which group consumed most alcohol. Provoked subjects drank most, the control group an intermediate amount and the anger-retaliation group drank least. Male and female subjects responded similarly although the women did more sipping and drank a lesser quantity than the men.

Experiments which have aroused a great deal of interest are those of Jones and his co-workers. Their findings indicate that with equivalent amounts of alcohol (adjusted to body weight), young women reach higher blood alcohol levels than do young men (Jones & Jones, 1976a). Women tested at various stages of the menstrual cycle show variation in blood alcohol concentration with amount of alcohol constant; higher levels are obtained at the premenstrual phase than at other times in the cycle (Jones & Jones, 1976b). Young women who are taking oral contraceptives show differences in the metabolism of alcohol when they are compared with women who do not take oral contraceptives (Jones, Jones, & Parades, 1976). Clearly there is a relationship between hormonal status and the effects of alcohol. Jones and his collaborators are now following through with research on sex differences in efficiency of cognitive functioning under alcohol conditions.

One obvious question which relates to sex difference in effects of alcohol is the effect of drinking on the fetus. The impact of the reported work and the attendant publicity about "the fetal alcohol syndrome" has been sizable. A recent issue of National Institute on Alcohol Abuse and Alcoholism Information and Feature Service contains this headline: "Social Drinking Affects Behavior of Newborns" (March 3, 1978). The news story goes on to state that,

> behaviors often reported present in babies with fetal alcohol syndrome or neonatal narcotic abstinence syndrome—excessive irritability and hyperactivity—were not observed in the babies of social drinkers, who, in fact, appeared to be less active on the first day of life (p. 3).

The evidence is not altogether clear and the limits of safe drinking during pregnancy are not known but the media's interest in this phenomenon, as well as in "addicted babies," has created, irresponsibly, an aura of anxiety. The complexities of the influence of parental alcohol ingestion on the offspring are manifest in a recent report of a study with rats (Pfeifer, MacKinnon, & Seiser, 1977). The experimenters in this study gave the alcohol to the *father* and they report that "alcohol consumption by males may adversely affect the growth, viability and behavior of their offspring" (p. 6).

DRUNKENNESS

The negative attitudes toward female intoxication have been discussed elsewhere (Gomberg, 1974). The findings are that attitudes of disapproval are widespread, expressed by both men and women and by people of different income levels. Cross-cultural comparison indicates that most societies limit drinking and drunkenness more for women than for men, and Child, Barry and Bacon (1965) conclude, "It seems reasonable . . . The general social roles of the sexes make drunkenness more threatening in women than in men" (p. 60). Knupfer (1964) suggests that such attitudes offer "cultural protection" for women, i.e. those taboos make alcoholism less likely. Further, she suggests that the greater disapproval of female drunkenness may be rooted in two perceptions: (a) that drunkenness in women involves loss of sensitivity to others' needs, and (b) that drunkenness in women involves the loss of customary sexual restraints.

It is interesting that this theme is echoed and supported in some recent observations. Although LeMasters (1975) is referring to women alcoholics rather than to intoxicated women in general, his observation is relevant: "It seems that the customers of the Oasis (bar) apply two tests: (1) does the woman neglect her children as a result of excessive drinking; and (2) does she become sexually promiscuous when drinking?" (p. 152). A footnote (p. 161) adds, "Note that they do not concern themselves about male promiscuity, only female."

Stafford and Petway (1977) interviewed white, middle-class urban people and concluded that there is little sex difference in the stigmatization of men versus women problem drinkers. However, their findings suggest that, "drunkenness in women may be more stigmatizing than drunkenness in men." This stigmatization was related by the respondents to selfishness and to immorality (insensitivity to others' needs and promiscuity?). In this study, attitudes toward problem drinking on the one hand and toward drunkenness on the other may be distinguished; could it be that public education has softened attitudes toward women alcoholics but that the double standard of feeling about *intoxication* of men and women remains untouched Nor is it clear that attitudes have softened: Women problem drinkers are rated as "significantly more hopeless" than male problem drinkers. The long-standing belief in the poorer prognosis of women alcoholics has not gone away.

Different attitudes toward male and female drunkenness will lead, obviously, to different courses of action. A study of enlisted women in the military services shows that many of the women who were hospitalized to sober up were not really diagnosable as alcoholic but had been intoxicated and engaged in a "mild rule infraction" which led to their hospitalization (Schuckit & Gunderson, 1975). The authors note that most servicemen or civilian men would not have been hospitalized under similar circumstances.

What are the deep hidden anxieties on which negative attitudes toward female intoxication are based? It is true that the realities of social role make the stronger taboo for women reasonable enough, but the feelings of antipathy associated with female drunkenness do seem to relate to some basic anxieties: Perhaps the perceived loss of sensitivity to others' needs is related to basic, childhood fears about abandonment by mother, or perhaps the perceived loss of customary sexual restraints is based on primitive anxieties about the carnality of women out of control?

Although there is not much recent work reported, we think that the dislike of female drunkenness is still strong. The limits of acceptable social/public behavior for women have certainly shifted: A half century ago, "nice" women did not live non-married with men (at least not openly), and drinking in public places by women was far less prevalent. Yet, even with change, there are attitudes which are resistant to change and it is probably safe to say that living-together-without-marriage is more acceptable but promiscuity and "sleeping around" are not. The right to drink and the right to drink publicly have become women's rights. Nevertheless, while female public drinking is accepted, it is still more characteristic of female drinking that it occurs in private settings, at home, at social gatherings. As societal perceptions and prohibitions change, we need more information about the perception of public and private intoxication—how people define drunkenness and how they feel about it.

An old phrase of Ogden Nash's, "Candy is dandy but liquor is quicker," does not appear to be outdated. I am surprised at the number of young women who tell me, often regretfully, that their first sexual encounter occurred after a party in which, lacking both drinking and sexual experience, they drank too much. Alcohol and sex are linked in people's minds. Apparently, many people still think of alcohol and seduction as linked. Further, as shown in Chapter 11, alcohol is certainly a critical factor in issues about rape.

PROBLEM DRINKING AND ALCOHOLISM

The terms *problem drinking* and *alcoholism will* be used interchangeably. The definition of alcoholism or problem drinking is not generally agreed upon, even by people working with alcoholic patients. Some therapists emphasize "loss of control." Many social scientists favor a definition which is based on social, medical, legal and economic problems which develop as a result of drinking excessively. Alcoholics Anonymous has a view of alcoholism as a disease and sets the goal of total sobriety as the definition of successful outcome. Others view alcoholism as a form of deviant behavior (which may have diagnosable medical consequences which constitute disease), raising the question of whether some problem drinkers might relearn drinking behavior and return to moderate social drinking. Alcoholism has been described as "an impulse neurosis," a disease, a rule-breaking deviant behavior, and a set of consequences which results from continued excessive drinking. For our purposes, it is worth noting that alcoholic behavior develops *over time* and in a reasonably predictable sequence. It is therefore possible to speak of *early* and *late* alcoholic stages. Alcoholism may vary along an acuteness-chronicity dimension, and persons who manifest diagnosable alcoholism may drink in a variety of ways: daily or on periodic binges, privately or publicly, to peak blood alcohol levels or to plateau blood alcohol levels. The way people drink is one of the many ways in which alcoholic people can be classified and it is used for such classification by Jellinek (1960).

Studies of female alcoholism make different kinds of comparison, i.e. the control group varies from study to study. Research comparisons fall into the following groupings: (a) studies which compare men and women alcoholics, usually at the same rehabilitation facility (Curlee, 1970; James, 1975; Lisansky, 1957; Mulford, 1977; Pemberton, 1967; Wanberg & Knapp, 1970); (b) studies which compare alcoholic women with non-alcoholic women (Belfer, Shader, Carroll, & Harmatz, 1971; McLachlan, Walderman, Birchmore, & Marsden, 1976; Wilsnack, 1973); and (c) studies which make comparison of subcategories within a general group of alcoholic women, e.g. alcoholic women at an outpatient clinic and in a state prison (Lisansky, 1957), remitted and unremitted women patients (Dunlap, 1961), women diagnosed as primary or secondary alcoholics (Schuckit, Pitts, Reich, King, & Winokur, 1969).

The Epidemiology of Problem Drinking

As with other deviance disorders like delinquency and narcotic addiction, alcoholism is more a male disorder than a female disorder. In any country in the world where data are available, the ratio involves more males. It is stated occasionally that there are now as many women alcoholics in the U.S. as male alcoholics but there is no real evidence of that. In looking at male/female ratios of alcoholism, there are a number of questions which must be raised: Are the ratios based on *estimates* of alcoholism in a community (as, for example, with the Jellinek statistical formula) or are ratios based on *numbers* derived from treatment facilities and doctors' offices? If ratios are based on census figures from treatment facilities, we know that the ratio of men to women patients varies widely depending on the type of facility (doctor's office, hospital, outpatient clinic, Alcoholics Anonymous). If we consider first estimates and surveys which relate to the number of men and women alcoholics in the U.S., estimates based on variations of the Jellinek formula (an equation based on frequency of death from liver cirrhosis) yield an estimate of five males for every one female. Surveys, dealing with alcoholism which is not officially diagnosed as such and varying somewhat in criteria for defining who is or is not an alcoholic, yield a 4:1 ratio of men to women alcoholics (Cahalan, Cisin, & Crossley, 1969; Rutledge, Carroll, & Perkins, 1974). A recent report on persons who came to alcoholism treatment programs in 45 community centers throughout the U.S. (Armor, Polich, & Stambul, 1976) finds a ratio of 4½:1. Recent New York State mental hospital statistics (New York State Department of Mental Hygiene, 1977) show a male to female ratio of alcoholism as primary diagnosis of 4½:1.

In general, the ratio of 4 to 5 male alcoholics for every female alcoholic appears to hold up, although this ratio will vary with setting, the highest proportion of female alcoholics being reported by physicians in private practice and the lowest proportion on Skid Row:

> 1:1 ratio—In a study of physicians in private practice, more than a third report that women comprise half or even more of their problem drinking patients (Jones & Helrich, 1972).
> 2:1 ratio—The 1974 survey of the membership of Alcoholics Anonymous shows that women alcoholics constituted 31% of those who joined A.A. in the three-year period before the survey (Norris, 1974).
> 3:1 ratio—A state hospital serving a high-income suburban area close to New York City reported this ratio for admissions for alcoholism (Oltman & Friedman, 1965).
> 4.4:1—The number of men and women alcoholics admitted to treatment facilities in Oklahoma during 1974 show the ratio for that state to be almost 4½ to 1 (Alcohol Technical Reports, 1975).
> A recent Iowa study of alcoholic men and women coming for treatment to community alcoholism centers shows a 9:1 ratio (Mulford, 1977) and a state hospital in Minnesota reports an 11:1 ratio (Hoffman & Noem, 1975).

To complicate matters further, there are quite different ratios depending on the criterion of alcoholism used. Edwards, Hensman and Peto (1972) point this up very effectively in comparing male/female ratios in the United Kingdom, based on different drinking problems. If "drunkenness arrests" are used for comparison, the male to female ratio is 14:1; if mental hospital admission for alcoholism is used, the ratio is 5:1; and if death from liver cirrhosis is used, the ratio becomes approximately 1:1.

Some interesting questions emerge from the epidemiological data.

When a social problem has public attention (and alcohol and the status of women are both matters of public concern), growing media attention gives an impression that the problem has magnified. Although more women engage in social drinking now and although the proportion who become problem drinkers may be slightly larger than it was a generation ago (and we can never be sure that we are not looking at increased willingness to come out of the closet), there is no real evidence of a large increase in rates of female alcoholism. Women have a longer life expectancy than do men, leading one to expect perhaps that there will be a change in male/female ratios of alcoholism in the geriatric population. A recent community survey of elderly persons (Rathbone-McCuan, Lohn, Levenson, & Hsu, 1976) shows a 5:1 ratio. If one argues that older persons are a population group socialized at a time when drinking was less acceptable among women, there are other data. Although the proportion of college women who drink socially has risen from 61% in 1950 surveys to 75% in 1977, while the proportion for college men has risen from 79% to 80% over the same time period, a recent study shows that five times as many men students are heavy drinkers (Engs, 1977). It is good to recognize a problem like female alcoholism which has been denied in the past but it is unnecessary to exaggerate its dimensions.

There is a consistent finding which merits further study. Cahalan, Cisin and Crossley (1969) reported a peak in proportion of heavy drinkers for women in the age group 21-24. The recent second survey of *Americans View Their Mental Health* (Veroff, 1978) included a question about family problems related to drinking. Although more men than women report such family problems, the percentage is higher among women respondents in the age group 21-24; 4% of the men and 5% of the women report family concern about their drinking (Table 3). It is not illogical: Perhaps parents are more concerned with a daughter's drinking than with a son's, perhaps a young husband is more concerned with his wife's drinking than the other way round. Certainly the young man who goes off on a drinking spree, gets drunk and acts out is less likely to be a source of concern to his family than the young woman who does the same. But there is more—if one examines the statistics about people admitted to New York state hospitals with primary diagnosis of alcoholism or with alcohol abuse checked in the admission problem list (New York State Department of Mental Hygiene, 1977), the proportions of male to female *under 20* are quite different from those *over 20*. Alcoholic admission of persons under 20 include a *higher* proportion of women than is true in the other age groups. It is not clear what this all means. A recent

TABLE 3

Male and Female Response About Drinking-Related Family Problems

QUESTION: Have there ever been problems between you and anyone in your family (spouse, parent, child or other close relative) because you drank alcoholic beverages?

	Percent responding Many Times or Sometimes Ages					
	21-24	25-34	35-44	45-54	55-64	65+
Male	4.0	8.7	9.2	10.3	9.1	8.0
Female	5.0	4.6	3.2	2.1	5.8	.4

Data from Veroff, J. Personal communication, March 1978. Replication of *Americans View their Mental Health*. Survey Research Center Project 462283, Institute for Social Research, University of Michigan, 1976.

analysis of alcoholism ward admissions (Selzer, Gomberg, & Nordhoff, in press) showed a very small number of admissions of persons under 20 (*N* of four), all female. Is it possible that we are dealing with different phenomena manifested by young women in relation to alcohol use? Are there some adolescent girls who get into trouble with alcohol and who are more likely to be hospitalized than their male counterparts? Is the peak of heavy-drinking-and-family-objection in the college, early working and dating years? Are we dealing with the same young women who might be narcotic addicts, and what determines choice of major substance? Are there problems relating to alcohol with some adolescent girls which link up with the increase in sexual behavior and pregnancies in that age group? Are there physiological differences which make heavy drinking among adolescent girls more serious from a medical point of view than heavy drinking among adolescent boys, or are we confronting again a double standard of acceptable limits so that drunken adolescent boys are "sowing wild oats" and drunken adolescent girls are more likely to be disturbing to others? There are all complex questions related to prevention and early casefinding, which need research attention.

WHAT DO WE KNOW ABOUT ALCOHOLISM IN MEN AND WOMEN?

There have been many reviews which summarize the research and clinical literature about alcoholic women (e.g. Gomberg, 1976; Johnson & Garzon, 1977; Lindbeck, 1972; Lisansky, 1957). In addition, there are annotated bibliographies (Women and Psychoactive Drug Use, 1976), proceedings of Congressional hearings (Alcohol Abuse Among Women: Special Problems and Unmet Needs, 1976) and conference proceedings (Workshop on Alcoholism and Alcohol Abuse Among Women: Research Issues, in preparation). We will here summarize the findings on antecedents of female alcoholism, on manifestations of male and female alcoholism, and on the consequences for men and for women.

Antecedents of Female Alcoholism

The literature on proneness or apparent high risk factors related to alcohol problems among women have been recently reviewed (Gomberg, in preparation) and will be here summarized:

1. Antecedents which are genetic in nature have not been clearly linked to the development of problem drinking in women (Goodwin, Schulsinger, Knop, Mednick, & Guze, 1977). A relationship exists between blood alcohol level and phase of menstrual cycle, probably with hormonal events in general, but we do not know how this relationship links to problem drinking. The incidence of gynecological obstetrical difficulties is reportedly high among alcoholic women (Kinsey, 1966; Wilsnack, 1973), but it is unclear whether these precede problem drinking and act as one sort of precipitant or whether the difficulties are consequential as a result of continued heavy drinking. There appears to be a relationship between age of onset of heavy drinking, female hormonal status and liver cirrhosis (Rankin, Schmidt, Popham, & deLint, 1975).

2. There is more disruption in early family history among women alcoholics than among men alcoholics. Table 4 shows the percentage of women alcoholics who report a parent missing, psychiatrically ill or alcoholic in various studies. An early history of family disruption is also true of women who manifest other forms of deviant behavior and it suggests that such history, in the absence of compensatory factors, produces a heightened vulnerability to psychological disorder. The woman alcoholic, as adolescent, has been described as depressed, distrustful and self-negating (Jones, 1971). Some adolescents who later become alcoholic appear to be overtly rebellious and to have impulse control problems; we would guess that these adolescents are likely to develop problem drinking relatively early, i.e. as young women. Another group of women alcoholics seem to have been, as adolescents, overtly compliant, passive and "feminine"; we would guess that these are the one who identify strongly with traditional roles, wife and mother, who find that marriage

Table 4

History of Disruption in Family of Origin: Percentages
Reported by Research Studies

Year	Investigator	% of female alcoholics	% of male alcoholics
Loss/parent absent			
1958	Rosenbaum	40%	
1964	deLint	37%	13%
1966	Kinsey	72%	
Parent absent or psychiatrically ill			
1968	Winokur & Clayton	39%	22%
Alcoholism/problem drinking in family of origin			
1937	Wall	50%	71%
1955	Sherfey	68%	50%
1957	Lisansky: clinic Ss	44%—either parent	35%
		24%—sibling	9%
	prison Ss	51%—either parent	
		19%—sibling	
1958	Rosenbaum	40%—fathers	
1964	Wood & Duffy	51%—fathers	
1966	Johnson et al.	34%—fathers	
		31%—sibling	
1966	Kinsey	34%—fathers	
1968	Winokur & Clayton	40%	24%
1970	Sclare	40%	females outnumbered males, difference not significant
1971	Jacob & Lavoie	42%	
		42%—sibling	
1971	Rathod & Thomson	60%	
1972	Jones, R. W.	30%	23%
1975	Hoffman & Noem	26%—fathers	24%
		6%—mothers	5%
1976	Browne-Mayers et al.	50%	

and motherhood do not yield the fantasies of happiness, who feel depressed and guilty. Later onset is probably more characteristic of the latter group. They are the ones who are seen most often in treatment facilities and the ones on whom most of the research literature is based.

3. Drinking behavior and conditions which are antecedent to later problem drinking include heavy/escape drinking and peer pressure for heavy drinking. Indicators of potential trouble seem to be traumatic life events or personal crises which act as stressors and early medical/health problems resulting from alcohol consumption (Cahalan, 1970). Fillmore (1974, 1975) has reported follow-up, 20 years later, of women subjects in a college drinking survey; most predictive of later drinking problems were "some degree of intoxication" and "psychological dependence" for women subjects.

4. Social environmental stresses generated within the family or from one's role and status in the community may lead to heavy drinking among women. Environmental stresses generated within the family include alcoholism in a significant other. This includes a heavy or problem drinking parent, sibling or other family-of-origin model and/or a heavy or problem drinking spouse. As an antecedent, the presence of a heavy drinking or alcoholic significant other in the woman's life, past or present, is almost universally reported to be present to a greater extent than is true of the general population and to a greater extent than is true of male alcoholics. Reflecting the role of stress from one's status in the community; it has been shown that women who are at high risk for depression and for mental disorder in general are those who are lower-class, nonwhite, separated or divorced, head of family, breadwinner with young children at home (Guttentag, Salasin, & Legge, 1976). We think that the same may be said for alcoholism and substance abuse. Very little has been written about the pressures of the workplace, about juggling multiple responsibilities, about minority group stresses as contributing antecedents to alcohol problems of women. Most research on female alcoholism has been about white, middle-class women. Epidemiological evidence suggests that low-income and minority group women tend to be abstainers to a greater extent than middle-class white women, but of those who drink, a higher proportion will be heavy drinkers. A higher proportion of black women than white are abstainers but of those who drink, 11% of the black women and 4% of the white women were heavy drinkers (Cahalan, Cisin, & Crossley, 1969). In a blue collar population (Siassi, Crocetti, & Spiro, 1973), the proportion of women abstainers is much higher than the national average: Three-quarters of the women

workers were non-drinkers. Of those who did drink, over a third were heavy drinkers. Does middle-class status offer women more alternatives between abstinence and heavy drinking?

5. Any high risk factor taken by itself is not predictive. Even women who drink heavily do not necessarily become alcoholic. But the summative effect of childhood deprivation, stormy adolescence, lack of trust in others or low self-esteem, peer pressure to drink, drinking for escape from problems, and heavy or alcoholic drinking engaged in by a significant other in the family is a much greater likelihood of alcohol problems.

Alcoholic Behaviors of Men and Women

Before we describe some of the comparisons between men and women's symptomatology and behaviors relating to alcohol, it is important to emphasize that alcoholism is *not* a single, unitary disorder and that generalizations made about one subgroup of alcoholic persons must be applied cautiously to others. There are alcoholics who live on Skid Row and alcoholics who are wealthy and powerful persons. There are alcoholics who are stormy people from childhood, constantly in one kind of difficulty or another, and there are alcoholic persons who have led exemplary lives, avoiding trouble until middle age. The heterogeneity among alcoholics has been responded to with classifications, i.e., Knight's (1937) essential vs. reactive distinction or primary vs. secondary alcoholism (Schuckit, Pitts, Reich, King, & Winokur, 1969).

It might be a good idea to start classification of women alcoholics something like this: Group A would consist of women alcoholics for whom onset occurs in their teens or twenties. They are more likely to have begun using alcoholic beverages recreationally, for pleasure, and they are more likely to have difficulties in impulse control; they may resemble other deviance groups of young women like delinquents or narcotic addicts, and they are closer to the *essential* or *primary* alcoholic than is Group B. Group B would include women with onset of alcoholism in their thirties and forties. They may have used alcohol recreationally at an earlier part of the life cycle but they have begun to use it medicinally to cope with feelings of depression, disappointment, abandonment and low self-esteem. Group B is closer to the *reactive* or *secondary* alcoholic. This classification does not deal with other variables, e.g., it omits social class differences, but it is a place to start in comprehending the complexities of female alcoholism.

Onset and precipitants. Research findings reported to date show that women begin their drinking somewhat later than men do but tend to seek out treatment at approximately the same age—duration is, therefore, shorter. This differential continues to show up in male/female alcoholic comparisons (Bromet & Moos, 1976; Mulford, 1977). Women report more frequently than men that a traumatic event like a divorce, a death or some kind of loss precipitated the alcoholic drinking. Since we have not systematically gathered life histories from women alcoholics, we have no way of verifying whether the stress is used defensively to explain away the alcoholism or whether the person reporting manifested no alcoholic behavior before the stressful event. A recent report (Mulford, 1977) about alcoholics at community treatment centers includes 395 women problem drinkers; compared to men, the women "evidenced more psychological stress," and more frequently reported, "an emotional crisis during the year prior to intake." If a heavy drinking or alcoholic significant other is considered a stressful precipitant, the evidence is clear that it occurs far more frequently in the history of female alcoholics than in the history of male alcoholics.

Early and later stages. A recent report (James, 1975) compares responses of men and women members of Alcoholics Anonymous on a questionnaire dealing with the sequence of various symptoms. Early stage behavior of women includes "personality change when drinking," "drinking before facing a new situation," and feeling "more intelligent and capable when drinking." These are not reported by men. The male alcoholics do report flashes of aggressiveness and grandiosity, and sneaking and gulping drinks earlier than do the women. Both sexes report increased tolerance, rationalizations, periods of abstinence, unwillingness to discuss drinking and blackouts as early stage signs, and both sexes report binges, morning drinking, tremors and a loss of tolerance as later stage symptoms. The progression of alcoholic behaviors of men and women is an important research area with implications for prevention, early case-finding and rehabilitation.

Quantity and contexts of drinking. Rimmer, Pitts, Reich and Winokur (1971) noted significant differences between hospitalized men and women alcoholics. Men, compared with women patients, showed the following:

    earlier onset of alcohol problems;
    younger age at first drink;
    more daily and morning drinking;
    more frequent weekly consumption of over 32 ounces of distilled
        spirits;
    more bender drinking;
    more histories of delirium tremens;

more blackouts;
more frequent loss of jobs and friends because of drinking;
more histories of school problems;
more histories of "reckless youth";
more alcohol-related arrests;
fewer suicide attempts.

A factor analytic study of 60 commonly reported alcoholism symptoms (Horn & Wanberg, 1973) found much similarity in men's and women's reports, but there were a number of items that significantly differentiated the sexes:

Women begin to drink and experience first intoxication later.
Women more often drink at home, alone or with spouse.
Women have shorter drinking bouts.
Women more often use alcohol to improve job performance.
Men lose jobs more frequently because of drinking.
Men are more often gregarious and women are more often solitary drinkers.
Women more often perceive their alcoholism as getting worse.

Certain findings keep appearing and reappearing: Women drink more frequently at home, alone or with spouse; men go on benders more; women seem to drink less distilled beverages; women are more often solitary drinkers.

The use of substances other than alcohol. The point was made earlier in the chapter that women generally are larger users of medically prescribed psychoactive drugs than are men. It follows with inexorable logic that alcoholic women are larger users of other substances, particularly tranquilizers and barbiturates, than are alcoholic men. The point has been extensively documented: For example, Curlee (1970) reported that 10% of the men and 25% of the women she interviewed in a private hospital were dependent on drugs other than alcohol, and a more recent report from the same hospital (Kammeier, 1977) found strong male/ female differences in regard to "alcohol and polydrug usage." Freed (1973) has reviewed studies of substance abuse by alcoholics and in the six research reports in which men and women alcoholics are compared, the percentage of men using tranquilizers and sedatives is smaller than the percentage of women in every instance. One conclusion which flows from this documented difference in use of other substances is that, other things being equal, women alcoholics are probably at high risk for the negative consequences of drug interactions and drug potentiations.

Other diagnostic features. Depression characterizes both male and female alcoholics. Separating depression as cause and depression as a concomitant or an effect of the alcoholism is another question but, at the time we see them in treatment facilities, a large majority of alcoholic patients, men and women, are depressed, and it is difficult to say whether it is more characteristic of one group than another.

There is a male alcoholism syndrome which includes an early history of hyperactivity (Tarter, McBride, Buonpane, & Schneider, in preparation); this syndrome has not been noted among women. Gomberg (in press) found sociopathic acting out behavior and defiance of authority in school and in the military to be more characteristic of early-onset male alcoholic veterans than late-onset older male alcoholic veterans. In this study, the history and psychological test performance of the younger men often resembled those of juvenile delinquents. This might be related to work reported by Cloninger and Guze (1970) with female delinquents in which they note, "a significant association between sociopathy and hysteria." We might hypothesize that the female early-onset alcoholic will manifest significantly more sociopathic behavior and the behavior patterns of the hysterical personality than will the older, late-onset alcoholic woman. Pattison (1976) has noted the frequency of "hysteric personality structure" in a sample of 50 women alcoholics; age of onset, however, is not noted. Hoffman and Jackson (1974) report that male alcoholics score significantly higher on scales for character disorders on a test inventory and female alcoholics score significantly higher on scales for neuroticism. These results are obtained in a state hospital setting. Perhaps the type of treatment facility, as well as the age of onset, must be considered in making any generalizations about samples of alcoholic men and women and their diagnostic characteristics.

It is difficult to say who is more depressed, men or women alcoholics. As is true in the general population, women report symptoms of depression more frequently when they are alcoholic. The differential in suicide which is true of men and women in general is apparently true of alcoholic men and women: Women make suicide attempts more often, but the suicide rates are higher for men.

Sex-role conflict. Research in sex-role conflicts has resulted in some interesting, parallel discoveries about male and female alcoholism. In 1960, the McCords wrote about "a façade of intense masculinity" to describe the alcoholics they were studying, and, in 1968, Jones, in a report of longitudinal follow-up of persons studied when they were younger, described male alcoholics—as adolescents—as overplaying the

active, masculine role (Gomberg, 1968). Work of the last few years has
found the same overidentification with traditional sexual role in alcoholic
women subjects (Kinsey, 1966; Wilsnack, 1973). There seem to be several
different issues here. First, it appears to be true that men and women who
become alcoholic tend to be strongly identified with *traditional sex roles*
and the development of their alcoholism appears to be related to their
difficulties in making it work. Second, what we see when we interview
alcoholics after they have become problem drinkers is a high degree of
conflict over sexual role. Whether this conflict existed from early life is
difficult to judge, but it seems more likely that the conflict develops over
their problems in making the traditional roles work out in a gratifying,
rewarding way. This is probably linked to the anger manifested by many
alcoholic persons—as though gratification which was supposed to be
delivered had failed to show. Third, there is a very special problem here
for women because "femininity," as measured by our test instruments
and defined in the culture, involves dependency and passivity, the anti-
thesis of independence and good coping skills. In a classic study, Broverman, Broverman, Clarkson, Rosenkrantz, and Vogel (1970) found that
clinical judgments of therapists involved a double standard with "greater
social value of masculine stereotypic characteristics." Some recent research has raised questions about the terms "masculine," "feminine," and
"androgynous," suggesting that the terms relate to self-esteem, competence
and social skills (Colten, 1978). What needs investigation now is the
relationship between (a) traditional and nontraditional sexual roles, (b)
the definition of such roles in terms of self-esteem, competence and problem-solving skills, and (c) the use of alcohol as a means of escaping
disappointment, frustration, conflict and feelings of failure.

   Isolation. Women drink alone and at home more than do men. This
has several important consequences. They are more likely to be called
"closet" or secret drinkers for the very good reason that their drinking is
less public; at the same time it is probably true that they are more secre-
tive about their drinking although it is not clear whether denial-of-alco-
holism is truer of one sex or the other. Repercussions for women are
more likely to be within the family while we know that for men one of
the main motivators in looking for treatment is work-related difficulties.

The Consequences of Alcoholism for Men and for Women

   It is arbitrary to divide antecedents from effects because there is a
smooth continuity to life, unlike isolated research events, and alcoholism
develops in phases over time in which causes and effects become inex-

tricably mixed. When we deal with issues like depression, premenstrual tension, low self-esteem, we have trouble separating, for example, a depression which *leads* to alcoholic drinking, a depression which *accompanies* a drinking bout, and a depression which *follows* a drinking episode and may lead into the next bout. A woman's heavy drinking may set into motion a sequence of denials (on her part and on the part of others surrounding her) and this may in turn lead to more drinking. Or the alcoholic woman, often looked upon with distaste ("female drunk!"), must cope with guilt, shame and isolation which are *consequences* of her drinking—these feelings may precipitate another drinking episode in spite of her good resolutions. The whole question of stigma is unresolved. As indicated above, disapproval and rejection for *drunkenness* are greater when it is a woman who is drunk than a man. Corrigan (1977) has raised the question of "the heavy burden of the alcoholic woman who apparently feels more stigmatized than her male counterpart because she drinks." Is the stigma for women alcoholics greater? Is it perceived as greater by the women themselves? My guess is that the answer to both questions is *yes*. As a society, we simply have less patience, less tolerance, and less sympathy for the female deviant than for the male. It does not mean that we are tolerant of male deviants but there does seem to be a difference in the degree of responsive irritation.

The consequences, or effects, of alcoholic drinking are effects in the sense that they follow upon or are an aftermath of the drinking. These consequences may be medical, legal, occupational, familial and social, and the different patterns (and similarities) of consequences for men and for women are an important and revealing research area. Here is where a double standard may operate clearly. In general, institutional consequences (e.g. arrests, hospitalizations) seem to be greater for men, and familial-social consequences greater for women. Institutional consequences usually follow from public visibility, i.e. it is more usual to know that men are drunk or having alcohol problems because they show up at work, in bars, or on the street. One of the most important differences between the outpatient women and the prisoner women alcoholics in Lisansky's work (1957) was this difference in the pattern of consequences. While women have to face familial-social consequences of their alcoholism regardless of class status, is there likely to be more institutional intervention (hospitalization, arrest) for lower-income women? We do not have the answer to that question.

Health and medical consequences. Edwards, Hensman and Peto (1972) compared problems related to drinking as reported for men and women in the United Kingdom. Compared for drunkenness arrests, the male/ female ratio is 14:1. Mental hospital admissions for alcoholism or alcoholic psychoses and deaths certified as due to alcoholism show a ratio of approximately 5:1. Deaths from cirrhosis of the liver show a ratio of 1:1. Perhaps the persistent finding that women rank health problems highest of drinking-related problems (Cahalan, 1970) is based on greater vulnerability. The question is whether alcohol does, indeed, have more devastating health effects for women than for men—in other words, do women mention health problems as alcohol-related only in part because they are more body-conscious or health-conscious than men? Do they indeed have more health problems connected with heavy alcohol intake? The work of Ben M. Jones and his colleagues suggests that there is a relationship between hormonal status and effects of alcohol. The work of Wilkinson and her colleagues (1971) suggests that women are more vulnerable to "physical disabilities"—in their study, the men and women show a similar proportion of physical disability but the women patients, who are somewhat older than the men, have a shorter duration of alcoholic drinking. A sex-related difference in liver disease associated with alcoholism has been noted again recently (Morgan & Sherlock, 1977). Are men perhaps more vulnerable to some alcohol-consequence medical problems and women to others?

Related to this, although not documented, are the reports by personnel in detoxification units of the toll taken by alcohol, the appearance and general state of the person on admission. Women, according to these reports, take longer than men to become presentable. If this is true, is the basis medical or psychological or both? If many of these women have indeed overidentified with traditional female roles and experience a sense of failure and frustration, might it not be that their anger is expressed in their neglect of appearance, in not giving a damn whether they look attractive or not? Like alcoholism, it serves the double purpose of self-abasement and anger toward others.

The occurrence of falls, bruises and injuries is still another question. Characteristically, it is more often men who appear at emergency rooms of hospitals with head and other injuries sustained while drunk. But James' (1975) female subjects reported "unexplained bruises" as an early stage sign of developing alcoholism, and Corrigan (1977) reported that many of her subjects had serious injuries because of falls or accidents.

Legal consequences. If arrests for driving under the influence and public intoxication are counted, men appear far more often. This has been the customary way of comparing legal consequences for men and women.

However, it might be useful to study the extent of alcohol-related problems among male and female delinquents and older criminals. A deviant behavior of women and girls, like heavy drinking, might be a concomitant of other deviant behaviors (sexual?) and thereby greatly increase the probability of arrest and punishment. But when legal consequences of alcoholism are discussed, the overwhelming number of arrests are made of the chronic drunkenness offender, i.e. the homeless man. How the decriminalization of public intoxication will affect those figures remains to be seen.

Occupational consequences. It seems to be a fact that younger alcoholics tend to have much poorer work records than alcoholics with later onset (Gomberg, in press). While there are changing norms about work and changing attitudes toward work performance, absenteeism and industrial accidents may be related to alcohol problems and to a wide variety of dissatisfactions of other sorts. The proportion of women in the work force is expanding but we tend to think of occupational consequences in terms of male job performance. A research comparison of women with alcohol and other substance abuse problems and men with similar problems in the work force has a number of problems. The male role is defined in terms of working and holding a job, but the situation for women working outside the home is still ambiguous. Women work outside the home for a variety of reasons, many of which are the same as men's reasons: They support the family. There are also women working outside the home in order to raise the family standard of living, because their maternal role has terminated, or simply because they enjoy the work, the contacts and the money. It will be important in the next years to study alcohol problems as manifested by women working outside the home and by housewives, to compare working male and female alcoholics in employee assistance programs, and to study working women in terms of comparison of hourly, salaried, skilled and unskilled, and professional status.

Marriage and family. The proportion of women seen in alcohol and substance abuse treatment facilities whose marriages have come apart is greater than the proportion of men with the same difficulties seen in these facilities. It is not always clear whether the alcoholism preceded the divorce or the other way around. The tolerance of the spouse for the drinking problems of his wife has been very little studied. The question is complicated by the fact that a considerably higher proportion of women are married to men with alcohol problems than vice versa. It is far more frequent that alcoholism develops because a woman drinks with her husband and far less frequent that a man develops alcohol problems because he is keeping his wife company in her drinking. We have an increasing number of systematic studies of marital interaction and an increasing amount of research into alcoholic marriages. It is true that "alcoholism is a family disease," that, in many significant ways, the non-alcoholic members of the family reinforce the alcoholic's drinking behavior. The study of alcoholic "family systems" is under way and promises much.

Let us again consider the matter of *isolation*. Men, even alcoholic men, tend to drink in groups. Women who drink infrequently or moderately will probably drink in groups. But when alcohol is a problem for a woman, she is much more likely to drink alone. Treatment manuals almost always deal with the question of substitute support systems because after one's drinking companions are gone, who is there? That seems to work out for male alcoholics, but, as a rule, not for female alcoholics. That is not to deny that there are alcoholic drinking groups which include women; such groups are almost invariably composed of men and women, not solely of women (except perhaps for Lesbian groups).

This is a description of women arrested for drunken driving in Boston (Argeriou & Paulino, 1976):

> . . . she is a woman . . . who is legally unattached and living alone. . . . Their social characteristics and circumstances of arrest appear to depict a group of isolated individuals seeking solutions or relief via the mechanism of local drinking establishments (p. 656).

And in the local drinking establishments, how does she do? This is a description of response to a few alcoholic women who appeared in a working-class tavern (LeMasters, 1975):

> One of these women died during this study while in her early forties. This woman would appear at The Oasis several times a week and drink beer until she could scarcely walk. She was not accepted by the other women at the tavern and was also avoided by most of the men. Several other women who might be labeled "alcoholics" . . . made their appearance at The Oasis at various times and disappeared. These were fringe members and not accepted by the regular customers (p. 152).

There are relatively few women on Skid Row but, studying these women, Garrett and Bahr (1973) observed:

Homeless women do not participate in the drinking institutions of Skid Row in the same way as men and their drinking activities, either in bars or public places, are considerably less group oriented than those of men. The results suggest that homeless women alcoholics may very well be the most isolated and disaffiliated residents of Skid Row (p. 1240).

Is the observation that women come to treatment facilities more often by themselves than men correct, and, if so, what are the implications for prognosis? Is the isolation antecedent or consequential? There is some evidence that the isolation is consequential: Tracey and Nathan's (1976) observations of a small sample of alcoholic women suggest that the solitary drinking of the woman alcoholic "may reflect social sanctions against women frequenting bars alone rather than a preference for seclusion by women alcoholics." Kammeier's (1977) follow-up of patients suggests that rehabilitation and improvement in social relationships have a higher correlation for women patients than for men.

The media and public response to the fetal alcohol syndrome reflects the general concern with the impairing effects of alcohol on maternal behavior. It has been stated often: The effect of maternal alcoholism is "worse" for the children than paternal alcoholism. In one study, however, when families in which the wife/mother is alcoholic are compared with those in which the husband/father is alcoholic, the results "fail to support a hypothesis about more negative social environments in families with alcoholic wives" (Bromet & Moos, 1977). The effect of parental alcoholism probably varies depending on whether one or both parents are drinking, the age and sex of the children, the family relationships, the alternative support systems for the children, and a host of other factors. It does appear to be true that generally women alcoholics show a good deal more concern and anxiety about their children than men alcoholics do about theirs. This is probably true of women and men in general. It would appear to be logically linked to the high value placed on traditional sex-role activities like mothering. It has been argued elsewhere that the woman who becomes an alcoholic already feels inadequate as a wife and a woman and that her role as mother becomes her last line of defense of her womanliness (Gomberg, 1976). We do not have real evidence that female alcoholism is harder on children in the family, but the belief relates, I think, to our disapproval of and anger at alcoholic women.

Treatment and Rehabilitation

Because so much research has focused on treatment outcome, on follow-up and evaluation, we can say something about the comparative prognosis for men and women. The information becomes very thin when we move to other questions: What are the reasons men/women seek out treatment? What are factors which help determine which facility they select? How effective is individual or group therapy for each of the sexes? How relatively effective are different treatment modalities? How relevant is the sex of the therapist?

A review of research on treatment and outcome (Blume, 1978) includes a summary by Emrick (1978) of studies which report no relationship between sex of patient and outcome, those which report a better outcome for women patients and those which report a better outcome for male patients. The weight of the evidence supports no significant difference in the prognoses of men and of women. This is hardly surprising when one considers the complex variables which determine prognosis (quite apart from the question of disagreements as to what constitutes successful outcome). But it was not very long ago that women were considered more difficult to treat, poorer patients with worse prognosis than men. There have been a number of additional recent reports where sex of the patient is unrelated to outcome. For example, a similar percentage of men and women patients completed the treatment program in a study by Heinemann, Moore, and Gurel (1976) and a two-year follow-up study of drug and alcohol abusers found no sex difference in rate of relapse (Barr, 1976). In fact, a recent summary of women client characteristics from the National Institute on Alcohol Abuse and Alcoholism Treatment Program Monitoring System (*Women in Treatment for Alcohol*, 1977) shows women with "greater improvement than men after 180 days of treatment."

Are there differences between men and women in the crises which drive them to seek help? Analysis of drinking-related problems experienced in the past year by men and women in treatment centers (Mulford, 1977) show that men more frequently report arrests and job troubles, and women more frequently report "illness other than hangover." Men report more often that the spouse has left or is threatening to leave but women seem to have more marital problems and, "A remarkably high proportion of the women alcoholics reported a 'heavy drinking' husband." An observation consistently made and supported by research is that women more often seek out treatment under familial and interpersonal pressures and men more often under legal, financial and occupational pressures.

How responsive are men and women clients to individual therapy and to group therapy? There is no clear answer to this question as yet. One study reports women as more responsive to individual therapy (Curlee, 1971), another reports women treated more effectively with group therapy (Battegay & Ladewig, 1970). The success of Alcoholics Anonymous with many women who are needful of a supportive network is a case in point. There are probably stages in treatment when a one-to-one contact is most needed and other stages where group work is vitally necessary. There may well be sex differences in the pattern of response to a treatment situation and there is a suggestion that women often drop out of treatment without its having the same predictive significance that it has for men.

One question on which there is more heat than light is the question of female therapists for women and treatment centers exclusively for women. At this point, the choice of treatment in a sex-integrated or all female facility is really a matter of opinion. Treatment centers for both men and women seem a more feasible idea to me but it would be very good if centers could offer women alcoholics a woman's group with a female therapist in addition to mixed groups with therapists of both sexes.

REFLECTION

Since I wrote about female alcoholism some years back (Lisansky, 1957), it is interesting to look at the progress made and not made in the last two decades. The epidemiological data have led us to a relatively new alcoholic phenomenon, the adolescent or young woman problem drinker who seems to be of more concern to her family and her society than her male counterpart. The biomedical data offer a challenge to learn more about the relationship of alcohol effects and hormonal status. The psychosocial data suggest that there are a number of variables in a woman's history, such as early family disruption, overidentification with traditional and dependent roles, and the presence of significant others with alcohol problems, which make some women more likely to develop alcohol problems than others.

The concern with health problems related to drinking and how this may be constructively utilized in early casefinding has not been explored. What will happen to the youngsters who begin experimenting with alcohol and intoxication early in adolescence is an important question which needs longitudinal study and follow-up planning. And we still know appallingly little about low-income women, minority group women, women on welfare, and women and girls caught up in the legal system. An important question concerns women with alcohol problems and how they differ from women with other kinds of problems: What determines symptom choice? Women seem more willing to be open about drinking problems at this time but we still have a long way to go in changing attitudes. We need to know more about treatments and therapists and what makes them effective. We have progressed a little but there is an enormous amount left to do.

REFERENCES

Alcohol Abuse Among Women: Special Problems and Unmet Needs, 1976. Hearing before the Subcommittee on Alcoholism and Narcotics, United States Senate, 94th Congress, September 1976. Washington, D. C.: Government Printing Office.

Alcohol and Other Drug Use and Abuse in the State of Michigan: Summary Report. Office of Substance Abuse Services, Department of Public Health, Lansing, Michigan, March, 1975.

Alcohol Technical Reports, Volume 4. Oklahoma State Department of Mental Health, Division on Alcoholism, 1975.

ARGERIOU, M. & PAULINO, D. Women arrested for drunken driving in Boston. *Journal of Studies on Alcohol,* 1976, 37, 648-658.

ARMOR, D. J., POLICH, J. M., & STAMBUL, H. B. *Alcoholism and Treatment.* Santa Monica, California: National Institute on Alcohol Abuse and Alcoholism, R-1739. Rand Corporation, 1976.

BALTER, M. B., LEVINE, J., & MANHEIMER, D. I. Cross-national study of the extent of anti-anxiety/sedative drug use. *The New England Journal of Medicine,* 1974, 290, 769-774.

BARR, H. *Some Data About Women.* Eagleville Hospital and Rehabilitation Center, Eagleville, Pennsylvania, February 21, 1976. Mimeographed, 4 pages.

BATTEGAY, VON R. & LADEWIG, G. Gruppentherapie und Gruppenarbeit mit Suechtigen Frauen. *British Journal of Addictions,* 1970, 65, 89-98.

BELFER, M. L., SHADER, R. I., CARROLL, M., & HARMATZ, J. S. Alcoholism in women. *Archives of General Psychiatry,* 1971, 25, 540-544.

BLACKFORD, L. S. Student trends in drug use—a basis for predicting the future of alcohol and drug related problems among women. *Drugs, Alcohol and Women: A National Forum.* National Institute on Drug Abuse, 1975.

BLACKFORD, L. S. The place of a continuing survey of adolescent alcohol use in defining "alcoholism." Is it an epidemic? Paper presented at Annual Forum of the National Council on Alcoholism, Washington, D. C., May, 1976.

BLUME, S. Researches on women and alcohol: Diagnosis, casefinding, treatment and outcome. In *Proceedings of the Workshop on Alcoholism and Alcohol Abuse Among Women, Research Issues.* National Institute on Alcohol Abuse and Alcoholism, April, 1978.

BRECHER, E. M. & THE EDITORS OF CONSUMER REPORTS. *Licit and Illicit Drugs: The Consumers Union Report on Narcotics, Stimulants, Depressants, Inhalants, Hallucinogens, and Marijuana—including Caffeine, Nicotine, and Alcohol.* Boston: Little, Brown and Co., 1972.

BROMET, E. & MOOS, R. Sex and marital status in relation to the characteristics of alcoholics. *Journal of Studies on Alcohol*, 1976, 37, 1302-1312.

BROMET, E. & MOOS, R. Environmental resources and the posttreatment functioning of alcoholic patients. *Journal of Health and Social Behavior*, 1977, 18, 326-338.

BROWNE-MAYERS, A. N., HAMILTON, F. J., SEELYE, E. E., & SILLMAN, L. Psychosocial study of hospitalized middle class alcoholic women in the U.S. *Proceedings of the 30th International Congress on Alcoholism and Drug Dependence*, September, 1972.

BROVERMAN, I. K., BROVERMAN, D. M., CLARKSON, F. E., ROSENKRANTZ, P. S., & VOGEL, S. R. Sex-role stereotypes and clinical judgments of mental health. *Journal of Consulting and Clinical Psychology*, 1970, 34, 1-7.

BUSH, P. J. & RABIN, D. L. Who's using nonprescribed medicines? *Medical Care*, 1976, XIV, 1014-1023.

CAHALAN, D. *Problem Drinkers*. San Francisco: Jossey-Bass, Inc., 1970.

CAHALAN, D., CISIN, I. H., & CROSSLEY, H. M. *American Drinking Practices: A National Study of Drinking Behavior and Attitudes*. New Haven: College and University Press, 1969.

CARPENTER, J. A. & ARMENTI, N. P. Some effects of ethanol on human sexual and aggressive behavior. In B. Kissin and H. Begleiter (Eds.), *The Biology of Alcoholism*, Volume 2. New York: Plenum Press, 1972.

CHAMBERS, C. D. *Differential Drug Use Within the New York State Labor Force*. Albany, N. Y.: New York Narcotics Addiction Control Commission, 1971.

CHILD, I. L., BARRY, H., III, & BACON, M. K. Sex differences in a cross-cultural study of drinking. *Quarterly Journal of Studies on Alcohol*, 1965, Supplement No. 3, 49-61.

CLONINGER, C. R. & GUZE, S. B. Psychiatric illness and female criminality: The role of sociopathy and hysteria in antisocial women. *American Journal of Psychiatry*, 1970, 127, 303-311.

COLTEN, M. E. A reconsideration of psychological androgyny: Self esteem, social skills and expectations rather than sex role identification. Unpublished doctoral dissertation, University of Michigan, 1978.

COOPERSTOCK, R. Sex differences in the use of mood-modifying drugs: An explanatory model. *Journal of Health and Social Behavior*, 1971, 12, 238-244.

COOPERSTOCK, R. Psychotropic drug use among women. *Canadian Medical Association Journal*, 1976, 115, 760-763.

CORRIGAN, E. M. Overview: The problem and its dimensions. In J. Newman (Ed.). *Counseling the Woman Alcoholic*. Pittsburgh, Pennsylvania: Western Pennsylvania Institute of Alcohol Studies, 1977. Pp. 1-16.

CURLEE, J. A comparison of male and female patients at an alcoholism treatment center. *The Journal of Psychology*, 1970, 74, 239-247.

CURLEE, J. Sex differences in patient attitude toward alcoholism treatment. *Quarterly Journal of Studies on Alcohol*, 1971, 32, 643-650.

DELINT, J. E. Alcoholism, birth rank and parental deprivation. *American Journal of Psychiatry*, 1964, 120, 1062-1065.

DUNLAP, N. G. Alcoholism in women: Some antecedents and correlates of remission in middle class members of Alcoholics Anonymous. Unpublished doctoral dissertation, University of Texas, 1961.

EDDY, N. B., HALBACH, H., ISBELL, H., & SEEVERS, M. H. Drug dependence: Its significance and characteristics. *Bulletin of the World Health Organization*, 1965, 32, 721-733.

EDWARDS, G., HENSMAN, C., & PETO, J. Drinking in a London suburb. III. Comparisons of drinking troubles among men and women. *Quarterly Journal of Studies on Alcohol*, Supplement No. 6, 1972, 120-128.

EDWARDS, G., HENSMAN, C., & PETO, J. A comparison of male and female motivation for drinking. *International Journal of Addictions*, 1973, 8, 577-587.

EMRICK, C. D. Aurora Community Mental Health Center, Aurora, Colorado. Personal communication, 1978.

ENGS, R. C. Drinking patterns and drinking problems of college students. *Journal of Studies on Alcohol*, 1977, 38, 2144-2156.

FILLMORE, K. M. Drinking and problem drinking in early adulthood and middle age: An exploratory 20-year follow-up study. *Quarterly Journal of Studies on Alcohol*, 1974, 35, 819-840.

FILLMORE, K. M. Relationships betwen specific drinking problems in early adulthood and middle age. *Journal of Studies on Alcohol*, 1975, 36, 882-907.

FREED, E. X. Drug abuse by alcoholics: A review. *The International Journal of the Addictions*, 1973, 8, 451-473.

GARRETT, G. R. & BAHR, H. M. Women on Skid Row. *Quarterly Journal of Studies on Alcohol*, 1973, 34, 1228-1243.

GOMBERG, E. S. L. Etiology of alcoholism. *Journal of Consulting and Clinical Psychology*, 1968, 32, 18-20.

GOMBERG, E. S. Women and alcoholism. In V. Franks and V. Burtle (Eds.), *Women in Therapy*. New York: Brunner/Mazel, 1974.

GOMBERG, E. S. Alcoholism in women. In B. Kissin and B. Begleiter (Eds.), *The Biology of Alcoholism*, Volume 4. New York: Plenum Press, 1976.

GOMBERG, E. S. The young male alcoholic—a pilot study. *Journal of Studies on Alcohol*, in press.

GOMBERG, E. S. Risk factors related to alcohol problems among women. In *Proceedings of the Workshop on Alcoholism and Alcohol Abuse Among Women: Research Issues*. National Institute on Alcohol Abuse and Alcoholism, April, 1978, In preparation.

GOODWIN, D. W., SCHULSINGER, F., HERMANSEN, L., GUZE, S. B., & WINOKUR, G. Alcohol problems in adoptees raised apart from biological parents. *Archives of General Psychiatry*, 1973, 28, 238-243.

GOODWIN, D. W., SCHULSINGER, F., KNOP, J., MEDNICK, S., & GUZE, S. B. Psychopathology in adopted and nonadopted daughters of alcoholics. *Archives of General Psychiatry*, 1977, 34, 1005-1009.

GURIN, G., VEROFF, J., & FELD, S. *Americans View Their Mental Health*. New York: Basic Books, 1960.

GUTTENTAG, M., SALASIN, S., & LEGGE, W. W. Women and mental health: A study in progress. Unpublished manuscript, Harvard University Graduate School of Education, 1976.

HEINEMANN, M. E., MOORE, B., & GUREL, M. Need patterns related to the treatment of alcoholism. Unpublished manuscript, University of Washington School of Nursing, Seattle, 1976.

HOFFMAN, H. & JACKSON, D. N. Differential personality inventory for male and female alcoholics. *Psychological Reports*, 1974, 34, 21-22.

HOFFMAN, H. & NOEM, A. A. Sex differences in a state of hospital population of alcoholics on admission and treatment variables. *Psychological Reports*, 1975, 35.

HORN, J. L. & WANBERG, K. W. Females are different: On the diagnosis of alcoholism in women. *Proceedings of the 1st Annual Alcoholism Conference of the National Institute on Alcohol Abuse and Alcoholism*. (NIH) 74-675. Washington, D. C.: Government Printing Office, 1973.

JACOB, A. G. & LAVOIE, C. A. A study of some characteristics of a group of women alcoholics. *Proceedings of the North American Association of Alcoholism Programs Conference*, Hartford, June 1971.

JAMES, J. E. Symptoms of alcoholism in women: A preliminary survey of A.A. members. *Journal of Studies on Alcohol*, 1975, 36, 1564-1569.

JELLINEK, E. M. *The Disease Concept of Alcoholism*. New Haven: Hillhouse Press, 1960.

JONES, B. M. & JONES, M. K. Male and female intoxication levels for three alcohol doses or do women really get higher than men? *Alcohol Technical Reports*, Oklahoma, 1976, 5, 11-14. (a)

JONES, B. M. & JONES, M. K. Alcohol effects on women during the menstrual cycle. *Annals of the New York Academy of Sciences*, 1976, 273, 576-587. (b)

JONES, B. M., JONES, M. K., & PARADES, A. Oral contraceptives and ethanol metabolism. *Alcohol Technical Reports*, Oklahoma, 1976, 5, 28-32.

JONES, M. C. Personality correlates and antecedents of drinking patterns in adult males. *Journal of Consulting and Clinical Psychology*, 1968, 32, 2-12.

JONES, M. C. Personality antecedents and correlates of drinking patterns in women. *Journal of Consulting and Clinical Psychology*, 1971, 36, 61-69.

JONES, R. W. Alcoholism among relatives of alcoholic patients. *Quarterly Journal of Studies on Alcohol*, 1972, 33, 810.

JONES, R. W. & HELRICH, A. R. Treatment of alcoholism by physicians in private practice: A national survey. *Quarterly Journal of Studies on Alcohol*, 1972, 33, 117-131.

JOHNSON, M. W., DEVRIES, J. C., & HOUGHTON, M. I. The female alcoholic. *Nursing Research*, 1966, 15, 343-347.

JOHNSON, S. & GARZON, S. R. Women and alcoholism: Past imperfect and future indefinite. Annual Research Conference of the Association for Women in Psychology, St. Louis, Missouri, 1977.

KAMMEIER, S. M. L. Alcoholism is the common denominator: More evidence on the male/female question, Hazelden Papers No. 2, Center City, Minn., 1977.

KELLER, M. & GURIOLI, C. *Statistics of Consumption of Alcohol and on Alcoholism*. Rutgers University Center of Alcohol Studies, 1976 edition.

KINSEY, B. A. *The Female Alcoholic: A Social Psychological Study*. Springfield, Ill.: Charles C Thomas, 1966.

KNIGHT, R. P. The psychodynamics of chronic alcoholism. *Journal of Nervous and Mental Disease*, 1937, 86, 538-548.

KNUPFER, G. & ROOM, R. Age, sex, and social class as factors in amount of drinking in a metropolitan community. *Social Problems*, 1964, 12, 224-240.

KNUPFER, G. Female drinking patterns. *Selected Papers Presented at the 15th Annual Meeting of the North American Association of Alcoholism Programs*, Washington, D. C., 1964, pp. 140-160.

LEMASTERS, E. E. *Blue-Collar Aristocrats*. Madison: University of Wisconsin Press, 1975.

LINDBECK, V. The woman alcoholic: A review of the literature. *The International Journal of Addictions*, 1972, 7, 567-580.

LISANSKY, E. S. (GOMBERG). Alcoholism in women: Social and psychological concomitants. *Quarterly Journal of Studies on Alcohol*, 1957, 18, 588-623.

MANHEIMER, D. I., MELLINGER, G. D., & BALTER, M. B. Psychotherapeutic drugs: Use among adults in California. *California Med.*, 1968, 109, 445-451.

MARLATT, G. A., KOSTURN, C. F., & LANG, A. R. Provocation to anger and opportunity for retaliation as determinants of alcohol consumption in social drinkers. *Journal of Abnormal Psychology*, 1975, 84, 652-659.

McCORD, W. & McCORD, J. *Origins of Alcoholism*. Stanford: Stanford University Press, 1960.

McLACHLAN, J. F. C., WALDERMAN, R. L., BIRCHMORE, D. F., & MARSDEN, L. R. The woman alcoholic: Summary of a report. Unpublished manuscript, 1976. The Donwood Institute, Toronto.

MORGAN, M. Y. & SHERLOCK, S. Sex-related differences among 100 patients with alcoholic liver cirrhosis. *British Medical Journal*, 1977, 1, 939-941.

MULFORD, H. A. Women and men problem drinkers: Sex differences in patients served by Iowa's community alcoholism centers. *Journal of Studies on Alcohol*, 1977, 38, 1624-1639.

MYERSON, A. Alcoholism: A study of social ambivalence. *Quarterly Journal of Studies on Alcohol*, 1940, 1, 13-20.

National Institute on Alcohol Abuse and Alcoholism Information and Feature Service, March 3, 1978.

New York State Department of Mental Hygiene Admission Statistics, Fiscal Year 1976-1977, 1977.

NORRIS, J. L. Alcoholics Anonymous' 1974 Membership Survey. North American Congress on Alcohol and Drug Problems, San Francisco, 1974.

OLTMAN, J. E. & FRIEDMAN, S. Trends in admissions to a state hospital, 1942-1964. *Archives of General Psychiatry*, 1965, 13, 544-551.

PARRY, H. J., BALTER, M. B., MELLINGER, G. D., CISIN, I. H., & MANHEIMER, D. I. National patterns of psychotherapeutic drug use. *Archives of General Psychiatry*, 1973, 28, 769-783.

PATTISON, E. M. Personality profiles of 50 alcoholic women. Personal communication, 1976. University of California, Irvine.

PEMBERTON, D. A. A comparison of the outcome of treatment in male and female alcoholics. *British Journal of Psychiatry*, 1967, 113, 367-373.

PFEIFER, W. D., MACKINNON, J. R., & SEISER, R. L. Adverse effects of paternal alcohol consumption on offspring in the rat. Paper presented at the 18th annual meeting of the Psychonomic Society, Washington, D. C., November, 1977.

RACHAL, J. V., WILLIAMS, J. R., BREHM, M. L., CAVANAUGH, B., MOORE, R. P., & ECKERMAN, W. C. *A National Study of Adolescent Drinking Behavior, Attitudes and Correlates. Final Report Summary.* Research Triangle Institute Project No. 23U-891. National Institute on Alcohol Abuse and Alcoholism, April, 1975.

RANKIN, J. G., SCHMIDT, W., POPHAM, R. E., & deLINT, J. Epidemiology of alcoholic liver disease—insights and problems. In J. M. Khanna, Y. Israel and H. Kalant (Eds.), *Alcoholic Liver Pathology.* Toronto: Addiction Research Foundation, 1975, pp. 31-41.

RATHBONE-McCUAN, E., LOHN, H., LEVENSON, J., & HSU, J. *Community Survey of Aged Alcoholics and Problem Drinkers* (Report No. NIAAA/NCALI 76/24). Baltimore: Levindale Geriatric Research Center, June 1976.

RATHOD, N. H. & THOMSON, I. G. Women alcoholics: A clinical study. *Quarterly Journal of Studies on Alcohol*, 1971, 32, 45-52.

RIMMER, J., PITTS, F. N., REICH, T., & WINOKUR, G. Alcoholism. II. Sex, socioeconomic status and race in two hospitalized samples. *Quarterly Journal of Studies on Alcohol*, 1971, 32, 942-952.

ROSENBAUM, B. Married women alcoholics at the Washingtonian Hospital. *Quarterly Journal of Studies on Alcohol*, 1958, 17, 77-89.

RUTLEDGE, C. C., CARROLL, G. B., & PERKINS, R. A. *A Socioepidemiological Study of Alcoholism in East Baton Rouge Parish.* Baton Rouge: Alcohol and Drug Abuse Section, Division of Mental Health, Louisiana Health and Social Rehabilitation Services Administration, 1974.

SCHUCKIT, M. A. & GUNDERSON, E. K. E. Alcoholism in Navy and Marine Corps women: A first look. *Military Medicine*, 1975, 140, 268-271.

SCHUCKIT, M., PITTS, F. N., REICH, T., KING, L. J., & WINOKUR, G. Alcoholism. I. Two types of alcoholism in women. *Archives of Environmental Health,* 1969, 18, and *Archives of General Psychiatry,* 1969, 20, 301-306.

SCLARE, A. B. The woman alcoholic. *Journal of Alcoholism,* London, 1975, 10, 134-137.

SELZER, M. L., GOMBERG, E. S. & NORDHOFF, J. A. The Michigan Alcoholism Screening Test: Use with men and women alcoholics. *Journal of Studies on Alcohol,* in press.

SHERFEY, M. J. Psychopathology and character structure in chronic alcoholism. In O. Diethelem (Ed.), *Etiology of Chronic Alcoholism.* Springfield, Ill.: Charles C Thomas, 1955.

SMART, R. G. & FEJER, D. Drug use among adolescents and their parents: Closing the generation gap in mood modification. *Journal of Abnormal Psychology,* 1972, 79, 153-160.

SIASSI, I., CROCETTI, G., & SPIRO, H. R. Drinking patterns and alcoholism in a blue-collar population. *Quarterly Journal of Studies on Alcohol,* 1973, 34, 917-926.

STAFFORD, R. A. & PETWAY, J. M. Stigmatization of men and women problem drinkers and their spouses: Differential perception and leveling of sex differences. *Journal of Studies on Alcohol,* 1977, 38, 2109-2121.

TARTER, R., MCBRIDE, H., BUONPANE, N., & SCHNEIDER, D. *Differentiation of Alcoholics, According to Childhood History of Minimal Brain Dysfunction, Family History and Drinking Patterns.* Bell Mead, New Jersey: Carrier Clinic (in preparation).

TRACEY, D. A. & NATHAN, P. E. Behavioral analysis of chronic alcoholism in four women. *Journal of Consulting and Clinical Psychology,* 1976, 832-842.

VEROFF, J. Personal communication, March 1978. Replication of *Americans View Their Mental Health,* Institute for Social Research, University of Michigan.

WALL, J. H. A study of alcoholism in women. *American Journal of Psychiatry,* 1937, 93, 943-952.

WANBERG, K. W. & KNAPP, J. Differences in drinking symptoms and behavior of men and women alcoholics. *British Journal of Addictions,* 1970, 64, 347-355.

WECHSLER, H. & MCFADDEN, M. Sex differences in adolescent alcohol and drug use. *Journal of Stuides on Alcohol,* 1976, 37, 1291-1301.

WILKINSON, P., KORNACZEWSKI, A., RANKIN, J. G., & SANTAMARIA, J. N. Physical disease in alcoholism: Initial survey of 1000 patients. *The Medical Journal of Australia,* 1971, 1, 1217-1223.

WILSNACK, S. C. Sex role identity in female alcoholism. *Journal of Abnormal Psychology,* 1973, 82, 253-261.

WILSON, G. T. & LAWSON, D. M. Expectancies, alcohol, and sexual arousal in women. *Journal of Abnormal Psychology,* 1978, 87, 358-367.

WINOKUR, G. & CLAYTON, P. Family history studies: IV. Comparison of male and female alcoholics. *Quarterly Journal of Studies on Alcohol,* 1968, 29, 885-891.

Women and Psychoactive Drug Use: An Interim Annotated Bibliography. Toronto: Addiction Research Foundation Series No. 11, 1976.

Women in Treatment for Alcoholism: A Profile, National Institute on Alcohol Abuse and Alcoholism Program Analysis and Evaluation Branch, February 1977.

WOOD, H. P. & DUFFY, E. L. Psychological factors in alcoholic women. *American Journal of Psychiatry,* 1964, 123, 341-345.

Workshop on Alcoholism and Alcohol Abuse among Women: Research Issues. Sponsored by the National Institute on Alcohol Abuse and Alcoholism, Jekyll Island, Georgia, April 2-5, 1978.

8

SEX DIFFERENCES
IN OBESITY

RICHARD B. STUART with BARBARA JACOBSON

Overweight is a condition in which one's weight is greater than that of the average person of the same sex, age, height, and body frame size. Obesity is a condition in which the percentage of one's body fat is greater than that shown for the average person of the same sex and age. Weight is measured by simply stepping on a scale. Obesity is measured by determining body composition. The simplest generally accepted means of doing this is by estimation of the thickness of fatfolds at various sites on the body. Because it is the most accessible site and because it correlates highly with measurements taken at other parts of the body, the triceps location on the upper arm is the point most frequently used to determine fatfold thickness. A fatfold greater than that found for the 85th percentile for one's age and sex cohort is generally accepted as indication of obesity. Weight is a poor index of obesity because one may be overweight and not obese, or one may be underweight and still be obese. For example, football players with huge muscle mass may be significantly heavier than the average man of their age and height and yet they may be leaner than the nonmuscular bookkeeper who, though light in weight, has less than the normal endowment of muscle mass.

Unfortunately, overweight and obesity are confused in much of the literature which will be reviewed in this paper. Generally, researchers index their subjects according to body weight and define heavier subjects as obese. Because this is not necessarily the case, some of the findings about "obesity" which will be reported here may best characterize the "overweight" rather than the obese.

Perhaps because measurement of obesity has been a controversial issue, or perhaps because sampling on a national scale is a highly complex

241

process, there is at this time no generally available study of the prevalence of obesity in the United States (U.S. Department of Health, Education, and Welfare, 1975a). It is known that female newborns have a higher percentage of fat than male newborns. We know, too, that females sustain their superior fat accumulation throughout life (Montoye, Epstein, & Kjelsberg, 1965). Boys are likely to lose a bit of their "baby fat" during adolescence only to begin to accumulate increasing amounts of fat after their late twenties. Girls' fat accumulation increases with the hormonal changes in puberty, again following childbirth, and a third time during their mid-thirties (Heald, 1972). Hormonal changes thus seem to affect males and females differently: Males lose fat during their adolescence, and females gain fat during adolescence and childbirth. Finally, men seem to begin their fat accumulation during their twenties when their food intake is constant but their physical activity declines. Because they are often active with child care responsibilities, this change is likely to be delayed until the mid-thirties for women.

It has been estimated that the percentage of men and women who are overweight is fairly comparable through the age of 40 when about one-third of all men and 40% of all women are overweight. However, 29% of all men and 45% of all women are obese by age 60 (Metropolitan Life Insurance Co., 1960). Sex and age are, therefore, important determinants of both obesity and overweight.

The accumulation of excess weight and/or fat is also under the influence of social class and race. For males, social class is correlated with obesity at all ages: Poorer males are thinner; richer males are fatter. For females, lower socioeconomic class standing is associated with leanness for girls and with fatness for women (Garn & Clark, 1976). Among adults, there are fewer obese black as opposed to white men at all ages and more obese black as opposed to white women at all ages (U.S. Department of Health, Education and Welfare, 1975a). Among those 20 to 44 years old, 16% of the white males are obese as opposed to 10.6% of the black males; and 18.9% of the white females are obese as opposed to 29.2% of the black females. Among those 45 to 75 years old, 13.4% of the white males are obese in contrast to 7.7% of the black males, and 24.7% of the white females have excessive fat stores as opposed to 32.4% of the black females.

When social class is considered, however, this age X sex X race relationship must be qualified. Table 1 summarizes data collected in the First Health and Nutrition Examination undertaken on a national scale by the U.S. Public Health Service (U.S. Department of Health, Educa-

TABLE 1

Percent of Older and Younger, Black and White Men and Women,
Above and Below the Poverty Line, Who Are Obese

		Age			
		20-44 Race		45-74 Race	
		White	Black	White	Black
Women	Below poverty line	25.1	35.0	29.6	32.9
	Above poverty line	18.6	25.0	24.7	32.4
Men	Below poverty line	9.3	10.9	15.4	5.1
	Above poverty line	17.0	11.3	13.3	9.7

Based upon data collected through the First Health and Nutrition Examination published in: U.S. Department of Health, Education and Welfare, *Anthropometric and Clinical Findings.* Rockville, Md.: National Center for Health Statistics, 1975.

tion and Welfare, 1975a). There it will be seen that, for both races, poorer young women are more likely to be obese than those with family incomes above the poverty line. Among older women, however, poorer whites have about a 20% greater probability of being obese when compared to their more well-to-do counterparts. However, the income difference all but vanishes for black women, one in three of whom is obese after reaching the age of 45 despite their family income level.

In summary, sex differences exert a strong influence on the tendency of individuals toward overweight and obesity. Females are endowed at birth with a higher percentage of their bodies as fat and this difference is likely to persist through life. But the relationship is not a simple one as both race and income level qualify sex differences throughout the cycle of life.

HEALTH CONSEQUENCES OF OBESITY

Many writers agree that obesity is often a key link in the chain leading from health to illness and death. Marks observed many years ago that:

In the long run, overweight even of relatively mild degree is harmful, and the penalty of overweight is largely reflected in the frequency of mortality through heart and other circulatory disorders, diabetes, liver and biliary tract disorders and some forms of arthritis.

Obviously, overweight is only one of the many factors in the situation. Nevertheless, as a practicable and relatively simple and widely applicable measure, control of body weight can contribute significantly to the retardation of the degenerative process as it affects the heart and circulatory system and to the prevention or postponement of onset of some other major disorders. (Marks, 1957, p. 423)

While some contemporary authors argue that obesity is not itself a cause of problems other than the mechanical difficulties created by excessive weight on the muscular, skeletal, cardiovascular, and respiratory systems, most medical researchers recognize that weight reduction can lead to significant improvement in blood chemistry, heart function, and related bodily functions.

The group which is least affected by the health hazards of obesity paradoxically enough is the group which is most committed to its management. It is well recognized that women are in the forefront of the dieting population. Yet among women the risks of mortality rise only slightly as a function of obesity while the risks for men rise precipitously. For example, the average man who lives to be 65 to 74 weighs exactly what he weighed between the ages of 18 and 24, but the average man who reaches the ages of 75 to 79 weighs some 6% less than he did in his early twenties. In contrast, the average woman who reaches the ages of 65 to 74 and 75 to 79 weighs some 13% and 7%, respectively, more than she did during her earliest adult years (U.S. Department of Health, Education and Welfare, 1965, p. 7). Among men the risk of death rises precipitously as a function of weight, but among women mortality does not appear to be significantly affected by excessive weight gain before later life. Men who are as little as 20% overweight seem to incur a serious risk of shortening their lives, beginning in their early twenties, but women who are 20% or more overweight do not reflect increased morality until their sixties (Dublin & Marks, 1958). It is therefore clear that while women are more prone to overweight and obesity, they are also far better able to bear its consequences. Obesity is thus a much greater hazard to the health of men than to the health of women.

BODY-CONCEPT, SELF-CONCEPT AND WEIGHT

Overweight and obesity are multiply determined. Beyond the influence of sex, age, and income, they may be brought on by genetic and traumatic forces, by cultural and social influences, and/or as a consequence of illness. In most instances several of these factors interact to create a condition in which more energy is taken in as food than is burned through activity, with the excess energy stored as fat in the body's adiposities (Stuart & Davis, 1972). Whatever the conditions of its accumulation, the accumulation of excess fat is believed to exert a profound effect upon the body concept and, hence, the self-concept of the afflicted.

It is virtually impossible to directly measure body and self-concept. Secord and Jourard (1953) developed what may be the simplest and most direct measures of body and self-concept. They presented subjects with a list of 55 body dimensions such as hair, width of shoulders, age, sex (male or female), and so forth, and a like number of personal attributes, such as "first name," "life goals," "self-understanding," and "sensitivity to opinions of others." Their subjects were asked to rate each of these items on a five-point Likkert-type scale ranging from "have strong feelings and wish change could somehow be made" at one end to "consider myself fortunate" at the other. Men and women valued their bodies and their selves at very comparable levels. For men, body and self-cathexis correlated at the level of .58 while for women the correlation was .66. Subjects low in body or self-regard tended to report greater anxiety, so that self-regard appeared to strongly influence subjects' sense of adequacy in coping with the world, regardless of sex. Interestingly, the only significant sex difference in this investigation was the fact that women tended to have stronger feelings about their body parts than did men. That is, women were more likely to select scores of great like or great dislike while men had a higher probability of choosing the middle alternative of "have no particular feelings one way or the other."

The more extreme reactions of women to their bodies may be expected to result from developmental experience during which selective attention to appearance develops. Two studies have shown that adolescent girls are highly sensitive to their weight and appearance. In Sweden Nylander (1971) studied 1,129 boys and 1,241 girls between the ages of 14 and 21. Most of the girls felt that they had been fat at some time, rising from 47% of the 14-year-olds to 72% of the 21-year-olds. In contrast, only 12% of the 14-year-old and 34% of the 21-year-old boys had considered themselves to be overweight at some time. Forty-six percent of the girls who were overweight attributed their weight to "weak character," but only 24% of the overweight boys offered this explanation. In addition, fully three-quarters of the overweight girls but only one-quarter of the overweight boys sought to lose weight by dieting. In the second study, conducted among 6,768 American youths between the ages of 12 and 17, approximately 12% of the boys of all ages perceived themselves as overweight, whereas from 21.7% of the 12-year-olds to 30.9% of the

17-year-old girls viewed themselves as overweight (U.S. Department of Health, Education and Welfare, 1975b). Overall, about one in five of the subjects considered themselves overweight while one in eight considered themselves underweight. In the latter category, boys significantly outnumbered girls: An average of 10.8% of the girls at all ages wished that they were heavier while from 20.4% of the 12-year-old boys to 34.6% of the 17-year-old boys preferred weight greater than their own. In the same vein, only about one-fifth of the girls, but one-half of the boys wished to be taller. Thus boys and girls as a group both expressed some dissatisfaction with their stature—boys with their height and weight because they equated bigness with strength, girls with their weight because they equated slimness with beauty.

There is some indication of sex-related age trends in self-acceptance among children and adolescents. Sallade (1973) studied third- and fifth-grade girls who were shown to be more secure than boys and eighth- and eleventh-grade girls who were shown to be less secure than boys. This shift in self-acceptance is very likely to be attributable to the girls' somatic concerns which appear to be greater than those of boys during adolescence.

Unfortunately, this differential sensitivity also carries over into adulthood. Johnson (1956) studied the level of self-acceptance among female nursing students and male seminary students with an average age of 20.2. She found that 42% of the men and 64% of the women reported dislike of their bodies. Surprisingly, only 13% of the seminarians and 2% of the nurses reported liking their bodies. Johnson speculated that both men and women have vague notions of ideal dimensions for their bodies, and they become upset when their proportions deviate from their ideal, even if the ideal is totally unrealistic.

In general, it was found in one large-scale study of adult Londoners (Ashwell & Etchell, 1974) that overweight people are more accurate in estimating their weight (81%) than those who were underweight (36%). But, within the overweight group, more women (89%) than men (69%) were accurate about their weight, with these percentages holding more or less constant across the social classes. However, another study which also asked Londoners' views of their weight (Silverstone, 1968) found that among those who were 30% or more overweight, one-third of the men and one-third of the women did not consider themselves to be too heavy. Thus, knowing one's weight does not necessarily mean that one will appropriately classify himself or herself as overweight, normal, or underweight. Indeed, Silverstone also found that 10% of the normal weight males and 33% of the normal weight females considered themselves to be overweight.

Therefore, it is clear that through adolescence girls become more sensitive to their body dimensions than boys. It is also clear that this differential concern with weight persists into adulthood for women, with more women than men weighing themselves often and interpreting information about their weight as an omen that reducing is necessary, even though their weight may be well within the normal range.

It is reasonable to speculate that this concern with weight, particularly when the self-reported news is bad, might lead the weight-conscious and the overweight to suffer from psychological stress not experienced by the more self-accepting and normal-weight adults. Although it has been shown that the overweight do perceive themselves to be stigmatized (Allon, 1976; Rodin & Slochower, 1974), no profile of the "obese personality" has been produced through scores of studies (Stuart, in press a). For example, Silverstone (1968) found women to be more psychologically disturbed than men, with over one-third of the women scoring in the "neurotic" range on the Cornell Medical Index. But in Silverstone's research, those with normal weight offered more symptomatic complaints than did those who were obese. In the same vein, Sallade (1973) and Wunderlich (1974) found sex differences but no obese/normal differences in their use of the California Psychological Inventory as a screening measure.

Sex differences were also found in a national survey of the prevalence of 12 psychological disturbances, including depression (U.S. Department of Health, Education and Welfare, 1970). Here, too, women were found to suffer more than men. But as with all generalizations, this one, too, must be qualified. Stuart and Lederer (in press) have found that women who work outside of their homes and who are single tend to be less depressed than women who are not employed in out-of-home occupations and who are married. Therefore, situation interacts with sex in producing the generalized finding that women tend more toward depression than men. Nonetheless, it may be this general tendency which influenced the outcome of another major British study in which normal and overweight men and women answered the questions posed by the Middlesex Hospital Questionnaire (Crisp & McGuiness, 1976). Here it was found that overweight men are both less anxious and less depressed than men of normal weight and that overweight women are less anxious but more depressed than women of normal weight. Thus, it is possible that in interaction with the social experiences which produce a tendency toward depression, overweight may be an exacerbating stress for women whose happiness is strongly and negatively affected by it.

THE DECISION TO LOSE WEIGHT

Thus far we have established that women have a higher percentage of body fat than men, that women can physically bear their extra weight more successfully than men, that women are more likely than men to be sensitive to their own weight, and that women are more likely than men to report feelings of unhappiness in their life adjustments. These factors may combine to create the conditions in which women surpass men in efforts to lose weight by any means, 75% as against 45% (Ashwell & Etchell, 1974). These forces may also explain the fact that the vast majority of participants in weight-reduction programs, at any moment in time, are women. For example, 92% of those who join both Weight Watchers and Diet Workshop (Berman, 1975) are women.

Dwyer, Feldman and Mayer (1970) have suggested a number of additional reasons for the greater likelihood of women's, as opposed to men's, joining weight-reduction programs, three of which seem to have particular significance. First, excessive weight may be more of a social liability to women than to men. Successful business women and the wives of successful men are rarely overweight; successful men may very well be overweight, however. Weight is thus more of a socioeconomic handicap to women than to men. Second, weight-related aspects of appearance may be more central to the self-concepts of women as opposed to men. In a culture which has generally depreciated the artistic, intellectual, and scientific contributions of women, women's success was for many years tied to their appearance. Hopefully, now that the talents of women are given more of their full due, it is possible that women's concepts of themselves may be tied more closely to their achievements than to their appearance. Third, obesity is more visible on women than men. Females begin with twice the percentage of body fat as men. Moreover, this fat is more conspicuously distributed on the extremities, hips, and chest. Any fat excess is therefore plainly in view on the bodies of women, while among men fat tends to mass less obtrusively on the torso.

The facts that women suffer more from the social liability of weight, that they experience cultural pressure to give appearance a central role in their self-concepts, and that excess fat is more visible on women probably all contribute to the conclusion that a desire to improve their appearance is pivotal in women's decisions to attempt to lose weight, while it is secondary in the decision matrix of men. For example, Berman (1975) found that a relatively constant 92% of the members of Diet Workshop joined that program because of a desire to improve their appearance in contrast to 56% who were at least partially motivated by a desire to improve their health. Unfortunately, the Berman report does not indicate sex differences in these goals nor does it suggest a priority of objectives. In a study of those who join Weight Watchers classes in North America, it was found that 85% of the men and 91% of the women saw improved appearance as an objective of their joining the program, while 82% of the men and 67% of the women had improved health as their objective. But, when they were asked to give priority to their choices, 41% of the men and 60% of the women were primarily motivated by the desire to improve their appearance while 48% of the men and only 20% of the women were primarily motivated to lose weight by the goal of achieving better health. Clearly, then, the desire to meet social rather than health challenges is differentially reflected in the structure of decisions reached by men and women. Although fewer women than men suffer risks of health hazards associated with obesity, it seems as though their desire for cosmetic change is socially rather than biologically motivated.

Data presented in Table 2 show other comparisons between the characteristics of men and women who come to Weight Watchers classes. Men are slightly better educated, they are slightly more hard drinking, they exercise more, and they are less dissatisfied with their jobs, all of which may be a reflection of secular trends in our society. Men also naturally tend to be heavier than women when they start a weight-loss program although the percent of excess weight is comparable to that of women. Finally, as measured by List D of the Lublin Depression Adjective Check Lists (Lublin, 1967), men tend to be less depressed than women when beginning the Weight Watchers program. Indeed, men are slightly less depressed than the norm for their sex, 9.12, and women are somewhat more depressed than their reference group, which averaged 7.87 on this test. Other than these differences, however, the men and women who join Weight Watchers are rather similar in characteristics such as age, marital status, and the age of onset of obesity, among others.

THE KINDS OF TREATMENT RECEIVED

When people enter a standardized program such as Weight Watchers, men and women receive the same service. Other programs which offer less standardized services may offer different programs to men and women. Most weight-conscious adults have experience with several differ-

TABLE 2

Comparison of the Characteristics and Experiences of Men and
Women Joining Weight Watchers Classes in North
America in 1975

	Men ($n = 72$)	Women ($n = 941$)	Significance
Age	36.4	36.2	*ns*
Married	74%	72%	*ns*
Some College	29%	13%	$\chi^2 = 14.84$*
Employed 31+ hours	68%	37%	*ns*
Age First Overweight	56%	53%	*ns*
Non-smokers	69%	74%	*ns*
Three or More Alcohol			
Drinks Each Week	64%	34%	$\chi^2 = 24.26$*
Number of Times Walk			
10+ Blocks Per Week	44%	23%	$\chi^2 = 17.41$*
Sources of Unhappiness			
Marriage	12%	20%	*ns*
Work	28%	44%	$\chi^2 = 7.91$*
Free Time	35%	46%	*ns*
Friendships	18%	20%	*ns*
First Choice Reason for			
Wishing to Lose Weight			
Appearance	41%	60%	$\chi^2 = 12.11$*
Health	48%	20%	$\chi^2 = 16.92$*
Achieve Self Control	0%	2%	*ns*
To Please Spouse	2%	9%	*ns*
Other Reasons	9%	9%	*ns*
Social Context of Weight			
Number of Overweight Parents			
or Siblings: 0 or 1	54%	57%	*ns*
Spouse Overweight	38%	50%	*ns*
Overweight Child	13%	16%	*ns*
Number of People Suggesting			
Weight Loss: 1-4	50%	50%	*ns*
Initial Weight	244.3	176.0	$t = 12.51$*
Initial Depression Level	8.2	10.1	$t = 2.82$*

* p < .05.

Reprinted with permission from: Henry J. Montoye, Frederick H. Epstein, & Marcus O. Kjelsberg. The measurement of body fatness: A study in a total community. *American Journal of Nutrition*, 1965, 16, 417-442.

ent weight-control programs. Among those who joined Weight Watchers classes, more than nine out of ten had made an attempt to curb their weight through use of a self-prescribed diet, three out of four sought a diet prescribed by their physician and/or a weight-management organization, and two out of three had asked their physicians for medication to control their appetites. This latter request may be a reflection of the ascription of obesity to biological causes by many of the afflicted. For example, slightly under half of the overweight male and female adolescents interviewed in a national study considered themselves to be overeaters (U.S. Department of Health, Education and Welfare, 1975b), but a study of adult obese in England found an even smaller percentage willing to own up to overeating as a cause of their corpulence (Silverstone, 1968).

The Weight Watchers data reflect the requests of the members as patients. Two studies conducted in England surveyed the kinds of service offered by physicians to their weight-conscious patients (Ashwell, 1973; Yudkin, 1968). Both researchers found that dietary prescriptions were the most common recommendation. Yudkin found that half of all patients were instructed to curb their carbohydrate consumption and one-third were instructed to curb their intake of carbohydrates and fats, with these recommendations being made equally to women and men. But Yudkin found that only 42.4% of the men were offered drugs in contrast to 57.8% of the women. Ashwell found an even greater disparity between the sexes in the likelihood that their recommended diets would be supplemented with medication. She found that drugs were prescribed in the cases of 18% of the men and 43% of the women. Hewitt (1974) has suggested that female dieters may be more likely to receive drugs than their male counterparts in part because the physician is concerned with offering women mood elevators to cope with depression, which is a less common problem among men. Finally, Ashwell also found that 16% of the men but only 4% of the women were advised to increase their exercise, and 7% of the women in contrast to only 1% of the men were advised to join a "slimming group." These differentials, along with that concerning the prescription of medication, are more likely to be a reflection of the cultural bias of the physicians than of the idiographic needs of the patients. Unfortunately, in the case of drugs at least, the bias may operate to the patient's disadvantage, for Bray (1974) has suggested that no drug currently used for the control of obesity has demonstrated the capacity to produce lasting weight loss, and many have some serious side effects.

Given ecological patterns in the prescription of these drugs, women are the more likely sufferers than men.

A vast majority of research concerned with the management of obesity is either addressed to women only or it has included a small number of male subjects without parceling results according to sex. Of the studies which do report data separately for the sexes, the preponderant finding is that men and women do about equally well in their weight-loss efforts when their different starting weights are taken into consideration.

In their self-ratings of the treatment which they received, some 42% of the men studied by Yudkin (1968) rated their treatment as "good" or "fairly good" whether they received diet instruction only or diet instruction in conjunction with drugs. Women in that study felt less well-served by their treatment: 15.1% gave "good" ratings to diet instruction and 20.3% considered their diet and drug treatment in the good range.

Cormier (1972) offered her subjects a well-designed nutrition education-oriented program lasting 12 weeks. The average initial weight of the women who participated in her program was 159.5 pounds and that of men was 205 pounds. Women lost an average of 1.46 pounds per week and men lost a weekly average of 1.79 pounds, both highly acceptable achievements for the small group and individual treatments which were employed. Cormier concludes that men outperformed women, but a re-analysis of her results, taking starting weight into account, yields a finding of no significant difference in the outcome for both sexes. Musante (1976) offered an intensive treatment program to subjects who lived in motel settings close to the treatment clinic where they spent large amounts of time every day. The women in his program weighed an average of 182.7 pounds initially, stayed in the program for an average of 10.4 weeks and lost an average of 2.3 pounds per week. The average man in this program, which combined nutrition education and instruction in the behavioral management of problem eating, weighed 259.6 pounds initially, stayed for 8.2 weeks and lost 3.5 pounds per week. These results are more positive than those reported by Cormier. They must, however, be qualified by three observations: First, the treatment offered by Musante is more intensive than any reported in the literature except for some studies of inpatient treatment. Second, Musante's subjects were heavier initially than were Cormier's, and those with the most to lose lose the most at first. Finally, the duration of Musante's observations was shorter than that of Cormier. This is important because weekly rates of weight loss are generally smaller as treatment progresses. Unfortunately, Musante's study does not provide sufficient data to permit a statistical analysis of the differences in the rate of weight lost by males and females in his project. By inspection, however, it would seem as though the differences are not sufficiently great to withstand analysis of covariance controlling for initial weight.

Musante found that women persisted in treatment a bit longer than men. Fifty-seven percent of the men in their study dropped out in comparison with 46% of the women. Their program was based in a hospital clinic and offered 1,000-calorie diets with biweekly contacts. Men and women did equally well in this study although the men who stayed for a particularly long time did lose a bit more weight than the women who stayed for the same period. In the same vein, sex differences were not found in three additional studies: one evaluating the effectiveness of covert sensitization as a means of reducing appetite (Elliott & Denney, 1975); a second evaluating the effectiveness of self-confrontation of problem eating (Gygi, Saslow, Sengstake, & Weitman, 1973); the third evaluating the effectiveness of inpatient treatment for obesity (Glennon, 1966).

Additionally, a study of the effectiveness of a behavioral self-management program introduced in a pilot test to 7,243 members of Weight Watchers classes revealed that men lost an average of 1.9 pounds per week and women an average of 1.5 pounds (Stuart, 1977). However, when their initial weights and length of time spent in the program were computed through use of the Feinstein Index (Stuart, 1976), it was found that there was no statistical difference in their average weekly rates of loss although men did remain in the program about 20% longer than women, giving men a greater overall loss of weight. Finally, in another study, also involving Weight Watchers members, it was found that while women are initially more depressed than men, within five weeks on the program both groups showed comparable and statistically significant changes in their level of depression: 2.2 points for men and 2.4 for women. Therefore, it appears possible to help weight losers to achieve at least some degree of the mood elevation which they seek by helping them to enjoy initial success in self-management.

CONCLUSION

It has been suggested that weight is a greater health hazard for men but that it is of greater cosmetic concern to women. There is no evidence that weight per se leads to psychological distress among men although women appear to be more sensitive to its social and, therefore, its psychological consequences. Given the consistent observation that women are far more likely than men to avail themselves of the services currently offered to the overweight, it would seem as though concern for appearance may be a more potent motivator toward action than concern for health—perhaps because cosmetic changes are somewhat more apparent and more immediate than the less tangible and often remote changes in general physical health. Once presented for treatment, women are more likely to be offered complex treatments involving diet and drugs, while men are offered a package involving diet and exercise. Once into their programs it appears as though women and men fare about equally well in losing weight. Regrettably, there are no studies which measure their respective success in sustaining their weight losses, nor are there careful studies which assess the long-term consequences of changed body weight and its potential sequelae, changed body image, psychological status, and social opportunity.

REFERENCES

ALLON, N. The stigma of overweight in everyday life. In G. A. Bray (Ed.), *Obesity in Perspective*. Bethesda, Md.: U.S. Department of Health, Education and Welfare, 1976.

ASHWELL, M. A. A survey of patients' views of doctors' treatment of obesity. *The Practitioner*, 1973, 211, 653-658.

ASHWELL, M. A. & ETCHELL, L. Attitude of the individual to his own body weight. In A. Howard (Ed.), *Recent Advances in Obesity Research: I*. London: Newman Publishing Company, 1974.

BERMAN, E. M. Factors influencing motivations in dieting. *Journal of Nutrition Education*, 1975, 7, 155-159.

BRAY, G. A. Pharmacological approach to the treatment of obesity. In G. A. Bray & J. E. Bethune (Eds.), *Treatment and Management of Obesity*. New York: Harper & Row, 1974.

CORMIER, A. Group versus individual dietary instruction in the treatment of obesity. *Canadian Journal of Public Health*, 1972, 63, 327-332.

CRISP, A. H. & McGUINNESS, B. Jolly fat: Relation between obesity and psychoneurosis in general population. *British Medical Journal*, 1976, 1, 7-9.

DUBLIN, L. I. & MARKS, H. H. Weight and longevity. In H. E. Ungerleider & R. S. Gubner (Eds.), *Life Insurance and Medicine*. Springfield, Ill.: Thomas, 1958.

DWYER, J. T., FELDMAN, J. J., & MAYER, J. The social psychology of dieting. *Journal of Health and Social Behavior*, 1970, 11, 269-287.

ELLIOTT, C. H. & DENNEY, D. R. Weight control through covert sensitization and false feedback. *Journal of Consulting and Clinical Psychology*, 1975, 6, 842-850.

GARN, S. M. & CLARK, D. Trends in fatness and the origins of obesity. *Pediatrics*, 1976, 57, 443-456.

GLENNON, J. A. Weight reduction: An enigma. *Archives of Internal Medicine*, 1966, 118, 1-2.

GUBNER, R. Overweight and health: Prognostic realities and therapeutic possibilities. In L. Lasagna (Ed.), *Obesity: Causes, Consequences and Treatment*. New York: Medcom Press, 1974.

GYGI, C., SASLOW, G., SENGSTAKE, C. B., & WEITMAN, M. Self-confrontation and weight reduction: A controlled experiment. *Psychotherapy: Theory, Research and Practice*, 1973, 10, 315-320.

HEALD, F. P. The natural history of obesity. *Advances in Psychosomatic Medicine*, 1972, 7, 102-115.

HEWITT, M. I. Negative mood, hunger and weight classification. *Obesity and Bariatric Medicine*, 1974, 3, 24-27.

JOHNSON, L. C. Body cathexis as a factor in somatic complaints. *Journal of Consulting Psychology*, 1956, 20, 145-149.

LUBLIN, B. *Manual for the Depression Adjective Check Lists*. San Diego: Educational and Industrial Testing Service, 1967.

MARKS, H. H. Relationship of body weight to mortality and morbidity. *Metabolism*, 6, 417-424.

METROPOLITAN LIFE INSURANCE COMPANY. Frequency of overweight and underweight. *Statistical Bulletin*, 1960, 41, 1-8.

MONTOYE, H. J., EPSTEIN, F. H., & KJELSBERG, M. O. The measurement of body fatness: A study in a total community. *American Journal of Clinical Nutrition*, 1965, 16, 417-427.

MUSANTE, G. J. The dietary rehabilitation clinic: Evaluative report of a behavioral and dietary treatment of obesity. *Behavior Therapy*, 1976, 7, 198-204.

NYLANDER, I. The feeling of being fat and dieting in a school population. *Acta Sociomedica Scandinavia*, 1971, 17-26.

RODIN, J. & SLOCHOWER, J. Fat chance for a favor: Obese-normal differences in compliance and incidental learning. *Journal of Personality and Social Psychology*, 1974, 29, 557-565 .

SALLADE, J. A comparison of the psychological adjustment of obese vs. nonobese children. *Journal of Psychosomatic Research*, 1973, 17, 89-96.

SECORD, P. F. & JOURARD, S. M. The appraisal of body-cathexis: Body-cathexis and the self. *Journal of Consulting Psychology*, 1953, 17, 343-347.

SILVERSTONE, J. T. Psychosocial aspects of obesity. *Proceedings of the Royal Society of Medicine*, 1968, 61, 371-375.

STUART, R. B. Behavioral control of overeating: A status report. In G. A. Bray (Ed.), *Obesity in Perspective*. Bethesda, Md.: U.S. Department of Health, Education and Welfare, 1976.

STUART, R. B. *Breaking the Chain: The Psychology of Weight Loss and Weight Maintenance*. New York: W. W. Norton, in press. (a)

STUART, R. B. Self help for self management. In R. B. Stuart (Ed.), *Behavioral Self Management: Behavioral Strategies, Tactics and Outcomes*. New York: Brunner/Mazel, 1977.

STUART, R. B. & DAVIS, BARBARA. *Slim Chance in a Fat World*. Champaign, Ill.: Research Press, 1976.

STUART, R. B. & LEDERER, W. J. *Caring Days: A Manual of Marriage Management Techniques*. New York: W. W. Norton, in press.

U.S. DEPARTMENT OF HEALTH, EDUCATION AND WELFARE. *Weight, Height, and Selected Body Dimensions of Adults: United States, 1960-1962*. Washington, D. C.: U.S. Government Printing Office, 1965.

U.S. DEPARTMENT OF HEALTH, EDUCATION AND WELFARE. *Selected Symptoms of Psycho-*

logical Distress: United States. Washington, D. C.: U.S. Government Printing Office, 1970.

U.S. DEPARTMENT OF HEALTH, EDUCATION AND WELFARE. *Anthropometric and Clinical Findings.* Rockville, Md.: National Center for Health Statistics, 1975. (a)

U.S. DEPARTMENT OF HEALTH, EDUCATION AND WELFARE. *Self Reported Health Behavior and Attitudes of Youths 12-17 Years: United States.* Rockville, Md.: National Center for Health Statistics, 1975. (b)

WUNDERLICH, R. A. Personality characteristics of super-obese persons as measured by the California Psychological Inventory. *Psychological Reports,* 1974, 35, 1029-1030.

YUDKIN, J. Doctors' treatment of obesity. *The Practitioner,* 1968, 201, 330-335.

9

HOMOSEXUALITY IN FEMALES AND MALES

BERNARD F. RIESS and JEANNE M. SAFER

INTRODUCTION

The current interest in homosexuality is more a product of socio-economic-political pressures than an evidence of genuine developments in establishing a data-based theory of sexual personality. Much mythology has accrued around the so-called sexual revolution (which is neither sexual nor revolutionary). Beyond the increased market value of overt and explicit sexual acts, there is a veneer of social activism, of a demand for equal rights and freedom to choose one's personal preference for a sexual partner. To make this statement does not imply a negative judgment. What we are saying is that, for psychologists and behavioral scientists, there is a noticeable dearth of hard data and sophisticated methodology.

Studies of sexual partnership choice are not merely esoteric investigations of allegedly deviant behavior. It is our belief that closer scrutiny, acquaintance, and knowledge of the various aspects of homosexuality will lead to a deeper understanding of how personal identification is achieved, particularly that identity which is based on sexual differentiation. This chapter does not pretend to present all the information from the numerous studies of homosexuality. We have selected those presentations which seem to be relatively free of experimental contamination and theoretical bias. In addition, we eschew purely clinical case history reports, interesting though they may be. What we are endeavoring to present is the broad scope of evidence that the development of choice of sexual partner is variably dependent on whether the decision-maker is woman or man.

Before facing the accumulation of data about like-sex choice of love partners, some methodological comments are necessary. It is also mandatory to assert some conclusions which should be axiomatic at this stage of our knowledge. We would first lay at rest and say *ave atque vale* to homosexuality as necessarily pathological. Those who still assert that it is so are wearing one or both of two blinders. The first is a theory-bound blindness which states that the development of sexual maturity necessarily demands a heterosexual endpoint. Second is the assumption that biology is destiny in the sense that continuity of the species requires heterosexual reproduction. It would be helpful if these blind theoreticians would follow in Freud's tradition and change the theory when it no longer fits the data obtained from observation of independent students of the phenomenon.

We also wish to point out that the term homosexuality has been so reified by its users that it has assumed both a diagnostic syndrome nature and a descriptive personality aspect. In his recent book, *Perversion: The Erotic Form of Hatred,* Robert Stoller (1975) effectively demolishes the diagnostic labeling of the so-called syndrome. He writes:

> To make a proper diagnosis in any branch of medicine there should be: (a) a syndrome—a constellation of signs and symptoms shared by a group of people visible to an observer; (b) underlying dynamics (pathogenesis)—pathophysiology or psychodynamics in psychiatry; (c) etiology—those factors from which the dynamics originate. When these exist we can save time by using shorthand . . . unfortunately for psychiatrists, we are usually not confronted with people whose thinking, feelings and behavior can be thus categorized . . . the conditions for which our speciality was developed do not usually fulfill these three criteria (p. 199).

Riess (1977) added to this:

> Homosexuality fails as a diagnosis because it does not describe a uniform set of signs and symptoms, because the dynamics of the preference vary among individuals rather than having a common core, and finally because the causes of the sex preference are so varied. In fact there would be no diagnosis of homosexuality—only the myriad forms of homosexual behavior would be recognized—if the bigotry of the righteous did not force the belief (shared even by homosexuals) that a distinct essence—homosexuality—exists.

From the above, it follows that homosexuality is behavior and must be so specified. It is clear, therefore, that we must reject the assertion of "latent" homosexuality. Congruently with this we must reject the implication that there is a mandatory homosexual drive or affect in all like-sexed groups. We use the word "homosocial" to describe the behavior of individuals in such aggregations. Homosexuality as a description must involve sexual behavior; otherwise it becomes meaningless.

Also we insist that, like other behaviors, there is no such single category as homosexuality. There are only male and female persons who have, for a variety of reasons, chosen a like-sexed love partner. As Kinsey (1948, 1953) many years ago pointed out, sexuality whether homo- or hetero- ranges from exclusive to merely random sporadic choice.

Since homosexuality is seen by us as the product of a developmental sequence in which early experiences, parental expectations, self-identification, and goal orientation are important ingredients, we attempt in the next section to sketch the major parameters of the growth of the individual to a firm, self-determined state of autonomy. The choice of direction for love-partnership is a function of the total growth process.

Elsewhere we have written (Gundlach & Reiss, 1968).

> The growth and development of the human being from infancy to maturity is largely a socializing process accomplished by parents and others who are themselves products of a specific culture. They use both conscious and unconscious pressures to mold the child and do so in varyingly effective ways. Development is a phased process, moving from stage to stage and, at each stage, dependent on the preceding one. Maslow (1962) has elaborated this concept as progressing from satisfaction of lower needs, instinctive-like in nature, to the gratification of more socialized needs. Angyal (1941) postulates movement toward autonomy as the first thematic element in maturation. Differentiation, acquisition of perceptual and motor skills, mastery of varying aspects of the environment and adaptation to other aspects are expressions of the development of autonomy. The second theme, found in later maturation, is that of homonomy.
>
> In a socio-psychological frame of reference in which values play a part, Loevinger (1964) distinguished at least six stages of maturation. The first is characterized by impulse-gratification with a consequent intolerance of frustration and fear of retaliation. In the second or opportunistic stage, security needs are dominant. The child understands the rules but finds out that it is being caught that matters. He moves away from dependency toward a "do it yourself" attitude and learns to manipulate the world and its persons. Third, the conformist era introduces a shift in response toward people as people are seen in the emergence of a desire for acceptance, belongingness, participation. Here, appearances, reputation, and moralisms such as "honesty is the best policy" represent the ethical system. As the fourth stage develops, the moralistic values of stage three become incorporated not as reactions to external pressures but as a set of

internalized rules. Capacity for guilt accompanies this stage. In the fifth period where considerable autonomy has been achieved by control over conflicts between duties and needs, one develops sufficient self-identity to make possible the recognition of the other and an appreciation of individual differences.

Those rare ones who achieve the sixth level of maturity are characterized by integration. They are balanced persons of depth, wisdom and humanity. Their achievements in autonomy are harmonized by homonomy, described Marston (1928), in terms of treatment of people not as things or as an audience but as people; not exploitively but with consideration, respect and understanding. Ideal marriages and family relationships are often seen in terms of mutuality, tenderness, cooperativeness, generosity, awareness of the other person, individuality, and the rich interaction and pleasures of the close association.

These levels may indicate a developmental sequence in which one can get to a higher level only by first growing through the lower levels. But they may also characterize the ultimate level of maturity of character achieved by adults. Examined in the social scene, one can classify the style of the man and his work; for instance the opportunistic (level 2) business man charges what the traffic will bear, the (level 4) conscientious public servant is devoted to carrying out certain conservation, or public interest principles. These levels also characterize the social and sexual relationships, from the (level 1) impulsive sexuality, expressed in indiscriminate petting to the search for quick and varying sexual partners, or (level 2) a marriage of convenience and mutual services; (level 3) a 'successful' marriage where the partners can glory in their social status, display of possessions, and rounds of publicized affairs, or to (level 6) complete relationships of some depth of feeling and mutuality (p. 205ff.).

PSYCHOANALYTIC THEORIES OF HOMOSEXUALITY

Because so much of the speculation and writing on homosexuals is derived from the varieties of psychoanalytic theory, the next section is an attempt to describe, in skeletal form, the ideological thinking about homosexuality as found in the major proponents of psychoanalysis.

An initial observation must be made here. Since most of the theorists were either men or had been trained by male analysts, there is much evidence that the theory explicitly or implicitly has an inherent male bias. In many instances, there is little separation of speculation about male homosexuality from that on women. Titles of articles rarely differentiate or specify whether the subjects are females or males. Where this is not so obvious, the assumption is often made that what is true of the male holds for women but in mirror-image form.

One of the most important humanizing and liberating contributions of psychoanalysis was the change it effected in attitudes toward sexuality in general and homosexuality in particular. The work of Freud and his followers—and their critics—has been a significant step in challenging the notion, virtually universal in Western culture since the Middle Ages, that homosexuality constitutes either moral depravity or constitutional abnormality and as such is a dread stigma. Careers and reputations were, and still are, routinely destroyed by even a suspicion of Wilde's "love that dare not speak its name." Even though, as we shall see, objective research has failed to substantiate many psychoanalytic formulations, an understanding of them is fundamental to the scientific study of homosexuality.

The following quotation from Freud's famous letter to the mother of a homosexual (Freud, 1957) demonstrates his scientific and compassionate viewpoint:

April, 9, 1935

DEAR MRS. . . . . :

I gather from your letter that your son is a homosexual. I am most impressed by the fact that you do not mention this term yourself in your information about him. May I question you, why you avoid it? Homosexuality is assuredly no advantage but it is nothing to be ashamed of, no vice, no degradation, it cannot be classified as an illness; we consider it to be a variation of the sexual function produced by a certain arrest of sexual development. Many highly respectable individuals of ancient and modern times have been homosexuals, several of the greatest men among them (Plato, Michelangelo, Leonardo da Vinci, etc.). It is a great injustice to persecute homosexuality as a crime and cruelty too. If you do not believe me, read the books of Havelock Ellis.

By asking me if I can help, you mean, I suppose, if I can abolish homosexuality and make normal heterosexuality take its place. The answer is, in a general way, we cannot promise to achieve it. In a certain number of cases we succeed in developing the blighted germs of heterosexual tendencies which are present in every homosexual, in the majority of cases it is no more possible. It is a question of the quality and the age of the individual. The result of treatment cannot be predicted.

What analysis can do for your son runs in a different line. If he is unhappy, neurotic, torn by conflicts, inhibited in his social life, analysis may bring him harmony, peace of mind, full efficiency, whether he remains a homosexual or gets changed. If you make up your mind he should have analysis with me—I don't expect you will—, he has to come over to Vienna. I have no intention of leaving here. However, don't neglect to give me your answer.

As this letter suggests, the central aspect of Freud's view of homosexuality is that it is a variation only in the choice of *object* of sexual desire; that is, the other two components of the sexual instinct, the source (libidinal energy) and the aim (genital union) of homosexual sexuality are identical with those of heterosexuality. Hence, homosexuality is seen as part of the continuum, and indeed part of the universal early experience, of innately bisexual human beings. As such it is pathological only because to psychoanalytic thinking it represents either a fixation at a pregenital stage of psychosexual development or a regression from the oedipal stage. In either event, homosexuals do not reach the stage of "post-ambivalent genitality"—rare enough among heterosexuals—where the oedipal conflict has been resolved and the necessarily opposite-sex partner is loved fully both tenderly and sexually.

According to the psychoanalytic formulation, choosing a lover of the same sex is necessarily narcissistic (self-referent) and therefore related to early developmental stages at which the child has not yet made a distinction between self and other, nor learned to tolerate enough ambivalence to make "object love" possible. The narcissistic object choice—which can be made by either homosexuals or heterosexuals—is loved more for the capacity to gratify needs than for any qualities of its own. Freud, therefore, felt that homosexuals of both sexes primarily love their partners as they themselves want to be loved by their mothers, from whom they are not adequately differentiated because of various traumas in early childhood.

Beyond the inclusion of homosexuality within the mainstream of human sexuality and the conviction that it is narcissistic and psychopathological, psychoanalytic theorists do not agree about the dynamics or the etiology of either male or female homosexuality. We shall examine the psychodynamic formulations of homosexuality in general and, where possible, views of sex differences in homosexuality in the work of Freud, Stekel, Klein, Sullivan, Jung, Adler, Horney and Thompson.

The most widely held Freudian formulation of male homosexuality, as summarized and investigated by Bieber (1962), is that it results from a confused sexual identity and exaggerated incestuous fears caused by a family in which the mother is close-binding and seductive and the father is weak or absent. This set of circumstances creates a particularly traumatic oedipal triangle in which the mother is feared because she is dangerously overstimulating and the father, who fails to give the boy the ego support he needs to withstand his own incestuous and murderous impulses or the real situation, is feared as a revengeful castrator. The child experiences a complex and terrifying mixture of desire for and dread of both parents, with concomitant ego weakness, confusions in his sexual identification, and deep ambivalence toward both sexes. Homosexual acts represent a denial of sex differences caused by castration anxiety and the associated fear of the mother which is transferred to all women.

In Wiedeman's (1962) summary of psychoanalytic interpretations of overt male homosexuality, anal fixations are explained as regressions from the overly intense oedipal conflict, the common preference for anonymous sex without stable partners as evidence of ego weakness, and acts of active or passive fellatio as either revenge or control of the paternal penis or oral incorporation of the maternal breast. The latter idea, as we shall see, is considered fundamental from the point of view of the object relations school of psychoanalysis. Anna Freud (1951) considers the resolution of the following issues as prerequisites for the successful treatment (i.e., conversion to heterosexuality) of homosexual males: fear of the castrating woman, fear of aggression and oral dependence on women, disgust with women as anal objects, fear of destruction and sadism toward women, fantasy fear of becoming a woman through intercourse. Freud's letter makes clear that he considered such conversions problematic, and many of his modern adherents have now come to question the desirability of such attempts.

Freud conceptualized female homosexuality as consisting of narcissistic, oral, and oedipal components. The choice of a female lover is seen primarily as a defense and a reaction formation against hatred of the mother, who deprived the daughter of her love, as well as an attempt to regain that love. Another possible dynamic in lesbianism is unconscious love and revengeful turning away from a disappointing father. Fenichel (1945) suggests that lesbians turn to other women as a means of denying castration through identification with their fathers. The principal dynamics of lesbianism from the classical psychoanalytic standpoint are either fixation at the oral stage of development or regression from the oedipal, and the same combination of mingled unconscious desire for and dread of both parents characterizes male and female homosexuals. Theory would therefore predict that lesbians particularly should manifest clinging dependency and oral rage in their love relationships.

One of the first of Freud's early adherents to study in depth the psychodynamics of sexuality, particularly sexual perversions, was Wilhelm Stekel (1920). His book on homosexuality presages much of the later psychoanalytic opinion on the subject and presents extensive case history material. While Stekel argues against a simplistic single-cause explanation of homosexuality, which he considers a deviation and a neurotic symptom, he emphasizes the relationship between homosexual behavior and unconscious sadism. Homosexuality he believes to be in many cases a substitute for "criminal heterosexual aggression" in both males and females. Homosexual behavior is therefore a flight necessary to protect both the self and the other from the acting-out of both murderous and incestuous impulses.

Stekel asserts that homosexuals of both sexes have similar psychodynamics, and that their feelings for the opposite sex are characterized by anxiety, disgust, and scorn, but never by indifference; these feelings are remnants of the oedipal period in which the opposite-sexed parent was the child's love object. One of Stekel's clinical observations supported by later analytic work with male homosexuals is that the narcissism and the identification with and fixation upon the mother may actually be a response to rejection by the father. Likewise—and this is noteworthy because it has been corroborated in the research of Gundlach and Riess (1968)—he suggests that lesbians may turn away from their fathers because of early rape by a family member which has resulted in hatred and a sense of betrayal.

The object relations school of psychoanalysis, as exemplified by the work of Melanie Klein (1948; Klein, Hermann, & Money-Kyrle, 1955), traces the roots of homosexuality, and of psychopathology in general, to the earliest experiences and stages of development; frustrations in the first months of life are felt to underlie and essentially determine all later personality traits, including sexual object choice. This approach emphasizes the primacy of primitive oral-sadistic and associated paranoid fantasies in the etiology of homosexuality. Unsatisfactory nurturing experiences cause massive anxieties and rage reactions which the child projects; he thereby comes to fear the world and its objects as potentially devouring. Klein interprets fellatio compulsions among male homosexuals as displacements of primitive oral incorporative fantasies of the mother's breast. The partner's penis represents a reassuringly visible breast substitute, and the vagina is equated with a castrating and devouring mouth. Like the Freudians, object relations analysts claim that male homosexuals have internalized a hated, destructive image of women and of the sexual act with women, but for the latter, the homosexual's turning to the father with the fantasy of taking continual nourishment from his penis is psychodynamically central. In addition, in the Kleinian view, females and the interior of the body represent the unconscious for the male homosexual; all that is terrifying and uncanny is seen as located inside the mother's body. Hence, choosing an object with a penis also allays fears of the unconscious, since the partner's penis represents consciousness and external reality. Male homosexuality is therefore considered to be a primitive mechanism by which the ego seeks to deny incapacitating anxiety and to control the unconscious by concentrating attention on the external and immediately perceivable.

The object relations view of homosexuality in women is that it involves a retreat from the terror of the father's bad and damaging penis. Loving women is also an attempt to make reparation to the mother for the fantasy of stealing the father's penis from her, as well as a reaction formation and undoing of oral-sadistic rage at the mother for oral deprivations the daughter suffered. The intense oral rage and paranoid fantasy which this school attributes to homosexuals of both sexes imply that they should manifest profound ambivalence in love relationships, distorted body image, and deeply disturbed functioning with primitive defenses predominating.

Harry Stack Sullivan, (1953), founder of the interpersonal school of psychoanalysis, has somewhat different and complementary ideas about the etiology of homosexuality. He believes that homosexuality in both sexes results from experiences which have "erected a barrier to integration with persons of the other sex." The development of close same-sex friendships in latency (the "chum") he regards as a favorable prognosis for heterosexuality; the failure to have chums forces the needs for same-sex intimacy to combine with sexuality, and homosexual attachments result from the "collisions of lust, security, and intimacy needs." In males, maturational retardation or attachment to an older male is often involved. Prohibitions against heterosexuality may additionally result in "primary genital phobia" forcing either sex to resort to homosexual outlets. Like the Kleinians, the Sullivanians believe that male homosexuals fear the vagina as alien and "not me," which implies serious dissociation of personality.

The expectations of the phenomenon of homosexuality in the works of Jung and Adler, Freud's early followers and later rivals, reflect their characteristic differences with him over the issue of the centrality of sexuality as a determinant of personality. According to Jung's (1974) analytical psychology, the unconscious of each sex contains a representation of the opposite sex (anima in men, animus in women) which, when it is projected upon an opposite-sexed love object, accounts for the power of the attraction to that person. In homosexuals, it is the persona, which represents the external, adaptive aspect of the personality, rather than the animus or anima, which is projected onto the same-sexed partner. The homosexual plays the role of the opposite sex with the love partner, which leaves her or him unconsciously identified with the animus or anima. Jung believed that such identifications "always involve a defective adaptation" to external reality and a lack of relatedness to the real object because the subject is predominantly oriented and absorbed in inner, rather than interpersonal, processes—a notion akin to Freudian narcissism in homosexuals.

Alfred Adler (1946), founder of individual psychology, viewed homosexuality as an unconscious form of antisocial rebellion akin to compulsion neurosis. The pains to which homosexuals go to explain away what Adler considered deviation from the compelling norm of heterosexuality indicates for him the degree of anxiety conformity to this norm excites for homosexuals, whom he regards as inordinately ambitious and afraid of life. Homosexuality represents a partial solution to this intolerable contradiction.

Adler traces homosexuality to childhood experiences of overprotection which lead to intense ambition, coupled with doubts about sexual identification and gender confusions (boys raised as girls, girls excluded from male company). He predicts that the condition should be more common in youngest children, who feel oppressed by their smallness and become intensely ambitious in an attempt to compensate. When their ambition is thwarted they are consumed with self-doubt which gets expressed in the sexual sphere. Male homosexuals, he concluded, experience heterosexual intercourse as an impossible performance and test of self-worth.

The etiology of female homosexuality from the standpoint of individual psychology is somewhat different. The salient factor is felt to be the little girl's conviction that her brother is preferred to her or that a male child would have been preferred, which creates an unattainable ambition to be the chosen one. He cites case histories where generalized experiences with brutal fathers and brothers cause the girl to withdraw fearfully. Fear and dread of the female role from traumatic losses or witnessing and misinterpreting childbirth can also contribute to sexual deviation. In addition, Adler cites the role of revenge motives against the mother and a low opinion of women's role vis-à-vis men.

In sum, homosexuals in Adler's opinion suffer from an "erroneous infantile evaluation of the demands of life, exaggerated because of their pessimistic outlook and fear of their inability to fulfill them." The task of psychological treatment of the homosexual is to make conscious her or his true motivation for the "flight from responsibility," which is the perception of normal sexuality as an impossible demand.

Karen Horney (1937), like Adler, stresses the importance of nonsexual motivation in sexual activities. In her view of the personalities of homosexuals, it is fear of injury to the neurotic pride which causes withdrawal from competition with same-sexed equals and inhibits heterosexual attraction.

The formulations of Clara Thompson (1947), a follower of Sullivan, take a quite different position than those of other psychodynamic theorists we have reviewed, a position more consonant to research findings in the area. She considers the homosexual diagnosis to be a "wastebasket into which all friendly and hostile feelings toward members of one's own sex are applied," and believes homosexuality to be not a clinical entity nor cause of behavior, but a symptom which appears in persons of different character structures and consequently has a multiplicity of meanings— rather like the role of headaches in medicine. She advocates investigating the type of relationship which any particular homosexual forms, the nature of any dependency, and the personality of the love object. In a radical departure from the thinking of most psychoanalytic theorists (and one corroborated by research), she finds female homosexuals more often normal than male homosexuals, with the behavior more often precipitated by isolation. She also goes so far as to entertain the possibility of adult and mature homosexual love relationships, and suggests the following areas for investigation in treatment: life situations which lead to homosexual choice, whether parents wanted child of opposite sex and/or treated child as such, presence of fear of opposite sex, and a simultaneous fear of intimacy and of loneliness. Homosexuality, like heterosexuality, can be either constructive or destructive, depending on which aspects of the parent/child relationship are recapitulated, she feels.

To summarize the psychodynamic views of homosexuality reviewed here, all (with the possible exception of Thompson) see it as a manifestation of psychopathology related in some way to early traumatic experiences and produced by certain family dynamics. However, as Thompson points out, many children grow up with similar conflicts and fail to become homosexual, while others with different family constellations do. There is also considerable disagreement even within the classical psychoanalytic camp over whether the phenomenon is predominantly a manifestation of arrested development and a fixation at the oral or the anal level (with much argument over whether it is predominantly oral or anal in nature), or whether it results from a regression away from the oedipal stage. Often one has the impression in reviewing the theories that they represent the fantasies of the theoretician more accurately than those of the subject. There is an unfortunate tendency, also, among theorists to look reductionistically for a single causative factor in so complex a phenomenon, and to assume that similar dynamics necessarily underlie similar behaviors. One could, and should, question instead the sense of treating all homosexuals as psychodynamically equivalent, as Lachmann (1975) has pointed out in a series of case studies where homosexuality as a presenting symptom has radically different meanings and functions for various patients.

METHODOLOGICAL CONSIDERATIONS

For those who are interested in scrutinizing what has been written about homosexuality, the best source, up to 1970, is the annotated bibliography by Weinberg and Bell (1970). This lists, describes, and briefly criticizes some 1200 scholarly publications in the general field. The reader's attention is also called to a relatively new, scientific magazine, the *Journal of Homosexuality*, begun in 1975 under the editorship of Charles Silverstein, Ph.D. Finally, for the reader more in search of a semi-popular resource, there is a fine brochure on homosexuality written by Elizabeth Ogg (1972) as one of the Public Affairs Institute Pamphlet series.

In what follows in this chapter, we shall deal mainly with major investigations of comparative material for male and female homophiles. These studies separate into three broad methodological categories. One includes paper-and-pencil questionnaires and other instruments administered to selected aggregations of self-identified male and female homosexuals and heterosexuals. The second involves the application of psychoanalytic interviews or the use of psychoanalytic therapy for small, specially selected samples. The third consists of comparisons between the researcher's sample population and a supposedly comparable group of the opposite sex whose data were collected by another investigator.

In all cases, the contents of the questionnaires, the focus of the depth interview and/or therapy and the instruments used vary with the theoretical bias or interest of the investigator. For some, the starting point is the axiomatic assumption that homosexuality is necessarily pathological, regressive or fixational. For others, the point of departure is concern for the formative influence of parental child-rearing practices, expectations, and attitudes. Still others start with an emphasis on emotional components of personality such as dependence-independence, dominance-submissiveness, hostility and aggression. Compounding this confusion is the lack of comparability among the groups of homosexuals in the most obvious demographic parameters. Hooker (1963) and Saghir and Robins (1973) used only urban California and Illinois homosexuals varying in age and ethnicity. Gundlach and Riess' (1968) subjects came from all over the U.S.A. and were all adult women from both urban and rural backgrounds. Weinberg and Williams (1974) gathered their data from members of homophile groups, private clubs and "gay" bars in New York City, San Francisco, Amsterdam, Holland and Copenhagen, Denmark. With this diversity of people and places, conclusions are necessarily tentative, limited, and subject to distortion and misinterpretation.

RESEARCH FINDINGS

This section on data derived from studies of female and male homosexuals and, in some instances, their heterosexual comparison subjects, starts with the least controversial and most objective methodological approaches. The first group of research studies cited consists of data on the frequency of the behavior in both sexes. Next we bring together material on birth-order and sibling status in relationship to later choice of partner. Finally we summarize social attitude differences about homosexuality in women and men.

Frequency of Homosexuality in Sample Population

First, as to frequency of the phenomenon in the two groups, the initial data come from Kinsey's (1953, p. 488) studies. He used his six-step classification ranging from entirely heterosexual to exclusively homosexual (Table 1).

The findings from countries like Sweden, Germany, and England are all in agreement in that female homosexuality occurred, in the past, about one-third as often as male homosexuality. Athanasiou and collaborators (1970) collected data on 20,000 upper-income, well educated men and women in the U.S.A. Of these, 33% of the males and 20% of the females had experienced at least one homosexual act. In comparison with a heterosexual group, both lesbians and male homosexuals tried heterosexual behavior at an earlier age than did the homosexuals. This is also in accord with the Gundlach and Riess study (1968).

So, too, the legal sanctions against like-sexed acts were very frequently not invoked against women. Kinsey (1953) found that, from 1896 to

TABLE 1

Category		In Females	In Males
		(in percentages)	
0	Entirely heterosexual experience		
	Single	61-72	53-78
	Married	89-90	90-92
	Previously married	75-80	
1-6	At least some homosexual experience	11-20	18-42
2-6	More than incidental homosexual experience	6-14	13-38
3-6	As much or more homosexual experience than heterosexual experience	4-11	9-32
4-6	Mostly homosexual experience	3-8	7-26
5-6	Almost exclusively homosexual experience	2-6	5-22
6	Exclusively homosexual experience	1-3	3-16

1952, there was no single sodomy conviction of a woman. Of all the arrests in New York City between 1940 and 1950, only three women were accused of homosexual acts as contrasted with "tens of thousands" of males.

Michael, Wilson, and Zumpe (1974) have made a recent survey of bisexuality among female monkeys. In addition, they have done research on rhesus monkeys in their own laboratory, studying female-female and female-male mounting behavior. They write:

> There was previously a lack of quantitative data on the expression of bisexual patterns of behavior in females of a primate species against which to evaluate the effects of experimental interventions. It now seems clear that male-like mounting behavior occurs as a part of the normal behavioral repertoire in about one-third of mature female rhesus monkeys that have been born and reared in the wild. However, bisexual behavior was observed with regularity only in about 12% of the females in our group. The occurrence of this behavior was influenced by the secretory activity of the ovaries: its incidence increased in intact animals near the expected time of ovulation and was greatly reduced by bilateral ovariectomy. Thus bisexual behavior was increased at those times and under those conditions when the heterosexual activity of the pair was maximal. These findings bring this primate species into line with several infraprimate mammals. Whether or not a given rhesus female would express any bisexual behavior was much influenced by the

reactions of her male partner and by his tolerance of her behavior. It was noteworthy that, as ejaculatory performance declined after castration, there was also a progressive increase in the expression of bisexual behavior by the female partners. Thus the hormonal status of both male and female influenced the expression and frequency of her mounting behavior (p. 410).

Birth Order

In another direction, interest has been developing in the differential aspects of birth order, sib order, and family size. Gundlach (1972) has treated the data from Bieber et al.'s (1962) sample of male homosexuals so as to relate frequency of appearance of homosexuality in the men and their comparison subjects to birth order. Here the homosexuals were more rarely only children than were the heterosexuals. Also, the homosexual male was more frequently found as the younger or youngest sib. So, too, Westwood (1960) reported that 102 of 127 homosexuals were only sons or youngest children.

In contrast, Gundlach and Riess (1968) report that their lesbian subjects were more frequently only children. Their results are presented in Table 2.

Schubert, Wagner, and Riess (1976) report data on 86 homosexuals drawn from a clinic population of 1040 male outpatients. These were compared to 217 male college entrants. The percentage of homosexuals among the outpatient males who had a younger sister or who were later-borns among all male sibships was in each case significantly higher than for contrasting heterosexual sibling constellations. These authors also summarize many relevant studies, most of which point to the primacy of child-rearing practices as determinative of later choice of sexual style.

All of these data seem to relate more to child-rearing practices and to parental expectations of sex-role differences in their children than to innate or constitutional factors. Gundlach (1972) concludes "Unlike the

TABLE 2

Numbers of Only, First-born and Last-born Children Among Lesbian
($N = 217$) and Non-Lesbian ($N = 231$) Groups

Group	Only	2, 3, 4 Siblings First-born	Last born	5, 6, 7 Siblings 1, 2, 3, or 4	5th, 6th or 7th
Homosexual	43	73	9	16	17
Comparison	31	63	62	32	5

only child or first-born in small families where being lesbians may in part be a function of rivalry with males, in large families the factor of omission and neglect seems crucial."

DIFFERENTIAL PUBLIC ATTITUDES TOWARD HOMOSEXUALS

The history of public acceptance of homosexual behavior seems to be in a state of rapid change. In 1949, Murdock cited evidence from 193 different world societies relating to differential attitudes toward male and female homosexuality. The former was acceptable to 28% of the societies studied whereas only 11% accepted the same behavior in women.

Cross-cultural and even biological reports deal almost exclusively with male acts. Ford and Beach (1951) in their book on 76 societies found only one group, the Mohave Amerindians, in which female-female relationships were tabooed while 36% of the societies disapproved of male relationships with males. As noted above in Michael et al.'s (1974) study of primate behavior, there are few observations on genuine female homosexuality in animals. The lack of data may be a function of the field scientist's preoccupation with male sexuality.

In two articles, Milham, San Miguel, and Kellogg (1976) and San Miguel and Milham (1976) develop a sound study of the structure of attitudes of the public toward homosexuality. Unfortunately their respondents were limited to 795 female and male undergraduates at the University of Houston. Despite the limitations of the sample, the conclusions fit into the general findings in the field. The authors constructed a test of 38 belief statements to which agreement or disagreement had to be indicated. The factorial analysis of the data turned up at least three factors which differentiated attitudes toward like-sexed behavior in women and men. The first factor, which accounted for 55% of the variance about male homosexuality and 14% for female behavior, had to do with the polarity of legal repression and danger. Both of these were more frequently chosen for male homosexuality. The authors conclude

> that persons express significantly more personal anxiety with respect to the same-sexed homosexuals than to opposite-sex homosexuals, that persons express greater preference for opposite-sexed over same-sexed homosexuals, that males advocate more repression than females against male homosexuals and that females attribute more cross-sexed mannerisms to male homosexuals than males attribute to female homosexuals (Milham et al., 1976, p. 6).

The most up-to-date data surveying public attitudes come from a Gallup poll conducted in June 1977 on a group of 1513 adults. The results are reported in an article in the *New York Times* on July 17, 1977. Once again, the pollsters do not differentiate female from male homosexuality nor female from male respondents. However, the significant conclusion is that there is still a large-scale resentment of homosexuality with 33% agreeing that homosexuals should not have equal rights in terms of job opportunities. An interesting finding was an apparent difference in homosexual job rights in differing job areas. For instance, elementary school teaching was seen by 65% of the respondents as a field in which not to hire homosexuals. Only 22% felt the same way about the sales field. Also, 54% were against homosexuals among the clergy.

PSYCHOLOGICAL TEST STUDIES

Space does not permit citations of the research on test signs of homosexual behavior or orientation. Most of the studies are contaminated by their origin in and dependence upon the specific analytic orientation of the tester. The material looked for in the test protocols is based on what the theory demands. So, if theory says that the male homosexual must have hostility towards other males, the protocols are examined and in many instances only inferentially treated from the bias of the theory. The same methodological error exists when comparisons are made of test indices of female and male homosexuality. Most of the studies of females use signs derived from material on males.

Even with these strictures, the data are nonsupportive of a complex of indicators for homosexual behavior or self-identification. That there are some obvious signs is axiomatic. For instance, the portrayal of two like-sexed lovers on a figure drawing test or an overtly homosexual story on the T.A.T. can be clear predictors. There are, however, very few such factors. For those interested in the field of projective and nonprojective testing of male and female homosexuals, there are three fairly recent surveys. Van den Aardweg (1967, 1969) has done an extensive literature search of test research including the Rorschach, T.A.T., figure drawings, Szondi, and M.M.P.I. His survey was limited to male homosexuality. Safer, Riess, and Yotive (1974) attempted to repeat van den Aardweg's search, but for female studies only. There are few valid studies of the lesbian. A significant step in developing this area would be to conduct a cross-validational testing of males with guidelines derived from the newer theories of women's personality. It is to be hoped that such studies will come from the women's movement.

As of now, van den Aardweg concludes that testing of males is non-predictive and that very few indices are in the direction of increased pathology in the homosexual group as compared to heterosexuals. Safer, Riess, and Yotive come to the same conclusion. In addition there is some evidence that lesbians are more like heterosexual males than they are like homosexual men or heterosexual women.

Direct comparisons by the same researchers of male and female homosexuals and comparison groups of heterosexuals are infrequent. Thompson, McCandless, and Strickland (1971) summarize their finding thus,

> The present study is an examination of the reported personal adjustment and psychological well-being of male and female homosexuals. Groups of white, well-educated, homosexual volunteers, matched for sex, age and education with heterosexual controls, did not differ in important ways from heterosexuals in Defensiveness, Personal Adjustment, or Self-Confidence (Adjective Check List); or Self-Evaluation (Semantic Differential). Male homosexuals were less defensive and less self-confident, female homosexuals more self-confident than their respective controls. Homosexuals were more self-concerned as there were more members of both homosexual groups who had undertaken psychotherapy. However, there were no adjustment differences in any groups between those who had and had not experienced psychotherapy (p. 78).

Loney (1972) also collected data from nonpatient homosexual volunteers. Her conclusions included findings of higher proportions of marriage among the women homosexuals, more expressed satisfaction with homosexual life and fewer homosexual partners than was true of male homosexuals. The groups consisted of 30 men and 40 men and women, all self-identified as homosexual.

Siegelman (1972) studied four groups of nonclinical (nonpatient) volunteers. There were 84 homosexual and 13 heterosexual women and 307 male homosexuals compared with 137 heterosexuals. The measuring instruments were the Scheir and Cattell Neuroticism Scale Questionnaire. Factor analytic processes were used. In general, the findings were: (a) Among the women, the homosexuals were as well adjusted as the heterosexuals; (b) the homosexual men were less well adjusted than their comparison males on four factors, better adjusted on three scales and no different on six scales; (c) the women homosexuals varied less in adjustment than the males.

We come then to three large-scale investigations of "normal" homosexuals. These studies make possible several entries into the better understanding of the so-called adjusted homosexual person. One of the three actually compares the responses of adult female and male homosexuals as well as of a group of female and male heterosexuals. By itself, this study of Saghir and Robins (1973) merits consideration because of its freedom from initial bias. From it alone, one can compare some male with some female homosexuals and with some heterosexuals. The generality of the findings is limited because of the kinds of persons selected as respondents.

However, the existence of Weinberg and Williams' (1974) book which deals with the male homosexual and the Gundlach and Riess (1968) paper on the female homosexual makes possible various tests of the generalizability of the findings of each study. Because of overlap with Bieber et al.'s (1962) discussion of male homosexual patients, the Gundlach and Riess study also makes feasible a comparison of self-labeled pathological male homosexuals who sought and were in psychotherapy with a similar group of women homosexual patients.

Looking first at what Saghir and Robins found for this group of subjects, it is essential to specify the nature of the sample and the method of studying the respondents. These authors chose their subjects from self-identified homosexuals who were members of or had friends in the Mattachine Society or one of its homophile organizations. Geographically, the subjects resided in Chicago or San Francisco. The heterosexuals, matched with homosexuals for marital status, age, socioeconomic standing, and religious background, were all from St. Louis county. The size of the obtained populations was 89 for the male homosexual, and 35 for the heterosexual counterpart. Women homosexuals were 57 in number, with 43 matched heterosexuals.

The nature of the sample is of considerable importance if one is to be able to draw conclusions from the data. In the Saghir and Robins groups, 82% of the male homosexuals and 86% of the heterosexual men were single persons. For the women, the comparable data are 75% single for both homo- and heterosexual groups. All of these people came from urban and larger city environments. Socioeconomic status was high for all respondents. The method used in this study was a structured interview covering the usual demographic variables and then focusing on psychopathological behavior, the evolution and development of sexual identity, family relationships, specific sexual practices, and involvements with people. The interviews with each member of all four groups lasted between three and four hours. Responses, usually of the yes or no type, were noted in a 50-page record booklet.

Judgment of pathology was based on manifest behavior and fell into well delineated categories: anxiety neurosis, antisocial personality, alcoholism, affective disorders, phobia, paranoia, psychophysiologic disturbances.

The authors of the study, like those of the other research studies, do not claim that their sample is representative of the total homosexual universe. Each investigation must initially be looked upon as unique. We shall therefore summarize whatever comparable data are found in each study and then indicate the similarities and differences across studies.

The basic conclusions arrived at by Saghir and Robins can be stated best in their own words.

> Homosexuals are not a priori sick. Many of them present little or no psychopathology and those who do are rarely disabled by their disorder. Homosexual men are psychopathologically very similar to single heterosexual men while homosexual women tend to show a greater degree of psychopathology than heterosexual women. This seems to be primarily related to excessive alcohol intake and drinking problems. However, manifest neurotic disorders do not seem to be more prevalent among homosexual men or women. . . Most often, the presenting psychopathology of both male and female homosexuals is depression and an underlying conflict involving the homosexual orientation . . . Psychotherapy, whether supportive or insight oriented, must be aimed realistically at the individual homosexual and not at homosexuality (p. 317).

The study and its statistical support are far too comprehensive to deal with in detail. We have extracted some data which, in our view, throw light on sex differences or non-differences. For instance, Saghir and Robins separated their subjects into those who, in childhood and adolescence, were called "sissies" or who displayed behavior which could be called sissyish and those who seemed to be "real" boys. Similarly, for the women, the groups were "tomboys" and girlish girls.

In both sexes, the frequency of opposite-sex orientation was about the same, two-thirds of the male homosexuals showing effeminancy and two-thirds of the women acting like tomboys. What are the characteristics and differentials of these four groups? Table 3, derived from several in Saghir and Robins, illustrates these factors.

There are many ways of looking at this table. First, in most respects the tomboy female homosexuals were more like the nontomboy homosexuals than the sissy males were like their noneffeminate comparisons. Tomboyishness was more frequent among women in adolescence regardless of

TABLE 3

Some Characteristics of Male and Female Homosexuals Divided
into Tomboys, Sissies, not Tomboys and not Sissies
(All in Percentages)

Items	Male sissie	Male not sissie	Female tomboy	Female not tomboy
During childhood and adolescence thought repeatedly about wanting to be the opposite sex.	45	5	73	38
As an adult considers status to be that appropriate to a person of the same sex.	38	88	46	40
Consider self to be like person of opposite sex or neuter	62	12	54	60
Cross-dressed in childhood more than once	25	9	5	0
Lost same sex parent by death or divorce before age 10	23	8	8	23
Identified primarily with cross-sexed parent	69	54	9	31
Identified primarily with same-sex parent	10	21	47	6
Identified equally with both parents	4	8	5	19
No identification with either parent	17	39	17	44

* Data from tables 2.2, 2.3, 10.1, 10.2 in Saghir & Robins (1973).

adult sexual status than is true of male sissyness. Again more male homosexuals identified with their mothers than the lesbians identified with
their fathers. The women also exceeded the males in their identification
with the parent of their own sex. Evidently for the lesbian, the father
was more potent as a negative factor than was the mother for the male
homosexuals. In general, then, tomboyishness is less predictive of lesbianism than effeminate behavior in males is of adult male homosexuality.

Saghir and Robins feel that their data indicate a major factor to be in
sibling sex. In male homosexual families there is a shortage of female
and an excess of male sibs which may account for the prevalence of sissyness. Among lesbians the same shortage and excess may operate to "mas-
culinize" the girls.

It is difficult to summarize a book in a few paragraphs. The following
statements are based on statistically significant differences in the material

on urban, single, educated and middle-income probands. First, comparing male homosexuals to heterosexuals, the former have more guilt and fear about sex, more active homosexual fantasies, do more "cruising," have earlier masturbation and genital arousal, poorer parental relationships, and more absent fathers.

Similar data for the women show that lesbians, in comparison to non-lesbians, show more attachments to a like-sexed teacher, later genitality, more "platonic" romances, greater frequency of homosexual fantasies, little guilt about sex, and greater self-identification as masculine or neuter. They more frequently drop out of college and drink more.

Finally, comparing men and women homosexuals, it is found that men are far more frequently beset by fear and guilt, have shorter affairs with more different partners, experience fewer heterosexual relationships, cruise much more, are much more hypersensitive to injury or insult, and are much more preoccupied with homosexuality as a form of behavior.

Sexual responsiveness in homosexual men parallels that in homosexual females. The age of onset of like-sexed attachments, of fantasies and dreams, and actual sexual arousal are about the same for both sexes. Although the differences are very small, there is some evidence that such affects develop later among women and are more often associated with a particular teacher. Genitality is also a differential between men and women, with more "platonic," nongenital relationships among lesbians.

Saghir and Robins conclude their study with a hope for research, a hope which depends for its realization on two social changes. These are reform in the laws restricting sexual choice and acts and improvement in the social climate. This is required in order for the research to be based on mutual trust and shared goals.

Somewhat paralleling the study above, Weinberg and Williams (1974) investigated the phenomenon of male homosexuality in three different cultures. Their focus is on the "ways in which the homosexual is affected by his social situation, for example, how the connotations and expectations surrounding homosexuality affect the homosexual's behavior and self-concept." As stated before, these authors selected male homosexuals in the U.S.A., Denmark, and Holland as respondents to an 11-page, 145-item questionnaire. In the U.S.A., the questionnaires were mailed to 3,667 people of whom 1,117 returned answers. Geographically they were concentrated around New York City and San Francisco. In Amsterdam, 1,077 questionnaires were returned of 2,794 sent out. Danish respondents numbered 303 of a total distribution of 1,916. It should be emphasized, since times and mores change, that the effective dates of the study were

1965 to 1970. In addition, the authors point to the selective nature of the large population, namely, that it consisted of self-identified males so committed to their way of life that they were active in its subculture. They were members of homophile organizations, frequented "gay" bars and belonged to the gay world. The heterosexuals in Europe were obtained by selection from telephone books. In the U.S.A., the source was Melvin Kohn's data on 3,101 males as described in his 1969 volume, *Class and Conformity* (p. 9). The European population was smaller, 34 in Amsterdam, 35 in Copenhagen. In general, the male homosexual studied by Weinberg and Williams is comparable to the man in the Saghir and Robins volume.

Again space does not permit citation of the approximately 100 data tables in the volume. As far as a sample comparison goes, we do not see significant differences in Weinberg and Williams' and Saghir and Robins' male cohorts. Weinberg and Williams draw some interesting and practical conclusions from their study. They believe that the homosexual is better known through his other characteristics than through his sexual deviance. So they list, among their conclusions, the following:

> Homosexuals in high-status occupations identify more with members of their own social class than other homosexuals, associate more with heterosexuals, and are more covert . . . social status apparently affects the way in which the person manages his homosexuality. Race also has an important effect. The fact that black homosexuals pass less and are more known about is associated with the greater tolerance of homosexuals shown by the black community. . . . Contrary to the expectations of many homosexuals and professionals, older homosexuals are found to be as well off psychologically as younger homosexuals. . . . Homosexuality should be conceptualized in terms of social statuses and roles rather than as a condition. . . . (It) is a social status and the role expectations surrounding it account for the types of homosexuals that any society produces" (p. 277).

Practical suggestions are an important innovation in a study of the male homosexual. Weinberg and Williams offer a rich menu. First, the homosexual should seek out the organizational apparatus of the subculture, the "gay" clubs, bars, organizations. He should room with another homosexual rather than with parents. Passing is not necessarily debilitating psychologically. What does hurt is the fear of exposure which is also exaggerated as to its bad psychological effects. Occupational goal-setting should take into account that homosexuals in higher-status occupations do better and have fewer adjustment problems than persons in lower-status jobs. Importantly, the homosexual needs to shed the notion that his behavior is sick and to learn that the usual picture of the "gay" person and his world is a caricature.

The last of the three major studies is that of Gundlach and Riess (1968) on lesbians. The population consisted of 226 women homosexuals and 234 heterosexuals matched for age, educational level, and geographical distribution. All the homosexuals were over 21 and had had, in adult life, like-sexed relationships of six months or more. These respondents were obtained with the cooperation of the Daughters of Bilitis, while the heterosexual group came from friends of the researchers. Geographic distribution was from North to South U.S.A. East, Midwest, and West Coast, urban, suburban, and rural.

At first the instrument used was a questionnaire of over 500 items on the course of family, educational, work, social, and sexual relationships and experiences. Later both sets of cohorts received paper and instructions for the Draw-A-Person Test and were given a modified semantic differential instrument. On this, six concepts were to be identified by 32 pairs of adjective polarities. The concepts were father, mother, man, woman, friend, and lover. This section was treated in a different way from other study materials. The S.D. responses of the total population, 460 adult women, were factor analyzed and the factor loading obtained. Each major factor was then examined to see whether the persons responding to its items were lesbians or comparisons. Only one group was found which consisted exclusively of either homosexuals or heterosexuals. The single group of lesbians so identified were those who were anti-man but pro-father and mother.

Since the data on women and the main findings from the study have been described elsewhere, we shall confine ourselves here to two comparisons, those of the Gundlach and Riess (1968) study with Bieber et al.'s (1962) cohort of male homosexual patients and with the Saghir and Robins (1973) female group. The questionnaires of Weinberg and Williams differ so significantly from the items of the Gundlach and Riess study that comparisons cannot easily be made. Tables 4, 5 and 6 are reprinted from previous publications. It should be stated that the population of women in the tables is drawn from the original 226 and 234 and includes those who had some psychotherapy.

These data presentations are not inconsistent with the propositions that (a) nothing like the patterns characterizing male homosexual patients' relations to mother, father, and family holds for the lesbians'; (b) a major characteristic of a large majority of male homosexuals is fear of

TABLE 4

Items in Which Only Male Homosexuals Differ Significantly
From All Other Groups

Items	N	Females H (90) %	Females C (98) %	Males H (106) %	Males C (100) %
1. Mother had contempt for father.		28	31	43	28*
2. Father regarded as inferior by mother.		26	31	43	29*
3. Parents shared similar interests.		30	39	20	37*
4. Mother confided in subject.		34	33	52	36*
5. Mother encouraged same sex role actions.		44	40	17	47*
6. Mother encouraged opposite sex role actions.		4	5	35	11**
7. Mother unduly protective from physical injuries.		28	34	58	38**
8. Mother restricted activities because of "health."		20	29	49	26**
9. Mother babied subject.		38	35	59	41*
10. Subject was father's favorite child.		29	26	7	22**
11. Brother was father's favorite child.		8	11	24	11*
12. Father sided with you before C.A. 12.		26	24	7	22**
13. Father sided with you after C.A. 12.		27	34	10	24*
14. Average to great deal of time spent with father.		37	48	13	40**
15. Subject wanted to be like same sex parent.		7	6	17	1**

* Significant at the .05 level.
** Signfiicant at the .01 level.
From Gundlach and Riess (1973).

TABLE 5

Selected Items Differentiating Between Total Female and
Total Male Therapy Groups

Items	Females (n = 188)	Males (n = 206)
1. There were overt family demonstrations of affection.	35	20
2. Which parent made the decisions?—Mother	32	56
Neither	31	3
3. Which parent sided with you before C.A. 12?		
Neither and mixed	30	10
4. Which parent sided with you after C.A. 12?		
Mother	35	58
Neither and mixed	25	8
5. Mother was physically demonstrative.	66	46
6. Mother was unduly concerned with my health.	32	52†
7. Subject was frightened of mother.	22	43
8. Subject was frightened of father.	27	60
9. Father babied subject.	32	7
10. Father was domineering.	57	41
11. Father confided in subject.	20	5
12. Subject confided in father.	26	4
13. Father discouraged opposite sex role activities in subject.	11	34
14. Father encouraged opposite sex role activities in subject.	13	2
15. Father was sexually seductive (sensuous kissing for females).	11	3
16. Father was overprotective.	23	5

All differences are significant at least at the .01 level.
† = N of 92 for male group.
From Gundlach and Riess (1973).

TABLE 6

Selected Items Differentiating Females from Males and, for at Least
One Sex, the Homosexuals from the Comparison Group

		Females		Males	
		H	C	H	C
Items	N	(90)	(98)	(106)	(100)
		%	%	%	%
1. Father made the decisions in the family.	12		27*	40	39
2. A sister was father's favorite child.	9		5	29	17*
3. Subject was mother's favorite child.	18		14	59	39**
4. Time spent with mother—great deal.	12		24*	56	27**
5. Mother was domineering.	48		60	81	65*
6. Mother was seductive.	24		19	57	34**
7. Subject was excessively dependent on mother.	24		37	58	40**
8. Subject had fear and/or aversion for opposite sex genitals.	35		4**	71	34**

* Significant at the .05 level.
** Significant at the .01 level.
From Gundlach and Riess (1973).

and/or aversion to the opposite sex genitalia, which is not nearly so for the female; (c) lesbians have been freer to engage in sexual behavior with both men and women; and (d) the two groups seem to have lived in a different family and world space.

Finally, we turn to a comparison of Saghir and Robins' females with those of Riess and Gundlach. This is made difficult because the samples studied are drawn from very different populations. However, there are some commonalities which can be cited. Both sets of lesbians showed ambivalence about femaleness in both childhood and adolescence. Tomboyishness characterized many subjects in both samples. Mother domination was true in each research. High frequency of parental discord and death or absence of one parent were seen by the two sets of authors. Significantly, overt psychopathology is rare in both groups. Saghir and Robins' respondents were more depressed and alcoholic than the larger group of lesbians. This may be an effect of the much higher frequency of unmarried, single, solitary-living women among the Saghir and Robins population, a situation quite different from the Riess and Gundlach groups.

CONCLUSIONS

From the surveys above, one can make the trite statement that women differ from men and therefore women homosexuals are different from male homosexuals. However, as in most cross-group studies, variations within the group are far greater than variations among groups. Homosexuality, like marriage among heterosexuals, is related to the social climate, expectations, and restrictions on the varieties of paired living.

Going beyond the obvious, one must reflect on the methodological difficulties and inadequacies in these studies of gender, sex, and gender-role differences. To start with, the definition of homosexuality has to be spelled out with specificity. Is it demonstrated in a casual, adolescent affair? Is it existent if the adult relationship is of short duration, taking place during a drunken moment or evening? Where does confinement or prison homosexuality fit into the overall picture?

From defining the behavior, one encounters the next difficulty, namely that of sampling bias. How does one construct an adequate sample of homosexuals which is free of the contaminating effect of self-identification? Are self-selected homosexuals different in demographic, developmental, familial, vocational and intrapsychic factors from the persons who are free to call themselves "gay" without the need to identify with a homophile group or institution? Again, when one seeks to research across sex to get comparable samples of men and women homophiles, is it sufficient to match for the common demographic data? What would happen if one were to take a large sample of persons of both sexes from the general population and ask for the sexual preferences of all those who had a close-binding mother and a rejecting father? Would the Bieber hypothesis stand? The use of varied studying materials is also a problem. Retrospective questionnaires need testing for validity. Riess and Gundlach checked their patient sample response by getting comparison data (with permission) from the respondents' therapists.

Finally, one must place the observed phenomenon in context and within a theory of personality which accounts for male and female differences. Here, at least, there are encouraging developments in the newer approaches to an understanding of woman's psychology by writers like Sherfey (1972) and others. One ends the search for better understanding of sex differences with a feeling of excitement and challenge to chart new paths into a significant territory.

REFERENCES

ADLER, A. *The Practice and Theory of Individual Psychology.* London: Kegan Paul, 1946.

ANGYAL, A. *Foundation for a Science of Personality.* New York: Commonwealth Fund, 1941.

ATHANASIOU, R., SHAVER, P., & TAVRIS, C. Sex. *Psychology Today.* July, 1970, 39-52.

BIEBER, I., DAIN, H., DINCE, P., DREILICH, M., GRAND, H., GUNDLACH, R., RIFKIN, A., WILBUR, C., & BIEBER, T. *Homosexuality: A Psychoanalytic Study.* New York: Basic, 1962.

FENICHEL, O. *The Psychoanalytic Theory of Neuroses.* New York: Norton, 1945.

FORD, C. S., & BEACH, F. A. *Patterns of Sexual Behavior.* New York: Harper & Row, 1951.

FREUD, A. Homosexuality. *Bulletin of the American Psychoanalytic Association,* 1951, 7, 117-118.

FREUD, S. *Three Essays on the Theory of Homosexuality* (1905). J. Strachey (Trans.), *Standard Edition.* London: Hogarth, 1953.

FREUD, S. *Leonardo da Vinci and a memory of his childhood* (1910). *Standard Edition.* London: Hogarth, 1953.

FREUD, S. A letter to a "Grateful Mother" dated April 9, 1935. *International Journal of Psychoanalysis,* Vol. 32, p. 331, 1951.

FREUD, S. Psychogenesis of a case of homosexuality in a woman (1920). *Collected Papers,* Vol. 2. London: Hogarth, 1953.

FREUD, S. Certain neurotic mechanisms in jealousy, paranoia and homosexuality. *Collected Papers,* Vol. 2. London: Hogarth, 1953.

GUNDLACH, R. H. Data on the relation of birth order and sex of siblings of lesbians oppose the hypothesis that homosexuality is genetic. *Annals of the New York Academy of Sciences,* 1972, 197, 179-181.

GUNDLACH, R. H. & RIESS, B. F. Self and sexual identity in the female: A study of female homosexuals. In B. F. Riess (Ed.), *New Directions in Mental Health.* New York: Grune & Stratton, 1968.

GUNDLACH, R. & RIESS, B. F. The range of problems in the treatment of lesbians. In D. Milman and G. Goldman (Eds.), *The Neurosis of Our Time: Acting Out.* Springfield, Illinois: Charles C Thomas, 1973.

HOOKER, E. The adjustment of the male overt homosexual. In H. M. Ruitenbeck (Ed.), *The Problems of Homosexuality in Modern Society.* New York: E. P. Dutton, 1963.

HORNEY, K. *The Neurotic Personality of Our Time.* New York: Norton, 1937.

JUNG, C. G. *Psychological Types. Collected Works,* Vol. 6. Princeton, 1974.

KINSEY, A. C., POMEROY, W. B., MARTIN, C. E., & GEBHARD, P. H. *Sexual Behavior in the Human Male.* Philadelphia: W. B. Saunders, 1948.

KINSEY, A. C., POMEROY, W. B., MARTIN, C. E., & GEBHARD, P. H. *Sexual Behavior in the Human Female.* Philadelphia: W. B. Saunders, 1953.

KLEIN, M. *Contributions to Psychoanalysis.* London: Hogarth, 1948.

KLEIN, M., HERMANN, P., & MONEY-KYRLE, R. W. *New Directions in Psychoanalysis.* London: Tavistock, 1955.

KOHN, M. L. *Class and Conformity. A Study in Values.* Illinois: Dorsey Press, 1969.

LACHMANN, F. Homosexuality: Some diagnostic perspectives and dynamic considerations. *American Journal of Psychotherapy,* 1975, 29(2), 254-260.

LOEVINGER, J. *The Meaning and Measurement of Ego Development.* St. Louis: Washington University, 1964.

LONEY, J. Background factors, sexual experiences and attitudes toward treatment in two "normal" homosexual samples. *Journal of Clinical and Consulting Psychology*, 1972, 38, 57-65.

MARSTON, W. M. *Emotions of Normal People*. New York: Harcourt, Brace, 1928.

MASLOW, A. H. *Toward a Psychology of Being*. Princeton: van Nostrand, 1962.

MICHAEL, R. P., WILSON, M. I., & ZUMPE, D. The bisexual behavior of female rhesus monkeys. In R. Friedman, R. Richard and T. van de Velde (Eds.), *Sex Differences in Behavior*. New York: Wiley, 1974.

MILHAM, J., SAN MIGUEL, C., & KELLOGG, R. A factor-analytic conceptualization of attitudes toward male and female homosexuals. *Journal of Homosexuality*, 1976, 2(1), 3-11.

MURDOCK, G. P. *Our Primitive Contemporaries*. New York: Macmillan, 1949.

OGG, E. Homosexuality in our society. *Public Affairs Institute Pamphlet #484*, 1972, New York.

RIESS, B. F. & STOLLER, R. J. Perversion: The erotic form of hatred. (Book Review) *Journal of Homosexuality*, 2(3), 290-291, 1977.

SAFER, J. & RIESS, B. F. Two approaches to the study of female homosexuality: A critical and comparative review. *International Mental Health Research Newsletter*, 1975, 17, 1, 11-14.

SAFER, J., RIESS, B. F., & YOTIVE, W. Psychological test data on female homosexuality: A review of the literature. *Journal of Homosexuality*, 1974, 1, 71-85.

SAGHIR, M. T. & ROBINS, E. *Male and Female Homosexuality*. Baltimore: Williams & Wilkins, 1973.

SAN MIGUEL, C. L. & MILHAM, J. The role of cognitive and situational variables in aggression toward homosexuals. *Journal of Homosexuality*, 1976, 2(11), 11-29.

SCHUBERT, H. J. P., WAGNER, M. E., & RIESS, B. F. Sibships size, sibsex, sibgap and homosexuality among male outpatients. *Transnational Mental Health Research Newsletter*, 1976, 18, 1-5.

SHERFEY, M. J. *The Nature and Evolution of Female Sexuality*. New York: Random House, 1972.

SIEGELMAN, M. Adjustment of homosexual and heterosexual women. *British Journal of Psychiatry*, 1972, 120, 558-563.

SIEGELMAN, M. Adjustment of male homosexuals and heterosexuals. *Archives of Sexual Behavior*, 1972, 2(1), 9-25.

STEKEL, W. *The Homosexual Neurosis* (1922). New York: Emerson, 1946.

STOLLER, R. J. *Perversion: The Erotic Form of Hatred*. New York: Pantheon, 1975.

SULLIVAN, H. S. *The Interpersonal Theory of Psychiatry*. New York: Norton, 1953.

THOMPSON, C. Changing concepts of homosexuality in psychoanalysis. *Psychiatry*, 1947, 10(2), 183-189.

THOMPSON, N., McCANDLESS, B. R., & STRICKLAND, B. R. Personal adjustment of male and female homosexuals and heterosexuals. *Journal of Abnormal Psychology*, 1971, 78, 237-240.

VAN DEN AARDWEG, G. Male homosexuality and psychological tests. *International Mental Health Research Newsletter*, 1969, 11(1), 6-13.

VAN DEN AARDWEG, G. *Homofilie, Neurose en Dwanzelfbeklag*. Amsterdam: Polak & van Gennep, 1967.

WEINBERG, M. S. & BELL, A. P. *Homosexuality: An Annotated Bibliography*. New York: Harper & Row, 1970.

WEINBERG, M. S. & WILLIAMS, C. J. *Male Homosexuals*. New York: Oxford, 1974.

WESTWOOD, G. *A Minority: A Report on the Life of the Male Homosexual in Great Britain*. London: Longmans Green, 1960.

WIEDEMAN, G. Survey of psychoanalytic literature on overt male homosexuality. *Journal of the American Psychoanalytic Association*, Vol. 10, April 1962, 386-409.

10

SEX DIFFERENCES IN SUICIDAL BEHAVIOR

DAVID LESTER

The basic sex difference in suicide is easily described: Men complete suicide more often than women, whereas women attempt suicide (and survive the attempt) more often than men.

It is extremely difficult to trace all completed and attempted suicides in a community. Some of the completed suicides get classified as accidental deaths or natural deaths and many of the attempted suicides never come to the attention of doctors or local health officials. The best attempt to trace all suicidal behavior in a community was carried out by Shneidman and Farberow in Los Angeles in 1957 (Faberow & Shneidman, 1961). They found 540 men who had killed themselves but only 228 women who had done so. At the same time, they found 1824 women who had atempted suicide but only 828 men who had done so.

To show that this sex difference is found in other cultures, I have extracted some figures from a study by Yap (1958) in Hong Kong whose population is mainly Chinese. Yap found 145 men who killed themselves but only 118 women; he found 508 women who had attempted suicide but only 386 men.

This sex difference in suicide has been found in white Americans and black Americans, in all age groups and in the single, married and divorced, and widowed.

COMPLETED SUICIDES

Since it is relatively easier to identify completed suicides than it is to trace attempted suicides, we have more information on people who kill themselves than on those who attempt suicide.

The ratio of men who kill themselves to women who kill themselves

287

is easily obtained from mortality statistics. Looking at these statistics, we find that the excess of males is found everywhere. In the United States in 1949-1951, the ratio ranged from 2.5 in Delaware to 5.6 in Vermont (Gibbs & Martin, 1964). Some cross-national figures are shown in Table 1, from which it can be seen that the ratio ranges from 1.5 in Japan to 7.4 in El Salvador. Bakwin (1957) found the same excess of men in teenagers in different countries. The only exception to this trend is in India where more women kill themselves than men, but this reversal occurs only in young adults.

The sex difference also appears to remain stable over time in the United States, as the figures in Table 2 show. However, a notable trend is that the suicide rate for women is rising and it is interesting to speculate about the effect of the changing roles of American women. A reasonable hypothesis is that the increasing opportunities in education and careers for women, though politically liberating, may entail an increase in stress and an accompanying rise in their suicide rate.

Although the sex difference in suicidal behavior is found at all ages,

TABLE 1

The Ratio of Male Suicides to Female Suicides in Various Nations Circa 1950

Nation	Sex ratio	Nation	Sex ratio
El Salvador	7.4	Belgium	3.1
Costa Rica	6.3	Switzerland	2.8
Finland	4.7	Australia	2.8
Norway	4.2	Venezuela	2.8
Chile	4.1	New Zealand	2.3
France	3.9	Austria	2.1
South Africa	3.6	West Germany	2.1
U.S.A.	3.6	Denmark	2.0
Ireland	3.4	Ceylon	2.0
Canada	3.3	England & Wales	1.9
Portugal	3.3	Netherlands	1.9
Sweden	3.2	Japan	1.5

From Gibbs & Martin, 1964, p. 183.

the excess of males varies with age. From Table 3, which shows the sex ratio for suicidal deaths for 1964, we see that the male suicide rate increases with age while the female suicide rate peaks at age 50. At the present moment we have no idea why this difference exists. It may be that menopause is the major crisis for women leading to increased stress in the late 40s and early 50s, whereas retirement is the major crisis for men, leading to stress in the late 60s and thereafter.

The sex difference in completed suicide is much less among professionals in the United States. In fact, female physicians have a *higher* suicide rate than male physicians (Ross, 1973). Among psychologists, chemists and nurses, although the male suicide rate is higher than the female suicide rate, the female suicide rate is higher than the rate for the general female population.

The increase in the female suicide rate in recent years appears to be worldwide. Burvill (1972) looked at nine nations and found that the female suicide rate had risen in each from 1955 to 1965, thereby causing

TABLE 2

The Sex Ratio for Completed in the U.S.A. from 1950 to 1973

| | Age-adjusted suicide rates (per 100,000 per year) | | | |
	Total	Male	Female	Male-Female Ratio
1950	11.0	17.3	4.9	3.5
1951	10.0	15.8	4.6	3.4
1952	9.7	15.3	4.3	3.6
1953	9.8	15.7	4.2	3.7
1960	10.6	16.6	5.0	3.3
1961	10.5	16.4	5.0	3.3
1962	11.0	16.8	5.6	3.0
1963	11.3	17.0	6.0	2.8
1970	11.8	17.3	6.8	2.5
1971	11.9	17.2	7.1	2.4
1972	12.1	17.9	6.9	2.6
1973	12.0	18.0	6.6	2.7

From Massey, 1967 and Robert Armstrong, personal communication.

the male-female ratio to decrease. It is perhaps a comment on modern civilization that the male suicide rate remains constant and the female rate rises. We seem inept at changing society so as to remove the suicidogenic stresses.

ATTEMPTED SUICIDE

In general, men who attempt suicide make more serious (that is, more damaging) suicide attempts than women (Lester, 1972a). In particular, it is much more common for women to make suicidal gestures, suicide attempts where there is absolutely no risk to life and everyone knows it. This fact has suggested to some investigators that the suicide attempt is in most cases a communication and it is made in that way because verbal communication has broken down or is too difficult. The incidence of suicidal attempts and suicidal gestures is relatively lower in black females than in white females (Pederson, Awad, & Kindler, 1973).

SUICIDAL IDEATION

So far, no differences have been found in the proportion of people in the population who think about suicide from time to time (Craig & Senter, 1972; Cameron, 1972). Cameron found, however, that men have

TABLE 3

Male and Female Suicide Rates by Age in the U.S.A. for 1964

Age	Male	Suicide rates Female	Ratio
5-14	0.4	0.1	4.0
15-24	9.2	2.8	3.3
25-34	16.9	7.0	2.4
35-44	21.3	10.1	2.1
45-54	29.9	11.6	2.6
55-64	36.1	10.2	3.5
65-74	37.0	9.8	3.8
75-84	47.5	6.4	7.4
85+	59.3	4.1	14.5

much more knowledge about how to kill themselves than women, which may in part explain why women survive their suicidal acts more than men.

It is clear that women complete suicide less than men, attempt suicide more, and think about it as much. Why is this so? What explanations can we suggest for these differences?

Methods for Suicide

Women use different methods for suicide from those used by men. For example, men shoot and hang themselves more than women, whereas women use drugs and poisons more than men (Farberow & Shneidman, 1961). Sex differences emerge even when the same method is used. For example, men shoot themselves in the head more while women shoot themselves in the body more. (One possible reason for this difference in choice of method is that women seem to be more concerned over how they will look when dead [Diggory & Rothman, 1961]. Women may therefore prefer suicide methods that preserve their beauty.) Lester (1972b) found sex differences in the methods used to mutilate bodies. Women prefer wrist-slashing and hair pulling. On the other hand, most people who mutilate their genitals are men. Incidentally, just as the suicide rate for women has risen in recent years, some investigators have claimed that women are more often using "traditionally male" methods for suicide (MacAulay, 1962), but the evidence for this is not too convincing at the moment.

One possible explanation for the sex difference in suicidal behavior is that women choose methods for suicide that are less lethal. For example, if you shoot yourself in the head your chances of survival and for rescue are poor. If you take an overdose of sleeping pills, your chances of survival are high, you have plenty of time to change your mind and go to an emergency room and there is a good chance that someone may happen by and intervene.

This explanation seems to be inadequate. First, if it were true, then the total number of suicidal actions (both attempted and completed) should be the same for men and women (Linehan, 1971). In fact, women make more suicidal actions than men. Secondly, if it were true, then the sex difference should not be found in countries where both sexes use poisons (Linehan, 1971). Again, the sex difference is found in those countries. Finally, the sex difference in suicide is found *within* each method for suicide (Lester, 1972a). For example, men die more often when jumping to their deaths while women survive more.

So, although there are sex differences in choice of method for suicide, this difference is not a complete explanation of the sex difference in suicidal behavior. And similarly, explanations based upon the mechanical incompetence and physical weakness of women are not adequate as explanations of the facts.

Mental Illness

Lester (1970) noted that psychotics tend to kill themselves more than neurotics and that neurotics tend to attempt suicide more than psychotics. One possible explanation for the sex difference in suicidal behavior, therefore, is that men and women differ in their likelihood of becoming psychotic. A search of community mental health surveys produced evidence that psychosis was indeed more common among men whereas neurosis was more common among women (for example, Roth & Luton, 1943). Thus, sex differences in suicidal behavior may be partly due to sex differences in psychiatric illness.

Physiological Factors

Lester (1969b) and Wetzel and McClure (1972) both reviewed a large number of studies and concluded that suicidal behavior is more frequent at some stages of the menstrual cycle than at others. Available data indicate no association between completed suicide and the menstrual cycle, but attempted suicide does seem to occur at the highest rate during the premenstrual phase (days 25-28) and the menstrual phase (days 1-5). Wetzel and McClure also found that women choose different methods for suicide at different phases of the menstrual cycle.

Thus, it is possible that the high rate of attempted suicide in women is due to the excess number of suicidal actions made by women in the premenstrual and menstrual phase of their cycle. (Although this seems reasonable, we must remember that we cannot tell whether there are too many suicidal actions premenstrually and menstrually or too few at other phases of the cycle [Parlee, 1973].)

It is noted that estrogen levels are low during pregnancy and the suicide rate is also low during this time (Rosenberg & Silver, 1965). Enovid has been used to treat a woman with suicidal ideation and psychotic symptoms (Kane, Daley, Wallach, & Keeler, 1966) and Lester (1969a) wondered whether women who use the birth control pill would have a lower suicide rate than those who do not.

The influence of the menstrual cycle upon the suicide rate is still speculative, but it does look to be a possible source of the high incidence of attempted suicide in women. Elsewhere (1969b, 1972a). I have already discussed possible mechanisms by which the levels of circulating estrogen might affect behavior.

Societal Expectations

Linehan (1973) asked what happens once a person has reached the crisis point where suicide is seen as a viable alternative. Then the social acceptability of suicidal behavior becomes a factor. If attempted suicide is seen as a "weak" or as a "feminine" behavior, then men may be less likely to choose that alternative. Men, therefore, may not have means of communicating mild levels of distress and so be more likely to suppress their depression and self-destructive impulses until they are so strong as to precipitate a lethal self-destructive behavior.

Do these societal expectations and evaluations exist? Linehan (1971, 1973) found some evidence that this was so. Completed suicide was seen as more masculine than attempted suicide. Attempted suicide, however, was as socially acceptable for men as for women. Linehan found that *sex role* rather than *sex* per se was a much more potent factor in social expectations. For example, Linehan presented students with character sketches of disturbed people and varied the sex of the person and the personality traits. The student judges had to predict which people would kill themselves. The students saw 71% of the masculine males as likely suicides, 62% of the masculine females, 43% of the feminine males and 22% of the feminine females.

Suggestibility

Motto (1970) tried to study whether suicide could be suggested to people as a possibility by examining the newspaper strike in Detroit during 1967 and 1968. During the newspaper blackout, when suicides went unreported by the press, the female suicide rate dropped while the male suicide rate remained unchanged. Motto speculated that women may be more influenced by news reports of suicides than men.

Manipulative Intent

Stengel (1964) proposed that women were more inclined to use suicidal behavior as an aggressive and defensive weapon and as a means of manipulating relationships. Although this makes sense, there is no evidence for it. In an earlier study, I found no differences in the motives of men and women who had killed themselves and left suicide notes (Shneidman & Farberow, 1959) and no differences in the degree to which men and women communicate their suicidal intent prior to their deaths. Thus, differences in manipulative intent do not account for the sex difference in completed suicide, but many account for some differences in attempted suicide.

Conclusion

It would seem that we have a number of factors contributing to the sex difference in suicide. There is some evidence to support the influence of choice of method, psychiatric illness, menstruation, societal expectations, and suggestibility and we cannot rule out manipulative intent. These explanations cover all levels of discourse (biological, psychological and societal) and what is impressive is that they are congruent. Since they each lead to the same predictions, it would appear that the sex difference in suicide has a multitude of forces operating to perpetuate it.

OTHER SEX DIFFERENCES IN SUICIDAL BEHAVIOR

So far in this chapter, the most basic difference between men and women who are suicidal has been discussed, and a number of proposed explanations have been reviewed. However, there are additional sex differences in suicidal behavior that are of interest, although considerably less research has been conducted on them. In this section we will briefly mention these minor differences.

Murder and Suicide

In England it has been reported that women who murder others are more likely to kill themselves after the murder than are men who murder others (West, 1966). In contrast, reports from the United States indicate that men who murder are more likely to kill themselves than women who murder (Wolfgang, 1958b). The source of this difference is obscure, except that we know that murder is much more common in the U.S.A. than in England and so may be differently determined.

Wolfgang (1958a) found that husbands who killed their wives were more likely to kill themselves than were wives who killed their husbands. Wolfgang speculated that husbands were more likely to provoke their their wives into murdering them (by beating them, for example) and so the murdering wives will feel less guilt than the murdering husbands and be less prone to suicide. Wolfgang found that 53% of the murdered husbands precipitated their own deaths as compared to only 11% of the murdered wives.

Incidentally, Resnick (1970) reported that parents who murder their children (and especially mothers) have a high incidence of suicide. This is particularly true where the motive for the murder is "altruistic," real or imagined.

Ascribed Versus Achieved Status

A number of investigators have argued that the more rigid a person's role is, the less likely suicidal behavior will be. Some writers phrase this in terms of the degree of external restraint on your behavior. The more external restraint, the less likely suicide is (and the more likely homicide is) whereas the opposite is true when external restraint is weak. Others phrase the argument in terms of ascribed versus achieved status (for example, MacAulay, 1962). Since in many societies, the role for women has in the past been more ascribed than achieved, it is argued that suicide will be less common in women than in men.

The suicide rate of women will change according to this argument as women become more liberated from their traditional ascribed roles, as we have discussed above. These changes take place to some extent during times of war, when women enter the labor force more and so change their roles. Lester (1972a) reviewed information on suicide rates during wartime and found some support for a relatively higher female suicide rate.

Related to this, Newman, Whittemore, and Newman (unpublished, a; unpublished, b) found that the suicide rate in census tracts in Atlanta and Chicago was higher the greater the proportion of women in the labor force. We (Lester, 1973; Diggory & Lester, 1975) failed to find this phenomenon in Buffalo. At the moment, therefore, we cannot determine whether Newman et al.'s results are reliable or whether the phenomenon they have described is unique to the two cities they studied.

Gove (1972a, 1972b), who discusses his research in Chapter 2, has argued that marriage is more stressful for women than for men. He has presented figures to demonstrate that rates for mental illness and suicide are higher in married women than in women living alone, while the opposite is true for men. The evidence is not completely consistent with Gove's argument (for example, he found the result only since the Second World War) but the phenomenon would prove of interest if it were found to be valid. It would, for example, conflict with expectations based on the differences between ascribed and achieved status discussed above.

Suicide, Pregnancy and Abortion

As we noted above, suicide is rare during pregnancy. In Minnesota, from 1950 to 1965, there were 1,301,745 live births and 658 maternal deaths, of which four were suicides during pregnancy and 11 were suicides in the first 11 weeks post partum (Barno, 1967). This means that pregnant women have a suicide rate of only 0.03 (per 100,000 per year). Rosenberg and Silver (1965) estimated that the completed suicide rate of pregnant women was about one-sixth of that of non-pregnant women.

Whitlock and Edwards (1968) found that attempted suicide was more common than completed suicide among pregnant women (about as common as it is for women in general), especially during the first two trimesters. However, some 57% of the attempts at suicide by pregnant women did not appear to be related to the pregnancy at all.

In estimating the suicidal risk of females requesting abortion, the figures are unreliable since a knowledgeable woman knew in the past that she had to talk of suicide in order to get her psychiatric excuse (Halleck, 1971). The majority of reports find suicidal behavior to be more common and more likely in women requesting abortions than in general psychiatric referrals (Kenyon, 1969).

CATEGORIES OF SUICIDAL PEOPLE

One final area of research that is worth reviewing is that which moves from the stark statistics toward a description of the kinds of people involved. Wold (1971) examined case files of callers to the Los Angeles Suicide Prevention Center who completed and attempted suicide and described several distinct types of suicidal people:

1. *Discarded women.* These women had experienced repeated rejection (for example, divorce) by men. They had a façade of femininity and hysterical personalities. They had felt rejected by their parents and felt that they were failures as women.

2. *Harlequin syndrome.* These women eroticize death. They have a masochistic life-style with a poor self-image, a façade of femininity, and a feeling of alienation from others. Death is seen as peaceful or pleasurable.

McClelland (1963) has noted that death and sexuality appear to be associated for women and he pointed out that this association was embodied in the figure of Harlequin, who was both lover and death.

Weisman (1967) has noted that occasional women find orgasm heightened by suffocation. (In males, hanging is associated with sexuality and some men hang themselves to heighten orgasm, often dying accidentally [Resnik, 1972].)

3. *Chaotic.* These people are psychotic, confused and impulsive. Some 80% were female.

4. *Middle-age depression.* About two-thirds of these cases were female.

5. *I can't live with you syndrome.* About two-thirds of these cases were women. Both partners are suicidal and they have a mutually destructive dependency on each other. They openly wish for the death of the partner. They are severely psychologically disturbed.

6. *I can't live without you syndrome.* About two-thirds of these cases were women. They become suicidal in response to threatened or actual break-up of an intense symbiotic relationship. They have a passive-dependent personality, but their life-style is reasonably stable.

7. *Adolescent family crisis.* These adolescents are equally often male and female. They have poor interpersonal communications with their parents. The parents are often destructive with respect to the child and may have death wishes for the child. The children have identity and independence problems.

8. *Old and alone.* These cases are old, have poor physical health and live alone. They are depressed and show the giving-up given-up syndrome (Engel, 1968). They are equally often male and female.

9. *The down and out syndrome.* These cases (about two-thirds are men) use alcohol and drugs a lot and have a downwardly mobile life course. They have a history of superficial relationships, low self-esteem and poor physical health.

10. *Violent men.* These men have episodes of rage. They are impulsive. They drink a lot, but their work record is good and they are rarely loners.

Several studies have compared male and females suicides and agree on several differences. Women who are suicidal tend to be diagnosed more often as neurotic and with affective disorders rather than schizophrenic or psychopathic (Davis, 1968). The motives for the suicidal actions of women tend to be interpersonal (Beck, Lester, & Kovacs, 1973; Farberow, 1970), whereas the motives for men tend to be intrapsychic and to be precipitated by factors such as job loss or legal problems.

Most suicide prevention centers use simple predictive scales in order to predict the suicidal risk of clients who call the centers. As the counselor acquires information about the client, he can complete the form and obtain a rough estimate of how serious a suicidal risk the client is. Formerly one form was used for all clients. In recent years, the growing awareness of the differences between men and women who are suicidal has led suicide prevention workers to devise separate predictor scales for each sex (Lettieri, 1974).

COMMENT

The fact that men kill themselves more than women while women attempt suicide more than men has been known for a long time. In the review above, we have seen that a number of explanations have been proposed for this difference and most of them seem plausible. We can expect to see some definitive studies in the near future that will confirm the role of these explanatory factors.

In more recent research, it is clear that investigators are moving towards a more complex and, therefore, more complete description of sex differences in suicidal behavior. For example, there is a possible difference in the relationship between marriage and suicidal behavior and another in the suicidal behavior of murderers. It would seem that many other differences remain to be identified and we can expect more to be described as research into suicidal behavior continues.

The topic of sex differences in suicidal behavior would appear to be a dynamic, growing and interesting area of research. The investigation of the sex difference should go far toward enlightening us about suicide.

REFERENCES

ARMSTRONG, R. Personal communication, February 20, 1976.

BAKWIN, H. Suicide in children and adolescents. *Journal of Pediatrics*, 1957, 50, 749-769.

BARNO, A. Criminal abortion deaths, illegitimate pregnancy deaths and suicides in pregnancy. *American Journa of Obstetrics and Gynecology*, 1967, 98, 356-367.

BECK, A., LESTER, D., & KOVACS, H. Attempted suicide by males and females. *Psychological Reports*, 1973, 33, 965-966.

BURVILL, P. Recent decreased ratio of male:female suicide rates. *International Journal of Social Psychiatry*, 1972, 18, 137-139.

CAMERON, P. Suicide and the generation gap. *Life Threatening Behavior*, 1972, 2, 194-208.

CRAIG, L. & SENTER, P. Student thoughts about suicide. *Psychological Record*, 1972, 22, 355-358.

CURLEE, J. A comparison of male and female patients at an alcoholism treatment center. *Journal of Psychology*, 1970, 74, 239-247.

DAVIS, F. Sex differences in suicide and attempted suicide. *Diseases of the Nervous System,* 1968, 29, 193-194.

DIGGORY, J. & LESTER, D. Suicide rates of men and women. *Omega,* 1975, 6, 383-389.

DIGGORY, J. & ROTHMAN, D. Values destroyed by death. *Journal of Abnormal and Social Psychology,* 1961, 63, 205-210.

ENGEL, G. A life setting conducive to illness. *Bulletin of the Menninger Clinic,* 1968, 32, 355-365.

FARBEROW, N. Self-destruction and identity. *Humanitas,* 1970, 6, 45-68.

FARBEROW, N. & SHNEIDMAN, E. *The Cry for Help.* New York: McGraw-Hill, 1961.

GABRIELSON, I., KLERMAN, L., CURRIE, J., TYLER, N., & JEKEL, J. Suicide attempts in a population pregnant as teenagers. *American Journal of Public Health,* 1970, 60, 2289-2301.

GIBBS, J. & MARTIN, W. *Status Integration and Suicide.* Eugene: University of Oregon Press, 1964.

GOVE, W. The relationship between sex roles, marital status and mental illness. *Social Forces,* 1972, 51, 34-44. (a)

GOVE, W. Sex, marital status and suicide. *Journal of Health and Social Behavior,* 1972, 13, 204-213. (b)

GOVE, W. & TUDOR, J. Adult sex roles and mental illness. *American Journal of Sociology,* 1973, 78, 812-835.

HALLECK, S. *The Politics of Therapy.* New York: Science House, 1971.

KANE, F., DALY, R., WALLACH, M., & KEELER, M. Amelioration of premenstrual mood disturbance with a progestational agent (Enovid). *Diseases of the Nervous System,* 1966, 27, 339-342.

KENYON, F. Termination of pregnancy on psychiatric grounds. *British Journal of Medical Psychology,* 1969, 42, 243-254.

LESTER, D. The antisuicide pill. *Journal of the American Medical Association,* 1969, 208, 1908. (a)

LESTER, D. Suicidal behavior in men and women. *Mentla Hygiene,* 1969, 53, 340-345. (b)

LESTER, D. Suicide, sex and mental disorder. *Psychological Reports,* 1970, 27, 61-62.

LESTER, D. *Why People Kill Themselves.* Springfield: Thomas, 1972. (a)

LESTER, D. Self-mutilating behavior. *Psychological Bulletin,* 1972, 78, 119-128. (b)

LESTER, D. Completed suicide and females in the labor force. *Psychological Reports,* 1973, 32, 730.

LETTIERI, D. Suicidal death prediction scales. In A. Beck, H. Resnik, & D. Lettieri (Eds.), *The Prediction of Suicide.* Bowie: Charles, 1974, pp. 163-192.

LINEHAN, M. Sex differences in suicide and attempted suicide. *Dissertation Abstracts International,* 1971, 32B, 3036.

LINEHAN, M. Suicide and attempted suicide. *Perceptual and Motor Skills,* 1973, 37, 31-34.

MACAULAY, I. Suicide and Social Integration. Master's thesis, University of Buffalo, 1962.

MASSEY, J. Suicide in the United States. *Vital and Health Statistics,* 1967, Series 20, #5.

MAUSNER, J. & STEPPACHER, R. Suicide in professionals. *American Journal of Epidemiology,* 1973, 98, 436-445.

McCLELLAND, D. The Harlequin complex. In R. White (Ed.), *The Study of Lives.* New York: Atherton, 1963, pp. 94-119.

MOTTO, J. Newspaper influence on suicide. *Archives of General Psychiatry,* 1970, 23, 143-148.

NEWMAN, J., WHITTEMORE, K., & NEWMAN, H. An Analysis of the Relation Between Suicide Rates and Community Characteristics. Unpublished. (a)

NEWMAN, J., WHITTEMORE, K., & NEWMAN, H. Community Characteristics as Predictors of Suicide Rates in Two Metropolitan Areas. Unpublished. (b)

PARLEE, M. The premenstrual syndrome. *Psychological Bulletin*, 1973, 80, 454-465.

PEDERSON, A., AWAD, G., & KINDLER, A. Epidemiological differences between white and nonwhite suicide attempters. *American Journal of Psychiatry*, 1973, 130, 1071-1076.

RESNICK, P. Murder of the newborn. *American Journal of Psychiatry*, 1970, 126, 1414-1429.

RESNIK, H. Eroticized repetitive hangings. *American Journal of Psychotherapy*, 1972, 24, 4-21.

ROSENBERG, A. & SILVER, E. Suicide, psychiatrists and therapeutic abortion. *California Medicine*, 1965, 102, 407-411.

ROSS, M. Suicide among physicians. *Diseases of the Nervous System*, 1973, 34, 145-150.

ROTH, W. & LUTON, F. The mental health program in Tennessee. *American Journal of Psychiatry*, 1943, 99, 662-675.

SENAY, E. Therapeutic abortion. *Archives of General Psychiatry*, 1970, 23, 408-415.

SHNEIDMAN, E. & FARBEROW, N. Suicide and death. In H. Feifel (Ed.), *The Meaning of Death*. New York: McGraw-Hill 1959, pp. 284-301.

STENGEL, E. *Suicide and Attempted Suicide*. Baltimore: Penguin, 1964.

WEISMAN, A. Self-destruction and sexual perversion. In E. Shneidman (Ed.), *Essays in Self-Destruction*. New York: Science House, 1967, pp. 265-299.

WEST, D. *Murder Followed by Suicide*. Cambridge, Mass.: Harvard University Press, 1966.

WETZEL, R. & McCLURE, J. Suicide and the menstrual cycle. *Comprehensive Psychiatry*, 1972, 13, 369-374.

WHITLOCK, F. & EDWARDS, J. Pregnancy and attempted suicide. *Comprehensive Psychiatry*, 1968, 9, 1-12.

WOLD, C. Subgroupings of suicidal people. *Omega*, 1971, 2, 19-29.

WOLFGANG, M. An analysis of homicide-suicide. *Journal of Clinical and Experimental Psychopathology*, 1958, 19, 208-217. (a)

WOLFGANG, M. Husband-wife homicides. *Journal of Social Therapy*, 1958, 2, 263-271. (b)

YAP, P. Suicide in Hong Kong. *Journal of Mental Science*, 1958, 104, 266-301.

11

RAPE AND PSYCHIATRIC VOCABULARIES OF MOTIVE

JOSEPH A. MAROLLA and DIANA H. SCULLY

For the past 50 years, the field of psychiatry has dominated the literature on rape and especially the literature on rapists. Not only have psychiatrists defined the problem from their particular perspective but they have also defined what constitutes "proper" treatment. The psychiatric model, like any other theory of human behavior, is not a description of what is but rather an interpretation of behavior based upon a set of logically related concepts. It is, then, an imposition in the sense that all theories impose an order on things that may or may not be real. Psychiatrists have imposed such an order on the study of rape and the elements that they have chosen to emphasize have become the generally accepted explanations for the behavior. This chapter will demonstrate the critical importance of understanding the inherent biases in any perspective that is allowed to dominate thought on a social problem.

VOCABULARIES OF MOTIVE

One approach to understanding the psychiatric rape literature is to examine it from a vocabulary of motive framework. This refers to the concept developed by Mills (1940) in which a motive is a linguistic device that functions to coordinate future actions of the parties concerned. According to Mills, "Rather than fixed elements 'in' an individual, motives are the terms with which interpretation of conduct by social actors proceeds" (Mills, 1940, p. 904). Appropriate vocabularies of motive exist within any given culture for specific groups of people who have broken a norm or set of norms. The question of the appropriateness of the motive is always defined by a particular reference group. There is no universal answer to the question "Why did you do that?" Rather the answer depends upon what a particular group or society will accept as appropriate. These "reasons" or motive statements must not only justify the past actions of the actor but, equally important, they must justify present and future behaviors of others.

In the literature influenced by the psychoanalytic approach, there are primarily four types of motive statements attributed to rapists. Although they are often found combined, for analytical purposes each will be treated as a separate category. They are: (a) uncontrollable impulse; (b) mental illness or disease; (c) momentary loss of control precipitated by unusual circumstances; (d) victim precipitation. Each of these explanations serves the similar function of providing a very insular view of rape. First, each is an individualistic explanation, thus negating the necessity of studying the problem of rape beyond the individual offender. Next, each one assumes that the behavior is strange or abnormal (with the exception of victim precipitation). Thus rape is removed from the realm of the everyday or "normal" world and is seemingly less threatening, especially to males. Additionally, each statement absolves everyone, except the victim, from responsibility. And finally, as Szasz (1963) pointed out in his discussion of the insanity plea, the effect is to avoid the study of society and/or social injustices. The psychiatric view of rapists has had the same consequence. It removes the necessity of investigating the elements within a society which precipitate violent aggression against women.

In the remainder of this chapter the logic behind each category and the consequences of each will be examined in greater detail. Our discussion is informed by a perspective which assumes that a relationship exists between interest and ideology and that the intellectual products of a group in power ultimately function in the interest of that group. In the case of rape, the psychiatric vocabulary of motive is the intellectual product of a male-dominated profession and a patriarchal society. It will become apparent that by labeling rape the product of individual pathology, one places the rapist outside the parameters of normal group membership and thus the connection between "normal" men and rape can be avoided. When an individual case cannot be made to fit the pathological model, other explanations, such as alcohol or victim precipitation, can be substituted. In the end, attention is forced away from the possibility that sexual aggression may be consistent with normative male sexual behavior.

Irresistible Impulse

In 1925 Glueck presented the argument that irresistible impulse and insanity affected an individual in similar ways. He argued that self-control involves the power to attend to distant motives and general principles of conduct. Disease of the brain weakens control and an irresistible impulse can result. The individual will not know that his behavior is wrong because he will not relate the particular act to the general rules forbidding it. Therefore, the behavior is not voluntary and the individual is not accountable. Glueck suggested expert (psychiatric) examination of these people because "the external symptoms are but indicative of a much deeper disturbance, the relation of which to the criminal act" can only be ascertained by mental analysis (Glueck, 1925, p. 323).

Since Glueck's writing, psychiatric literature has been filled with the assertion that irresistible impulse is at the root of rape. For example:

> Whether it is comparatively mild as in the case of simple assault, or whether it is severely aggravated assault, it is, as a rule, an expression of an uncontrollable urge, committed without logic or rationale, under the influence of a strong, overpowering drive (Karpman, 1951, p. 185).

> It is not intended to suggest that all recidivous sex offenders are physically dangerous, but experience shows that some of them are compulsively so, and that most of them are driven by uncontrollable impulsions that do not respond to customary procedures (Reinhardt & Fisher, 1949, p. 734).

And Guttmacher and Weihofen (1952) list "explosive expression of pent up impulse" as a primary motivation for rape.

It is important to note the consequences of this particular vocabulary of motive. Not only does it abdicate responsibility for the act, but it also removes the behavior from legal jurisdiction. "There is little doubt that the reactions that are attributed to sexual psychopaths are beyond the sphere of conscious control and appear as irresistible impulses, which explains why in practice these cases do not profit by punishment; uncontrollable instinct is beyond punishment" (Karpman, 1951, p. 191).

Sutherland (1950) questioned the logic of the uncontrollable impulse theory. He noted that most convicted rapists were between the ages of 20 to 29 and asked why the impulse seldom occurred before or after that point. Furthermore, reporting a recidivism rate of 5.3% in a 1937 study of rape, he questioned whether the impulse came but once in a lifetime.

Recently Gibbens, Way, and Soothill (1977) also reported a low recidivism rate for rape, 3% over a 12-year period. Recidivism was defined as a subsequent conviction after release for a previous rape conviction. They reported that rapists tend to have records of nonsexual offenses and are more likely to be convicted of a subsequent nonsexual offense. Socioeconomic status was not given but one must assume that since the sample consisted of convicted rapists, it was biased in the direction of lower socioeconomic class. Even if this was the case the finding is still interesting in its lack of congruence with the Reinhardt and Fisher (1949) position and general impulse theory.

In order for a crime to be prosecuted, the element of volition or criminal intent is often critical. When an act is attributed to irresistible impulse, the volitional element and, thus, responsibility are removed. Spirer (1942) noted that most things that are called impulses can be resisted up to a point and therefore irresistible is a relative, not absolute, term. Further, from a strict behaviorist view, almost all behavior might be considered irresistible. "But, as we well know, not every person who is thus emotionally stimulated finds a release in an aggressive act, for if this were so, the incidence of violent crimes would be tremendously greater than is now the case" (Spirer, 1942, p. 459). Spirer argued that criminal habituation need not be viewed as deep-seated pathology but rather arises in the same manner as non-criminal habituation. The psychological processes involved in learning are the same whether the outcome is a criminal act or a legal one. If the courts were to extend the logic of irresistible impulse to its limits, no one would be responsible for anything!

The impulse theory lacks empirical support. We have already noted the lack of fit between the theory and recidivism rates. Even more critical is Amir's (1971) finding that 71% of the rapes he studied were premeditated. If the act was impulsive, by definition, the offender should not have been able to delay his response. Finally, since impulse theory could hypothetically be applied to any behavior, it is interesting to question why it has been used as an appropriate motive for crimes against women and not for other types of criminal behavior. The motive does not necessarily explain rape, but it does fit psychiatric assumptions about male and female sexuality.* In more recent literature, irresistible impulse is often replaced by mental illness, a more sophisticated vocabulary of motive.

---

* For a discussion of this point see Albin, R. Psychological studies of rape. *Signs,* 1977, 3, 423-435.

Disease

Irresistible impulse theory differs from the disease model in at least one significant way. Irresistible impulse does not necessarily imply a character disorder and is often associated, in the literature, with special circumstances. Sexual deprivation, for example, is believed to remove the normal social constraints which usually prevent aggressive sexual attacks. In contrast, when psychoanalysts employ the disease model, one or more of the following assumptions are usually made. Rape is directly or indirectly sexual in nature. It is perpetrated by a perverted or sick individual who often has latent homosexual tendencies. He has experienced an abnormal childhood which has resulted in a sadistic personality. And finally, rape is often an attack on a mother figure and should be considered as symptomatic of inner conflicts which are the real problem. While it is tempting to place all writers who have employed the disease model into one category, such an approach would obscure the broader implications of the particular psychoanalytic models used. Consequently, an examination of each assumption is warranted.

A Sexual Act. Albin (1977) writes that M. L. Cohen stated in 1977, "I have never studied a rapist where there was not present, together with many other problems, a rather severe sexual disorder." Cohen's statement derives from Freud's dual instinct theory in which sexual and aggressive drives are combined. "A sexual act becomes dynamically an act of aggression towards the partner, while aggression may readily have a disguised sexual meaning" (Fine, 1965, p. 149). In psychoanalytic theory the act of sexual intercourse is intricately tied to aggression. Fine (1965) interpreted Freud's sexual stages of development in terms of hostility "in the oedipal situation, as rivalry towards the parent of the opposite sex; in the anal phase as the anal-sadistic wish; in all infantile sexuality as the partial instinct of sadism; and as a result of frustration" (Fine, 1965, 149). East hinted at the element of power in rape but only within a sexual context. "Psychoneurotic persons sometimes show their sexual inferiority and striving for superiority by committing a sexual murder or other sexual crime" (East, 1946, p. 540). He related this to Freud's stages of sexual pleasure and early childhood sexual traumas.

Karpman (1951), firmly committed to a sexual interpretation of rape, took issue with the legal definition. "Rape, clearly a sexual crime, is regarded by law as an assault on a person" (Karpman, 1951, p. 185). In Karpman's view, incest and homosexuality were the real problems, and rape was merely symbolic of these "greater crimes." Guttmacher and

Weihofen (1952) were in partial agreement. They maintained that the "true" sex offender was motivated by "an explosive expression of a pent up impulse" (Guttmacher & Weihofen, 1952, p. 116) and a strong latent homosexual component.

By 1965 the influence of psychiatry was evident as 30 states and the District of Columbia had sexual psychopath laws in which the offender was defined in sexual terms. "The sexual psychopath is usually defined as a person unable to control his sexual impulses or having to commit sex crimes" (Bowman & Engle, 1965, p. 758). The psychiatric profession had successfully claimed a new territory. They became the expert consultants in cases of suspected sexual psychopathy. This encroachment on the legal profession undoubtedly was facilitated by the desire of some judges to be relieved of the responsibility of making difficult decisions.

The major research efforts in this tradition primarily consisted of elaborate discussions of early childhood sexual behavior and later adult sexual habits.* Research also concentrated on individual characteristics of rapists and seldom moved beyond a discussion of sexual practices.

A number of implications arise from viewing rape as a sexual act. First, it implies the presence of impulsive or uncontrollable drives. The rapist's responsibility for the behavior is abated by the justification that peculiar circumstances precipitated an unusual arousal which could not be controlled. This presumes a belief about the uncontrollable nature of male sexuality which is as outdated as the Victorian belief in universal female frigidity.

When rape is viewed as a sexual act, victim seduction becomes a possible element in the crime. Since sex is generally thought of as a reciprocal process, the role of the other and the issue of consent become relevant. However, when rape is defined as physical assault, the word motive "sexual provocation" is hardly appropriate. Unless it could be proven that the woman was a practicing masochist there would be no case. When defined sexually a husband cannot be accused of rape nor can a prostitute or allegedly "promiscuous" woman be victimized since in both cases consent has been brought or exchanged for material goods.**

---

* See Ellis, A. and Brancale, R. *The Psychology of Sex Offenders.* Springfield: C. Thomas, 1956; Gebhard, P., Gagnon, J., Pomeroy, W. and Christensen, C. *Sex Offenders.* New York: Harper and Row, 1965; Abrahamsen, D. *The Psychology of Crime.* New York: John Wiley, 1960.

** For a Marxian interpretation see Kasinsky, R. Rape: A normal act? *Canadian Forum,* 1975, Sept., 18-22.

All of these arguments appear absurd when rape is viewed as a violent attack against a person.

Disordered individuals. Another assumption frequently made by psychoanalysts is that rapists are sick, and, therefore, their behavior is really symptomatic of a mental disorder. Although research comparing convicted rapists to other groups, including convicts, other sex offenders, and college males, has been, at best, inconclusive and, at worst, from the disease model perspective, nonsupportive of psychological differences,* many writers still assume that differences do exist.

Early works on mental disorders and criminal behavior were simplistic and straightforward. Glueck (1925) described sexual aggression as the result of a "disease of the brain which so weakens the sufferer's powers as to prevent him from attending or referring to "general principles of conduct" (Glueck, 1925, p. 243). Disease was used in the literal sense to mean a physical problem which affects behavior. In the same tradition, Leppmann (1941), based on personal experience in prisons, arrived at three types of rape-related diseases: (a) twilight state—offender is unaware of what he is doing; (b) general paresis—organic disease occurring mostly in middle-aged men; and (c) schizophrenia—delusions with sexual intonations.

Karpman (1951) presented a slightly different use of the disease model. Whereas Glueck, Leppmann, and others referred to mental illness as an organic disease of the brain, Karpman argued that most sex offenders were really suffering from a neurosis rather than a psychosis and separated "paraphilliac neurosis," defined as developmental, from sexual psychopathy, defined as organic.** Karpman reflected the beliefs of others (Reinhardt & Fisher, 1949) when he stated that sex offenders were sick and therefore not responsible for their behavior. "Sexual psychopaths are, of course, a social menace, but they are not conscious agents deliberately and viciously perpetrating these acts; rather they are victims of a disease

---

* For example see Cohen, M., Seghorn, T., and Calmas, W. Sociometric study of the sex offender. *Journal of Abnormal Psychology*, 1969, 74, 249-255; Hammer, E. A comparison of H-T-P of rapists and pedophiles. *Journal of Projective Techniques*, 1954, 18, 346-354; Kanin, E. An examination of sexual aggression as a response to sexual stimuli. *Journal of Marriage and the Family*, 1967, 29, 428-433.

** Hollingshead, A. B. and Redlich, F. *Social Class and Mental Illness.* New York: John Wiley, 1958, found that clinical diagnosis varies by social class and that the middle class is more likely to be labeled neurotic while the lower class is more likely to be labeled psychotic. There is a similar potential for class bias in the disposition of rape cases. Since sexual psychopathy is believed to be deteriorating, sentencing is indeterminate, but since neurosis is considered treatable, the offender has a better chance for release.

from which many suffer more than their victims." (Karpman, 1951, p. 190). Thus, a direct consequence of placing rapists in the sick role is to alleviate them of responsibility for their behavior.

Following a set of categories developed in 1952 by Guttmacher and Weihofen, Cohen et al. (1971) used the descriptive features of the rape act to categorize rapists. Although the possibility that other factors may contribute to rape was considered, their approach was primarily psychoanalytic and "sex offenders" were treated as sick people who could be cured with psychotherapeutic techniques.

In 1973, the *Police Law Quarterly* referred to an article by analyst Littner as "one of the finest psychological studies of the sex offender ever published." In it Littner argued, "The single most important item we need to know about the sex offender is how sick he is emotionally. This is far more important than the nature of the crime that he has committed" (Littner, 1973, p. 7). He reasoned that if the degree of illness was known, recovery could be predicted. Yet in the same article he stated that there are no personality characteristics common to all rapists and that the only universal was the act itself. Furthermore, he noted that there was little difference in recidivism among treated and non-treated first offenders and, with regard to repeat offenders, the prognosis was usually poor. Consequently, his argument has no significance for first offenders and usually fails when applied to repeat offenders.

The ability to predict recovery is undoubtedly linked to the ability to diagnose sexual psychopathy. Relevant to this point, Bowman and Engle (1965) argued that sexual psychopathy "subsumes a long, broadly descriptive list of personality traits and is not a specific diagnostic label based on scientific data" (Bowman & Engle, 1965, p. 766). They pointed out that legal definitions mixed with psychiatric terms have proven to be ineffective administratively and suggested that psychiatrists should return to a consultant role. Supporting this position, Ellis and Brancale (1956) demonstrated that individuals who would be defined as having more serious emotional disturbances quite often commit minor offenses and vice versa.

Wenger and Fletcher (1969) have demonstrated the effect of legal counsel on psychiatric recommendations for commitment. They suggest that if the decision to commit is based on medical diagnosis the presence of legal counsel should not have an impact on the outcome. However, in a study of 81 cases, they demonstrated that the presence of legal counsel did affect the psychiatrist's recommendation and concluded that the use of psychiatric categories to determine legal responsibility is dangerous.

Further evidence for the view that categorizing of rapists has traditionally been subject to social, class, and racial bias is the fact that, of all men executed for rape in the United States since 1930, 89% have been black. "Heavier sentences imposed on blacks for raping white women is an incontestable historic fact" (Brownmiller, 1975, p. 216). If the problem were purely a medical one, sentencing would not, presumably, be distributed differentially across social classes.

The disease model has several obvious functions. It places the behavior in a "special" category and thus protects the interest of "normal" males. Additionally, it casts offenders in the sick role. Behavior attributed to incapacity beyond the individual's control carries the obligation of admitting illness and seeking professional help. Ultimately, the offender is returned to psychiatry's domain.

Symptomatic behavior. Given the presumption of illness, many psychiatrists conclude that rape is merely symptomatic of the real disorder or disease. Psychiatrists often read into behavior hidden motives such as latent homosexuality or hostility toward a mother figure. This leads to an investigation that has, for the most part, ignored an analysis of the behavior itself. Littner (1973), for example, claimed that the nature of the illness is far more important than the crime, which is only a symptom.* Guttmacher and Weihofen also believed that "sex offenses are symptoms of mental disorders" (1952, p. 116). They argued that the actual behavior cannot be taken seriously because very often a sex offense is not really committed by a sexual deviate. Rather, poorly organized egos and "noxious circumstances can momentarily break down defenses" (Guttmacher & Weihofen, 1952, p. 112). To illustrate their point they discuss the case of a man who while riding on a bus became very nervous and agitated. He resolved his problem by getting off the bus and approaching a woman who he demanded have oral sex with him. The analysts explained that the man had a claustrophobic experience (noxious circumstance) on the bus and was merely trying to get his mind off his "self." This type of interpretation is frequently found in psychiatric literature. They do not explain why the man chose to free his psyche by assaulting a woman rather than a man.

Finally, Littner (1973) epitomized the application of the pyschoanalytic model to sexual offenders and the current belief in rape as symptom.

---

* For a critique of the behavior-as-symptom logic see Szasz, T. *The Myth of Mental Illness.* New York: Harper and Row, 1961.

"Similarly when we talk about rape we are describing an act that is the symptom of a mental illness; we are not indicating what the mental disease is. We must study the rapist carefully in order to understand his underlying mental disease" (Littner, 1973, p. 6). The consequence of emphasizing the secondary nature of the behavior is clear in this passage. The act is attributed to a particular, individualistic disease and is not associated with the cultural context in which it occurs. However, Szasz (1961), among others, has argued that behavior always communicates a set of beliefs and values. Consequently, the origin and substance of these beliefs and values are relevant to understanding the behavior.

Homosexuality. The idea that rapists are often latent homosexuals frequently appears in psychiatric literature. For example, Guttmacher and Weihofen (1952) listed latent homosexuality as one of two sources of motivation for the "true" sex offender. Implicit in other psychoanalytic discussions of rape, even after homosexuality was redefined in the American Psychiatric Association *Diagnostic and Statistical Manual,* is the belief that homosexuality is the root of the "evil" (East, 1946; Guttmacher, 1951; Karpman, 1951; Littner, 1973).

The linkage between homosexuality and rape can be explained in the same way that Szasz (1973) interpreted the use of homosexuality in general as "the model psychiatric scapegoat," subhuman, defective and in need of repair. Obviously this places rapists in a group that historically has been composed of outsiders and therefore assures minimal identification with "normal" men. Thus, using a homosexual "scapegoat" protects the interests of the dominant group in our society.

Alcohol and Unusual Circumstances

The use of alcohol by rapists prior to the act is mentioned throughout the literature. While alcohol is not claimed to cause rape, most writers maintain that it removes social constraints (disinhibition thesis) and leaves men at the mercy of their sexual drives. Overwhelmed by these drives, they attack a convenient victim.

This belief is based on very limited empirical research. Carpenter and Armenti (1972, p. 509) noted that "the amount of experimental evidence for opinions about the actions of ethyl alcohol on either sexual behavior or aggression is extremely small." In an extensive review of the literature they show that the relationship between alcohol and sexual desire has not been empirically established. Experiments with animals and with humans have failed to demonstrate a positive relationship. "Sexual desire may or may not be increased by alcohol. At present there is no real evidence for or against such an idea" (Carpenter & Armenti, 1972, p. 524). With regard to aggression, the authors concluded that "the generalization that alcohol increases aggression is tenuous" (p. 532). Only one study they reviewed suggested that disinhibition was a reasonable thesis. However, so many writers have reported a correlation between alcohol and rape that some type of association must exist (Amir, 1971; East, 1946; Guttmacher, 1951; Leppmann, 1941; Rada, 1975).

Rada (1975) presented an alternative explanation. Noting the widespread acceptance of disinhibition theory, he suggested that rapists may be using alcohol as an excuse for their behavior. In vocabulary of motive terms, alcohol has become an acceptable excuse for deviant behavior in our culture. Supporting this hypothesis, McCaghy (1968) found that child molesters used alcohol as a technique for neutralizing their deviant identity.

Equally interesting, while alcohol consumption is often used to the advantage of rapists, it has the opposite effect for victims. In fact, victim intoxication is a primary cause for declaring rape complaints unfounded. For example, LeGrand (1973) found that among the rape complaints filed by victims who had been drinking, 82% were classified unfounded. Although he does not feel drunkenness can be used as an excuse for rape, Judge Morris Ploscowe stated "when a woman drinks with a man to the point of intoxication, she practically invites him to take advantage of her person. She should not be permitted to yell when she is sober, 'I was raped' " (1968, p. 215). Surely, attorneys, as well as offenders, are aware of the utility of a defense based on alcohol consumption and that it can be used to shift responsibility to the victim.

The use of alcohol is a classic example of the differential application of vocabularies of motive. Females are discredited for the same act which males can use to justify their behavior.

Victim Precipitation

Victim precipitated rape is another major theme within psychiatric literature. Traditionally, support came from victimology, a subfield of criminology, in which the victim's contribution to the genesis of crime was the object of study. Recently victimology has also focused on crime from the victim's perspective.

Criminologist von Hentig was one of the first to articulate the victimologists' position. Writing in 1940, he argued that "the human victim in many instances seems to lead the evil doer actively into temptation. The predator is—by varying means—prevailed to advance against the prey" (von Hentig, 1940, p. 303). If there are born criminals, he argued, there are born victims who are self-harming and self-destructive. Central to his thesis is the question of why a particular victim was chosen. In the case of incest and rape, seduction played a prominent role, leading him to question whether rape may not be considered a case of "the oversexed on the oversexed" (von Hentig, 1940, p. 209).

The work of sociologist Amir (1972) is a more contemporary example of the application of victimology to rape. Amir made a distinction between victim precipitative behaviors through acts of commission and through acts of omission. Commissive behavior included "last moment retreating from sexual advancement" or "agreeing voluntarily to drink or ride with a stranger" (Amir, 1972, p. 155). Omission referred to a lack of preventive measures such as failing to react strongly enough to sexual suggestions or "when her outside appearance arouses the offender's advances which are not staved off" (Amir, 1972, p. 155). Amir stated that under these circumstances, "the victim becomes functionally responsible for the offense by entering upon and following a course that will provoke some males to commit crimes" (Amir, 1972, p. 155). Thus Amir argued that attention should be focused upon the victim-offender relationship, the moral character of the victim, and the "victim's personality makeup which may orient her toward the offender and the offense" (Amir, 1972, p. 132). While the field of victimology can be accused of overidentifying with offenders, in the case of rape psychoanalytic theory has provided the vocabulary of motive with which victims could be discredited.

In psychoanalytic terms the core female personality consists of three characteristics: narcissism, masochism, and passivity. The masochistic element accounts for women's alleged unconscious desire to be raped. In her summary and critique of the psychoanalytic view of female personality, Horney stated:

> The specific satisfactions sought and found in female sex life and motherhood are of a masochistic nature. The content of the early sexual wishes and fantasies concerning the father is the desire to be mutilated, that is, castrated by him. Menstruation has the hidden connotation of a masochistic experience. What the woman secretly desires in intercourse is rape and violence, or in the mental sphere, humiliation. . . . This swinging in the direction of masochism is 'part of the woman's anatomical destiny' (Horney, 1973, p. 22-24).

While many analyses of the psychoanalytic view of women have been made,* with the exception of Albin (1977) no one has noted how easily it can be translated into a rationalization for male sexual aggressive behavior.

Masochism. In the psychiatric literature, victims are frequently sorted into categories on the basis of personal or circumstantial characteristics. Analyst Littner distinguished between true "victims," those who do not consciously or unconsciously wish to be raped, and "professional victims," those who have an inner masochistic need to be raped. According to Littner, "professional victims" have an inner need to be sexually molested or attacked even though consciously they are totally unaware of their motivation (Littner, 1973, p. 23). Because of these unconscious desires, they "unwittingly cooperate with the rapist in terms of covertly making themselves available to the rapist" (Littner, 1973, p. 28).

Likewise, similar assumptions are made about the masochistic needs of sex offenders' wives. Abrahamsen (1960), in his discussion of eight wives who had been subjected to sexual aggression by their rapist husbands, stated, "The offender needs an outlet for his sexual aggression and finds a submissive partner who unconsciously invites sexual abuse and whose masochistic needs are being fulfilled" (Abrahamsen, 1960, p. 163). The fact that these women divorced their rapist-husbands didn't alter Abrahamsen's belief in the psychoanalytic model. Instead he argued that the wives were also latently aggressive and competitive. In Abrahamsen's scheme the rapist was the innocent victim of his wife, his mother, and the women whom he raped. "There can be no doubt that the sexual frustration which the wives caused is one of the factors motivating the rape which might be tentatively described as a displaced attempt to force a seductive but rejecting mother into submission. The sex offender was not only exposed to his wife's masculine and competitive inclinations, but also, in a certain sense, was somehow 'seduced' into committing the crime" (Abrahamsen, 1960, p. 165).

Seduction. Seduction by the victim frequently appears in psychiatric literature as an explanation for rape. Used in this way a criminal attack takes on the appearance of a normal sexual encounter. For example, Hollander stated, "Considering the amount of illicit intercourse, rape of women is very rare indeed. Flirtation and provocative conduct, i.e. tacit if not actual consent, is generally the prelude to intercourse" (Hollander, 1924, p. 130).

---

* See Chesler, P. *Women and Madness.* New York: Doubleday and Co., 1972; Miller, J. (Ed.). *Psychoanalysis and Women.* New York: Brunner/Mazel, 1973.

Since psychiatrists view rape as a sexual act and since women are supposed to be coy about their sexual attractions, a refusal has little meaning. The fact that violence and often a weapon are used to accomplish the act is not considered.

> The conscious or unconscious biological and psychological attraction between man and woman does not exist only on the part of the offender toward the woman but also on her part toward him, which in many instances may to some extent be the impetus for his sexual attack. Often a women (sic) unconsciously wishes to be taken by force—consider the theft of the bride in *Peer Gynt* (Abrahamsen, 1960, p. 161).

Even more interesting than what psychiatrists say about women is what they say about female children who are the victims of rape and or incest. Girls are alleged to have the same motives as their adult counterparts. For example, Abrahamsen presented the thesis that sexual trauma was often unconsciously desired by the child and that it represented a form of infantile sexual activity. "If there is an underlying unconscious wish for it, the experiencing of sexual trauma in childhood is a masochistic expression of the sexual impulse. . . . We can say that children belonging to this category show an abnormal desire for obtaining sexual pleasure, and in consequence of this undergo sexual traumas" (Abrahamsen, 1960, p. 54).

A frequently quoted psychiatric study of girls (Weiss, Rogers, Darwin, & Dutton, 1955) who were the victims of adult sex offenders distinguished between "accidental" victims and "participating" victims, "those who took part in initiating and maintaining the relationship." Half or 23 out of the 44 victims labeled "participating" were under age 10, and some were as young as four or five years of age. Furthermore, "participation" was determined on the basis of psychiatric evaluations of the victims' personality rather than on the objective facts of the case. The authors concluded that the girls had severe emotional problems which motivated the initiation and participation in their own victimization, but they never considered the possibility that these problems might be the result, not the cause of the rape or incest. Elsewhere in the literature (Bender, 1965), girl victims are described as very attractive, charming, appealing, submissive, and seductive.

Boys as well as girls are sexually victimized by adult men. However, discussions of males lack the suggestion that masochism, seduction, or promiscuity are causative factors. For example, Halleck stated, "Most girl victims are familiar with the offender and many are willing or passive participants in the sexual act" (Halleck, 1965, p. 681). About males he stated, "A significant number of male victims may be considered as truly 'accidental' in the sense that they did not know the attacker and did not willingly participate in the act" (Halleck, 1965, p. 680).

"Nice Girls Don't Get Raped." Perception of fault in rape is also affected by the belief that "nice girls don't get raped." The victim's reputation as well as characteristics or behavior which violate normative sex-role expectations are perceived as contributing to the commission of the act. For example, hitchhike rape is defined as a victim precipitated offense (Nelson & Amir, 1975). The inherent injustice of this position is compounded by the criteria which have been used to determine the victim's reputation. For example, one indication used by the President's Commission on Crime in Washington, D.C. was "substantiated statements by offenders that the victim was generally known to be a loose or easy object of sexual assault" (Curtis, 1974, p. 600). Reputation has been used to discredit the victim, to present her as the legitimate object of sexual attack, and it ultimately functions to deny women legal protection. Von Hentig obviously echoed the opinion of others in the criminal justice system when he stated, "The victim could be held unworthy of being protected by the law, either not being a female 'of previous chaste character' or succumbing to false pretenses which would not deceive 'a man of ordinary intelligence and caution'" (von Hentig, 1940, p. 307).

The psychiatric assumptions which underscore allegations of victim precipitated rape are a clear example of how vocabularies of motive can be constructed without empirical data and used to discredit the powerless, in this case women and girls. Equally important, when this vocabulary is used, attention is focused on the behavior and motives of the victim rather than on the offender. Consequently, responsibility for the act is also shifted to the victim. The power and influence of this vocabulary extend beyond psychiatric journals. As numerous observers have noted, in court it is the rape victim who appears to be on trial. Perhaps feminist psychiatrists like Hilberman, whose book, *The Rape Victim* (1976), was approved by the American Psychiatric Association, will begin to correct these damaging beliefs.

CONCLUSION

A review of the psychiatric rape literature has revealed several trends worthy of emphasis. First is the dramatic, concurrent growth of the psychiatric profession and sexual psychopath legislation. By 1965, 30 states and the District of Columbia had specific laws under which rapists could be defined as persons unable to control sexual impulses or as having the propensity to commit sex crimes.

Within the span of 50 years, psychiatry moved from the desire to be consulted in sexual offense matters to a position in which they could control the labeling and, consequently, the sentencing and release of sex offenders. To accomplish this they claimed a professional monopoly over a body of relevant "expert" knowledge. Thus they established the idea that rape was symptomatic of other, more serious, emotional problems and that individual rapists were sick. Once the medical model had been accepted, psychiatry could also argue that if rape was an individual illness, psychotherapy was the preferred cure. As Mills (1940) noted, word motives function to coordinate and serve the interests of others as well as the person who has broken a norm.

This review has also demonstrated the biases inherent in the motive statements generated by the pyschiatric perspective. Each motive functions to emphasize the individual, idiosyncratic nature of the problem. When rapists are defined as sick and in need of help, individual responsibility is removed. When offenders are placed in the category of "outsider," the connection with "normal" men is eliminated. Finally, much of the blame can be placed on the victim. Each motive functions, as Mills pointed out, to justify or excuse the past behavior of the actor and, as a result, the social and cultural conditions within the society which might be the source of the problem are not examined.

A sociological alternative to the psychiatric perspective views criminal behavior as learned behavior. There is little reason to believe that learning to rape is different from learning to do anything else. But when rapists are labeled pathological for what they have learned, many questions remain unanswered.

The psychiatric model assumes that sex offenders have somehow distorted the input that normal men receive throughout their lives. But it is equally relevant to ask if rather than distortion, rapists may not represent one end of a quasi-socially sanctioned continuum of male sexual aggression. In this view, rapists may be conforming to their perception of male sex-role expectations. When interviewed, rapists often claim that they are normal and have done nothing wrong. Psychiatrists interpret this as a rationalization. But Mills' point, that rationalization to one group is reason to another, should also be considered. This is especially reasonable in light of the ambiguity of the research which has attempted to empirically verify that rapists are psychologically different from other men.

The pyschiatric model also cannot explain the low recidivism rates for first offenders. While a number of questions can be raised concerning the accuracy and interpretation of these statistics, it is also possible to suggest that first offenders define their behavior as normal until they are convicted. If the rapist's perspective is developed socially in interaction with signfiicant others and reference groups, it might take drastic action such as a conviction to alter that perspective. At least the data suggest such a hypothesis.

The psychiatric perspective will continue to dominate thought on rape until challenged by research predicated on a different set of assumptions. Until then, the model will continue to protect the interests of psychiatry and white middle-class men in general and will continue to work to the detriment of women, especially those who have been victimized.

REFERENCES

ABRAHAMSEN, D. *The Psychology of Crime.* New York: John Wiley & Sons, 1960.

ALBIN, R. Psychological studies of rape. *Signs*, 1977, 3, 423-435.

AMIR, M. *Patterns in Forcible Rape.* Chicago: University of Chicago Press, 1971.

AMIR, M. The role of the victim in sex offenses. In H. Resnik & M. Wolfgang (Eds.), *Sexual Behavior: Social, Clinical, and Legal Aspects.* Boston: Little, Brown, 1972.

BENDER, L. Offended and offender children. In R. Slovenko (Ed.), *Sexual Behavior and the Law.* Springfield, Ill.: Charles C Thomas, 1965.

BOWMAN, K. & ENGLE, B. Sexual psychopath laws. In R. Slovenko (Ed.), *Sexual Behavior and the Law.* Springfield, Ill.: Charles C Thomas, 1965.

BROWNMILLER, S. *Against Our Will.* New York: Simon & Schuster, 1975.

CARPENTER, J. & ARMENTI, N. Some effects of ethanol on human sexual and aggressive behavior. In B. Hessin & H. Begleiter (Eds.), *The Biology of Alcoholism* (Vol. 2). New York: Plenum Press, 1972.

COHEN, M., GAROFALO, R., BOUCHER, R., & SEGHORN, T. The psychology of rapists. *Seminars in Psychiatry*, 1971, 3, 307-327.

CURTIS, L. Victim precipitation and violent crime. *Social Problems*, 1974, 21, 594-605.

EAST, W. Sexual offenders—A British view. *Yale Law Review*, 1946, 55, 527-557.

ELLIS, A. & BRANCALE, R. *The Psychology of Sex Offenders.* Springfield: C. Thomas, 1956.

FINE, R. Psychoanalytic theory of sexuality. In R. Slovenko (Ed.), *Sexual Behavior and the Law.* Springfield, Ill.: Charles C Thomas, 1965.

GIBBENS, T., WAY, C., & SOOTHILL, K. Behavioral types of rape. *British Journal of Psychiatry*, 1977, 130, 32-42.

GLUECK, S. *Mental Disorders and the Criminal Law.* New York: Little Brown, 1925.

GUTTMACHER, M. *Sex Offenses: The Problem, Causes, and Prevention.* New York: Norton, 1951.

GUTTMACHER, M. & WEIHOFEN, H. *Psychiatry and the Law.* New York: Norton, 1952.

HALLECK, S. Emotional effects of victimization. In R. Slovenko (Ed.), *Sexual Behavior and the Law.* Springfield, Ill.: Charles C Thomas, 1965.

HILBERMAN, E. *The Rape Victim.* New York: Basic Books, 1976.

HOLLANDER, B. *Psychology of Misconduct, Vice and Crime.* New York: Macmillan, 1924.

HORNEY, K. The problem of feminine masochism. In J. Miller (Ed.), *Psychoanalysis and Women.* New York: Brunner/Mazel, 1973; Baltimore: Penguin (paper), 1973.

KARPMAN, B. The sexual psychopath. *Journal of Criminal Law and Criminology,* 1951, 42, 184-198.

LEGRAND, C. Rape and rape laws: Sexism in society and law. *California Law Review,* 1973, 61, 919-941.

LEPPMANN, F. Essential differences between sex offenders. *Journal of Criminal Law and Criminology,* 1941, 32, 366-380.

LITTNER, N. Psychology of the sex offender: Causes, treatment, prognosis. *Police Law Quarterly,* 1973, 3, 5-31.

McCAGHY, C. Drinking and deviance disavowal: The case of child molesters. *Journal of Social Problems,* 1968, 16, 43-49.

MILLS, C. Situated actions and vocabularies of motive. *American Sociological Review,* 1940, 5, 904-913.

NELSON, S. & AMIR, M. The hitchhike victim of rape. In I. Drapkin & E. Viano (Eds.), *Victimology: A New Focus* (Vol. 5). Massachusetts: Lexington Books, 1975.

PLOSCOWE, M. Rape. In E. Sagarin & D. MacNamara (Eds.), *Problems of Sexual Behavior.* New York: Thomas Crowell, 1968.

RADA, R. Acoholism and forcible rape. *American Journal of Psychiatry,* 1975, 132, 444-446.

REINHARDT, J. & FISHER, E. The sexual psychopath and the law. *Journal of Criminal Law and Criminology,* 1949, 39, 734-742.

SPIRER, J. Psychology of irresistible impulse. *Journal of Criminal Law and Criminology,* 1942, 33, 457-462.

SUTHERLAND, E. Sexual psychopathy laws. *Journal of Criminal Law and Criminology,* 1950, 40, 543-554.

SZASZ, T. *Law, Liberty and Psychiatry.* New York: Macmillan, 1963.

SZASZ, T. *The Manufacture of Madness.* Frogmore, St. Albans: Paladin, 1973.

SZASZ, T. *The Myth of Mental Illness.* New York: Harper and Row, 1961.

VON HENTIG, H. Remarks on the interaction of perpetrator and victim. *Journal of Criminal Law and Criminology,* 1940, 31, 303-309.

WEISS, J., ROGERS, E., DARWIN, M., & DUTTON, C. A study of girl sex offenders. *Psychiatric Quarterly,* 1955, 29, 1-29.

WENGER, D. & FLETCHER, C. The effects of legal counsel on admission to a state mental hospital: A confrontation of professions. *Journal of Health and Social Behavior,* 1969, 10, 66-72.

Part IV
FUNCTIONAL DISORDERS

12

GENDER AND SCHIZOPHRENIA

FLORENCE SCHUMER

Schizophrenia, thought to be the most prevalent of all mental disorders, remains a baffling problem to researchers and clinicians. There is still little consensus as to etiology, treatment, or even management. The mysteries of this disease continue to elude us. We are sure only about the hard facts of human waste and anguish.

The actual counting of heads—patients about whom a diagnosis of schizophrenia has been made—does not represent the extent of schizophrenia, for the uncounted cases—those who do not come to the attention of any facility or institution and leave no record of themselves—are estimated to be almost three times the number of recorded cases (Deming, 1968). The distribution of male and female frequencies in this vast unknown population is of course also unknown.

The recorded figures for schizophrenia are staggering, with estimates ranging from about 2% of the general population (predicted to have schizophrenia at some point in their lifetime) to about 6% in urban slums. At any given time, about half the beds in mental facilities are occupied by patients diagnosed as schizophrenics ("Schizophrenia, is there an answer?", 1974). These figures are strikingly high in the light of the drop in hospital inpatients because of the widespread use of psychoactive drugs.

It is likely that more research attention has been focused on schizophrenia than on any other clinical entity. Yet, questions of etiology continue to baffle researchers. Schizophrenia remains difficult to treat. There is no consensus as to its diagnosis. Theories of schizophrenia continue to burgeon. And no two schizophrenias are truly alike, although we talk of schizophrenia as if it were a single disease. These problems multiply our difficulties in understanding what schizophrenia is all about.

To make matters worse, there are only meager attempts to explore sex

321

differences in the theoretical, experimental, and clinical literature on schizophrenia (Wahl, 1977). The prevalence of this practice of ignoring the sex distribution of a phenomenon or failing to look at gender influences on findings is an important social as well as scientific problem. However, despite sparse substance in this area, there is still something to talk about, as we shall see.

DIAGNOSIS: SOME PROBLEMS

Although there is moderate agreement about some of its clinical features, there is much disagreement as to the diagnosis and measurement of schizophrenia. Among some of the symptoms associated with schizophrenia are: bizarre behavior, acutely obsessional thinking, bizarre body sensations and ruminations, grandiosity, hallucinations, delusions, waxy flexibility, word salads, grimacing, apathy and loss of motivation, withdrawal into a subjective world, mutism, negativism, catatonic stupor, attentional and perceptual difficulties, flattening of or inappropriate affect, paranoid ideation, occasional violence, and communication and language difficulties.

The sad facts are that many other pathological conditions, especially those that accompany various types of CNS dysfunctions, can also yield some of the above symptomatology. Further, the foregoing qualities are not uniformly present when a diagnosis of schizophrenia is made. The complex array of symptoms and the lack of homogeneity of the clinical picture have impeded scientific progress in the field of schizophrenia for years.

No matter what the symptoms, however, there is more than ample evidence to indicate that it is the *behavioral* expression of the labeled patient that becomes troublesome or that draws the attention of others: oddness, queerness, eccentricity in behavior; peculiar or inappropriate response to people; unconventional dress or role-behavior; unpredictability as to social conventions in speech, mannerism, posture. Although schizophrenia may well be a tangible disease process, decisions as to who gets labeled, shunted aside by society, or hospitalized are social decisions. The terrifying self-doubts and fears about competence (loss of job; inability to run the household) that many patients experience could reflect social and cultural factors. For schizophrenia, as a label, is not only a disease, but also a social diagnosis; it seems powerfully related to social factors. This theme will underlie much of this chapter.

The traditional clinical division of schizophrenia into simple, hebephrenic, catatonic, and paranoid subtypes (see American Psychiatric

Association *DSM-II*, 1968) is being severely criticized by many scientists in the light of validity and reliability considerations. Overall, there is not much evidence concerning sex distribution of incidence figures in these categories. Perhaps it is just as well, because the unreliability of these diagnoses and problems concerning untreated cases would obscure "true" prevalence. Stereotypes about the simple type are likely to be male: the hobo, vagrant, or "peeping Tom," who ends up on Skid Row or in the inner-city hotel as a bum or alcoholic. But many women are simple schizophrenics. And although our thinking has been shaped by theorists like Freud to think of paranoid symptoms as expressions of male pathology (in response to homosexual panic), it seems that twice as many females as males show paranoid ideation (Freedman, Kaplan, & Sadock, 1972), at least in recorded cases.

A word about infantile autism: When a "nonorganic" diagnosis of infantile autism is made, an interesting gender relationship appears—a much higher percentage of mothers than of fathers is schizophrenic (Rosenthal, 1971). It is not clear whether this is a result of environmental or genetic factors or an interaction of both, since little is known about the exact etiology of infantile autism. Later, however, we shall refer to some intriguing possibilities concerning the ways in which schizophrenic mothers relate to their babies, and to findings that show that the incidence of pregnancy and birth complications (PBCs) increases with the pathology of the mothers.

Current Classifications

Dissatisfaction with the usual nosological system stemmed largely from considerations concerning its unreliability or poor reliability. A good diagnostic system should be capable of consistent use and objective application in a wide variety of settings and crosscultural contexts; it should also be capable of predicting outcome and even contain some maps for treatment. Unfortunately, there is ample evidence that suggests that these criteria are not successfully met by the old system (Zubin, 1967).

The process-reactive classification was developed in attempts to meet some of these problems. Essentially, the process-reactive framework contains some elements that predict prognosis, whether a patient gets better or worse. This distinction rests heavily on the premorbid characteristics of the patient: In process schizophrenia, there is a long history of poor interpersonal and social adjustment with a gradual, insidious onset and a worsening picture of deterioration with poor prognosis; in reactive schizophrenia, there is a picture of relatively good premorbid adjustment with sudden onset, dramatic symptomatology, and favorable prognosis, usually in a relatively brief period of time.

There is much empirical support for the belief that the reactive-process classification is a meaningful one in terms of outcome variables, cognitive factors, hospital and treatment status, and other related and measurable factors. Its measurement is generally based on scales of premorbid functioning, such as the Phillips Scale (1953), which attempts to assess the interpersonal adjustment and competence of the patient. An interesting sidelight of this widely used method is that it weights rather heavily the sexual experiences of the premorbid individual, with the less favorable classification and poorer prognosis (process schizophrenia) emerging from background factors such as having had homosexual experiences, being of single marital status, and the like. Since these social and sexual roles are indicative of poor adjustment only in the light of the cultural and social times and contexts, it is highly likely that as role expectations and acceptable standards change, they will no longer reflect the kinds of poor premorbid adjustments that predict or are associated with chronic (process) schizophrenia.

Many empirical studies have clearly indicated that various premorbid characteristics of the patient are powerful determinants of outcome. These premorbid characteristics are apparently interwoven with role behaviors, role expectations, marital status, sexual fears, and various other socioculturally-induced stresses; being a woman or man in our culture is also very much enmeshed with these same social variables—with all their attendant conflicting expectations and confusions. It seems likely that gender influences on premorbid competence are present. The precise nature of these influences would have to be teased out by highly sophisticated research methods, since they (the influences) are probably also interacting with social class variables (see later section). Poor premorbids of lower classes will more likely become chronic, process schizophrenics than poor premorbids of higher social classes because of the social supports that are available to the latter.

SOCIOCULTURAL FACTORS, SOCIOECONOMIC STATUS (SES), AND SCHIZOPHRENIA

Although incidence figures suggest that (a) rates have remained about the same in this country for about 100 years, (b) all cultures report some form of schizophrenia, and (c) incidence cuts across all SES groups, there are some challenges to these statements.

Although rates may be the same, we cannot know this definitely. It could be that schizophrenia is actually decreasing, but our diagnostic tools—and vigilance about competence—are more powerful. Life is longer (at both ends), providing more opportunities for pathology to become evidenced. And, because of technological advances in perinatal care, we are permitting babies to be born who may be neurologically and developmentally handicapped, perhaps more vulnerable to stress and schizophrenia. Further, we do not necessarily apply the same diagnostic criteria from one century to the next.

Second, recent evidence (e.g., Torrey, 1973) suggests that schizophrenia is less universal among cultures than was thought to be the case; but if universality is true, it probably holds only for process schizophrenia.

Third, some strong possibilities are raised that social norms and myths, especially prevailing attitudes toward insanity and its etiology, determine actual prevalence figures from culture to culture, especially for chronic cases. Murphy (1968) predicts, for example, that in societies in which insanity is attributed to external causes such as poisoning or witchcraft, there would be fewer chronic cases than in those societies in which personal and individual variables are felt to be the cause. It would be expected, then, that women are especially vulnerable to chronic or process pathology in those societies such as ours in which guilt about role competence and duties as a woman prevails.

Overall, even if prevalence, for whatever reasons, is stable through time or from culture to culture, there is virtually uniform agreement that incidence of schizophrenia is related to social class, with higher rates found among lower SES levels (Dohrenwend & Dohrenwend, 1969, 1974; Garmezy & Streitman, 1974; Kohn, 1973; Torrey, 1973). And further, *within* this extremely strong association, we can find some gender differences, as predicted, since the social class-schizophrenia association is most in evidence among women (Freedman et al., 1972).

There appear to be ethnic, as well as social class, variations, so that even within the lowest of SES groups incidence of schizophrenia varies along ethnic lines (e.g., in New York City, persons of Puerto Rican origin have a higher rate of schizophrenia than matched lower SES subjects of non-Puerto Rican origin—Rendon, 1974).

In sum, most evidence suggests that there is a strong association between socioeconomic conditions, cultural norms, and related sociocultural factors and incidence of schizophrenia. It is suggested that such factors also play a significant role in the actual expression of the disease and its symptoms, despite any uniform baseline in etiology such as genetic predisposition.

GENDER AND SCHIZOPHRENIA: A SURVEY

Women tend to report more psychiatric symptoms than men (Phillips & Segal, 1969). In a review of some of the literature, Garai (1970) noted that there are also differences in content: Among the differences noted are that women express more anxiety, a greater number of psychosomatic symptoms, and more concern about interpersonal relationships and self-image than men, who apparently are more concerned about occupational achievement and success. Women report being more unhappy; when there is a "breakdown," men assume more feminine and women more masculine behaviors.

What does this tell us about schizophrenia? Are there gender differences in the incidence, expression, and outcome for schizophrenia? As might already be expected, there is evidence suggesting that the number of first admissions of females with the diagnosis of schizophrenia is somewhat greater than that of men. In New York State, one female in 62 and one male in 68 was admitted for schizophrenia at any point in time. Overall, the chances for first admissions at any age are one in 39 for females and one in 46 for males (Deming, 1968). Why is this so? Is it easier for men to "drift" within the community? Are women more liable to get into "trouble" with society or with their families or communities in terms of role expectations and therefore become labeled and hospitalized more quickly? Are there genetic differences?

In general, many investigators believe that more women than men in our society become mentally ill (e.g., Gove & Tudor, 1973). The suggestion is that there are more problems, conflicts, and confusions attendant to being a woman, and that women have poorer self-images. It would follow, therefore, that the foregoing incidence figures are to be expected.

It should be noted, however, that some investigators do not agree with this generalization. For example, Dohrenwend and Dohrenwend (1974) found only inconclusive evidence for such a relationship. True prevalence figures, however, are difficult to obtain, and the number of untreated cases or unrecognized cases is an unknown factor.

Judging by some first admission data, however, women do appear to be more susceptible to becoming schizophrenic, being labeled as such, being incarcerated, and all the other things that happen to psychiatric patients. However, the empirical data do not always consistently support this point. And some data are actually contradictory. For example, according to Rosenthal (1970), first admissions for schizophrenia are higher for younger males; as age increases, however, rates are higher for females.

Does this suggest that the rising complexity of life for older females, such as family and work and child-rearing functions, when impinging on a poor premorbid personality, contributes to the expression of the disease? Or are there endocrinological variables at work? On the other hand, some of the literature notes that male schizophrenics tend to be admitted to inpatient care more often than females; under age 18, however, female schizophrenics are more likely than males to be hospitalized (Taube & Redick, 1973).

Gender differences in admission data obviously exist. But in which direction? Both age and social class variables, as well as the community's tolerance for absorbing or dealing with deviance, apparently influence admission data. Since this is the case, if one subscribes to the interpretation that there are rising admission rates for females with age, an intriguing hypothesis presents itself. Perhaps the interaction between gender and social class variables is strongest at lower age levels. That is, it may well be that young women in lower SES groups are picked up and labeled more easily as "sick" than young men. Marginally competent premorbids or "sick" young women from upper-income groups may be protected, even hidden, by their families. Higher age levels often mean marriage, especially for women, even with poor premorbid backgrounds. When married, does disorganization become more apparent for women in both lower and upper SES groups because of the demands and responsibilities made upon them—so that women from both lower and upper SES groups become equally vulnerable? And therefore, do female first admission rates increase over males as age increases no matter what the SES level?

GENDER AND THEORIES OF ETIOLOGY

Genetic Approaches

A genetic "explanation" for schizophrenia is viewed with increasing favor by many investigators. Schizophrenia occurs in all areas of the world, as already noted, even though process rather than reactive cases might be involved—and apparently its incidence is about equally distributed between the sexes (Rosenthal, 1971).

Most evidence does indeed point to genetic components in schizophrenia; the evidence is based in part on concordance of schizophrenia in monozygotic twins (MZ—identical) reared apart. The data do not indicate 100% concordance, however, leaving room for a good amount of variation to be accounted for by environmental factors (Rosenthal, 1971), especially those related to stress. The percentage can be as low as

25% (Allen, Cohen, & Pollin, 1972)—a high concordance rate, neverthe-less. Highest rates (up to 75%) are found among hospitalized twins. Presumably, the chronic deteriorated twin is likely to have a chronic deteriorated twin somewhere else with the same diagnosis. These are likely to be poor premorbids, and poor premorbids may well be the expression of a special type of strong predisposition for schizophrenia that has a higher genetic component than other types of schizophrenia. That is, the more severe cases may have a stronger genetic component than milder forms.

With increasing closeness of blood relationship, a higher concordance of schizophrenia is found. Of this there is no doubt. But the symmetry of the relationship stops right here. For the quantitative findings simply do not conform to a pure genetic hypothesis.

Since no evidence can be found that females are more genetically prone to schizophrenia than males, it is interesting to note that much evidence points to the fact that female MZ twins are more likely to have a higher rate of concordance than male MZ twins (as high sometimes as twice as much discordance for males as for females—see Wahl's review, 1976). That is, among females, if one of a pair of MZ twins develops schiz-ophrenia, the chances are greater that the other twin will develop schizophrenia than if they were male MZ twins. The greater incidence in the expression of this disease among female MZ twins is a fascinating research problem, opening up many possibilities for exploration as to the precise nature of the stresses, strains, sense of competence, powerlessness, frailty, failure, and conflicts that females experience, so that, if overlaid on genetic predisposition, higher rates of schizophrenia emerge.

Biochemical and Autonomic Variables

Genetic predisposition ultimately reduces itself to biochemical and physiological components. Possible relevant indices have been studied through blood chemistry, urine analysis, examinations of spinal fluid, autopsy, and various autonomic indicators. Unfortunately, except for longitudinal studies that predict on the basis of factors that are dis-covered on an a priori basis, one can never know whether or not differ-ences are due to changes that take place as a result of the schizophrenic process rather than the other way around. That is, are these differences actually precursors or results of schizophrenia?

Although there is increasing evidence implicating biochemical factors in schizophrenia, the complexities of considering their effect on the different kinds of schizophrenia (for example, acute vs. chronic), solving the problem of which came first, and the effect of hospitalization and diet on biochemistry are only now being considered. Sex differences in biochemical variables are understandably not the prime considerations in these studies; however, there is some evidence suggesting that female schizophrenics tend to have a slightly higher platelet MAO activity than male schizophrenics (Wyatt & Murphy, 1976). Why this is so is not yet clear. Certainly, a rich field is opened up for further study, especially in connection with hormonal and endocrinological differences between males and females and their role in disordered or disorganized behavior.

As for autonomic and other physiological variables, such as yielded by the galvanic skin response (GSR), cardiovascular, and EEG and evoked potential methods, most studies disclose differences between normal and schizophrenic groups (Mirsky, 1969), and sometimes even among certain schizophrenic subtypes (Payne & Shean, 1975). Reviews of the literature, however, have not always yielded consistent results as to the nature of these differences.

Male-female differences are reported in some of this literature. Gunderson, Autry, Mosher, and Buchsbaum (1974), for example, reported work by Shagass, who found chronic female patients more responsive than chronic male patients in terms of evoked potential responses to painless stimulation at the wrist—while normal females generally show *less* responsiveness in contrast to normal males. The restricted CNS responsiveness of chronic schizophrenics apparently applies to males, rather than females, according to Shagass. The precise meaning of such differences and the relationship to chronicity are not clear; however such findings open up the possibility that some autonomic differences between male and female chronic patients exist.

Psychoanalytic Theory

Freud and his followers had much difficulty in treating schizophrenics, but much less difficulty in theorizing about its etiology. Although paranoia was described by Freud as resulting from panic over homosexual fantasies or impulses in males (on the basis of the famous Schreber case), more generally (see Fenichel, 1945) schizophrenia was thought to represent some defect in regard to the patient and his or her object relationships; a breakdown of ego functions, regression to narcissism, and a parting from reality are all results of rising id forces that dominate the patient's behavior without the usual restraints of ego and superego. Regression to infantile forms of thinking and behavior is an essential ingredient of the schizophrenic process, accompanied by primitiveness, dominance of id impulses, and primary process characteristics.

In this general way of thinking, the relationship of mother and child in their primary intense symbiosis during infancy has been implicated: As the child develops, a disturbing traumatic event throws him or her back to earlier forms or prevents further development. To repeat, regression is the primary dynamic in this approach to schizophrenia. Beyond these statements, there is little literature in the Freudian approach that is specific in regard to gender differences.

Family Forces

Family theories implicate nonverbal as well as verbal communication systems, pathways, and ways of interacting among family members that can create a pathological milieu thought capable of generating schizophrenia in one of its members. The "rules" imposed by family members in such families are contradictory, double-binding, and bewildering, creating pathology in the perceptions, thought processes, and communications of the family member most vulnerable to the confusion thus infused into the family environment.

Family approach studies and case histories take many paths, as might be expected. There are occasional attempts to link role problems— generational and sex, in the Parsonian sense—to the development of schizophrenia. Some approaches implicate gender confusions in schizophrenogenic families. There are mothers who raise a boy as a girl or who occasionally act out incestuous impulses with a son, or who sleep in the same bed with a teenage son, or who constantly examine his penis for "defects"; sexuality between fathers and daughters and incestuous and homosexual acts between fathers and sons are also described in the literature. The fluidity of sexual roles and role confusions between generational lines as well as sexual identity lines are well known to observers of pathological families. These observations do not necessarily tell us about male-female differences in schizophrenia. Rather, they suggest that the confusing expectations and relationships that may exist in some families—specifically, incestuous expectations and fantasies, sexual guilts, and failure of parents to act out parental roles (in some of these families, it is the children who take care of their pathological parent)—may create the kind of atmopshere as a child is growing up in which the confusions, terrors, and perplexities of the world around him or her become "built-in" features of an unstable, disordered world, to be handled in disordered ways.

Some family hypotheses have specifically suggested that schizophrenogenic families may have parents showing role reversals. In reviewing studies of verbal activities, dominance, and other objective observational data, Goldstein and Rodnick (1975) have concluded that this evidence is inconclusive and often contradictory. For example, findings in an earlier study by Farina (1960) that indicated a tendency for fathers to show dominant patterns in families of good premorbid schizophrenics while mothers tended to show dominance in families of poor premorbid schizophrenics washed out in a later replicated study (Farina & Holzberg, 1968).

Contradictory or double-bind messages in schizophrenogenic families (Bateson, Jackson, Haley, & Weakland, 1956, 1963) are not specifically limited to male or female roles, but some of the work of Lidz and his co-workers (Lidz, 1958, 1973; Lidz & Lidz, 1949) does specifically concern itself with gender. One of these sex-related concepts is that of *schism*, in which parental battles and conflicts and opposing expectations for children contribute to the emergence of a schizophrenic child, usually female. In *skewed* families, there is a heavy focus on the problems, values, wishes, and distortions of only one of the parents, usually the mother. The family members in skewed families maintain a myth of support for the irrationality of this parent, with a wide variety of distortions and illogical, unreal perceptions generated. The patient in such families is usually a boy.

Overall, then, the vast literature on family forces—for example, the work of Wynne and his colleagues (see Morris & Wynne, 1965; Wynne & Singer, 1964)—does not necessarily call attention to role, male-female differences, and gender problems. Rather, this work stresses the milieu, especially the communicational system, within these families.

An extensive review of empirical studies of normal and schizophrenic families (Jacob, 1975) (that is, families having one schizophrenic member) yielded few consistent findings concerning dominance or power of a mother or father over a member, or differences in general levels of mood or expression of affect. Some communicational difficulties were evidenced, however. More disagreement and much less clarity of communication were found in schizophrenic families.

Mothers and Sometimes Also Fathers

In much of the literature—not necessarily psychoanalytic and not necessarily family-oriented—mothers are implicated in the rearing of their schizophrenic child. One specific hypothesis relates to the aversive qualities of the so-called schizophrenogenic mother, who, no matter what the biochemistry or genetics of the situation are, brings forth the kinds of responses in her child that add up to schizophrenia. One upholder of this view is Heilbrun (1973): Aversively controlling, demanding mothers, or mothers perceived as such by their children, tend to produce children who become schizophrenic. But which came first? The mother's aversive responses may have been in part attempts to control or shape the behavior of a child who in some way was not considered "normal." Further, the clinical literature is replete with an opposite picture—of an unusually enmeshed, interdependent relationship bewteen mother and child—a disturbed symbiosis—in which a child never develops a sense of self or motivation for mastery and independence.

One early "classic" attempt to observe parental behaviors in families containing a schizophrenic patient is the work of Cheek (1964a, 1964b, 1965) in the early sixties. Cheek observed and reliably evaluated the interactions of mothers and fathers in 67 families containing a young male or female schizophrenic patient and compared these responses to similar data for 56 families with nonpsychotic young adults. In observations, the mothers in families of schizophrenics appeared to be detached and removed although their questionnaire data yielded reports of permissiveness and support. Similar analyses for fathers of these families indicated that their behaviors differed more from fathers in normal families than did the mothers. Although fathers were generally "peripheral," fathers of schizophrenic males tended to be "passive and ineffectual," while fathers of schizophrenic females tended to be "narcissistic and proud."

Generally, small samples and failure to shed light on whether the schizophrenic patient elicited such behaviors from parents rather than the other way around limit the generalizations we can make on the basis of this and similar studies. However, some interesting hypotheses emerged concerning sex roles and sex-role enforcement from these data. Parents of schizophrenics seemed less successful in instituting or implementing role-specific behaviors (male-female). Perhaps their schizophrenic children were less successful in performing these behaviors. Even so, the intricate relationship between role behavior and society's expectations for patients and the stress involved in meeting these expectations might be involved here. We shall return to this question in a later section.

By and large, it does seem that maternal responses play an important role in the production of schizophrenia. And as a matter of fact, in a group of children diagnosed as "nonorganic schizophrenics" (childhood schizophrenics often display a variety of neurological dysfunctions), Gold-farb (1968) reported that 44% of the mothers and only 8% of the fathers were classified as schizophrenic. One possible explanation is that schizophrenic mothers have higher marriage rates and produce more children than schizophrenic fathers (Bleuler, in press).

Pregnancy and Birth Complications (PBCs)

In longitudinal studies, children who develop schizophrenia tend to have had pregnancy and birth complications (PBCs), including prematurity, delivery complications, anoxia, etc. Pollin and Stabenau (1968) report that in MZ twins discordant for schizophrenia, the twin who became schizophrenic was likely to have had a perinatal complication; and Mednick, Mura, Schulsinger, and Mednick (1971) report that schizophrenic women tend to have a greater number of PBCs in their offspring. Schizophrenic mothers also tend to have a greater number of fetal and neonatal deaths in their offspring (Rieder, Rosenthal, Wender, & Blumenthal, 1975). Perhaps schizophrenic women have had too much medication, or their emotional disorders affect their physiological ability to have children through biochemical factors as a product of their own stress.

However, some investigators (e.g., Sameroff & Zax, 1973) view these findings as a result of the unhealthy transactions that take place between an emotionally disordered mother and her offspring—with severity and chronicity of emotional disorder, rather than schizophrenia per se as the crucial variable. According to these authors, the child has been affected by the transactions that have taken place early in its life; even if adopted into other houses, these offspring might elicit behaviors from their caretakers conducive to the development of pathology, especially since such offspring bring with them certain predisposing constitutional factors.

Children born to schizophrenic mothers have a higher mortality rate than children in the general population. For the latter, there is an infant mortality rate of about 2-3% (Wegman, 1968). Children born to schizophrenic mothers in mental hospitals have as high a mortality rate as 8% (Sobel, 1961). Perinatal complications, medications, hospitalization, and motivational, genetic, and biochemical factors may all contribute to this higher rate.

Other Characteristics of Schizophrenia

A sizable body of theoretical and empirical work is currently being accumulated concerning the ways in which schizophrenic patients respond in cognitive, perceptual, and attentional situations. These studies have stressed various cognitive functions and thinking processes; attention and set; reaction time to various simple and complex stimuli; verbal and language processes; memory and recall; and the "processing" of stimuli (e.g., the ways in which information is utilized and stored). Attentional deficits have received special emphasis.

In these explorations, especially in reaction-time studies, large differences in the performance between schizophrenic and normal subjects have been reported. In addition, many differences between subgroups of schizophrenics have also been reported, especially between reactive and process schizophrenics and paranoid and nonparanoid ones.

Despite an increasing reservoir of interesting experimental findings, there is a caveat: Differences in attention, memory, recall, and perception may result from or accompany the schizophrenic process. And often, especially in earlier studies, effects of medication, diet, motivation, hospitalization, and chronicity were not considered in the experimental design.

By and large, in this sizable body of what has become well-designed research, female-male differences were not sought and so there is little evidence that indicates whether or not these exist.

Specific Learning Mechanisms as Etiology for Schizophrenia

Several approaches that attempt to link the development of schizophrenia with certain faulty mechanisms of learning are found in the literature. These include an early model by Mednick (1958) which suggested that schizophrenics operate under a higher drive state (anxiety) so that conditioning for simple tasks is made easier but conditioning for more complex tasks more difficult because of competing responses. It is suggested that among schizophrenics anxiety responses and avoidance learning are more frequently generalized because of the physiological differences between schizophrenics and nonschizophrenics. Broen and Storms (1966) present a related view suggesting that schizophrenics function under higher levels of arousal, while Ullmann and Krasner (1969) describe the schizophrenic's retreat from, or avoidance of, socially reinforcing stimuli—an extinction of attentional responses to social stimuli.

A learning approach to the study of schizophrenia, while extremely straightforward, does not tell us the specific mechanism by which women or men, in the light of their experiences, experience a schizophrenic break. Presumably, within the life history of each individual, male or female, one can find the specific conditions by which this learning takes place.

Broad Environmental View

The general view that environmental factors alone—extreme deprivation, maternal separation, stress, near-death experiences—can cause a schizophrenic breakdown is not currently held in high regard. The broad environmental view that a patient has learned to deal with severe conflict by adopting a schizophrenic posture has been proposed by many theorists, including those who adopt a family view that implicates the mother through inadequate mothering (for example, R. D. Laing, 1960), or who hold other psychodynamic or Freudian positions. The view that harsh, brutalizing experiences with a schizophrenic parent might cause a retreat into a schizophrenic process is not supported by the evidence that demonstrates that the majority of children who have suffered in this way do not become schizophrenic (see Bleuler, 1974).

A strictly environmental view must also explain the remission experienced by many schizophrenics and the frequent development of schizophrenia later in life. Finally, a strictly environmental approach fails to account for the impressive genetic and biochemical data that are beginning to emerge.

Environmental variables are necessary but not sufficient in the development of schizophrenia. Instead, the diathesis-stress approach, described below, seems to make the most sense.

Diathesis-Stress

The view supported here—diathesis-stress—holds that there are genetic, predispositional variables which, in the context of stress and trauma in the life of the individual, induce a schizophrenic process. The events in an individual's life, his or her social circumstances, social supports, educational level, resources for coping, and general premorbid history provide the stage for the unfolding of this drama.

The concept of stress—its definition and measurement—is only now receiving some systematic attention (see, for example, a review of methodological problems in research concerning life events, stress, and illness by Rabkin & Struening, 1976). Social stressors, life events such as those associated with marriage, childbirth, divorce, death, accidents, jobs, and interpersonal relationships, and the individual's coping responses in the context of these events are presumably related to onset of illness.

Here, more broadly, we describe stress and stressor agents in the unfolding of a life as those events from birth on which require special coping responses on the part of the individual. We include not only the more obvious kinds of experiences such as near-death accidents, loss of a parent (especially the caretaking parent) early in life, harsh and cruel experiences, bewildering sets of instructions and communications in some families, but also the kinds of stressor agents that are associated with the ghetto and with poverty: hunger; harsh exposure to cold; the witnessing of brutality, violence, raw and open sexuality; being victimized sexually and physically; and other kinds of physical and psychological assault and abuse at home or on the street. We include, also, pregnancy and birth complications—the toxicity and anoxia induced in the newborn, say, by a junkie giving birth; or the physical and neurological impairment of an infant born to an impoverished, nutritionally deprived, psychiatrically ill, ghetto mother. Babies born in these circumstances are experiencing stress: They lack a reservoir of strength—physical, neurological, and emotional—and the possibilities for normal development and maturation to cope with life even from the very beginning.

In this context, then, one would suspect that gender plays an important role. For there is little doubt that in our society women experience special conflicts, sense of powerlessness, confusion over mastery, and stress and guilt with regard to family competence that mold their perceptions and experiences of stress (see, for example, Hoffman, 1972, who outlines the differences in maternal responses, attitudes, and expectations toward boys and girls in our culture). Men, too, are burdened with confusing pressures for mastery, aggression, and financial and sexual prowess. Predisposition, in the genetic sense, perhaps does not recognize gender. Stressors, however, are often culturally and socially defined; women and men are trained to respond to these agents differently and to have differing concepts as to appropriate coping responses. For example, independence, mastery, and achievement in girls—in response to a stressful situation—are not generally encouraged in our culture. We are only beginning to explore these differences in response; to understand them in the context of schizophrenia is an enigma yet to be explored.

Although the diathesis-stress approach comes closest to organizing the vast complexities of data in schizophrenia research, the puzzle remains. Why do only some people with all of the necessary ingredients develop schizophrenia? Vulnerable children (see below) with genetic potential and extremely stressful environments and economic deprivation do not always develop schizophrenia. The exact nature of the interaction between predisposition and environment is still not known.

Children at Risk

We spoke above of vulnerable children. Who are these vulnerables? An intriguing research strategy—designed to answer this question—has become increasingly popular. If we come up with the answers, perhaps the next step is possible: to equip and strengthen the (identified) vulnerables so that the inevitability of a schizophrenic episode is challenged or prevented. The basic question is: What are the antecedents of schizophrenia?

If we randomly select an extremely large group of children and observe and rate them as to various neurological, behavioral, physical, and developmental variables and as to a variety of social ones such as aggression, social competence, and peer-relatedness, and then follow these children for decades, we can assume that some of them will become clinically schizophrenic; we will also find ourselves in a position to relate our earlier observations and measurements to that fact. We would be in a position of saying that these but not those variables are associated with the later development of schizophrenia. We would be able to describe some of the antecedents of schizophrenia. For example, are babies later to become schizophrenic more withdrawn?

Such longitudinal research, unfortunately, is barely worthwhile, since only a small fragment of the large initial pool will become schizophrenic. High risk research attempts to stack the cards so that more of the initial population actually becomes schizophrenic. That is, children at greater risk are chosen to begin with on an assumption that many more of them than from a random population will become schizophrenic. Even so, only a small percentage actually develop schizophrenia.

The greater risk children are generally selected from samples with disordered parents (especially schizophrenic mothers); such children show unsocialized, aggressive behavior, have had perinatal complications, and often come from socioeconomically deprived backgrounds with accompanying nutritional difficulties. They may have intellectual limitations and disabilities (see Rolf & Harig, 1974). (Actually, Rosenthal, 1966, reports that 10-16% of offspring of families in which one of the parents is schizophrenic become schizophrenic; there seems to be no difference as to whether the mother or father is schizophrenic; when both are schizophrenic, the rates go up to 35-44%.)

Although there are now many ongoing, extensive high risk studies in this country and abroad, the earliest researches along these lines were the Danish investigations of Mednick and his associates (Mednick, 1970; Mednick & Schulsinger, 1968) in the early sixties.

In these studies, high risk children were selected on the basis of having schizophrenic mothers. These children and matched controls were then evaluated and followed up on a variety of tasks and measures. The high risk children who became schizophrenic were called the "sick" group, while the high risk children who did not become schizophrenic were called the "well" group.

Here are some major findings, briefly noted. One unexpected finding was a physiological one. Children who later became "sick" showed autonomic differences from the other children. There was a quicker galvanic skin response (GSR) and quicker return to basal levels. These fast latencies did not habituate, as expected, with continued trials. These findings suggest that such children are physiologically different from the other children.

Two-thirds of the "sick" group also had had pregnancy and birth complications—a much larger proportion than was found in either the "well" or the control group. The possibility of anoxia and consequent brain impairment in the "sick" group was suggested (Mednick, 1970). Additional analysis of the data indicated more stress during pregnancy of the mothers, more frequent separations from the mother, less substitute "mothering," and more mentally ill fathers in the "sick" group (all had schizophrenic mothers) than in the other groups (Mednick, 1973).

Characteristics of Preschizophrenics and Gender

Because of the increased use of longitudinal studies, it is now possible to talk with greater accuracy than in prior years about the characteristics of children later to become schizophrenic. Some of this research is based on retrospective analysis of data that society collects on its population, such as school, army, and job records, and some data are collected as an ongoing cumulative history of a subject as he or she progresses through life. Our current concern is whether there are gender differences to be found as these data are emerging.

Overall, children who later become schizophrenic show a declining pattern of achievement, tend to drop out of school more, and are described as showing unusual personality traits (but these are not evidenced early in childhood). The expected pattern of withdrawal and social isolation is not found. In general, preadolescent as well as adolescent patterns of behavior tend to distinguish the later schizophrenic population from the nonschizophrenic one, but the disease process may already be at work, rather than the "precursor" process.

Impressive, detailed retrospective reports by Watt and his associates

(Watt, 1972, 1974; Watt, Stolorow, Lubensky, & McClelland, 1970) yielded some interesting relevant findings. These researchers developed a method for quantifying teachers' records of a large group of Massachusetts patients (over 15,000) between the ages of 15 to 34, all of whom had been admitted to Massachusetts mental institutions between 1958 and 1965. Equivalent data from a matched group of controls were also analyzed.

These data show that preschizophrenic boys and preschizophrenic girls differ significantly, with boys showing more aggression, and generally more unsocialized behavior, less achievement, less agreeableness, less cooperativeness, less dependability, less self-control, and more "nervousness" than girls. Role-reversal differences were not found. Boys tended to conform to male-stereotyped behavior and girls to female-stereotyped behavior along lines of aggression or expression.

While other identifying patterns of the matched control vs. preschizophrenic group were distinguished that were not based on gender (greater number of parental deaths, or more severe physical disorder in the preschizophrenic group) (Watt, 1974), two significant distinguishing characteristics (among five that comprised an index of risk) actually differentiating gender were extreme introversion for females and extreme disagreeableness for males.

In the generations ahead, as sex-role stereotyping, expectations, and differences in educational and training approaches to boys and girls disappear (and there is little indication that this will occur in the immediate future), it would be interesting to note whether or not these differences in preschizophrenic boys and girls tend to hold up. It may be that preschizophrenic boys and girls become "more so" in terms of society's expectations for boy or girl role, but find it increasingly difficult to do so because of the beginning of pathology. Perhaps such differences will wash out as changes take place in what is expected of a boy or a girl.

Offspring of Schizophrenic Mothers and Fathers

The children of male schizophrenics tend to grow up in more "favorable" circumstances and have more of a family life than the children of schizophrenic females, according to Bleuler (in press). Stated another way, a healthy mother with a "sick" father is more able to keep her family intact than a "sick" mother with a healthy father (see, also, Rogler & Hollingshead, 1965)—undoubtedly a sign of the culture and the times, rather than of anything intrinsic to the disease process. And apparently this holds for mental illnesses other than schizophrenia (Rutter, 1966).

It is important to note that the vast majority of schizophrenics do not have a schizophrenic parent and only a small percentage of offspring with a schizophrenic parent (10-16%) develop schizophrenia (see, also, Garmezy & Streitmen, 1974). To link psychiatric status of parents to that of their offspring, therefore, does not necessarily follow on a one-to-one basis. Schizophrenic parents may produce normal children or those with a wide range of mental illness. And yet, the sharing of disturbed fantasies and the abuse children suffer at the hands of their mentally ill parents cannot fail to alter their behavior in the world around them, as well as their self-images and their strategies in dealing with life. And upset behavior on the part of the mother, especially, often engenders guilt in the child (Rutter, 1966). Helping a child to perceive aberrant, illogical, and inconsistent behavior as an aspect of illness (a kind of cognitive restructuring) would help, according to most authorities, to offset some of the confusion and internalized anxiety and guilt engendered by the disordered behavior by either the mother or the father in the disordered family setting.

Despite the disorganized lives of children with schizophrenic parents, especially the mother, speculations about their ultimate doom apparently are not completely founded in empirical study (see "No worse," 1976); children reared by schizophrenic mothers did not fare any more poorly and were perhaps even better off than children raised in orphanages and foster homes. On the whole, however, the picture is more complicated than some of the foregoing suggests, since duration of contact with the schizophrenic mother, as well as her premorbid status, apparently influences outcome for her offspring.

There is some research evidence suggesting that only the good premorbid mothers (after discharge) can effectively take care of their children, while poor premorbid mothers continue to show extremely poor caretaking skills (Goldstein & Rodnick, 1972). This makes sense in that even after discharge and with continued medication, poor premorbid mothers return to levels of competence which at best are marginal and crude.

Another long-term follow-up Danish study (Reisby, 1967), in connection with the life histories (to adulthood) of children born to schizophrenic women, indicates that the duration of contact with a disturbed mother was an important factor in determining the nature of the schizophrenic impairment, if indeed the offspring did develop schizophrenia (there was a morbidity risk of 10.5% in the pool of offspring). That is, offspring who became schizophrenic developed a more chronic and severe form if they lived with their mothers for a mean of 13 years; offspring with a less severe form lived with their mothers for a mean of ten years and five months. Once again, these data suggest that despite genetic predisposition (for which there is great evidence), there are long-range, disturbing effects of the family environment on the developing child.

Marriage rates. Schizophrenics, especially male schizophrenics, have among the lowest marriage rates—indeed, much lower than other psychiatric patients (Dube & Kumar, 1972). Female schizophrenics tend to have higher marriage rates and, thus, higher fertility rates, probably because of (in our culture) the more passive, less responsible female role in pursuing a courtship and marriage than the male. Once the female schizophrenic is married, however, and bears children, her pathology is more disruptive to the family's intactness than if her husband were the schizophrenic, as already noted.

Mothering behaviors under supervision. For several decades, various attempts have been made to study the effects of admitting psychotic and specifically schizophrenic mothers and their babies jointly to a hospital setting; results are generally favorable insofar as comparisons to the behavior of children and mothers not jointly admitted. Garmezy and Streitman's review (1974) of these projects underscores the many methodological problems in these studies, especially those in connection with the sample of mothers who do get admitted. Overall, however, this material suggests that schizophrenic mothers in supervised settings can take care of, "mother," and feel responsible for their babies in ways which materially and positively affect the children's development, especially after their return home. However, they continue to have difficulty with school-age children at home.

Overall, this section suggests that schizophrenic mothers and their premorbid status—at least in our culture—are more significant in the fates of their offspring than schizophrenic fathers. The modifiability of these mothers' behavior patterns seems entirely possible. But only the barest beginnings of attempts to understand this area have been made.

GENDER IDENTITY, ROLE, AND PREFERENCE; SELF-CONCEPT

In recent years, researchers have come to concern themselves with how people behave with regard to their society's expectations regarding male and female role, how they identify themselves as males or females subjectively, and the kinds of preferences, confusions, and distortions they experience regarding their own gender. One thing is clear: Even among so-called normals, questions of identity, role assignment, preference, and behavior are not clear-cut; nor is the simple anatomic presence of male or female genitalia in an individual a sufficient criterion for establishing the nature of these parameters. The extensive work of John Money in this area (see, for example, Money & Erhardt, 1972) makes this point amply clear. Further, the assignment of sex at birth, the gender role (overt behavior) played out in life, the gender identity experienced (subjective experience and sense of being male or female), and gender preference may differ from one another in any individual in baffling ways. To further confuse the matter, the choices in sexual partners, activity to reach orgasm, and fantasies, images and behaviors an individual seeks for sexual arousal may not coordinate in expected ways with the assignment, role, and identity parameters already noted.

Further, how does one measure these variables? The validity and reliability of measurements now in use are open questions. It is thus with considerable tentativeness that conclusions can be drawn about how schizophrenic men and women differ in regard to such variables. And yet, a pool of literature is emerging on just this issue, reviewed in considerable detail by LaTorre (1976).

Most of the studies reviewed employ self-inventories (often based on sex-stereotyped notions as to occupational choice—nursing, for example, is regarded as female), checklists about satisfaction or dissatisfaction with body parts, and projective methods such as figure drawings (about which an assumption is made that the first drawn figure represents the unconscious gender identity of the subject) and drawing completions with or without objective checklists for scoring details (such as size of breasts, curve of hips, whether a penis is drawn, etc.). These techniques, as noted, are replete with measurement difficulties.

Nevertheless, this already sizable literature indicates (according to LaTorre's review) that while gender identity of male or female schizophrenics does not differ from that of male or female normal subjects, differentiation (distinctiveness of attributes assigned) between the sexes does, in that schizophrenics tend to show less differentiation than normals in the attributes (verbal or in drawings) assigned to male or female. As for body-parts satisfaction, the evidence is difficult to summarize since it is contradictory and unclear. There is some evidence that male and female schizophrenics tend to prefer the gender role of the opposite sex, with the findings more consistent and conclusive in the case of male schizophrenics. Although the evidence does seem to point to some gender problems in schizophrenia, closer examination of the literature, according to LaTorre, implies that this is related to degree of pathology or length of hospitalization, and to the paranoid status of many of the subjects used in these studies. Failure to match groups for degree of pathology in many of these studies is a further confounding element in interpreting these results. A still further complicating fact is the empirical evidence that suggests that many other pathological groups of patients also show gender impairment. LaTorre proposes, after a careful analysis of these studies, that gender confusions may be one of the stressor agents that *induce* a schizophrenic episode (in the context of a diathesis-stress approach). In other words, gender problems precede, rather than result from, the schizophrenic process.

That expectations about social roles and guilt and confusion about achievement might characterize schizophrenic women was noted quite early by Cheek (1964b) in the context of a large-scale observational study (noted earlier) of parental interactions with their young adult schizophrenic child in comparison to a matched group of families. Through both observational and questionnaire data, Cheek unexpectedly found differences in the interaction profiles between male and female schizophrenics. She expected to find that both male and female subjects would show withdrawal, passivity, and emotional constraint, but she did not find this to be the case. From interview and questionnaire data, she found instead that during childhood female schizophrenics were more active in recreational choices and activities than normal females, while male schizophrenics were less active in choices and activities than normal males, this distinction continuing for the males, but not the females, through adolescence.

Cheek also found reversal of "expected" gender roles in the behavior of male and female schizophrenics when family group behavior was observed. Reversal of sex roles—as "cultural anomaly"—according to Cheek, may well be related to hospitalization and labeling. That is, schizophrenics who do not show role reversals may have a better chance of remaining in the community. They are more conforming, more molded to social expectation, less deviant in behavior.

That women schizophrenics may differ from male schizophrenics with regard to role, self-concept, and how they view the world around them was not always a feature of research in schizophrenia. As noted earlier, such differences were largely ignored in the field of psychopathology, not only by Freud, but also by his followers.

An exception was provided by the work of Holzberg (1963), using

psychological methods like the semantic differential technique. Working
with schizophrenic male, female, and control subjects, Holzberg found
that female schizophrenics—compared to male schizophrenics or male
and female controls—in judging 48 commonplace behaviors as morally
right or wrong, showed more extreme judgments and more "morally
wrong" judgments. That is, they showed a more severe conscience
("superego"). Schizophrenic females viewed their fathers as weak and
their mothers as powerful (on a semantic-differential rating method), and
both mothers and fathers as bad—that is, mothers were rated as powerful
and evil and fathers as weak and evil. Among additional results was a
particularly interesting one: In ideal-self ratings, all women apparently
wished themselves to be less strong and more passive, but this was much
more so for schizophrenic women.

TREATMENT

This chapter makes no attempt to review the vast literature on treatment effects and outcome on schizophrenia. The premorbid status of the
patient and the length of hospitalization, age of onset, and the SES context of the patient and his or her family are all related to prognosis.
Criteria used for judging effectiveness of treatment are complex and
also determine findings. These criteria include: length of hospitalization;
number of relapses; length of community stay between hospitalization;
and self-reports of symptoms.

The purpose of this chapter is to look for differences, if any, or relationship, if any, to male and female status. With this as a goal, despite
the impressive literature on treatment of schizophrenia, there is strikingly
sparse gender literature to summarize.

First, overall, if one is to make any kind of empirical summary statement, the literature suggests that psychotherapy—verbal, nonverbal, supportive, group, alone or in combination—is never superior to medication
(phenothiazines). Medication alone (e.g., see Hogarty, Goldberg, Schooler,
& Ulrich, 1974) or in combination with any of the other methods is
superior—judging by any number of criteria—to the variety of methods
available (Feinsilver & Gunderson, 1972).

Within this context, however, it appears that the social supports, family
requirements, guilts and fears, pressures, and economic strengths that a
remitted schizophrenic experiences are very much essential to the effectiveness of various programs. And it is here, possibly, that being male or
female (or poor or black) plays a role.

Community programs, facilities, and interdisciplinary social supports can be dramatically effective in sustaining an ex-patient in the community—and in keeping many people out of the dehumanized, prison-like hospital settings to which they have been doomed. Davis, Dinitz, and Pasamanick (1974), in an extensive follow-up to their attempt to keep over 200 patients in the community rather than in hospitals, found that medication, social services, home care, and clinic attendance could sustain people in the community, even though improvement in their emotional and symptomatic status was not necessarily found.

An examination of the kinds of patients requiring readmission to hospitals yields some provocative speculations. These included a high proportion of low SES patients of single status and a high proportion of blacks and females. Why are women less likely to remain in the community? Sociocultural considerations and role behavior problems may be relevant.

OVERVIEW: GENDER AND SCHIZOPHRENIA—SOME FINAL THOUGHTS

The thrust of this chapter was to survey an extraordinarily vast literature to search for relationships, if any, of gender to schizophrenia. The harvest was not a rich one, but it may yield some seeds for the future. One dominant thread that seems to bind any number of empirical findings in this area is that there is some genetic, biochemical predisposition to schizophrenia that—given certain social and life-history circumstances—can result in the expression of the disease in any given individual. These genetic components apparently do not bear any relationship to gender, nor is there an inevitable association between genetic vulnerability and disease expression. The specific life-experience and life-events crises of an individual—gender-related or not—such as near-death accidents, child-bearing, menopause, separations, and various hormonal events, also do not bear a precipitating relationship to the expression of the disease; that is, they do not operate alone, independently of vulnerability.

Another dominant thread in this burgeoning literature is that there is a decided relationship of incidence of schizophrenia to SES factors: Poverty and schizophrenia, like poverty and many other pathologies, are inextricably related to each other.

Within this diathesis-stress perspective it is proposed that the relationship of an individual to his or her world and all the pressures, conflicting role expectations, drives, and socially-induced goals that are woven into this relationship very much affect that individual's life history. And this is where we run into questions of gender.

1. *Schizophrenia as a social (possibly gender-related) diagnosis.* No matter what the etiology, it is the peculiarity of the individual, the queerness of his or her thinking, the flaunting of social expectations, the illogical misperceptions, and the social withdrawal, eccentricity, or bizarreness that enter into the labeling process and the eventual incarceration. In this social appraisal, the literature suggests that, even though role reversals and role-identity problems are not apparent in young children, later on the struggle to fulfill the sexual role that society imposes is a losing struggle for many schizophrenics, who show problems of identity, conflict, and related concerns. Some investigators have even suggested that role confusions may serve as stressor-agents in this society, combining with other variables as precursors to or causes of schizophrenia.

As a matter of fact, some of this literature indicates that young preschizophrenic children behave in ways that are very much gender-specific to expectations within our culture. The question was raised: Do preschizophrenic boys desperately try to behave in role-specific "boy-behavior" and preschizophrenic girls in role-specific "girl-behavior" but have great difficulty in doing so, eventually failing, but in the process becoming distressed, "different," and emotionally conflicted?

2. *Sexual role and gender preoccupations and behaviors clinically characterize many schizophrenics.* We will not belabor the point: The clinical and empirical literature is dramatically replete with illustrations of how body perceptions, sexual fantasies, and taboo primary material run through the hallucinations, delusions, and misperceptions of a schizophrenic. Society's harsh and punitive views about bodily and sexual content and gender-related physiological processes (menstruation, ejaculation, body fluids, and so on) seep through the distortions, fears, and anguishes of the suffering schizophrenic, subjectively and behaviorally.

Both schizophrenic men and women are penalized by their sense of inadequately filling their sexual roles, are plagued by fears and guilts about their nonconforming role behavior, and suffer, in general, at the hands of social pressures for rigid conformity. Many schizophrenics are obsessed—literally torn apart—by sexual preoccupations and by bizarre sex-related behaviors.

The schizophrenic's fears, feeling of lack of competence, and poor self-image are undoubtedly related to society's expectations about role, gender, and "right" and "wrong." For a schizophrenic, the sense of guilt and failure tends to be profoundly more extreme than for members of other pathological groups. And because society's sexual attitudes are so intricately involved in generating guilt, one would suspect that a schizophrenic feels much more self-punitive for the fantasies (incestuous? homosexual? violently sexual?) he or she might harbor. One dramatic illustration of this point lies in the empirical evidence that schizophrenic males are among those with the highest rates of genital self-mutilation and castration (Mendez, Kiely, & Morrow, 1972).

3. *Premorbid status, morbid status, and gender considerations.* In our society, women tend to view themselves as less competent, less able, less capable of coping than men (see review by Mednick & Weissman, 1975). One would suspect that a prevailing sense of powerlessness and incompetence exists in the ghetto. That is, women who are trapped in the binds of poverty experience an intense sense of incompetence to do anything about their problems. This would seem especially true for premorbidly incompetent females, preschizophrenics who are beginning to flounder without the social supports and reinforcements that sustain their healthier peers.

We often find that female borderline or simple schizophrenics, like some of their sisters, look to men for supports—in prostitution, to the pimp—sometimes suffering emotional and physical abuse and degradation in exchange for so-called support. Many pre- or borderline schizophrenic females may marry for the same reasons.

They have more children than male schizophrenics. And they apparently affect their offspring more dramatically and pathologically than schizophrenic fathers. They are often abandoned to (incompetently) raise their children, and, failing to do even a moderately good job, are picked up and sent away, again and again. The schools, welfare agencies, neighbors, relatives, and husbands have "fingered" them.

Being a woman, biologically, is not apparently related to schizophrenia. Childbirth, for example, is not necessarily implicated. But a woman's sense of role, guilt about her failures, responses to her offspring, and the perinatal complications that surround the birth of her baby attendant to poverty, drugs, and disease may be very much associated. And her sense of competence—and whom she can turn to for supports if she is schizophrenic—is very much related to eventual outcome.

4. *Course of illness and gender: hospitalizations and remissions.* There is strong reason to believe that under current social conditions, being a woman and being schizophrenic shapes the hospitalization-recovery path-

ways in ways which differ from those available to men in similar circumstances. These social conditions are changing, but the prevailing stereotypes and role expectations continue to be crucial determinants of what happens to patients.

Three capsule family histories come to mind. Each family contains or contained a schizophrenic patient and several school-age children.

In the first family, the patient was the wife and mother. She was hospitalized again and again by her perplexed, unhappy, and rigidly "macho" husband. The children were cared for by a succession of relatives, until they were old enough to be on their own. The husband finally abandoned his wife who died in a state hospital, wasted and forgotten.

The second family contained a schizophrenic husband and father. He was hospitalized several times, too. His discharges were accompanied by support and concern on the part of his wife. During his hospitalizations, she not only cared for the children and worked full-time, but also visited him regularly. The family remained intact and the children continued to live at home, faring moderately well. The patient finally was able to remain at home, with limited employment, on continuous medication, until the end of his days.

In the third family, the repeated hospitalizations of the schizophrenic mother did not result in the expected family disorganization. The father was "androgynous" in the way he viewed his role. He worked, took care of the children, saw that they went to school, helped them with homework, and nurtured his wife when she was discharged. She continues to take her medication and has been able to remain outside of the hospital, emotionally limping a bit perhaps, but certainly contributing to family care in ways that represent a real, even if moderate, contribution to family life.

In each family setting, the different sets of role expectations and the rigidity or flexibility of role behaviors helped to sustain the family and its patient or to disorganize the family and bury its patient.

Genetics, yes. But the life course of the patient and what becomes of him or her—and we are talking about outcome—are very much determined by the social supports and structures that the community and nuclear family provide, the degree to which the culture forces its members to feel "freaky," nonconforming, peculiar, or unable to fill rigid role and gender expectations, and the degree to which individuals can tolerate deviance in role expectations and role behaviors in themselves as well as others.

5. *Outlook for the future.* There is little doubt that women's expectations for themselves, attitudes toward power and achievement, acceptance and use of abilities, and role expectations are undergoing dramatic changes. If role confusions and conflicts, sex-stereotyped reversals, sexual preoccupations and fantasies, premorbid incompetence, and being an impoverished female schizophrenic on the maternity ward bear even a tangential relationship to admission data, future risks for offspring, the clinical picture, and outcome, then a natural laboratory is emerging.

As social circumstances change, will the picture for schizophrenia change? Women are having fewer children, getting married later in life, and bearing children later. There are increasing numbers of households headed by women; these household heads are younger (black women have a median age of about nine years younger than white women; one-third more women have joined the labor force over a recent 25-year period (Van Dusen & Sheldon, 1976). Women are adopting roles that are changing—and even outside of middle-class, verbally-oriented "consciousness-raising" groups or similar supportive settings (such as on college campuses), social and sex roles are rapidly changing. As this happens, one would suspect that gender confusions, anxieties about role and competence, sexual preoccupations and attitudes and guilts toward oneself will play less dramatic roles in the enactment of a schizophrenic drama. Will women handle stress more effectively? Will their sense of achievement, competence, ability to handle conflict change? Or will women—coping on their own—experience more stress? If so, will these changes eventually be reflected in the epidemiological charts? Or will changes cancel themselves out? It is difficult to say.

One change that can be expected arises from the changing profile—hopefully, the decrease or demise—of poverty in our culture. The relationship between SES and incidence of schizophrenia might undergo some modifications as the starkness of contrast between the very rich and the very poor and between the tree-lined streets of the suburb and the debris-line streets of the ghetto diminishes.

We can probably expect that as educational levels, public health awareness, and the number of public health facilities increase, prenatal and perinatal care will change. And as this happens, it might not be too much to expect that the pregnancy and birth complications that are associated with schizophrenia will become less virulent as determinants of risk in the newborn.

Thus, despite the strong evidence for biochemical and genetic predisposition in the etiology of schizophrenia, much of our survey has implicated the stress of poverty and the marginal physical, nutritional, and emotional resources that being born into the ghetto or into a disorganized family automatically signifies. We have been describing the pregnancy and birth complications, anoxia, and the toxicity associated with childbirth in poverty conditions. Females (and blacks and other minority groups) find it more difficult to remain in the community after hospital discharge. Their families are more disorganized when they are "sick" and their husbands well than the other way around. Both male and female future and current schizophrenics tend to show role confusions, guilts, fears, and reversals, as an expression of disease, as precursor to it, or as a stressor that adds to the risk of a schizophrenic breakdown.

We have been describing cultural variables. Attitudes and expectations of males and females toward themselves and each other are significant if not core elements in this cultural substance.

REFERENCES

ALLEN, M., COHEN, S., & POLLIN, W. Schizophrenia in veteran twins: A diagnostic review. *American Journal of Psychiatry*, 1972, 128, 939-945.

AMERICAN PSYCHIATRIC ASSOCIATION. *DSM-II. Diagnostic and Statistical Manual of Mental Disorders* (2nd ed.). Washington, D. C.: American Psychiatric Association, 1968.

BATESON, G., JACKSON, D. D., HALEY, J., & WEAKLAND, J. H. Toward a theory of schizophrenia. *Behavioral Science*, 1956, 1, 251-264.

BATESON, G., JACKSON, D. D., HALEY, J., & WEAKLAND, J. H. A note on the double bind theory—1962. *Family Process*, 1963, 2, 154-161.

BLEULER, M. The long-term course of the schizophrenic psychoses. *Psychological Medicine*, 1974, 4, 244-254.

BLEULER, M. *The Schizophrenic Disorders*. New Haven: Yale University Press, in press.

BROEN, W. E., JR. & STORMS, L. H. Lawful disorganization: The process underlying a schizophrenic syndrome. *Psychological Review*, 1966, 73, 265-279.

CHEEK, F. The "schizophrenic mother" in word and deed. *Family Process*, 1964, 3, 3, 155-177. (a)

CHEEK, F. A serendipitous finding: Sex roles and schizophrenia. *Journal of Abnormal and Social Psychology*, 1964, 69, 392-400. (b)

CHEEK, F. The father of the schizophrenic. *Archives of General Psychiatry*, 1965, 13, 336-345.

DAVIS, A. E., DINITZ, S., & PASAMANICK, B. *Schizophrenics in the New Custodial Community: Five Years After the Experiment*. Columbus: Ohio State University Press, 1974.

DEMING, W. E. A recursion formula for the proportion of persons having a first admission as schizophrenic. *Behavioral Science*, 1968, 13, 467-476.

DOHRENWEND, B. P. & DOHRENWEND, B. S. *Social Status and Psychological Disorder*. New York: Wiley, 1969.

DOHRENWEND, B. P. & DOHRENWEND, B. S. Social and cultural influences on psychopathology. *Annual Review of Psychology*, 1974, 25, 417-452.

DUBE, K. C. & KUMAR, N. An epidemiological study of schizophrenia. *Journal of Biosocial Sciences*, 1972, 4, 187-195.

FARINA, A. Patterns of role dominance and conflict in parents of schizophrenic patients. *Journal of Abnormal Psychology,* 1960, 61, 31-38.

FARINA, A. & HOLZBERG, J. D. Interaction patterns of parents and hospitalized sons diagnosed as schizophrenic or nonschizophrenic. *Journal of Abnormal Psychology,* 1968, 73, 114-118.

FEINSILVER, D. B. & GUNDERSON, J. G. Psychotherapy for schizophrenics—is it indicated? A review of the relevant literature. *Schizophrenia Bulletin,* 1972, No. 6, 11-23.

FENICHEL, O. *The Psychoanalytic Theory of Neurosis.* New York: Norton, 1945.

FREEDMAN, A. M., KAPLAN, H. I., & SADOCK, B. J. *Modern Synopsis of Comprehensive Textbook of Psychiatry.* Baltimore: Williams & Wilkins, 1972.

GARAI, J. E. Sex differences in mental health. *Genetic Psychology Monographs,* 1970, 81, 123-142.

GARMEZY, N. & STREITMAN, S. Children at risk: The search for the antecedents of schizophrenia. Part I. Conceptual models and research methods. *Schizophrenia Bulletin,* 1974, No. 8, 14-90.

GOLDFARB, W. The subclassification of psychotic children: Application to a study of longitudinal change. In D. Rosenthal & S. S. Kety (Eds.), *The Transmission of Schizophrenia.* London: Pergamon Press, 1968.

GOLDSTEIN, M. J. & RODNICK, E. H. Phenothiazine effects on acute schizophrenic behavior. Progress report to the schizophrenia research committee of the Scottish Rite, September, 1972.

GOLDSTEIN, M. J. & RODNICK, E. H. The family's contribution to the etiology of schizophrenia: Current status. *Schizophrenia Bulletin,* 1975, No. 14, 48-63.

GOVE, W. R. & TUDOR, J. F. Adult sex roles and mental illness. *American Journal of Sociology,* 1973, 78, 812-835.

GUNDERSON, J. G., AUTRY, J. H., III, MOSHER, L. R., & BUCHSBAUM, S. Special report: Schizophrenia, 1974. *Schizophrenia Bulletin,* 1974, No. 9, 16-54 .

HEILBRUN, A. B. *Aversive Maternal Control: A Theory of Schizophrenic Development.* New York: Wiley, 1973.

HOFFMAN, L. W. Early childhood experiences and women's achievement motives. *Journal of Social Issues,* 1972, 28, 129-155.

HOGARTY, G. E., GOLDBERG, S. C., SCHOOLER, N. R., & ULRICH, R. F. The collaborative study group. Drug and sociotherapy in the aftercare of schizophrenic patients. II. Two-year relapse rates. *Archives of General Psychiatry,* 1974, 31, 603-608.

HOLZBERG, J. D. Sex differences in schizophrenia. In H. Beigel (Ed.), *Advances in Sex Research.* New York: Harper, 1963.

JACOB, T. Family interaction in disturbed and normal families: A methodological and substantive review. *Psychological Bulletin,* 1975, 82, 33-65.

KOHN, M. L. Social class and schizophrenia: A critical review and a reformulation. *Schizophrenia Bulletin,* 1973, No. 7, 60-79.

LAING, R. D. *The Divided Self.* London: Tavistock Publications, 1960.

LATORRE, R. A. The psychological assessment of gender identity and gender role in schizophrenia. *Schizophrenia Bulletin,* 1976, 2, 266-285.

LIDZ, R. W. & LIDZ, T. The family environment of schizophrenic patients. *Ameircan Journal of Psychiatry,* 1949, 106, 332-345.

LIDZ, T. Schizophrenia and the family. *Psychiatry,* 1958, 21, 21-27.

LIDZ, T. *The Origin and Treatment of Schizophrenic Disorders.* New York: Basic Books, 1973.

MEDNICK, B. R. Breakdown high-risk subjects: Familial and early environmental factors. *Journal of Abnormal Psychology,* 1973, 82, 469-475.

MEDNICK, M. T. S. & WEISSMAN, J. J. The psychology of women—selected topics. *Annual Review of Psychology,* 1975, 26, 1-18.

MEDNICK, S. A. A learning theory approach to research in schizophrenia. *Psychological Bulletin*, 1958, 55, 315-327.

MEDNICK, S. A. Breakdown in individuals at high risk for schizophrenia: Possible predispositional perinatal factors. *Mental Hygiene*, 1970, 54, 50-63.

MEDNICK, S. A., MURA, E., SCHULSINGER, F., & MEDNICK, B. Perinatal conditions and infant development in children with schizophrenic parents. *Social Biology*, 1971, 18 (Suppl.), S103-S113.

MEDNICK, S. A. & SCHULSINGER, F. Some premorbid characteristics related to breakdown in children with schizophrenic mothers. In D. Rosenthal and S. S. Kety (Eds.), *The Transmission of Schizophrenia*. London: Pergamon Press, 1968.

MENDEZ, R., KIELY, W. F., & MORROW, J. W. Self-emasculation. *Journal of Urology*, 1972, 107, 981-985.

MIRSKY, A. F. Neuropsychological bases of schizophrenia. *Annual Review of Psychology*, 1969, 20, 321-348.

MONEY, J. & EHRHARDT, A. A. *Man and Woman, Boy and Girl: The Differentiation and Dimorphism of Gender Identity from Conception to Maturity*. Baltimore: Johns Hopkins Press, 1973.

MORRIS, G. O. & WYNNE, L. C. Schizophrenic offspring and parental styles of communication. *Psychiatry*, 1965, 28, 19-44.

MURPHY, H. B. M. Sociocultural factors in schizophrenia: A compromise theory. In J. Zubin & F. A. Freyhan (Eds.), *Social Psychiatry*. New York: Grune & Stratton, 1968.

No Worse. *APA Monitor*, 1976, 7, 11.

PAYNE, P. & SHEAN, G. Autonomic responses of paranoid, nonparanoid schizophrenic, and normal subjects to affective visual stimulation. *Journal of Nervous and Mental Disease*, 1975, 161, 123-129.

PHILLIPS, D. L. & SEGAL, B. E. Sexual status and psychiatric symptoms. *American Sociological Review*, 1969, 34, 58-72.

PHILLIPS, L. Case history data and prognosis in schizophrenia. *Journal of Nervous and Mental Disease*, 1953, 117, 515-525.

POLLIN, W. & STABENAU, J. R. Biological, psychological, and historical differences in a series of MZ twins discordant for schizophrenia. In D. Rosenthal and S. S. Kety (Eds.), *The Transmission of Schizophrenia*. New York: Pergamon Press, 1968.

RABKIN, J. G. & STRUENING, E. L. Life events, stress, and illness. *Science*, 1976, 194, 1013-1020.

REISBY, N. Psychoses in children of schizophrenic mothers. *Acta Psychiatrica Scandinavica*, 1967, 43, 8-20.

RENDON, M. Transcultural aspects of Puerto Rican mental illness in New York. *International Journal of Social Psychiatry*, 1974, 20, 18-24.

RIEDER, R. O., ROSENTHAL, D., WENDER, P., & BLUMENTHAL, H. The offspring of schizophrenics—fetal and neonatal deaths. *Archives of General Psychiatry*, 1975, 32, 200-211.

ROGLER, L. H. & HOLLINGSHEAD, A. B. *Trapped: Families and Schizophrenia*. New York: Wiley, 1965.

ROLF, J. E. & HARIG, P. T. Etiological research in schizophrenia and the rationale for primary intervention. *American Journal of Orthopsychiatry*, 1974, 44, 538-554.

ROSENTHAL, D. The offspring of schizophrenic couples. *Journal of Psychiatric Research*, 1966, 4, 169-188.

ROSENTHAL, D. *Genetic Theory and Abnormal Behavior*. New York: McGraw-Hill, 1970.

ROSENTHAL, D. *Genetics of Psychopathology*. New York: McGraw-Hill, 1971.

RUTTER, M. Children of sick parents: An environmental and psychiatric study. *Maudsley Monograph*, No. 16, 1966.

SAMEROFF, A. & ZAX, M. Schizotaxia revisited: Model issues in the etiology of schizo-phrenia. *American Journal of Orthopsychiatry,* 1973, 43, 744-754.

Schizophrenia: Is There An Answer? U.S. Department of Health, Education, and Welfare, Public Health Service: Publication No. (HSM) 73-9086, 1974.

SOBEL, D. E. Infant mortality and malformations in children of schizophrenic women. *Psychiatric Quarterly,* 1961, 35, 60-65.

TAUBE, C. A. & REDICK, R. W. *Utilization of Mental Health Resources by Persons Diagnosed with Schizophrenia.* U.S. Department of Health, Education, and Welfare, Public Health Service: Publication No. (HSM) 73-9110, 1973.

TORREY, E. F. Is schizophrenia universal? An open question. *Schizophrenia Bulletin,* 1973, No. 7, 53-59.

ULLMANN, L. P. & KRASNER, L. *A Psychological Approach to Abnormal Behavior.* Engle-wood Cliffs, N. J.: Prentice-Hall, 1969.

VAN DUSEN, R. A. & SHELDON, E. B. The changing status of American women: A life cycle perspective. *American Psychologist,* 1976, 31, 106-116.

WAHL, O. F. Monozygotic twins discordant for schizophrenia: A review. *Psychological Bulletin,* 1976, 83, 91-106.

WAHL, O. F. Sex bias in schizophrenia research: A short report. *Journal of Abnormal Psychology,* 1977, 86, 195-198.

WATT, N. F. Longitudinal changes in the social behavior of children hospitalized for schizophrenia as adults. *Journal of Nervous and Mental Disease,* 1972, 155, 42-54.

WATT, N. F. Childhood roots of schizophrenia. In D. F. Ricks, A. Thomas, & M. Roff (Eds.), *Life History Research in Psychopathology.* Vol. 3. Minneapolis: University of Minnesota Press, 1974.

WATT, N. F., STOLOROW, R. D., LUBENSKY, A. W., & McCLELLAND, D. C. School adjust-ment and behavior of children hospitalized for schizophrenia as adults. *American Journal of Orthopsychiatry,* 1970, 40, 637-657.

WEGMAN, M. Annual review of vital statistics. *Pediatrics,* 1968, 42, 1005-1008.

WYATT, R. J. & MURPHY, D. L. Low platelet monoamine oxidase activity and schizo-phrenia. *Schizophrenia Bulletin,* 1976, 2, 77-89.

WYNNE, L. C. & SINGER, M. T. Thinking disorders and family transactions. Paper presented at joint meeting of the American Psychiatric Association and the American Psychoanalytic Association, 1964.

ZUBIN, J. Classification of the behavior disorders. *Annual Review of Psychology,* 1967, 18, 373-406.

13

THE POLITICS OF HYSTERIA:
THE CASE OF THE WANDERING WOMB

PAULINE B. BART and DIANA H. SCULLY

> *All good women are a little hysterical, that's why we marry them and pay for their therapy.*

Clinical director of a major psychiatric teaching hospital*

Hysteria is a highly protean illness and, like the mythological figure Proteus, its form varies. But there is one constant. From the time of Hippocrates, who coined the name, to the present day, hysteria has been a gender-linked affliction uniquely or predominantly characteristic of females. It is a label that is a mark of oppression since men who are termed hysterical are almost always gay, third world, lower class, or in the armed forces. But its origin is *hystera,* the Greek term for uterus, for women's reproductive equipment has been considered to dominate their experience whereas this has not been the case with men.

THE HISTORY OF HYSTERIA

Antiquity

Hippocrates, drawing on Egyptian Papyri, considered the womb's wandering to be the cause of hysteria. A more graphic description can be found in Plato's Timaeus:

> If it remains barren too long after puberty it is distressed and sorely disturbed and straying about in the body and cutting off the passages

---

We are indebted to Lenore Gay for the valuable assistance she gave us in the preparation of this paper.

* From Pleck, 1976.

of the breath, it impedes respiration and brings the sufferer into extreme anguish and provokes all manner of diseases. (Veith, 1965, p. 7-8)

It was felt that, because of the nature of women, these symptoms could only be allayed through passion and love (Veith, 1965); thus, widows were advised to remarry and spinsters to marry.

Although the term hysteria is derived from the term for uterus, Aretaeus, "the latin Hippocrates," as well as Galen, spoke of another form of hysteria known as catochus (Aretaeus, 1856, p. 286). Aretaeus, like Plato, believed the uterus was an animal—in fact, Aretaeus stated, "an animal within an animal"—and he reasoned, "for it is moved of itself hither and thither in the flanks . . . it is altogether erratic. It delights, also, in fragrant smells, and advances toward them; and it has an aversion to the fetid smells, and flees from them" (Aretaeus, 1856, p. 285) .

Soranus of Ephesus stated that the uterus was not an animal, although it was "similar in certain respects, having a sense of touch" (Soranus, 1956, p. 286). Galen (A.D. 129-199), who influenced subsequent ages, agreed with Soranus that the womb did not wander. He hypothesized that the uterus secreted a fluid analogous to semen and when either this or menses was retained, for example by formerly fertile and ardent widows who were currently abstinent, they were poisoned. The result was an hysterical fit. Galen, however, thought that when men retained semen through sexual abstinence, particularly if they led an idle life, they would fall into a torpor or become melancholic (Veith, 1965). He apparently cured one of his widowed patients by clitoral manipulation. "Following the warmth of the remedy and arising from the touch of the genital organs required by the treatment, there followed twitchings, accompanied at the same time by pain and pleasure after which she emitted turbid and abundant amounts of sperm. From that time on she was freed of all the evil she felt" (Veith, 1965, p. 38).

Middle Ages

The Middle Ages was a period of femicide; many women accused of witchcraft were killed (Ehrenreich & English, 1973). Some women designated witches may have been hysterics since they suffered from symptoms of conversion hysteria, mutism, blindness, convulsion, regional anesthesia, and sexual delusions (Veith, 1965). This contention can be supported by the description in *Malleus Maleficarum,* the witch-hunter's handbook, of the test for insensitivity on the skin. The authors justified their focus on women by referring to their proneness to evil superstition:

What else is woman but a foe to friendship, an unescapable punishment, a necessary evil, a natural temptation, a desirable calamity, a domestic danger, a delectable detriment, an evil of nature, painted with fair colours! Therefore, if it be a sin to divorce her when she ought to be kept, it is indeed a necessary torture; for either we commit adultery by divorcing her, or we must endure daily strife (Malleus Maleficarum, 1928, p. 43).

Presaging some of the later comments on hysterical females, they added that "the tears of a woman are a deception, for they may spring from true brief, or they may be a snare" (Malleus Maleficarum, 1928, p. 43). In addition, strict control of women was advocated because, "when a women thinks alone, she thinks evil" (Malleus Maleficarum, 1928, p. 43). By the end of the Middle Ages the "afflicted persons," most of whom were hysterics, Veith (1965) states, were considered medically rather than spiritually sick.

The Renaissance

Ambroise Paré, a sixteenth century physician, described and treated many "diseases of the womb" and thus was concerned with hysteria. Adding to the ideas of Hippocrates and Galen, he spoke of strangulation of the uterus, caused mainly by the "corruption of the seed" (Paré, 1649, p. 632), with less grievous symptoms coming from the the menstrual blood. The resulting madness was "furor uterinus" (Paré, 1649, p. 633). Men could be cured of the accumulation of male sperm by "great and violent exercise" but his treatment of women was more violent:

> The sick woman must presently bee placed on her back, haveing her breast and stomach loos; and all her cloaths and garments slack and loos about her, whereby shee may take breath the more easily and shee must be called on by her own name, with a loud voice in her ears; and pulled hard by the hair of the temples and neck, but yet especially by the hairs of the secret parts, that by provokeing or causing pain in the lower parts, the patient may not onley bee brought to her self again, but also that the sharp and malign vapor assending upwards, may bee drawn downwards . . . and let this pessarie following bee put into the womb (Paré, 1649, p. 634).

Married women were encouraged to have frequent and "wanton copulation with their husbands" (Paré, 1649; p. 639) to relieve their suppressed menses. Virgins had to resort to walking, riding, and dancing. In addition, he designed a gold or silver instrument "into the form of a pessarie . . . that end which goeth up into the neck of the womb, let there bee made manie holes on each side" (Paré, 1649, p. 634) presumably to fumigate the uterus.

The Renaissance physicians such as Paré (1510-1590) and Jordon (1578-1632) believed that both physical and mental diseases were based on natural changes and thus should be treated by physicians rather than clerics. Jordon transferred the seat of hysteria from the uterus to the brain, which constituted a major turning point in the history of hysteria, and suggested treating hysteria by attempting to relieve emotional tensions with the aid of the patient's friends and relations. In addition, Robert Burton (1577-1640) in his *The Anatomy of Melancholy* included hysteria which he believed was a malady of "ancient maids, widows, and barren women" (Burton, 1927, p. 353). Offenses to the various organs resulted from the "vicious vapours which come from menstrous blood" (Burton, 1927, p. 353). He believed the best cure was to "see them well placed and married to good husbands" (Burton, 1927, p. 355). Rather than blame the woman, however, he blamed parents, guardians, friends and "popish monasteries" who bound people with celibacy and chastity. Thomas Sydenham, writing in the seventeenth century, stated that hysteria was the most common disease next to fever and could afflict men as well as women. Unless she leads a hard and hardy life, no woman is wholly free of hysteria, he claimed. While women are more subject to it, male subjects who lead a studious, sedentary life are also vulnerable, but he termed their syndrome hypochondriasis, a distinction which continued into the nineteenth century, although by then the term connotated a preoccupation with one's physical health. While the modal prescription for hysteria was marriage, Bernard de Mandeville (Veith, 1965) preferred horseback riding, exercise, and massage, because such a marriage could harm the children. Apparently he was not concerned with any harm such a marriage could cause the woman.

The Enlightenment

By the eighteenth century, a number of physicians such as Robert Whytt in England, who treated hysteria with opium, and Francois de Sauvage in France considered hysteria a disorder of the nervous system. Since the etiology did not rest in the uterus, both sexes could be afflicted with it. The term "vapors," originally referring to the emanations coming from the ailing uterus, itself became a euphemism for hysteria. Veith (1965) quotes a French physician of that period who discarded the uterine grounding of the term and extensively studied hysterical males or, as he termed them, "vaporous men" with the sensation of a globus. While he added that "men are by no means exempt from the effects of the imagination," like the previous writers he believed it to occur predominately in women because of their "feminine sensitivity that responded to the slightest stimulus . . ."

The uterine theory returned in the work of the neurologist William Cullen (1712-1790) who considered hysteria common in females "libel to the Nymphomania" and aptly called it "Hysteria Libidinosa" (Veith, 1965). The famous Philippe Pinel, humanizer of the treatment of the mentally ill, associated hysteria with nymphomania which he described under the rubric "Genital Neuroses of Women." Thus he prescribed marriage for a 17-year-old hysterical girl (Veith, 1965). The etiology of nymphomania was "lascivious reading . . . severe restraint and secluded life . . . masturbation, an extreme sensitivity of the uterus, and a skin eruption upon the genital organs" (Veith, 1965, p. 179). One of his two examples was a young woman who reacted in a violent, hysterical manner to her marriage to an impotent husband while the second described a postpubescent girl who was separated from her lower-class male lover. Although Pinel described the physical symptoms of hysterics, he considered hysteria a genital neurosis of women and reintroduced sex as the major factor in hysteria, leading to later developments and ultimately the work of Freud.

Baron Ernst von Feuchtersleben (1806-1849), who first differentiated psychosis from neurosis, considered hysteria a sister sickness to the male illness hypochondriasis. Women with the male malady would be generally masculine and Amazonian. Applying the same principle to men he stated, "When men are attacked by genuine hysterical fits, which certainly does occur, they are, for the most part, effeminate men" (von Feuchtersleben, 1847, p. 228). In women, education was the culprit because education "combines everything that can heighten sensibility, weaken spontaneity and give a preponderance to the sexual sphere" (von Feuchtersleben, 1847, p. 228). His prognosis was discouraging for it could lead to "consecutive diseases . . . namely nymphomania, somnambulism, idiomagnetism, and violent neurosis" (von Feuchtersleben, 1847, p. 229).

"The Nervous Century"*

The nineteenth century is particularly interesting for our discussion of gender differences and hysteria. Caroll Smith-Rosenberg's (1972) work

---

* This term was used by Haller, J. and Haller, R. *The Physician and Sexuality in Victorian America*. Urbana: University of Illinois Press, 1974.

on the female sex role and hysteria addresses the conditions of women of this era. Freud laid the roots of the psychoanalytic conceptualization of hysteria and, as the century closed, the classic case study of a hysteric, his analysis of Dora, began, only to abruptly terminate in three months.

Veith's pro-psychoanalytic bias is apparent in her discussion of the nineteenth-century British physician Robert Brudenell Carter (1828-1918) who "clearly integrated hysteria with the emotions and skillfully dissected the emotional patterns of human beings in relation to predisposition to and manifestation of hysterical phenomena" (Veith, 1965, p. 201).

Carter spoke of the role of temperament as a cause of hysteria. "The relative intensity of different kinds of feeling will be found to depend . . . upon peculiarities of individual temperament" (Carter, 1853, p. 21). He believed that "sexual passion is more concerned than any other single emotion" and that the reproductive system or specifically "morbid conditions of the uterus and faulty menstruation" were most responsible (Carter, 1853, p. 35-36). He entertained the bizarre belief, which makes no sense to any woman who has undergone a standard gynecological examination, that women avidly sought to be examined by speculum and caused vaginal lesions in order to obtain this procedure. He wrote that:

> No one who has once realized the amount of moral evil wrought in girls . . . whose prurient desires have been increased by Indian hemp and partially gratified by medical manipulation, can possibly deny that remedy . . . is worse than disease. I have . . . seen young unmarried women, of the middle classes of society, reduced by the constant use of the speculum, to the mental and moral condition of prostitutes; seeking to give themselves the same indulgence by the practice of solitary vice; and asking every medical practitioner . . . to institute an examination of the sexual organs (Carter, 1853, p. 69).

Carter's discussion of the distinction between primary, secondary, and tertiary hysteria makes manifest his primary, secondary and tertiary misogyny. Primary hysteria was the initial convulsive paroxysm. Secondary hysteria referred to subsequent attacks following induced or spontaneous recall of the emotions to which the primary fit was due. Tertiary hysteria was indulged in for secondary gains. The woman who feels neglected displays "selfishness and deceptivity allied in order to indulge that desire for sympathy . . ." (Carter, quoted by Veith, 1965, p. 203) He advised moral treatment which "has been put in practice against hysteria in a very large number of cases" because "neither the cold dash, nor the infliction of pain, will exert the smallest influence over the course of a convulsive attack of average severity" (Carter, 1853, p. 96). However, most important, Carter believed that "we must look for a degree of perversion of the moral sense" (p. 106).

The misogynistic tradition prominent in writings on hysteria was continued by Alfred Hegar (1830-1914) and his pupils who performed ovariectomies on hysterics, and by the students of Nikolaus Friedrich (1825-1882) who cauterized the clitorises of patients who had "immoderate" sexual demands (Veith, 1965).

Woman-hating knows no national boundaries. While Carter was English and Hegar and Friedrich were German, the French psychiatrist Jean-Pierre Falret considered hysteria a common variety of "moral" or psychogenic insanity and stated that all hysterical women are characterized by duplicity and falsehood. His source of information was the husbands of these women (Veith, 1965).

The American expert on hysteria was psychiatrist S. Weir Mitchell (1829-1914). His treatment is explicated in his book *Fat and Blood: and How to Make Them* (1877) which describes his famous rest cure. Charlotte Perkins Gilman (1973), a patient of Mitchell and a prominent feminist, describes this rest cure treatment for "Neurasthenia" (hysteria) in the novel *The Yellow Wallpaper*. This important work, the first description of the relationship between the psychiatrist and madness, notes how the paternalistic collusion between the psychiatrist and the physician-husband destroyed the female protagonist. It was not accidental that the room in which she had to be confined for her rest cure was the nursery.

Caroll Smith-Rosenberg (1972) sets women's behavior socioculturally and demonstrates that hysteria, among nineteenth century women, was *structurally induced,* primarily caused by role discontinuity in their female socialization. Such an analysis does not end up blaming the victim as do works locating the source of the problem within the individual without reference to the social context.* She calls hysteria the classic protean disease of the nineteenth century characterized by paraplegia, aphonia, hemianesthesia, and violent epileptic seizures. Under its rubric, physicians treated ailments which today might be called neurasthenia, hypochondriasis, depression, conversion reaction, and ambulatory

---

* Note the similarity to the analysis of depression in middle aged women in the 1960s in Bart, P. Depression in middle aged women. In V. Gornick and B. Moran (Eds.), *Woman in Sexist Society.* New York: Basic Books, 1971.

schizophrenia. Noting that in Western culture there has always been some clinical entity with a pejorative implication called hysteria considered particularly relevant to the female experience, she adds that male hysterics have been considered "somehow different from other men." In the nineteenth century they were new immigrants and blacks while in contrast, female hysterics carried femininity to its ultimate conclusion (Smith-Rosenberg, 1972). I (Bart) might add that on a "masculinity-femininity continuum" they would be three standard deviations out on the femininity side.

The physicians who treated hysterics were ambivalent at best, but usually caustic and punitive. Because the women did not fulfill their female roles, they threatened the physicians as professionals and as men.* Although these physicians, notably S. Weir Mitchell, George Beard and Charles Dana, sympathized with their patients, any description of middle-class hysterics emphasized their self-indulgence and craving for sympathy. Generally, the physicians believed "hysteria commenced with puberty and ended with menopause" since it was caused by reproductive ailments and women, but not men, were controlled by their reproductive systems. Indeed, Smith-Rosenberg points out that Thomas Laycock thought hysteria was "the natural state" in a female but a "morbid state" in the male: In lower-class women and prostitutes it was the result of masturbation and "sexual excess." Extended virginity and sterility could also be the cause of hysteria. Epitomizing the hostile view of hysterics is Oliver Wendell Holmes' famous statement: "A hysterical girl is a vampire who sucks the blood of the healthy people around her."

Caroll Smith-Rosenberg (1972) points to the social changes which cause stress within the family and the new role alternatives for women. She states, "Hysteria can be seen as an alternative role option for particular women incapable of accepting their life situation." She notes significant discontinuities between ideals of feminine socialization and women's tasks in the real world. For example, the ideal mother had to be strong, self-reliant, protective, an efficient manager, and able to withstand bodily pain, disease, and death, serving as the emotional support and strength of her family. Victorian women were ill-prepared for childbirth and child-rearing. Moreover, social changes made her particular socialization inappropriate. Women spent less time in primary processing of

---

* For a contemporary example of a similar phenomenon, see Scully, D. and Bart, P. A funny thing happened on the way to the orifice: Women in gynecology texts. *American Journal of Sociology,* 1973, 78, 1045-1050.

food and clothing. She adds that poor women were also hysterical because this condition followed gender rather than class lines.

Smith-Rosenberg (1972) argues that the socially accepted chronic sick role of hysteria furnished an alleviation of conflict and tension but at a cost of pain, disability, and "an intensification of women's traditional passivity and dependence. Indeed, a complex interplay existed between the character traits assigned women in Victorian society and the characteristic symptoms of the nineteenth century hysteric: dependency, fragility, emotionality, narcissism." Thus, hysteria can be considered a stark caricature of femininity, with the hysteric's passive aggression and exploitive dependence eliciting hostility from the men who lived with or cared for her. Accordingly, "the hysterical woman can be seen as both product of and indictment of her culture."

Smith-Rosenberg (1976) stated that by the late nineteenth century the disease symptoms of hysteria and hypochondriasis appeared to be interchangeable for the most part and were so used by S. Weir Mitchell. In general, while middle- and upper-class men were called neurasthenic, lower-class ethnic or gay men were labeled hysteric. Upper-class educated women were also termed neurasthenic rather than hysterical. While hysteria may have been ovarian in etiology, neurasthenia was believed to flower from a too highly developed nervous system which, needless to say, characterized the higher but not the lower orders.

Unlike Smith-Rosenberg, social historian Barbara Sicherman (1977) differentiates neurasthenia, characterized by "languor," from the "bizarre symptoms" of hysteria in the nineteenth century. Because physicians considered neurasthenics more moral than hysterics, she continues, it is not surprising that the diagnosis of neurasthenia was more generally applied to men. The label neurasthenia was useful since it gave men permission to exhibit weakness. It was less pejorative than either hysteria or hypochondria. Men suffered from it in response to difficulties in choosing the right profession, while educated women had problems if they wanted a profession at all, e.g., Jane Addams and Charlotte Perkins Gilman. Jane Addams improved when she founded a settlement house, while Gilman had a more severe breakdown postpartum. Both are among the most conspicuous failures of S. Weir Mitchell, for neither responded to his paternalistic therapy.

It should be noted that S. Weir Mitchell studied male hysterics during the Civil War, documenting many cases of "nostalgia and homesickness." Note the different flavor of these adjectives from his descriptions of female hysteria. What reasonable person would not be homesick and nostalgic when away from home in the armed forces during a war?

Jean-Martin Charcot (1825-1893), chief of medical services at the Salpetriere and professor of pathological anatomy at the University of Paris, believed that "the word hysteria means nothing, and little by little you will acquire the habit of speaking of hysteria in a man without thinking in any way of the uterus" (Veith, 1965, p. 232). However, since the Salpetriere was a hospital for women, he developed a theory of "hysterogenic zones," among which were the ovaries and mammary glands. He developed an ovary compressor to treat the "hysterogenic zones" because "more energetic compression is capable of stopping the development of the attack when beginning, or even of cutting it short when the evolution of the convulsive accident is more or less advanced" (Charcot, 1879, p. 223). He expressed concern for his colleagues because "the operation, if it require to be prolonged for some minutes, is always rather fatiguing to the physician" (Charcot, 1879, p. 224). In the spirit of medicine, he recommended experimentation and stated, "You may besides vary the experiment and at your pleasure, by removing the compression and again applying it, you can stop the seizure or allow it to recur as often almost as you like" (Charcot, 1879, p. 224).

As a leading neuropsychiatrist, his recognition of the role of emotions in hysteria was significant, and it is notable that, like many subsequent psychiatrists whose etiological theories are characterized by father absence, he thought the mother's influence in hysteria in children was "particularly pernicious." Hypnosis was involved in both diagnosis and treatment.

Charcot's influence on Freud was positive because the former considered hysteria a psychic rather than an organically related phenomenon and this was the beginning of Freud's formulation of the theory of hysteria. Freud credited Charcot with recognizing this phenomenon in males. But when he reported to the Viennese Medical Society that he saw male hysterics in Paris, one physician said, "But my dear Sir . . . hysteron . . . means the uterus, so how can a man be hysterical" (Veith, 1965, p. 263). After the rejection of this paper it is unlikely that Freud ever again spoke of hysteria associated with males.

Freud's early interest in hysteria, kindled by visiting Charcot and watching his demonstrations in Paris, formed the starting point of psychoanalysis. He translated Charcot and worked with Breuer who had used hypnosis in treating Anna O., "the ur-patient of psychoanalysis" (Reiff, 1959). Although Breuer, at that time, had no new explanation "for the enigma of hysteria," he simply tried replacing contempt with lengthy

observation, and indifference with sympathy (Reiff, 1959). He used hypnosis to treat hysterical patients. It is interesting to note that Anna O.,
the prominent social worker Bertha Pappenheim, never spoke of this
period in her life and violently opposed any suggestion of psychoanalytic
therapy for someone for whom she was responsible, to the surprise of her
co-workers (Echinger, 1968). Szasz (1961), who considers hysteria a language, commented on Anna O., who fell "ill" while nursing her father,
as follows:

> Anna O. thus started to play the hysterical game from a position of
> distasteful submission: she functioned as an oppressed, unpaid, sick-
> nurse, who was coerced to be helpful by the very helplessness of a
> (bodily) sick patient. The women in Anna O.'s position were—as
> are their counterparts today, who feel similarly entrapped by their
> small children—insufficiently aware of what they valued in life and
> how their own ideas of what they valued affected their conduct. For
> example, young middle-class women in Freud's day considered it
> their duty to take care of their sick fathers. They treasured the value
> that it was their role to take care of father when he was sick. Hiring
> a professional servant or nurse for this job would created a conflict
> for them, because it would have symbolized to them as well as to
> others that they did not love (care for) their fathers. (Notice how
> similar this is to the dilemma in which many contemporary women
> find themselves, not, however, in relation to their fathers, but rather
> in relation to their young children.) Today, married women are
> generally expected to take care of their children; they are not sup-
> posed to delegate this task to others. The old folks can be placed in a
> home: it is alright to delegate their care to hired help. This is an
> exact reversal of the social situation which prevailed in upper
> middle-class European circles until the First World War and even
> after it. Then, children were often cared for by hired help, while
> parents were taken care of by their children now fully grown (Szasz,
> 1961, p. 216-17).

Freud and Breuer, writing about the hysterical attack, said it was the
"recurrence of the event which caused the outbreak of the trauma—the
psychical trauma" (Freud & Breuer, 1950, p. 28). Furthermore, they
stated that "sexual life is especially well suited to provide this content
. . . owing to the very great contrast it presents to the rest of the
personality . . ." (Freud & Breuer, 1950, p. 32). By 1895 he and Breuer
published *Studies in Hysteria* which elucidated the symptoms of hysteria,
notably in the case of Anna O., and used catharsis as the therapeutic
method. Freud, in the tradition of Plato, contributed the sexual aspect to
the etiology of hysteria and gradually transferred the method of catharsis

to psychoanalysis (Veith, 1965). In "Fragment of an Analysis of a Case of Hysteria" (The Story of Dora), Freud stated that "the causes of hysterical disorders are to be found in the intimacies of the patient's psycho-sexual life, and that hysterical symptoms are the expression of their secret and repressed wishes . . ." (Freud, 1963). In *Studies in Hysteria,* he used an electrical system as a metaphor for the nervous system, speaking about overloading from excitation which is then "converted into hysterical symptoms" (Reiff, 1959). Freud and Breuer maintained that the "key to curing the hysterical symptom was to give these blocked repressed memories and the feelings attached to them free expression. They freed the concept of hysteria from the ancient concept of the wandering uterus as well as the medieval concept of possession by the devil (Reiff, 1959).

Freud described two types of hysterical neuroses: conversion hysteria, which was similar to what the Greeks and Egyptians identified as hysteria, and anxiety hysteria. In conversion hysteria, a phyical conflict is expressed somatically through paralysis, lumps in the throat (globus), etc. Anxiety hysteria resulted "from the ego's defending itself against some incompatible idea by attaching anxiety to an external object. As long as the person avoids the phobic object he/she avoids the anxiety attached to the idea that the object symbolically represents" (Satow, 1976). The similarity between anxiety and conversion hysteria is that in both cases repression separates painful affect from ideas (Satow, 1976).

To return to the case of Dora, Dora's father visited Freud, complaining of migraine and a nervous cough. Four years later Dora first visited with symptoms that did not seem severe. Phyllis Chesler (1971), in her perceptive analysis of Freud's treatment of Dora, states that Dora was brought to Freud for a nervous cough, depression and fatigue but suggests there is a question as to whether she had a crisis or her father had a crisis. Dora's situation was as follows. Her father was having an affair with the wife of a Mr. K. Mr. K. made sexual advances to Dora. "Freud knew that she was the bait in a monstrous sexual bargain her father had concocted. This man, who during an earlier period in his life, had contracted syphillis and apparently infected his wife . . . was using Dora to appease Mr. K and Freud was fully aware of this" (Simon, 1970). In spite of this, Freud interpreted Dora's symptoms as a response to her repression of her own sexual feelings for Mr. K. and his rape-like kissing of her. That she denied it only made him more certain of his interpretation.

Although Freud eventually conceded (but not to Dora) that her insights into her family situation were correct he still concluded that these insights could not make her "happy." Freud's own insights, based on self reproach rather than on Dora's reproaching of those around her, would hopefully help her discover her own penis envy and the Electra complex; somehow this would magically help her to adjust to, or at least to accept, her only alternative in life: housewife's psychosis. If Dora had not left treatment (which Freud considered an act of revenge) her cure, presumably would have involved her regaining . . . a grateful respect for her patriarch father; loving and perhaps serving him for years to come: or getting married and performing these service functions for a husband or surrogate-patriarch (Chesler, 1971, p. 755).

Another Freudian, Felix Deutch, reported that later, as a 42-year-old hysterical married woman:

> she started a tirade about her husband's indifference toward her offerings and how unfortunate her marital life had been . . . resentfully she expressed her conviction that her husband had been unfaithful to her . . . tearfully she denounced men in general as selfish, demanding, and ungiving . . . (she recalled that) her father had been unfaithful even to her mother . . . From (an) informant, I learned the additional pertinent facts about the fate of Dora. She clung to her son with the same reproachful demands she made on her husband who had died of coronary disease—slighted and tortured by her almost paranoid behavior. Strangely enough, he had preferred to die rather than divorce her. Without question only a man of this type would have been chosen by Dora for a husband . . . Dora's death from a cancer of the colon, which was diagnosed too late for a successful operation, seemed a blessing to those who were close to her. She had been, as my informant phrased it, "one of the most repulsive hysterics" he had ever met (Deutch, 1957, p. 26).

Because of the focus on intrapsychic variables, nowhere is the reality of Dora's existence as a brilliant woman in a society that afforded her no outlets, and as a woman who was betrayed by her father and not protected from this betrayal by her mother, discussed. Rather, in a classic example of "blaming the victim," she is made responsible for all her problems.

To what extent this approach represents progress over the one which attributes women's problems to the wanderings of their wombs, we will leave to the reader to decide. (For a summary of these various viewpoints, see Table 1.)

Twentieth Century

Although the term hysteria has been in existence for almost 4000 years, a review of contemporary psychiatric literature reveals that psychiatrists

TABLE 1

Historical Chart of Hysteria

Women only	Primarily Women	Women and Men
Hippocrates		
Plato		Aretaeus
	Paré, Ambroise	Galen
Burton	Jordan	Le Pois
Harvey	Willis	
		Sydenham
		Whytt
Pinel	Cullen	Sauvage
von Feuchtersleben		
Hegar	Carter	
Friedrich		
Falret	Charcot	
Beard and Dana	Breuer	Laycock
	S. Weir Mitchell	
	Freud (almost completely female)	

have not been able to agree upon what it is or upon what criteria should be used for diagnosis (Alarcon, 1973; Berger, 1971; Chodoff & Lyons, 1958; Cleghorn, 1969; Guze & Perley, 1963; Lazare, 1971; Slater, 1965). Hysteria has been characterized as having the attributes of both a fossil and a chameleon (Chodoff & Lyons, 1958), referred to as a delusion and a snare, a disguise for ignorance and a fertile source of clinical error (Slater, 1965), and considered analogous to the story of the wise men of Chelm (Berger, 1971) who attempted to capture sunlight in sacks only to find it had disappeared at night. Alarcon (1973) derived 28 characteristics attributed to hysterical personality from 22 authors and Cleghorn (1969) argues that the entire history of hysteria is marked by confused thinking. Lazare (1971) recalls his perplexity as a medical student with the concept and adds he has subsequently learned the confusion is widely shared by his teaching colleagues.

Despite confused thinking and lack of consensus among psychiatrists, the label hysteric continues to be applied albeit to a somewhat different set of behaviors than in Freud's time. Hysteria is now more frequently presented as a personality type rather than the earlier "vapors" or classical conversion reaction of Freud's Dora. But while hysteria shows remarkable instability over time and lacks an objective or even uniform clinical picture which can be translated into diagnostic terms, certain notable consistencies do emerge. Throughout the history of the concept, as well as in contemporary literature, and despite Freud's dictum regarding male hysteria, it is almost exclusively seen as a female problem. The bias is so pervasive that contemporary researchers often either eliminate males from their sample (Blinder, 1966) or select symptoms into a syndrome which by definition exclude males. For example, Guze, Woodruff, and Clayton (1972) require a history of at least 25 symptoms in nine out of ten groups of symptoms before a diagnosis of hysteria can be made. However, of the ten groups, one group of symptoms includes dysmenorrhea, menstrual irregularity, amenorrhea and excessive bleeding, while another includes sexual indifference, frigidity, dyspareunia, other sexual difficulties, vomiting during pregnancy and hospitalization for hyperemesis gravidarum. Even Guze (1972) admits that with these criteria, it would be difficult to diagnose a male hysteric.

Not only are women believed to be hysterics, but consistently the hysterical personality is stereotyped through the biased eyes of male psychiatrists as a loathsome, childlike caricature of femininity whose primary purpose is to cause trouble. A few examples from the literature will illustrate this point. From his clinical observations, Wittels (1930) states:

> Hysteria appertains to women as fear does to a child, and coercive mechanisms to man. . . . As an actress, the hysteric is capable of achievements that cannot be surpassed. But she is unreliable, and at times will prove to be unsupportably bad in the same or some other role . . . Even as a saint the hysteric cannot be relied upon, and occasionally lapses into the diabolic. As a loving woman she represents a veritable martyrdom for the serious, compulsive male who, enwrapped in love and enjoyment in an hour of happiness, sees himself betrayed the following day. The hysterical character never frees itself from its fixation on the infantile level. Hence it cannot attain its actuality as a grown-up human being; it plays the part of a child and also of the women . . . (p. 186-87).

Allen and Houston (1959) describe hysterics as

> The young women patients we have in mind almost always overdress and use too much make-up; they are physically provocative, as if inviting one to play sexual games with them; and they often look younger than their actual age . . . these women are the counterpart of the Don Juan character—the "Dona Juanita" if you will or . . .

the coquette. . . . These women are small children in adult's clothing but they deny themselves and others their need for maternal care—for protection, succor, reassurance, and firm benign limit-setting. Likewise their response to frustration is like that of a child, with emotional outbursts, spiteful actions, and poorly directed demanding attitudes. They have often succeeded in getting various people to provide their maternal needs. They are past masters at creating turmoil among friends and family (p. 41).

Interestingly, two American Psychiatric Association Diagnostic and Statistical Manuals have not included a definition of hysterical personality. Once committee members couldn't agree on a definition (Chodoff & Lyons, 1958) and in the latest draft edition, DSM-III (in press), histrionic personality has been substituted for hysterical personality though Hysterical Disorders remain. DSM-II (1968), however, defined hysterical personality as,

These behavior patterns are characterized by excitability, emotional instability, overreactivity and self-dramatization. This self-dramatization is always attention seeking and often seductive, whether or not the patient is aware of its purpose. These personalities are also immature, self-centered, often vain, and usually dependent on others (p. 43).

Chodoff and Lyons' (1958) definition of hysterical personality derived from an analysis of the most recurrent characteristics mentioned in the psychiatric literature is frequently quoted. Thus hysterical personality has come to mean

persons who are vain and egocentric, who display labile and excitable but shallow affectivity, whose dramatic, attention seeking and histrionic behavior may go to the extremes of lying and even pseudologia phantastica, who are very conscious of sex, sexually provocative yet frigid, and who are dependently demanding in interpersonal situations (Chodoff & Lyons, 1958, p. 736).

The gestalt that emerges in the literature is best summarized by one author who commented, "You're talking about a prick-teasing, whining, frigid, manipulative, freeby Southern Belle type, out of the bayous, who's hung up on Dear Old Dad" (Lewis, 1974, p. 147).

It is evident that hysterical personality within psychiatry is used as an opprobrious label to indicate an exaggerated version of the characteristics that men in our culture are likely to use when talking about women. One can only speculate with Chodoff and Lyons (1958) upon what type of personality disorder might be defined if psychiatrists were female and spent their time observing the foibles of male clients?

Consistent with the descriptions of hysteria, men are infrequently referred to in the contemporary psychiatric literature and when they are it is in terms of their feminine characteristics with the suggestion that the male hysterical personality would be a passive homosexual. For example, Halleck (1967) states that men diagnosed as hysterical personality have some comfort with the "feminine role" and "often are homosexuals." Likewise some attempts to separate the concept of hysterical personality from conversion reaction (Chodoff & Lyons, 1958; Guze & Perley, 1963; Blinder, 1966)—a source of considerable confusion—seems to stem from the feeling that men are prone to conversion reactions,[*] especially in the armed forces where secondary gains are particularly beneficial, but with the exception of a rare "feminine" male, do not have hysterical personalities.

Female hysterics are described in the literature as frigid but seductive and provocative and often as youthful and attractive. For example, one author stated,

> When the hysterical patient presents herself to the physician, he is often charmed by her femininity. . . . He is therefore likely to invest himself heavily in pleasing her. Unfortunately, the patient's youth and attractiveness are often crucial variables in influencing the doctor's attitude. The young attractive hysteric is likely to be viewed as an interesting patient, while the less attractive middle-aged woman is more likely to be viewed as a hopeless hypochondriac (Halleck, 1967, p. 754).

And Allen and Houston (1959) state: "In therapy these patients are appealing at first. They are not only sexually provocative, but may be seductive toward the therapist in other ways . . . flattering him and making him feel professionally competent" (p. 42). As expected, when male hysterics are described, seductive appearance is rarely mentioned by their male therapists (Luisada, Peele, & Pittard, 1974). Canadian psychiatrist Berger (1971), noting the persistent and recurring association between female hysterics and provocative and seductive sexuality, states that the best definition of hysteria historically and at present is "behavior or symptoms which arouse unconscious sexual feelings in the observer." Berger (1971) predicts that if it were studied, a positive correlation

---

[*] For a discussion of conversion hysteria in Appalachian men in which symptoms are described as a "language of violence" see Weinstein, E., Eck, R. and Lyerly, O. Conversion hysteria in Appalachia. *Psychiatry*, 1969, 32, 334-341.

would be found between the relative attractiveness of the female hysteric to her psychiatrist and the tendency to use the term hysterical to describe her. In psychiatric terms, evidence suggests that male therapists experience countertransference, i.e., unconsciously react sexually to the patient resulting in what is sometimes jokingly referred to in psychiatric circles as "sticky transference." Under these circumstances, therapists experience difficulty controlling the therapeutic relationship but rather than admit complicity, blame the patient. For example, Golden (1968) talks of feeling "manipulated and castrated," and Halleck (1967) states,

> Any doctor who has ever dealt with an hysterical patient, who has had the experience of feeling strongly indebted to her, or uncomfortably trapped by her deceptive helplessness, can appreciate the depth of this power. Her sexual charms are suitable weapons in a quest for power since she is less dominated by a need to gratify erotic drives than she is interested in ultimate control of the sexual object (p. 750-51).

While the female hysteric is described as seductive, it is also generally agreed among psychiatrists that she is frigid. In fact, hysteria and frigidity are linked in the Freudian tradition which views hysteria as the consequence of repression necessary to shift libido from clitoral to vaginal erotogeneity and to repress masculine tendencies. While most contemporary psychiatrists are undoubtedly aware that the myth of the vaginal orgasm has been shattered, they may still lack insight into female sexuality. Winokur and Leonard's (1963) study of female hysterics found a large range of sexuality, including multiorgasmic women, similar to that of a "normal" population defined by Kinsey's study of female sexuality (Kinsey, Pomeroy, Martin, & Gebhard, 1953). Yet on the psychiatrist's couch, normalcy can translate into orgasmic difficulty. Many "normal" women do not achieve orgasm in heterosexual intercourse when vaginal penetration is the only technique. Many can experience multiple orgasms when masturbation is used either in self-stimulation or with a partner. That psychiatrists have defined their female clients as frigid is not surprising since the techniques of heterosexual intercourse have traditionally functioned to assure the male an orgasm.

A report by Prosen (1967) reveals another bias in male therapists' interpretation of female sexuality. Rather than frigidity, Prosen's concern is with two cases of "hypersexual" hysteria—women who he claimed were capable of enjoying "an unusual amount of sexual pleasure in heterosexual relationships," defined as "wanting intercourse every night" and "having several orgasms." Though this is normal by current standards, Prosen (1967) stated that the condition was the result of pregenital fixation and oral dependency on the father but that after therapy "their sexual life became much more that of a usual adult female." About one of the women he commented, "A remarkable change also occurred in the patient's sexual life . . . The ecstasy and extreme pleasure have gone. She gets what she and her husband describe as an acceptable amount of gratification and is satisfied with her sexual life. She does, however, miss the intense pleasure and transportation from reality that she previously achieved" (p. 144). About the second case he remarked, "At this time (during therapy) the patient's intense sexual desires began to diminish, and the frequency of sexual relations decreased from nightly to several times a week . . . she described it as feeling as though she had been married for many years with the romance and initial intensity of feeling gone" (p. 145). One can only hope that most therapy does not function to rob women of their sexuality.

While psychiatrists accuse female hysterics of sexualizing their interactions, a similar charge can be applied to analysts. Standard Freudian interpretations are essentially sexual, and when the client is female, neurosis is likely to be interpreted as resulting from feelings of biologic inferiority and penis envy. Thus, the story goes, if she cannot possess one of her own, she will attempt to possess those who do. It is the therapist's construction of reality which views the male penis as the measure of all things and which reduces the behavior and motives of women to a sexual level, sometimes so extreme as to be absurd. For example, Fenichel (1945) interpreted two cases of conversion hysteria as follows:

> At the height of her fits, a woman patient used to have jerking convulsions in her arms. Analysis revealed that they portrayed the spasmodic contractions of the penis during ejaculation. A similar significance became evident in the sneezing spells of a hysterical woman patient; her nose represented her fantasied penis (p. 218).

Likewise, Jaffee (1971), in an extensive article on the analysis of a case of hysteria, interprets his female client's anger at him as "seeking omnipotence through a quest for a penis she could control" (p. 389).

It is worth noting that while females are alleged to unconsciously desire male castration, evidence indicates that women are the ones actually castrated. Barker-Benfield (1976) supplies data which show that beginning in the 1870s and continuing into the first decade of the twentieth century "female castration" or oophorectomy and to a lesser degree clitoredectomy was frequently performed by male gynecologists as a remedy for female masturbation as well as psychological disorders. The hysterectomy has now superseded these procedures and is estimated to be among the most frequently performed unnecessary operations in the U.S. (McCarthy, 1977).

While hysteria has come to be a pejorative label representing a psychiatric double standard, it is also true that women, because of their relatively powerless positions in society, do develop compensatory symptomatology. Szasz (1961), though he failed to connect it with the restrictions of the female sex role, did identify conversion hysteria as body language, or the vocabulary of the powerless, used in an attempt to communicate unacceptable external conditions to an unresponsive audience. The powerful shout or threaten to make themselves heard but the powerless weep or develop symptoms.

Also significant is the fact that hysterical personality traits are closer to what is considered the "normal" female expressive personality than they are to the "normal" male instrumental personality. Female socialization is likely to produce emotional, dependent women. Indeed at least some therapists consider these qualities normal in adult females. Broverman, Broverman, Clarkson, Rosenkrantz, and Vogel (1970) administered a sex-role stereotype questionnaire to 79 clinically trained therapists, including psychologists, psychiatrists, and social workers, with instructions to describe a healthy, mature, socially competent (a) adult, sex unspecified, (b) man, and (c) woman. Findings were along predicted lines; the characteristics of healthy individuals differed as a function of sex and paralleled sex-role stereotypes. Further, therapists displayed a double standard by specifying behavior and characteristics for a healthy adult which were similar to the standard for males but different from the standard for females. Of greater interest here, the characteristics attributed to healthy mature adult females strongly resemble descriptions of hysterical personality. Healthy women differed from healthy men by being more submissive, less independent, less adventurous, more easily influenced, less aggressive, less competitive, more excitable in minor crises, having their feelings more easily hurt, being more emotional, more conceited about their appearance, less objective and disliking math and science.* Thus, for a female to be considered healthy, she must conform to norms for her sex even though these behaviors are generally

---

* Recent attempts to replicate Broverman's findings have failed. However, it is not clear whether mental health professionals have changed or their rhetoric has become more sophisticated.

less socially desirable and considered to be less healthy than the male standard for adult behavior. If she acts according to the mandates of her sex role, she risks a deviant label, but so also does she by rejecting femininity and acting according to the male standard. The hysterical personality can be viewed as accepting the former alternative. And as Wolowitz (1972) correctly observes, in a society which regards passivity and dependency as acceptable in women but not in men, hysterical characteristics are likely to persist more frequently in women.

There is some suggestion in the literature that hysteria as a diagnosis is on the decline, possibly due to an increasing tendency for hysteria and depression to occur jointly (Alarcon & Covi, 1973). Also, as Bart (1968) found, some hysterics, who lacked psychiatric vocabularies of motive, sought relief from their symptoms from neurologists rather than from psychiatrists. However, Lewis and Berman's (1965) ten-year study of one large hospital showed no tendency toward decreasing use of hysteria as a diagnosis. We must therefore assume that women are still being labeled hysterical and, in light of the pejorative implications of the label, question the consequences.

Some contemporary psychiatrists continue in the tradition of Freud, who didn't like Dora, and Deutsch, who referred to her as "one of the most repulsive hysterics" he had ever met. Several authors note that hysteria, used as an epithet, is often heard in the coffee rooms and corridors of hospitals and in some of the less official conversations of analysts (Chodoff & Lyons, 1958; Lewis, 1974). Supporting this accusation, a study by Lazare and Klerman (1968) found that staff characterized hysterical women as "demanding, flamboyant, causing turmoil, bitchy and armtwisting." Further, they distinguished between nonhysterical patients who were seen as "the helpless child" and hysterical patients who were seen as "the bad child." And Golden (1968) writes that of the many attitudes which the therapist may develop towards the hysterical personality, the attitudes chosen are, in general, negative.

While Fenichel (1945) listed hysteria as most favorable to treatment, a number of contemporary analysts disagree. Some of the negative affect associated with hysteria derives from the analysts' perception of their clients as noncooperative in analysis (Knapp, Levin, McCarter, Wermer, & Zetzel, 1960; Zetzel, 1968). For example, Allen and Houston (1959) state that hysterical patients often can stir up enough negative feeling in the therapist to interfere with objective clinical thinking and "are often able to make a fool of the therapist." Among other maneuvers they list "the good pal" in which the female hysteric tries to relate to the therapist "man to man." In the male therapist's view this violates the norm which requires women "to know their place" and also implies these hysterics don't have the stereotyped feminine characteristics they are alleged to have.

Abuses associated with hysteria are not confined to psychiatry. In an excellent review, Lewis (1974) discusses the types of subversive effects a hysterical label can have in other treatment milieus. He states that "to be labeled hysteric today can put one in a position which, in extreme cases, reminds one of the plight of a person in Pilgrim Salem suspected of being a witch" (p. 150). As used on medical and surgical wards, it often labels a "difficult" patient with misunderstood symptoms who can then be referred to a psychiatrist. As with conversion hysteria, this can result in misdiagnosis of organically ill patients who are, as a consequence, deprived of necessary medical treatment. While the actual incidence of these types of errors is unknown, evidence indicates they do occur. One 20-year follow-up study of 66 female hospitalized patients diagnosed as hysteric found that central nervous system diseases, particularly epilepsy, were frequently mistaken for hysteria (Ziegler & Paul, 1954). The most extensive study was done by Slater (1965) in 1962 and involved a follow-up of 85 patients, 32 men and 53 women, admitted to a hospital in 1951, 1953, and 1955 who had received a diagnosis of hysteria. Most surprising were his findings regarding the gravity of their post-hospital history and the frequency of misdiagnosis. Though the mean age for men was 42 and for women 37, after only nine years 12 had died (four deaths were from suicide but in two cases organic disease had been missed in the prior hospitalization), 14 became totally disabled, and 16 became partially disabled, 43 remained independent and of these only 19 were actually symptom-free at the time of follow-up. Slater concludes that as a diagnosis, hysteria "is used at peril."

There is another hazard associated with hysteria. Lewis (1974) notes that physicians can also fail to correctly identify symptoms as lacking an organic base. Surgeons, and especially gynecologists, seem to be susceptible to this type of error. A number of authors have noted the correlation between hysteria and surgery (Blinder, 1966; Lazare & Klerman, 1968; Purtell, Robins, & Cohen, 1951; Robins, Purtell, & Cohen, 1952). In fact excessive hospitalization and surgery are so common that Guze and Perley (1963) and Guze, Woodruff, and Clayton (1972) included it in their definition of hysteria. One of the most thorough studies by Purtell, Robins, and Cohen (1951) analyzed the medical histories of 50 women diagnosed as hysteric admitted to a New England hospital and compared them to three control groups consisting of healthy women, women with chronic medical illness, and healthy hospitalized postpartum women.

The hysterics were found to have undergone a total of 190 major operations as opposed to 59 in the healthy control group. A mean of 3.8 operations was obtained in the hysteria group compared to 1.2 operations in the healthy control group and 2.0 operations in the medical control group. Gynecologic operations, such as dilation and curettage, salpingo-oophorectomy, and hysterectomy had been performed on 72% of the hysteria patients compared to 18% of the healthy controls. Furthermore, not only were the female hysterics more likely to have surgery, but their operations were more likely to involve removal of more than one organ. Six operations on healthy women compared to 42 operations on hysterical women involved removal of multiple organs, typically the appendix plus a tube and ovary or multiple internal female genital organs.

These findings raise questions about the medical histories of male hysterics. Robins, Purtell, and Cohen (1952) located 38 men diagnosed as hysteric in Veterans Administration hospitals where, in contrast to civilian hospitals, hysteria is an acceptable diagnosis for men. Replicating the Purtell study, the medical histories of the male hysterics were compared to three control gorups—healthy men, men with chronic medical illness, and men with anxiety neurosis. The male hysterics were also compared to 25 female hysterics. The findings indicate that while male hysterics were hospitalized more frequently and had more complaints and symptoms than the male control subjects, they did not have significantly more surgery. Male hysterics had a mean of 1.6 major surgical procedures compared to a mean of 1.3 in the healthy controls. Female hysterics, however, were found to have approximately twice as many major surgical operations as the male hysterics—the mean per woman was 2.9 operations compared to 1.6 for men. These findings lead to the conclusion that male hysterics can be distinguished from female hysterics in at least one major way: Hysteria in men, despite multiple physical complaints, does not lead to an excess of surgical procedures. While it may be true that some female hysterics seek gynecologic operations, it is also true that surgeons can refuse if they are unnecessary. Furthermore, patients are not usually given the option of specifying which organs or the number of organs to be removed. For multiple removal of organs, surgeons alone are culpable.

Contemporary literature no longer attributes hysteria to a "wandering womb" or to witchcraft and some psychiatrists part with Freud and demonstrate laudable sensitivity to the politics of hysteria. The American Psychiatric Association is changing hysterical personality to histrionic personality, thus removing the long association with uterus. However, stereotypes, especially functional ones, are difficult to remove. Women continue to receive harmful labels for behavior with roots in the social structure and they continue to be blamed for their own victimization. "Vapors" have disappeared along with other artifacts of the Victorian era. Twentieth century women, as their sisters before them, manifest their powerlessness in ways consistent with the current sociocultural milieu. Throughout history "woman's place" has caused her problems, and interpretations from a male perspective by the "helping professions" have resulted in complications rather than solutions. The long history of hysteria demonstrates this well.

CONCLUSIONS

Psychiatry, like other institutions in our sexist society, has been used as a method of social control in general and of women in particular (e.g., Bart, 1972; Chesler, 1972). Some of this control stems from pejorative labeling. This paper has focused on the diagnostic label "hysteria" which, as Lewis (1974) states, has had a "subversive effect on treatment." The term "conversion hysteria" has been used to invalidate women since it is assumed that all female illnesses or physical discomforts are psychogenic until proven otherwise, (e.g., Campbell, 1973; Lennane & Lennane, 1973). Terms such as "hysterical" double bind women. On the one hand, women are rewarded for having many of the traits considered "hysterical," traits embedded in traditional female socialization, and punished when they lack those "feminine" qualities. On the other hand, when those "feminine" qualities make life difficult for men, they are "put down" for being "hysterical." As Caroll Smith-Rosenberg (1972) noted, ". . . the hysterical woman can be seen as both product of and indictment of her culture."

In fact, it is possible that the problem mental health professionals have treating hysterical women is a result of "sticky transference." These women are so "feminine" that the therapists become sexually aroused and can do little about this arousal ethically. Their anger at their "hysterical" patients, manifest in the review of the literature presented above, may in fact stem from their own frustration.

The historical review sheds light on the contemporary use of the term. Hysteria was originally thought to be caused by the wandering womb, the term itself stemming from the Greek work for uterus. Originally considered physiologically based on women's reproductive tracts, it was later located in the "brain" and thus men could also be diagnosed "hysterical." However, it was always primarily a woman's disease. Misogyny at worst and paternalism at best were manifested in many descriptions of hysterics as well as in the cruel treatment they received. Since the etiology frequently involved inadequate sexual outlet, marriage as soon as possible was a frequent prescription.

Wolowitz (1972) has mentioned the role of a sense of personal injustice characteristic of hysterical women. This "sense" may in fact reflect reality—the actual structural injustice encountered by women in this society, in childhood vis-à-vis their brothers, in marriage vis-à-vis their husbands, and in the workplace vis-à-vis men generally.

It is no accident that women suffering from "involutional depression," the existential depression found in middle-aged women who have followed the cultural scripts (Bart, 1971), have MMPI's high on hysteria as well as on hypochondriasis and depression. These women who suffer from "learned helplessness" (Seligman, 1974), do in fact have a limited response repertoire and are in fact relatively powerless, for they were taught that powerful women cannot attract men or hold them and they learned their lesson too well. Of course they experience a sense of injustice. Who wouldn't?

Freud said that hysterics suffer from reminiscences. Having reviewed the literature on hysteria, let us hope that in the future the pervasive misogyny we found will only be reminiscences of things past.

REFERENCES

ALARCON, R. Hysteria and hysterical personality: How come one without the other. *Psychiatric Quarterly*, 1973, 47, 258-275.

ALARCON, R. & COVI, L. Hysterical personality and depression: A pathogenetic view. *Comprehensive Psychiatry*, 1973, 14, 121-132.

ALLEN, D. & HOUSTON, M. The management of hysteroid acting-out patients in a training clinic. *Psychiatry*, 1959, 22, 41-49.

ARETAEUS. *The Extant Works of Aretaeus, the Cappaducian.* London: Sydenham Society, 1856.

BARKER-BENFIELD, G. *The Horrors of the Half-Known Life.* New York: Harper and Row, 1976.

BART, P. Depression in middle-aged women. In V. Gornick and B. Moran (Eds.), *Woman in Sexist Society.* New York: Basic Books, 1971.

BART, P. Social structure and vocabularies of discomfort: What happened to female hysteria. *Journal of Health and Social Behavior*, 1968, 9, 188-193.

BART, P. The myth of a value free psychotherapy. In W. Bell and J. Mau (Eds.), *The Sociology of the Future.* New York: Russell Sage Foundation, 1972.

BERGER, D. Hysteria: In search of the animus. *Comprehensive Psychiatry*, 1971, 12, 277-286.

BLINDER, M. The hysterical personality. *Psychiatry*, 1966, 29, 227-235.

BROVERMAN, I., BROVERMAN, D., CLARKSON, F., ROSENKRANTZ, P., & VOGEL, S. Sex role stereotypes and clinical judgments of mental health. *Journal of Consulting and Clinical Psychology*, 1970, 34, 1-7.

BURTON, R. *The Anatomy of Melancholy.* New York: Tudor Publishing Co., 1927.

CAMPBELL, M. *Why Would a Girl Go Into Medicine?* Old Westbury, N.Y.: The Feminist Press, 1973.

CARTER, R. *On the Pathology and Treatment of Hysteria.* London: John Churchill, 1853.

CHARCOT, J. *Lectures on the Diseases of the Nervous System.* Philadelphia: Henry C. Lea, 1879.

CHESLER, P. *Women and Madness.* New York: Doubleday and Co., 1972.

CHESLER, P. Women as psychiatric and psychotherapeutic patients. *Journal of Marriage and the Family,* 1971, 33, 746-755.

CHODOFF, P. & LYONS, H. Hysteria, the hysterical personality and "hysterical" conversion. *American Journal of Psychiatry,* 1958, 114, 734-740.

CLEGHORN, R. Hysteria—multiple manifestations of semantic confusion. *Canadian Psychiatric Association Journal,* 1969, 14, 539-551.

DEUTCH, F. A footnote to Freud's "fragments of an analysis of a case of hysteria." *The Psychoanalytic Quarterly,* 1957, 26, 159-167.

Diagnostic and Statistical Manual of Mental Disorders II. Washington, D. C.: American Psychiatric Association, 1968.

Diagnostic and Statistical Manual of Mental Disorders III. Washington, D. C.: American Psychiatric Association, in press.

ECHINGER, D. *Bertha Pappenheim—Freud's Anna O.* Highland Park, Illinois: Congregation Solel, 1968.

EHRENREICH, B. & ENGLISH, D. *Witches, Midwives, and Nurses, A History of Women Healers.* New York: The Feminist Press, 1973.

FENICHEL, O. *The Psychoanalytic Theory of Neurosis.* New York: W. W. Norton, 1945.

FREUD, S. & BREUER, J. *Collected Papers.* London: Hogarth Press, 1950.

FREUD, S. *The Standard Edition of the Complete Works of Sigmund Freud* (Vol. 7). London: Hogarth Press, 1963.

GILMAN, C. *The Yellow Wallpaper.* New York: The Feminist Press, 1973.

GOLDEN, R. Hysterical personality and the psychiatric trainee. *Virginia Medical Monthly,* 1968, 95, 689-693.

GUZE, S. & PERLEY, M. Observations on the natural history of hysteria. *American Journal of Psychiatry,* 1963, 119, 960-965.

GUZE, S., WOODRUFF, R., & CLAYTON, P. Sex, age and the diagnosis of hysteria. *American Journal of Psychiatry,* 1972, 129, 745-748.

HALLECK, S. Hysterical personality traits, psychological, social, and iatrogenic determinants. *Archives of General Psychiatry,* 1967, 16, 750-757.

JAFFE, D. The role of ego modification and the task of structural change in the analysis of a case of hysteria. *International Journal of Psychoanalysis,* 1971, 52, 395-399.

KINSEY, A. C., POMEROY, W. B., MARTIN, C. E., & GEBHARD, P. H. *Sexual Behavior in the Human Female.* Philadelphia: W. B. Saunders, 1953.

KNAPP, P., LEVIN, S., McCARTER, R., WERMER, H., & ZETZEL, E. Suitability for psychoanalysis: A review of one hundred supervised analytic cases. *Psychoanalytic Quarterly,* 1960, 29, 459-477.

KRAMER, H. & SPAENGER, J. *Malleus Maleficarum.* M. Summers (trans.) London: Pushkin, 1928.

LAZARE, A. The hysterical character in psychoanalytic theory. *Archives of General Psychiatry,* 1971, 25, 131-137.

LAZARE, A. and KLERMAN, G. Hysteria and depression: The frequency and significance of hysterical personality features in hospitalized depressed women. *American Journal of Psychiatry,* 1968, 124, 48-56.

LENNANE, K. & LENNANE, R. Alleged psychogenic disorders in women—a possible manifestation of sexual prejudice. *The New England Journal of Medicine,* 1973, 288, 288-292.

LEWIS, W. Hysteria. The consultant's dilemma: Twentieth century demonology, pejorative epithet, or useful diagnosis. *Archives of General Psychiatry*, 1974, 30, 145-151.

LEWIS, W. & BERMAN, M. Studies of conversion hysteria. *Archives of General Psychiatry*, 1965, 13, 275-282.

LUISADA, P., PEELE, R., & PITTARD, E. The hysterical personality in men. *American Journal of Psychiatry*, 1974, 131, 518-522.

McCARTHY, E. Second Opinion Surgical Program: A Vehicle for Cost Containment? Unpublished report to the American Medical Association's Commission on Cost of Medical Care, 1977.

MITCHELL, S. W. *Fat and Blood: And How to Make Them.* Philadelphia: Lippincott & Co., 1878.

PARE, A. *The Works of the Famous Chirurgion Ambrose Paré.* T. Johnson (Trans.). London: R. Cotes and W. Dugard, 1649.

PLECK, J. Sex roles in clinical training. *Psychotherapy: Theory, Research, and Practice,* 1976, 13, 17-19.

PROSEN, H. Sexuality in females with "hysteria." *American Journal of Psychiatry,* 1967, 124, 687-692.

PURTELL, J., ROBINS, E., & COHEN, M. Observations on clinical aspects of hysteria. *Journal of the American Medical Association,* 1951, 146, 902-909.

REIFF, P. *Freud, the Mind of a Moralist.* New York: Doubleday, 1959.

ROBINS, E., PURTELL, J., & COHEN, M. Hysteria in men. *New England Journal of Medicine,* 1952, 246, 678-685.

SATOW, R. Where Has All the Hysteria Gone? Paper presented at the Conference on Women in Midlife Crisis, Cornell University, 1976.

SELIGMAN, M. Fall into helplessness. *Psychology Today,* 1974, 7, 43-53.

SICHERMAN, B. The uses of diagnosis: Doctors, patients, and neurasthenia. *Journal of the History of Medicine and the Allied Sciences,* 1977, 32, 33-54.

SIMON, L. The political unconscious of psychology: Clinical psychology and social change. Unpublished manuscript, 1970. Quoted in P. Chesler, Women as psychiatric and psychotherapeutic patients. *Journal of Marriage and the Family,* 1971, 33, 746-755.

SLATER, E. Diagnosis of "hysteria." *British Medical Journal,* 1965, May, 1395-1399.

SMITH-ROSENBERG, C. The hysterical woman: Sex roles and role conflict in 19th century America. *Social Research,* 1972, 39, 652-678.

SMITH-ROSENBERG, C. Personal communication, December 1976.

SORANUS. *Soranus' Gynecology.* O. Temkin (Trans.). Baltimore: Johns Hopkins Press, 1956.

SZASZ, T. *The Myth of Mental Illness.* New York: Harper & Row, 1961.

VEITH, I. *Hysteria: The History of a Disease.* Chicago: University of Chicago Press, 1965.

VON FEUCHTERSLEBEN, E. *The Principles of Medical Psychology.* London: Sydenham Society, 1847.

WINOKUR, G. & LEONARD, C. Sexual life in patients with hysteria. *Diseases of the Nervous System,* 1963, 24, 337-343.

WITTELS, F. The hysterical character. *Medical Reviews of Reviews,* 1930, 36, 186-190.

WOLOWITZ, H. Hysterical character and feminine identity. In J. Bardwick (Ed.), *Readings on th Psychology of Women.* New York: Harper & Row, 1972.

ZETZEL, E. The so-called good hysteric. *International Journal of Psychoanalysis,* 1968, 49, 256-260.

ZIEGLER, D. & PAUL, N. On the natural history of hysteria in women. *Diseases of the Nervous System,* 1954, 15, 301-306.

14

SEX DIFFERENCES AND THE EPIDEMIOLOGY OF DEPRESSION

MYRNA M. WEISSMAN and GERALD L. KLERMAN

A frequent observation in epidemiologic studies of depression is that women predominate. Observations of a sex difference in the frequency of any disease is an epidemiologic finding which attracts attention and stimulates explanations. Depression has recently gained the attention of biologists, sociologists, feminists, and the educated public. Is it a "true" finding that women are more prone to depression? Or are the observations the result of confounding factors in case reporting or some aspect of the organization of the health care system? If the finding is "real," what processes, biological or psychosocial, can best explain the differences between men and women in predisposition to depression?

The topic is timely for a number of reasons. All aspects of women's roles are currently under close scrutiny. Demographic changes in the past century have increased longevity for women more than for men. Although these changes have resulted in a larger population of women in the sixth, seventh, and eighth decades, and considering the increased rates of depression after middle age, the aging of the female population in itself cannot account for the predominance of women in epidemiologic studies. For one thing, the preponderance of women is not just in absolute numbers of depressed patients but, more significantly, in rates per population group adjusted for age. At every age group, rates of depression are higher for women. Moreover, the recent increases are occurring among younger adults in the second and third decade. If anything, there is evidence for a shift in the peak age of onset of depression. Whereas pre-World War II textbooks and reports characterized onset of

---

Reprinted, in part, from the *Archives of General Psychiatry*, Vol. 34, 98-111, January, 1977. Copyright 1977, American Medical Association.

depression as rising after the fourth decade of life, recent reports emphasize depressions in young adults, again with a predominance of females.

A number of explanations for the female predominance have been offered (Table 1). One set of explanations questions whethers the findings are "real" and hypothesizes that they are more likely an artifact accounted for by women's perceptions of stress and life changes and their emotional and coping response to stress, their willingness to acknowledge and express affective symptoms, and the high frequency with which they seek medical help for any discomfort or distress. Alternately, the finding is considered a real phenomenon and attributed to female biological susceptibility due to genetic or endocrine differences, or to social causes such as longstanding social discrimination or the recent changes in women's role.

In this chapter, we first review the evidence for differing rates of depression between the sexes and then critically analyze the various explanations offered.

METHODOLOGICAL ISSUES

In any discussion of epidemiological issues such as differing rates of an illness between men and women, it is customary to express cautions about the methodological problems in gathering data about illness and the consequent difficulties in comparing findings across studies. These difficulties include uncertainty as to the adequacy of the sampling of the population under study, reliability of the diagnostic measures and classification categories, and variations in the method of calculating the measures, among others. A detailed discussion of these methodological issues can be found in several recent reviews (Klerman & Barrett, 1973; Kramer, 1969; Silverman, 1968; Winokur, Clayton, & Reich, 1969).

TABLE 1

Why Women Have Higher Rates of Depression

An Artifactual Finding	A Real Finding
Perception of Stress	Genetic Sex Linked Transmission
Response Set	Female Endocrine Physiology
Acknowledgment	Disadvantages of Being a Woman
Help Seeking	Social Discrimination
	Recent Social Change

One major source of discrepancy is that of case definition. There are at least three meanings of the term depression—a mood, a symptom, a syndrome. As a *mood*, depression is part of the human condition. Feelings of sadness, disappointment, and frustration are within the vicissitudes of the normal human experience. The boundary between "normal" mood and clinical depression is not always clear, and psychiatrists do not agree on the full range of affective phenomena to be diagnosed as pathological (Katz, 1971; Weissman, Pincus, & Prusoff, 1975).

As a *symptom*, pathological depression often occurs in association with other psychiatric disorders such as alcoholism or schizophrenia, and medical illnesses such as endocrine dysfunction, viral infections, and drug reactions. The clinician may not regard these symptomatically depressed patients as suffering a primary affective disorder, and researchers may or may not exclude such patients from their studies.

Beyond the symptom level, there is a more specific meaning, that of the *syndrome*, a cluster of symptoms, behaviors, and functional disturbances that occur together and may vary together over time. Syndromes usually share some common mechanism in symptom formation and pathogenesis but may or may not have multiple etiologies. Psychiatrists and epidemiologists usually will be concerned with the syndrome of clinical depression.

Although the boundaries between mood, symptom, and syndrome are not always clear, in this paper we will be interested in the depressive syndrome of primary affective disorders. We will not be focusing on normal mood states or demoralization as reported, for example, in the studies on happiness by Bradburn and Caplowitz (1965), or on secondary depressions associated with medical or psychiatric disorders.

Some of the variations in rates can be explained by variations in methodology, particularly in case definition. The problems in methodological difficulties notwithstanding, it is striking that the findings show amazing consistency—the preponderance of females among depressives.

THE EVIDENCE THAT WOMEN PREDOMINATE AMONG DEPRESSIVES

The available evidence for the predominance of females among depressives comes from four sources: (a) clinical observations of patients coming for medical treatment; (b) surveys of persons not under treatment; (c) studies of suicide and suicide attempters; (d) studies of grief and bereavement. These sources, from which a number of trends have emerged, are reviewed in Tables 2, 3, and 4. The data are arranged by place and time of reporting (Adelstein, Downham, & Stein, 1964; Aitken,

Buglass, & Kreitman, 1969; Bash & Bash-Liechti, 1969, 1974; Bazzoui, 1970; Benfari, Beiser, & Leighton, 1972; Bridges & Koller, 1966; Buchan, 1969; Cannon & Redick, 1973; Clayton, Halikas, & Maurice, 1972; Clendenin & Murphy, 1971; Collomb & Zwingelstein, 1961; Cooper, Lemkau, & Tietze, 1942; Dube & Kumar, 1973; Dupont, Videbech, & Weeke, 1974, Duvall, Kramer, & Locke, 1966; Edwards & Whitlock, 1968; Ellis, Comish, & Hewer, 1966; Essen-Moller & Hagnell, 1961; Freeman, Ryan, & Beattie, 1970; Gardner, Bahn, & Miles, 1963; Gershon & Liebowitz, 1975; Gold, 1966; Grewel, 1967; Hershon, 1968; Hetzel, 1971; Hinkle, Redmont, & Plummer, 1960; Hirsh, Zauder, & Drolette, 1961; Hogarty & Katz, 1971; Hudgens, deCastro, & deZuniga, 1970; Ianzito, 1970; Jacobson & Tribe, 1972; James, Derham, & Scott-Orr, 1963; Juel-Nielson, Bille, & Flygenring, 1961; Kielholz, 1959; Krupinski, Stoller, & Polke, 1966; Lehmann, 1971; Martin, Brotherston, & Chave, 1957; Miller & Schoenfeld, 1971; Modan, Nissenkorn, & Lewkowski, 1970; Odegaard, 1961; Oliver, 1971; Parkin & Stengel, 1965; Patel, Roy, & Wilson, 1972; Paykel & Dienelt, 1971; Paykel, Myers, & Lindenthal, 1974; Pedersen, Barry, & Babigian, 1972; Rice & Kepecs, 1970; Rin, Schooler, & Caudill, 1973; Roberts & Hooper, 1969; Rosen, Bahn, & Kramer, 1964; Rosenthal, 1966; Sartorious, 1975; Schwab, McGinnis, & Warheit, 1973; Sclare & Hamilton, 1963; Sethi, 1974; Siessi, Crocetti, & Spiro, 1974; Smith & Davison, 1971; Sorenson & Stromgren, 1961; Tarnower & Humphries, 1969; Teja, Aggarwal, & Narang, 1971; Tongyonk, 1971; Torrey, 1973; Venkoba, 1965, 1966, 1970, 1971; Weschler, 1961; Weeke, Videbeck, & Dupont, 1975; Weissman, 1974; Weissman, Paykel, & French, 1973).

Most Diagnosed Depressives Are Women

Rates of diagnosed or treated depressions are underestimates, subject to the availability of treatment facilities, the individual's willingness to seek medical care, ability to afford treatment, and other factors related to utilization of health care. Therefore, such rates do not represent true estimates of the prevalence of the disorder.

Table 2 summarizes reported findings of the sex ratios for treated depressives for the United States and elsewhere between 1936 and 1973. Looking first at the United States, a 2:1 sex ratio is fairly consistent over the time period. When a specific diagnosis is given, the ratios are lower for manic depressives (1.2:1) and higher for neurotic depressives. Countries other than the United States report similar predominances of females, with the exception of a number of developing countries such as India, Iraq, New Guinea, and Rhodesia. Interesting exceptions to the

TABLE 2

Sex Ratios in Depression: Treated Cases

PLACE AND TIME	SEX RATIOS (Female/Male)	Investigators
United States		
Baltimore, Maryland 1942	2:1 (Psychoneurosis, including depression and manic depressive)	Cooper et al.
Boston, Massachusetts 1945; 1955; 1965	Marked increase in young females with diagnosis of depressive reaction	Rosenthal
Pittsfield, Massachusetts 1946-1968	2.4:1 (Patients treated with ECT)	Tarnower
New York State 1949	1.7:1	Lehmann
Massachusetts 1957-1958	2.5:1 (All depressives)	Weschler
Ohio 1958-1961	First Admissions: 1.9:1 (white) 2.7:1 (non-white)	Duvall et al.
Madison, Wisconsin 1958-1969	Increase in depression for women over decade (patients referred for psychological testing)	Rice & Kepecs
Monroe County, New York 1960	2.1:1 (Affective psychosis)	Gardner et al.
United States 1961	Outpatient Admissions: 1.4:1 (Psychotic depression) 1.2:1 (Manic depression) 1.8:1 (Involutional psychosis) 1.6:1 (Depressive reactions)	Rosen et al.
Monroe County, New York 1961-1962	1.6:1 (Prevalence) 1.3:1 (Incidence)	Pederson et al.
New Haven, Connecticut 1966	3:1 (All depressions)	Paykel & Dienelt
United States 1970	Admissions to all Psychiatric Facilities: 2.1:1 (All depressive disorders)	Cannon & Redick
Outside United States		
Amsterdam 1916-1940	2.3:1 Ashkenazim Jews 2.4:1 Gentiles	Grewel

TABLE 2 *(continued)*

PLACE AND TIME	SEX RATIOS (Female/Male)	Investigators
Gaustad, Norway 1926-1955	Life Time Risk of First Admission: 1.37:1 (1926-1935) 1.36:1 (1946-1950) 1.33:1 (1951-1955)	Odegaard
Buckinghamshire, England 1931-1947	1.8:1 (1931-1933) 1.9:1 (1945-1947)	Lehmann
Basel, Switzerland 1945-1957	1.5:1 (approximately)	Kielholz
1965-1971	First admissions of manic-depres- sives; involutional melancholia, and affective psychosis	Sartorious

	1965	1967	1969	1971	
Canada	1.8:1	1.7:1	1.8:1	1.7:1	
Czechoslovakia	2.1:1			2.1:1	
Denmark	2.4:1	1.9:1	1.8:1	1.8:1	
Finland*	1:1	1.3.1			
France			1.7.1	1.6:1	
Norway	1.2:1	1.2.1	.9:1	1.5:1	
Poland*	1.4:1	1.4:1	1.4:1		
Sweden**	1.8:1	1.8:1			
Switzerland*	1.6:1	1.3:1	1.4:1		
England and Wales	1.9:1	1.9:1	1.8:1		
New Zealand	1.5:1	2.2:1	1.8:1		

PLACE AND TIME	SEX RATIOS (Female/Male)	Investigators
London, England 1947-1949	2:1	Lehmann
Scania, Sweden 1947; 1957	1.8:1 (Life time prevalence of severe depression)	Essen-Moller & Hagnell
England and Wales 1952; 1960	1.6:1 (1952) 1.7:1 (1960)	Lehmann
Aarhus County, Denmark 1958	2:1 (Endogenous depression) 4:1 (Psychogenic depression) 3:1 (Depressive Neurosis)	Juel-Nielson et al.
Salford, England 1959-1963	1.9:1 (Depressive Psychosis)	Adelstein et al.
Dakar, Guinea 1960-1961	0.5:1	Collomb & Zwingelstein

TABLE 2 (continued)

PLACE AND TIME	SEX RATIOS (Female/Male)	Investigators
Madras and Madurai, India 1961-1963	0.2:1	Venkoba Rao
Tokyo, Japan and Taiwan, China 1963-1964	Women have more depressive symptoms	Rin et al.
Madurai, India 1964-1966	0.56:1 (Endogenous depression)	Venkoba Rao
Bulaways, Rhodesia 1965-1967	1.1:1 (N = 76)	Buchan
Baghdad, Iraq 1966-1967	1.1:1	Bazzoui
Honduras 1967	1.6:1 (Admissions) 6.7:1 (Outpatients)	Hudgens et al.
New Delhi, India 1968	0.55:1	Teja et al.
Jerusalem, Israel 1969-1972	2.1:1 (Affective disorders)	Gershon & Liebowitz
Papua, New Guinea 1970-1973	0.4:1 (Based on a few cases)	Torrey
Denmark 1973	1.9:1 (First admission for manic depression)	Dupont et al.
Bangkok, Thailand (Time not indicated)	1.3:1 (Far East Orientals) 0.8:1 (Occidentals)	Tongyonk

* Manic depressives only.
** Discharges only.

sex ratios among highly industrialized countries are Finland in 1965 and Norway in 1969, where reports describe sex ratios nearly equal. The excess of male depressives reported among Westerners living in Thailand probably reflects the excess of such men who immigrated to Thailand alone in search of work, and the relatively smaller population of Western women.

Do More Women Get Depressed?

Since rates of treated cases do not represent true prevalence, epidemiologic analysis requires data from community surveys. Such surveys usually involve a random sample drawn from a total community, and therefore provide information on many persons who have the disorder but have not received treatment.

Table 3 summarizes data from community surveys in the U.S.A. and elsewhere. In clinical studies of diagnosed cases, the sex ratios show minor variations, but in the community surveys there are no variations, with the exception of bereaved widows (which will be discussed separately). Women predominate in all countries and over all time periods.

Suicide and Suicide Attempters

Since Stengel's work (1964), it is conventional to distinguish between persons who die from suicide (completers) and those who make attempts (suicide attempters), because these two groups differ. Suicide attempters tend to be young females while completers are older males. Rates of suicide attempts are an indirect index of depression since most, but not all, suicide attempters are depressed.

The sex ratios reported for suicide attempters in recent years are especially interesting because of the rise in rates among youthful adults (mostly under 30 years of age), a consistent trend reported internationally (Weissman, 1974). All countries report an increase in suicide attempts over the last decade, which persists even after correcting for population growth or for changes in reporting methods. Reviewing the figures (Table 4) from Australia, Great Britain, United States, Israel, and India, the sex ratio in suicide attempts is about 2:1. The only exception is India, where the sex ratios are reversed. This reversal is consistent with the ratios of treated cases of depression but not with data from community surveys, suggesting that this may be due to a national pattern of help-seeking. In Poland the sex ratios are nearly equal for suicide attempts but this is consistent with the data from first admissions (see Table 2), and no community survey data from Poland could be found.

The Depression of Bereavement: Is It Normal?

The data on the bereaved spouse from community surveys deserves special mention since the sex ratios found in studies of bereavement are different from those found in clinical depression. The naturally occurring depression accompanying bereavement, usually called grief, has been universally noted in almost all societies (Clayton, Halikas, & Maurice 1971; Klerman & Izen, in press).

Lindemann (1944) intensively studied the grief reactions of survivors of the Coconut Grove Disaster in which hundreds were burned to death

Table 3

Sex Differences in Depression: Community Surveys

PLACE AND TIME	SEX RATIOS (Female/Male)	Investigators
United States		
Brooklyn and Queens, New York 1960	Women were more depressed	Benfari et al.
Baltimore, Maryland 1968	1.6:1 (Includes wives of blue collar workers only)	Siessi et al.
Northern Florida 1968	1.8:1	Schwab et al.
Carroll County, Maryland 1968	Women were more nervous, helpless, anxious	Hogarty & Katz
New Haven, Connecticut 1969	2:1 (Suicidal feelings)	Paykel et al.
St. Louis, Missouri 1968-1969	No significant sex differences in depression in bereaved spouse	Clayton et al.
New York, New York 20 Year Period	More referrals for minor depression in female employees in one company	Hinkle et al.
Outside United States		
Iceland 1910-1957	1.6:1 (All depressions)	Juel-Nielson et al.
Samso, Denmark 1960	3.5:1 (All depressions)	Sorenson & Stromgren
Ghiraz, Iran 1964	3.6:1 (N = 23)	Bash & Bash-Liechti
Luchnow, India 1969-1971	2:1	Sethi
Herfordshire, England 1949-1954	2.4:1	Martin et al.
Agra, India (Time not indicated)	1.6:1 (Manic depression)	Dube & Kumar
Aarhus County, Denmark	1.6:1 (Manic depression) 3.8:1 (Psychogenic depression) 2.9:1 (Neurotic depression)	Weeke

TABLE 4

Sex Ratios in Suicide Attempts

PLACE AND TIME	SEX RATIO Female/Male	Investigators
United States		
New York, New York 1960	3:1	Hirsh et al.
Window Rock, Arizona 1968	2:1	Miller & Schoenfeld
St. Louis, Missouri 1968-1969	2:1	Clendenin & Murphy
Providence, Rhode Island 1968	3:1	Ianzito
New Haven, Connecticut 1970	2:1	Weissman et al.
Israel		
Israel 1962-1963	1.5:1	Modan et al.
Jerusalem, Israel 1967-1969	2.1:1	Gershon & Liebowitz
India		
New Delhi, India 1967-1969	.8:1	Venkoba Rao
Madurai, India 1964	.8:1	Venkoba Rao
Poland		
Krakow, Poland 1960-1969	1.5:1 (1960) .6:1 (1962) 1.0:1 (1966) 1.2:1 (1967) .8:1 (1969)	Weissman
Poznania, Poland 1970	1.1:1	Weissman
Australia		
Western Australia 1961	2:1	James et al.

TABLE 4 (continued)

PLACE AND TIME	SEX RATIO Female/Male	Investigators
Northeast Tasmania 1961-1963	1.7:1	Gold
Victoria 1963	1.3:1	Krupinski et al.
Melbourne 1963-1968	2.4:1	Hetzel
Brisbane 1965-1966	2.5:1	Edwards & Whitlock
Southern Tasmania 1968-1969	2.5:1	Freeman et al.
Melbourne 1970	2.2:1	Oliver et al.
Great Britain		
Glasgow, Scotland 1960-1962	1.3:1	Sclare & Hamilton
Sheffield, England 1960-1961	1.7:1	Parkin & Stengel
Edinburgh, Scotland 1962 and 1967	2.1 (1962) 1.6 (1967)	Aitken et al.
Leicester, England 1961	2.4:1	Ellis et al.
London, England 1963	2.1:1	Bridges & Koller
Bristol, England 1964-1965	2:1	Roberts & Hooper
Shropshire, Montgomeryshire, England 1965-1966	2.3:1	Hershon
Brighton, England 1967	2:1	Jacobson & Tribe
Newcastle-upon-Tyne, England 1962-1964; 1966-1969	2.5:1	Smith & Davison
Glasgow, Scotland 1970	1.4:1	Patel et al.

Engel (1961) has described the three stages of uncomplicated grief following bereavement. In the first stage, shock and disbelief predominate as the bereaved person tries to deny the loss as an insulation against the emotional shock. In the second stage there is a developing awareness of the loss with the effect of sadness, guilt, shame, accompanied by a loss of interest and pleasure in usual activities as well as appetite and sleep disturbances. This stage is most similar to clinical depression. In the third stage, restitution and recovery, the grief subsides and health and well-being are reestablished.

Whereas the clinical depressive syndrome is maladaptive and requires treatment, the depression of grief may be normal and adaptive. Lindemann and others hypothesized that those who did not grieve were at higher risk for a variety of psychosomatic illnesses.

The fact that there are few differences between men and women in frequency or types of depressive symptoms in the first year following bereavement lends support to the view that regards grief as qualitatively different from clinical depression. Longer-term studies are required to determine possible delayed consequences of bereavement, per se, or whether absent, delayed, or atypical grief predisposes to psychosomatic, medical, or psychiatric illness. Such studies may show male-female differences, but the current evidence is that there are no differences between the sexes in the frequency of depressive symptoms following bereavements.

Summary of Evidence for Female Predominance

To summarize, the evidence from international comparisons of diagnosed and treated depressed patients and from community surveys which include both treated and untreated "cases" is consistent. Women predominate in the rates of depression.

IS THE PREPONDERANCE OF FEMALE DEPRESSIVES AN ARTIFACT
OF SEX DIFFERENCES IN REPORTING STRESS AND DISTRESS?

In accepting the evidence for female preponderance, it is necessary to assess the possibility that the trends are not "real" but are spurious due to artifacts produced by methods of reporting symptoms. The "artifact" hypothesis proposes that women perceive, acknowledge, report, and seek help for stress and symptoms differently from men, and these factors account for the sex ratio findings. Put another way, the "artifact" hypothesis would hold that response set and labeling processes serve to overestimate the female depressives.

Are Women Under More Stress?

Before the sex differences in rates of depression can be regarded as an artifact, the possibility must be considered that women are under more stressful life events and therefore are at greater risk for depression. There is an extensive research literature concerning the relationship between stress and general illness.

Many clinicians have observed stressful events, especially loss and separation, occurring before the onset of clinical depression and, therefore, have concluded that they serve as precipitating events. In spite of this clinical conviction relating stress to depression, until recently there had been relatively little systematic research testing these hypotheses. Holmes and Rahe (1967) provided great impetus to these studies by developing a simple quantitative scale for assessing life events. These techniques have been used extensively in both epidemiologic and clinical studies. The results support the hypothesized relationship between stressful life events and the onset and severity of numerous medical illnesses and psychiatric disorders, particularly depression. No consistent sex differences in stress reports have appeared (Horowitz, 1975).

Uhlenhuth and his colleagues have conducted a series of elegant studies to examine the relationship between actual or perceived stress, using newer life events scales and the report of symptoms among patients in both psychiatric settings and normal populations in community studies (Uhlenhuth & Paykel, 1973a, 1973b). They found a direct relationship between stress and symptom intensity but did not find that women reported more stressful life events. At the same levels of stress, women reported symptom intensities about 25% higher than men. This study was repeated in a probability sample of all households in Oakland, California, with similar results (Uhlenhuth, Lipman, & Balter, 1974). Again, the findings were that women report more symptoms than men, even when the level of stress is controlled.

One possible criticism of these studies is that most stress scales, such as the life events schedule, emphasize discrete life events and acute changes in life conditions. They are relatively insensitive to certain chronic conditions such as poverty, the impact of large family size, or health problems, which might differentially impact to a greater extent upon women than men. However, pending empirical research to test these possibilities, the available evidence is that women do not experience or report more stressful events.

Do Women Weigh Events as More Stressful?

While women may not report more stressful life events, they may evaluate or judge events as more stressful. To study the weighing given to stress, Paykel, Prusoff and Uhlenhuth (1971) asked patients and their relatives to judge the degree to which various life events were upsetting. They found no sex differences. Men and women do not appear to evaluate the standard lists of life events as having different impacts upon their lives.

Women Report More Symptoms, Especially Affective Distress

One hypothesis proposed to account for the excess of symptoms among women is that women respond to stress with affective distress because they feel freer to acknowledge symptoms, whereas men are reluctant to publicly admit symptoms and unpleasurable feelings (Blumenthal, 1975). Clancy and Gove (1974) examined the possible role of social disapproval in affecting the reporting of symptoms and they found no significant sex difference. Women did not report more desire for social approval and did not judge having psychiatric symptoms as less undesirable. Women did tend to "naysay," i.e., report more items negatively, overlooking that the meaning of the sentence had been reversed. This tendency would have led to an underestimate of the degree of symptoms in the female subjects. Clancy and Gove conclude that sex differences in symptom reporting appear to reflect actual differences and are not an artifact of response bias. Therefore, women reacted to the same level of stress with greater acknowledgment of symptoms than men, and this does not appear to be due to their perception of these events as more stressful, or their valuation of having the symptoms as less undesirable, or their wish to please the interviewer. Women experienced more symptoms.

Women Go to Doctors More Often

Men and women may utilize different coping techniques. Women cope with problems by visiting doctors and, by every measure of utilization of the general health care system, women predominate. Women have increased rates of use of outpatient facilities, of visiting physicians, of prescriptions and of psychotropic drug use (Mazer, 1974; Parry, Balter, & Mellinger, 1973). Hinkle, Redmont, & Plummer (1960) in a 25 year study of over 200 telephone company employees in New York City, found that women had more visits to the doctor and were away from work for health reasons more frequently, but these differences were accounted for almost entirely by minor illnesses such as colds. On the other hand, serious life-endangering illness occurred among men. Analysis of the risk of death based upon expected case fatality rates led to an estimate that, over a 20-year period, men experienced a greater risk of death from illness than did women, in a ratio of about 4:3. Based on this evidence, Hinkle inferred that men and women probably experience a similar variety of minor illnesses but men do not seek medical attention. The male-female differences in attendance at doctor or loss of days due to illness, they concluded, were largely the result of socially determined sex differences in what constitutes sickness behavior, including seeking medical care and absenting oneself from work.

There is a consistency in the findings for help-seeking. Women come for help for minor complaints of all kinds, and mortality rates show that men die sooner. For depression, women seek treatment more often and men have a higher suicide rate (Silverman, 1968). In our society the public assumption of the sick role is interpreted by men as a sign of weakness. Moreover, the health care system is organized in ways that make it economically difficult for most men to come for treatment, i.e., office hours usually conflict with hours of employment.

Help-seeking patterns alone cannot account for the predominance of depressed women in community surveys. The majority of persons assessed in community surveys and judged depressed have not been treated in psychiatric clinics. Therefore they have not been included in any official treatment rates. Consequently, health-care-seeking behavior cannot account for the female predominance.

Men Use More Alcohol

While depression is more common in women, alcohol use and abuse are considerably more common in men (Gomberg, 1974). It has been hypothesized that depression and alcoholism are different but equivalent disorders. Women get depressed. Men are reluctant to admit being depressed or to seek treatment for such feelings and mitigate this by drinking. Thus, men self-prescribe alcohol as a psychopharmacological treatment for depression.

Winokur and Clayton (1967) noted that environmental factors may render it difficult for women to drink excessively. In families that discourage drinking in women, the same "illness" might manifest itself as depression rather than alcoholism. This hypothesis holds that alcoholism and depression are different manifestations of the same familial-genetic disorder.

While alcohol in moderate to high amounts is a central nervous system pharmacologic depressant (Mayfield, 1968; Mayfield & Coleman, 1968), in small amounts it is a psychic relaxant. Moreover, the social context of the consumption can provide emotional and social support. The working-class man seeks the local pub, while middle- and upper-class men seek the country club or cocktail lounge; all settings provide a socially sanctioned group atmosphere for psychopharmacological self-treatment. The psychosocial supports provided by these group situations should not be overlooked as powerful reinforcers for participation, synergistically reinforcing the pharmacological actions of alcohol itself upon mood and self-esteem.

Many treated alcoholics have symptoms of depression. Tyndel (1974), in a study of 1,000 alcoholic patients, found serious depressive symptoms either at interview or in the past history of approximately 35% of alcoholics. Studies of outpatients coming for treatment of alcoholism in New Haven found that over 50% had depressive disorders of sufficient magnitude to require antidepressant treatment. These results are consistent with earlier reports by Winokur who described that 53% of patients diagnosed as alcoholic had a secondary depression (Winokur, 1972). However, studies of frequency of depression among alcoholics coming for treatment are not suitable for assessing the true incidence of depression among alcoholics, since people with two serious conditions (in this case alcoholism and depression) have a greater probability of coming for treatment (Lilienfeld, Pedersen, & Dowd, 1967).

As further evidence for an association between alcoholism and depression, excessive alcohol use has been reported in patients with bipolar illness (Reich, Davies, & Himmelhoch, 1974). Female depressed patients who have an early onset of depression have an increased rate of alcoholism in their first-degree relatives (Winokur & Clayton, 1968). Suicide and suicide attempts frequently occur in the context of alcohol abuse. Depression is associated with alcohol post-withdrawal states (Butterworth, 1971), and antidepressants and other psychotropic drugs have suggested therapeutic value in the treatment of detoxified alcoholics (Mayfield, 1968; Overall, Brown, & Williams, 1973; Rosenberg, 1974; Wren, Kline, & Cooper, 1974).

These studies have not successfully sorted out causes from consequences. Two processes certainly operate. Alcohol is used by men to mitigate their symptoms of depression. For others, chronic alcohol abuse and the consequent social impairment can lead to depression. Whether cause (primary) or effect (secondary), the hypothesis that a substantial portion of depressed men appear under the diagnostic rubric of alcoholism cannot be ruled out.

Males Predominate in the Law Enforcement and Correctional Systems

In most industrial nations women predominate in the health care system and men in the law enforcement system and correctional institutions. It is hypothesized, therefore, that depressed men may show up in the courts rather than the clinics, e.g., a depressed man may get drunk, get into a fight, and end up in court. Mazer's intensive epidemiological study of Martha's Vineyard showed that adult men and adolescent boys were more likely to show their affective distress by coming to the attention of legal and social agencies rather than mental health clinics (Mazer, 1974).

If these hypotheses are verified, epidemiological studies of rates of depression must include more extensive case reporting from law enforcement and correctional institutions. Where this has been done in studies ascertaining rates of suicide attempts, a higher number of male attempters than is usually reported have been found (Clendenin & Murphy, 1971; Whitehead, Johnson, & Ferrence, 1973).

Summary of the Evidence for Female Preponderance

Women do not have more stressful life events and do not judge life events as more stressful. While women acknowledge having symptoms and affective distress more frequently, this does not seem to be because they feel less stigma in having symptoms or because they wish to win approval from the interviewer. Women and men have different help-seeking patterns. Women attend doctors and use clinics more frequently than men for all illnesses, both minor and major, not just for psychiatric disorders. In general, women do not get involved in legal difficulties, either as a result of psychiatric problems or otherwise. While their tendency for attendance at health care facilities may inflate rates of treated depressed patients, increased female utilization would not account for the preponderance of depressed women in community surveys, since most survey "cases" are not in psychiatric treatment either at the time of the interview or in the past.

There is no question that more males than females have alcohol abuse problems, so that some unknown proportion of depressed men appears in the alcoholism rates and are not identified as depressed. There could be debates, however, as to whether or not these men are really depressed. Accurate diagnostic assessments are required to determine the morbid risk of depression and the time sequence of onset in relationship to alcoholism. Similar considerations apply to the possibility that the depressed men are to be found in the law enforcement system. Pending future research to test this possibility, it remains an interesting, but unproven, hypothesis. When all these possibilities are considered, our conclusion is that the female preponderance is not an artifact.

THE FEMALE PREPONDERANCE IS REAL

We must regard the sex differences as real findings and examine the possible explanations. These explanations include hypotheses involving biological susceptibility and others involving social discrimination and its psychological consequences. Among the biological hypotheses, possible genetic transmission and female endocrine physiological processes have been investigated.

Is There a Genetic Transmission for Depression?

The possibility of a genetic factor in the etiology of depression has regularly attracted attention. There are four main sources of evidence for the genetic hypothesis: (a) family aggregation studies which compare illness rates within and between generations of a particular family based on the fact that members of the same family share the same genes to varying degrees; (b) studies of twins comparing illness rates in monozygotic twins with those of dizygotic twins; (c) general population surveys comparing illness rates of relatives of depressed patients with those of the general population; (d) cross-rearing studies; and (e) linkage studies in which known genetic markers are used to follow other traits through several generations or in siblings. The majority of genetic studies in depression are concerned with evidence from the first two types of studies. Cross-rearing studies in affective disorders are currently under way by Kety, Rosenthal and Schulsinger in Scandinavia.

The available evidence summarized by several investigators (Gershon, Dunner, & Goodwin, 1971; Klerman & Barrett, 1973; Slater & Cowie, 1971) shows an increased morbid risk of affective disorder in the first-degree relatives of diagnosed patients as compared with the general population and a higher concordance rate for affective disorders in monozygotic than dizygotic twins. Considering all the studies, there is reasonable evidence for a genetic factor operating in depressive illness.

A greater frequency of a disorder in one sex is a genetically interesting phenomenon. One possible explanation is X-linkage, that is, the location of the relevant locus on the X chromosome. For X-linked locus, if the trait is dominant, females (with two X chromosomes) will be more commonly affected. A rare X-linked recessive trait will seldom appear in the parents or children of an affected male but will always be found in both the father and all sons of an affected female. A rare X-linked dominant trait will usually appear in the mother and all of the daughters of an affected male and will occur in at least one parent and at least half of the children (both male and female) of an affected female. The exact frequencies with which first-degree relatives are affected is also a function of the allele frequency in the population and of the mating pattern. Based on assumptions of random mating and X-linked dominant, Slater and Cowie (1971) calculated that for every affected male sibling of an affected female there would be three affected female siblings.

The examination of possible X-linkage in depression has been accelerated by the identification of at least two groups of affective disorders: unipolar which includes persons only with a major depressive illness, usually of a recurring nature (although the definition varies); and bipolar which includes persons with episodes of both mania and depression (Leonhard, 1957; Leonhard, Korff, & Schulz, 1962; Perris, 1966; Winokur & Clayton, 1967a). Bipolars differ also by an earlier age of onset (median about 30 years), and a pharmacologic response to lithium carbonate (Goodwin & Ebert, 1973). The results of family studies investigating X-linkage are conflicting. Data consistent with X-linked transmission have been shown for unipolar but not for bipolar depression by Perris (1971). However, Helzer and Winokur (1974) and Reich, Clayton, and Winokur (1969) found data suggesting X-linkage for bipolar but not for unipolar depression. The inconsistency of studies has continued into recent work as well. Gershon, et al. (in press) have found no evidence for X-linkage of bipolar affective disorder in a study in Jerusalem, Israel; Goetzl (1974) had similar results in a study conducted in New Hampshire.

Another possible explanation of the different incidences in the two sexes is a differential interaction of genotype and environment depending on sex. Kidd, Reich, and Kessler (1973, 1974) have shown that a sex effect can be treated as a differential threshold with the less commonly affected sex having a higher threshold. The underlying liability is determined by a combination of genetic and environmental factors. They have considered two types of inheritance: a polygenic model and a single major autosomal locus. While they have not applied these models to data on depression, they have shown that many of the commonly observed aspects of the sex effect could be explained by these models. The results of Uhlenhuth and Paykel (1973a, b) suggest that at the same level of stress females have more symptoms than males. This is consistent with the concept of females having a lower threshold.

At this stage the findings are in need of further examination. It is possible that the mode of transmission is much more complex than originally hypothesized. Winokur has suggested that for bipolar depressives there may be one group of families in which the illness is transmitted as an X-linked dominant and another group in which the transmission is different and may involve one or more autosomal genes.

Currently the samples studied are small, and the family-genetic patterns of depressives who may not fit either the unipolar or bipolar classification are not available. There is insufficient evidence from genetic studies yet to draw conclusions about the mode of transmission or to explain the sex differences in depression.

CAN THE FEMALE ENDOCRINE PHYSIOLOGY CAUSE DEPRESSION?

In psychiatry, interest in the possible relationships between female sex hormones and affective states derive from observations that clinical depression tends to occur in association with events in the reproductive cycle. Included are the menstrual cycle, use of contraceptive drugs, the postpartum period, and the menopause. Four questions are raised for each event: (a) are depressive symptoms more likely to be associated with these events; (b) do they occur with sufficient frequency to account for the excess of depressed woman; (c) is there a specific clinical syndrome associated with the event; and (d) is any specific female hormone implicated as mediating the depression?

Premenstrual Tension

Mood changes associated with hormonal fluctuation during the normal menstrual cycle have received much attention (Bardwick, 1974; Neu & DiMascio, 1974; Shader & Ohly, 1970; Sommer, 1973; Tonks, 1968). Many women undergo physical, mental, and behavioral changes concomitant with different phases of the menstrual cycle, particularly during the four to five days before the onset of the menses. The syndrome, usually called premenstrual tension, includes irritability, anxiety, depression, bloated feelings, headaches, etc. It can be hypothesized that if a substantial number of women undergo such changes on a regular monthly basis, this could account for some of the excess of female depressives. Moreover, it would suggest that some aspect of female hormonal balance plays a role in pathogenesis of depression.

The frequency of premenstrual tension as a real phenomenon has received systematic study, and a few careful clinical studies are available. Sommer (1973), in a critical review, has identified the major methodologic problem inherent in these studies, including variations in the cycle phase and response bias, and notes that studies which ask the subject to report behavior changes associated with menses are positive, whereas studies which use actual objective performance measures generally fail to demonstrate menstrual cycle-related changes. Morton et al. noted premenstrual tension in 80% of a volunteer sample of women prisoners, 5% of whom reported severe symptoms. Lamb et al. found such symptoms in 73% of a sample of student nurses. McCance, on the other hand, in a study of 167 women who gave daily information about mood, found great discrepancies between what they claimed were their symptoms related to menstruation and what was actually reported on the forms (Tonks, 1968). Consistent cycles of irritability related to the menses or otherwise are rare.

Numerous etiological hypotheses, both physiological and psychological, have been offered to explain premenstrual tension. These hypotheses have been summarized by Tonks (1968). The physiological hypotheses have implicated high blood levels of estrogens; deficiency of progestational hormones relative to estrogens; allergic sensitivity to estrogens; direct effect of progesterone; allergic sensitivity to progesterone; water and sodium retention due to sex hormones; increased antidiuretic hormone; increased aldosterone; a hypothalmic lesion, or increased capillary permeability to protein; hypoglycemia; menotoxin; pelvic congestion; increased blood levels of serotonin synergist. The psychogenetic explanations have included feminine role conflict; inability to accept femininity as symbolized by menstruation; frightened attitude towards menarches and menses; childhood family tensions. After reviewing the evidence, Tonks concluded that no definitive conclusions can be drawn.

There may be a tendency for some symptoms to be more common premenstrually and perhaps menstrually. Rarely does it happen with regularity, although it happens often enough so that women may believe it is regular. There may be different mechanisms, both physiologic and psychologic, responsible for a variety of premenstrual manifestations (Bardwick, 1974). The psychological changes associated with the menstrual cycle are probably subtle, subject to measurement error, and a wide range of responses probably can be found both between and within women. Although many of the hypotheses have been investigated, few are more than speculation and no one sex hormone can be implicated.

Oral Contraceptives

The use of oral contraceptives, which provide exogenous gonadal steroids, is associated with increased depression. This hypothesis is supported by findings from a number of case reports, uncontrolled studies, studies of small samples, and overall side effect incidence rates. Careful, adequately controlled studies are lacking because of the problems inherent in their design. For example, ideal control groups are difficult to establish since contraceptives cannot easily be randomly assigned or compared to placebos. Moreover, the suggestibility attendant to use of all medication requires placebo controls to differentiate the psychological from the pharmacologic effects of oral contraceptives.

Weissman and Slaby (1973) have reviewed the available evidence and conclude that there are insufficient data to justify the conclusion that oral contraceptives cause depressive symptoms on a pharmacologic basis. There is evidence that women with a prior psychiatric history and those with an expectation of adverse side effects tend to develop more depressive symptoms while on oral contraceptives. One well-controlled study (Weissman & Slaby, 1973) showed that mild psychiatric disturbances may develop during the first four weeks of use with high estrogen preparations. These symptoms, however, gradually disappear.

While these studies do not exclude the hypothesized physiological basis to psychiatric symptoms associated with oral contraceptives use, such an association is probably of low incidence. For example, Adams, Rose, Folkard et al. (1973) and Winston (1973) have suggested that a small number of women taking steroid hormones may become depressed due to the inhibition of the synthesis of biogenic amines in the central nervous system. This is the result of a functional pyridoxine deficiency caused by the estrogens in the oral contraceptive and may be alleviated or prevented by supplementary Vitamin B_6. Both studies agree that this occurs in a small number of women.

Evidence based on experiences with oral contraceptive use, like that from premenstrual tension, is not conclusive. In summary, the amount of female depression which could be attributed to the possible psychopharmacologic effects of oral contraceptives is small.

Postpartum Depression

In the postpartum period, significant hormonal changes occur, and depressive mood changes have been described. Transient emotional disturbances in the first weeks following delivery, commonly referred to as the "new baby blues," occur with such frequency as to be considered normal. These mild depressive states are benign and resolve without treatment (Yalom, Lunde, Moos et al., 1968). However, there is overwhelming evidence that the longer postpartum period (up to six months) carries an excess risk for more serious psychiatric disorders (Asch & Rubin, 1974; Brown & Shereshefsky, 1972; Butts, 1969; Gordon & Gordon, 1959; Thuwe, 1974). The most comprehensive studies on the risk of mental illness in the pre- and postpartum periods were reported by Paffenberger and McCabe (1966) and by Pugh, Jerath, and Schmidt (1963). Paffenberger and McCabe studied the medical records of all women in Cincinnati during a two-year period, aged 15 through 44, who were inpatients on any psychiatric service. They found that age adjusted rates of mental illness were low for married women in general, but they were highest for women in the postpartum period and lowest for pregnant women. The peak rates of mental illness occurred in the first months following delivery. Moreover, about half of the women who suffered a postpartum illness had a recurrence in one-third of their subsequent pregnancies.

Paffenberger and McCabe's results were very similar to those of Pugh et al. who studied all females, aged 15-44, who were first admissions to Massachusetts mental hospitals during 1950. Pugh et al. also found a large excess of psychosis, especially the manic-depressive type, during the first three months postpartum. While all authors agree that endocrine changes are involved in the postpartum psychiatric illness, in a previous era many acute psychotic states, including delirium, may have been related to infections, fevers, dehydration, and hemorrhaging following childbirth. However, with better medical care, these are rare occurrences in industrialized countries. Currently, the severe psychiatric reactions of postpartum are almost all of a depressive nature. It must be concluded that women are at greater risk for psychiatric disorders, particularly depression, in the postpartum period, although, if any specific endocrine abnormality is involved, the mechanism is not understood.

The Menopause

The menopausal period is widely presumed to produce an increased risk of depression, and depressions occurring in this period are supposed to have a distinct clinical entity. It is believed that women who are normally symptom-free experience depressive changes during this period. Moreover, the depression occurring in the menopause is described as a separate entity and involutional melancholia appears in the official APA diagnostic classification. Involutional depression is purported to include an overconscientious and obsessive personality and a clinical picture dominated by agitation, guilt, and hypochondriasis.

In regard to the supposedly characteristic clinical picture, Rosenthal (1968) reviewed 30 years of studies and concluded that involutional melancholia never existed as a separate entity. The early clinical studies were poorly controlled and contained small samples, and the recent studies find new patients with the characteristic symptom pattern. If such an entity existed in the past, its relative absence now may have to do with the availability of better case finding and effective treatments so that depressed patients are seen earlier before the full blown "involutional" syndrome emerges.

In regard to the possible increased risk of depression around the menopause, Winokur (1973) found that there was no greater risk for depression during the menopause than during other times of the life span. Similar findings have been noted by others (Adelstein, Downham, Stein et al., 1964; Juel-Neilson, Bille, & Flygenring, 1961; Juel-Neilson & Stromgren, 1965; Silverman, 1968; Sorenson & Stromgren, 1961). McKinlay and Jeffreys (1974), conducted a community survey of over 600 women in the premenopausal and menopausal age range to ascertain the prevalence of depressive symptoms. They found that hot flushes occurred more frequently in women whose menstrual flow showed evidence of change or cessation, but few of the women sought treatment for this symptom. There was no direct relationship between depression and menopausal status. Moreover, the majority of respondents did not anticipate or experience any difficulties at menopause and only 10% expressed regret at the cessation of menses. These conclusions have also been reported by Neugarten (1968), although this may vary in rural cultures, and by Hallstrom (1973).

The most definitive epidemiologic study of mental disorders in the climacteric was recently completed in Sweden (Hallstrom, 1973). Between 1968 and 1970, over 800 women, aged 38-60, were surveyed to determine possible changes in mental health status during the climacteric. No significant differences were observed in the incidence rates for mental illness, depressive states, or psychiatric morbidity in the different age strata as a function of menopause. Moreover, there was no evidence that characteristic personality or emotional changes took place.

The psychologic impact of the menopause has also been implicated along with the hypothesized hormonal changes. Deykin, Jacobson, and Klerman (1966), Bart (1970) and others have pointed out that the period coinciding with the menopause may be associated with other life events such as departure of children from the home. These psychosocial changes may have more of an impact on women than the cessation of the menses itself.

In summary, there is no evidence that women are at greater risk for depression during the menopausal period or that depressions occurring in this period have a distinct clinical pattern.

Summary of the Endocrine Evidence

The pattern of the relationship of endocrine to clinical states is inconsistent. There is good evidence that premenstrual tension and use of oral contraceptives have an effect to increase rates but these effects are probably of small magnitude. There is excellent evidence that the postpartum period does induce an increase in depression. Contrary to widely-held views, there is good evidence that the menopause has no effect to increase rates of depression.

There is little evidence to relate these mood changes and clinical states to altered endocrine balance or specific hormones. However, it must be emphasized that no study could be located which correlated clinical state with female endocrines, utilizing modern endocrinological methods or sensitive quantitative hormonal assays. Here is an area for fruitful collaboration between endocrinology and psychiatry. While some portion of the sex differences in depression, probably during the child-rearing years, may be explained endocrinologically, this factor is not sufficient to account for the large differences.

PSYCHOSOCIAL EXPLANATIONS

Sociologists, psychologists, psychiatrists, feminists, and others concerned with women have become increasingly concerned to explain why more women become depressed. The conventional wisdom is that the long-standing disadvantaged social status of women has psychological consequences that are depressing, and the persistence of social status discrimination is proposed to explain the long-term trends of female predominance in depression. In addition to this hypothesis based on social status differences, there are explanations offered based on psychoanalytic theories of female personality and historical changes associated with rapid social stress.

Psychological Disadvantages of the Woman's Social Status

Various hypotheses have been proposed specifying the pathways whereby women's disadvantaged status might contribute to clinical depression. Our review of these hypotheses indicates two main proposed pathways (Figure 1). One pathway emphasizes the low social status, legal and economic discrimination of women; while the other pathway emphasizes women's internalization of role expectations which results in a state of learned helplessness.

The first pathway, which we will call the *social status hypothesis*, is widely accepted in the recent discussions on social discrimination against women. Many women find their situation depressing since the real social discriminations make it difficult for them to achieve mastery by direct action and self-assertion, further contributing to their psychological distress. Applied to depression, it is hypothesized that these inequities lead to legal and economic helplessness, dependency on others, chronically low self-esteem, low aspirations, and, ultimately, clinical depression.

The second pathway, which we call the *learned helplessness hypothesis,* proposes that socially conditioned, stereotypical images of men and women

FIGURE 1

Possible Social Processes Leading to Depression in Women

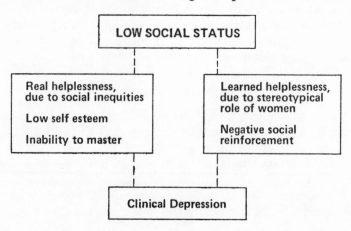

produce in women a cognitive set against assertion and independence which is reinforced by societal expectations. In this hypothesis, the classic "femininity" values are redefined as a variant of "learned helplessness," characteristic of depression (Seligman, 1974). Young girls learn to be helpless during their socialization and thus develop a limited response repertoire when under stress. These self-images and expectations are internalized in childhood so that the young girl comes to believe that the stereotype of femininity is expected, valued, and normative (Bart, 1975; Beck & Greenberg, 1974; Broverman, Broverman, & Clarkson, 1970; Chesler, 1972; Cole, Pennington, & Buckley, in press; Friedman, Richart, & Vande Wiele, 1975; Gove & Lester, 1974; Gove & Tudor, 1973; Keller, 1974; Maccoby & Jacklin, 1975; Menaker, 1974).

Marriage and Depression

In the few attempts to test this hypothesis that the high rates of depression are related to the disadvantages of the woman's social status, particular attention has been given to differential rates of mental illness among married and unmarried women. If this hypothesis is correct, marriage should be of greater disadvantage to the woman than to the man, since married women are likely to embody the traditional stereotyped role and should, therefore, have higher rates of depression. Gove, in particular, has focused his research on examining whether rates of mental illness among married women compared to other women and married men. Gove (1972, 1973) and his associates found that the higher overall rates of many mental illnesses for females are largely accounted for by higher rates for married women. In each marital status category, single, divorced, and widowed women have lower rates of mental illness than men. He concludes that being married has a protective effect for males but a detrimental effect for females. Similar conclusions were reached by Radloff (in press) from data from a community survey of depressive symptoms conducted in Kansas City, Missouri, and Washington County, Maryland; by Porter in a study of depressive illness in a Surrey, England general practice (Bachrach, 1975); by a National Health Survey of psychological distress (Bachrach, 1975); and by Manheimer, Mellinger, and Balter in a California survey of factors related to psychotropic drug use (Bachrach, 1975).

Gove and others attribute the disadvantages of the married female to: role restriction (most men occupy two roles as household head and worker and, therefore, have two sources of gratification, whereas women have only one); housekeeping being frustrating and of low prestige; the role of housewife is unstructured and invisible allowing time for brooding; even if the married women works, she is usually in a less favorable position than a working man; the expectations confronting women are unclear and diffuse; the female role encompasses a low self-image.

Additional, but indirect, support for the hypothesized disadvantage of the female role comes from experimental research on boredom in humans and in animals. Ramsey (1974) presented evidence for the negative effect of boredom which characterized the life of many married women. In one experiment, when human subjects were exposed to a uniformly uninteresting environment, their reaction time, sensory acuity, power of abstract reasoning, verbal ability, space visualization, and internal motivation to move, to daydream, or to think, all decreased. In a separate experiment, rats were similarly placed in "boring" situations. After three months, the animals began to act like "caricatures of the lonely housewife." They became jumpy, irritable, and aggressive. They nibbled at food constantly and became fatter than their peers out in the exciting world, and developed nervous twitches. Like rats, the author notes, humans who are bored place a heavy load on our medical care delivery system because boredom, with its accompanying depression, guilt, and anxiety, affects functioning of many organ systems.

Boredom and role restriction may not be the major or only risk factors in marriage; other intervening factors such as family size, financial resources, etc. must also be taken into account. An elegant study of the interaction of some of these factors was recently reported by Brown, Bhrolchain, and Harris (1975). Using data collected from a community survey in London, Brown and associates examined the relationship between psychosocial stress and subsequent affective disorders and found that working-class married women with young children living at home had the highest rates of depression. Subject to equivalent levels of stress, working-class women were five times more likely to become depressed than middle-class women. Four factors were found which contributed to this class difference: loss of a mother in childhood; three or more children under 14 living at home; absence of an intimate and confiding relationship with husband or boyfriend; lack of full- or part-time employment outside of home. The first three factors were more frequent among working-class women. Confidants other than spouse or boyfriend did not have a protective effect. Access to a confidant per se was not sufficient; rather, the general levels of satisfaction and intimacy in the relationship with the husband or boyfriend and the amount of emotional support he gave the woman in her role were the important factors in preventing depression in the face of life stress. Employment outside the home, it was suggested, provided a protective effect by alleviating boredom, increasing self-esteem, improving economic circumstances, and increasing social contacts.

The association of poor interpersonal relations within the marriage and clinical depression is further supported by studies of depressed women during psychiatric treatment. The New Haven group found that marital discord was the most common event in the previous six months reported by depressed patients compared to normals (Paykel, Myers, Dienelt et al., 1969). Wiessman and Paykel (1974) found that acutely depressed women as compared to matched normal controls reported considerably more problems in marital intimacy, especially ability to communicate with the spouse. Moreover, these marital problems often were enduring and did not completely subside with symptomatic remission of the acute depression. Furthermore, the data that unmarried women have lower rates of mental illness than unmarried men but that married women have higher rates than married men, are cited as evidence that the excess of symptoms noted currently are not entirely due to biological factors intrinsic to being female, but are contributed to by the conflicts generated by the traditional female role.

Psychoanalytic Explanations

Among mental health clinicians, the most widely-held explanations for the high rates of depression among women locate the cause in female intrapsychic conflicts. It is of interest that two parallel psychoanalytic theories related to this issue were developed in the early decades of this century but were not linked together until recently with the emergence of the feminist critique. These two theories are (a) the psychoanalytic theory of female psychological development, and (b) the psychodynamic theory of the psychogenesis of depression.

As regards the psychoanalytic theory of the psychology of women, Freud, Deutsch, and others proposed that the personality of adult women, normal and neurotic, is characterized by narcissism, masochism, low self-esteem, dependency, and inhibited hostility as a consequence of the young girl's special resolution of her oedipal complex. The postulated crucial event in the sequence of the girl's childhood experience is her penis envy, which derives from her accidental awareness of the anatomical differences, combined with her necessity to shift her intrapsychic identifications and object love from the initially-held mother to her oedipal father. As is widely known, this theory has been extensively criticized, recently by

Kate Millet (1970), but earlier by Clara Thompson and Karen Horney. The psychological consequences of Freud's dictum, "anatomy is destiny," is, in fact, contingent upon the young girl's becoming consciously aware of this anatomical difference. The crucial test of this hypothesis would be to study young girls who, for one reason or another, did not have an awareness of, or were delayed in observing, anatomical differences.

Parallel with the theory of femininity, but not explicitly linked to it, the classic psychodynamic theory of depression emphasized that individuals prone to depression were characterized by difficulties in close relationships, excess dependency, early childhood deprivation, excessive guilt, and tendency to turn hostility against themselves. The immediate precipitant for the overt clinical depression was hypothesized to be a loss, either actual or symbolic.

Interestingly, these two theories developed in parallel with each other for almost 50 years, and relatively few psychoanalysts attempted to deal with the epidemiologic fact that women predominate among depressives by linking the predisposition to depression among women to their presumed characteristic psychic conflicts related to childhood experiences of penis envy, narcissism, low self-esteem, dependency, etc.

Although these two theories in one form or another have been widely accepted among clinicians, empirical evidence for their support has been meager. As Chodoff (1972) points out in a recent review of personality and depression, there are relatively few systematic studies in support of the hypothesis that depression-prone individuals are excessively dependent for the maintenance of self-esteem.

The Mental Health System's Contribution

The predominance of these psychodynamic views among clinicians has contributed to criticism of the mental health system by feminists. It is claimed that the feminine stereotype behavior has been reinforced by the ideology and practices of professionals in health settings. It is further claimed that women find difficulty in freeing themselves from the feminine stereotype because it has been consistently reinforced in public by "experts" on child development and psychology who are quoted by the press and other media.

Keller (1974), Kirsh (1974) and others state that psychotherapeutic treatment too often reinforces the negative self-image of women and perpetuates the problems of women who suffer symptoms from their life situation. Psychotherapy, it is claimed, promotes dependency by reinforcing stereotypical roles.

The most pertinent work supporting the existence of sex-role stereotype among mental health professionals is that of Broverman et al. (1970), who asked mental health clinicians what behaviors they considered healthy in men, women, and adults with sex unspecified. These researchers found a powerful negative assessment of women. The standard for a healthy adult was the same for a healthy man, but *not* for a healthy woman. Healthy women were seen as differing from healthy men in that the healthy women were supposed to be submissive, dependent, subjective, nonaggressive, emotional, and easily hurt. Thus, a double standard of mental health was found which parallels the sex-role stereotypes in our society. Moreover, both sexes incorporated the better or worse aspects of the stereotypical role in their image of themselves and women tended to have a more negative self-concept than men.

Feminist critics have been intense in their assertions that psychiatry and psychology are male-oriented professions which have perpetuated male-dominated theories. Attempts have been made to encourage women to seek female therapists and to join groups for consciousness-raising. Before these assertions can be accepted, the results of some recent studies on the attitudes and views of female mental health practitioners need to be appraised (Schwartz & Abramovitz, 1975). In response to various case histories, male psychotherapists actually judged protocols of female patients less stringently than did female counselors. Male mental health professionals were not necessarily bound by their ideology to discriminate against women.

Historical Change, Rising Expectations, and Changing Rates of Depression

Any attempt to understand the female predominance in depression must explain both the long-term and the short-term trends. Conventional explanations have assumed that the female predominance in depression has been a long-term trend. Most of the studies do support this and the data that exist from the nineteenth century indicate a female predominance of depression. These enduring trends can be interpreted as supporting either the biological or the social status theories.

On the other hand, recent evidence suggests short-term trends in addition to the long-term one. There has been an increase in the rates of depression (Secunda, Katz, Friedman et al., 1973), especially among young women, manifested especially by rising suicide attempt rates among young women (Weissman, 1974) and by high attendance by women at psychiatric outpatient clinics (Zonana, Henisz, & Levine, 1973). This has prompted speculation about the possible role of recent historical changes, especially the presumed pathogenic pressures of modern life.

Rising expectations, increased life events, separations, and loss of attachment bonds are all risk factors of depression which have been suggested as mechanisms by which social change can be psychic stressors (Klerman, 1974). These stressors are proposed to have a greater impact on women because of their more vulnerable social position.

Rate increases in depression have been reported to have occurred during earlier periods of rapid social change. Schwab (1970) has pointed to possible historical parallels to the current era in the late Elizabethan and early seventeenth century England when depression was described to have reached epidemic proportions. At that time, political and social conditions were characterized by the lack of cohesive value systems, loss of shared sentiments, and the upheavals of the English Civil War. Similarly, Rosen (1959), citing the example of late eighteenth century England, quotes Edgar Shepherd (1773) who, attributing the rise in mental illness to the "wear and tear of a civilization," speculated on the reasons for the differential prevalences of mental disorder between the sexes.

Rising expectations, access to new opportunities as created by the women's movement, and efforts to redress the social inequalities of women have been suggested as further explanation for the recent increase in depression among women. Depressions may occur not when things are at their worst, but when there is a possibility of improvement and a discrepancy between one's rising aspirations and the likelihood of fulfilling these wishes. The women's movement, governmental legislation, and efforts to improve educational and employment opportunities for women have created higher expectations. Social and economic achievement often have not kept pace with the promises, especially in a decreasing job market, and where long-standing discriminatory practices perpetuate unequal opportunities.

These new role expectations may also create intrapsychic personal conflicts, particularly for those women involved in traditional family tasks but who also desire employment and recognition outside the family. While the women's movement has mainly involved middle- and upper-class and educated women, it has had an impact on women from other social classes where opportunities for work outside the home, management of money, dominance in the marriage, etc. may be crucial. Even for the educated and economically comfortable women, ambivalence and conflict continue about careers not conventionally seen as feminine (Horner, 1972; Weissman, Pincus, Radding, et al., 1973). The documented increase in suicides and suicide attempts among women in the United States and Great Britain suggests that social changes may be exacting psychological costs for many young women. In this regard, Gove and Tudor (1973) note that communities which are extremely close-knit, stable, traditional family-oriented, and culturally isolated, such as the Acadian French village studied by Leighton, have lower rates of mental illness in general, with the women having even lower rates than the men.

Although support can be adduced for the hypothesis that participation in the women's movement is associated with psychological distress, it is highly unlikely that this is the major factor for the excess of depression among women. The differing rates substantially predate the women's movement. The short-term changes may be disruptive, but in the long-term a new equilibrium may be reached and the high female rates may begin to decrease. Such a reduction in the rate of depression would be indirect confirmation of the hypothesis that the female excess of depression is due to psychological disadvantages of the female role. As behaviors and expectations become more similar between the sexes, females may begin to employ modes of coping with stress that are similar to those used by men. There are some indications that this may be occurring in that the female rates of alcoholism, suicide, and crime (predominantly male behaviors) have begun to rise. Alternatively, the sex ratios for depression could become equal because of an increase in depression among men due to the stress produced by the change in the roles of women, and the uncertainty of the male role. In this regard, it would be interesting to determine the rates of depression among educated and emanicipated women or in countries where women have achieved emancipation, such as Scandinavia. Similarly, are the rates of depression equalized between the sexes in cultural subgroups whose sex-role allocations are less rigid or nonconventional?

Summary of the Psychosocial Explanations

The most convincing evidence that social role plays an important role in the vulnerability of women to depression is the data that suggest that marriage has a protective effect for males but a detrimental effect for women. This supports the view that elements of the traditional female role may contribute to depression. Further understanding of social stress and its interactions with components of the female vulnerability in the traditional role is a promising area of research. This research would need to take into account intervening variables such as women's employment and the quality of the marriage. Any comprehensive theory, including biological ones proposed to account for the predominance of depression among women, must explain both long-term rates and recent changes in rates.

The male-female differences in rates of depression are real. The evidence in support of these differential rates is best established in Western industrialized societies. Further studies in non-Western countries, particularly in Africa and in Asia, are necessary before any conclusions can be drawn as to the universality of this differential rate.

Given evidence that the sex difference in rates of depression is real, the qeustion then arises: "Why is this is so?" The biological evidence is compelling but not entirely comprehensive. As regards genetic explanations, the evidence supports the hypothesis that some forms of depression are genetically transmitted. Genetic factors are most likely involved in bipolar forms of manic-depressive illness, but even if a sex linked gene transmission is substantiated for this and other severe affective disorders, it is unlikely to account for all depressions.

Similar conclusions pertain to the evidence about endocrine factors. During the postpartum period and with oral contraceptive use, women are at greater risk for depression, probably due to endocrine influence, but this higher risk does not seem to prevail during the menopause. In any event, while postpartum and some other endocrine-linked episodes do increase risk of depression, they do not appear to be associated with unique clinical syndromes, so that no specific clinical form of depression can be considered to be exclusively endocrine-determined. More research using advanced biochemical and endocrinological techniques is needed to identify possible aberrant endocrines or altered balance of female hormonal metabolism in patients with depressive syndromes.

Female Sensitivity to Disruption of Attachment Bonds

The biological evidence suggests that a single-factor theory is insufficient. At least a second factor related to psychosocial change is required. Preferably it should be a factor embodying a concept bridging biological and behavioral domains and consistent with the findings from the diverse areas.

Attachment bonding, a concept derived from ethological studies, meets the criteria of an integrating and bridging concept. It has been proposed by several investigators (Akiskal & McKinney, 1973; Klerman, 1974;

Hamburg, 1963; Rutter, 1972) as possibly related to depression. The common denominator of these diverse views is that depression is associated with a loss, or anticipation of loss of significant attachment bonds or related social affiliative reinforcers. The study of attachment has identified powerful behavioral mechanisms in mammals, but especially primates, which have evolutionary bases and which have served for phylogenetic survival of groups and adaptive success of individuals. The disruption of these bonds evokes in all mammalian species, especially in primates, changes accompanied in humans by cognitive, perceptual, and social responses, perhaps uniquely human, and influenced by culturally-learned patterning.

Most attention has been focused on various psychosocial stress explanations. The currently used techniques for assessing psychosocial stress indicate that women are not under greater stress. However, the likelihood exists that there are specific stressors impacting on women which are not being evaluated by the currently used techniques.

We propose that there is a specific interaction between characteristics of women, biological and/or learned, and their sensitivity to specific stressors, both psychosocial and bio-developmental. The specific stressors would be those related to disruption of attachment bonding.

If this attachment bonding hypothesis is correct, women would be more vulnerable either for biological or historical reasons. By natural selection, on an evolutionary basis, females would have acquired stronger attachments which were biologically reinforced by endogenous neuro-endocrine as well as environmentally interactive reward processes to fulfill their reproductive functions. Historically, due to social training and their traditional roles in societies, as well as fewer real opportunities for independence, women may be more vulnerable to the loss of bonds (Rutter, 1972). Disruption of bonds, e.g., by moves, divorce, separation, and the dimunition of family ties and church supports, have occurred with increasing frequency.

Modern industrial society with its social, psychological, and geographical mobility is increasingly likely to disrupt attachment bonding. For example, geographic mobility is high in industrial society. Nearly 20% of all Americans relocate annually, requiring adaptation to separation from family and familiar friends (disruption of bonds). Such moves may be more stressful to women than men; the moves are most often initiated by the men for economic gain and may be experienced by them as positive due to employment advancement (Weissman & Paykel, 1972). The increasing divorce rate represents another loss of bonds and may consequently have a greater impact on women. As noted before, marital difficulties are the most frequent event reported by female depressed patients in the six months prior to the depression (Paykel, Myers, Dienelt, et al., 1969). The extended family and church have increasingly diminished as sources of support in modern industrial society.

Lastly, the high mortality rate in males leads women to be at a higher risk for bereavement and loneliness in advancing years. There is currently a seven-year differential mortality between the sexes in the United States. While Clayton has shown that the sex ratios for depressions following bereavement are equal, in fact more women, because of their greater longevity, are at risk for bereavement (Clayton, Halikas, & Maurice, 1971).

Moreover, the trends in rates of depression may provide clues as to the relative importance of biological and social factors in depression. If the attachment theory is correct, we should expect a decrease in rates of depression among Western women over the next decade, as society moves towards greater social equality and less pressure for reproduction. These events should decrease the female vulnerability to the disruption of attachment bonds. To test these hypotheses, measures of attachment bonding and psychosocial stress are required. The currently existing scales for assessing life events and stress do not seem adequate in our opinion to calculate this specific form of stress.

Testing Alternative Hypotheses

There is little doubt that the sex differences found in depression are a promising lead which requires considerably broader based inquiry in epidemiology. It is highly unlikely that any one of the explanations already described will be the sole factor accounting for the phenomena or that all types of depressions will be associated with the same risk factors. As was shown, the explanations cross such a wide variety of disciplines and disparate points of view that rarely are all interactions entertained by any one group of investigators. In this field, there has been an unfortunate tendency for fragmentation so that the investigators in genetics, social psychology, or endocrinology are not specifically aware of attempts by their scientific colleagues to deal with similar phenomena. The purpose of this review has been to assess different positions and to guide future research. The salient areas for future research include: broad community-based epidemiologic studies which use consistent and operationalized diagnostic criteria and which overcome the problem of reporting and response set; further research on the genetics of depression including the nonbipolar and less severe forms of the disorder, and examining the rates of depression in first-degree relatives of depressed patients to see if they fit frequencies and patterns consistent with a particular mode of inheritance; endocrine studies on the relationship between hormones and mood; cross-cultural epidemiologic studies using consistent and similar diagnostic criteria which examine the suggestion that depression may be less frequent in females in nonindustrialized countries; longitudinal studies of the help-seeking pattern and rates of depression of women who do not assume the traditional female roles and especially in countries where women have achieved increased emancipation, and close surveillance of changes in rates controlling for potential artifacts.

In summary, we have reviewed the evidence critically and believe that the sex differences in depression in Western society are, in fact, real and not an artifact of reporting or health care behavior. Various alternative suggestions have been explored and the strengths and weaknesses of various theories have been critically examined. As an integrating guide we have proposed that, by virtue of evolutionary selection, historical changes, and social training, women are more sensitized to those psychosocial changes which disrupt attachment bonding and are, therefore, more vulnerable to depression.

REFERENCES

ADAMS, P. W., ROSE, D. P., FOLKARD, J., et al. Effect of pyridoxine hydrochloride (Vitamin B₆) upon depression associated with oral contraception. *The Lancet,* 1973, April 28, 897-904.

ADELSTEIN, A. M., DOWNHAM, D. Y., STEIN, Z., et al. The epidemiology of mental illness in an English city: Inceptions recognized by Salford Psychiatric Services. *Soc. Psychiatry,* 1964, 3, 455-468.

AITKEN, R. C. B., BUGLASS, D., & KREITMAN, N. The changing pattern of attempted suicide in Edinburgh, 1962-1967. *Brit. J. Prev. Soc. Med.,* 1969, 23, 111-115.

AKISKAL, H. & McKINNEY, W. Depressive disorders: Towards a unifying hypothesis. *Science,* 1973, 182, 20-29.

ASCH, S. S. & RUBIN, L. J. Postpartum reactions: Some unrecognized variations. *American J. Psychiatry,* 1974, 131, 870-874.

BACHRACH, L. Marital status and mental disorder: An analytical review. U.S. Dept. Health, Education and Welfare, PHC DHEW Publication No. (ADM) 75-217, 1975.

BARDWICK, J. M. The sex hormones, the central nervous system and affect variability in humans. In V. Franks and V. Burtle (Eds.), *Women in Therapy.* New York: Brunner/Mazel, 1974.

BART, P. Mother Portnoy's complaints. *Trans-Action,* November-December, 1970, 69-74.

BART, P. Unalienating abortion, demystifying depression, and restoring rape victims. Paper presented at American Psychiatric Association, Anaheim, Cal., May 7, 1975.

BASH, K. W. & BASH-LIECHTI, J. Studies on the epidemiology of neuropsychiatric disorders among the rural population of the province of Khuzestran, Iran. *Social Psychiatry*, 1969, 4, 137-143.

BASH, K. W. & BASH-LIECHTI, J. Studies on the epidemiology of neuropsychiatric disorders among the population of the city of Shiraz, Iran. *Social Psychiatry*, 1974, 9, 163-171.

BAZZOUI, W. Affective disorders in Iraq. *British Journal of Psychiatry*, 1970, 117, 195-203.

BECK, A. T. & GREENBERG, R. L. Cognitive therapy with depressed women. In V. Franks and V. Burtle (Eds.), *Women in Therapy*. New York: Brunner/Mazel, 1974.

BENFARI, R. C., BEISER, M., LEIGHTON, A. H., et al. Some dimensions of psychoneurotic behavior in an urban sample. *Journal of Nervous and Mental Disease*, 1972, 155, 77-90.

BLUMENTHAL, M. D. Measuring depressive symptomatology in a general population. *Archives of General Psychiatry*, 1975, 32, 971-978.

BRADBURN, N. & CAPLOWITZ, A. *Reports on Happiness: A Pilot Study on Four Small Towns*. Chicago: Aldine Publishing Co., 1965.

BRIDGES, P. K. & KOLLER, K. M. Attempted suicide. A comparative study. *Comprehensive Psychiatry*, 1966, 7, 240-247.

BROVERMAN, I. K., BROVERMAN, D. M., CLARKSON, F. E., et al. Sex-role stereotypes and clinical judgments of mental health. *Journal of Consulting and Clinical Psychology*, 1970, 34, 1-7.

BROWN, G., BHROLCHAIN, M., & HARRIS, T. Social class and psychiatric disturbance among women in an urban population. *Sociology*, 1975, 9, 225-254.

BROWN, W. A. & SHERESHEFSKY, P. Seven women: A prospective study of postpartum psychiatric disorders. *Psychiatry: Journal for the Study of International Processes*, 1972, 35, 139-159.

BUCHAN, T. Depression in African patients. *South African Medical Journal*, 1969, 43, 1055-1058.

BUTTERWORTH, A. T. Depression associated with alcohol withdrawal: Imipramine therapy compared with placebo. *Quarterly Journal of Studies in Alcoholism*, 1971, 32, 343-348.

BUTTS, H. F. Postpartum psychiatric problems. *Journal of National Medical Association*, 1969, 61, 136-139.

CANNON, M. & REDICK, R. *Differential Utilization of Psychiatric Facilities by Men and Women: U.S. 1970*. DHEW, Surveys & Reports Section, Statistical Note 81 (June) 1973.

CHESLER, P. *Women and Madness*. New York: Doubleday & Co., 1972.

CHODOFF, P. The depressive personality: A critical review. *Archives of General Psychiatry*, 1972, 27, 666-673.

CLANCY, K. & GOVE, W. Sex differences in mental illness: An analysis of response bias in self-reports. *American Journal of Sociology*, 1974, 80, 205-216.

CLAYTON, P. J., HALIKAS, J. A., & MAURICE, W. L. The bereavement of the widowed. *Diseases of the Nervous System*, 1971, 32, 597-604.

CLAYTON, P. J., HALIKAS, J. A., & MAURICE, W. The depression of widowhood. *British Journal of Psychiatry*, 1972, 120, 71-77.

CLENDENIN, W. W. & MURPHY, G. E. Wrist cutting: New epidemiological findings. *Archives of General Psychiatry*, 1971, 25, 465-469.

COLE, J. D., PENNINGTON, B. F., & BUCKLEY, H. H. Effects of situational stress and sex roles on the attribution of pyschological disorder. *Journal of Consulting and Clinical Psychology*, in press.

COLLOMB, H. & ZWINGELSTEIN, J. Depressive states in an African community, from

First Pan-African Psychiatric Conference Report, Lamba, J. (Ed.), Abeokuta, Africa, 1961.

COOPER, M., LEMKAU, P., & TIETZE, C. Complaint of nervousness and the psychoneuroses: An epidemiological viewpoint. *American Journal of Orthopsychiatry,* 1942, 12, 214-223.

DEYKIN, E. Y., JACOBSON, S., KLERMAN, G. L., et al. The empty nest: Psychosocial aspects of conflict between depressed women and their grown children. *American Journal of Psychiatry,* 1966, 122, 1422-1426.

DUBE, K. C. & KUMAR, N. An epidemiologic study of manic-depressive psychosis. *Acta Psychiatrica Scandinavica,* 1973, 49, 691-697.

DUPONT, A., VIDEBECH, T., & WEEKE, A. A cumulative national psychiatric register: Its structure and application. *Acta Psychiatrica Scandinavica,* 1974, 50, 161-173.

DUVALL, H. J., KRAMER, M., & LOCKE, B. Z. Psychoneuroses among first admissions to psychiatric facilities in Ohio, 1958-1961. *Community Mental Health Journal,* 1966, 2 (3), 237-243.

EDWARDS, J. E. & WHITLOCK, F. A. Suicide and attempted suicide in Brisbane: I. *Medical Journal of Australia,* 1968, 1, 932-938.

ELLIS, G. G., COMISH, K. A., & HEWER, R. L. Attempted suicide in Leicester. *Practitioner,* 1966, 196, 557-561.

ENGEL, G. Is grief a disease? *Psychosomatic Medicine,* 1961, 23, 18-22.

ESSEN-MOLLER, E. & HAGNELL, O. The frequency and risk of depression within a rural population in Scania. *Acta Psychiatrica Scandinavica (Suppl.),* 1961, 162, 28-32.

FREEMAN, J. W., RYAN, C. A., & BEATTIE, R. R. Epidemiology of drug overdosage in Southern Tasmania. *Medical Journal of Australia,* 1970, 57, 1168-1172.

FRIEDMAN, R. C., RICHART, R. M., & VANDE WIELE, R. L. (Eds.). *Sex Differences in Behavior.* New York: J. Wiley & Sons, 1975.

GARDNER, E. A., BAHN, A. K., MILES, H. C., et al. All psychiatric experience in a community. *Archives of General Psychiatry,* 1963, 9, 365-378.

GERSHON, E. S., BUNNEY, W. E., LECKMAN, J. F., et al. The inheritance of affective disorders: A review of data and of hypotheses. *Behavioral Genetics,* in press.

GERSHON, E. S., DUNNER, D. L., and GOODWIN, F. K. Toward a biology of affective disorders. *Archives of General Psychiatry,* 1971, 25, 1-15.

GERSHON, E. S. & LIEBOWITZ, J. H. Sociocultural and demographic correlates of affective disorders in Jerusalem. *Journal of Psychiatric Research,* 1975, 12, 37-50.

GOETZL, U., GREEN, R., WHYBROW, P., et al. X linkage revisited. *Archives of General Psychiatry,* 1974, 31, 665-672.

GOLD, N. Attempted suicide with chlorpromazine. *Medical Journal of Australia,* 1966, 1, 492-493.

GOMBERG, E. S. Women and alcoholism. In V. Franks and V. Burtle (Eds.), *Women in Therapy.* New York: Brunner/Mazel, 1974.

GOODWIN, F. K. & EBERT, M. H. Lithium in mania: Clinical trials and controlled studies. In S. Gershon and B. Shopsin (Eds.), *Lithium: Its Role in Psychiatric Research and Treatment.* New York: Plenum Press, 1973.

GORDON, R. & GORDON, K. Social factors in the prediction and treatment of emotional disorders of pregnancy. *American Journal of Obstetrics and Gynecology,* 1959, 77, 1074-1083.

GOVE, W. R. The relationship between sex roles, marital status, and mental illness. *Social Forces,* 1972, 51, 34-44.

GOVE, W. R. Sex, marital status, and mortality. *American Journal of Sociology,* 1973, 79, 45-67.

GOVE, W. R. & LESTER, B. J. Social position and self-evaluation: A reanalysis of the Yancy, Rigsby, and McCarthy data. *American Journal of Sociology,* 1974, 79, 1308-1314.

GOVE, W. R. & TUDOR, J. F. Adult sex roles and mental illness. *American Journal of Sociology,* 1973, 78, 812-835.

GREWEL, F. Psychiatric differences in Ashkenazim and Sephardim. *Psychiat. Neurol. Neurochir.,* 1967, 70, 339-347.

HALLSTROM, T. *Mental Disorder and Sexuality in the Climacteric.* Goteberg, Sweden: Orstadius Biktryckeri AB, 1973.

HAMBURG, D. A. Emotions in the perspective of human evolution. In P. H. Knapp (Ed.), *Expression of Emotions in Man.* New York: International Universities Press, 1963.

HELZER, J. E. & WINOKUR, G. A family interview study of male manic depressives. *Archives of General Psychiatry,* 1974, 31, 73-77.

HERSHON, H. I. Attempted suicide in a largely rural area during an eight year period. *British Journal of Psychiatry,* 1968, 114, 279-284.

HETZEL, B. S. The epidemiology of suicidal behavior in Australia. *Australia and New Zealand Journal of Psychiatry,* 1971, 5, 156-166.

HINKLE, L. E., REDMONT, R., PLUMMER, N., et al. II. An explanation of the relation between symptoms, disability, and serious illness in two homogeneous groups of men and women. *Women in Industry,* 1960, 50, 1327-1336.

HIRSH, J., ZAUDER, H. L., & DROLETTE, B. M. Suicide attempts with ingestants. *Archives of Environmental Health,* 1961, 3, 94-98.

HOGARTY, G. E. & KATZ, M. M. Norms of adjustment and social behavior. *Archives of General Psychiatry,* 1971, 25, 470-480.

HOLMES, T. H. & RAHE, R. H. The social readjustment rating scale. *Journal of Psychosomatic Research,* 1967, 11, 213-218.

HORNER, M. Towards an understanding of achievement related conflicts in women. *Journal of Social Issues,* 1972, 28, 157-175.

HOROWITZ, M. New directions in epidemiology. Review of books by E. Gunderson, R. H. Rahe; and by B. S. Dohrenwend, B. R. Dohrenwend. *Science,* 1975, 188, 850-851.

HUDGENS, R., deCASTRO, M. I., & deZUNIGA, E. A. Psychiatric illness in a developing country. A clinical study. *American Journal of Psychiatry,* 1970, 60, 1788-1805.

IANZITO, B. M. Attempted suicide by drug ingestion. *Diseases of the Nervous System,* 1970, 31, 453-458.

JACOBSON, S. & TRIBE, P. Deliberate self-injury (attempted suicide) in patients admitted to hospital in Mid-Sussex. *British Journal of Psychiatry,* 1972, 121, 379-386.

JAMES, I. P., DERHAM, S. P., & SCOTT-ORR, D. N. Attempted suicide: A study of 100 patients referred to a general hospital. *Medical Journal of Australia,* 1963, 1, 375-380.

JUEL-NIELSON, N., BILLE, M., FLYGENRING, J., et al. Frequency of depressive states within geographically delimited population groups. *Acta Psychiatrica Scandinavica,* 1961, 162, 69-80.

JUEL-NIELSON, N. & STROMGREN, E. A five-year survey of a psychiatric service in a geographically delimited rural population given easy access to this service. *Comprehensive Psychiatry,* 1965, 6, 139-165.

KATZ, M. M. The classification of depression: Normal, clinical and ethnocultural. In R. R. Fieve (Ed.), *Depression in the 70s.* The Hague: Excerpta Medica, 1971.

KELLER, S. The female role: Constants and change. In V. Franks and V. Burtle (Eds.), *Women in Therapy.* New York: Brunner/Mazel, 1974.

KIDD, K. K., REICH, T., & KESSLER, S. A genetic analysis of stuttering suggesting a single major locus. *Genetics,* 1973, 74 (2, pt. 2), s137 (Abstract).

KIDD, K. K., REICH, T., & KESSLER, S. Sex effect and single gene: The relevance of sex effect in discriminating between genetic hypotheses. Unpublished manuscript, 1974.

KIELHOLZ, P. Drug treatment of depressive states. *Canadian Psychiatric Association Journal,* 1959, 4, S129-137.

KIRSH, B. Consciousness-raising groups as therapy for women. In V. Franks and P. Burtle (Eds.), *Women in Therapy.* New York: Brunner/Mazel, 1974.

KLERMAN, G. L. Depression and adaptation. In R. Friedman and M. Katz (Eds.), *The Psychology of Depression: Contemporary Theory and Research.* Washington, D. C.: V. H. Winston & Sons, 1974.

KLERMAN, G. L. & BARRETT, J. E. The affective disorders: Clinical and epidemiological aspects. In S. Gershon and B. Shopsin (Eds.), *Lithium: Its Role in Psychiatric Research and Treatment.* New York-London: Plenum Press, 1973.

KLERMAN, G. & IZEN, J. The effects of grief and bereavement on physical health and general well being. In F. Reicksman (Ed.), *Advances in Psychosomatic Medicine.* Basel, Switzerland: S. Karger, in press.

KRAMER, M. Cross-national study of diagnosis of the mental disorders: Origin of the problem. *American Journal of Psychiatry,* 1969, 125 (Suppl. 10), 1-11.

KRUPINSKI, J., STOLLER, A., & POLKE, P. Attempted suicides admitted to the mental health department, Victoria, Australia: A sociodemiological study. *International Journal of Social Psychiatry,* 1966, 13, 5-13.

LEHMANN, H. E. The epidemiology of depressive disorders. In R. R. Fieve (Ed.), *Depression in the 70s.* The Hague: Excerpta Medica, 1971.

LILIENFELD, A., PEDERSEN, E., & DOWD, J. E. *Cancer Epidemiology: Methods of Study.* Baltimore, Md.: Johns Hopkins Press, 1967.

LINDEMANN, E. The symptomatology and management of acute grief. *American Journal of Psychiatry,* 1944, 101, 141-148.

LEONHARD, K. *Aufteilung der Endogenen Psychosen.* First Edition. Berlin: Akademie-verlag, 1957.

LEONHARD, K., KORFF, I., & SCHULZ, H. Die temperamente in den familien der monopolaren und bipolaren phasischen psychosen. *Psychiatric Neurology,* 1962, 143, 416-434.

MACCOBY, E. E. & JACKLIN, C. N. *Psychology of Sex Differences.* Palo Alto, Cal.: Stanford University Press, 1975.

MARTIN, F. F., BROTHERSTON, J. H. F., & CHAVE, S. P. W. *British Journal of Preventive Social Medicine,* 1957, 11, 196-202.

MAYFIELD, D. G. Psychopharmacology of alcohol: I. Affective change with intoxication, drinking, behavior and and affective state. *Journal of Nervous and Mental Diseases,* 1968, 146, 314-321.

MAYFIELD, D. G. & COLEMAN, L. L. Alcohol use and affective disorder. *Diseases of the Nervous System,* 1968, 29, 467-474.

MAZER, M. People in predicament: A study in psychiatric and psychosocial epidemiology. *Social Psychiatry,* 1974, 9, 85-90.

McKINLAY, S. M. & JEFFREYS, M. The menopausal syndrome. *British Journal of Preventive Social Medicine,* 1974, 28, 108-115.

MENAKER, E. The therapy of women in the light of psychoanalytic theory and the emergence of a new view. In V. Franks and V. Burtle (Eds.), *Women in Therapy.* New York: Brunner/Mazel, 1974.

MILLER, S. I. & SCHOENFELD, L. S. Suicide attempt patterns among the Navajo Indians. *International Journal of Social Psychiatry,* 1971, 17, 180-193.

MILLET, K. *Sexual Politics.* New York: Doubleday & Co., 1970.

MODAN, B., NISSENKORN, I., & LEWKOWSKI, S. R. Comparative epidemiologic aspects of suicide and attempted suicide in Israel. *American Journal of Epidemiology,* 1970, 91, 393-399.

NEU, C. & DiMASCIO, A. Variations in the menstrual cycle. *Medical Aspects of Human Sexuality,* February, 1974, 164-180.

NEUGARTEN, B. *Middle Age and Aging.* Chicago: University of Chicago Press, 1968.

ODEGAARD, O. The epidemiology of depressive psychoses. *Acta Psychiatrica Scandinavica,* 1961, 162, 33-38.

OLIVER, R. G., et al. The epidemiology of attempted suicide as seen in the casualty department, Alfred Hospital, Melbourne. *Medical Journal of Australia,* 1971, 1, 833-839.

OVERALL, J. E., BROWN, D., WILLIAMS, J. D., et al. Drug treatment of anxiety and depression in detoxified alcoholic patients. *Archives of General Psychiatry,* 1973, 29, 218-221.

PAFFENBERGER, R. S. & McCABE, L. J. The effect of obstetric and perinatal events on risk of mental illness in women of childbearing age. *American Journal of Public Health,* 1966, 56, 400-407.

PARKIN, D. & STENGEL, E. Incidence of suicidal attempts in an urban community. *British Medical Journal,* 1965, 2, 133-138.

PARRY, H. J., BALTER, M. B., MELLINGER, G. D., et al. National patterns of psychotherapeutic drug use. *Archives of General Psychiatry,* 1973, 28, 769-783.

PATEL, A. R., ROY, M., & WILSON, G. M. Self-poisoning and alcohol. *Lancet,* 1972, 2, 1099-1102.

PAYKEL, E. S. & DIENELT, M. N. Suicide attempts following acute depression. *Journal of Nervous and Mental Diseases,* 1971, 153, 234-243.

PAYKEL, E. S., MYERS, J. K., DIENELT, M. N., et al. Life events and depression: A controlled study. *Archives of General Psychiatry,* 1969, 21, 753-760.

PAYKEL, E. S., MYERS, J. K., LINDENTHAL, J. J., et al. Suicidal feelings in the general population: A prevalence study. *British Journal of Psychiatry,* 1974, 124, 1-10.

PAYKEL, E. S., PRUSOFF, B. A., & UHLENHUTH, E. H. Scaling of life events. *Archives of General Psychiatry,* 1971, 25, 340-347.

PEDERSEN, A. M., BARRY, D. J., & BABIGIAN, H. M. Epidemiological considerations of psychotic depression. *Archives of General Psychiatry,* 1972, 27, 193-197.

PERRIS, C. A study of bipolar (manic-depressive) and unipolar recurrent depressive psychoses. *Acta Psychiatrica Scandinavica,* 1966, 42 (Suppl. 194), 1-89.

PERRIS, C. Abnormality on paternal and maternal sides: Observations in bipolar (manic-depressive) and unipolar depressive psychoses. *British Journal of Psychiatry,* 1971, 118, 207-210.

PUGH, T. F., JERATH, B. K., SCHMIDT, W. M., et al. Rates of mental disease related to childbearing. *New England Journal of Medicine,* 1963, 268, 1224-1228.

RADLOFF, L. Sex differences in depression: The effects of occupation and marital status. *Sex Roles: A Journal of Research,* in press.

RAMSEY, E. R. Boredom: The most prevalent American disease. *Harpers,* 1974, 249, (Nov), 12-22.

REICH, L. H., DAVIES, R. K., & HIMMELHOCH, J. M. Excessive alcohol use in manic-depressive illness. *American Journal of Psychiatry,* 1974, 131, 83-86.

REICH, T., CLAYTON, P., & WINOKUR, G. Family history studies: V. The genetics of mania. *American Journal of Psychiatry,* 1969, 125, 1358-1369.

RICE, D. G. & KEPECS, J. G. Patient sex differences and MMPI changes—1958 to 1969. *Archives of General Psychiatry,* 1970, 23, 185-192.

RIN, H., SCHOOLER, C., & CAUDILL, W. Symptomatology and hospitalization: Culture, social structure and psychopathology in Taiwan and Japan. *Journal of Nervous and Mental Diseases,* 1973, 157, 296-312.

ROBERTS, J. & HOOPER, D. The natural history of attempted suicide in Bristol. *British Journal of Medical Psychology,* 1969, 42, 303-312.

ROSEN, B. F., BAHN, A. K., & KRAMER, M. Demographic and diagnostic characteristics of psychiatric clinic outpatients in the U.S.A., 1961. *American Journal of Orthopsychiatry,* 1964, 34, 455-468.

ROSEN, G. Social stress and mental disease from the 18th century to the present: Some origins of social psychiatry. *Milbank Memorial Fund Quarterly*, 1959, 37, 5-32.

ROSENBERG, C. Drug maintenance in the outpatient treatment of chronic alcoholism. *Archives of General Psychiatry*, 1974, 30, 373-377.

ROSENTHAL, S. H. Changes in a population of hospitalized patients with affective disorders, 1945-1965. *American Journal of Psychiatry*, 1966, 123 (6), 671-681.

ROSENTHAL, S. H. The involutional depressive syndrome. *American Journal of Psychiatry* (Suppl.), 1968, 124, 21-35.

RUTTER, M. *Maternal Deprivation Reassessed*. Middlesex, England: Penguin Books, 1972.

SARTORIOUS, N. Data provided by the World Health Organization, Geneva, Switzerland. Personal communication, 1975.

SCHWAB, J. Coming in the 70s—An epidemic of depression. *Attitude*, 1970, 1, 2-6.

SCHWAB, J. J., McGINNIS, N. H., & WARHEIT, G. J. Social psychiatric impairment: Racial comparisons. *American Journal of Psychiatry*, 1973, 130, 183-187.

SCHWARTZ, J. & ABRAMOVITZ, S. Value related effects on psychiatric judgment. *Archives of General Psychiatry*, 1975, 32, 1525-1529.

SCLARE, A. B. & HAMILTON, C. M. Attempted suicide in Glasgow. *British Journal of Psychiatry*, 1963, 109, 609-615.

SECUNDA, S., KATZ, M., FRIEDMAN, R., et al. The depressive disorders. U.S. Department of Health, Education and Welfare, Special Report, 1973.

SELIGMAN, M. E. Depression and learned helplessness. In R. J. Friedman and M. M. Katz (Eds.), *The Psychology of Depression: Contemporary Theory and Research*. Washington, D. C.: V. H. Winston, 1974.

SETHI, B. B. Personal communication, Lucknow, India, 1974.

SHADER, R. I. & OHLY, J. I. Premenstrual tension, femininity, and sexual drive. *Medical Aspects of Human Sexuality*, April, 1970, 42-49.

SIESSI, I., CROCETTI, G., & SPIRO, H. Loneliness and dissatisfaction in a blue collar population. *Archives of General Psychiatry*, 1974, 30, 261-265.

SILVERMAN, C. *The Epidemiology of Depression*. Baltimore: The Johns Hopkins Press, 1968.

SLATER, E. & COWIE, V. *The Genetics of Mental Disorders*. Oxford Monographs on Medical Genetics. London: Oxford University Press, 1971.

SMITH, J. S. & DAVISON, K. Changes in the pattern of admissions for attempted suicide in Newcastle-upon-Tyne during the 1960s. *British Medical Journal*, 1971, 4, 412-415.

SOMMER, T. The effect of menstruation on cogintive and perceptual-motor behavior: A review. *Psychosomatic Medicine*, 1973, 35, 515-534.

SORENSON, A. & STROMGREN, E. Frequency of depressive states within geographically delimited population groups. *Acta Psychiatrica Scandinavica*, 1961, 37, 32-68.

STENGEL, E. *Suicide and Attempted Suicide*. Middlesex, England: Penguin Books, 1964.

TARNOWER, S. M. & HUMPHRIES, M. Depression: A recurring, genetic illness more common in females. *Diseases of the Nervous System*, 1969, 30, 601-604.

TEJA, J., AGGARWAL, A. K., & NARANG, R. L. Depression across cultures. *British Journal of Psychiatry*, 1971, 119, 253-260.

THUWE, I. Genetic factors in puerperal psychosis. *British Journal of Psychiatry*, 1974, 125, 378-385.

TONGYONK, J. Depression in Thailand in the perspective of comparative-transcultural psychiatry. *Journal of the Psychiatric Association of Thailand*, 1971, 16, 337-354.

TONKS, C. Premenstrual tension. *British Journal of Hospital Medicine*, 1968. 7. 383-387.

TORREY, E. F. Is schizophrenia universal? An open question. (NIMH). *Schizophrenia Bulletin*, 1973, 7, 53-59.

TYNDEL, M. Psychiatric study of one thousand alcoholic patients. *Canadian Psychiatric Association Journal*, 1974, 19, 21-24.

UHLENHUTH, E. H., LIPMAN, R. S., BALTER, M. B., et al. Symptom intensity and life stress in the city. *Archives of General Psychiatry*, 1974, 31, 759-764.

UHLENHUTH, E. H. & PAYKEL, E. S. Symptom configuration and life events. *Archives of General Psychiatry*, 1973, 28, 744-748. (a)

UHLENHUTH, E. H. & PAYKEL, E. S. Symptom intensity and life events. *Archives of General Psychiatry*, 1973, 28, 473-477. (b)

VENKOBA RAO, A. Attempted suicide (An analysis of 114 medical admissions into the Erskine Hospital, Madurai). *Indian Journal of Psychiatry*, 1965, 7, 253-264.

VENKOBA RAO, A. *Depression in Southern India*. Excerpta Medica International Congress, Series No. 150, 1966, pp. 1882-1885.

VENKOBA RAO, A. A study of depression as prevalent in South India. *Transcultural Psychiatric Research*, 1970, 7, 166-168.

VENKOBA RAO, A. Suicide attempters in Madurai. *Journal of the Indian Medical Association*, 1971, 57, 278-284.

WEEKE, A. B., VIDEBECK, TH., DUPONT, A., et al. The incidence of depressive syndromes in a Danish County. *Acta Psychiatrica Scandinavica*, 1975, 51, 28-41.

WEISSMAN, M. M. The epidemiology of suicide attempts. *Archives of General Psychiatry*, 1974, 30, 737-746.

WEISSMAN, M. M. & PAYKEL, E. S. Moving and depression in women. *Society*, 1972, 9, 24-28.

WEISSMAN, M. M. & PAYKEL, E. S. *The Depressed Woman: A Study of Social Relationships*. Chicago: University of Chicago Press, 1974.

WEISSMAN, M. M., PAYKEL, E. S., FRENCH, N., et al. Suicide attempts in an urban community, 1955 and 1970. *Social Psychiatry*, 1973, 8, 82-91 .

WEISSMAN, M. M., PINCUS, C., & PRUSOFF, B. Symptom patterns in depressed patients and depressed normals. *Journal of Nervous and Mental Diseases*, 1975, 160, 15-23.

WEISSMAN, M. M., PINCUS, C., RADDING, R., et al. The educated housewife: Mild depression and the search for work. *American Journal of Orthopsychiatry*, 1973, 43, 565-573.

WEISSMAN, M. M. & SLABY, A. E. Oral contraceptives and psychiatric disturbance: Evidence from research. *British Journal of Psychiatry*, 1973, 123, 513-518.

WESCHLER, H. Community growth, depressive disorders, and suicide. *American Journal of Sociology*, 1961, 67, 9-16.

WHITEHEAD, P. C., JOHNSON, F. G., & FERRENCE, R. Measuring the incidence of self-injury: Some methodological and design considerations. *American Journal of Orthopsychiatry*, 1973, 43, 142-148.

WINOKUR, G. Family history studies. VIII. "Secondary depression is alive and well, and. . . ." *Diseases of the Nervous System*, 1972, 33, 94-99.

WINOKUR, G. Depression in the menopause. *American Journal of Psychiatry*, 1973, 130, 92-93.

WINOKUR, G. & CLAYTON, P. Family history studies. I. Two types of affective disorders separated according to genetic and clinical factors. In I. J. Wartis (Ed.), *Recent Advances in Biological Psychiatry*. New York: Plenum Press, 1967. (a)

WINOKUR, G. & CLAYTON, P. Family history studies. II. Sex differences and alcoholism in primary affective illness. *British Journal of Psychiatry*, 1967, 113, 973-979. (b)

WINOKUR, G. & CLAYTON, P. Family history studies. IV. Comparison of male and female alcoholics. *Quarterly Journal on the Studies of Alcohol*, 1968, 29, 885-891.

Winokur, G. W., Clayton, P. J., & Reich, T. *Manic Depressive Illness.* St. Louis: C. V. Mosby Co., 1969.

Winston, F. Oral contraceptives, pyridoxine, and depression. *American Journal of Psychiatry,* 1973, 130, 1217-1221.

Wren, J. C., Kline, N. S., Cooper, T. B., et al. Evaluation of lithium therapy in chronic alcoholism. *Clinical Medicine,* 1974, 81, 33-36.

Yalom, I. D., Lunde, T. T., Moos, R. H., et al. Postpartum blues syndrome. *Archives of General Psychiatry,* 1968, 18, 16-27.

Zonana, H., Henisz, J., & Levine, M. Psychiatric emergency service a decade later. *Psychiatric Medicine,* 1973, 4, 273-290.

15

GENDER DIFFERENCES IN PSYCHOPHYSIOLOGICAL ILLNESS

ANNE M. SEIDEN

One might well expect that gender differences would be one of the most prominent considerations in the conceptualization of psychosomatic disorders and that, conversely, psychosomatic disorders would be seen as one of the most promising arenas for the elucidation of gender differences. After all, women and men have bodies which differ in certain important characteristics and differ also in the kinds of stresses to which they are exposed and the behavioral patterns with which they are normatively expected to cope with stress. Yet, surprisingly, recent conceptualizations of psychosomatic illness give little systematic attention to gender differences: They are not mentioned in a recent overview article for psychiatrists (Lipowski, 1977) and a major two-volume collection of papers on "society, stress, and disease" does not even index sex differences (Levi-Lennart, 1975). This is in marked contrast to the popular stereotypic view that women often go to physicians for non-serious psychogenic complaints, whereas men avoid physicians but suffer from serious, often fatal illnesses such as cardiovascular disease, which are thought to have major psychophysiologic components.

Before examining some of the reasons for these differences between popular conceptions of psychosomatic illness and recent systematic theoretical accounts, it will be useful to look at some basic concepts in psychosomatic theory and some of the history of that theory. We will then examine some of the existing data on gender differences in illnesses which are thought to be psychosomatic and some of the differences in "illness behavior" between the genders. Finally, we will look at some of the implications of these data and concepts for attempts to increase the general health and well-being of both men and women.

426

CONCEPTS AND CLASSIFICATION IN PSYCHOSOMATIC ILLNESS

In classical psychoanalytic theory there was no hard and fast separation between psychosomatic and psychological symptoms (Freud, 1926). "Energy" was seen as flowing freely into behavior or being damned up or diverted by the various defenses and, when diverted, taking alternative routes through behavioral or somatic discharge.

Similarly, in behavior therapy behaviors are generally seen as conditionable or as changing in frequency after appropriate reinforcement, whether the behavior in question appears to be a psychosomatic symptom or a more purely behavioral one (LeBow, 1975).

However, clinical medicine tends to make a sharp theoretical distinction (in practice it is more elusive) between those illnesses having a somatic etiology—implying a somatic treatment—and those which mimic these but result from social or psychological stress. Since Koch's postulates were accepted, illnesses more or less caused by tissue trauma, such as infections and injuries, became the classical models of disease. Closely related to these has been the recognition of illnesses which are initiated by tissue trauma, but in which the main manifestations of the disease are not the direct results of trauma but rather the body's acute or chronic response set in motion by the trauma. Examples of this kind of illness include the allergic disorders, presumably the collagen disorders, and probably many, if not most, of the malignant disorders.

"Psychosomatic" symptoms in principle could bear several kinds of relationships to these classical "medical" illnesses:

1. Psychosocial factors could be involved in vulnerability to, or proneness to receiving tissue trauma (as in accident proneness, risk-taking behavior, patterns of sexaul behavior increasing the probability of exposure to venereal disease, poor nutritional patterns reducing the resistance to infectious disease, and the like).

2. Psychosomatic factors could be involved in the body's responses to tissue trauma or other stress (Selye, 1966), thus perhaps making one person less resistant than another to the development of allergic, malignant, or chronic inflammatory disease.

3. Personality factors might obviously be involved in the *psychological* response to physical illness or trauma: All persons do not necessarily respond to similar kinds or magnitude of stress in the same way. This perhaps more properly terms "somatopsychic" than "psychosomatic" illness, but in practice, the same clinicians are often called upon to treat both kinds of interrelated problems, in the same settings.

4. Psychosocial factors are obviously involved in the generation of factitious disease—whether "unconsciously" mediated as in the so-called "conversion reactions," "secondary gain phenomena," and the like—or more obviously factitious as in the case of suicide, homicide, child abuse, sub-lethal self-inflicted injury, and direct attempts to cause or mimic illness.

5. Psychological factors are obviously involved in the extent to which one's "illness behavior" in response to physical illness is appropriate and adaptive in limiting the extent of the disease as opposed to making it worse.

6. There are of course the classical "stress disorders" in which the illness itself is seen as an exaggeration of, or a result of, the chronic presence of some variant of the classical physiological preparation for "fight or flight."

7. Psychological factors at times determine the amount of stressful circumstance an individual seeks in life. Some individuals seek challenges, regardless of stress; others avoid stress at all costs.

8. Finally, there is always the residual category of disease with "no organic causes found," where the presence of illness leads to the assumption that there might be a psychological cause, for lack of finding an acceptable organic one.

In summarizing these eight patterns of psychosomatic relationship, one is immediately struck by the ways in which biological sex differences and social gender differences enter at every point. For example: risk-taking behavior is clearly gender-linked in many of its manifestations—as evidenced by higher rates for automobile insurance for young men. Vulnerability or resistance to certain chronic illnesses is clearly linked to both gender and psychology—as, for example, prostate cancer, whose spread is clearly linked to testosterone levels which are themselves highly sensitive to sexual behavior and even to sexual anticipations (Rose, Gordon, & Bernstein, 1972). In terms of psychological responses to illness, depression and help-seeking behavior have long been regarded as sex-linked, with women more prone to seek treatment both for depression and anxiety and for somatic complaints. "Conversion reaction" or old-fashioned hysteria was so clearly regarded as gender-linked that a female anatomic name was given to the syndrome.

POSSIBLE PSYCHOSOMATIC MECHANISMS

Classically, two basic mechanisms have been proposed for psychosomatic illness. Conversion symptoms (classical "hysteria"; see Chapter

14) are those in which the somatic symptom has some symbolic meaning: The body is used "intentionally" to express an important idea, although the intentionality might be outside the scope of awareness. Hysterical blindness prevents seeing something unwelcome; hysterical paralysis prevents carrying out some action which is unacceptable, or hysterical convulsions mimic sexual behaviors, actions which are unacceptable in their direct form, and so on. The "voluntary" or skeletal muscle system is involved.

By contrast, psychophysiological symptoms are supposed to be unsymbolically mediated by the autonomic nervous system. Anger which is recognized or unrecognized seems to raise the blood pressure, quickens (or inhibits) respiration and heart beat, contracts and empties the gut, and so on (Cannon, 1929). But the unrecognized emotion is less likely to be carried on into effective action which solves the problem. The body is prepared for a fight or flight which never happens, and because it never happens, the preparation may continue longer. These responses may be conditioned to new stimuli, as in classical Pavlovian conditioning, but in principle they serve no useful function for the behaving organism. They might have, had fight or flight been useful in the situation, but then we would not be speaking of an illness.

In this sense, conversion reactions are diseases of *expression*, albeit an expression which is distorted by a prior repression of knowledge of what the conflict is all about. In the same sense, psychophysiological symptoms proper are diseases of *reaction*.

In terms of their social context, psychosomatic disorders can be classified in several other ways. Sometimes they are diseases of social adaptation; sometimes diseases of social maladaptation (Kellam, Brareh, Agrawal, & Ensminger, 1975). For example, the classical hysterical symptoms were those of *over-adaptation*: Proper social behavior dictated repression of emotions such as anger or sexual feelings, and the denied affect was veiwed as returning in the form of the symptom; classically the symptom is a "compromise formation" which expresses both the affect and the barrier against it. By contrast, most psychophysiological complaints (and some behavior problems) are disorders of *maladaption*. The individual who is not performing a social role as adequately as she/he would like to suffers added stresses—fear of failure, fear of criticism, fear of ostracism. The body responds with the same autonomic discharge which follows more concrete threats—the classical "fight or flight" response (usually with inhibition of its motor components). Thus, there is a rough, but by no means one-to-one, correlation between disorders of adaptation and conversion symptoms on the one hand, and disorders of maladaption and psychophysiological responses on the other. Women in cultural circumstances which dictated greater denial of sexual or aggressive feelings would understandably be expected to be more prone than men to conversion reactions. Both sexes might be expected to have psychophysiological symptoms since either sex may be placed in situations which elicit the "fight or flight" response.

A third conceptualization, differing only somewhat from the first two, is seen in the extensive literature on scaling of life crises. Life events require an adaptation; the magnitude of the adaption varies with the event. It turns out that in general these magnitudes can be scaled despite the obvious objection that they may "mean" different things to different people symbolically. Thus the birth or death or severe illness of a family member is a major adaptive demand (whether mourned or welcomed) whereas receiving a traffic ticket is a minor adaptive demand. Empirically it is observed that (a) the magnitude of these demands can be scaled across persons and across cultures, and (b) persons having a large number of such demands within any given year are at higher risk of developing a subsequent illness. However, (a) the nature of the illness varies with individuals, and (b) there appear to be individuals who are exceptions in terms of having higher tolerance to large amounts of life stress. These individuals have some distinctive characteristics which will be discussed more fully below. A final observation is that there appear to be levels of optimal adaptive demand: The literature on sensory deprivation (more properly deprivation of sensory variation) demonstrates a tendency for psychological disorganization in the absence of sufficient novelty.

In Rahe's review (1975) of epidemiological studies of life change and illness, recent experiences of life change were correlated with subsequent illness; statistically significant but usually low-order correlations have been found in a number of other studies (Hawkins, Davies, & Holmes, 1957; Holmes & Rahe, 1967; Rahe & Holmes, 1965; Rahe, 1969; Rahe & Arthur, 1968; Rahe, McKean, & Arthur, 1967; Rahe, Mahan, & Arthur, 1970; Rahe, Biersner, Ryman, & Arthur, 1972). These scales were first constructed in the early 1950s in reference to the study of tuberculosis (Hawkins et al., 1957). Five major categories are generally used: health, work, home and family, personal-social, and financial events.

It is immediately apparent that all of these conceptualizations assume some kind of relationship between "mind" and "body," with "emotion" usually playing a central or mediating role; also, all have both mental and somatic aspects. Often the nature of these relationships are not spelled out. Aristotle's (1907) theory of emotion was that events caused feelings, which in turn caused behaviors (including those behaviors which come to be called symptoms). This framework corresponds closely to a naive phenomenological perception and has been the usual conceptualization in Western thought, being highly elaborated in both Thomistic (Arnold, 1960) and psychoanalytic systems (Freud, 1933). Something happens; it "makes" me sad; therefore I cry. And, if suitably predisposed, I may inhibit or displace my tears, and I may develop psychosomatic symptoms as part of an expressed (or more likely denied) grief reaction. If gender differences affect the probability of denial, they may affect the probability of symptoms, but this is not a very serious or interesting theoretical problem: The therapy would consist of overcoming the denial regardless of the patient's gender.

In contrast, the James-Lange theory of emotion (Cannon, 1927; Mandler, 1976) holds that the affect (subjective part of the emotion) *results* from a physical part of the emotion rather than causing it. Something happens; I cry; I recognize my crying and *then* feel sad. My bodily reactions to the situation precede rather than follow my subjective affective experience.

The Aristotelian theory is obviously compatible with Cartesian dualism. It has the advantage of more often feeling phenomenologically correct—at least to post-Cartesian Westerners!—but falls short at the interfaces. It is never clear just how emotion leaps across the gap from psyche to soma and, therefore, it is unclear how an affect which is unfelt could exist or cause disease.

The James-Lange theory seems to reverse the order of phenomenologically experienced reality, but in its more sophisticated versions is more compatible with attempts to bring modern knowledge of neurochemistry to bear on psychophysiological illness. Events impinge on the organism, are perceived, and stimulate greater activity in certain neural circuits, which then may or may not lead to bodily and/or behavioral change. Somewhere along the line there may occur the subjective experience of an affect, but this does not pose a major mind-body problem greater than that posed by any perceptual process. Affect is viewed as representing a sort of interoception, in principle not different from the appreciation of pain or any other sensation. Tissue trauma—say a pin-prick—ordinarily elicits a series of response, including increased autonomic activity (heart rate and galvanic skin response) and a quick reflex or voluntary withdrawal of the pricked extremity. Whether these responses would occur in the absence of subjective pain would depend on at what level the subjective perception was blocked. Local or general anesthesia would abolish both responses; habituation to the pin-prick might diminish them without eliminating them; a voluntary decision not to flinch might abolish the behavioral but not the autonomic components, and so on.

Similarly, a "decision" to be stoic in the face of bereavement (whether consciously acknowledged or not) might abolish the behavioral but not the autonomic components of grief. No major theoretical problems are posed by this, only a practical question of working out the mechanisms by which the usual responses are inhibited at varying levels. The affect is viewed as the interoceptive recognition that a loss has occurred. The threshold for making such a recognition might be high or low, depending on factors which in principle can also be studied both neurochemically and behaviorally. Increased affective lability as well as inhibited affect can be easily handled by this theory. Thus, a person might be more irritable (i.e. have a lower threshold for subjective and behavioral manifestations of anger) at a time when there are already higher levels of those neurotransmitters which mediate fight responses. This would be equally true, regardless of whether the higher neurotransmitter level resulted from prior stimuli of the same sort (i.e. the additive effect of life change units) or from quite different sources such as circulating levels of sex hormones (Sachar, 1975).

Since affect in this theory is regarded as a basically perceptual response rather than a separate category of mental event, it can be studied in the same way that other perceptions can, i.e. by the classical methods of psychophysics. An elaboration of classical psychophysics, signal detection theory, holds that reinforcement conditions systematically affect the detection and reporting of ambiguous percepts; this would be as true for affects as for pain or for differences between weights (McNicol, 1972).

But if there were systematic gender differences in the reinforcement conditions for detecting and reporting various affects, one would expect corresponding differences in their expression and in related behaviors. Meanwhile, the neurochemical response to the stimulus continues unabated. The "denied" affect is more likely to be associated with greater autonomic responses than the recognized affect, not because the affect is a fluid which if blocked takes another channel (the leap from mind to body), but rather because the individual who denies the affect thereby does not use that information to detect and remedy a noxious situation.

The implication for this model, with respect to gender differences in psychophysiological symptoms, is very different from that of the Aristotelian and psychoanalytic ones. In the earlier model, therapy occurs by helping the patient remove the denial so that the affect can take its "natural" course; gender does not affect the treatment in its essential conceptualization. But in this model gender might affect treatment in two ways: (a) Real differences between the sexes, in sex hormone levels, might affect the levels of certain neurotransmitters and therefore the thresholds for various affects and their related behaviors. (b) Different gender-role socialization might materially affect the reinforcement conditions for detection and expression of affect and performance of related behaviors.

Recognizing these factors, the therapy might in principle be quite different for individuals of the two sexes, since the therapist in general does not control all of the reinforcers which would be relevant. Furthermore, training an individual to run counter to her/his prior gender-role socialization is in principle different from training to enhance it. The therapist undertaking such a treatment contract—as well as the patient doing so with fully informed consent—would need to consider such potentially loaded issues as possibly having to abandon certain familiar sources of reinforcement in favor of potential other ones whose reliability and availability are unknown. The possible role of both therapists' and patients' values in prioritizing kinds and sources of reinforcement becomes explicit in ways that the earlier model does not foresee. The earlier metaphor, which held that the therapist was merely helping remove blocks from a clogged channel, made the task appear to be a technical one which was more or less value-neutral (but, see Bart, 1971). The latter model cannot make such an assumption.

GENDER DIFFERENCES IN PSYCHOSOMATIC DISORDERS:
THEORETICAL ASPECTS

Epidemiologists make a distinction between the incidence and prevalence of disorders. Operationally, incidence is usually expressed as the number of new cases diagnosed per year, while prevalence is expressed as the number of all cases, new or old, currently carrying the diagnosis in question. The concept of "true" incidence or prevalence refers to the hypothetical number of persons in the population who "actually" have the condition, regardless of whether they have been diagnosed. Except for conditions which are rampantly overdiagnosed, the "true" incidence and prevalence are always larger than the operational incidence and prevalence, sometimes by a very large margin if there is a low frequency of help-seeking for the particular illness in question. Obviously, an illness of high incidence and short duration (as in the nearly universal childhood infectious diseases) may have a low prevalence in the population, while a disorder of great chronicity may come to be prevalent even though the incidence is low. And a disorder which quickly kills all or most of its victims cannot have a high prevalence at all—thus successful suicide is a condition which by definition has incidence but no prevalence, since there are no live victims.

In principle, gender differences in the operationally defined *incidence* of illness could arise in at least the following ways:

1. *Intrinsic anatomical differences.* Only women could suffer a psychogenic interruption of labor, because only women give birth. And while male lactation exists in some disease states and as an exotic curiosity, in general only women would be seen as having a psychogenic inhibition of lactation. Only men could suffer a psychogenic inhibition or acceleration of ejaculation. Only women could experience a psychogenic amenorrhea, dysmenorrhea, or menorrhagia.

2. *Different vulnerability to illness on the basis of sex-hormone differences.* Thus, for example, if estrogens exert a protective effect against heart disease, premenopausal women would be less vulnerable even though suffering similar stresses which otherwise increase risk. If female hormones increase vulnerability to depression, women would be more likely than men to have it (and, indeed, there is an excess prevalence of depression among women, particularly in child-bearing years) Weissman & Klerman, 1977).

3. *Sex-linked genes.* If psychosomatic factors, for example, are important in modifying or exacerbating the course of a sex-linked disease such as hemophilia, these will obviously only affect the largely male population having hemophilia. If one kind of depression is related to sex-linked dominant genes, women would have more chance than men of suffering from it.

4. *Social gender roles in relationship to stresses and risk factors.* If certain personality types or persistent behaviors are associated with greater vulnerability to certain kinds of psychogenic illness and the behavioral or personality factors in question are gender-linked, one would find an impact on the epidemiology of the illness in question. For example, one would expect more males to have coronary thrombosis, *if* the risk of that illness is associated with fast-paced competitive work and cigarette smoking and *if* these behaviors are more characteristic of males.

5. *Social gender roles in relationship to "illness behavior."* Sex-stereotyped patterns of response to identified or suspected symptoms may affect

the course of an illness. Thus, if seeing doctors is associated with other help-seeking behaviors which are traditionally female and is seen as antagonistic to the male role, more women will see more doctors earlier in the course of illnesses. This would tend to be beneficial for those illnesses which are helped by early detection and harmful for those illnesses where iatrogenic complications outweigh medical benefits of treatment.

If "cutting back" and "taking it easy" are beneficial responses to a stress overload, and if these patterns are more acceptable for women, one might expect women in general to suffer less stress-induced disease.

6. *Exaggerations and distortions of stereotypic gender roles.* Persons with anxieties about gender identity or adequacy of gender role performance may engage in high-risk behaviors to "prove something," thus increasing risks of illnesses or trauma.

Thus, male expectations of "courage" may lead to accident-proneness; male expectations of "sexual prowess" might lead to increased risk of venereal disease. Attempts to "prove femininity" by increased sexual behavior would lead to increased exposure to the medical risks of contraceptives, pregnancies, and/or abortions, as well as venereal disease.

7. *Inappropriate diagnosis of psychosomatic disorders.* If there are more poorly understood conditions affecting women, and there is a tendency to use psychogenic explanations for any illness which is poorly understood, then one would expect to see more diagnoses of psychogenic disorders in women. Indeed, for a variety of reasons conditions affecting women may be poorly understood by individual physicians. Lenane and Lenane (1973) pointed out the extent to which a number of common conditions affecting women, particularly in their reproductive functions, such as dysmenorrhea, labor pain, postpartum depression, and colic in infants, are commonly attributed almost entirely to psychological difficulties on the woman's part.

Large scale studies of psychiatric epidemiology, as, for example, reviewed by the Dohrenwends (Dohrenwend & Dohrenwend, 1974) almost invariably show a higher prevalence of diagnosis of "neurosis" in women and "personality disorder" in men. If the patient who is perceived as neurotic also has undiagnosed somatic symptoms, the *post hoc* fallacy would lead to an excess diagnosis of psychosomatic conditions in women, even when the somatic symptoms actually bear no relationship to the neurotic ones.

Besides differences in *incidence* of psychosomatic disorders, gender may contribute to added differences in *prevalence*. For example:

1. The same illness may have different manifestations in the male and female, for either biological or social reasons. Thus, for example, the same somatic infection, gonorrhea, has the same behavioral beginning for both genders—intercourse with an infected person. But the male is more likely to have such a painful urethritis that he is driven to seek help, while a higher proportion of women have "silent" infections. And similarly, for example, alcoholism might be associated with conspicuous aggressive behavior and inability to hold a job in males, but with much quieter and less conspicuous drinking behaviors and others behaviors in women. Fewer women would thus be diagnosed as alcoholic, even if they drank as much as men. Those writers who regard alcoholism as a "depressive equivalent" are saying in effect that the social manifestations of the same condition may be so different between the genders as to lead to different naming and failure to recognize that we have the "same disease" in both.

2. The genders may differ in their willingness to seek or avoid help for illness in general, or a specific condition in particular. This has several interesting consequences: For example, if both genders have headaches, but women are more likely to seek treatment, the known prevalence would be more of an underestimate for men than for women. On the other hand, if treatment is effective in curing the condition, the prevalence for women would drop as they got cured, while the "true prevalence" for men would rise as they continued to suffer the illness in silence, unmodified by potentially effective treatment.

3. These very errors in estimating true prevalence might affect the accuracy of diagnosis: If, for example, a disease is thought to be more prevalent in women than in men, that becomes a self-fulfilling prophecy —when in doubt doctors will be likely to overdiagnose this disease in women and underdiagnose it in men. And if psychosomatic disease in general is known or thought to be more common in women than men, then doctors are more likely to diagnose it in women.

4. Prevalence may be affected differentially in the genders if and when there are differential treatment customs for male and female patients, with differing effectiveness. Thus, if outpatient psychotherapy is prescribed (or self-prescribed) more often for women than men, women would be expected to increase the *operational* prevalence, but decrease the *true* prevalence, of those kinds of psychosomatic illnesses which tend to respond to psychotherapy.

Before we move from a theoretical to an empirical consideration of gender differences in the psychosomatic disorders, there are two further areas of methodological concern which we will need to consider:

1. It is extremely hard to determine or estimate the true incidence and prevalence of psychosomatic disorders in the community—much harder than it is to determine prevalence or incidence of a reportable infectious disease like smallpox or measles or even a classical psychiatric illness like depression. At the least, the following considerations confuse the data and its interpretation:

(a) There are major problems of shifting diagnosis in this area—both genuine differences of opinion on the part of sufferers and clinicians and different reinforcement contingencies for shifting the diagnosis one way or the other. Depression with severe headaches may be called "depression" in a psychiatric clinic (that is, entered on the clinic face sheet by the primary psychiatric diagnosis with the somatic symptom not listed, though perhaps mentioned elsewhere in the chart). It may be called "headache" as such in a general medical or neurological clinic (that is, entered on the records by the primary medical diagnosis). The internist may call it "psychogenic headache," "tension headache" etc. if he/she wishes to get rid of the patient, either by referral to psychiatry or simply by discouraging the patient from returning. This is not an uncommon attitude among those physicians who construe the proper high priority use of their time as screening for serious organic illness with potentially treatable and otherwise dangerous outcomes. The patient may strenuously wish to have it defined as "medical" rather than "psychiatric" illness if he/she is ashamed of psychiatric or psychosomatic illness, or has insurance which pays more completely for medical than psychiatric conditions or care, or has a work supervisor who sees the insurance forms and has negative attitudes towards psychosomatic or psychiatric illness.

(b) Surveys of a clinic population may yield data on the number of patients who have varying kinds of symptoms, the proportion of those which have been clinically determined to have major psychogenic determinants, and the like; but of course this sample is biased by help-seeking behaviors and says nothing about the larger population which has not entered that clinic or any clinic for similar symptoms.

(c) However, household surveys, while potentially yielding data on the proportions of patients who have varying kinds of symptoms (if they are willing to report them), often do not help clarify the etiology. The survey field worker is rarely able to determine whether a headache is a symptom of brain tumor or emotional tension, or histamine sensitivity, or undetected allergy, or all the rare and common conditions which have been found to be associated with headache. The study's principal investigators can of course assume that the majority of headaches in the un-treated population result from emotional tension, as do the majority of headaches in the treated population, but in a sense that weakens the argument for adding field studies to clinical ones. The assumption cannot be tested.

(d) Even household surveys, although they eliminate the variable of help-seeking behavior, do not eliminate other aspects of reporting bias. Conditions which are known to have, or popularly assumed to have, major psychological components in their etiology are often ones which people are particularly embarrassed to report—sexual dysfunctions, bowel troubles, menstrual difficulties, presumed tension syndromes—all are conditions about which there are various degrees of reporting taboos.

(2) In any case, getting down to the nitty-gritty of classification of the individual case highlights the extent to which the very concept of psychosomatic disorder is a rough category of convenience rather than a precise diagnostic category. *All* illness is psychosomatic in the sense that feelings emerge around any somatic symptom, may precede it, and may affect its handling or its course. In the treatment of the individual case, the recognition of a somatic component to a depression, say, or of a psychosocial stress factor in headache or belly pain may indeed be an illuminating insight which might tip the balance in favor of effective treatment. But this says nothing at all about which component is "major" in any causative sense. In the classical epidemiological triad of host, agent, and environment, in treating the individual case one is grateful for the discovery of any factor in any one of the three that yields to treatment.

Informally one tends to think of causation in terms of the factors related to the currently most effective treatment, but this is very different at different levels of analysis or treatment and at different times in medical history. Thus, prior to the availability of effective chemotherapy for tuberculosis, treatment heavily depended on providing long-term hospitalization in a setting with adequate nutrition and as little stress as possible. It was known to be a disease "caused" by a bacillus but a then untreatable one. Epidemiology tended to stress the social environment, since tuberculosis was thought of as an infectious disease that was particularly associated with poverty and stress. Today it is more simply thought of as an infectious disease since the available treatments are directed at the bacillus. Was it a psychosomatic disease then and not one now? Should a field survey team, attempting to assess the prevalence of psychosomatic disorders in the community, record those instances in which there was a high contribution from the psychosocial side of things but not others? How would they know, on the basis of any kind of data which, could be economically gathered?

Because of these many factors, the following section on available epidemiological data pertinent to the incidence and prevalence of psychosomatic conditions between the genders will be shorter and more closely tied to sketchily interpreted symptoms than we might wish. It will be difficult to expect that such data will be substantially better in the near future.

GENDER DIFFERENCES IN PSYCHOSOMATIC ILLNESSES: EMPIRICAL STUDIES

With the large number of reservations about methodology and availability of data which have been reviewed above, what findings are in fact reasonably well established?

1. Psychosomatic conditions are widely believed to be quite common among patients receiving medical care for all causes, with estimates in prior studies ranging from 15-50% (Gardner, 1970).

2. Symptoms generally regarded as psychophysiological are extremely common in the population at large, with one representative study finding that more than half of the population (51.6%) reported having at least one such symptom "regularly" while an even greater proportion have them sometimes (Schwab, Fennell, & Warheit, 1974). And 17.3% had two or more of the conditions "regularly." (The symptoms inquired about were headaches, indigestion, constipation, nervous stomach, stomachaches, diarrhea, hypertension, asthma, ulcers, colitis, and weight trouble.)

3. Sex differences in these conditions are quite common. For example, Schwab et al. (1974) found that females were significantly more likely than males to report headaches, constipation, nervous stomach, weight difficulties, or hypertension; males were significantly more likely to report ulcers and asthma. Of those who had two or more psychosomatic conditions regularly, there were significantly more females than males, significantly more blacks than whites, more old than young, more of the poor than the well-off. Not only is there a gender difference in the incidence of specific psychosomatic symptoms, but there is also a general female preponderance in almost all studies, as discussed in Kessel and Munro's review (1964). Pasamanick (1961) found an overall female/male ratio of 3 to 1; Watts (1962) reported a 3 to 2 ratio; however, Leighton, Harding, Macklin, MacMillan, & Leighton (1963) reported a 3 to 3 ratio. Halliday (1967) noted apparent changes in the sex ratios for a variety

of psychosomatic conditions, especially peptic ulcers and thyrotoxicosis, which were becoming more common in males than females, and diabetes, where the reverse was occurring. Halliday, in fact, considered a characteristic sex ratio to be one of his seven defining conditions for a psychosomatic illness.

4. Psychophysiological symptoms are not necessarily regarded by the respondent as evidence of ill health; for example Schwab et al. (1974) found that 25% of those who rated their own physical or mental health as excellent or good reported having two or more of the psychophysical symptoms regularly.

5. Psychophysiological illness does *not* appear to serve as an alternative to directly expressed psychiatric illness, as a naive reading of psychodynamic theory would suggest. Rather, there is a concurrence. People who have a greater number of somatic illnesses, regardless of their nature and etiology, as a group also have a greater number of psychiatric symptoms (Doust, 1952; Hinkle & Wolf, 1957). And conversely, people having a higher number of psychiatric complaints also have a higher number of medical ones (Matarrazzo, Matarrazzo, & Saslow, 1961; Roessler & Greenfield, 1961). Schwab (1971) reported that about 35% of his community sample showed some degree of mental impairment; almost 70% of these reported upper gastrointestinal symptoms and 60% reported headaches (vs. 40% and 25% respectively by those who were adjudged not psychiatrically impaired). In other words, those adjudged psychiatrically ill were about twice as likely as those felt to be psychiatrically well to also have psychophysiological symptoms.

6. The general acceptance of the concept of psychophysiological illness has not resulted either in most physicians in medical specialties being trained in management of the psychological component or in referral of such patients to psychiatrists (Schwab, 1970). Indeed, Schwab found that about 20% of medical patients were referred for psychiatric consultation, but that in the medical patients who were not referred, almost the same proportion displayed sufficient psychopathology to indicate a referral.

7. Patients referred for psychiatric treatment of somatic symptoms who later turn out to have serious unrecognized somatic disease do not show much specificity of relationship between the pyschiatric diagnosis and the type of medical illness later found (Rossman, 1963).

8. In medical practice, physicians and nurses show demographic differences in the correspondence between their ratings of patient's anxiety levels and the patients' own self-ratings (Schwab, Warheit, & McGinnis, 1970). Thus, patients with lower incomes, lower socioeconomic status, and

less education rated themselves as significantly more anxious than higher status patients, while doctors rated middle- and upper-class patients as more anxious, and nurses showed no trend in either direction. Doctors and nurses both rated younger patients as more anxious, though self-ratings showed no age trends. Male doctors rated women patients as being much more anxious than did the nurses. Both doctors and nurses significantly underrated the anxiety levels of black patients.

Thus, in general, the doctors and nurses overrated the anxiety levels of patients with demographic characteristics similar to their own, and consistently underrated the anxiety levels of patients who differed from them—but gender acted in an opposite way from all of the other demographic variables, in that male doctors rated women patients as more anxious than did female nurses (unfortunately, the absence of female doctors and male nurses from the sample prevents separating the effects of sex and occupation).

9. Psychiatric illness itself is quite common, depending on one's cut-off point for diagnosis. For example, Leighton et al. (1963) found that 50% of the sample studied would be cases as defined by the DSM-I, but only 3% had what they felt was a "mandatory" need for psychiatric attention. In the Dohrenwends' review (1974), rates varied from .4 to 69% of the populations interviewed! But the higher rates are not useful for our purposes, since the studies include physical symptoms as part of the definition of psychiatric morbidity.

10. Modes of expressing psychiatric distress vary with cultures, as reviewed by the Dohrenwends (1974). This poses an important problem: Women report psychological distress in terms of somatic symptoms more frequently than men do (and lower-class subjects do so more than middle- and upper-class persons) (Crandell & Dohrenwend, 1967; Hollingshead & Redlich, 1958). But when is this best understood as a different vocabulary of distress as opposed to a differential incidence of an illness? The fact, as noted above, that so many subjects reporting the symptoms did not consider themselves ill makes it clear that the point is not moot.

Repeatedly, writers on epidemiological aspects of psychosomatic illnesses point to reservations about the quality of the data and/or the methodological problems involved in obtaining or interpreting it. The problems of definition often imply problems of philosophy which are sometimes merely implied by these authors and sometimes extensively discussed. For example, one recent paper indicates how epidemiologic research is hampered by the fact that the "same" illness will be charted as, for example, "mucous colitis" in the gastrointestinal clinic and "psychophysiological gastrointestinal disorder" in psychiatry (Looney, Lipp, & Spitzer, 1978). Nonpsychiatric physicians are often criticized by psychiatrists for ignoring psychosomatic aspects of etiology either from prejudice or from habit. It is implied that they regard it as softheaded (thus perhaps 'unmasculine"?) to take social or psychological causality seriously. Undoubtedly, many sources enter into one's philosophy of medical causality and hence diagnosis.

One is inclined to digress a bit here and look at the history of Western medicine. Primitive societies vary considerably in the extent to which medicine is distinguished from religion and, indeed, from the state or tribal governmental authority. Within most ethnomedicines many illnesses are attributed to social and/or supernatural causes (which again may be not clearly differentiated) (Landy, 1976). Thus, these illnesses are viewed as the equivalent of what we would call psychosomatic, though the term as such is not used because one has to differentiate and reify the psyche and the soma in a particular way before it is possible to think of the impact of the "one" on the "other." In actual fact, of course, either the position of monism or of dualism is an abstraction from the facts, and confusing this abstraction with the reality gives rise to a host of the kinds of problems which are dealt with in general semantics theory (Hayakawa, 1972; Korzybski, 1933).

Primitive cultures do distinguish the spirit from the body, using the concept of spirit initially to refer to that which is absent from the body after death. Ideas that the spirit can leave the body in conditions other than death are common in many cultures, appear to have been arrived at independently, and show a number of enduring themes which are probably phenomenologically nearly universal. Thus, the spirit is seen as leaving in sleep, in dreams, in hallucinogenic drug "trips," in madness, and perhaps in a host of other kinds of altered states of consciousness. Related ideas pertinent to the concepts of illness are that one can also be possessed by additional spirits or have one's own spirit replaced by one or more others. And, of course, the spirit may persist after death to affect the lives and health of others. Indeed, much of what we today consider to be primitive medicine consists of practices conceptualized as affecting either the spirit of the sick individual or of those who may be possessing him.

It should be emphasized that "primitive" medicine is so designated from the standpoint of modern medicine, and until recently our own ethnocentrism has led to radical rejection of traditional medical conceptualizations. Actually, there is often a sharp distinction between the acuteness of clinical observation and the theoretical framework within which it is organized. In recent years a number of drugs and practices from "primitive" medical systems have entered modern practice, though often with a different rationale or understanding of mechanism. For example, rauwolfia preparations, widely used in African and Indian medical systems for treatment of psychosis, became the first of the modern major tranquilizers and are still in use for treatment of some cases of hypertension. Ancient psychoactive drugs such as opiates and cannabis are used recreationally or for self-treatment today and have new medical uses as well as the older ones. Social network involvement in therapy, a bulwark of much tribal medicine, is taken with increased seriousness today.

The forerunners of modern Western medicine, as seen in the writings of Hippocrates and Galen, were much more monistic. These writers repeatedly pointed out the essential unity of spirit and body and accounted for both psychological and psychosomatic illness on the basis of "humors," bodily fluids which were more or less predominant in different individuals, affected the heart and brain, and accounted for differences in temperament as well as specific diseases. Treatments such as blood-letting or purging for a variety of what we would today consider physical, mental, or psychosomatic ills were rational derivatives of this theory (and had for most conditions limited effectiveness).

Modern medical philosophy has major philosophical underpinnings in Cartesian dualism. It is only in this framework that the concept of a purely somatic disease has been developed. And it has been developed to such an extent that a writer like Mary Baker Eddy, who radically denies even the existence of somatic illness or evil, can nevertheless allow for medical treatment of a "purely mechanical problem," such as a broken leg (Eddy, 1906).

Cartesian dualism, of course, was developed within a Catholic framework, and it allowed for the separation of soul and body—during the same historical epoch that eventually developed the political doctrine of the separation of church and state. According to this doctrine, illnesses of the soul could be seen as the province of the church, to be treated by exorcism or punishment or penance, and to be prevented by avoidance of sin and proper upbringing to accomplish that. Bodily illness then was to be allowed to be the province of the physician, to be studied and treated in a scientific and morally neutral manner. By giving up in general the sphere of illness of the soul, medicine obtained greater freedom to treat illnesses of the body with less religions interference in practices and conceptualizations.

This freedom has never been complete, and has never been sustained without some fighting. And there have been important areas of exceptions or controversies about both the propriety of the morally neutral physician role and the extent to which this can be carried out. Thus, there continue to be limitations in, for example, the kinds of drugs which physicians can legally prescribe, or the situations in which they may do so, where the public at large suspects that these drugs may be used for "immoral" purposes. Interestingly, the major areas of controversy about the moral neutrality of the physician role (and, therefore, the freedom of the physician to operate untrammeled by church or state) are often particularly within the scope of this paper—psychiatric and psychosomatic illnesses and issues having to do with gender, particularly direct reproductive issues.

Thus it is argued—by psychiatrists as well as other physicians (cf. Szasz, 1974)—that the use of the "medical model" for psychiatric illness is inappropriate, depriving the individual soul of its own responsibility for behavior and "problems of living." Sometimes the degree of personal responsibility which the individual is to carry is an issue of the patient's or therapist's personal philosophy or treatment strategy. But at other times it becomes a major public issue around medico-legal concerns, such as the definition of sanity for purposes of assigning or exempting criminal responsibility. There are similar issues with respect to otherwise relatively minor psychophysiological illnesses. For example, should a worker or student who has an attack of functional but severe gastrointestinal distress with diarrhea—on precisely the days when schools or work demands are heavy—be considered as having a legitimate medical illness, or as handling his/her responsibilities in an ineffective way? What about the patient whose psychophysiological problems are aggravated at times of increased marital conflict? Is the gastroenterologist as responsible for working with the spouse about this, as the gynecologist diagnosing a vaginal infection would be in considering the likelihood that the husband (or a secret other partner) may be the carrier? And even if one feels the gastroenterologist does have this responsibility, how is it to be discharged if medical school and gastroenterology training have not provided the conceptual and therapeutic skills?

It is perhaps not surprising, even if it is viewed as regrettable, that a high proportion of physicians in non-psychiatric specialties have dealt with emotional complexities by taking the classic Dragnet position: "I just want the facts, ma'am." The fear of re-opening the Pandora's box of moral and emotional responsibility, of losing the hard-won freedom of separation of church and medicine, of moral and scientific authority, is considerable. The fact that "scientific neutrality" is a myth, that medical decisions do have moral and emotional consequences whether the physician recognizes them or not, does not remove the fact that this *fiction* of scientific neutrality has been in many other ways beneficial to medicine and to patients. The physician's ethical dilemmas are easier and freedom for action greater whenever it is possible to take the position that "we just treat illness—someone else will have to worry about moral issues." The consequence is that illness itself is conceptualized in a concrete and mechanical way. The body is to be repaired much as the automobile may be repaired—how the driver feels, or what the conditions under which the accident occurred, or the purposes for which the driver intends to use the car are not the province of the skilled mechanic.

A further consequence is that for something to be defined as part of the core responsibility of the physician it must usually be defined or at least treated as an illness, even when the mechanical illness model does not fit the facts very well. Writers and workers in the field of psychosomatic medicine quickly observe that this model becomes a sort of procrustean bed, which, if followed strictly, lops off important aspects of clinical observation and potentially effective treatment. Nowhere is this more evident than in the kinds of issues discussed here. Normal physiological processes —such as sexual functioning, menstruation and menopause, and particularly childbirth—are treated as illnesses, and indeed as mechanical illnesses, in order to bring them within the rubric of medicine. This has been viewed as necessary in order to provide the real benefits which medicine has developed for the pathologies of these conditions which can and do occur and which are the source of much human misery.

There is a major revolution occurring today in the public's attitude towards medicine, supported by the growing strength of consumer movements, the women's health movement, and the increasing public support for national health insurance (the latter brought about precisely because the real benefits conveyed by scientific medicine have come to be seen as valuable enough that they should be available to all). Increased empathy for the patient's emotional feelings is coming to be seen again as part of the humane expectations for good medical care. And increased clinical skills in recognizing, diagnosing, and appropriately handling or treating the psychosocial aspects of the patient's illness are again coming to be seen as part of ordinary good clinical medicine. The movement to increase the number of physicians trained in primary care specialties is part of this, as is the increased sensitivity to the need for some primary care skills for all specialists.

But we cannot expect that the compleat psychophysiologically oriented physician can be easily achieved within the philosophical framework which Western medicine has so far developed. And we cannot expect that the dilemmas which center around the issues of "scientific neutrality" can be easily resolved. There are problems on the alternative side as well. Western medicine may never have achieved its goals of scientific moral neutrality, and should perhaps consider that a guiding fiction rather than something to be fully expected. But as a widely accepted goal, physicians can be held accountable to it. If physicians are found to be, for example, defining sexual behavior of female adolescents as illness, and collaborating with their parents in coercively hospitalizing them for it, they can be held accountable for distorting the definition of illness in what is essentially a moral or political way. This would not be true in a society in which the use of psychiatric diagnosis or hospitalization for political purposes was defined as an acceptable act, rather than a perversion of the process. If physicians are found to be going along with advertising and prescribing Valium for the woman with a master's degree who is unhappy with a housewife role, and developing psychophysiological symptoms under the resultant stresses, they can be and are being called to task for it.

Value-free clinical medicine in general, like value-free psychotherapy, is surely a myth (Bart, 1971). But it has been a guiding mythology which has served its useful purposes. As physicians become more accountable for dealing with the psychosocial realm, they will be dealing with issues about which it is not possible to avoid having ones own values stirred, challenged, and expressed—often in an authoritarian way unless we can learn new ways of handling values within medicine. It is possible to cling to an objectivity about values within the framework of a mechanical medical model—appendicitis is always bad, pneumonia is almost always to be cured (unless perhaps the patient is being maintained on a respirator after loss of cerebral functioning). If the wife's headaches however come from the adjustments she has tried to make to support her husband's career—or to carry out her own while doing a disproportionate amount of the housework—the physician's own evaluation of those adaptations will inevitably be aroused. The old medical ethical issues— not abandoning the patient, not forcing unnecessary treatment for personal gain, not treating the patient without genuine informed consent— difficult as they have been to achieve, may seem simpler by comparison.

REFERENCES

ARISTOTLE. *DeAnima* with translation, introduction, and notes by R. D. Hicks. Cambridge: Cambridge University Press, 1907.

ARNOLD, M. *Emotion and Personality, Vol. 1: Psychological Aspects* and *Vol. 2: Neurological and Physiological Aspects.* New York: Columbia University Press, 1960.

BART, P. The myth of a value-free psychotherapy. In W. Bell & J. Man (Eds.), *The Sociology of the Future.* New York: Russell Sage Foundation, 1971, pp. 113-159.

CANNON, W. B. The James-Lange theory of emotion. *American Journal of Psychology,* 1927, 39, 106-124.

CANNON, W. B. *Bodily Changes in Pain, Hunger, Fear and Rape* (2nd ed.). New York: Appleton-Century, 1929.

CRANDELL, D. L. & DOHRENWEND, B. P. Some relations among psychiatric symptoms, organic illness and social class. *American Journal of Psychiatry,* 1967, 123 (12), 1527-1538.

DOHRENWEND, B. P. & DOHRENWEND, B. S. Social and cultural influences on psychopathology. *Annual Review of Psychology,* 1974, 25, 417-452.

DOUST, J. W. L. Psychiatric aspects of somatic immunity: Differential evidence of physical disease in histories of psychiatric patients. *British Journal of Social Medicine,* 1952, 6, 49-67.

EDDY, M. B. *Science and Health with Key to the Scriptures.* Boston: Trustees under the Will of Mary Baker G. Eddy, 1906.

FREUD, S. Inhibitions, symptoms and anxiety. *Standard Edition,* 20:77 (see especially editor's introduction, pp. 77-86), 1926.

FREUD, S. Anxiety and instinctual life. Lecture 32 in New introductory lectures on psychoanalysis. *Standard Edition,* 1933, 22, 81.

GARDNER, E. Emotional disorders in medical practice. *Annals of Internal Medicine,* 1970, 73 (4), 651.

HALLIDAY, T. L. *Psychosocial Medicine: A Study of the Sick Society.* London: Heinemann, 1963.

HAWKINS, N. G., DAVIES, R., & HOLMES, T. H. Evidence of psychosocial factors in the development of pulmonary tuberculosis. *American Review of Tuberculosis Pulmonary Diseases,* 1957, 75, 5.

HAYAKAWA, S. I. *Language and Thought in Action* (3rd ed.). New York: Harcourt, Brace, Jovanovich, 1972.

HINKLE, L. E. & WOLF, H. G. The nature of man's adaptation to his total environment and the relation of this to illness. *Archives of Internal Medicine,* 1957, 99, 442.

HOLLINGSHEAD, A. B. & REDLICH, F. C. *Social Class and Mental Illness.* New York: John Wiley & Sons, 1958.

HOLMES, T. H. & RAHE, R. H. The social readjustment rating scale. *Journal of Psychosomatic Research,* 1967, 11, 213.

KELLAM, S. G., BRAREH, J. D., AGRAWAL, K. C., & ENSMINGER, M. E. *Mental Health and Going to School.* Chicago: University of Chicago Press, 1975.

KESSEL, N. & MUNRO, A. Epidemiological studies in psychosomatic medicine. *Journal of Psychosomatic Research,* 1964, 8, 67-81.

KORZYBSKI, A. *Science and Sanity: An Introduction to Non-Aristotelian Systems and General Semantics.* New York: International Non-Aristotelian Library Public Co., 1933.

LANDY, D. (Ed.). *Culture, Disease and Healing: Studies in Medical Anthropology.* New York: Macmillan, 1977.

LeBow, M. D. Operant condition-based behavior modification: One approach to treating somatic disorders. *International Journal of Psychiatry in Medicine,* 1975, 6 (1/2), 241-254.

LEIGHTON, D. C., HARDING, J. S., MACKLIN, D. B., MACMILLAN, A. M., & LEIGHTON, A. H. *The Character of Danger: Psychiatric Symptoms in Selected Communities.* New York: Basic Books, 1963.

LENANE, K. J. & LENANE, R. J. Alleged psychogenic disorders in women: A possible manifestation of sexual prejudice. *New England Journal of Medicine,* 1973, (6), 288-292.

LEVI-LENNART, L. *Society, Stress and Disease* (Vols. 1 & 2). London, New York, Toronto: Oxford University Press, 1975.

LIPOWSKI, Z. J. Psychosomatic medicine in the seventies: An overview. *American Journal of Psychiatry,* 1977, 134, 233-244.

LOONEY, J. G., LIPP, M. R., & SPITZER, R. L. A new method of classification for psychophysiological disorders. *American Journal of Psychiatry,* 1978, 135, 304-308.

MANDLER, G. The search for emotion. In L. Levi (Ed.), *Emotions—Their Parameters and Measurements.* New York: Raven Press, 1975.

MATARRAZZO, R. G., MATARRAZZO, J. D., & SASLOW, G. The relationship between medical and psychiatric symptoms. *Journal of Abnormal Social Psychology,* 1961, 62 (1), 55.

McNICOL, D. *A Primer Signal Detection Theory.* London: George Allen & Unwin Ltd., 1972.

PASAMANICK, B. A survey of mental disease in an urban population. V: An approach to total prevalence by diagnosis and sex. *Journal of Nervous and Mental Disorders,* 1961, 133, 519.

RAHE, R. H. Life crisis and health change. In P. R. A. May and J. R. Wittenborn (Eds.), *Psychotropic Drug Responses: Advances in Prediction.* Springfield: Charles C Thomas, 1969.

RAHE, R. H. Epidemiological studies of life change and illness. *International Journal of Psychiatry,* 1975, 6 (1/2), 133-146.

RAHE, R. H. & ARTHUR, R. J. Life change patterns surrounding life experiences. *Journal of Psychosomatic Research,* 1968, 11, 341.

RAHE, R. H., BIERSNER, R. J., RYMAN, D. H., & ARTHUR, R. J. Psychosocial predictors of illness behavior and failure in stressful training. *Journal of Health and Social Behavior,* 1972, 13, 393-397.

RAHE, R. H. & HOLMES, T. H. Social, psychologic and psychophysiologic aspects of inguinal hernia. *Journal of Psychosomatic Research,* 1965, 8, 487.

RAHE, R. H., MAHAN, J., & ARTHUR, R. J. Prediction of near-future health change from subjects' preceding life changes. *Journal of Psychosomatic Research,* 1970, 14, 401.

RAHE, R. H., McLEAN, J., & ARTHUR, R. J. A longitudinal study of life change and illness patterns. *Journal of Psychosomatic Research,* 1967, 10, 355.

ROESSLER, R. & GREENFIELD, N. S. Incidence of somatic disease in psychiatric patients. *Psychosomatic Medicine,* 1961, 23, 413.

ROSE, R. M., GORDON, T. P., & BERNSTEIN, L. S. Plasma testosterone levels in the male rhesus: Influence of sexual and social stimuli. *Science,* 1972, 178, 643-645.

ROSSMAN, P. L. Organic diseases simulating functional disorders. *Archives of General Psychiatry,* 1963, 28, 78.

SACHAR, E. Hormonal changes in stress and mental illness. *Hospital Practice,* July 1975, pp. 49-55.

SCHWAB, J. J. Comprehensive medicine and the concurrence of physical and mental illness. *Psychosomatics,* 1970, 11, 591-595.

SCHWAB, J. J. Depressive illness: A sociomedical syndrome. *Psychosomatics,* 1971, 12, 385-389.

SCHWAB, J. J., FENNELL, E. B., & WARHEIT, G. J. The epidemiology of psychosomatic disorders. *Psychosomatics,* 1974, 15, 88-93.

SCHWAB, J. J., WARHEIT, G. J., & McGINNIS, N. H. Current perspectives on social psychiatry. *Psychosomatics*, 1970, 11, 18-23.

SELYE, H. *Stress of Life*. New York: McGraw-Hill, 1956.

SZASZ, T. S. *The Myth of Mental Illness*. New York: Harper & Row, 1974.

WATTS, C. A. H. Psychiatric disorders. In The Research Committee of the Council of the College of General Practitioners. *Morbidity Statistics from General Practice*, No. 14, Vol. 3. London: HORSO, 1962, pp. 35-52.

WEISSMAN, M. M. & KLERMAN, G. L. Sex differences and the epidemiology of depression. *Archives of General Psychiatry*, 1977, 34 (1), 98-111.

Part V

PSYCHOTHERAPY ISSUES

16

GENDER AND PSYCHOTHERAPY

VIOLET FRANKS

Sooner or later, the burgeoning literature on women, sex roles and sex differences will filter through to the traditional practice of psychotherapy. Psychotherapists are a diversified group, trained in different disciplines (psychiatry, psychology, psychoanalysis, social work, counseling, etc.), offering allegiance to diverse orientations and working in settings ranging from private practice to a variety of institutional facilities. Nevertheless, all share a responsibility for understanding contemporary problems in the light of the prevailing *Zeitgeist* if they are to alleviate suffering.

To review the complexities of gender and psychotherapeutic interactions within such diverse modalities in one chapter is clearly impractical. Fortunately, other chapters deal with therapy from epidemiological or institutional points of view (cf. Chapters 2, 6 and 14). Here, we limit ourselves, in the main, to the more typical one-to-one client-therapist interactions encountered by the psychotherapist in daily practice.

Under the rubric of therapy we could include methods dealing with a client's physiology, biochemistry, interpersonal reactions, inner dynamics, life-style and a multitude of behaviors and thoughts requiring interventions and value judgments by the therapist. Though we cannot determine the precise relevance of therapist or patient gender, it is still possible to examine the existing state of knowledge. It is particularly important to update our viewpoint and examine recent theories and findings.

According to radical therapists such as Szasz and radical feminists such as Chesler, emotional malaise is a societal problem. Mental disorders are not illnesses *per se;* the "patient" is reacting to the inability of society or the family to cope with the individual's deviant behavior. As far as radical feminists are concerned, it is a "sexist" society which is primarily responsible for emotional maladjustment in women.

Gender as it relates to psychotherapy is rarely discussed by traditional therapists at all other than to reiterate nebulous pyschoanalytic clichés such as penis envy and oedipal desire. For example, Marmor's (1975) well-balanced article on the nature of the psychotherapeutic process rightly concluded that, regardless of orientation, all therapists aim at enabling the patient to have meaningful and satisfying social and sexual relationships, to love and work effectively and be a responsible and productive human being. But at no stage in his thesis are the parameters of patient gender delineated. For example, what constitutes a satisfactory social or sexual relationship differs in more than obvious ways for male and female clients. Even the definition of "productive human being" must be considered with the sex of the client in mind. Men and women have traditionally held different goals with regard to their concepts of productiveness. Their previous learning experiences and their self-concepts may differ (Deaux & Farris, 1977; Horner, 1972). Even when we consider the changing roles of men and women, how many men today feel "fulfilled" because they have scrubbed the kitchen floor and taken care of the children? Yet this may be an acceptable and satisfying accomplishment for some female clients.

One does not have to belabor the fact—the measuring sticks are different, even today, for men and women. Changing roles confuse matters further. For example, a woman may feel depressed and emotionally upset because she cannot handle a high level executive job, whereas 10 years ago she may have been exhilarated at creating a good cheese soufflé. Therapeutic goals are often situation specific. Men and women deal with different situations and at different times in their lives.

Marmor points out that all therapists purvey their values to the patient by what they refuse to comment on and by what they react to as healthy or neurotic. Therapeutic objectives of most psychotherapists are essentially similar and reflect the culture's normative ideals. Psychotherapy must be understood in relation to the prevailing cultural norms. Marmor further points out that the most important element for therapeutic improvement is the *relationship* between therapist and client. This is true whether one is using a behavioral, classical analytic, Gestalt or any other theoretical system. If we accept Marmor's views, then it would appear to be especially important to consider the effects of gender on the relationship between client and therapist as well as the individual's acceptance or rejection of contemporary cultural normative ideals. It is also not unlikely that the nature of the *relationship* between a male therapist and a female client may differ in alternative dyads, male-male, female-female, or female-male. All things considered, it is difficult to see how a therapist can ignore his or her own attitude to gender- and sex-role identification during the therapeutic process. Unfortunately, all things are rarely, if ever, considered, and ignorance of gender influence is the rule rather than the exception at the present time.

As the contents of this book indicate, men and women often present different problems in a therapeutic situation. They have different life-styles and they suffer in different ways. It is important, therefore, to fit treatment and disorder to both therapist and patient. As yet, there is much we do not understand about creating optimum conditions in a therapy situation, and we must study the complexities involved. While our state of knowledge does not permit definitive and premature rulings (such as "women should not go to male therapists"), to ignore the obvious would be equally foolhardy. For example, it is possible to examine the effects of gender role, whether certain patients do better with men or women therapists and which specific factors determine optimal therapeutic progress.

It is significant that the seventies have seen the growth of journals devoted to therapy issues as they affect women. *Sex Roles* and the *Psychology of Women Quarterly* deal with psychological issues facing women. *Signs* has an excellent section on the psychology of women. In addition, traditional publications such as the *Quarterly Journal of Psychoanalysis*, *Voices*, the *Journal of Counseling Psychology*, and *Social Work* have recently devoted whole issues to the therapy of women. Growth in the interests of women as separate consumers of the therapeutic process is one result of the women's movement. There will be a lag, one assumes, in applying these findings to the special needs of men. Though journals such as *Sex Roles* do study the male role, it is difficult at this time to find material geared specifically to the male. Of course, one could accept the feminist allegation that all therapy, and even all psychology, has been formulated with the male stereotype in mind. Nevertheless, as we single out one sex we may discover that men, too, have needs which are unique to them and which require understanding.

Certainly, most therapists have been male and most psychotherapy books have been written by men; it is only in recent years that women have started contributing significantly to this body of knowledge. Most clients and consumers are still women and the male doctor-female client dyad is still the norm.

This chapter starts with a brief historical survey of the effects of gender on psychotherapy. This leads to consideration of some emerging new viewpoints about psychotherapy and gender in the seventies as well as shifts in concepts about sex roles which may have significant implications for psychotherapists. Finally, certain new approaches will be reviewed which are being incorporated into therapy techniques and which are related to change in gender roles (such as assertiveness training and training for androgeny).

SOME HISTORICAL NOTES: A PERSPECTIVE

If we view the influence of gender on psychotherapeutic techniques from a historical point of view, we gain a sense of perspective. Obviously, attitudes toward gender depend on the state of knowledge during any given period, as well as prevalent sexist viewpoints and the needs of society.

Much of the early literature was contributed by physicians. S. Weir Mitchell, an eminent nineteenth century American psychiatrist, emphasized the "rest-cure." We are fortunate to have a written account by one of his patients, Charlotte Perkins-Gilman (1935), a noted feminist and author of "The Yellow Wallpaper." Her book was a response to Mitchell's therapeutic strategem for her postnatal depression: Go home, stay in bed and restrict all activities. She became even further depressed by her inactivity and was able to counteract her depression only by her own prescription of planned activity, leaving behind the "yellow wall-paper" of the nursery and the traditional role of the female. Mitchell's model of generic rest-cures was possibly more suitable to his upper middle-class male patients, taking on, then as now, a heavy burden of responsibilities. Future "masculine revolution" may well emphasize techniques and goals aimed at helping men have a longer life span (women now outlive men in America by an average of seven years), and reducing stress, excessive responsibility, competition and emphasis on success.

The nineteenth century considered hysteria to commence with puberty and end with menopause, since it was then thought that hysteria was related to reproductive ailments (see Chapter 13). The twentieth century adds the menopause as a vulnerable period for women (since we now know more about the "raging hormones"). It is easier to apply biological interpretations to women because we can pinpoint observable phenomena (men do not menstruate, give birth or go through an observable menopause). How many women today are diagnosed as having a postpartum depression or menopausal depression? How many biochemical remedies are being advocated without real evidence that there is a biochemical disorder?

It is tempting to use *post hoc* reasoning. For example, because a woman is going through menopausal change, her depression is *due* to the menopause. Examining more recent findings, we can see fallacies in *post hoc* conclusions. Winokur and Cadoret (1975) point out that there is no increase in depressive illness among females in the years from 45 to 55. The largest absolute increase for depressive psychosis and suicide rate occurs between the age period of 20 to 34 years of age. They conclude that there are few data to support the concept that the menopause is particularly relevant to depressive illness. Taking a nonbiological viewpoint, Melges (1975) presents strong evidence that psychological conflict over mothering is important in postpartum depression. We do not know the extent to which psychological changes contribute to depression in childbirth. A study using a control group of fathers who assumed a full parenting role after the birth of a child might help unravel the relative contributions of physiological and psychological factors. To date, I know of no such study.

Gender stereotypes in medical practice can be hazardous to both men and women. Contemporary medical viewpoints of the biochemical aspects of emotional disabilities may be obsolete within the next couple of decades. In the last five years, for example, looking to the "magic" estrogens to cure emotional disabilities in women has fallen into disrepute.

A danger exists for women who may be experiencing more surgical interventions than absolutely necessary. They may be encouraged to adopt a sick role. Their health may be impaired. By contrast, there is a tendency for men and their physicians to delay seeking medical help. If we are still viewing men and women with sexist bias (e.g., men have to be strong and women can be weaker, seek medical help more often and be treated with more radical surgery) then we are doing a disservice to both sexes. We are reacting to historically rooted stereotypes rather than to facts and findings.

THE IMPACT OF THE FEMINIST ORIENTATION ON THERAPY

If it were not for the feminist thrust in psychotherapy, there would be little reason for this chapter. At the turn of the sixties a significant new body of literature emerged. There may be a cultural lag. Research has not kept up with changing conditions. Conventional mental health training programs rarely include explicit coursework on changing sex roles. Nevertheless, the feminist orientation and the study of the influence of gender on therapy needs *have* influenced a number of such programs, particularly those in social work and counseling.

More radical viewpoints continue to have an impact. Let us consider some of the earlier literature. In the early seventies, Chesler (1972a) claimed that both psychotherapy and marriage were to be viewed as vehicles for the social control and oppression of women. Her attitudes towards therapy are reflected in such widely disseminated statements, reaching lay person, feminist and professional alike, as "She wants from a psychotherapist what she wants—and often can't get—from a husband: Attention, understanding, merciful release, a personal solution—in the arms of the 'right' husband, on the couch of the 'right' therapist" (1972b).

The radical feminist outcry in the seventies produced arguments such as, "In medicine, a woman with clogged sinuses is seen as some woman with a sinus problem, not an air-pollution problem" (Krakauer & Becker, 1972). As radical feminists, Krakauer and Becker view depression and despair as "understandable reactions to a system that promises opportunity to all and delivers little to many." They demand that society be reorganized along new lines so that psychotherapy will not be kept going by "myths." With Szasz, they regard psychotherapy as an institution which helps people conform. The therapist is someone who wants to keep a privileged position, a low risk taker who is unaware of the special needs that women may have. All traditional therapeutic concepts are being constantly challenged by more radical thinkers. For many feminists, the vaginal orgasm and Erikson's once widely accepted "empty-space syndrome" are being rapidly relegated to the realm of the mythological where they belong. Traditional therapists will have difficulty providing any objective data to support a number of pet theories which feminist therapists are rejecting.

We must consider seriously the possibility that therapy can make personal problems out of political issues. Tennov (1975) emphasizes that clients are misled by being encouraged to take blame for situations over which they have no control. This is particularly the problem with women, as well as any other group, for whom environmental oppression still exists. Such individuals should not be in conventional intrapsychic-oriented therapy at all.

It is proposed that the authoritarian, hierarchial therapy-client relationship model does not facilitate feminine emancipation from male authority figures. Feminist therapists encourage the therapist to explore personal values and to receive negative as well as positive feedback from clients concerning the process and goals of therapy. For many feminist therapists, feminine labels are valued to the extent that they contribute to the notion of "personhood." Mental health is viewed as competence for change and as acquisition of skills and competency rather than adjustment per se. Flexibility of roles (androgeny) and flexibility of life-styles are also emphasized. In this value system, egalitarian rather than power-based relationships and sensitivity to human rights are the ideals.

Rawlings and Carter's (1977) edited book deals with feminist-oriented psychotherapy. Their targeted sexist therapist is Houck (1972), whose point of view they paraphrase as follows: "The husband should be helped to become dominant in a relationship and to control his wife, who should be submissive and dependent in a relationship" (p. 84). Houck, their straw man sexist therapist, accepts marriage as the only life-style for his female patient and her need to be submissive as paramount. Articles such as this openly flourished in the sixties but still exist today (less obviously so and more subtly expressed). The concept of an egalitarian relationship between male and female partners is beginning to receive "lip service" in traditional psychotherapy literature. Most therapists now tend to agree that a woman's mental health depends upon her having personal power and controlling her own life. But to what extent they actually "walk the walk" rather than "talk the talk" in the reality of the therapeutic session remains less certain.

In evaluating the claims of feminist therapists, it may be helpful to refer back to some of the chapters in the present volume. It is of interest to note that even such "establishment" and objective researchers as Gove, Weissman and Sarri are forced to take into consideration the role of gender in the understanding of deviant behavior. Their findings and observations could lend support to the need to consider gender in formulating therapeutic interventions with women as well as men. Feminist therapists have given impetus for expanding our knowledge about the influence of gender on therapeutic practice.

Feminist criticisms of traditional psychotherapy will have far-reaching reverberations, with an impact which is not as yet fully felt. Traditional values are being questioned and there is a growth of research studies, panels and theories to probe the existing state of affairs. Unfortunately, these developments are only sparsely filtering through to the settings where professionals train and practice.

One outgrowth may be nonsexist therapy for men and we may envision a growth of literature which deals with problems peculiar to men due to culturally (and biologically) imposed conditions. Nevertheless, to date, there is no significant body of literature dealing with "masculine" therapy and we are forced to examine only the emerging theories of feminist therapy and thinking.

Some writers point out that there is a distinction between feminist therapy and nonsexist therapy (e.g., Maracek & Kravetz, 1977). This distinction is important to our understanding of gender and psychotherapy. A feminist approach emphasizes a sociopolitical component in therapy for women. In nonsexist therapy, treatment focuses on *individual* change and change in *personal* behavior without undue influence of sex-role stereotypic values. Criticisms of society and social institutions is a focal point in feminist therapy and societal change an essential ingredient for personal change. The overlap is obvious. It is doubtful if one could be a nonsexist therapist without being aware of feminist philosophy, and vice versa. However, differences in actual therapeutic practice can be crucial. Some feminists will not treat a client unless the client is committed to feminist dogma. I have always felt committed to feminism and against sexism in psychotherapy. Nevertheless, it is important, as a therapist, to separate politics from therapeutic practice. For many women who are grappling with personal problems, adding a mandatory political credo to the therapeutic structure could be overburdening. Each client is a unique individual and merits an individualized approach.

THERAPY AND CHANGING SEX ROLES

People do not usually consult therapists when their behavior is maintaining a balance in their lives. They come only when the behavior patterns are breaking down, when new adjustments have to be made and new life crises are to be faced. The therapist does not usually have to consider values for the contented, dependent housewife conforming to a feminine role in a protected nest. Neither does the therapist have to be concerned about the successful, authoritarian male functioning well at his job and within his family. However, when traditional roles break down due to divorce, sudden unemployment, loss of mate or other life crises, a more flexible and androgenous adjustment may become necessary. Behaviors and social competencies may then need to include a wider range of less sex-role stereotypic behavior.

Bernard (1973) views the current restructuring of sex roles as "no less epochal than the restructuring of the class system which was one of the first consequences of the industrial revolution" (p. 1). If Bernard is correct, we are at the threshold of a paradigm shift of major importance and many of our sex-related stereotypes and norms about behavior would have to be changed—but in reality little has changed and it would be premature for therapists to contemplate any drastic restructuring of sex roles.

An examination of demographic data does show a current drop in birth rates and a marked rise in the number of working women. Nevertheless, though one out of four students in professional schools (law and medicine) are women, we continue to maintain a constant differential between men and women with respect to salary and entry into more prestigious jobs. As yet, little fundamental change is occurring. If political pulses are accurate, the current status of the anti-abortion movement and the fight against ERA legislation indicate that change is evident more in theory than in practice. Bernard's optimistic comment about "change in our total society no longer calling for the sex specialization of the past" may well be premature. Society has not changed to such an extent that therapists can safely disregard differentiated sex roles. For some avant-garde clients who are considering these options, therapy can be very helpful in freeing clients from "shoulds" and stereotypes. But for the more traditional-minded, therapist and client alike, this may be completely inappropriate. Theories will change; therapy will evolve. The therapist must look at significant changes within a realistic light and help the client deal with the current situation rather than with any far-reaching dream.

In a much cited article, Broverman, Broverman, Clarkson, Rosenkrantz and Vogel (1970) studied the stereotypes of mental health workers and concluded that there is a double standard involved in assessing feminine and masculine behavior. Mental health workers considered masculine behaviors to be more synonymous with mental health than behaviors characterized as predominantly feminine. Mentally healthy traits as agsiveness, independence, objectivity, activity and logic were rated as masculine. Traits viewed as mentally unhealthy, such as dependency, submissiveness, and passivity, were rated as feminine. Criticisms of the experimental design notwithstanding (see Stricker, 1977), the impact of this article is vast. The notion that sex-role stereotypes permeate judgments about mental health has challenged therapists who are interested in the influences of gender on the therapeutic process. We cannot escape the mounting evidence that when we deal with the terms "masculine" and "feminine" there are numerous changing stereotypes with which we must contend. There is no therapist who can honestly say that he or she does not have a value judgment stereotype in mind when thinking of the terms "feminine" or "masculine." Even if it is sincerely believed that the goal is to help a female client become more "masculine" or a male client more "feminine" in order to conform with the changing norms of society, a political stance with a value judgment is already taken.

We are living in an era which involves changing values for the nuclear family. As these values change, so do our concepts of psychopathology and family dynamics. The fifties and sixties, for example, saw the schizophrenogenic mother cited as an important factor in the development of schizophrenia. The father was rarely an important figure in the development of childhood disorders. Nowadays, the role of the father is becoming more prominent. Nevertheless, it is a myth to view the average family as one in which the fathering role is of equal importance with that of the mother with respect either to time or quality. The structure of American society, though more flexible in role assignments than many more traditional societies, leaves much room for ambiguity and frustration. Few women can be the principal breadwinners; few men share equally in child-rearing and in housekeeping. When people delude themselves into believing that we already have a new society in which stereotypic sex roles no longer prevail, they may break the structure of their marriage only to find that no viable alternative is available.

Single-parent families are rapidly increasing. Birth rate is declining, more women are employed, many marriages are delayed. Effective therapy must take these developments and their consequences into full consideration. For example, both divorced women and women who are delaying marriage are looking for new self-concepts. Children often have to share parents who have remarried. Frequently, the divorced couple are living in a world where the traditional balance between male and female is being assailed. Such children and their parents constitute a not inconsiderable proportion of the population who go to therapists. Unfortunately, there are few models and few traditions for either the therapist or client to follow in their quests for healthy solutions. It would appear that the new emphasis is pointing in the direction of more role flexibility. Ideally, good psychotherapy could lead to decreasing dependency, greater adaptability and less differentiation of roles within the martial situation. The goal may be a more flexible choice of appropriate ways of expressing dependency needs. Will the therapist of the eighties be dealing with these issues? Is the therapist of the seventies aware of these issues?

SEX OF THERAPIST IN RELATION TO SEX OF PATIENT: RESEARCH FINDINGS

Research studies are at last emerging. According to Billingsley (1977), the sex of the client is *not* related to the therapist's stated goals. (She notes, however, that her findings might have been different had the therapist's actual behavior rather than declared intent been studied.) The sex of the therapist was the more important variable: Male therapists chose more feminine treatment goals for all their clients and female therapists chose more masculine treatment goals. Nevertheless, the issues are complex and, as Billingsley points out, the client's sex may affect therapists' treatment goal choices when the pathology presented is less severe than that prevailing in her study. It might further be noted that Billingsley relied upon case histories and questionnaires to elicit responses from therapists. To date, there is a dearth of direct observational data. The development of a sophisticated coding system and the videotaping of therapy sessions would seem to be the logical next step in trying to understand gender variables in psychotherapy.

The therapist's behavior may influence the value system of the client in subtle ways. A nod, a smile, a reinforcement may display an attitude which the therapist may not be able to appreciate intellectually or of which he may not even be aware. For example, a male therapist may indicate in a questionnaire that he values independence behavior for female clients. Nevertheless, during an actual therapy session he may smile approvingly or nod when the female client is more dependent upon him and, by the same token, he may fail to signal his approval of her moves towards independence. Similarly, in an interactional situation, if a female client becomes assertive, he may feel that she is being aggressive and react by emitting disapproval behavior or negative reinforcement. He may be totally unaware of this tendency, and quite oblivious of this bias when asked to assess his attitudes on an "objective" questionnaire. In private, male therapists are usually willing to reveal their stereotypic attitudes towards women. But these same therapists who sincerely present themselves in public and on questionnaires as being very flexible and liberated may, in fact, not have flexible liberated attitudes at all when they are off guard. (Of course, a similar argument applies to female therapists.)

An interesting paper by Delk and Ryan (1977) discusses the differences between what they call Type A and Type B therapists. Type A therapists are more successful in treating schizophrenic disorders, whereas Type B therapists achieve greater success with neurotics (see Heaton, Carr and Hampson, 1975, for a more extensive discussion of research on A-B status and psychotherapy outcome). There may be identifiable patterns among both male and female therapists which identify the sort of person who would support change in sex-role stereotypes. It should be possible to match therapist and patient according to the way each scores on some form of A-B status scale. Considerable effort has gone into exploring personality characteristics related to the A-B therapist distinction. It appears that B as compared to A therapists are more field independent, have more masculine interests and are perceived as being more dominant, persistent and risk-taking. (This fits in with the typical male sex-role stereotype!) By contrast, A therapists are seen as more cautious, submissive, less persistent and, in general, less well adjusted. It would be of interest to determine how male and female therapists differ on these scales. Within both Delk and Ryan's patient and therapist groups, male subjects stereotyped significantly more than their female counterparts.

Delk and Ryan's patients sex-role stereotyped significantly more than therapists. This supports the hypothesis that androgyny is a better predictor of good mental health than sex-role stereotyping. Since the study found that Type "A" therapists stereotype sex roles more than Type "B" therapists, the psychotherapist who structures therapy may be better with schizophrenic types of patients (who do not know the guidelines and may be looking for more structure). Neurotics may need the flexibility of "B" Type therapists, who do not sex-role stereotype as much. Type "A" therapists, more bound by cultural traditions and values, may provide a definitive role model of culturally valued, socially acceptable behavior. This may be necessary for working with very severely disturbed patients who have poor reality contact, such as schizophrenics. By contrast, the less culturally restricted behavioral style of the "B" therapist would be indicated as the role model of choice for neurotics, who are too inhibited and have difficulty expressing feelings and need to have a therapist who will be more relaxing and allow them to express themselves freely. The authors pose the question "Can one assume that a female 'B' therapist would be better able to treat a female schizophrenic patient than a male 'A' therapist simply because of her sex?" Extending this logic, regardless of sex, "B" therapists who put little reliance on sex-role stereotypes may be excellent therapists for a woman striving for self-actualizing or for rigid men having difficulty adjusting to a rapidly changing culture.

This avenue of thinking presents fruitful research possibilities and may help us further understand the complexities of the situation. One must take into consideration the many multiple personalities that fall within the population of male and female therapists, as well as male and female clients—a simplistic model cannot suffice. The rigid sex-role stereotyped person can be either male or female. Regardless of the gender of the person involved, the emerging literature on the measurement of androgeny may shed light on this issue.

If we consider traits as fixed, then we will have to think in terms of assigning different patients to different types of therapists. If we believe that people react according to the situation in which they find themselves, then we can permit more flexibility and emphasize the importance of training therapists to cue into their personality types, the personality types of their patients, and how they can deal with their own stereotyped attitudes.

Another viewpoint to examine is the hypothesis that the greater the *similarity* between therapist and patient, the more effective the therapeutic interaction. This could lead to attempts to match personality types in arranging dyadic patient-therapist interactions. Unfortunately, we do not know whether the similarity hypothesis or the complementary differences hypothesis is valid and under what circumstances. The issues are not simple; one must look into the multitude of interactions that go on between therapist and patient and the needs of the particular patient at a particular time. The demography of the therapeutic relationship is complex and it would be premature to make sweeping generalizations about the male-female dyad in therapy.

The complexity of the situation may account for the obtained discrepancies in assessing the effects of therapist and client gender. For example, in examining the questions of sex-related countertransference and bias in psychotherapy, Abramowitz, Roback, Schwartz, Yasuna, Abramowitz and Gomes (1976) found that the sex of the patient made little difference to the therapist's response. Sex-related counter transference problems may not be as prevalent as had been previously thought. However, the sex of the therapist does seem to have some influence on the therapeutic process. For example, female therapists tended to empathize more strongly with female patients than with male. They also showed more empathy than male therapists, regardless of how the case materials were labeled.

It is necessary that investigators of male and female therapists emphasize other variables which may be important to therapists, such as expectancy and degree of training. Orlinsky and Howard (1976) found that single depressed women did better with female therapists whereas older women did well with male therapists, and younger married women showed only initial differences due to the sex of the therapist.

Cowan (1976) studied the tendency to sex-role stereotype patients. A male or adult standard of mental health is being applied to female clients rather than a double standard. Women in therapy are seen as too feminine, whereas men's problems are not seen in terms of sex-role at all. Cowan points out that therapists may view acceptance of femaleness as important to health, but clearly do not see stereotypic femininity as healthy. While Chesler (1972) suggests overinvestment in femininity as one way women become "mad," Cowan's findings do not support her further contention that male therapists are invested in keeping women feminine. In fact, male therapists may be overly invested in masculine values in treating female patients and may undervalue positive female behaviors.

In summary, it is difficult to point to any firm data which demonstrate that the sex of either therapist or patient consistently or systematically affect psychotherapy. Nevertheless, it may be that our research is too simplistic. We may have to look further to see if there are certain personality types which are more sex-role stereotyped or if the raising of consciousness in women reduces stereotypic behavior and effects therapeutic issues. It is difficult to believe that the research to date reflects the true situation and the question remains: Will women therapists change their stereotypes more rapidly than males?

A recent study by Aslin (1977) reexamined the double standard theory of mental health and expanded the Broverman et al. (1970) findings. Aslin studied psychotherapists' perceptions of healthy wives and mothers as well as perceptions of all healthy adults as compared with those of healthy female adults. In addition, Aslin explored the perceptions of feminist therapists, raising a number of pertinent issues along the way. She finds that judgments of "mental health" of wives did not differ from judgments of mentally healthy adults, whereas male perceptions of mentally healthy characteristics of women in general and of mothers as a group differed from those perceived by both female and feminist therapists. Aslin hypothesizes that the women's movement has influenced women more than men. Female therapists (whether feminist or not) accept a wide range of options and behaviors as appropriate for women. Male therapists accept more sex-role stereotypes.

Furthermore, male therapists' expectations vary according to the nature of the term used. "Wife" is viewed in a more egalitarian manner than "mother" or "single female." The concept of "women" itself evokes different standards according to the role we expect the women to assume. Male therapists may have an idealized concept of a woman when thinking of a wife. Steinmann (1974), for example, also finds discrepancies between male expectations for their ideal woman and their choice in the real situation.

Female therapists in Aslin's study valued competence and independence for *all* mentally healthy wives or mothers. The Broverman et al. findings were not entirely replicated and there does appear to be a shift in attitude since 1970 for female therapists, in particular.

GENERAL RESEARCH FINDINGS ON SEX DIFFERENCES AND SEX ROLE STEREOTYPES: THERAPEUTIC IMPLICATIONS

There does not appear to be any research which pinpoints therapist bias or differences according to patient/therapist gender. However, inferences can be drawn both from the developmental literature pertaining to sex differences and the large body of information about sex roles which is now emerging. Eventually, we will have clinically derived research data which we will be able to apply in the therapy situation. But, for the time being, we have to rely primarily upon nonclinical data such as that derived from research on sex-role stereotypes. If men and women have been trained to be stereotypic in their thinking, and if both have learned to view the world and themselves in different ways (according to their gender), this may well influence the interactions which occur in the therapy situation. If women tend to be more nurturant, then even the very few indications to date that female therapists are becoming more positive and accepting towards their female clients may actually reflect a major trend. If men tend to be more dominant and more self-confident, then these traits may also affect therapy to a greater extent than we can now possibly assess.

If present techniques do not demonstrate gender differences and interactions, we must determine if we are missing important variables or whether we can assume that therapists are so very sophisticated and well-trained that they do not put forth the same cues as the general population. This latter possibility is unlikely. It is true that, in some studies, the more skilled therapists showed less sex-role stereotypic behaviors and were less influenced by gender (at least on questionnaires). Nevertheless, at this stage of knowledge, it is very unlikely that the typical male or female therapist is so free of social conditioning that there will be no difference in interaction because of gender identity.

Other possibilities are important and should be further researched, even if this leads us to areas not usually considered by therapists, such as attribution theory or systems analysis. Zanna and Pack (1975), for example, showed that female students are affected by stereotypes particularly when they are interacting with a desirable male. The students actually moderated their behavior on a performance task and presented themselves as more conventionally feminine (using the Broverman sex-role stereotypes—tender, sentimental, not aggressive, etc.) when anticipating interactions with desirable or attractive males, depending on whether the males presented themsleves as sexist or nonsexist. Men also behave in ways so as to confirm others' expectations or desires when highly motivated to impress the other person. We can hypothesize from such findings that a female patient who is anxious to please a sexist male therapist may present herself as the woman she feels the therapist will value the most highly. This is particularly true if we accept a "transference" hypothesis. If she senses that the male therapist prefers women to be gentle, dependent, kind and emotional rather than independent, logical, assertive and intelligent, it is likely that she will conform with the therapist's values and gain acceptance. A male patient, by contrast, may be highly motivated to impress either a male or female therapist by behaving in ways that will confirm the therapist's expectancies and desires.

Some clinicians, such as Rice and Rice (1977), are already applying nonsexist methods in their therapy situations. Yet most therapists see no need to become aware of sexist issues and the impact of gender on their therapy approach. If we take, for example, a contemporary theory, such as Seligman's (1974, 1977) learned helplessness model, we can hypothesize that the theory might have a different effect depending upon whether one is dealing with women or men. Some researchers have recognized this (e.g., Radloff, 1975) and there is literature emerging which tends to view these theories from a more feminist viewpoint. Interestingly, Seligman has not examined male-female differences with respect to learned helplessness. Using a logical sequence and following Seligman's reasoning, if 80% of depressed patients are women and if depression is explained in behavioral terms (i.e., the patient has learned that his or her responses are ineffective and is therefore emitting fewer responses and developing depressive symptoms), then women may learn these behaviors at a different rate than do men. Seligman (1977) has recently hypothesized a mediating cognitive component: Self-statements further reinforce the depressive tendency. We must determine now whether women and men make similar self-statements. Men tend to attribute their failure to outside causes, luck, etc., whereas women attribute their failures to inner deficiencies (Deaux & Farris, 1977). If this is true, then the woman's self-statement might well be that she is a failure because she is inadequate, whereas the man might say that he fails because of poor luck or because things are against him. According to Seligman, self-statements which attribute failure to long-range situations (such as inadequacy feelings related to self-image) lend themselves to more severe depressions and are much more depression inducing. Again, the therapist may want to become aware of the more typical female self-statement, of the literature on fear of success (Horner, 1972), of attribution theory, of male and female self-concepts, and of a multitude of other behaviors which appear to differ in men and women in our society.

Since women have already begun to question both standard therapeutic techniques and their roles as females in society, their male counterparts may have little alternative but to reexamine their motives for achievement and success. We are still going through the early stages in this questioning process. There are many indications that gender stereotypes will continue to evolve and that the feminist movement did not start a temporary revolt. Social and political accommodations are developing slowly but inevitably. The initial feminist protests have generated counterreactions from some men who are questioning whether they wish to enter a highly competitive, success-oriented society while leaving their wives at home to a more feminine adjustment (e.g., Farrell, 1975). Women are now entering the work field in increasing numbers. Today, a woman's employment history is likely to be close to that of a man's simply because she has many more years which do not involve child-rearing.

The therapist of the seventies doing therapy as he or she did in the sixties will find the therapeutic process inappropriate. In this transitional era, many new and different therapeutic problems will be presented to therapists by both men and women. Ignoring contemporary issues and remaining with traditional issues may indeed be destructive. For example, attitudes towards homosexuality as a viable life-style are changing rapidly. At the same time, attitudes towards traditional male and female models are also changing rapidly. How will the therapist deal with the marriage which is breaking up? With the male who wants to stay home? With the female who is career-oriented? With the couple who do not want to have children? What will the therapist do with the middle-aged, very traditional male, with all the associated sex-role stereotypes, whose wife has changed suddenly? What will the therapist do with the depressed female who sees herself only in the traditional way and has learned "helplessness" to such an extent that she is in a retarded depression? What will the therapist do with the "hysterical" female who has learned that the only way to function is by using indirect manipulative methods —while married to a chauvinist spouse? What will the therapist do with the righteous, chauvinistic male alcoholic who cannot express emotion, who uses alcohol as a way of blunting his emotions?

Examining the chapters which appear in this book and considering the contemporary issues, the therapist is ethically obliged to think not only in terms of changing times but of the different types of problems that may affect men and women. Hopefully, we will be able to develop more sophisticated methods in our therapeutic approaches and a more stable body of knowledge. In the meantime, one can hope that the therapy of the eighties will be more advanced than the therapy of the seventies in understanding the influence of gender on therapeutic issues. In the sections that follow I will deal with therapy and related findings concerned with actively changing sex-role stereotyped behavior.

If contemporary analytic viewpoints receive short shrift in this chapter it is because even the most recent and avant-garde viewpoints deal lightly with the changing roles of men and women. For example, Ticho (1977) critically reviews Freud's concepts with respect to female psychology but accepts unconditionally the concept of the oedipal complex as part of normal development: Environmental or biological crises become nonthreatening when the self is integrated enough "to allow a regressive revival of the Oedipus complex to subject its previous solutions to further revisions and transformations" (p. 143). The unquestioning Freudian assumptions of universal Oedipal and latency periods is no longer tenable. Though Ticho acknowledges the change in society and the frustrations involved when women strike out for independence and equal pay, she does not evaluate the phenomenon of oedipal phase in a generation which may be dealing with different types of parent-child interactions. To accept a dated Viennese oedipal phase in contemporary American society may be as unrealistic as accepting this phase as universal in African tribal families. Remarriage and separated parents may involve more than one father figure or even no father figure at all.

Menaker (1974) gives a more modern analytic point of view without uncritical acceptance of dogma, but her approach is rare in analytic literature and vulnerable to attack by more traditional psychoanalysts. She writes, "I see a major task of psychoanalytic therapy in its contemporary garb to be the freeing of the individual from conflict-producing identifications in order to make room for the incorporation of new values" (p. 244). For Menaker, terms such as "penis envy" lose their old meaning; her approach can be consistent with a nonsexist orientation. The therapeutic methods to be explored in the following sections, which examine innovations for a nonsexist therapy, would probably produce little conflict with her interpretation of a "psychoanalytic" approach. It is difficult, if not impossible, to find traditional analytic literature, however, which takes into consideration changing gender roles without falling back on unproven, nebulous sex-role stereotyped theories of a bygone age.

ANDROGYNY AS NONSEXIST THERAPY

Androgyny signifies behavior that is not delimited or constrained by prevailing sex-role stereotypes about what is or is not proper for each sex (Kaplan, 1976). Psychotherapy can be utilized to augment or counterbalance an incomplete socialization process, and the client helped to broaden his or her sense of what is appropriate or acceptable. Psychotherapy then becomes a sort of resocialization. Kaplan specifically focuses on the emotions of anger and dependency and considers ways in which psychotherapy can ameliorate inappropriate anger and dependency. The feminist movement points out deficiencies in women's abilities to express emotions in assertive, non-angry but effective ways. Since the socialization process can lead to increased female dependency, new androgynous approaches are needed if mature, responsible independence is to be achieved. It therefore becomes a logical sequences for the therapist to add new models of androgyny to changing values and goals as part of this new concept of mental health.

Kelly, O'Brien, Hosford and Kisinger (1976) likewise emphasize a blending of instrumental masculine and expressive feminine social skills into an androgynous repertoire of effective interpersonal styles. The forward thrust, then, stemming from the feminist rebellion against traditional values, is to deal with both masculine and feminine stereotypes in order to develop a healthier model. Much psychological attention has been given to defining and assessing the terms masculinity and femininity, but sex-role style on a more basic level reflects certain sex-correlated social skills. Therefore, the goal is to increase the repertoire of effective social behaviors which men and women can use to obtain and maintain successful personal outcomes. As Kelly et al. put it, "From this perspective, and in light of our current findings, what has been called androgynous roles probably represents a diverse, extensive behavioral repertoire of social competencies across situations." For the therapist, this may be particularly important. For example, a man whose masculine authority remains unchallenged both at home and at work is not likely to seek therapy. But during a crisis, perhaps when his job is threatened or his family no longer accepts his masculine authoritarian role, he will seek therapy and become the "patient," that is, present symptoms such as depression, alcoholism, or other stress-related symptoms. The therapist may then find an androgynous model to be useful in helping the client readjust to new life goals and situations. It is not the political credo per se that is important for therapy, i.e., that androgyny is the wave of the future and an essential political dogma. It is the usefulness of the androgyny model in our changing society and its implications for therapy that the therapist must consider.

The concept of androgyny continues to be researched at a more sophisticated level. We are not dealing with simple polarities—i.e., masculine versus feminine identification. As discussed previously, we can assume that, regardless of gender, sex-role orientation is highly correlated with a number of personality traits, attributes and attitudes. Both male and female androgynous individuals rate well on measures related to high self-esteem (Spence, Helmreich, & Stopp, 1975; Bem, 1977; Wetter, 1975). Undifferentiated or indeterminate people (those who score *low* on feminine and *low* on masculine scales using measures such as the Bem Androgyny Scale and the Wetter ANDRO Scale) will also have lower self-esteem scores and show behavioral deficits (Bem, Martyna, & Watson, 1976; Bem, 1977; Spence, Helmreich, & Stopp, 1975). Certain androgynous subjects don't score significantly different in self-esteem from those who are masculine-typed, and feminine-typed subjects fare consistently worse in research related to self-esteem, behavioral correlates of adjustment and even in histories associated with parental encouragement (Kelly & Worrell, 1976; Spence, Helmreich, & Stopp, 1975; Bem, 1977; Bem, Martyna, & Watson, 1976; Orlofsky, 1977). In our society as it is today, high self-esteem seems to be closely and positively related to "male" traits such as toughness, independence and logic. If society were to change, the emphasis might shift to valuing expressive female traits rather than the more instrumental (action-oriented) masculine traits. Male self-esteem rarely depends on mastering a good fathering role. Good fathering may be dependent on traits such as warmth, sympathy and gentleness (female-oriented traits). If shifts in family structure necessitate this type of behavioral repertoire, future studies may reflect a shift of values from instrumental to expressive behavior (at least within the family as opposed to the work environment; executive requirements may also, in the future, value a less authoritarian pattern).

Kelly and Worrell (1977) pose the possibility that androgynous people may have a potential for greater behavioral conflict. They cite the example of a high level executive who has difficulty making decisions because of conflict between aggressive, competitive behavior and compassion-for-the-underdog behavior. Nevertheless, a wider, more adaptive response pattern could help the conflicted person choose a response appropriate to a particular situation. For example, compassion-for-the-underdog behavior could well be coupled with aggressive competition and need to make profits. Hence, an effective executive may refer an alcoholic colleague to an appropriate agency but not allow this colleague to engage in behaviors which would endanger the firm's profits and, eventually the alcoholic's well-being. The advantage of an androgynous model is that it offers options and choices to people who may be locked into a blocked and helpless script.

An important contribution of the androgyny concept as an approach to better mental health is that the clinician can view masculinity and femininity as orthogonal and nonexclusive approaches which are not restricted to sex-typed stereotypes carried by clinicians and clients. Hence, we can help patients obtain appropriate reinforcements of social competencies by dealing with their environment in a more adaptive manner. Hopefully, research will continue to uncover useful concepts which the clinician will then be able to apply.

In turn, the client will benefit from social skills training which enables a broader repertoire of high positive feminine and high positive masculine behavior. Kaplan's emphasis on training women to be more androgynous can be extended to both male and female clients. Future models may look to many options: to train men and women to understand each other's masculinity and femininity, to break down barriers which limit behavior to masculinity for men and femininity for women. A group therapy session of the future may well include training women to be more masculine and men to be more feminine, while accepting the high masculine positive qualities in men and the high feminine positive qualities in females. To cope with crises, both men and women will be able to call upon a range of behaviors suited to the situation. That is, men and women can break through the stereotype barrier and become more gentle, or less gentle, according to the situation; more dominant and more submissive, according to the situation. Qualities such as sympathy, kindness, logic, understanding, loyalty, warmth, friendliness, competitiveness, tact, and ambition will be distributed equally among men and women as groups. A Broverman type of study in the 1980s will perhaps show no polarity in thinking among mental health workers and both the mentally healthy male and mentally healthy female will be considered well adjusted if they have a broad repertoire of healthy male stereotyped as well as healthy female stereotyped behavior, regardless of gender assignment. If Aslin's (1977) findings indicate that female therapists are becoming less stereotyped in considering healthy female behavior, can we expect the trend to continue, and will male therapists also change their stereotypes in the same direction?

ANDROGYNY AND ASSERTIVENESS TRAINING: A THERAPY PACKAGE

According to Maccoby and Jacklin (1974) there are biological sex differences in the aggression of males and females as well as learned passivity in women. If this is so, then the clinician who is aware of these differences may wish to monitor therapy to maximize adaptive behavior with an eye to developing techniques which will introduce assertive rather than aggressive responses for males, and assertive rather than passive responses for females. Assertiveness training can be applied in a nonsexist manner to help both men and women deal with problems. However, the clinician should be cued into sex differences and the literature on sex differences in order to evaluate methodology. One may not use the same assertiveness training techniques with women as one would use with men. An awareness of cognitive self-statements would be particularly important to see why men may become more aggressive and why women may become passive in certain situations. Women often report a cognitive self-statement to the effect that they believe they should behave ladylike and gently, even though they do not want to behave this way. Men may posit a cognitive self-statement that they are expected to behave manly and effectively and therefore they may become aggressive because they feel threatened, even though they do not want to assume an aggressive role.

Therapists may thus have to deal with new issues in the future. Permission to change style and cognitive restructuring to change self-statements may be important interventions for the nonsexist therapist. Although assertiveness training has long been regarded as a viable behavior therapy technique, it is only within recent years that it has achieved widespread popularity. However, with this revival the focus now includes the changing of female behaviors to cope more effectively with new situations in their lives. Though the focus has been mainly on women (Baer, 1976; Bloom, Coburn, & Pearlman, 1975), there are also a number of books geared to both men and women (Alberti & Ammons, 1978; Fensterheim & Baer, 1975).

There is a difference in expressiveness between males and females. Men may seek therapy less frequently because it is difficult for them to express their feelings or to admit that they are suffering any emotional problem. However, they may, in fact, have many more internalized problems than they can talk about. Eisler et al. (1975) had 60 hospitalized male psychiatric patients role-play 32 assertive situations involving various interpersonal contexts. They found that behavior in assertive situations varied as a function of social context. In situations which required expression of anger (for example, where an individual had to stand up for personal rights), male subjects evidenced greater assertion towards women than towards men. In situations requiring positive assertion, subjects were more likely to offer praise and appreciation to female than to male partners. Their findings are consistent with the general belief that men normally have less difficulty in expressing their demands and women have less difficulty in expressing feelings. With these findings in mind, therapists may deal with men so that they can practice giving assertive *feeling* statements whereas they may need to deal with women by training them to defend their personal rights and deal with their lives in a generally more effective manner. Gove (Chapter 2) and Weissman and Klerman (Chapter 14) emphasize the female's less powerful position which makes her more vulnerable to psychopathology.

If we take into consideration research findings on stereotypical sex roles, therapy may be directly aimed at helping women who are unable to use flexible behavior and who are overwhelmed by needs to remain within the sex-role stereotypes of passivity, dependence, noncompetitive behavior and overly sensitive behavior. The best therapy package to date which can deal with this type of approach may consist of effective and broadly defined assertiveness training. By considering therapy in the context of detrimental sex-role conditioning, we may be able to ameliorate mental distress much more effectively.

A study by Tolar and Brannigan (1975) is concerned with attitudinal dimensions of sex-role stereotyping and self-concept related to differences in assertiveness in both sexes. Low sex-role stereotyping women have more favorable self-concept than low sex-role stereotyping men. There are indications, therefore, that women who can behave in a more assertive fashion are better adjusted. Men do not necessarily follow this pattern. In assertiveness training, it is important to consider that men who behave in a more feminine direction (which is less valued in our society) may have enough dissonance so that their self-concept is not improved. And in seeking assertiveness training, the goals for men and for women may not be similar. A change in sex-role stereotypes in the future *may* reinforce men for being able to behave and have stereotypes in a less rigid fashion. However, based upon the research findings, clinicians may not wish, at this time, to teach men to be androgynous in the same way that they may want to teach women.

From a developmental point of view, the clinician should realize that the socialization process encourages more assertive behavior for men but discourages this behavior for women. This can be highlighted by looking at longitudinal studies in girls and boys. Nevertheless, Block (1973), a developmental psychologist, emphasizes that the ideal would be to broaden behavioral and experiential options to become "whole and human." Assertiveness training is a tool clinicians have available to broaden the behavioral and experiential options. Eventually, we hope, more clinical tools along these lines will evolve so that gender deficits in socialization processes can be minimized.

Statistics shows that there is a rise in single-parent families. It then becomes necessary for the clinician to think in terms of the social milieu of the individual patient. The patient cannot be seen in isolation from society and the family unit in which he or she lives. The single-parent mother will need to learn independency skills and to profit from assertiveness training as well as other therapies which help deal with everyday real-life situations. If the patient has cognitive deficits which emphasize stereotypic adjustment—if the women, for example, believes that she must remain gentle, kind, meek and mild to preserve her feminine image—then she will make an ineffective head of a single-parent family. Legislation has already been introduced to alter the concept of the male as head of the household, since there are so many women heads of households. By the same token, there are now a number of men who are given custody of children. Many of these men will have to learn how to be nurturing and caring. These may have previously been female-oriented traits which men do not like to include in their repertoires because they may think of them as threats to their masculinity. It is a responsibility of the therapist to deal with these issues in helping a man adjust to a new life situation.

Many men are fathers and are coping with divorces in which they will have to take more responsibility in the fathering role since they are no longer living with their wives, whether they are fathering on weekends or full-time. It will cause a male client considerable grief if he is unable to behave as a good parent, and a good parent must have parenting skills. All these issues come under the province of therapeutic responsibility. A therapist does not work in a vacuum. Therefore, in considering the effects of gender role on the client's adjustment, it will be necessary to evaluate very carefully whether a particular gender role is adaptive or maladaptive, according to the life sitaution in which the client is placed. This does not mean that androgyny as a model for therapeutic change (and assertiveness training as a tool) needs to be considered in all therapy cases. Nevertheless, it is a potentially viable hypothetical structure for those clients who are changing life-styles, questioning value systems and are having difficulty with their identification if they identify too rigidly as male or female.

Insight-oriented therapists, as well as behavior therapists, could incorporate a model of androgyny and behavioral change into their models to help their clients adapt more readily to a changing world and changing self-concepts. Though gender role may have little importance when dealing with a Middle-Eastern Moslem small-town community where such roles are clearly differentiated and fixed, in our more complex American society, during this particular period when gender roles are not as clearly differentiated, it is vital that we help clients assess their situations in a more flexible manner.

It is probable that social changes will bring mass confusion. Some parents, for example, will still be using old concepts and be very concerned about little boys who are too gentle and little girls who do not conform to the stereotype. Other parents may be concerned in an opposite fashion. It is up to the therapist to understand the "here and now" of each client's experience. Some of the dissonance may be quite subtle. The working wife with a good job (and the increase in working wives is manyfold) may appear to be well-adjusted because she is handling her life extremely well, as a mother, wife and professional. Yet, this same woman may be suffering from a number of unspoken frustrations and conflicts. The astute clinician must assess whether this woman is really putting too many "shoulds" onto herself and has too much of a drive for perfection. The term "role-proliferation" which has emerged in recent literature may have some bearing here. One person trying to deal with too many roles may be suffering from a great deal of tension and conflict. Therefore, the more feminist-oriented therapist may need to assess the client's situation and figure out how to help some clients "ease off."

On the other hand, one may be dealing with a woman, for example, who is quite satisfied with only one or two main roles (i.e., the more traditional woman) yet feels uncomfortable because this is no longer valued in her community. Again, the therapist has to determine carefully the individual needs of each client. To push a feminist political philosophy on a woman who is feeling conflict, or perhaps even being pushed by friends, neighbors, relatives or husband, will only add to her pressures and will not be therapeutically valuable. The clinician must not only be an astute clinician, understanding the behavioral dynamics of each client, but he or she must also understand the dynamics of the *Zeitgeist*.

Each era produces its own change. The seventies have produced a great change in gender stereotypes. The well-functioning clinician keeps up with the values, techniques and changes in the therapy field, just as the well-trained physician understands recent advances in medical knowledge.

GENDER AND FUTURE PROSPECTIVE: CRITIQUE AND SUMMING UP

How one views the plight of women and the finding that women seek psychiatric help much more frequently than do men depends on one's orientation. Rice and Rice (1973), radicals, feel that the therapist can be harmful to the client if he or she supports the status quo. An extremely radical point of view takes the position of refusing to "diagnose" patients as "sick." Strict conformity to this position leads to the invidious conclusion that no one is schizophrenic and that no one can be treated with medication. Since so much of the literature is based upon sweeping generalizations and subjective conclusions, it is essential to consider the issue of gender and psychotherapy from a data-based point of view.

The therapist must consider the current status of the field with respect to understanding how therapy can or cannot help a particular patient. To refuse all medication to female patients because this will be furthering a political system whereby male therapists sedate female patients could be destructive—sometimes literally so. To deny that schizophrenia exists when faced with a patient who is hallucinating, grimacing, acting inappropriately (whether male or female) shows schizophrenic thinking on the part of the therapist.

We welcome *logical* articles on sex bias in psychological research. As Favreau (1977) points out, many psychological studies set up experimental hypotheses which look for differences rather than similarities between males and females. The fact is that there is much overlap, and by far the larger part of the research on sex differences consists essentially in comparing group performances. If differences are found the results are published. When abilities are unequally distributed among the sexes, we do not seek to understand the effects of independent variables other than sex. Therapists may find it interesting to know that variables which are correlated with sex, such as independence training and role identification, may have much influence on the so-called sex differences that are observed by researchers. For the therapist, Favreau's conclusion on the issue of sex differences is significant: "What is far more important is to understand how to help change behavior, if changing it is socially desirable" (p. 65).

The issues of sex bias are also complex for the practitioner. For example, consider the allegation some feminist therapists have made that there is a kind of tacit collusion between therapist and patient. The female patient feels safe and secure in the dependent role and the male therapist feels safe in the authoritarian role. Therefore, both encourage this type of relationship, being unaware of any possible interactions in therapy which induce an authoritarian independent/dependent variable. Such an arrangement is, of course, covert. If this type of therapy proves not to be beneficial to the person's state of mind and the patient does not learn skills which will help generalize to her everyday world, then, despite his good intentions, the therapist is interfering with the therapeutic process. It is difficult to measure this type of sex bias and it has rarely appeared in the literature. Similarly, learned sex bias may also exist between male therapist and male patient, but the prevailing pattern is probably one of women learning to be passive and dependent, and men to be powerful and authoritarian. Researchers may have to broaden their concepts in order to help clinicians grapple with significant issues concerning sex bias which may be less evident in carefully controlled studies and more evident when one looks into the real world.

Now that a few male therapists, such as Pleck (1976), are beginning openly and honestly for themselves to observe that clinical training involves sex bias, clinicians as a group may be ready to benefit from being able to assess the importance of these issues in their own training. Anecdotal and subjective material cannot be too readily dismissed at this stage of our knowledge. In evaluating his internship, Pleck comments that he found it to be "a remarkable example of how gender determines the careers and experiences that people have in institutions, even though they enter the institution with identical training and assigned identical institutional roles." He gives as one example a female patient who had been raped and found herself unable to return to her apartment or be alone. His male supervisor gave him a strategy. From his therapeutic experience, it was obvious that the woman kept remembering the rape experience because "some part of her liked it and found it pleasurable and exciting" (p. 18). As Pleck points out with dismay, this was in 1970, when he found the reasoning to be "plausible" and "suitably dynamic" and began to work with his female patient based on this information. If similar assumptions are still being made by male therapists and female therapists regarding dynamic processes (and we believe they are!), then for many clients the therapeutic process may indeed be destructive.

A recent article in the *American Psychologist* (Stricker, 1977) makes a cogent and detailed analysis of the literature on sex bias and women. In particular, Stricker criticizes the Broverman type of research as well as other milestone researchers in this area. In discussing the American Psychological Association Task Force findings (1975), he rightly concludes that the recommendations are virtually data-free, but he then goes on to make some data-free recommendations of his own. His conclusions about how women are treated in psychotherapy may be summarized as follows:

> Sexual relations do occur and provide blatant examples of sexism and exploitation in psychotherapy, but they are probably infrequent.

> The sex of the therapist per se is of little consequence with regard to sexist practice.

> Double standards of mental health and negative evaluations of women are premature in light of the data.

> Sex role stereotyping is widespread in our society but well-trained therapists dealing with specific patients are less likely to stereotype.

If we examine his conclusions we may find that some of them are premature. We have not yet grappled in an objective manner with the problem of sexism in psychotherapy. Some of the studies cited in this chapter show the possibility of certain types of sexist interventions by therapists (cf. Tolar & Brannigan, 1975). Also, at this stage, we cannot dismiss the consequence of the sex of the therapist in many therapeutic interventions. Androgyny research tends to indicate that female-valued traits are less adaptive in our society at this time and there may be a realistic basis for assuming a double standard for mental health. Perhaps we are helping female clients by adopting a double standard and helping them develop male, valued traits such as independence and assertiveness.

Stricker's conclusions that women should be made aware of what they should and should not expect from therapy so that they are not placed in a position of accepting authority blindly is certainly a valuable one. What is important when we consider the implications of gender as it relates to psychotherapy is that this article has appeared in the *American*

Psychologist, the most widely distributed journal in the field of psychology.

Prior to now an article of this nature would not have been considered significant. We are at the beginning of an era which may well involve radical changes in the practice of psychotherapy as far as sex-role stereotypes are concerned. Whether the growth of therapeutic practice keeps up with the research findings and the more advanced thinking in this field remains to be seen. There is always a lag between research and practical implementation. Many traditional therapy training programs fail to take into consideration the research literature with respect to gender identification, the influence of stereotypes and sex bias on the therapeutic process. Neither the psychology of women nor the psychology of gender is included in most conventional psychotherapeutic internships or doctoral clinical training programs.

It is hoped that the sudden and large growth in the literature on the psychology of women and the emerging research in the area of sex differences, gender identification, sex bias and sex stereotyping will influence more establishment practices. It was virtually impossible to ignore loud cries made at the turn of the seventies by the militant feminists but we are now able to consider our position, contemplate the current scene, examine the data, generate research hypotheses, and assess our present status. The radical cries against establishment therapists may be becoming more moderate or more demanding, but the subjective statements are at long last being reexamined. It is unlikely that the increasing number of panels at therapy conferences, the numerous papers, the growth in the literature will fail to have some positive impact on the psychotherapeutic processes.

The Task Force findings cited in the *American Psychologist* in 1975 indicate that sexism was indeed prevalent in psychotherapeutic interventions. We may feel, from a more enlightened position, that most therapists (male or female) would not assume today that the resolutions of a woman's problems would come from perfecting the role of wife or mother. However, it is premature to ignore the Task Force allegation that many therapists are inadvertently reinforcing undesirable and maladaptive sex-role stereotypes and are unaware of the changing status of men and women in our society and the changing behaviors that will have to be emphasized for a healthy adjustment. The themes emphasized in this chapter may not be confirmed in research surveys, but the clinician will need to be alerted to the issues presented. Future research will perhaps be more refined and geared to objective evaluation of what is taking place in actual therapy situations rather than based upon analogue studies or data inferred from questionnaires completed by sophisticated clinicians well able to avoid revealing their more covert stereotypic attitudes. For example, we cannot dismiss the notion that, in dealing with a particular client's assertiveness, the therapist may be labeling appropriate assertive behavior as overaggressive and using a covert (penis envy) model in reinforcing behaviors and setting goals for his female patient. The therapist may have a covert, nonconscious double standard for male and female clients. This double standard may work against either the male or the female client.

It is hoped that the Task Force recommendation for workshops for therapists and therapists in training to raise awareness of sex-role stereotyping in psychotherapeutic practice and to increase sensitivity and awareness will become a prominent goal. The therapist, keeping an eye on the contemporary scene with a view to future changes, will always have to assess the individual patient's needs in the light of new options, new keys, and new scripts that will alleviate stress in both men and women who feel locked into the old regime. It is the therapist's responsibility to evaluate the situation correctly and to understand the changes that are going on. However, it is not by quoting political dogma alone that the therapist will best be able to alleviate distress. It is only by dealing with the conflicts, values and problems of the individual client in relation to a changing society that the therapist can most effectively help expedite the therapeutic process.

REFERENCES

ABRAMOWITZ, S., ROBACK, H., SCHWARTZ, F., YASUNA, A., ABRAMOWITZ, C., & GOMES, B. Sex bias in psychotherapy: A failure to confirm. *American Journal of Psychiatry*, 1976, 133, 706-709.

ALBERTI, R. E. & EMMONS, M. L. *Your Perfect Right: A Guide to Assertive Behavior* (3rd ed.), San Luis Obispo, CA: Impact Press, 1978.

AMERICAN PSYCHOLOGICAL ASSOCIATION. Report of the task force on sex bias and sex-role stereotyping in psychotherapeutic practice. *American Psychologist*, 1975, 30, 1169-1175.

ASLIN, A. L. Feminist and community mental health center psychotherapist's expectations of mental health. *Sex Roles*, 1977, 3, 537-544.

BAER, J. *How to Be An Assertive (Not Aggressive) Woman in Life, in Love and on the Job: A Total Guide to Self-Assertiveness*. Chicago, IL: Signet, 1976.

BEM, S. L. On the utility of alternative procedures for assessing psychological androgeny. *Journal of Consulting and Clinical Psychology*, 1977, 215, 196-205.

BEM, S. L. & LENNEY, E. Sex typing and avoidance of cross-sex behavior. *Journal of Personality and Sexual Psychology*, 1976, 33, 48-54.

BEM, S. L., MARTYNA, W., & WATSON, C. Sextyping and androgeny: Future explorations of the expressive domain. *Journal of Personality and Social Psychology*, 1976, 34, 1016-1023.

BERNARD, T. *The Future of Marriage.* New York: Bantam Books, 1973.

BILLINGSLEY, D. Sex bias in psychotherapy: An examination of the effects of client sex, client pathology, and therapist sex on treatment planning. *Journal of Consulting and Clinical Psychology,* 1977, 45, 250-256.

BLOCK, J. H. Conceptions of sex role: Some cross cultural and longitudinal perspectives. *American Psychologist,* 1973, 28, 512-526.

BLOOM, L. Z., COBURN, K., & PEARLMAN, J. *The New Assertive Woman.* New York: Delacorte Press, 1975.

BLUM, H. P. (Ed.). *Female Psychology: Contemporary Psychoanalytic Views.* New York: International Universities Press, 1977.

BROVERMAN, I. K., BROVERMAN, D. M., CLARKSON, F. E., ROSENKRANTZ, P. S., & VOGEL, S. Sex role stereotypes and clinical judgments of mental health. *Journal of Consulting and Clinical Psychology,* 1970, 34, p. 1.

CHESLER, P. *Women and Madness.* New York: Doubleday, 1972. (a)

CHESLER, P. *Marriage and Psychotherapy.* Know, Inc., 1972. (b)

COWAN, G. Therapist judgments of clients' sex-role problems. *Psychology of Women Quarterly,* 1976, 1, 115-124.

DEAUX, K. & FARRIS, E. Attributing causes for one's own performance: The effects of sex, norms and outcome. *Journal of Research on Personality,* 1977, 11, 59-72.

DELK, J. L. & RYAN, T. T. A-B status and sex stereotyping among psychotherapists and patients. Toward a model for maximizing therapeutic potential. *Journal of Nervous and Mental Disease,* 1977, 164, 253-262.

EISLER, R. M., HERSEN, M., MILLER, P. M., & BLANCHARD, E. F. Situational determinants of assertive behaviors. *Journal of Consulting and Clinical Psychology,* 1975, 43, 330-340.

FARRELL, W. *The Liberated Male.* New York: Bantam Books, 1975.

FAVREAU, O. E. Sex bias in psychological research. *Canadian Psychological Review,* 1977, 18, 56-65.

FENSTERHEIM, H. & BAER, J. *Don't Say Yes When You Want to Say No.* New York: David McKay Co., 1975.

GILMAN, C. P. *The Living of Charlotte Perkins Gilman: An Autobiography.* New York: D. Appleton-Century-Croft, 1935.

HEATON, R. K., CARR, J. E., & HAMPSON, J. L. A-B therapist characteristics vs. psychotherapy outcome: Current status and prospects. *J. Nervous and Mental Diseases,* 1975, 160, 229-309.

HORNER, M. S. Femininity and successful achievement: A basic inconsistency. In J. M. Bardwick, E. Douvan, M. S. Horner & D. Gutman, *Feminine Personality and Conflict.* Belmont, CA: Brooks/Cole, 1972.

HOUCK, J. H. The intractable female patient. *American Journal of Psychiatry,* 1972, 129, 27.

KAPLAN, A. G. Androgyny as a method of mental health for women: From theory to therapy. In A. G. Kaplan & F. P. Bean (Eds.), *Beyond Sex-Role Stereotypes: Readings Toward a Psychology of Androgyny.* Boston: Little, Brown & Co., 1976.

KAPLAN, A. G. & BEAN, J. P. *Beyond Sex-Role Stereotypes: Readings Toward a Psychology of Androgyny.* Boston: Little, Brown & Co., 1976.

KELLY, J. A., O'BRIEN, C. G., HOSFORD, R. L., & KISINGER, E. G. Sex roles and social skills: A behavioral analysis of "Masculinity," "Femininity," and "Psychological androgeny." Paper presented to the Association for Advancement of Behavior Therapy, Tenth Annual Convention, New York City, December 1976.

KELLY, J. A. & WORRELL, J. New formulation of sex roles and androgyny: A critical review. *Journal of Consulting and Clinical Psychology,* 1977, 45, 1101-1115.

KELLY, J. A. & WORRELL, L. Parent behaviors related to masculine, feminine, and androgynous sex role orientations. *Journal of Consulting and Clinical Psychology*, 1976, 44, 843-851.

KRAKAUER, A. & BECKER, M. Politics of therapy for women. *Journal of Liberation*, 1972, 3, 2-6.

MACCOBY, E. & JACKLIN, E. (Eds.). *The Psychology of Sex Differences*. Stanford, CA: Stanford University Press, 1974.

MARACEK, J. & KRAVETZ, D. Women and mental health: A review of feminist change efforts. *Psychiatry*, 1977, 40, 323-329.

MARMOR, J. The nature of psychotherapeutic process revisited. *Canadian Psychiatric Association Journal*, 1975, 20, 557-565.

MELGES, F. T. Postpartum psychiatric syndrome. In R. K. Unger & F. L. Denark (Eds.), *Woman: Dependent or Independent Variable*. New York: Psychological Dimensions, 1975.

MENAKER, E. The therapy of women in the light of psychoanalytic theory and the emergence of a new view. In V. Franks & V. Burtle (Eds.), *Women in Therapy: New Perspectives for a Changing Society*. New York: Brunner/Mazel, 1974.

ORLINSKY, D. E. & HOWARD, K. I. The effects of sex of therapist on the therapeutic experience of women. *Psychotherapy: Theory, Research & Practice*, 1976, 13, 82-88.

ORLOFSKY, J. L. Sex-role orientations, identity formation and self-esteem on college men and women. *Sex Roles*, 1977, 3, 561-575.

PERSELY, G., JOHNSON, J. H., & HORNSBY, L. G. Effects of profession, sex and prognostic expectancies on therapists' comments in a psychotherapeutic analogue. *Psychological Reports*, 1975, 37, 455-459.

PLECK, J. H. Sex role issues in clinical training. *Psychotherapy: Theory, Research & Practice*, 1976, 13, 17-19.

RADLOFF, L. Sex differences in depression: The effects of occupation and marital status. *Sex Roles*, 1975, 1, 249-265.

RAWLINGS, E. I. & CARTER, D. K. *Psychotherapy for Women*. Springfield, Ill.: Charles C Thomas, 1977.

RICE, D. G. & RICE, I. K. Non-sexist "marital" therapy. *Journal of Marriage and Family Counseling*, 1977, 3, 3-10.

RICE, I. K. & RICE, D. G. Implications of the woman's liberation movement for psychotherapy. *American Journal of Psychiatry*, 1973, 130, 191-196.

SACHAR, E. J. (Ed.). *Hormones, Behavior and Psychopathology*. New York: Raven Press, 1976.

SALTER, A. *Conditioned Reflex Therapy*. London: Allen and Unwin, 1952.

SELIGMAN, M. E. Depression and learned helplessness. In R. J. Friedman & M. M. Katz (Eds.), *The Psychology of Depression: Contemporary Theory and Research*. Washington, D. C.: V. H. Winston, 1974.

SELIGMAN, M. E. Learned Helplessness and Cognition. Paper presented to European Congress of Behaviour Therapy, Uppsala, Sweden, August 1977.

SPENCE, F. T., HELMREICH, R., & STOPP, J. Ratings of self and peers on sex role attributes and their relation to self-esteem and conceptions of masculinity and femininity. *Journal of Personality and Social Psychology*, 1975, 32, 29-39.

STEINMANN, A. Cultural values, female role expectancies and therapeutic goals: Research and interpretation. In V. Franks and V. Burtle (Eds.), *Women in Therapy: New Psychotherapies for a Changing Society*. New York: Brunner/Mazel, 1974, pp. 51-82.

STRICKER, G. Implications of research for psychotherapeutic treatment of women. *American Psychologist*, 1977, 32, 14-22.

TENNOV, D. *Psychotherapy: The Hazardous Cure*. New York: Abelard-Schuman, 1975.

TICHO, G. R. Female autonomy and young adult women. In H. P. Blum (Ed.),

Female Psychology: Contemporary and Psychoanalytic Views. New York: Universities Press, 1977.

TOLAR, A. & BRANNIGAN, G. G. Sex differences reappraised: A rebuttal. *Journal of Genetic Psychology,* 1975, 127, 319-321.

WETTER, R. E. Levels of self-esteem associated with four sex role categories. In R. Bednar (chair.), Sex roles: Masculine, feminine, androgynous or none of the above? Symposium presented to the American Psychological Association, Chicago, August 1975.

WINOKUR, G. & CADORET, R. The irrelevance of the menopause to depressive disease. In E. J. Sacher (Ed.), *Topics in Psychoendocrinology.* New York: Grune & Stratton, 1975.

WOLF, T. A field experience of live-modeled sex-inappropriate play behavior. Paper presented at the Eastern Psychological Association Convention, 1972.

WOLPE, J. & LAZARUS, A. A. *Behavior Therapy Techniques.* New York: Pergamon Press, 1966.

WYCKOFF, H. Radical psychiatry for women. In E. I. Rawlings & D. K. Carter (Eds.), *Psychotherapy for Women, Treatment Toward Equality.* Springfield, Ill.: Charles C Thomas, 1977.

ZANNA, M. P. & PACK, S. J. On the self-fulfilling nature of apparent sex differences in behavior. *Journal of Experimental Social Psychology,* 1975, 11, 585-591.

17

REFLECTIONS

EDITH S. GOMBERG and VIOLET FRANKS

The origins of this book go back at least 20 years. In 1957, one of the editors wrote:

The research problem of sex differences in psychopathology is a neglected one. The psychological studies of sex differences in general yield little; a review of the major findings presents a substantial amount of material on intellectual functions and school achievement, but information about sex differences in social and emotional behavior is sparse. There is little information about adult sex roles or about the different parental behaviors and attitudes that shape the "masculine" character of the boy and the "feminine" character of the girl. In psychopathology, the problem of sex differences is rarely raised. This is not, of course, to say that a psychotherapist is unaware of differing sex norms of behavior and adjustment in American society. But there is implicit assumption in much of the literature of psychopathology that any particular psychological disorder is much the same among women as among men, that etiology, psychodynamics and symptom patterns are probably alike for both sexes. This may be a valid assumption but we do not know. An occasional study suggests that it is not. (Lisansky-Gomberg, 1957, p. 588).

It is curious to note that, at this time, with so much consciousness-raising activity relating to the status and role of women, with books on sex-role socializations and the war between the sexes multiplying rapidly and with a good deal of research activity relating to masculinity and femininity, there is still little attention paid to the research possibilities inherent in comparison of male and female mental disorders and deviant behaviors. If one views schizophrenia, for example, the fact that both men and women manifest hallucinations during a paranoid episode is important and it is equally important to study the *content* of the hallucinatory experience and the likelihood of hospitalization for each of the sexes.

486

Both men and women attempt and commit suicide but it is highly relevant to prevention efforts that the ages at which suicide attempts peak and decline are different for the two sexes. Both men and women engage in alcoholic drinking but people's perception of intoxication and attitudes toward such intoxication have been different depending on whether the intoxicated/alcoholic person is a man or a woman. A sensitive therapist must be aware of social perceptions and attitudes and their impact on the person to be helped.

The other editor, concerned with the needs of women in therapy, wrote more recently:

> Traditionally, and even understandably in a man's world, psychotherapy for women has been viewed from a male vantage point. Ironically, the majority of clients who consult therapists are women and the majority of therapists they consult are men. If therapy is carried out primarily by men in a male-oriented society, then it is tempting—as certain prominent feminists have recently done—to draw the seemingly obvious conclusion that therapy as it now exists fails to take into account the special needs of women. Questioning the validity of this conclusion . . . a carefully selected series of papers . . . (result in) a searching examination of women, their changing roles and identities, their problems, and what happens when they seek professional help. (Franks & Burtle, 1974, p. xi)

Coming from research and clinical backgrounds, the need seemed obvious. If men and women who manifest disordered behavior which is diagnosably similar are compared, perhaps information can come from such comparison which will be pertinent to the understanding of the disorder and to more effective interventions. The goal of this book was set forth: to present a series of reviews of the *current state of knowledge* about male/female comparisons in problem behaviors in different stages of the life cycle, in different life crises, and in traditional psychiatric diagnostic categories. Since work oriented toward developmental comparison of the sexes and their behaviors in crises at different stages of the life cycle is needed, we have included chapters dealing with sex comparisons in adolescent problems, in coping with divorce, and in the aging process and its attendant problems. We need to look carefully at the meaning of gender differences. Although it is apparently true that women manifest more clinically diagnosed depression, is this true of the age group over 50? Over 60? Does the peak of women's depression years come when her children are young or when they leave home? And why do suicide rates for women drop from age 55 on while climbing for men?

From childhood to old age, such comparison could tell us a good deal about adaptive behavior and difficulties at different stages of the life cycle that are common to both sexes or unique to one of the sexes.

THE DIMENSIONS OF MALE/FEMALE COMPARISON

We have avoided the term "sex differences" as much as possible because the term has come to have a meaning and an influence in behavioral research and clinical practice which is ambiguous and unclear. It is more than possible that there are people doing research who consider their data as non-findings if, in comparing performance of the two sexes, the differences are minimal and not significant. The term *comparison* is preferred here because this permits as much importance to be attached to similarities and to overlap as to the discovery of differences.

In dealing with disordered behavior, we must somehow keep two perspectives in balance. When disordered behavior of the sexes is compared in terms of incidence and prevalence, etiology, symptoms, treatment, etc., we are usually making reference to the *person manifesting the disordered behavior*. That is one perspective. The other is *societal response to the disordered behavior*. From this perspective, disordered behavior is viewed as differentially responded to and differentially rejected. Labeling and stigma theory have made a valuable contribution in heightening the awareness of the behavioral sciences that people do not manifest breakdown or disordered behavior in a vacuum but that they participate in families, neighborhoods and institutions that respond to the breakdown. Neither the person-centered view of disordered behavior nor the societal response view is sufficient by itself to deal with the complexities of human breakdown.

Norms which define the range from acceptability to nonacceptability of a given behavior vary from society to society, from one period of time to another, from one subculture within a society to another. Some norms change rapidly; others remain immutable. We are not always sure which changes are superficial and more a matter of lip-service than a real shift in attitudes. We are, in fact, not always sure what the new norms are. This problem of shifting norms and the uncertainties of contemporary life was played out recently in the trial of a woman defendant who had murdered a man who had raped her. The old "unwritten law" of the frontier accepted a man's seeking vengeance if a woman was "dishonored" but does that apply to the woman seeking vengeance? The defendant was first found guilty, later acquitted.

The same disordered behavior may be viewed by society as more severe or more benign depending on the person manifesting the behavior. Heavy drinking by an upper-class executive may be viewed as a reflection of the strains and responsibilities of his job, while the same heavy drinking by a lower-class man may be seen as reflecting how shiftless and irresponsible he is. Both may be responding to the stresses of their lives but the same behavior may be differently labeled. Sexual promiscuity manifested by a young man may be described as "tom catting" or "sowing wild oats" (old-fashioned terms); when young women act out sexually, it is viewed far from benignly and may become the basis of female juvenile delinquency charges.

The dimensions of male/female comparison of disordered behavior seem best ordered into a number of categories: First, epidemiology—the incidence and prevalence of various disorders among men and among women, the size and location of the disorder among different groups; second, the points of view which exist about the causes, antecedents, onsets of disordered behavior and whether theorists have offered etiological viewpoints about both sexes; third, the clinical manifestations, the symptomatic behaviors, the observable and measurable acts, moods, thoughts of men and women who show disordered behavior; and fourth, the patient role as it is perceived and acted out by men and by women.

Epidemiology

The term "epidemiology" was originally used for infectious diseases but it has been used to describe the incidence and prevalence of non-infectious disease states and it has been extended to cover behaviors of all sorts which are considered social problems, e.g. we speak of the epidemiology of schizophrenia or of alcoholism. As Knupfer (1967) has pointed out, the dependent variables which are the subject of epidemiology include infectious diseases, noninfectious diseases, nonphysical diseases and behavioral problems. Independent variables, originally factors in the physical environment which influenced contagion, now include almost *any* population characteristic: early history, demographic information, psychological test results, anthropometric measurements, survey research items, and so on.

Epidemiology has therefore come to mean the statistical study of the magnitude and correlates of any medical or social problem. It refers to research in which particular populations are counted and studied, and it deals with problematic socially undesirable behaviors as well as with tuberculosis, malaria and cholera.

The chapter by Walter Gove in this book reviews the literature describing the incidence and prevalence of mental disorder as manifested by men and by women. Generally, this kind of information is available as a by-product of epidemiological study of disturbed behavior (Dohrenwend & Dohrenwend, 1969); the sex of subjects is the most obvious subject characteristic, with age ranking as next most obvious. In the epidemiology of mental disorder, there are a number of problems of which we will mention a few.

First, there is a history of diagnosis within psychiatry which includes the diagnoser's training, set and expectations. Women are more often diagnosed as hysterical disorders than are men; men are more often called character disorders, women are more frequently characterized with the diagnostic term "depression." It is not easy to separate the extent to which diagnostic differences of the sexes are valid and the extent to which the diagnoser's expectations are operating. It does appear to be true that little boys get into trouble for aggressive and acting-out behaviors more than do little girls, and it appears to be true that more men are reported as manifesting the acting-out disorders, delinquency and alcoholism. Sex differences in psychiatric diagnosis do relate to *actual* behaviors, but they relate to the socially and professionally conditioned perceptions and attitudes of the diagnosers as well.

Second, as we have noted above, the place of the disturbed person in the social scheme—sex, age, socioeconomic class, etc.—plays an important role in the acquisition of the label "psychiatrically disturbed." We have known this for some time now (Hollingshead & Redlich, 1958). How do gender and socioeconomic status interact in the labeling process? A recent study found little evidence of consistent sex-linked bias in labeling someone as psychiatrically disturbed but reported some suggestive findings that there are *class* differences and that upper status persons have more of a double standard with regard to sex than lower income persons (Coie & Costanzo, 1977). If such results are consistently found, it raises some interesting questions: Does a woman's strange behavior evoke more response in a well-to-do community than in a poor community? And how do gender and age interact in the labeling process?

A third point has more to do with the *correlates* of mental disorder than with the incidence and prevalence. A high proportion of people who manifest disordered behaviors are brought to hospitals, clinics and therapists *by others,* and many come *by themselves* (children must be excluded from this question since they are, almost without exception, brought by others). To what extent are men/women likely to be brought by others and to what extent does sexual role, e.g. wage-earner for a family or mother of young children, relate to the decision to seek help or to submit to hospitalization? To what extent are men/women more likely to come by themselves, having made the decision to seek help? Is the question of whether *others* are family, neighbors or police a matter of social class? We know that women report more psychological symptoms (Garai, 1970; Selected Symptoms of Psychological Distress, 1970) and we know that they seek out medical attention and counseling and therapy more than do men—*on their own.*

Considering how relatively simple it is to collect such data, it seems surprising that the decision to seek help and the presence or absence of others accompanying a patient have been so little studied. The very small amount of information available suggests, for example, that with alcoholic admissions whether relatives accompany a patient to the hospital or whether he comes alone is a potent predictor of whether he will stay in the alcoholism program (Bowen & Twemlow, 1977). It is a common observation made by alcoholism and substance abuse clinic workers that women tend to come more often alone and that men tend to come accompanied by spouse more frequently.

We need to study the decision to seek help: Has it been made by the client alone, by significant others, by the police and courts, by a physician? What behaviors precipitate such a decision by others or by the self? It is often clear in the history of hospital or clinic or private practice admissions that the difficulties have existed for a long period; it is, therefore, important to know what precipitated such an important decision. Are men and women similar in the ways these decisions are made? Are women more vulnerable to pressure from others or are they more self-aware? Do families of men and women play similar roles when the decision is made? Who comes—if anyone—to the hospital or therapist with the disturbed person?

Is seeking help for anxiety and unhappiness a middle- and upper-class phenomenon? We know from many surveys that a sizable percentage of the general population presents symptomatic behavior but never seeks help (e.g., Srole, Langner, Michael, Opler, & Rennie, 1962). Survey research might include more questions about what people perceive as disordered behavior and the conditions under which they would or would not seek out help. We know that some groups, e.g., distressed elderly persons, minority group individuals, are underrepresented in community mental health centers (Sue, 1977). What are the conditions under which some populations will look for help and where will they look for it? If they turn to folk healers, for example, they will not enter into the statistics of mental health and mental disorder.

Viewpoints about Etiology of Disordered Behavior

This area of theory is a difficult one in which to compare the two sexes since there is so little agreement about etiological variables in general. The history of such theorizing, oversimplified, has been something like this: After World War II there was a period of psychological explanation (first, more psychoanalytic, later more behavioristic). The 1960s was a decade in which social stress explanations and sociological debate over labeling, stigma and consequences were prominent. And we seem to be in a period now in which genetic-biological-neurochemical explanations are popular. All such viewpoints coexist but do seem to take turns in being center stage.

There is difficulty in making comparisons of the sexes in theories of etiology, pointed out many times in recent writing: Most theorizing has been about male disorder and women have been more or less ignored. This is something of an exaggeration because women's psychological disorders have been very readily attributed to their hormonal status or their greater sensitivity or fragility. Serious and scholarly attempts to evolve a theory of human behavior and malfunctioning have been primarily about *male* development and malfunctioning with women brought in as a kind of afterthought (like the product of Adam's rib).

We will divide viewpoints about etiology into physiological, psychological and social viewpoints, for a cursory look at theory relating to women's/men's disorders.

In *physiological explanations,* particularly endocrine theories, women are well represented. The presumed relationship between uterus and hysteria is an ancient idea which is still around. Middle aged depression is related to the menopause. Suicide attempts may be a manifestation of premenstrual tension or at least related to the menstrual cycle. Explanations in terms of genetic endowment seem more evenhanded but endocrinological explanations seem to deal more often with women than with men.

Psychological explanations of breakdown and mental disorder may be psychoanalytic or behavioristic with many variations. Behavioristic theories would seem to be more evenhanded in explaining disordered behavior because assessment and modification of behavior are, presumably, more or less independent of the sex of the behaving person. Concepts of behavior as fixed by reinforcement contingencies do not seem to be primarily about either sex. On the other hand, psychoanalytic explanations have their origin in a view of development which was primarily about the male. The work of Gregory Zilboorg, Karen Horney,

Clara Thompson, and more recent writers indicates that there have been psychoanalysts who were concerned with the question of female development.

Some psychological explanations are not so much in terms of whole theories of development as they are of particular traits or patterns or conflicts. One recent example of such a psychological explanation is difficulty-in-adjustment-to-sexual-role as an etiological agent of various disorders. Sexual role is assumed to be culturally defined and socially learned—although it may be based on biological factors as well—and difficulty in learning and accepting one's sexual role in an adaptive, balanced way has recently been offered as an explanation of various disorders. There are sexual politics in this position because the assumption which is implicit is that the "traditional" female role is not wholesome but an androgynous role is. This work has been recently reviewed and evaluated (Locksley & Colten, in press).

Sex role is seen as an etiological agent in a variety of ways: (a) over-acceptance or exaggeration of the traditional female sex role is seen as a primary explanation for hysterical or depressive disorders (Wolowitz, 1972; Lewis, 1976); (b) rejection of the role and reversal or "sex-role alienation" is linked with schizophrenia in women (Cheek, 1964; McClelland & Watt, 1968); and (c) conflict about masculinity vs. femininity has been posited as a primary basis for phobic disorder (Fodor, 1974) and alcoholism among women (Wilsnack, 1973).

There are several problems with sex-role explanations. First, there is the question of definition of masculinity or femininity: Sometimes the definition seems to be in terms of passivity or dependency, at other times in terms of problem-solving competence and independence. Second, it is highly probable that the acceptable female sex role varies from place to place, class to class, time to time, yet the assumption implicit in all this work is that there is something called "traditional" sex role which is universal and eternal. Third, the research instruments which have measured sex-role identity and sex-role conflict have been rather limited in the aspects of behavior and attitude sampled by the instrument (Colten, 1978). Fourth, if sex-role conflict is indeed part of the etiology of mental disorder, might this not be part of *conflict in general* as contributing to the etiology of mental disorder, i.e. might sex-role conflict be one of a number of complex approach-avoidance conflicts which prove to be unbearable stresses for some individuals? This was the direction of some early work (Conger, 1951) and merits reexamination. Finally, does not sex-role conflict apply to men as well as to women as an etiological factor? Both sexes have conflicts about passivity, assertiveness, independence, aggressive feelings, expression of tenderness and achievement drives. *Both* men and women alcoholics, for example, report early histories of strongly traditional attitudes about how men or women should behave and both sexes seem to have difficulties living with these attitudes and behaviors (Gomberg, 1976).

Social stress theories about disordered behavior tend to look for explanations in the social environment of the poor, the ghetto dweller, the discriminated-against minority, and those persons who are disadvantaged by the social structure. We can hardly doubt that stresses, poverty and low status play a significant role in the etiology of disordered behavior, but social stress *alone* cannot account for mental breakdown. There are groups in which some mental illness appears although social stresses appear to be minimal (Hostetler & Huntington, 1967) and, of course, there are many members of stressed groups who do *not* manifest mental illness. Such stress theories relate to sex comparison in suggesting that women are a more stressed group in American society but this seems far too broad a generalization. Women are, by government fiat, a "minority group"—but are they more stressed? While women are in many ways second class citizens, it is also true that there are many cultural protections for women and achievement drive stress may be less for them than for men. Although there are high rates of depression among adult women, there are also greater longevity and a much lower suicide rate among older women than among older men.

The subjective vs. objective definition of stress needs exploration: Might women report more stress than men while actually experiencing less stress? Is stress defined by objective conditions, e.g. discrimination in an employment situation, or is stress the internalized feelings of low self-esteem which may result from being discriminated against? When one speaks of minorities or the poor or "the disadvantaged," is there not a note of condescension?

Labeling theory has dealt with a variety of deviant behaviors including those which are ascribed (minority group status) and those which are chosen (alcoholism, criminal activity). Although these theories have dealt with a wide variety of behaviors, there is no *explicit* statement about different norms of behavior for men and women and we must assume that they are dealing with rule-breaking behavior common to men and women. Nonetheless, recognition of sex differences in normative standards of behavior (e.g., sexual) and sex differences in social definition of deviance would probably be acceptable to labeling theorists. This point of view raises many interesting issues: For example, it appears that of female deviant behaviors, sexual acting out is a major source of concern to society, and although women murderers are hardly viewed with approbation, most of societal activity concerns itself with sexual acting out. In some situations, women are more stigmatized than men for similar behavior, e.g., adultery. Other behaviors, like alcoholism, may reflect the lesser likelihood that women will be labeled as deviant; this seems to be particularly true in the aura of denial which surrounds the woman alcoholic. Stigma is a very useful concept for clearly it is not only *aberrant behavior* which men or women manifest but the *negative valuation* that society places on these behaviors which determines the response of others. For instance, being poor and on welfare is a form of stigmatized behavior for both men and women. However when the attitudes of welfare workers toward men and women clients were compared in a recent study, the data showed that welfare workers had more negative attitudes toward *male* welfare recipients (Day, 1976).

Clinical Manifestations or Symptoms

It seems evident that the content of hallucinations will vary with *historical period*. The religiosity and guilt-loading of hallucinatory content have varied, we are reasonably certain, from one nation to another and from one historical period to another. Except for some work in transcultural psychiatry (Kiev, 1972) and in crosscultural comparisons of schizophrenic symptoms, there does not appear to have been much systematic work in this area. But it does seem clear that the paranoid patient who tells of lasers which threaten him or the sexually impotent man threatened by the abundance of assertive women in his social environment is manifesting clinical disturbance which, in its form, relates to a time and place. Life expectancy is considerably longer than it was a half century ago but we have not worked out socially useful roles for older persons and depression apparently appears often among older persons, sometimes misdiagnosed as organic brain syndrome. Gerontological depression may well be a phenomenon of our time.

There has been interesting work in *ethnic differences* in clinical symptoms (Opler & Singer, 1956; Kelleher, 1972), but it has not been strenuously pursued as a research subject. One comes close to a literature of ethnic/racial difference in the attempts to relate the stresses of particular groups, e.g. discrimination against blacks or Chicanos, persecution of Jews, etc., and the patterns of breakdown such groups manifest. There does not seem to be a contradiction between recognition of such differences, on the one hand, and the point of view of Murphy (1976) and others that similar kinds of disturbed behavior are labeled abnormal in diverse cultures on the other. Murphy says, in fact,

> Almost everywhere a pattern composed of hallucinations, delusions, disorientations, and behavioral aberrations appear to identify the idea of "losing one's mind" even though the content of these manifestations is colored by cultural beliefs (p. 1027).

Social class differences have been explored for some time. Beginning with the work of Hollingshead and Redlich (1958), the Stirling county studies (Leighton, 1959), the Midtown project (Srole, Langner, Michael, Opler, & Rennie, 1962), and the work of the Dohrenwends (1969), there has been clear recognition of the differences between social classes in distribution among the different diagnostic categories. We do not know of any work which explores social class differences in the content of symptoms in the different disorders although such information could readily be gathered in comparisons of patients in state, community and private hospitals.

Sex differences in the different kinds of disturbed behavior have not been a very active research area. There have been male/female comparisons in the problem behaviors of children (MacFarlane, Allen, & Honzik, 1954) and, more recently, Phillips (1968), writing of "a social view of psychopathology" includes a section on "sex." He observes that, "Fairly consistent sex differences in pathological reactions have been observed among both children and adults" (p. 438). These differences are conspicuously absent in almost all recent textbooks of psychopathology.

In general, available comparison of age group six to 11 suggests that little boys are much more likely to exhibit problem behavior in school and to get into difficulty than are little girls. Aggressive behavior, inattentiveness, and "excessive motor activity" are characteristically the problem behaviors of boys. From parents' reports, boys manifest speech defects and bedwetting more often than girls but girls show more thumbsucking, fear of the dark, and eating problems (Parent Ratings of Behavioral Patterns of Children, 1971; Parent Ratings of Behavioral Patterns of Youths 12-17, 1974). This is consistent with earlier findings that boys tend to act out in motor ways more than girls, who are reported as showing "personality" problems rather than conduct disorders.

Government survey data show that in the age group 12 to 17, girls seem to be well adjusted to school more frequently than boys (Behavior Patterns in School of Youths 12-17 years, 1974). Maccoby and Jackin

(1974) have reviewed the research literature relating to sex differences in temperament, sociability, and power relationships. Chapter 3 of this book reports on problem behavior of adolescents and makes the telling point that most of the research literature about adolescents tends to come from psychiatric facilities. Locksley and Douvan suggest that there are shifts during the adolescent years. Chapter 2 by Gove also makes reference to data showing that during adolescence girls may overtake and surpass boys in the incidence of behavior problems and psychopathology.

Phillips (1968) stated that men express deviance more readily in "action" and women in "thought." Male symptomatic behavior is more likely to be destructively hostile and female symptomatic behavior more manifest in self-critical and even self-destructive attitudes. This differentiation is supported by a state mental hospital report which compares symptom frequency by sex (Eaton, Sletten, Kitchen, & Smith, 1971). This report found women to have been hospitalized more frequently, cry more frequently, attempt suicide more often, report more feelings of being incapable, and have more religious interests and activities than men patients. Male patients more frequently report serious accidents, get into fights, cause injury to others, get arrested and go to prison, have histories of alcoholism; they also more frequently report positive family histories of alcoholism. Garai (1970), reviewing sex differences reported in mental health literature, indicates that women patients express more anxiety and more disturbance in interpersonal relationships, affect and self-image.

There are problems in comparing the sexes in clinical symptoms and in diagnoses. There are stereotypes and biases in observing, reporting, and diagnosing. Acting-out behaviors may be defined with reasonable objectivity, but societal responses to such acting-out behaviors may be quite different for the two sexes. The expectation of the person making the observation and diagnosis plays a significant role; for example, the diagnosis of hysteria is more readily applied to women than to men. There may, indeed, be more women than men who manifest hysterical symptoms, but hysteria is underemphasized as a male symptom even when it appears frequently in combat neuroses and among men under stress. There are apparently real differences between men and women in their choice of symptomatic behaviors, but the diagnostician must remain as free of stereotype as possible if he is to observe the patient, male or female, accurately.

Rather than relating particular sexual roles and stress, there is a point of view that both sexes have stresses which impinge on them and that response to stress relates to styles of behaving learned by each sex. Dohrenwend and Dohrenwend (1969) see no greater magnitude of social stress impinging on one sex or the other, although each sex reacts differentially to stresses. In a recent study of sex differences in the expression of depressed responses on the Beck Depression Inventory, Hammen and Padesky (1977) found no sex differences in *degree* of depression but clear sex differences in the *patterns* of symptom expression of young, unmarried, college student subjects. With the current state of knowledge, it is probably best to assume that both sexes have similar magnitudes of social stress impinging on them and to get on with the business of studying the different ways in which the two sexes cope or break down. We assume that men and women both lead lives of quiet desperation, and go on from there.

The Patient Role

Although the patient role in physical and mental disorder as it relates to sexual role would seem to be a reasonable research area in which men and women could be compared, there is very little work on this and very little agreement. Is the patient role more consistent with the socially prescribed "traditional" feminine role or masculine role? There has been some research in recent years on therapists' view of patients and views about mental health. Sorely needed are studies of help-seeking behavior, motives and events that precipitate help-seeking, patient compliance (particularly in following medical or chemotherapeutic regimes), and styles of response to treatment. There appears to be very little literature on help-seeking decisions and, as far as we know, none on sex comparison in help-seeking. One theory, an additive stress theory, has been offered about women by Guttentag, Salasin, and Legge (1976), who describe the woman who is at high risk for depression. She is separated or divorced from her husband, poorly educated, of low economic status, non-white, and coping with ". . . the combined stresses of raising young children and of being the breadwinner, together with a low income." Perhaps one important line of research would be to pursue the *sum* of additive stresses that bring the experience of helplessness and depression to the point of unbearability and precipitate help-seeking behavior. Would the sum and its component parts be the same for different groups of men and women?

The behavior of hospitalized patients is an accessible area of study. What are the differences in the way men and women play the patient role in the hospital? Is the patient role, including compliance with hospital routine, an extension of socially defined female role? Or is being taken care of a rewarding regression for male patients? There are some authors who believe that women are better patients; Garai (1970) noted that women accept being mental patients more readily. There are also a number of reports which suggest that women's psychiatric wards are noisier and more characterized by disruptive behavior and belligerence than men's wards (Chesler, 1972). We are not sure what we mean by *better* or *worse* patients—are better patients more conforming or do they have a better prognosis for healthy functioning? Many people working with alcoholics, addicts or delinquents hold the belief that women are more difficult to deal with as patients and one wonders about self-fulfilling prophecies and the attitudes of caretakers. Some hold the view that being a hospitalized patient is more consistent with women's dependent role, while others hold the view that mental disorder is frequently characterized by a reversal in sexual-role-prescribed behavior. Cheek (1964), for example, described male schizophrenic patients as withdrawn and passive in interacting with their families whereas female schizophrenic patients were active and dominating. McClelland and Watt (1968) describe women schizophrenics are more assertive and male schizophrenics as more "sensitive."

Is the hospital a male-dominated or female-dominated institution? From a hierarchal or authority point of view, it is more male-dominated because more physicians and executives are men. But the caretakers who work directly with patients are more often women and the hospital is frequently seen as a woman-dominated institution as in Kesey's book, *One Flew Over The Cuckoo's Nest*. The behavior of any patient, man or woman, is likely to vary with the status of the different caretakers in the system and with the sex of the caretaker as well.

One research approach to the patient role is to study length of hospitalization. Doherty (1976) found that those patients, men or women, who conformed to hospital rules and to staff expectations were released earlier. He noted, however, that " . . . longer staying women seemed more negatively oriented toward the ward normative expectations, themselves, and their family situations . . ." (p. 91). Doherty's findings suggest that compliance (feminine?) behavior led to earlier release for both men and women but that women are released less readily when they manifest negative (masculine?) behavior.

Still another research approach is comparative study of who remains in therapy, who drops out, and the predictive significance of dropping out.

We have some data about alcoholic women indicating that they tend to terminate more readily than do male patients but there are also indications that such dropping out is not as predictive of final termination as is true among men. Women alcoholics appear to go in and out of therapy more readily than do men and we need to know more about this: Are there different demands of the socially prescribed sexual role including the needs of children and family at home? Is there more ambivalence about the treatment process? Or does dropping out of therapy reflect wariness and less trust on the part of women patients who have more difficulty in making rapport and forming a transference, or more acting out of conflicting feelings and more difficulty in decision behavior?

It is of interest that, in the welter of research and discussion of treatment and psychotherapy, so much is written about the process of therapy and so relatively little about the patient and his/her behavior in treatment, starting with the decision to seek help.

COMPARISONS OF DISORDERED BEHAVIOR

A few decades ago, black vs. white results on intelligence tests were commonly subject to research. It was an issue of differences and comparisons and many social scientists argued that in spite of differences in mean scores, it was more important to note that the *range* within each group was much greater than the difference between the means and that the *overlap* of the two groups' scores was being overlooked. The same reasoning bears application to studies which compare men and women. Kanter (1976), in fact, argues that many studies of female socialization and sex differences make the same errors of comparison as was true in the past:

> Despite the large amount of overlap between the sexes in most research, the tendency to label and polarize and thus to exaggerate differences remains in much reporting of data, which may, for example, report the mean scores of male and female populations but not the degree of overlap (p. 284).

A question raised by this book is: Which are the universal phenomena of disordered behavior which characterize all persons, regardless of age, sex, social class, ethnic background, etc., and how do these phenomena differ among groups? Both men and women manifest autistic thinking, thought distortion, and poor ego boundaries when they are schizophrenic. Both men and women report blackouts as one of the early signs of alcoholism. In raising this question, we hope to learn more about the nature of disordered behavior.

A book about gender comparisons may seem to imply that such comparisons stand alone. It seems important to emphasize the limitations of such a view. We believe that gender differences interact with differences in age, social class, ethnicity and other sociocultural variables. Gender comparison is only one step in the analysis of group differences in disordered behavior. But there is no way of comparing populations in terms of the parameters delineated above without a basic understanding of gender differences and similarities. After all, what is the universal basic and probably first question asked about a human being: Is it a boy or is it a girl?

REFERENCES

Behavior Patterns of Children in School. National Center for Health Statistics. Series 11. No. 113. Vital and Health Statistics, Department of Health, Education and Welfare Publication No. (HRA) 76-1042, 1972.

Behavior Patterns in School of Youths 12-17 Years. National Center for Health Statistics. Series 11. No. 139. Vital and Health Statistics, Department of Health, Education and Welfare Publication No. (HRA) 74-1621, 1974.

BOWEN, W. T. & TWEMLOW, S. W. People who accompany alcoholics to the hospital as a predictor of patient dropout. *Hospital and Community Psychiatry,* 1977, 28, 880-881.

CHEEK, F. A serendipitous finding: Sex roles and schizophrenia. *Journal of Abnormal and Social Psychology,* 1964, 69, 392-400.

CHESLER, P. *Women and Madness.* New York: Doubleday and Co., 1972.

COIE, J. D. & COSTANZO, P. R. Sex roles and mental illness labeling: A subcultural study. Paper presented at the meeting of the American Psychological Association, San Francisco, August 1977.

COLTEN, M. E. A reconsideration of psychological androgyny: Self esteem, social skills and expectations rather than sex role identification. Unpublished doctoral dissertation, Department of Psychology, University of Michigan, 1978.

CONGER, J. T. The effects of alcohol on conflict behavior in the albino rat. *Quarterly Journal of Studies on Alcohol,* 1951, 12, 1-29.

DAY, P. J. P. Sex, race, and work ethic stereotypes: Effects of organizational structure on perspectives of public welfare workers. Unpublished doctoral dissertation in Social Work and Sociology, University of Michigan, 1976.

DOHERTY, E. G. Length of hospitalization on a short-term therapeutic community: A multivariate study by sex across time. *Archives of General Psychiatry,* 1976, 33, 87-93.

DOHRENWEND, B. P. & DOHRENWEND, B. S. *Social Status and Psychological Disorder.* New York: Wiley, 1969.

EATON, M. E., SLETTEN, I. W., KITCHEN, A. D., & SMITH, R. J. The Missouri automated psychiatric history: Symptom frequencies, sex differences, use of weapons and other findings. *Comprehensive Psychiatry,* 1971, 12.

FODOR, I. G. The phobic syndrome in women: Implications for treatment. In V. Franks & V. Burtle (Eds.), *Women in Therapy.* New York: Brunner/Mazel, 1974.

FRANKS, V. & BURTLE, V. (Eds.). *Women in Therapy.* New York: Brunner/Mazel, 1974.

GARAI, J. E. Sex differences in mental health. *Genetic Psychology Monographs,* 1970, 81, 123.

GOMBERG, E. S. The female alcoholic. In R. E. Tarter & A. A. Sugerman (Eds.), *Alcoholism: Interdisciplinary Approaches to An Enduring Problem.* Reading, Mass.: Addison-Wesley, 1976.

GUTTENTAG, M., SALASIN, S., & LEGGE, W. W. Women and mental health: A study in progress. Unpublished manuscript, Harvard University, 1976.

HAMMEN, C. L. & PADESKY, C. A. Sex differences in the expression of depressive responses on the Beck Depression Inventory. *Journal of Abnormal Psychology,* 1977, 86, 609-614.

HOLLINGSHEAD, A. B. & REDLICH, F. C. *Social Class and Mental Illness.* New York: Wiley, 1958.

HOSTETLER, J. A. & HUNTINGTON, G. E. *The Hutterites in North America. Case Studies in Cultural Anthropology Series.* New York: Holt, Rinehart & Winston, 1967.

KANTER, R. M. Presentation VI. In M. Blaxall & B. Reagan (Eds.), *Women and the Workplace.* Chicago: University of Chicago Press, 1976.

KELLEHER, M. J. Cross-national (Anglo-Irish) differences in obsessional symptoms and traits of personality. *Psychological Medicine,* 1972, 2, 33-41.

KESEY, K. *One Flew Over the Cuckoo's Nest.* New York: Viking Press, 1962.

KIEV, S. *Transcultural Psychiatry.* New York: Free Press, 1972.

KNUPFER, G. V. The epidemiology of problem drinking. *American Journal of Public Health,* 1967, 57, 973-986.

LEIGHTON, A. H. *My Name Is Legion.* New York: Basic Books, 1959.

LEWIS, H. B. *Psychic War in Men and Women.* New York: NYU Press, 1976.

LISANSKY-GOMBERG, E. S. Alcoholism in women: Social and psychological concomitants. I. Social History data. *Quarterly Journal of Studies on Alcohol,* 1957, 18, 588-623.

LOCKSLEY, A. &. COLTEN, M. E. Psychological androgyny: A case of mistaken identity? Manuscript submitted for publication, 1978.

MACCOBY, E. E. & JACKLIN, C. N. *The Psychology of Sex Differences.* Stanford, California: Stanford University Press, 1974.

MACFARLANE, J. W., ALLEN, L., & HONZIK, M. P. *A Developmental Study of the Behavior Problems of Normal Children Between 21 Months and 14 Years.* Berkeley, California: University of California Press, 1954.

McCLELLAND, D. C. & WATT, N. F. Sex role alienation in schizophrenia. *Journal of Abnormal Psychology,* 1968, 73.

MURPHY, J. M. Psychiatric labeling in cross-cultural perspective. *Science,* 1976, 191, 1019-1028.

OPLER, M. K. & SINGER, J. L. Ethnic differences in behavior and psychopathology: Italian and Irish. *The International Journal of Social Psychiatry,* 1956, II, 11-22.

Parent Ratings of Behavior Patterns of Children. National Center for Health Statistics. Series 11. No. 108. Vital and Health Statistics. U.S. Department of Health, Education and Welfare, 1971.

Parent Ratings of Behavior Patterns of Youths 12-17 Years. National Center for Health Statistics. Series 11, No. 137. Department of Health, Education and Welfare Publication No. (HRA) 74-1619, 1974.

PHILLIPS, L. A social view of psychopathology. In P. London and D. Rosenhan (Eds.), *Foundations of Abnormal Psychology.* New York: Holt, Rinehart & Winston, 1968.

Selected Symptoms of Psychological Distress. National Center for Health Statistics. Series 11, No. 37. Vital and Health Statistics, U.S. Department of HEW. Public Health Service Publication No. 1000, 1970.

SROLE, L., LANGNER, T. S., MICHAEL, S. T., OPLER, M. K., & RENNIE, T. A. C. *Mental Health in the Metropolis: The Midtown Study*, Vol. 1. New York: McGraw-Hill, 1962.

SUE, S. Community mental health services to minority groups: Some optimism, some pessimism. *American Psychologist*, 1977, 32, 616-624.

WILSNACK, S. Sex-role identity in female alcoholism. *Journal of Abnormal Psychology*, 1973, 82, 253-261.

WOLOWITZ, H. M. Hysterical character and feminine identity. In J. M. Bardwick (Ed.), *Readings on the Psychology of Women*. New York: Harper & Row, 1972.

SUBJECT INDEX

505

NAME INDEX